OUR NATIONAL INCOME ACCOUNTS AND CHAIN WEIGHTED REAL GDP SINCE 1929*

In this table we see historical data for the various components of nominal GDP. These are given in the first four columns. We then show the rest of the national income accounts going from GDP to NDP to NI to PI to DPI. The last column gives chain-weighted real GDP.

	The Sum of These Expenditures				Equals	Less	Equals	Plus	Less	Equals	Less			Plus	Equals	Less	Equals	
Year	Personal Consumption Expenditures	Gross Private Domestic Investment	Government Purchases of Goods and Services	Net Exports	Gross Domestic Product	Depreciation	Net Domestic Product	Net U.S. Income Earned Abroad	Indirect Business Taxes and Transfers	National Income	Undistributed Corporate Profits	Social Security Taxes	Corporate Income Taxes	Transfer Payments and Net Interest Earnings	Personal Income	Personal Income Taxes and Nontax Payments	Disposable Personal Income	Chain-Weighted Real GDP (1996 dollars)
1977	1278.4	361.3	415.3	-23.7	2031.4	232.0	1799.4	20.7	184.7	1635.4	91.2	155.4	73.0	321.3	1637.1	201.2	1436.0	4455.7
1978	1430.4	436.0	455.6	-26.1	2295.9	261.9	2034.0	22.1	196.3	1859.8	110.6	177.0	83.5	359.6	1848.3	233.5	1614.8	4709.9
1979	1596.3	490.6	503.5	-24.0	2566.4	301.0	2265.4	32.9	223.3	2075.0	124.6	204.2	88.0	423.3	2081.5	273.3	1808.2	4870.1
1980	1762.9	477.9	569.7	-14.9	2795.6	346.1	2449.5	35.3	242.7	2242.1	102.6	225.0	84.8	494.2	2323.9	304.2	2019.8	4872.3
1981	1944.2	570.8	631.4	-15.0	3131.3	395.8	2735.5	34.7	274.1	2496.1	86.0	261.6	81.1	532.0	2599.4	351.5	2247.9	4993.9
1982	2079.3	516.1	684.4	-20.5	3259.2	437.5	2821.7	36.5	256.3	2601.9	56.2	280.6	63.1	566.4	2768.4	361.6	2406.8	4900.3
1983	2286.4	564.2	735.9	-51.7	3534.9	457.2	3077.7	36.9	319.2	2795.4	70.5	301.9	77.2	601.1	2946.9	360.9	2586.0	5105.6
1984	2498.4	735.5	800.8	-102.0	3932.7	483.5	3449.2	35.3	323.3	3161.2	81.0	345.5	94.0	634.1	3274.8	387.2	2887.6	5477.4
1985	2712.6	736.3	878.3	-114.2	4213.0	517.7	3695.3	25.3	341.4	3379.2	61.0	375.9	96.5	669.2	3515.0	428.5	3086.5	5689.8
1986	2895.2	747.2	942.3	-131.9	4452.9	552.9	3900.0	15.5	391.0	3524.5	30.6	402.0	106.5	727.0	3712.4	449.3	3262.5	5885.7
1987	3105.3	781.5	997.9	-142.3	4742.5	587.4	4155.1	13.7	366.8	3802.0	75.3	423.3	127.1	786.2	3962.5	503.0	3459.5	6092.6
1988	3356.6	821.1	1036.9	-106.3	5103.8	628.9	4474.9	18.4	343.7	4149.6	115.2	462.8	137.2	837.7	4272.1	519.7	3752.4	6349.1
1989	3596.7	872.9	1100.2	-80.7	5489.1	678.7	4810.4	20.4	440.2	4390.6	30.2	491.2	141.5	872.1	4599.8	583.5	4016.3	6568.7
1990	3831.5	861.7	1181.4	-71.4	5803.2	712.5	5090.7	29.0	478.8	4640.9	95.3	518.5	140.6	1016.7	4903.2	609.6	4293.6	6683.5
1991	3971.2	800.2	1235.5	-20.7	5986.2	749.1	5237.1	24.7	506.3	4755.5	104.1	543.5	133.6	1111.1	5085.4	610.5	4474.8	6669.2
1992	4209.7	866.6	1270.5	-27.9	6318.9	788.7	5530.2	23.5	560.0	4993.7	122.9	571.4	143.1	1234.1	5390.4	635.8	4754.6	6891.1
1993	4454.7	955.1	1293.0	-60.5	6642.3	813.6	5828.7	24.3	601.9	5251.1	141.9	592.9	165.4	1259.1	5610.0	674.6	4935.3	7054.1
1994	4716.4	1097.1	1327.9	-87.1	7054.3	875.7	6178.6	16.8	639.3	5556.1	151.8	628.3	186.7	1298.7	5888.0	722.6	5165.4	7337.8
1995	4969.0	1143.8	1372.0	-84.3	7400.5	912.2	6488.3	20.4	632.5	5876.2	203.3	656.6	211.0	1395.6	6200.9	778.3	5422.6	7537.1
1996	5237.5	1242.7	1421.9	-89.0	7813.2	956.4	6856.8	18.1	664.7	6210.2	205.0	676.8	223.6	1442.6	6547.4	869.7	5677.7	7813.2
1997	5524.4	1383.7	1481.0	-88.3	8300.8	1009.7	7291.1	4.2	660.4	6634.9	223.9	701.2	238.3	1479.6	6951.1	968.3	5982.8	8165.1
1998	5848.6	1531.2	1529.7	-149.6	8759.9	1066.9	7693.0	-9.9	646.7	7036.4	193.1	721.1	240.2	1476.9	7358.9	1072.6	6286.2	8516.3
1999	6254.9	1621.6	1628.7	-256.8	9254.6	1141.2	8113.4	-10.1	633.2	7470.1	207.8	739.6	251.5	1520.0	7791.2	1152.0	6639.2	8867.0
2000[a]	6661.5	1727.0	1734.6	-273.6	9849.5	1215.4	8634.1	-22.3	762.1	7849.7	219.2	760.2	257.3	1629.3	8242.3	1253.2	6989.1	9256.2

*Note: Except for real GDP, all figures in billions of dollars. Some rows may not add up due to rounding errors.
[a]Estimates based on preliminary data.

ECONOMICS TODAY

The Macro View

2001–2002 EDITION

Roger LeRoy Miller

Institute for University Studies, Arlington, Texas

Addison
Wesley

Boston San Francisco New York
London Toronto Sydney Tokyo Singapore Madrid
Mexico City Munich Paris Cape Town Hong Kong Montreal

Photo Credits

Pages 3 and 14, ©Grant LeDuc/Stock Boston; pages 26 and 43, ©Annie Griffiths Belt/CORBIS; pages 48 and 71, ©Keren Su/Stock Boston; pages 75 and 90, ©Tony Freeman/Photo Edit; pages 95 and 115, ©Bill Aron/Photo Edit; pages 120 and 135, ©CORBIS; pages 145 and 164, ©Miladinovic/Sygma CORBIS; pages 168 and 190, PN/The Slide File; page 170 left, Frank Siteman/The Picture Cube; page 170 right, Bernsau/The Image Works; pages 195 and 215, ©Bruce Forster/Tony Stone Images/Chicago Inc.; pages 225 and 241, ©Lee Snider/CORBIS; pages 246 and 265, ©Ilkka Uimonen/Sygma CORBIS; pages 269 and 292, ©Susan Van Etten; pages 298 and 314, ©Mark Richards/Photo Edit; pages 327 and 348, ©Grant LeDuc/Stock Boston; pages 353 and 378, ©Rob Crandall/Stock Boston; pages 383 and 398, ©Susan Van Etten; pages 402 and 419, ©AFP/CORBIS; pages 425 and 445, ©Tony Freeman/Photo Edit; pages 783 and 800, ©Paul Conklin/Photo Edit; pages 805 and 827, ©Miladinovic/Sygma CORBIS.

Executive Editor: Denise Clinton
Acquisitions Editor: Victoria Warneck
Developmental Editor: Rebecca Ferris
Editorial Assistant: Christine Houde
Managing Editor: James Rigney
Senior Production Supervisor: Nancy Fenton
Marketing Manager: Dara Lanier
Senior Media Producer: Melissa Honig
Designer: Regina Hagen
Senior Manufacturing Buyer: Hugh Crawford
Cover Collage Images: ©Digital Vision/PictureQuest; © Robert Cattan/Index Stock Imagery; ©PhotoDisc.
Composition: WestWords, Inc.
Art Studio: ElectraGraphics, Inc.
Printer and Binder: Quebecor World
Cover Printer: Lehigh Lithographers

Library of Congress Cataloging-in-Publication Data

Miller, Roger LeRoy.
  Economics today. The macro view / Roger LeRoy Miller. — 2001-2002 ed.
    p.   cm. — (The Addison-Wesley series in economics)
  Supplemeneted by a companion Web site and a multi-media package, including a CD-ROM.
  Includes index.
  ISBN 0-201-07817-9 (pbk.)
    1. Macroeconomics.   2. Economics.   I. Title. II. Series.
  HB172.5.M54   2000
339—dc21   00-038120

ISBN 0-321-07817-9
12345678910—RNT—0403020100

To David VanHoose,

*Whose help for the past
decade has shown no limits
and for which I remain
eternally grateful.*

R. L. M.

Contents in Brief

IN THIS VOLUME, CHAPTER 18 IS FOLLOWED BY CHAPTER 32.

CONTENTS IN DETAIL

Acknowledgments

I am the most fortunate of economics textbook writers, for I receive the benefit of literally hundreds of suggestions from those of you who use *Economics Today*. I continue to be fully appreciative of the constructive criticisms that you offer. There are some professors who have been asked by my publisher to participate in a more detailed reviewing process of the 2001–2002 Edition. I list them below. I hope that each one of you so listed accepts my sincere appreciation for the fine work that you have done.

Bill Adamson, South Dakota State University

John Allen, Texas A&M University

John Baffoe-Bonnie, Pennsylvania State University

Kevin Baird, Montgomery County Community College

Daniel Benjamin, Clemson University

Abraham Bertisch, Nassau Community College

John Bethune, University of Tennessee

R. A. Blewett, St. Lawrence University

Melvin Borland, Western Kentucky University

James Carlson, Manatee Community College

Robert Carlsson, University of South Carolina

K. Merry Chambers, Central Piedmont Community College

Catherine Chambers, Central Missouri State University

Marc Chopin, Louisiana Tech University

Curtis Clarke, Mountain View College

Jerry Crawford, Arkansas State University

Andrew J. Dane, Angelo State University

Carl Enomoto, New Mexico State University

Abdollah Ferdowsi, Ferris State University

James Gale, Michigan Technical University

Neil Garston, California State University, Los Angeles

William Henderson, Franklin University

Charles W. Hockert, Oklahoma City Community College

Yu Hsing, Southeastern Louisiana University

Scott Hunt, Columbus State Community College

Joseph W. Hunt Jr., Shippensburg University of Pennsylvania

John Ifediora, University of Wisconsin, Platteville

Allan Jenkins, University of Nebraska, Kearney

Alan Kessler, Providence College

James C. McBrearty, University of Arizona

Diego Méndez-Carbajo, Florida International University

Khan Mohabbat, Northern Illinois University

Zuohong Pan, Western Connecticut State University

Ginger Parker, Miami-Dade Community College

Bruce Pietrykowski, University of Michigan, Dearborn

Mannie Poen, Houston Community College

Robert Posatko, Shippensburg University of Pennsylvania

Jaishankar Raman, Valparaiso University

Richard Rawlins, Missouri Southern State College

Charles Roberts, Western Kentucky University

Larry Ross, University of Alaska, Anchorage

Stephen Rubb, Providence College

Henry Ryder, Gloucester County College

Swapan Sen, Christopher Newport University

Garvin Smith, Daytona Beach Community College

Alan Stafford, Niagara County College

Thomas Swanke, West Virginia State College

Lea Templer, College of the Canyons

David VanHoose, University of Alabama

Craig Walker, Delta State University

Mark Wohar, University of Nebraska, Omaha

Tim Wulf, Parkland College

Alex Yguado, Los Angeles Mission College

I also thank the reviewers of previous editions:

Esmond Adams
John Adams
John R. Aidem
Mohammed Akacem
M. C. Alderfer
Ann Al-Yasiri
Leslie J. Anderson
Fatima W. Antar
Aliakbar Ataiifar
Leonard Atencio
Glen W. Atkinson
Thomas R. Atkinson
James Q. Aylesworth
Charley Ballard
Maurice B. Ballabon
G. Jeffrey Barbour
Daniel Barszcz
Robin L. Bartlett
Kari Battaglia
Robert Becker
Charles Beem
Glen Beeson
Charles Berry
Scott Bloom
M. L. Bodnar
Mary Bone
Karl Bonnhi
Thomas W. Bonsor
John M. Booth
Wesley F. Booth
Thomas Borcherding
Tom Boston
Barry Boyer
Maryanna Boynton
Ronald Brandolini
Fenton L. Broadhead
Elba Brown
William Brown
Michael Bull
Maureen Burton
Conrad P. Caligaris
Kevin Carey
Dancy R. Carr
Doris Cash
Thomas H. Cate
Richard J. Cebula
Richard Chapman
Young Back Choi
Carol Cies
Joy L. Clark
Gary Clayton
Marsha Clayton
Warren L. Coats
Ed Coen
Pat Conroy
James Cox
Stephen R. Cox

Eleanor D. Craig
Joanna Cruse
John P. Cullity
Thomas Curtis
Mahmoud Davoudi
Edward Dennis
Carol Dimamro
William Dougherty
Barry Duman
Diane Dumont
Floyd Durham
G. B. Duwaji
James A. Dyal
Ishita Edwards
Robert P. Edwards
Alan E. Ellis
Mike Ellis
Steffany Ellis
Frank Emerson
Zaki Eusufzai
Sandy Evans
John L. Ewing-Smith
Frank Falero
Frank Fato
Grant Ferguson
David Fletcher
James Foley
John Foreman
Ralph G. Fowler
Arthur Friedberg
Peter Frost
E. Gabriel
Steve Gardner
Peter C. Garlick
Alexander Garvin
Joe Garwood
J. P. Gilbert
Otis Gilley
Frank Glesber
Jack Goddard
Allen C. Goodman
Richard J. Gosselin
Edward Greenberg
Gary Greene
Nicholas Grunt
William Gunther
Kwabena Gyimah-
    Brempong
Demos Hadjiyanis
Martin D. Haney
Mehdi Haririan
Ray Harvey
E. L. Hazlett
Sanford B. Helman
John Hensel
Robert Herman
Gus W. Herring

Charles Hill
John M. Hill
Morton Hirsch
Benjamin Hitchner
R. Bradley Hoppes
James Horner
Grover Howard
Nancy Howe-Ford
R. Jack Inch
Christopher Inya
Tomotaka Ishimine
E. E. Jarvis
Parvis Jenab
Mark Jensen
S. D. Jevremovic
J. Paul Jewell
Frederick Johnson
David Jones
Lamar B. Jones
Paul A. Joray
Daniel A. Joseph
Craig Justice
Septimus Kai Kai
Devajyoti Kataky
Timothy R. Keely
Ziad Keilany
Norman F. Keiser
Randall G. Kesselring
E. D. Key
M. Barbara Killen
Bruce Kimzey
Philip G. King
Terrence Kinal
E. R. Kittrell
David Klingman
Charles Knapp
Jerry Knarr
Faik Koray
Janet Koscianski
Peter Kressler
Michael Kupilik
Larry Landrum
Margaret Landman
Keith Langford
Anthony T. Lee
George Lieu
Stephen E. Lile
Lawrence W. Lovick
Akbar Marvasti
Warren T. Matthews
Robert McAuliffe
Howard J. McBride
Bruce McClung
John McDowell
E. S. McKuskey
James J. McLain
John L. Madden

Mary Lou Madden
Glen Marston
John M. Martin
Paul J. Mascotti
James D. Mason
Paul M. Mason
Tom Mathew
Warren Matthews
G. Hartley Mellish
Mike Melvin
Dan C. Messerschmidt
Michael Metzger
Herbert C. Milikien
Joel C. Millonzi
Glenn Milner
Thomas Molloy
Margaret D. Moore
William E. Morgan
Stephen Morrell
Irving Morrissett
James W. Moser
Martin F. Murray
George L. Nagy
Jerome Neadly
James E. Needham
Claron Nelson
Douglas Nettleton
Gerald T. O'Boyle
Lucian T. Orlowski
Diane S. Osborne
Jan Palmer
Gerald Parker
Randall E. Parker
Norm Paul
Raymond A. Pepin
Martin M. Perline
Timothy Perri
Jerry Petr
Maurice Pfannesteil
James Phillips
Raymond J. Phillips
I. James Pickl
Dennis Placone
William L. Polvent
Reneé Prim
Robert W. Pulsinelli
Rod D. Raehsler
Kambriz Raffiee
Sandra Rahman
John Rapp
Gautam Raychaudhuri
Ron Reddall
Mitchell Redlo
Charles Reichhelu
Robert S. Rippey
Ray C. Roberts
Richard Romano

Duane Rosa
Richard Rosenberg
Barbara Ross-Pfeiffer
Philip Rothman
John Roufagalas
Patricia Sanderson
Thomas N. Schaap
William A. Schaeffer
William Schaniel
David Schauer
A. C. Schlenker
Scott J. Schroeder
William Scott
Dan Segebarth
Augustus Shackelford
Richard Sherman Jr.
Liang-rong Shiau
David Shorow
Vishwa Shukla
R. J. Sidwell
David E. Sisk
Alden Smith
Howard F. Smith
Lynn A. Smith
Phil Smith
Steve Smith
William Doyle Smith
Lee Spector
George Spiva
Richard L. Sprinkle
Herbert F. Steeper
Columbus Stephens
William Stine
Allen D. Stone
Osman Suliman
J. M. Sullivan
Rebecca Summary
Joseph L. Swaffar
Frank D. Taylor
Daniel Teferra
Gary Theige
Robert P. Thomas
Deborah Thorsen
Richard Trieff
George Troxler
William T. Trulove
William N. Trumbull
Arianne K. Turner
Kay Unger
John Vahaly
Jim Van Beek
Lee J. Van Scyoc
Roy Van Til
Robert F. Wallace
Henry C. Wallich
Milledge Weathers
Robert G. Welch

Terence West	Mark A. Wilkening	Travis Wilson	Donald Yankovic	Ed Zajicek
Wylie Whalthall	Raburn M. Williams	Ken Woodward	Paul Young	Paul Zarembka
Everett E. White	James Willis	Peter R. Wyman	Shik Young	William J. Zimmer Jr.
Michael D. White	George Wilson	Whitney Yamamura	Mohammed Zaheer	

No major textbook revision can be undertaken without the help of numerous participants. I was fortunate enough to have the assistance of a sterling group of professionals at Addison-Wesley. The executive editor, Denise Clinton, kept the project on point at all times. My developmental editor, Rebecca Ferris, turned out to be a constant source of support, constructive criticism, and innovation. She also took over the job of managing the many new supplements as well as the revisions of the old ones. Nancy Fenton, my tried-and-true production editor, pushed the project through to the very end. Melissa Honig undertook the oversight of all of the multimedia supplements, including the major task of getting the CD-ROM out on time and without errors. I was again blessed by the copyediting efforts of Bruce Emmer, who now seems a permanent part of this book.

Many of my colleagues helped revise the numerous supplements to this text. David Van Hoose undertook developing the new version of the interactive CD-ROM. He not only finished it on time but also did an amazingly complete job of expanding this valuable learning tool. He also helped with the revision of the *Study Guide*. Andrew J. Dane continued to develop the ever-improving *Instructor's Manual* and *Lecture Outlines with Transparency Masters*. I also extend my continuing thanks for his day-to-day support of the Web site. John Ifediora and James Carlson worked tirelessly on new test questions and revisions of old for Test Banks 1 and 2, respectively. Scott Hunt, John Baffoe-Bonnie, and Diego Méndez-Carbajo developed multiple on-line quizzes for each chapter. To all these professors I extend a special note of appreciation.

K&M Consulting, operated by Suzanne Jasin, undertook manuscript preparation and the development of camera-ready copy for many of the supplements. This organization continues to offer the highest quality service and the best turnaround time in the business. I wish to thank the entire K&M staff for their excellent work.

Always more can be done. Contact me with any suggestions at **www.econtoday.com**.

Roger LeRoy Miller

Preface

The 2001–2002 Edition of *Economics Today* presents economic principles within the context of the sweeping changes occurring in the economic landscape, including the Internet explosion and the e-commerce boom, the East Asian recession, the expansion of global trade and investment, and concerns about inflation and rising interest rates closer to home. *Economics Today* clearly outlines the core principles of economics so that students can fully understand and analyze these and other developments.

Economics Today is based on the belief that students learn more when they are involved and engaged. All of the 150 new examples have been selected to grab and hold students' attention. These examples serve one basic purpose—to drive home the application of the theory just presented. You will find the latest theoretical concepts in this 2001–2002 Edition presented in a logical manner for ease of understanding. For more specific details on the presentation of theory, see "Content Changes in the 2001–2002 Edition."

One of the keys to the success of *Economics Today* is that it is suitable for many teaching styles. Instructors who wish to stress theory can do so. Those who wish to stress applications and examples can do that. Those who wish to incorporate technology into the class can do so with ease.

WHAT'S NEW IN THE 2001–2002 EDITION?

- **Chapter 6,** "Your Future with Social Security" This pressing national issue is the subject of a complete chapter that examines the economic problems Social Security and Medicare systems face and possible ways that these programs may be reformed.

- **Chapter 16,** "Electronic Banking" This new chapter focuses on the implications of applications of information technologies in the nation's banking and payment systems. It reviews the recent surge in stored-value and debit cards, the potential for expanded applications of smart-card technologies, and the likely effects of digital cash on the money multiplier.

- **Compelling New Pedagogy NETNOMICS** boxes probe how technological innovations change economic theory and behavior. *FAQ* boxes foster economic intuition by outlining answers to real-world questions. Economics on the Net activities guide students to a Web site and provide a structured assignment for both individual and group work. **TYING IT ALL TOGETHER** case applications wrap up each part by demonstrating the relevance of concepts in a business decision-making context.

- **New Release of Economics in Action** Conveniently packaged with the text, the Economics in Action, 2001–2002 Edition, CD-ROM includes two new modules—on labor economics and on payment systems and electronic banking. New marginal icons in the text direct students to corresponding software modules.

● **www.econtoday.com** The text's dynamic **companion Web site** provides numerous testing resources with tutorial feedback, timely news articles with ready-made discussion questions, an on-line syllabus builder, and virtual office hours. WebCT and Black-Board versions are available.

● **Wired Test Bank** This indispensable aid for professors who are using *Economics Today*'s many technology resources includes test questions based on the Economics in Action modules, end-of-chapter Economics on the Net activities, and Tying It All Together cases' Internet feature.

● **Econ Tutor Center** Order the Econ Tutor Center Edition of *Economics Today* to give your students access to qualified economic instructors via phone, fax, and e-mail.

CONTENT CHANGES IN THE 2001–2002 EDITION

Building on the success of previous editions, the 2001–2002 Edition offers thoroughly updated coverage throughout and two all-new chapters. Every chart, table, and graph has been revised to reflect the most recent data available.

● **Revised and Updated Macro Coverage** The discussion of economic growth in **Chapter 9** is now followed by a focused examination of long-run macroeconomic equilibrium in **Chapter 10**. This lays a solid foundation for evaluating the sources of short-run macroeconomic fluctuations in **Chapter 11**. The coverage of macroeconomic policy-making in the subsequent chapters now has a broader international focus. **Chapters 14, 15, and 33** have been significantly revised to provide more complete and up-to-date discussions of worldwide developments in banking, payment systems, and monetary policy.

● **Revised and Updated Micro Coverage** Here there is also increased emphasis on globalization of markets, particularly in the coverage of the financial environment of business in **Chapter 21** and discussions of market behavior in **Chapters 23–25** and of regulation and antitrust in **Chapter 26**. In addition, **Chapter 21** reviews the growth of electronic securities trading and evaluates economics issues posed by on-line financial trading.

PEDAGOGY WITH PURPOSE

Economics Today, 2001–2002 Edition, provides a fine-tuned teaching and learning system. This system is aimed at capturing student interest through the infusion of examples that capture the vitality of economics. Each of the following features has been carefully crafted to enhance the learning process:

◉ **Chapter-Opening Issues** Each chapter-opening issue whets student interest in core chapter concepts with compelling examples.

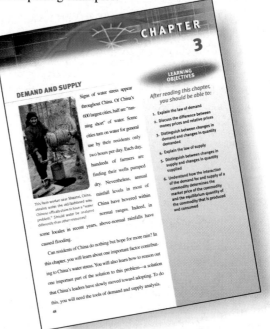

◉ **Did You Know That . . . ?** Each chapter starts with a provocative question to engage students and to lead them into the content of the chapter.

Did You Know That... more than 75 million people currently own portable cellular phones? This is a huge jump from the mere 200,000 who owned them in 1985. Since 1992, two out of every three new telephone numbers have been assigned to cellular phones. There are several reasons for the growth of cellular phones, not the least being the dramatic reduction in both price and size due to improved and cheaper computer chips that go into making them. There is something else at work, though. It has to do with crime. In a recent survey, 46 percent of new cellular phone users said that personal safety was the main reason they bought a portable phone. In Florida, for example, most cellular phone companies allow users simply to dial *FHP to reach the Florida Highway Patrol. The rush to cellular phones is worldwide. Over the past decade, sales have grown by nearly 50 percent every year outside the United States.

We could attempt to explain the phenomenon by saying that more people like to use portable phones. But that explanation is neither satisfying nor entirely accurate. If we use the economist's primary set of tools, *demand and supply*, we will have a better understanding of the cellular phone explosion, as well as many other phenomena in our world. Demand and supply are two ways of categorizing the influences on the price of goods that you buy and the quantities available. As such, demand and supply form the basis of virtually all economic analysis of the world around us.

As you will see throughout this text, the operation of the forces of demand and supply take place in *markets*. A **market** is an abstract concept referring to all the arrangements individuals have for exchanging with one another. Goods and services are sold in markets, such as the automobile market, the health market, and the compact disc market. Workers offer their services in the labor market. Companies, or firms, buy workers' labor services in the labor market. Firms also buy other inputs in order to produce the goods and services that you buy as a consumer. Firms purchase machines, buildings, and land. These markets are in operation at all times. One of the most important activities in these markets is the setting of the prices of all of the inputs and outputs that are bought and sold in our complicated economy. To understand the determination of prices, you first need to look at the law of demand.

- **Learning Objectives** A clear statement of learning objectives on the first page of the chapter focuses students' studies.

- **Chapter Outline** The outline serves as a guide to the chapter coverage.

- **Graphs** Precise, four-color graphs clearly illustrate key concepts.

- **Key Terms** To simplify the task of learning the vocabulary of economics, key terms are printed in bold type and defined in the margin of the text the first time they appear.

- **Policy Examples** Students are exposed to important policy questions on both domestic and international fronts in over 40 policy examples.

POLICY EXAMPLE

Should Shortages in the Ticket Market Be Solved by Scalpers?

If you have ever tried to get tickets to a playoff game in sports, a popular Broadway play, or a superstar's rock concert, you know about "shortages." The standard ticket situation for a Super Bowl is shown in Figure 3-12. At the face-value price of Super Bowl tickets (P_1), the quantity demanded (Q_2) greatly exceeds the quantity supplied (Q_1). Because shortages last only so long as prices and quantities do not change, markets tend to exhibit a movement out of this disequilibrium toward equilibrium. Obviously, the quantity of Super Bowl tickets cannot change, but the price can go as high as P_2.

Enter the scalper. This colorful term is used because when you purchase a ticket that is being resold at a price that is higher than face value, the seller is skimming an extra profit off the top. If an event sells out, ticket prices by definition have been lower than market clearing prices. People without tickets may be willing to buy high-priced tickets because they place a greater value on the entertainment event than the face value of the ticket. Without scalpers, those individuals would not be able to attend the event. In the case of the Super Bowl, various forms of scalping occur nationwide. Tickets for a seat on the 50-yard line have been sold for more than $2,000 a piece. In front of every Super Bowl arena, you can find ticket scalpers hawking their wares.

In most states, scalping is illegal. In Pennsylvania, convicted scalpers are either fined $5,000 or sentenced to two years behind bars. For an economist, such legislation seems strange. As one New York ticket broker said, "I look at scalping like working as a stockbroker, buying low and selling high. If people are willing to pay me the money, what kind of problem is that?"

For Critical Analysis
What happens to ticket scalpers who are still holding tickets after an event has started?

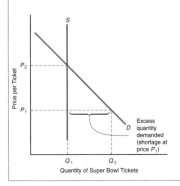

FIGURE 3-12
Shortages of Super Bowl Tickets
The quantity of tickets for any one Super Bowl is fixed at Q_1. At the price per ticket of P_1, the quantity demanded is Q_2, which is greater than Q_1. Consequently, there is an excess quantity demanded at the below-market-clearing price. Prices can go as high as P_2 in the scalpers' market.

- **International Examples** Over 30 international examples emphasize the interconnections of today's global economy.

INTERNATIONAL EXAMPLE

The High Relative Price of a U.S. Education

In 1993, about 40 percent of all college students classified as "international students"—students working toward degrees outside their home countries—were enrolled in U.S. colleges and universities. This figure has shrunk to just over 30 percent today, and it gradually continues to decline.

Have foreign students decided that the quality of American higher education is diminishing? Some may have made this judgment, but a more likely explanation for the falling U.S. share of international students is the higher relative price of a U.S. college education. Throughout the 1990s, tuition and other fees that U.S. colleges and universities charged for their services rose much faster than the average price of other goods and services. They also rose faster than tuition and fees at foreign universities. For instance, even before the sharp 1997–1998 economic contraction in Southeast Asia, increasing numbers of students from this region had begun studying at Australian universities. Colleges in Australia are not only closer to home but also less expensive.

For Critical Analysis
If the relative price of education at U.S. universities continues to increase, what other means could these universities use to try to regain their lost share of international students?

● **Examples** More than 50 thought-provoking and relevant examples highlight U.S. current events and demonstrate economic principles.

EXAMPLE

Garth Brooks, Used CDs, and the Law of Demand

A few years ago, country singer Garth Brooks tried to prevent his latest album from being sold to any chain or store that also sells used CDs. His argument was that the used-CD market deprived labels and artists of earnings. His announcement came after Wherehouse Entertainment, Inc., a 339-store retailer based in Torrance, California, started selling used CDs side by side with new releases, at half the price. Brooks, along with the distribution arms of Sony, Warner Music, Capitol-EMI, and MCA, was trying to quash the used-CD market. By so doing, it appears that none of these parties understands the law of demand.

Let's say the price of a new CD is $15. The existence of a secondary used-CD market means that to people who choose to resell their CDs for $5, the cost of a new CD is in fact only $10. Because we know that quantity demanded is inversely related to price, we know that more of a new CD will be sold at a price of $10 than of the same CD at a price of $15. Taking only this force into account, eliminating the used-CD market tends to reduce sales of new CDs.

But there is another force at work here, too. Used CDs are substitutes for new CDs. If used CDs are not available, some people who would have purchased them will instead purchase new CDs. If this second effect outweighs the incentive to buy less because of the higher effective price, then Brooks is behaving correctly in trying to suppress the used CD market.

For Critical Analysis
Can you apply this argument to the used-book market, in which both authors and publishers have long argued that used books are "killing them"?

● **For Critical Analysis** At the end of each example, students are asked to "think like economists" to answer the critical analysis questions. The answers to all questions are found in the Instructor's Manual.

● **Concepts in Brief** Following each major section, "Concepts in Brief" summarizes the main points of the section to reinforce learning and to encourage rereading of any difficult material.

● **FAQ** All-new sidebars encourage analysis by providing answers to frequently asked questions based on economic reasoning.

> **FAQ**
>
> **_Isn't postage a lot more expensive than it used to be?_**
>
> No, in reality, the _relative price_ of postage in the United States has fallen steadily over the years. The absolute dollar price of a first-class stamp rose from 3 cents in 1940 to 33 cents at the beginning of the twenty-first century. Nevertheless, the price of postage relative to the average of all other prices has declined since reaching a peak in 1975.

See how the U.S. Department of Agriculture seeks to estimate demand and supply conditions for major agricultural products at **http://usda.mannlib. cornell.edu/reports/ waobr/wasde-bb**

● **Internet Resources** Margin notes identify interesting Web sites that illustrate chapter topics, giving students the opportunity to build their economic research skills by accessing the latest information on the national and global economy.

Putting
Economics in Action
to Work

To study market equilibrium in more detail, start the _EIA_ CD, and click on "Demand and Supply." Then click on "Putting Demand and Supply Together."

● **Economics in Action Icon** This marginal element directs students to "Economics in Action" modules corresponding to chapter content.

● **Netnomics** The new "Netnomics" feature explores how innovations in information technology are changing economic theory and behavior.

NETNOMICS

Stealth Attacks by New Technologies

Successful new products often get off to a slow start. Eventually, however, consumers substitute away from the old products to the point at which demand for the old products effectively disappears. Consider handwritten versus printed manuscripts. For several years in the mid-fifteenth century, printed books were a rarity, and manuscript-copying monks and scribes continued to turn out the bulk of written forms of communication. By the 1470s, however, printed books were more common than handwritten manuscripts. By the end of the fifteenth century, manuscripts had become the rare commodity.

A more recent example involves train engines. Just before 1940, after the diesel-electric engine for train locomotives was invented, an executive of a steam-engine company declared, "They'll never replace the steam locomotive." In fact, it only took 20 years to prove the executive wrong. By 1960, steam engines were regarded as mechanical dinosaurs.

To generate the bulk of its profits, the U.S. Postal Service relies on revenues from first-class mail. To keep its first-class customers satisfied, it recently deployed a $5 billion automation system that reads nine addresses per second and paints envelopes with bar codes to speed sorting. Yet the postal service has lost about $4 billion in first-class mail business since 1994. Around that time, people began to compare the 25-cent cost of a one-minute phone call with the 32-cent cost of first-class postage. Then they began to substitute away from first-class letters to faxes. Other people got access to the Internet and began to send messages by electronic mail, at no additional charge. First-class mail increasingly looks like a steam-engine dinosaur.

Some observers of the software industry think the same sort of thing could happen to a powerhouse of the present: Microsoft Windows. Today the code for this program is on most personal computers on the planet. Competing operating system applications offered by Sun Microsystems's Java software and others currently run more slowly than Windows. But they consume many fewer lines of computer code and hence promise swift accessibility via the Internet. It is conceivable that someday people may log on to the Internet and pay by the minute to use such software to run their computers, thereby freeing up their hard drives for other uses. Thus today's dominant operating system may someday look a lot like a handwritten manuscript does to generations accustomed to reading printed books instead of handwritten manuscripts.

● **Issues and Applications** Linked to the chapter-opening issue, the all-new "Issues and Applications" features are designed to encourage students to apply economic concepts to real-world situations. Each outlines the concepts being applied in the context of a particular issue and is followed by several critical thinking questions that may be used to prompt in-class discussion. Suggested answers to the critical thinking questions appear in the Instructor's Manual.

- **Summary Discussion of Learning Objectives** Every chapter ends with a concise, thorough summary of the important concepts organized around the learning objectives presented at the beginning of each chapter.

- **Key Terms** A list of key terms with page references is a handy study device.

- **Problems** A variety of problems support each chapter. Answers for all odd-numbered problems are provided at the back of the textbook.

- **Economics on the Net** Internet activities are designed to build student research skills and reinforce key concepts. The activities guide students to a Web site and provide a structured assignment for both individual and group work.

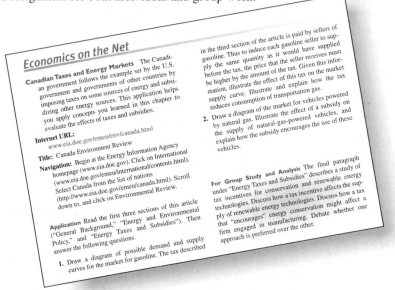

- **Tying It All Together** This new feature captures the themes of each part in an extensive case application that demonstrates the relevance of concepts in a business decision-making context. Accompanying questions probe students to assess key issues and do additional research on the Internet. (The answers to all questions are found in the Instructor's Manual.)

AN EXPANSIVE, INNOVATIVE TEACHING AND LEARNING PACKAGE

Economics Today is accompanied by a variety of technologically innovative and useful supplements for instructors and students.

TO THE INSTRUCTOR

The following supplementary materials are available to help busy instructors teach more effectively and to incorporate technological resources into their principles courses.

- **Instructor's Resource Disk (IRD) with PowerPoint Lecture Presentation** Fully compatible with the Windows NT, 95, and 98, and Macintosh computers, this CD-ROM provides numerous resources.

- The PowerPoint Lecture Presentation was developed by Jeff Caldwell, Steve Smith, and Mark Mitchell of Rose State College and revised by Andrew J. Dane of Angelo State University. With nearly 100 slides per chapter, the PowerPoint Lecture Presentation animates graphs from the text; outlines key terms, concepts, and figures; and provides direct links to **www.econtoday.com** for in-class Internet activities.

- For added convenience, the IRD also includes Microsoft Word files for the entire content of the Instructor's Manual and Computerized Test Bank files. The easy-to-use testing software (**TestGen-EQ with QuizMaster-EQ** for Windows and Macintosh) is a valuable test preparation tool that allows professors to view, edit, and add questions.

- **www.econtoday.com** The *Economics Today* **companion Web site** provides on-line access to innovative teaching and learning tools.

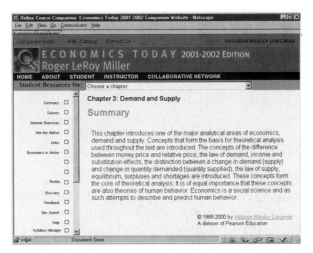

- A number of testing resources are available for your students, including four **multiple-choice quizzes** per chapter and **practice exams** that test their readiness for midterm and final exams. **Tutorial feedback** guides students to the appropriate text sections for further study when they answer questions incorrectly.

- The Companion Web site system provides an **on-line syllabus builder** that allows you to create a calendar of assignments for each class and to track student activity and quiz grades with an electronic gradebook.

● Before class, visit the Web site and print off a **timely news article with ready-made discussion questions** for your students. And a weekly quiz rewards students who follow the news with prizes.

● For added convenience, many of the instructor supplements are available for downloading from the site, including the PowerPoint Lecture Presentation, Computerized Test Bank files, and Instructor's Manual. Please contact your sales representative for the instructor resources password and information on obtaining the **Web content in WebCT and BlackBoard versions**.

● **"Ask the Author"** gives professors and students round-the-clock access to the author.

Economics in Action, 2001–2002 Edition, CD-ROM This interactive tutorial software has been developed by Michael Parkin and Robin Bade of the University of Western Ontario. Adapted by David VanHoose of the University of Alabama for use with *Economics Today*, the software is conveniently packaged with the text and includes two all-new modules on labor economics and on payment systems and electronic banking. The market leader in principles of economics software, Economics in Action aids students' mastery of concepts through review, demonstration, and interaction. Step-by-step tutorials guide students in their discovery of the relationship between economic theory and real-world applications, while the Draw Graph palette tests their graphing abilities. Detailed, customizable quizzes help students prepare for exams by testing their grasp of concepts.

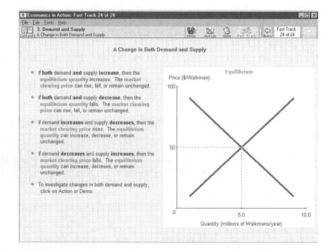

● **Instructor's Manual** Prepared by Andrew J. Dane of Angelo State University, the Instructor's Manual provides the following materials:
   ● Chapter overviews, objectives, and outlines
   ● Points to emphasize for those who wish to stress theory
   ● Answers to "Issues and Applications" critical thinking questions
   ● Further questions for class discussion
   ● Answers to even-numbered end-of-chapter problems
   ● Detailed step-by-step analysis of end-of-chapter problems
   ● Suggested answers to "Tying It All Together" case questions
   ● Annotated answers to selected student learning questions
   ● Selected references

- **Test Bank 1** This Test Bank provides over 3,000 multiple-choice questions and more than 250 short-essay questions with answers. Revised by John Ifediora of the University of Wisconsin, the questions have been extensively classroom-tested for a number of years.

- **Test Bank 2** Revised by James R. Carlson of Manatee Community College, this test bank includes over 3,000 multiple-choice questions and more than 250 short-essay questions. These questions have been class-tested by many professors, including Clark G. Ross, coauthor of the National Competency Test for economics majors for the Educational Testing Service in Princeton, New Jersey.

- **NEW** **Wired Test Bank** This all-new, innovative supplement is an indispensable aid for professors who are incorporating *Economics Today*'s many technology resources into their courses. It includes questions that allow you to test students on the "Economics in Action" modules, end-of-chapter "Economics on the Net" activities, and "Tying It All Together" cases' Internet feature.

- **Lecture Outlines with Transparency Masters** Prepared by Andrew J. Dane of Angelo State University, this lecture system features more than 500 pages of lecture outlines and text illustrations, including numerous tables taken from the text. Its pages can be made into transparencies or handouts to assist student note taking.

- **Four-Color Overhead Transparencies** One hundred of the most important graphs from the textbook are reproduced as full-color transparency acetates. Many contain multiple overlays.

- **Economics Experiments in the Classroom** Developed by Denise Hazlett of Whitman College, these economics experiments involve students in actively testing economic theory. In addition to providing a variety of micro and macro experiments, this supplement offers step-by-step guidelines for successfully running experiments in the classroom.

- **Additional Homework Problems** For each text chapter, more than 20 additional problems are provided in two separate sets of homework assignments that are available for download from **www.econtoday.com**. Each homework problem is accompanied by suggested answers.

- **Regional Case Studies for the East Coast, Texas, and California** Additional case studies, available at **www.econtoday.com**, can be used for in-class team exercises or for additional homework assignments.

- **Pocket Guide to Economics Today for Printed and Electronic Supplements** The Pocket Guide is designed to coordinate the extensive teaching and learning package that accompanies the 2001–2002 Edition of *Economics Today*. For each chapter heading, the author has organized a list of print and electronic ancillaries with page references to help organize lectures, develop class assignments, and prepare examinations.

- **NEW** **Econ Tutor Center** Order the Econ Tutor Center Edition of *Economics Today* to give your students help when you are not available. Five days a week, qualified economics instructors answer questions via phone, fax, and e-mail, all at no additional cost for students who purchase a new textbook. Contact your local sales representative for details.

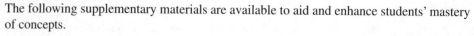

TO THE STUDENT

The following supplementary materials are available to aid and enhance students' mastery of concepts.

- **Study Guide** Available in micro, macro, and complete versions, the Study Guide has been written by the author and updated by David VanHoose. This valuable guide offers the practice and review students need to succeed. It has been thoroughly revised to take into account the significant changes in many of the chapters of the 2001–2002 Edition. Review questions now are focused on issues appropriate for the 2000s, and the Study Guide is firmly oriented toward helping students learn what they need to know to succeed in the course—and in life.

- **Student Study Notes for PowerPoint Lecture Presentation** Developed by Jeff Caldwell of Rose State College and updated by Andrew J. Dane of Angelo State University, the Student Study Notes are a valuable note-taking and study device.

- **www.econtoday.com** The *Economics Today* **companion Web site** provides on-line access to effective learning tools.
  - Test your mastery of concepts by taking the four multiple-choice quizzes per chapter that offer instant results and tutorial feedback. Practice exams gauge your readiness for midterm and final exams.
  - Keep up to date with news headlines with the "Economics Today" article feature—and win prizes by taking a weekly current events quiz.
  - "Ask the Author" gives you round-the-clock access to the author. For added convenience, all the in-text Internet references and "Economics on the Net" activities are on the Web site for easy navigation.

- **Economics in Action, 2001–2002 Edition, CD-ROM** This interactive tutorial software is conveniently packaged with the text. The market leader in principles of economics software, Economics in Action aids mastery of concepts through review, demonstration, and interaction. See how changing conditions cause curves to shift. Test your graphing abilities with the Draw Graph palette. And prepare for exams with detailed, customizable quizzes. New to the 2001–2002 Edition of Economics in Action are units on labor economics and electronic banking and payments.

- **Your Economic Life** Available at **www.econtoday.com**, this booklet offers numerous practical applications of economics and guidance for analyzing economic news.

Part 1
Introduction

THE NATURE OF ECONOMICS

Men who are married earn, on average, higher incomes than those who are not married. Does this marriage premium mean that if you are single and decide to get married, you will automatically make a higher income?

After reading this chapter, you should be able to:

1. Discuss the difference between microeconomics and macroeconomics

2. Evaluate the role that rational self-interest plays in economic analysis

3. Explain why the study of economics is a science

4. Distinguish between positive and normative economics

In 1911, Edgar Watson Howe wrote, "Marriage is a good deal like a circus: There is not as much in it as is represented by the advertising." Nevertheless, for men (but not, apparently, for women), marriage has a concrete payoff: earnings 10 to 20 percent higher than those of unmarried men. Economists call this wage differential the "marriage premium."

One rationale for the marriage premium is that by settling down, men are able to be more successful in their careers. Another theory, however, is that the women do a good job of selecting their husbands. That is, women choose to marry men who are more successful than the men they choose not to marry.

Whether it is men deciding to marry for the good of their careers or women selecting a successful marriage partner, both make *choices*. A fundamental aspect of the science of economics is seeking to understand how people make choices.

Did You Know That... since 1989, the number of fax machines in U.S. offices and homes has increased by over 10,000 percent? During the same time period, the number of bike messengers in downtown New York City *decreased* by over 65 percent. The world around us is definitely changing. Much of that change is due to the dramatically falling cost of communications and information technology. Today the computers inside video games cost only about $100 yet have 50 times the processing power that a $10 million IBM mainframe had in 1975. Not surprisingly, American firms have been spending more on communications equipment and computers than on new construction and heavy machinery.

Cyberspace, the Internet, the World Wide Web—call it what you want, but your next home (if not your current one) will almost certainly have an address on it. The percentage of U.S. households that have at least one telephone is close to 100 percent, and those that have video game players is over 50 percent. Over half of homes have personal computers, and more than two-thirds of those machines are set up to receive and access information via phone lines. Your decisions about such things as when and what type of computer to buy, whether to accept a collect call from a friend traveling in Europe, and how much time you should invest in learning to use the latest Web browser involve an untold number of variables: where you live, the work your parents do, what your friends think, and so on. But as you will see, there are economic underpinnings for nearly all the decisions you make.

THE POWER OF ECONOMIC ANALYSIS

Knowing that an economic problem exists every time you make a decision is not enough. You also have to develop a framework that will allow you to analyze solutions to each economic problem—whether you are trying to decide how much to study, which courses to take, whether to finish school, or whether America should send troops abroad or raise tariffs. The framework that you will learn in this text is based on the *economic way of thinking*.

This framework gives you power—the power to reach informed conclusions about what is happening in the world. You can, of course, live your life without the power of economic analysis as part of your analytical framework. Indeed, most people do. But economists believe that economic analysis can help you make better decisions concerning your career, your education, financing your home, and other important matters. In the business world, the power of economic analysis can help you increase your competitive edge as an employee or as the owner of a business. As a voter, for the rest of your life you will be asked to make judgments about policies that are advocated by a particular political party. Many of these policies will deal with questions related to international economics, such as whether the U.S. government should encourage or discourage immigration, prevent foreigners from investing in domestic TV stations and newspapers, or restrict other countries from selling their goods here. Finally, just as taking an art, music, or literature appreciation class increases the pleasure you receive when you view paintings, listen to concerts, or read novels, taking an economics course will increase your understanding when watching the news on TV or reading the newspaper.

DEFINING ECONOMICS

What is economics exactly? Some cynics have defined *economics* as "common sense made difficult." But common sense, by definition, should be within everyone's grasp. You will encounter in the following pages numerous examples that show that economics is, in fact, pure and simple common sense.

Economics is part of the social sciences and as such seeks explanations of real events. All social sciences analyze human behavior, as opposed to the physical sciences, which generally analyze the behavior of electrons, atoms, and other nonhuman phenomena.

> Economics is the study of how people allocate their limited resources in an attempt to satisfy their unlimited wants. As such, economics is the study of how people make choices.

To understand this definition fully, two other words need explaining: *resources* and *wants*. **Resources** are things that have value and, more specifically, are used to produce things that satisfy people's wants. **Wants** are all of the things that people would consume if they had unlimited income.

Whenever an individual, a business, or a nation faces alternatives, a choice must be made, and economics helps us study how those choices are made. For example, you have to choose how to spend your limited income. You also have to choose how to spend your limited time. You may have to choose how much of your company's limited funds to spend on advertising and how much to spend on new-product research. In economics, we examine situations in which individuals choose how to do things, when to do things, and with whom to do them. Ultimately, the purpose of economics is to explain choices.

Economics
The study of how people allocate their limited resources to satisfy their unlimited wants.

Resources
Things used to produce other things to satisfy people's wants.

Wants
What people would buy if their incomes were unlimited.

MICROECONOMICS VERSUS MACROECONOMICS

Economics is typically divided into two types of analysis: **microeconomics** and **macroeconomics.**

> Microeconomics is the part of economic analysis that studies decision making undertaken by individuals (or households) and by firms. It is like looking through a microscope to focus on the small parts of our economy.

> Macroeconomics is the part of economic analysis that studies the behavior of the economy as a whole. It deals with economywide phenomena such as changes in unemployment, the general price level, and national income.

Microeconomics
The study of decision making undertaken by individuals (or households) and by firms.

Macroeconomics
The study of the behavior of the economy as a whole, including such economywide phenomena as changes in unemployment, the general price level, and national income.

Microeconomic analysis, for example, is concerned with the effects of changes in the price of gasoline relative to that of other energy sources. It examines the effects of new taxes on a specific product or industry. If price controls were reinstituted in the United States, how individual firms and consumers would react to them would be in the realm of microeconomics. The raising of wages by an effective union strike would also be analyzed using the tools of microeconomics.

By contrast, issues such as the rate of inflation, the amount of economywide unemployment, and the yearly growth in the output of goods and services in the nation all fall into the realm of macroeconomic analysis. In other words, macroeconomics deals with **aggregates,** or totals—such as total output in an economy.

Be aware, however, of the blending of microeconomics and macroeconomics in modern economic theory. Modern economists are increasingly using microeconomic analysis—the study of decision making by individuals and by firms—as the basis of macroeconomic analysis. They do this because even though in macroeconomic analysis aggregates are being examined, those aggregates are the result of choices made by individuals and firms.

Aggregates
Total amounts or quantities; aggregate demand, for example, is total planned expenditures throughout a nation.

THE ECONOMIC PERSON: RATIONAL SELF-INTEREST

Economists assume that individuals act *as if* motivated by self-interest and respond predictably to opportunities for gain. This central insight of economics was first clearly articulated by Adam Smith in 1776. Smith wrote in his most famous book, *An Inquiry into the*

To explore whether it is in a consumer's self-interest to shop on the Internet, go to **www.ecominfocenter.com**, and click on "To e-shoppers."

Nature and Causes of the Wealth of Nations, that "it is not from the benevolence of the butcher, the brewer, or the baker that we expect our dinner, but from their regard to their own interest." Otherwise stated, the typical person about whom economists make behavioral predictions is assumed to act as though motivated by self interest. Because monetary benefits and costs of actions are often the most easily measured, economists most often make behavioral predictions about individuals' responses to ways to increase their wealth, measured in money terms. Let's see if we can apply the theory of rational self-interest to explain an anomaly concerning the makeup of the U.S. population.

EXAMPLE

The Increasing Native American Population

Look at Figure 1-1. You see that the proportion of Native Americans increased quite dramatically from 1970 to 1990. Can we use Adam Smith's ideas to understand why so many Native Americans have decided to rejoin their tribes? Perhaps. Consider the benefits of being a member of the Mdewakanton *(bday-WAH-kan-toon),* a tribe of about 100 that runs a casino in which gamblers in a recent year wagered over $500 million. Each member of the tribe received over $400,000 from the casino's profits. There is now a clear economic reason for Native Americans to return home. Over 200 of the nation's 544

tribes have introduced gambling of some sort, and almost half of those have big-time casinos. Reservations are grossing almost $6 billion a year from gaming. Tribe members sometimes get direct payments and others get the benefits of better health care, subsidized mortgages, and jobs. Self-identified Native Americans increased in number by 150 percent between 1970 and 2000.

For Critical Analysis
What nonmonetary reasons are there for Native Americans to rejoin their tribes?

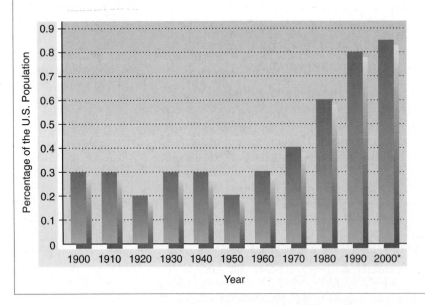

FIGURE 1-1
Native American Population of the United States
The percentage of the U.S. population identifying itself as Native American has increased substantially in recent decades. Is there an economic explanation for this demographic trend?

* Data for 2000 based on author's estimate

The Rationality Assumption

Rationality assumption
The assumption that people do not intentionally make decisions that would leave them worse off.

The **rationality assumption** of economics, simply stated, is as follows:

We assume that individuals do not intentionally make decisions that would leave them worse off.

The distinction here is between what people may think—the realm of psychology and psychiatry and perhaps sociology—and what they do. Economics does *not* involve itself in analyzing individual or group thought processes. Economics looks at what people actually do in life with their limited resources. It does little good to criticize the rationality assumption by stating, "Nobody thinks that way" or "I never think that way" or "How unrealistic! That's as irrational as anyone can get!"

Take the example of driving. When you consider passing another car on a two-lane highway with oncoming traffic, you have to make very quick decisions: You must estimate the speed of the car that you are going to pass, the speed of the oncoming cars, the distance between your car and the oncoming cars, and your car's potential rate of acceleration. If we were to apply a model to your behavior, we would use the rules of calculus. In actual fact, you and most other drivers in such a situation do not actually think of using the rules of calculus, but to predict your behavior, we could make the prediction *as if* you understood the rules of calculus.

In any event, when you observe behavior around you, what may seem irrational often has its basis in the rationality assumption, as you can see by the following example.

EXAMPLE

When It May Be Rational *Not* to Learn New Technology

The standard young person's view of older people (particularly one's parents) is that they're reluctant to learn new things. The saying "You can't teach an old dog new tricks" seems to apply. Young people, in contrast, seem eager to learn about new technology—mastering computers and multimedia, playing interactive games, surfing the Internet. But there can be a rational reason for older people's reduced willingness to learn new technologies. If you are 20 years old and learn a new skill, you will be able to gain returns from your invest-

ment in learning over the course of many decades. If you are 60, however, and invest the same amount of time and effort learning the same skill, you will almost certainly not be able to reap those returns for as long a time period. Hence it can be perfectly rational for "old dogs" not to want to learn new tricks.

For Critical Analysis

Some older people do learn to use new technologies as they emerge. What might explain this behavior?

Responding to Incentives

If it can be assumed that individuals never intentionally make decisions that would leave them worse off, then almost by definition they will respond to different incentives. We define **incentives** as the potential rewards available if a particular activity is undertaken. Indeed, much of human behavior can be explained in terms of how individuals respond to changing incentives over time.

Incentives
Rewards for engaging in a particular activity.

Schoolchildren are motivated to do better by a variety of incentive systems, ranging from gold stars and certificates of achievement when they are young to better grades with accompanying promises of a "better life" as they get older. There are, of course, negative incentives that affect our behavior, too. Children who disrupt the class are given after-school detention or sent to the vice principal for other punishment. Young people, like adults, respond to incentives.

For instance, consider the juvenile criminal justice system. Between the late 1970s and the mid-1990s, the number of arrests of adults for murder fell by 7 percent, but juvenile murder arrests increased by 177 percent. Arrests of juveniles for all violent crimes rose by 79 percent during the period, nearly three times the increase in adult arrests for these crimes.

Steven Levitt of the University of Chicago examined the incentives that juvenile criminals face. While the average number of adults incarcerated per violent crime rose by

60 percent over the same period, the corresponding ratio of juveniles imprisoned in youth detention centers *declined* by 20 percent. Levitt concluded that the probability of a juvenile offender's being jailed was less than half the probability of imprisonment that an adult faced.

Levitt also found changes in criminal behavior when youths face adult criminal justice at age 18. In states where incarceration rates for youths are high but those for adults are low, violent crimes committed by 18-year-olds rise by 23 percent. But crimes committed by 18-year-olds *fall* by 4 percent in states where incarceration rates for adults are relatively high.

Implicitly, all people, including juveniles contemplating crime, react to changing incentives after they have done some sort of rough comparison of the costs and benefits of various courses of action. In fact, making rational choices invariably involves balancing costs and benefits.

The linked concepts of incentives and costs and benefits can be used to explain much human behavior in the world around us. It can also explain how government policies can *induce* people to break the law.

INTERNATIONAL POLICY EXAMPLE

Chinese Smuggling

Recently, China's leaders announced the formation of a new antismuggling police force to try to stop the annual flow of tens of billions of dollars in illegal contraband.

One example of "illegal contraband" is cigarettes. Domestic taxes on cigarettes are so high that many Chinese cigarette manufacturers export half of their output, which they then smuggle back into China. Another example is diesel oil, the price of which the Chinese government sets at levels above prices elsewhere in the world. This gives consumers of diesel oil an incentive to smuggle foreign-produced diesel oil into the country.

Why does China need an antismuggling police force when it already has an army of border guards and customs inspectors? The answer is that the returns to smuggling are so high that many existing border guards and customs inspectors have become smugglers themselves. Thus the government feels that new police are needed in part to watch over the existing cadre of "law enforcers."

For Critical Analysis
What actions could the government take to end the incentives to smuggle cigarettes and diesel oil?

Defining Self-Interest

Self-interest does not always mean increasing one's wealth measured in dollars and cents. We assume that individuals seek many goals, not just increased wealth measured in monetary terms. Thus the self-interest part of our economic-person assumption includes goals relating to prestige, friendship, love, power, helping others, creating works of art, and many other matters. We can also think in terms of enlightened self-interest whereby individuals, in the pursuit of what makes them better off, also achieve the betterment of others around them. In brief, individuals are assumed to want the right to further their goals by making decisions about how things around them are used. The head of a charitable organization will usually not turn down an additional contribution because accepting it gains control over how that money is used, even if it is for other people's benefit.

Otherwise stated, charitable acts are not ruled out by self-interest. Giving gifts to relatives can be considered a form of charity that is nonetheless in the self-interest of the giver. But how efficient is such gift giving?

EXAMPLE

The Perceived Value of Gifts

Every holiday season, aunts, uncles, grandparents, mothers, and fathers give gifts to their college-aged loved ones. Joel Waldfogel, an economist at Yale University, surveyed several thousand college students after Christmas to find out the value of holiday gifts. He found that compact discs and outerwear (coats and jackets) had a perceived intrinsic value about equal to their actual cash equivalent. By the time he got down the list to socks, underwear, and cosmetics, the stu-

dents' valuation was only about 85 percent of the cash value of the gift. He found out that aunts, uncles, and grandparents gave the "worst" gifts and friends, siblings, and parents gave the "best."

For Critical Analysis

What argument could you use against the idea of substituting cash or gift certificates for physical gifts?

CONCEPTS IN BRIEF

● Economics is a social science that involves the study of how individuals choose among alternatives to satisfy their wants, which are what people would buy if their incomes were unlimited.

● Microeconomics, the study of the decision-making processes of individuals (or households) and firms, and macroeconomics, the study of the performance of the economy as a whole, are the two main branches into which the study of economics is divided.

● In economics, we assume that people do not intentionally make decisions that will leave them worse off. This is known as the rationality assumption.

● Self-interest is not confined to material well-being but also involves any action that makes a person feel better off, such as having more friends, love, power, affection, or providing more help to others.

ECONOMICS AS A SCIENCE

Economics is a social science that employs the same kinds of methods used in other sciences, such as biology, physics, and chemistry. Like these other sciences, economics uses models, or theories. Economic **models,** or **theories,** are simplified representations of the real world that we use to help us understand, explain, and predict economic phenomena in the real world. There are, of course, differences between sciences. The social sciences—especially economics—make little use of laboratory methods in which changes in variables can be explained under controlled conditions. Rather, social scientists, and especially economists, usually have to examine what has already happened in the real world in order to test their models, or theories.

Models, or theories
Simplified representations of the real world used as the basis for predictions or explanations.

Models and Realism

At the outset it must be emphasized that no model in *any* science, and therefore no economic model, is complete in the sense that it captures *every* detail or interrelationship that exists. Indeed, a model, by definition, is an abstraction from reality. It is conceptually impossible to construct a perfectly complete realistic model. For example, in physics we cannot account for every molecule and its position and certainly not for every atom and subparticle. Not only is such a model impossibly expensive to build, but working with it would be impossibly complex.

The nature of scientific model building is such that the model should capture only the *essential* relationships that are sufficient to analyze the particular problem or answer the particular question with which we are concerned. *An economic model cannot be faulted as unrealistic simply because it does not represent every detail of the real world.* A map of a city that shows only major streets is not necessarily unrealistic if, in fact, all you need to know is how to pass through the city using major streets. As long as a model is realistic in terms of shedding light on the *central* issue at hand or forces at work, it may be useful.

A map is the quintessential model. It is always a simplified representation. It is always unrealistic. But it is also useful in making (refutable) predictions about the world. If the model—the map—predicts that when you take Campus Avenue to the north, you always run into the campus, that is a (refutable) prediction. If our goal is to explain observed behavior, the simplicity or complexity of the model we use is irrelevant. If a simple model can explain observed behavior in repeated settings just as well as a complex one, the simple model has some value and is probably easier to use.

Assumptions

Every model, or theory, must be based on a set of assumptions. Assumptions define the set of circumstances in which our model is most likely to be applicable. When scientists predicted that sailing ships would fall off the edge of the earth, they used the *assumption* that the earth was flat. Columbus did not accept the implications of such a model. He assumed that the world was round. The real-world test of his own model refuted the flat-earth model. Indirectly, then, it was a test of the assumption of the flat-earth model.

EXAMPLE

Getting Directions

Assumptions are a shorthand for reality. Imagine that you have decided to drive from your home in San Diego to downtown San Francisco. Because you have never driven this route, you decide to get directions from the local office of the American Automobile Association (AAA).

When you ask for directions, the travel planner could give you a set of detailed maps that shows each city through which you will travel—Oceanside, San Clemente, Irvine, Anaheim, Los Angeles, Bakersfield, Modesto, and so on—and then, opening each map, show you exactly how the freeway threads through each of these cities. You would get a nearly complete description of reality because the AAA travel planner will not have used many simplifying assumptions. It is

more likely, however, that the travel planner will simply say, "Get on Interstate 5 going north. Stay on it for about 500 miles. Follow the signs for San Francisco. After crossing the toll bridge, take any exit marked 'Downtown.'" By omitting all of the trivial details, the travel planner has told you all that you really need and want to know. The models you will be using in this text are similar to the simplified directions on how to drive from San Diego to San Francisco—they focus on what is relevant to the problem at hand and omit what is not.

For Critical Analysis

In what way do small talk and gossip represent the use of simplifying assumptions?

The *Ceteris Paribus* Assumption: All Other Things Being Equal.   Everything in the world seems to relate in some way to everything else in the world. It would be impossible to isolate the effects of changes in one variable on another variable if we always had to worry about the many other variables that might also enter the analysis. As in other sciences, economics uses the ***ceteris paribus*** **assumption.** *Ceteris paribus* means "other things constant" or "other things equal."

Ceteris paribus [KAY-ter-us PEAR-uh-bus] assumption
The assumption that nothing changes except the factor or factors being studied.

Consider an example taken from economics. One of the most important determinants of how much of a particular product a family buys is how expensive that product is relative to other products. We know that in addition to relative prices, other factors influence decisions about making purchases. Some of them have to do with income, others with tastes, and yet others with custom and religious beliefs. Whatever these other factors are, we hold them constant when we look at the relationship between changes in prices and changes in how much of a given product people will purchase.

Deciding on the Usefulness of a Model

We generally do not attempt to determine the usefulness, or "goodness," of a model merely by evaluating how realistic its assumptions are. Rather, we consider a model good if it yields usable predictions and implications for the real world. In other words, can we use the model to predict what will happen in the world around us? Does the model provide useful implications of how things happen in our world?

Once we have determined that the model does predict real-world phenomena, the scientific approach to the analysis of the world around us requires that we consider evidence. Evidence is used to test the usefulness of a model. This is why we call economics an **empirical** science, *empirical* meaning that evidence (data) is looked at to see whether we are right. Economists are often engaged in empirically testing their models.

Empirical
Relying on real-world data in evaluating the usefulness of a model.

Consider two competing models for the way students act when doing complicated probability problems to choose the best gambles. One model predicts that based on the assumption of rational self-interest, students who are paid more money for better performance will in fact perform better on average during the experiment. A competing model might be that students whose last names start with the letters *A* through *L* will do better than students with last names starting with *M* through *Z,* irrespective of how much they are paid. The model that consistently predicts more accurately is the model that we would normally choose. In this example, the "alphabet" model did not work well: The first letter of the last name of the students who actually did the experiment at UCLA was irrelevant in predicting how well they would perform the mathematical calculations necessary to choose the correct gambles. On average, students who received higher cash payments for better gambles did choose a higher percentage of better gambles. Thus the model based on rational self-interest predicted well.

Models of Behavior, Not Thought Processes

Take special note of the fact that economists' models do not relate to the way people *think;* they relate to the way people *act,* to what they do in life with their limited resources. Models tend to generalize human behavior. Normally, the economist does not attempt to predict how people will think about a particular topic, such as a higher price of oil products, accelerated inflation, or higher taxes. Rather, the task at hand is to

 FAQ

Can economists rely on opinion polls to understand what motivates behavior?

No, most economists are leery of trying to glean much from opinion polls. For instance, a psychology study once revolved around polls asking people at various income levels how "happy" they were, based on a scale of 1 to 10. The researchers who conducted the study received responses that appeared to indicate that many rich people were less happy, leading the researchers to conclude that wealth can be associated with lower satisfaction. Economics is a science of *revealed* preferences, however. We find out virtually no useful information by asking people to rate their happiness levels on an arbitrary scale. In response to this particular study, a typical economist would note that if "too much" wealth makes people unhappy, they can always give it away. No one forces them to keep it. The fact that we rarely observe people disposing of their wealth causes an economist to infer that higher wealth must be preferred to lower wealth.

predict how people will act, which may be quite different from what they *say* they will do (much to the consternation of poll takers and market researchers). The people involved in examining thought processes are psychologists and psychiatrists, not typically economists.

EXAMPLE

Incentives Work for Pigeons and Rats, Too

Researchers at Texas A&M University did a series of experiments with pigeons and rats. They allowed them to "purchase" food and drink by pushing various levers. The "price" was the number of times a lever had to be pushed. A piece of cheese required 10 pushes, a drop of root beer only one. The "incomes" that the animals were given equaled a certain number of total pushes per day. Once the income was used up, the levers did not work. The researchers discovered that holding income con- stant, when the price of cheese went down, the animals purchased more cheese. Similarly, they found that when the price of root beer was increased, the animals pur- chased less root beer. These are exactly the predictions that we make about human behavior.

For Critical Analysis
"People respond to incentives." Is this assumption also usable in the animal world?

POSITIVE VERSUS NORMATIVE ECONOMICS

Economics uses *positive analysis,* a value-free approach to inquiry. No subjective or moral judgments enter into the analysis. Positive analysis relates to statements such as "If A, then B." For example, "If the price of gasoline goes up relative to all other prices, then the amount of it that people will buy will fall." That is a positive economic statement. It is a statement of *what is.* It is not a statement of anyone's value judgment or subjective feelings. For many problems analyzed in the hard sciences such as physics and chemistry, the analy- ses are considered to be virtually value-free. After all, how can someone's values enter into a theory of molecular behavior? But economists face a different problem. They deal with the behavior of individuals, not molecules. That makes it more difficult to stick to what we consider to be value-free or **positive economics** without reference to our feelings.

When our values are interjected into the analysis, we enter the realm of **normative economics,** involving *normative analysis.* A positive economic statement is "If the price of gas rises, people will buy less." If we add to that analysis the statement "so we should not allow the price to go up," we have entered the realm of normative economics—we have expressed a value judgment. In fact, any time you see the word *should,* you will know that values are entering into the discussion. Just remember that positive statements are con- cerned with *what is,* whereas normative statements are concerned with *what ought to be.*

Each of us has a desire for different things. That means that we have different values. When we express a value judgment, we are simply saying what we prefer, like, or desire. Because individual values are diverse, we expect—and indeed observe—people express- ing widely varying value judgments about how the world ought to be.

Positive economics
Analysis that is strictly limited to making either purely descriptive statements or scientific predic- tions; for example, "If A, then B." A statement of *what is.*

Normative economics
Analysis involving value judg- ments about economic policies; relates to whether things are good or bad. A statement of *what ought to be.*

A Warning: Recognize Normative Analysis

It is easy to define positive economics. It is quite another matter to catch all unlabeled nor- mative statements in a textbook, even though an author goes over the manuscript many times before it is printed. Therefore, do not get the impression that a textbook author will be able to keep all personal values out of the book. They will slip through. In fact, the very choice of which topics to include in an introductory textbook involves normative economics. There is no value-free, or objective, way to decide which topics to use in a textbook. The author's values ultimately make a difference when choices have to be made. But from your own standpoint, you might want to be able to recognize when you are engaging in normative as opposed to positive economic analysis. Reading this text will help equip you for that task.

CONCEPTS IN BRIEF

- A model, or theory, uses assumptions and is by nature a simplification of the real world. The usefulness of a model can be evaluated by bringing empirical evidence to bear on its predictions.

- Models are not necessarily deficient simply because they are unrealistic and use simplifying assumptions, for every model in every science requires simplification compared to the real world.

- Most models use the *ceteris paribus* assumption, that all other things are held constant, or equal.

- Positive economics is value-free and relates to statements that can be refuted, such as "If A, then B." Normative economics involves people's values, and normative statements typically contain the word *should*.

NETNOMICS

Is It Irrational for People to Pay Amazon.com More for a Book They Can Buy for Less at Books.com?

To try to understand how consumers respond to changing incentives they face now that they can purchase goods and services on the Internet, Erik Brynjolfsson and Michael Smith of the Massachusetts Institute of Technology gathered more than 10,000 observations of the prices charged by traditional brick-and-mortar bookstores and Internet booksellers. What they found was what most economists would predict: The lower costs faced by Internet booksellers allowed them to charge about 8 percent less for a given book than traditional bookstores. Furthermore, the cost advantage of Internet booksellers allowed them to gain market share at the expense of traditional stores. (Indeed, some brick-and-mortar bookstores initially included in the study went out of business before the study ended.)

One finding seemed surprising, however. Amazon.com, which garnered an 80 percent share of all Internet-based book sales, charged an average of $1.60 more per book than Books.com, another Internet bookseller (now part of barnesandnoble.com). Yet Books.com could not seem to push its market share much above 2 percent during the period of the study. On the surface, this seemed to imply irrational consumers. After all, wouldn't everyone want to choose Books.com and save $1.60 per book?

As the authors point out, this would be true only if the *ceteris paribus* assumption had been satisfied. In their study, however, it was not. For one thing, Amazon.com spent a considerable amount on advertising and got a jump start on its Internet competitors. Indeed, even today, a great many Internet users have heard of Amazon.com but are unfamiliar with its competitors. This made Brynjolfsson and Smith wonder if perhaps people felt confident that Amazon.com really would deliver but might not have as much faith in less well-known Internet companies. Thus part of the $1.60 difference in the average price of a book might amount to a "trust premium." Furthermore, Brynjolfsson and Smith's study did not take into account differences in features of the two companies' Web sites. If people already knew how to use the Amazon.com Web site, then a legitimate question to ask is, would the average person consider $1.60 enough to compensate for having to learn how to order a book from another Web site?

Marriage Isn't a Marxist Utopia, but It Can Pay Off

Concepts Applied

Decision Making

Rational Self-Interest

Incentives

Karl Marx was a German economist who wrote a treatise called *Das Kapital* (Capital), in which he proposed that labor is the fundamental source of all value. With Friedrich Engels, he wrote an even more famous book, *The Communist Manifesto,* in which he promoted the virtues of state socialism. Economists largely have rejected his theory of value as overly narrow, and communism is on the decline worldwide. Nevertheless, Marx left a lasting legacy: the idea that people could achieve a perfect world, commonly called a *utopia.* The word was coined by Sir Thomas More in his book about a fictitious island by that name. More called his land Utopia (Greek for "no place") because he knew that a perfect world is impossible to achieve.

Nevertheless, on their wedding day, many women and men think they are entering a personal utopia: They convince themselves that they are embarking on the "perfect marriage." Jennifer Roback Morse of the Hoover Institution has written, "Utopianism in politics is destructive: Perfectionism in human relationships can be, too. The Marxist search for a perfect society has cost millions of lives. The American yearning for perfect marriages probably has ruined many lives."

Marriage as an Exercise in Self-Interest

A number of couples, however, remain married for decades even when they know that their marriages are imperfect. To outsiders looking at such a married couple and observing one spouse silently suffering for years while the other spouse continually behaves in some socially unacceptable manner, the rationality of the marriage can be hard to fathom. To an economist, this makes the institution of marriage an especially interesting case study of human choice.

Throughout history, literally billions of people have chosen to be married and to put up with the faults of their matrimonial partners. Why do they do this? One reason that economists have offered is that spouses show consideration for their marriage partners in the hope or expectation that the favor will be returned. This is self-interest at work. In addition, by entering into and staying faithful to a marriage, one spouse establishes a reputation with the other. By honoring their commitment to the marriage, they show more broadly that they are not afraid of commitments. This gives both a greater incentive to trust each other when they make joint financial decisions. By pooling their resources, both marriage partners can thereby make themselves better off than they would be alone. This is also an example of people responding in a self-interested way to incentives they face.

"Shotgun Weddings" and the Marriage Premium

Economists have evidence that there is something to this story. Recall from the opening to this chapter that most married men earn more than unmarried men. Donna Ginther of Washington University and Madeline Zavodny of the Federal Reserve Bank of Atlanta tried to evaluate whether this marriage premium is simply due to beneficial effects of marriage for men or instead results from careful spousal choices by women seeking committed husbands. To do this, they compared the wages of men married in so-called shotgun weddings—marriages followed within, say, seven months by the birth of a child—with the wages of men whose wives did not bear children until later on. After controlling for other factors, they found that men married in shotgun weddings typically did not earn a marriage premium. Presumably, many men in such situations are less committed to the marriage. Nevertheless, women expecting children may feel that their choices are constrained, so they are less likely to reject the marriage partner in a shotgun wedding. Thus it appears that in most instances, the marriage premium applies to the husbands of women who feel less constrained in choosing their mates.

FOR CRITICAL ANALYSIS

1. So far there is little evidence of a marriage premium for women. Can you think of any reasons why this is so?

2. What is the economic role of love in marriage?

SUMMARY DISCUSSION OF LEARNING OBJECTIVES

1. **Microeconomics Versus Macroeconomics:** In general, economics is the study of how individuals make choices to satisfy wants. Economics is usually divided into microeconomics, which is the study of individual decision making by households and firms, and macroeconomics, which is the study of nationwide phenomena, such as inflation and unemployment.

2. **Self-Interest in Economic Analysis:** Rational self-interest is the assumption that individuals behave in a reasonable (rational) way in making choices to further their interests. That is, economists assume that individuals never intentionally make decisions that would leave them worse off. Instead, they are motivated primarily by their self-interest, keeping in mind that self-interest can relate to monetary and nonmonetary objectives, such as love, prestige, and helping others.

3. **Economics as a Science:** Like other scientists, economists use models, or theories, that are simplified representations of the real world to analyze and make predictions about the real world. Economic models are never completely realistic because by definition they are simplifications using assumptions that are not directly testable. Nevertheless, economists can subject the predictions of economic theories to empirical tests in which real-world data are used to decide whether or not to reject the predictions.

4. **The Difference Between Positive and Normative Economics:** Positive economics deals with *what is,* whereas normative economics deals with *what ought to be.* Positive economic statements are of the "if . . . then" variety; they are descriptive and predictive and are not related to what "should" happen. By contrast, whenever statements embodying values are made, we enter the realm of normative economics, or how individuals and groups think things ought to be.

Key Terms and Concepts

Aggregates (5)

Ceteris paribus assumption (10)

Economics (5)

Empirical (11)

Incentives (7)

Macroeconomics (5)

Microeconomics (5)

Models, or theories (9)

Normative economics (12)

Positive economics (12)

Rationality assumption (6)

Resources (5)

Wants (5)

Problems

Answers to the odd-numbered problems appear at the back of the book.

1-1. Some people claim that the "economic way of thinking" does not apply to issues such as health care. Explain how economics does apply to this issue by developing a "model" of an individual's choice.

1-2. In a single sentence, contrast microeconomics and macroeconomics. Next, categorize the following issues as either a microeconomic issue, a macroeconomic issue, or not an economic issue.
   a. The national unemployment rate
   b. The decision of a worker to work overtime or not
   c. A family's choice of having a baby
   d. The rate of growth of the money supply
   e. The national government's budget deficit
   f. A student's allocation of study time across two subjects

1-3. One of your classmates, Sally, is a hardworking student, serious about her classes, and conscientious about her grades. Sally is also involved, however, in volunteer activities and an extracurricular sport. Is Sally displaying rational behavior? Based on what you read in this chapter, construct an argument supporting the conclusion that she is.

1-4. You have 10 hours in which to study for both a French test and an economics test. Construct a model to determine your allocation of study hours. Include as assumptions the points you "gain" from an hour of study time in each subject and your desired outcome on each test.

1-5. Use the model you constructed in Problem 1-4 to determine the allocation of study time across subjects.

1-6. Suppose you followed the model you constructed in Problem 1-4. Explain how you would "grade" the model.

1-7. Write a sentence contrasting positive and normative economic analysis.

1-8. Based on your answer to Problem 1-7, categorize the following conclusions as the result of positive analysis or normative analysis.

   a. Increasing the minimum wage will reduce minimum wage employment opportunities.
   b. Increasing the prospects of minimum wage employees is desirable, and raising the minimum wage is the best way to accomplish this.
   c. Everyone should enjoy open access to health care.
   d. Heath care subsidies will increase the demands for health care.

1-9. Consider the following statements, based on a positive economic analysis that assumes that all other things remain constant. List one other thing that might change and offset the outcome stated.

   a. Increased demand for laptop computers will drive up their price.
   b. Falling gasoline prices will result in additional vacation travel.
   c. A reduction of income tax rates will result in more people working.

1-10. Alan Greenspan, chairman of the U.S. Federal Reserve, referred to the high stock market prices of the late 1990s as a result of "irrational exuberance." Counter this statement by considering the rationality of stock market investors.

Economics on the Net

The Usefulness of Studying Economics This application helps you see how accomplished people benefited from their study of economics. It also explores ways in which these people feel others of all walks of life can gain from learning more about the economics field.

Internet URL:
   http://woodrow.mpls.frb.fed.us/pubs/region/98-12/quotes.html

Title: Economics in *The Region* on Their Student Experiences and the Need for Economic Literacy

Navigation: Start at the Federal Reserve Bank of Minneapolis homepage (woodrow.mpls.frb.fed.us). Under Publications, click on *The Region* (woodrow.mpls.frb.fed.us/region). Page down to and click on December 1998 (woodrow.mpls.frb.fed.us/region/98-12). Select the last article of the issue, Economics in *The Region* on Their Student Experiences and the Need for Economic Literacy.

Application Read the interviews of the six economists, and answer the following questions.

1. Based on your reading, what economists do you think other economists regard as influential? What educational institutions do you think are the most influential in economics?

2. Which economists do you think were attracted to microeconomics and which to macroeconomics?

For Group Study and Analysis Divide the class into three groups, and assign the groups the Blinder, Yellen, and Rivlin interviews. Have each group use the content of its assigned interview to develop a statement explaining why the study of economics is important, regardless of a student's chosen major.

APPENDIX A

READING AND WORKING WITH GRAPHS

Independent variable
A variable whose value is determined independently of, or outside, the equation under study.

Dependent variable
A variable whose value changes according to changes in the value of one or more independent variables.

TABLE A-I
Gas Mileage as a Function of Driving Speed

Miles per Hour	Miles per Gallon
45	25
50	24
55	23
60	21
65	19
70	16
75	13

Direct relationship
A relationship between two variables that is positive, meaning that an increase in one variable is associated with an increase in the other and a decrease in one variable is associated with a decrease in the other.

Inverse relationship
A relationship between two variables that is negative, meaning that an increase in one variable is associated with a decrease in the other and a decrease in one variable is associated with an increase in the other.

A graph is a visual representation of the relationship between variables. In this appendix, we'll stick to just two variables: an **independent variable,** which can change in value freely, and a **dependent variable,** which changes only as a result of changes in the value of the independent variable. For example, if nothing else is changing in your life, your weight depends on the amount of food you eat. Food is the independent variable and weight the dependent variable.

A table is a list of numerical values showing the relationship between two (or more) variables. Any table can be converted into a graph, which is a visual representation of that list. Once you understand how a table can be converted to a graph, you will understand what graphs are and how to construct and use them.

Consider a practical example. A conservationist may try to convince you that driving at lower highway speeds will help you conserve gas. Table A-1 shows the relationship between speed—the independent variable—and the distance you can go on a gallon of gas at that speed—the dependent variable. This table does show a pattern of sorts. As the data in the first column get larger in value, the data in the second column get smaller.

Now let's take a look at the different ways in which variables can be related.

DIRECT AND INVERSE RELATIONSHIPS

Two variables can be related in different ways, some simple, others more complex. For example, a person's weight and height are often related. If we measured the height and weight of thousands of people, we would surely find that taller people tend to weigh more than shorter people. That is, we would discover that there is a **direct relationship** between height and weight. By this we simply mean that an *increase* in one variable is usually associated with an *increase* in the related variable. This can easily be seen in panel (a) of Figure A-1.

Let's look at another simple way in which two variables can be related. Much evidence indicates that as the price of a specific commodity rises, the amount purchased decreases—there is an **inverse relationship** between the variable's price per unit and quantity purchased. A table listing the data for this relationship would indicate that for higher and higher prices, smaller and smaller quantities would be purchased. We see this relationship in panel (b) of Figure A-1.

FIGURE A-I
Relationships

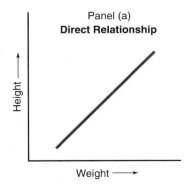

Panel (a)
Direct Relationship

Height → / Weight →

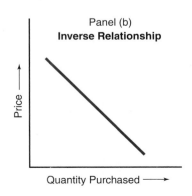

Panel (b)
Inverse Relationship

Price → / Quantity Purchased →

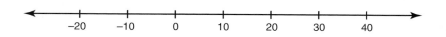

FIGURE A-2
Horizontal Number Line

CONSTRUCTING A GRAPH

Let us now examine how to construct a graph to illustrate a relationship between two variables.

A Number Line

The first step is to become familiar with what is called a **number line.** One is shown in Figure A-2. There are two things that you should know about it.

1. The points on the line divide the line into equal segments.
2. The numbers associated with the points on the line increase in value from left to right; saying it the other way around, the numbers decrease in value from right to left. However you say it, what we're describing is formally called an *ordered set of points.*

On the number line, we have shown the line segments—that is, the distance from 0 to 10 or the distance between 30 and 40. They all appear to be equal and, indeed, are equal to $\frac{1}{2}$ inch. When we use a distance to represent a quantity, such as barrels of oil, graphically, we are *scaling* the number line. In the example shown, the distance between 0 and 10 might represent 10 barrels of oil, or the distance from 0 to 40 might represent 40 barrels. Of course, the scale may differ on different number lines. For example, a distance of 1 inch could represent 10 units on one number line but 5,000 units on another. Notice that on our number line, points to the left of 0 correspond to negative numbers and points to the right of 0 correspond to positive numbers.

Of course, we can also construct a vertical number line. Consider the one in Figure A-3. As we move up this vertical number line, the numbers increase in value; conversely, as we descend, they decrease in value. Below 0 the numbers are negative, and above 0 the numbers are positive. And as on the horizontal number line, all the line segments are equal. This line is divided into segments such that the distance between −2 and −1 is the same as the distance between 0 and 1.

Combining Vertical and Horizontal Number Lines

By drawing the horizontal and vertical lines on the same sheet of paper, we are able to express the relationships between variables graphically. We do this in Figure A-4.

Number line
A line that can be divided into segments of equal length, each associated with a number.

FIGURE A-3
Vertical Number Line

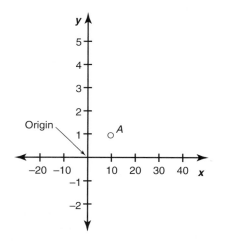

FIGURE A-4
A Set of Coordinate Axes

We draw them (1) so that they intersect at each other's 0 point and (2) so that they are perpendicular to each other. The result is a set of coordinate axes, where each line is called an *axis*. When we have two axes, they span a *plane*.

For one number line, you need only one number to specify any point on the line; equivalently, when you see a point on the line, you know that it represents one number or one value. With a coordinate value system, you need two numbers to specify a single point in the plane; when you see a single point on a graph, you know that it represents two numbers or two values.

The basic things that you should know about a coordinate number system are that the vertical number line is referred to as the **y axis,** the horizontal number line is referred to as the **x axis,** and the point of intersection of the two lines is referred to as the **origin.**

Any point such as A in Figure A-4 represents two numbers—a value of x and a value of y. But we know more than that; we also know that point A represents a positive value of y because it is above the x axis, and we know that it represents a positive value of x because it is to the right of the y axis.

Point A represents a "paired observation" of the variables x and y; in particular, in Figure A-4, A represents an observation of the pair of values x = 10 and y = 1. Every point in the coordinate system corresponds to a paired observation of x and y, which can be simply written (x, y)—the x value is always specified first, then the y value. When we give the values associated with the position of point A in the coordinate number system, we are in effect giving the coordinates of that point. A's coordinates are x = 10, y = 1, or (10, 1).

y axis
The vertical axis in a graph.

x axis
The horizontal axis in a graph.

Origin
The intersection of the y axis and the x axis in a graph.

GRAPHING NUMBERS IN A TABLE

Consider Table A-2. Column 1 shows different prices for T-shirts, and column 2 gives the number of T-shirts purchased per week at these prices. Notice the pattern of these numbers. As the price of T-shirts falls, the number of T-shirts purchased per week increases. Therefore, an inverse relationship exists between these two variables, and as soon as we represent it on a graph, you will be able to see the relationship. We can graph this relationship using a coordinate number system—a vertical and horizontal number line for each of these two variables. Such a graph is shown in panel (b) of Figure A-5.

TABLE A-2

T-Shirts Purchased

(1) Price of T-Shirts	(2) Number of T-Shirts Purchased per Week
$10	20
9	30
8	40
7	50
6	60
5	70

FIGURE A-5

Graphing the Relationship Between T-Shirts Purchased and Price

Panel (a)

Price per T-Shirt	T-Shirts Purchased per Week	Point on Graph
$10	20	I (20, 10)
9	30	J (30, 9)
8	40	K (40, 8)
7	50	L (50, 7)
6	60	M (60, 6)
5	70	N (70, 5)

Panel (b)

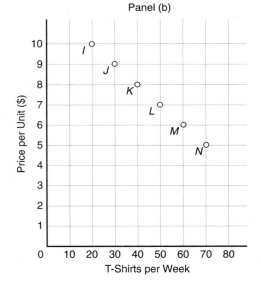

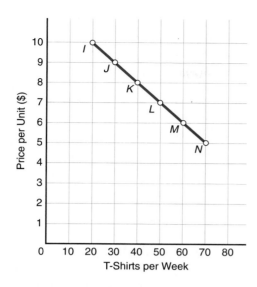

FIGURE A-6
Connecting the Observation Points

In economics, it is conventional to put dollar values on the *y* axis. We therefore construct a vertical number line for price and a horizontal number line, the *x* axis, for quantity of T-shirts purchased per week. The resulting coordinate system allows the plotting of each of the paired observation points; in panel (a), we repeat Table A-2, with a column added expressing these points in paired-data (*x, y*) form. For example, point *J* is the paired observation (30, 9). It indicates that when the price of a T-shirt is $9, 30 will be purchased per week.

If it were possible to sell parts of a T-shirt ($\frac{1}{2}$ or $\frac{1}{20}$ of a shirt), we would have observations at every possible price. That is, we would be able to connect our paired observations, represented as lettered points. Let's assume that we can make T-shirts perfectly divisible so that the linear relationship shown in Figure A-5 also holds for fractions of dollars and T-shirts. We would then have a line that connects these points, as shown in the graph in Figure A-6.

In short, we have now represented the data from the table in the form of a graph. Note that an inverse relationship between two variables shows up on a graph as a line or curve that slopes *downward* from left to right. (You might as well get used to the idea that economists call a straight line a "curve" even though it may not curve at all. Much of economists' data turn out to be curves, so they refer to everything represented graphically, even straight lines, as curves.)

THE SLOPE OF A LINE (A LINEAR CURVE)

An important property of a curve represented on a graph is its *slope*. Consider Figure A-7, which represents the quantities of shoes per week that a seller is willing to offer at different prices. Note that in panel (a) of Figure A-7, as in Figure A-5, we have expressed the coordinates of the points in parentheses in paired-data form.

The **slope** of a line is defined as the change in the *y* values divided by the corresponding change in the *x* values as we move along the line. Let's move from point *E* to point *D* in panel (b) of Figure A-7. As we move, we note that the change in the *y* values, which is the change in price, is +$20, because we have moved from a price of $20 to a price of $40 per pair. As we move from *E* to *D,* the change in the *x* values is +80; the number of pairs of shoes willingly offered per week rises from 80 to 160 pairs. The slope calculated as a change in the *y* values divided by the change in the *x* values is therefore

Slope
The change in the *y* value divided by the corresponding change in the *x* value of a curve; the "incline" of the curve.

$$\frac{20}{80} = \frac{1}{4}$$

FIGURE A-7
A Positively Sloped Curve

Panel (a)

Price per Pair	Pairs of Shoes Offered per Week	Point on Graph
$100	400	A (400,100)
80	320	B (320, 80)
60	240	C (240, 60)
40	160	D (160, 40)
20	80	E (80, 20)

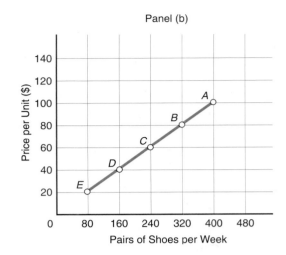

Panel (b)

It may be helpful for you to think of slope as a "rise" (movement in the vertical direction) over a "run" (movement in the horizontal direction). We show this abstractly in Figure A-8. The slope is measured by the amount of rise divided by the amount of run. In the example in Figure A-8, and of course in Figure A-7, the amount of rise is positive and so is the amount of run. That's because it's a direct relationship. We show an inverse relationship in Figure A-9. The slope is still equal to the rise divided by the run, but in this case the rise and the run have opposite signs because the curve slopes downward. That means that the slope will have to be negative and that we are dealing with an inverse relationship.

Now let's calculate the slope for a different part of the curve in panel (b) of Figure A-7. We will find the slope as we move from point B to point A. Again, we note that the slope, or rise over run, from B to A equals

$$\frac{20}{80} = \frac{1}{4}$$

A specific property of a straight line is that its slope is the same between any two points; in other words, the slope is constant at all points on a straight line in a graph.

We conclude that for our example in Figure A-7, the relationship between the price of a pair of shoes and the number of pairs of shoes willingly offered per week is *linear,* which simply means "in a straight line," and our calculations indicate a constant slope. Moreover, we calculate a direct relationship between these two variables, which turns out to be an

FIGURE A-8
Figuring Positive Slope

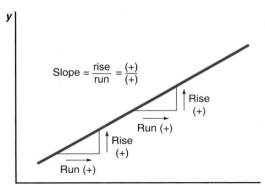

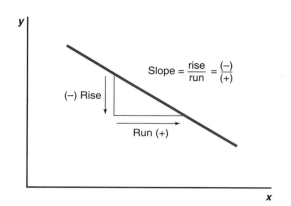

upward-sloping (from left to right) curve. Upward-sloping curves have positive slopes—in this case, it is $+\frac{1}{4}$.

We know that an inverse relationship between two variables shows up as a downward-sloping curve—rise over run will be a negative slope because the rise and run have opposite signs, as shown in Figure A-9. When we see a negative slope, we know that increases in one variable are associated with decreases in the other. Therefore, we say that downward-sloping curves have negative slopes. Can you verify that the slope of the graph representing the relationship between T-shirt prices and the quantity of T-shirts purchased per week in Figure A-6 is $-\frac{1}{10}$?

Slopes of Nonlinear Curves

The graph presented in Figure A-10 indicates a *nonlinear* relationship between two variables, total profits and output per unit of time. Inspection of this graph indicates that at first, increases in output lead to increases in total profits; that is, total profits rise as output increases. But beyond some output level, further increases in output cause decreases in total profits.

Can you see how this curve rises at first, reaches a peak at point *C,* and then falls? This curve relating total profits to output levels appears mountain-shaped.

Considering that this curve is nonlinear (it is obviously not a straight line), should we expect a constant slope when we compute changes in *y* divided by corresponding changes in *x* in moving from one point to another? A quick inspection, even without specific numbers, should lead us to conclude that the slopes of lines joining different points in this curve, such as between *A* and *B, B* and *C,* or *C* and *D,* will *not* be the same. The curve slopes upward (in a positive direction) for some values and downward (in a negative direction) for

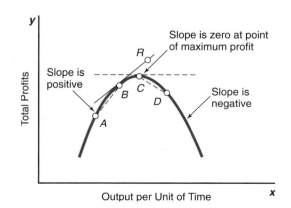

other values. In fact, the slope of the line between any two points on this curve will be different from the slope of the line between any two other points. Each slope will be different as we move along the curve.

Instead of using a line between two points to discuss slope, mathematicians and economists prefer to discuss the slope *at a particular point*. The slope at a point on the curve, such as point *B* in the graph in Figure A-10, is the slope of a line *tangent* to that point. A tangent line is a straight line that touches a curve at only one point. For example, it might be helpful to think of the tangent at *B* as the straight line that just "kisses" the curve at point *B*.

To calculate the slope of a tangent line, you need to have some additional information besides the two values of the point of tangency. For example, in Figure A-10, if we knew that the point *R* also lay on the tangent line and we knew the two values of that point, we could calculate the slope of the tangent line. We could calculate rise over run between points *B* and *R,* and the result would be the slope of the line tangent to the one point *B* on the curve.

Appendix Summary

1. Direct relationships involve a dependent variable changing in the same direction as the change in the independent variable.
2. Inverse relationships involve the dependent variable changing in the opposite direction of the change in the independent variable.
3. When we draw a graph showing the relationship between two economic variables, we are holding all other things constant (the Latin term for which is *ceteris paribus*).
4. We obtain a set of coordinates by putting vertical and horizontal number lines together. The vertical line is called the *y* axis; the horizontal line, the *x* axis.

5. The slope of any linear (straight-line) curve is the change in the *y* values divided by the corresponding change in the *x* values as we move along the line. Otherwise stated, the slope is calculated as the amount of rise over the amount of run, where rise is movement in the vertical direction and run is movement in the horizontal direction.
6. The slope of a nonlinear curve changes; it is positive when the curve is rising and negative when the curve is falling. At a maximum or minimum point, the slope of the nonlinear curve is zero.

Key Terms and Concepts

Dependent variable (18)	Inverse relationship (18)	Slope (21)
Direct relationship (18)	Number line (19)	*x* axis (20)
Independent variable (18)	Origin (20)	*y* axis (20)

Problems

Answers to the odd-numbered problems appear at the back of the book.

A-1. Explain which is the independent variable and which is the dependent variable for the following examples.

    a. Once you determine the price of a notebook at the college bookstore, you will decide how many notebooks to buy.

    b. You will decide how many credit hours to register for this semester once the university tells you how many work-study hours you will be assigned.

    c. You are anxious to receive your economics exam grade because you studied many hours in the weeks preceding the exam.

A-2. For the following items, state whether a direct or an inverse relationship is likely to exist.

a. The number of hours you study for an exam and your exam score
b. The price of pizza and the quantity purchased
c. The number of games the university basketball team won last year and the number of season tickets sold this year

A-3. Review Figure A-4, and then state whether the following paired observations are on, above, or below the *x* axis and on, to the left of, or to the right of the *y* axis.

a. $(-10, 4)$
b. $(20, -2)$
c. $(10, 0)$

A-4. State whether the following functions are linear or nonlinear.

a. $y = 5x$
b. $y = 5x^2$
c. $y = 3 + x$
d. $y = -3x$

A-5. Given the function $y = 5x$, complete the following schedule and plot the curve.

y	x
	-4
	-2
	0
	2
	4

A-6. Given the function $y = 5x^2$, complete the following schedule and plot the curve.

y	x
	-4
	-2
	0
	2
	4

A-7. Calculate the slope of the function you graphed in Problem A-5.

A-8. Indicate at each ordered pair whether the slope of the curve you plotted in Problem A-6 is positive, negative, or zero.

A-9. State whether the following functions imply a positive or negative relationship between *x* and *y*.

a. $y = 5x$
b. $y = 3 + x$
c. $y = -3x$

SCARCITY AND THE WORLD OF TRADE-OFFS

This harried father tries to balance the demands of work with those of child rearing. Why does it typically cost more for higher-income-earning parents to raise children than for those earning less income?

In Chapter 1, you learned that men and women can have good economic reasons to marry. Because children traditionally shared the family workload, couples have also had a strong incentive to have children. In most developed nations, however, this incentive for having children has largely disappeared. Even on today's "family farms," many tasks are now mechanized and even automated.

At the same time, the costs of raising children have increased. Of course, parents have always housed, fed, and clothed their children. In addition, they have sacrificed to provide "quality time" with their children. For many people today, the value of that time is greater than it was in years past. In this chapter you will learn how to put a value on time spent with children. This will help you understand why children are a more costly "commodity" than they used to be.

LEARNING OBJECTIVES

After reading this chapter, you should be able to:

1. Evaluate whether even affluent people face the problem of scarcity

2. Understand why economics considers individuals' "wants" but not their "needs"

3. Explain why the scarcity problem induces individuals to consider opportunity costs

4. Discuss why obtaining increasing increments of any particular good typically entails giving up more and more units of other goods

5. Explain why society faces a trade-off between consumption goods and capital goods

6. Distinguish between absolute and comparative advantage

Did You Know That... Chris Van Horn, president of CVK Group in Washington, D.C., grosses over $200,000 a year for having people wait in line? Adam Goldin loves working as a "line waiter" because he gets paid for "doing nothing." His job is to arrive early in the morning on Capitol Hill to hold places for lobbyists who must attend congressional hearings. Van Horn charges his more than 100 lobbyists and law firm clients $27 an hour and pays his part-time line waiters like Mr. Goldin $10 an hour. For example, when Congress was going to hold hearings for the proposed 1997 tax cut, $10-an-hour professional standees arrived to hold places for $300-an-hour lobbyists who would not show up until hours later. After all, lobbyists do not have an unlimited amount of time. Their time is scarce. It is worth more than what they are charged to "save" it.

SCARCITY

Whenever individuals or communities cannot obtain everything they desire simultaneously, choices occur. Choices occur because of *scarcity*. **Scarcity** is the most basic concept in all of economics. Scarcity means that we do not ever have enough of everything, including time, to satisfy our *every* desire. Scarcity exists because human wants always exceed what can be produced with the limited resources and time that nature makes available.

What Scarcity Is Not

Scarcity is not a shortage. After a hurricane hits and cuts off supplies to a community, TV newscasts often show people standing in line to get minimum amounts of cooking fuel and food. A news commentator might say that the line is caused by the "scarcity" of these products. But cooking fuel and food are always scarce—we cannot obtain all that we want at a zero price. Therefore, do not confuse the concept of scarcity, which is general and all-encompassing, with the concept of shortages as evidenced by people waiting in line to obtain a particular product.

Scarcity is not the same thing as poverty. Scarcity occurs among the poor and among the rich. Even the richest person on earth faces scarcity because available time is limited. Low income levels do not create more scarcity. High income levels do not create less scarcity.

Scarcity is a fact of life, like gravity. And just as physicists did not invent gravity, economists did not invent scarcity—it existed well before the first economist ever lived. It exists even when we are not using all of our resources.

Scarcity
A situation in which the ingredients for producing the things that people desire are insufficient to satisfy all wants.

Scarcity and Resources

The scarcity concept arises from the fact that resources are insufficient to satisfy our every desire. Resources are the inputs used in the production of the things that we want. **Production** can be defined as virtually any activity that results in the conversion of resources into products that can be used in consumption. Production includes delivering things from one part of the country to another. It includes taking ice from an ice tray to put it in your soft-drink glass. The resources used in production are called *factors of production,* and some economists use the terms *resources* and *factors of production* interchangeably. The total quantity of all resources that an economy has at any one time determines what that economy can produce.

Production
Any activity that results in the conversion of resources into products that can be used in consumption.

Factors of production can be classified in many ways. Here is one such classification:

1. Land. **Land** encompasses all the nonhuman gifts of nature, including timber, water, fish, minerals, and the original fertility of land. It is often called the *natural resource.*
2. Labor. **Labor** is the human resource, which includes all productive contributions made by individuals who work, such as steelworkers, ballet dancers, and professional baseball players.
3. Physical capital. **Physical capital** consists of the factories and equipment used in production. It also includes improvements to natural resources, such as irrigation ditches.
4. Human capital. **Human capital** is the economic characterization of the education and training of workers. How much the nation produces depends not only on how many hours people work but also on how productive they are, and that in turn depends in part on education and training. To become more educated, individuals have to devote time and resources, just as a business has to devote resources if it wants to increase its physical capital. Whenever a worker's skills increase, human capital has been improved.
5. Entrepreneurship. The factor of production known as **entrepreneurship** (actually a subdivision of labor) involves human resources that perform the functions of organizing, managing, and assembling the other factors of production to make business ventures. Entrepreneurship also encompasses taking risks that involve the possibility of losing large sums of wealth on new ventures. It includes new methods of doing common things and generally experimenting with any type of new thinking that could lead to making more money income. Without entrepreneurship, virtually no business organization could operate.

Goods Versus Economic Goods

Goods are defined as all things from which individuals derive satisfaction or happiness. Goods therefore include air to breathe and the beauty of a sunset as well as food, cars, and CD players.

   Economic goods are a subset of all goods—they are goods derived from scarce resources about which we must constantly make decisions regarding their best use. By definition, the desired quantity of an economic good exceeds the amount that is directly available at a zero price. Virtually every example we use in economics concerns economic goods—cars, CD players, computers, socks, baseball bats, and corn. Weeds are a good example of *bads*—goods for which the desired quantity is much *less* than what nature provides at a zero price.

   Sometimes you will see references to "goods and services." **Services** are tasks that are performed for someone else, such as laundry, cleaning, hospital care, restaurant meal preparation, car polishing, psychological counseling, and teaching. One way of looking at services is thinking of them as *intangible goods.*

WANTS AND NEEDS

Wants are not the same as needs. Indeed, from the economist's point of view, the term *needs* is objectively undefinable. When someone says, "I need some new clothes," there is no way to know whether that person is stating a vague wish, a want, or a lifesaving necessity. If the individual making the statement were dying of exposure in a northern country

Land
The natural resources that are available from nature. Land as a resource includes location, original fertility and mineral deposits, topography, climate, water, and vegetation.

Labor
Productive contributions of humans who work, involving both mental and physical activities.

Physical capital
All manufactured resources, including buildings, equipment, machines, and improvements to land that is used for production.

Human capital
The accumulated training and education of workers.

Entrepreneurship
The factor of production involving human resources that perform the functions of raising capital, organizing, managing, assembling other factors of production, and making basic business policy decisions. The entrepreneur is a risk taker.

Goods
All things from which individuals derive satisfaction or happiness.

Economic goods
Goods that are scarce, for which the quantity demanded exceeds the quantity supplied at a zero price.

Services
Mental or physical labor or help purchased by consumers. Examples are the assistance of doctors, lawyers, dentists, repair personnel, housecleaners, educators, retailers, and wholesalers; things purchased or used by consumers that do not have physical characteristics.

during the winter, we might argue that indeed the person does need clothes—perhaps not new ones, but at least some articles of warm clothing. Typically, however, the term *need* is used very casually in most conversations. What people mean, usually, is that they want something that they do not currently have.

Humans have unlimited wants. Just imagine if every single material want that you might have were satisfied. You can have all of the clothes, cars, houses, CDs, tickets to concerts, and other things that you want. Does that mean that nothing else could add to your total level of happiness? Probably not, because you might think of new goods and services that you could obtain, particularly as they came to market. You would also still be lacking in fulfilling all of your wants for compassion, friendship, love, affection, prestige, musical abilities, sports abilities, and so on.

In reality, every individual has competing wants but cannot satisfy all of them, given limited resources. This is the reality of scarcity. Each person must therefore make choices. Whenever a choice is made to do or buy something, something else that is also desired is not done or not purchased. In other words, in a world of scarcity, every want that ends up being satisfied causes one or more other wants to remain unsatisfied or to be forfeited.

CONCEPTS IN BRIEF

- Scarcity exists because human wants always exceed what can be produced with the limited resources and time that nature makes available.

- We use scarce resources, such as land, labor, physical and human capital, and entrepreneurship, to produce economic goods—goods that are desired but are not directly obtainable from nature to the extent demanded or desired at a zero price.

- Wants are unlimited; they include all material desires and all nonmaterial desires, such as love, affection, power, and prestige.

- The concept of need is difficult to define objectively for every person; consequently, we simply consider that every person's wants are unlimited. In a world of scarcity, satisfaction of one want necessarily means nonsatisfaction of one or more other wants.

SCARCITY, CHOICE, AND OPPORTUNITY COST

The natural fact of scarcity implies that we must make choices. One of the most important results of this fact is that every choice made (or not made, for that matter) means that some opportunity had to be sacrificed. Every choice involves giving up another opportunity to do or use something else.

Consider a practical example. Every choice you make to study one more hour of economics requires that you give up the opportunity to do any of the following activities: study more of another subject, listen to music, sleep, browse at a local store, read a novel, or work out at the gym. Many more opportunities are forgone also if you choose to study economics an additional hour.

Because there were so many alternatives from which to choose, how could you determine the value of what you gave up to engage in that extra hour of studying economics? First of all, no one else can tell you the answer because only you can *subjectively* put a value on the alternatives forgone. Only you know what is the value of another hour of sleep or of an hour looking for the latest CDs. That means that only you can determine the highest-valued, next-best alternative that you had to sacrifice in order to study economics one more hour. It is you who come up with the *subjective* estimate of the expected value of the next-best alternative.

Opportunity cost
The highest-valued, next-best alternative that must be sacrificed to obtain something or to satisfy a want.

The value of the next-best alternative is called **opportunity cost.** The opportunity cost of any action is the value of what is given up—the next-highest-ranked alternative—because a choice was made. When you study one more hour, there may be many alternatives available for the use of that hour, but assume that you can do only one other thing in that hour—your next-highest-ranked alternative. What is important is the choice that you would have made if you hadn't studied one more hour. Your opportunity cost is the *next-highest-ranked* alternative, not *all* alternatives.

In economics, cost is always a forgone opportunity.

One way to think about opportunity cost is to understand that when you choose to do something, you lose. What you lose is being able to engage in your next-highest-valued alternative. The cost of your choice is what you lose, which is by definition your next-highest-valued alternative. This is your opportunity cost.

Let's consider a real-world example: the opportunity cost of a national monument.

POLICY EXAMPLE

The Trillion-Dollar Canyon

In September 1996, the U.S. government established the Grand Staircase/Escalante National Monument. If you visit the Monument's Web page (http://www.gorp.com/gorp/resource/US_nm/ut_escal.htm), you will learn all about various activities available to visitors to the cliffs and canyons encompassed within the monument.

What the Web page does not tell you is that this 1.8 million-acre park in the southern Utah desert lies above the largest known reserve of coal in the United States: an underground bank of nearly 7 billion tons of coal with an estimated market value of about $1 trillion. That is the opportunity cost of this particular national monument.

For Critical Analysis
Recall that opportunity cost is the value of the next-best alternative. What does this tell us about the perceived social value of the Grand Staircase/Escalante National Monument?

THE WORLD OF TRADE-OFFS

Whenever you engage in any activity using any resource, even time, you are *trading off* the use of that resource for one or more alternative uses. The value of the trade-off is represented by the opportunity cost. The opportunity cost of studying economics has already been mentioned—it is the value of the next-best alternative. When you think of any alternative, you are thinking of trade-offs.

Let's consider a hypothetical example of a one-for-one trade-off between the results of spending time studying economics and accounting. For the sake of this argument, we will assume that additional time studying either economics or accounting will lead to a higher grade in the subject studied more. One of the best ways to examine this trade-off is with a graph. (If you would like a refresher on graphical techniques, study Appendix A at the end of Chapter 1 before going on.)

Graphical Analysis

In Figure 2-1, the expected grade in accounting is measured on the vertical axis of the graph, and the expected grade in economics is measured on the horizontal axis. We simplify the world and assume that you have a maximum of 10 hours per week to spend studying these two subjects and that if you spend all 10 hours on economics, you will get an A in the course. You will, however, fail accounting. Conversely, if you spend all of your 10 hours studying accounting, you will get an A in that subject, but you will flunk economics. Here the trade-off is a special case: one to one. A one-to-one trade-off means that the opportunity cost of receiving one grade higher in economics (for example, improving from a C to a B) is one grade lower in accounting (falling from a C to a D).

The Production Possibilities Curve (PPC)

The graph in Figure 2-1 illustrates the relationship between the possible results that can be produced in each of two activities, depending on how much time you choose to devote to each activity. This graph shows a representation of a **production possibilities curve (PPC).**

Consider that you are producing a grade in economics when you study economics and a grade in accounting when you study accounting. Then the graph in Figure 2-1 can be related to the production possibilities you face. The line that goes from A on one axis to A on the other axis therefore becomes a production possibilities curve. It is defined as the maximum quantity of one good or service that can be produced, given that a specific quantity of another is produced. It is a curve that shows the possibilities available for increasing the output of one good or service by reducing the amount of another. In the example in Figure 2-1, your time for studying was limited to 10 hours per week. The two possible outputs were grades in accounting and grades in economics. The particular production possibilities curve presented in Figure 2-1 is a graphical representation of the opportunity cost of studying one more hour in one subject. It is a *straight-line production possibilities curve,* which is a special case. (The more general case will be discussed next.) If you decide to be at point *x* in Figure 2-1, 5 hours of study time will be spent on accounting and 5 hours will be spent on economics. The expected grade in each course will be a C. If you are more interested in getting a B in economics, you will go to point *y* on the production possibilities curve, spending only 2.5 hours

Production possibilities curve (PPC)

A curve representing all possible combinations of total output that could be produced assuming (1) a fixed amount of productive resources of a given quality and (2) the efficient use of those resources.

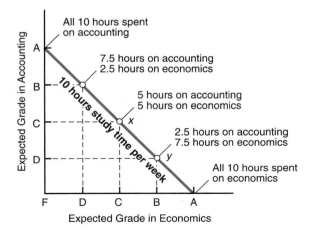

FIGURE 2-1

Production Possibilities Curve for Grades in Accounting and Economics (Trade-Offs)

We assume that only 10 hours can be spent per week on studying. If the student is at point *x*, equal time (5 hours a week) is spent on both courses and equal grades of C will be received. If a higher grade in economics is desired, the student may go to point *y*, thereby receiving a B in economics but a D in accounting. At point *y*, 2.5 hours are spent on accounting and 7.5 hours on economics.

on accounting but 7.5 hours on economics. Your expected grade in accounting will then drop from a C to a D.

Note that these trade-offs between expected grades in accounting and economics are the result of *holding constant* total study time as well as all other factors that might influence a student's ability to learn, such as computerized study aids. Quite clearly, if you wished to spend more total time studying, it would be possible to have higher grades in both economics and accounting. In that case, however, we would no longer be on the specific production possibilities curve illustrated in Figure 2-1. We would have to draw a new curve, farther to the right, to show the greater total study time and a different set of possible trade-offs.

CONCEPTS IN BRIEF

- ● Scarcity requires us to choose. Whenever we choose, we lose the next-highest-valued alternative.
- ● Cost is always a forgone opportunity.
- ● Another way to look at opportunity cost is the trade-off that occurs when one activity is undertaken rather than the next-best alternative activity.
- ● A production possibilities curve (PPC) graphically shows the trade-off that occurs when more of one output is obtained at the sacrifice of another. The PPC is a graphical representation of, among other things, opportunity cost.

THE CHOICES SOCIETY FACES

The straight-line production possibilities curve presented in Figure 2-1 can be generalized to demonstrate the related concepts of scarcity, choice, and trade-offs that our entire nation faces. As you will see, the production possibilities curve is a simple but powerful economic model because it can demonstrate these related concepts. The example we will use is the choice between the production of network computers and digital televisions (DTVs). We assume for the moment that these are the only two goods that can be produced in the nation. Panel (a) of Figure 2-2 gives the various combinations of computers and DTVs that are possible. If all resources are devoted to computer production, 25 million per year can be produced. If all resources are devoted to DTV production, 30 million per year can be produced. In between are various possible combinations. These combinations are plotted as points A, B, C, D, E, F, and G in panel (b) of Figure 2-2. If these points are connected with a smooth curve, the nation's production possibilities curve is shown, demonstrating the trade-off between the production of computers and DTVs. These trade-offs occur *on* the production possibilities curve.

Notice the major difference in the shape of the production possibilities curves in Figures 2-1 and 2-2. In Figure 2-1, there is a one-to-one trade-off between grades in economics and in accounting. In Figure 2-2, the trade-off between computer production and DTV production is not constant, and therefore the PPC is a *bowed* curve. To understand why the production possibilities curve for a society is typically bowed outward, you must understand the assumptions underlying the PPC.

Assumptions Underlying the Production Possibilities Curve

When we draw the curve that is shown in Figure 2-2, we make the following assumptions:

1. Resources are fully employed.
2. We are looking at production over a specific time period—for example, one year.

For one perspective on whether society's production decisions should be publicly or privately coordinated, visit **www.public-policy.org/~ncpa/pd/**

FIGURE 2-2
Society's Trade-Off Between Network Computers and Digital Televisions

The production of network computers and digital televisions are measured in millions of units per year. The various combinations are given in panel (a) and plotted in panel (b). Connecting the points A–G with a relatively smooth line gives the society's production possibilities curve for network computers and digital televisions. Point *R* lies outside the production possibilities curve and is therefore unattainable at the point in time for which the graph is drawn. Point *S* lies inside the production possibilities curve and therefore represents an inefficient use of available resources.

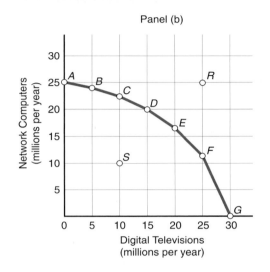

Panel (a)

Combination	Network Computers (millions per year)	Digital Televisions (millions per year)
A	25.00	0
B	24.00	5
C	22.50	10
D	20.00	15
E	16.50	20
F	11.25	25
G	0	30

3. The resource inputs, in both quantity and quality, used to produce computers or digital televisions are fixed over this time period.
4. Technology does not change over this time period.

Technology is defined as society's pool of applied knowledge concerning how goods and services can be produced by managers, workers, engineers, scientists, and artisans, using land and capital. You can think of technology as the formula or recipe used to combine factors of production. (When better formulas are developed, more production can be obtained from the same amount of resources.) The level of technology sets the limit on the amount and types of goods and services that we can derive from any given amount of resources. The production possibilities curve is drawn under the assumption that we use the best technology that we currently have available and that this technology doesn't change over the time period under study.

Technology
Society's pool of applied knowledge concerning how goods and services can be produced.

Putting
Economics in Action
to Work

For additional work with production possibilities curves, start the *EIA* CD, and click on "Scarcity and the World of Trade-Offs." Then click on "Production Possibilities Curve: Introduction."

Being off the Production Possibilities Curve

Look again at panel (b) of Figure 2-2. Point *R* lies *outside* the production possibilities curve and is *impossible* to achieve during the time period assumed. By definition, the production possibilities curve indicates the *maximum* quantity of one good given some quantity of the other.

It is possible, however, to be at point *S* in Figure 2-2. That point lies beneath the production possibilities curve. If the nation is at point *S*, it means that its resources are not being fully utilized. This occurs, for example, during periods of unemployment. Point *S* and all such points within the production possibilities curve are always attainable but usually not desirable.

Efficiency

The production possibilities curve can be used to define the notion of efficiency. Whenever the economy is operating on the PPC, at points such as *A, B, C,* or *D,* we say that its production is efficient. Points such as *S* in Figure 2-2, which lie beneath the production possibilities curve, are said to represent production situations that are not efficient.

Efficiency can mean many things to many people. Even within economics, there are different types of efficiency. Here we are discussing productive efficiency. An economy is productively efficient whenever it is producing the maximum output with given technology and resources.

A simple commonsense definition of efficiency is getting the most out of what we have as an economy. Clearly, we are not getting the most that we have if we are at point *S* in panel (b) of Figure 2-2. We can move from point *S* to, say, point *C,* thereby increasing the total quantity of network computers produced without any decrease in the total quantity of digital televisions produced. We can move from point *S* to point *E,* for example, and have both more computers and more DTVs. Point *S* is called an **inefficient point,** which is defined as any point below the production possibilities curve.

We can relate the concept of economic efficiency to how goods are distributed among different individuals and entities. In an efficient economy, people who value specific goods relatively the most end up with those goods. If you own a vintage electric Fender guitar but I value it more than you, I can buy it from you. Such trading benefits you and me mutually. In the process, the economy becomes more efficient. The maximum efficiency an economy can reach is when all such mutual benefits through trade have been exhausted.

Efficiency
The case in which a given level of inputs is used to produce the maximum output possible. Alternatively, the situation in which a given output is produced at minimum cost.

Inefficient point
Any point below the production possibilities curve at which resources are being used inefficiently.

The Law of Increasing Relative Cost

In the example in Figure 2-1, the trade-off between a grade in accounting and a grade in economics is one to one. The trade-off ratio was fixed. That is to say, the production possibilities curve was a straight line. The curve in Figure 2-2 is a more general case. We have re-created the curve in Figure 2-2 as Figure 2-3. Each combination, *A* through *G,* of network computers and digital televisions is represented on the production possibilities curve. Starting with the production of zero DTVs, the nation can produce 25 million units of computers with its available resources and technology. When we increase production of DTVs from zero to 5 million per year, the nation has to give up in computers that first vertical arrow, *Aa.* From panel (a) of Figure 2-2 you can see that this is 1 mil-

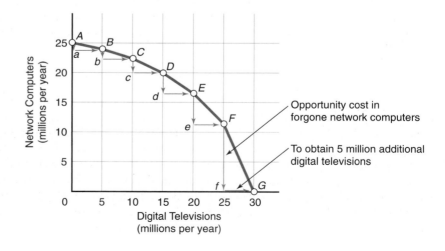

FIGURE 2-3
The Law of Increasing Relative Cost
Consider equal increments of digital television production, as measured on the horizontal axis. All of the horizontal arrows—*aB, bC,* and so on— are of equal length (5 million). The opportunity cost of going from 25 million DTVs per year to 30 million (*Ff*) is much greater than going from zero units to 5 million (*Aa*). The opportunity cost of each additional equal increase in DTV production rises.

Opportunity cost in forgone network computers

To obtain 5 million additional digital televisions

lion computers a year (25 million − 24 million). Again, if we increase production of DTVs by 5 million units per year, we go from *B* to *C*. In order to do so, the nation has to give up the vertical distance *Bb,* or 1.5 million computers a year. By the time we go from 25 million to 30 million digital televisions, to obtain that 5 million increase, we have to forgo the vertical distance *Ff,* or 11.25 million computers. In other words, we see an increase in the opportunity cost of the last 5 million digital televisions—11.25 million computers—compared to an equivalent increase in DTVs when we started with none being produced at all—1 million computers.

What we are observing is called the **law of increasing relative cost.** When society takes more resources and applies them to the production of any specific good, the opportunity cost increases for each additional unit produced. The reason that, as a nation, we face the law of increasing relative cost (which causes the production possibilities curve to bow outward) is that certain resources are better suited for producing some goods than they are for other goods. Resources are generally not *perfectly* adaptable for alternative uses. When increasing the output of a particular good, producers must use less suitable resources than those already used in order to produce the additional output. Hence the cost of producing the additional units increases. With respect to our hypothetical example here, at first the computer hardware specialists at computer firms would shift over to producing digital televisions. After a while, though, computer networking technicians, workers who normally build hard drives, and others would be asked to help design and manufacture television components. Clearly, they would be less effective in making televisions than the people who specialize in this task.

As a rule of thumb, *the more specialized the resources, the more bowed the production possibilities curve.* At the other extreme, if all resources are equally suitable for digital-television production or network computer production, the curves in Figures 2-2 and 2-3 would approach the straight line shown in our first example in Figure 2-1.

Law of increasing relative cost
The observation that the opportunity cost of additional units of a good generally increases as society attempts to produce more of that good. This accounts for the bowed-out shape of the production possibilities curve.

● Trade-offs are represented graphically by a production possibilities curve showing the maximum quantity of one good or service that can be produced, given a specific quantity of another, from a given set of resources over a specified period of time—for example, one year.

● A PPC is drawn holding the quantity and quality of all resources fixed over the time period under study.

● Points outside the production possibilities curve are unattainable; points inside are attainable but represent an inefficient use or underuse of available resources.

● Because many resources are better suited for certain productive tasks than for others, society's production possibilities curve is bowed outward, following the law of increasing relative cost.

CONCEPTS IN BRIEF

Putting Economics in Action to Work

For more practice with the concept of the law of increasing relative cost, start the *EIA* CD, and click on "Scarcity and the World of Trade-Offs." Then click on "The Bowed-Out Curve."

ECONOMIC GROWTH AND THE PRODUCTION POSSIBILITIES CURVE

Over any particular time period, a society cannot be outside the production possibilities curve. Over time, however, it is possible to have more of everything. This occurs through economic growth. (An important reason for economic growth, capital accumulation, is discussed next. A more complete discussion of why economic growth occurs is discussed in Chapter 9). Figure 2-4 shows the production possibilities curve for network computers and digital televisions shifting outward. The two additional curves shown represent new choices open to an economy that has experienced economic growth. Such economic growth

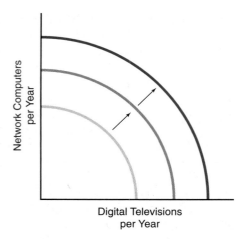

FIGURE 2-4
Economic Growth Allows for More of Everything
If the nation experiences economic growth, the production possibilities curve between network computers and digital televisions will move out, as is shown. This takes time, however, and it does not occur automatically. This means, therefore, that we can have more network computers and more DTVs only after a period of time during which we have experienced economic growth.

occurs because of many things, including increases in the number of workers and productive investment in equipment.

Scarcity still exists, however, no matter how much economic growth there is. At any point in time, we will always be on some production possibilities curve; thus we will always face trade-offs. The more we want of one thing, the less we can have of others.

If a nation experiences economic growth, the production possibilities curve between network computers and digital televisions will move outward, as shown in Figure 2-4. This takes time and does not occur automatically. One reason it will occur involves the choice about how much to consume today.

THE TRADE-OFF BETWEEN THE PRESENT AND THE FUTURE

Consumption
The use of goods and services for personal satisfaction.

The production possibilities curve and economic growth can be used to examine the trade-off between present **consumption** and future consumption. When we consume today, we are using up what we call consumption or consumer goods—food and clothes, for example. And we have already defined physical capital as the manufactured goods, such as machines and factories, used to make other goods and services.

Why We Make Capital Goods

Why would we be willing to use productive resources to make things—capital goods—that we cannot consume directly? For one thing, capital goods enable us to produce larger quantities of consumer goods or to produce them less expensively than we otherwise could. Before fish are "produced" for the market, equipment such as fishing boats, nets, and poles are produced first. Imagine how expensive it would be to obtain fish for market without using these capital goods. Catching fish with one's hands is not an easy task. The price per fish would be very high if capital goods weren't used.

Forgoing Current Consumption

Whenever we use productive resources to make capital goods, we are implicitly forgoing current consumption. We are waiting for some time in the future to consume the fruits that will be reaped from the use of capital goods. In effect, when we forgo current consumption to invest in capital goods, we are engaging in an economic activity that is forward-looking—we do not get instant utility or satisfaction from our activity. Indeed, if we were to produce only consumer goods now and no capital goods, our capacity to produce consumer goods in the future would suffer. Here we see a trade-off.

The Trade-Off Between Consumption Goods and Capital Goods

To have more consumer goods in the future, we must accept fewer consumer goods today. In other words, an opportunity cost is involved. Every time we make a choice for more goods today, we incur an opportunity cost of fewer goods tomorrow, and every time we make a choice of more goods in the future, we incur an opportunity cost of fewer goods today. With the resources that we don't use to produce consumer goods for today, we invest in capital goods that will produce more consumer goods for us later. The trade-off is shown in Figure 2-5. On the left in panel (a), you can see this trade-off depicted as a production possibilities curve between capital goods and consumption goods.

Assume that we are willing to give up $1 trillion worth of consumption today. We will be at point *A* in the left-hand diagram of panel (a). This will allow the economy to grow. We will have more future consumption because we invested in more capital goods today. In the right-hand diagram of panel (a), we see two goods represented, food and recreation. The production possibilities curve will move outward if we collectively decide to restrict consumption each year and invest in capital goods.

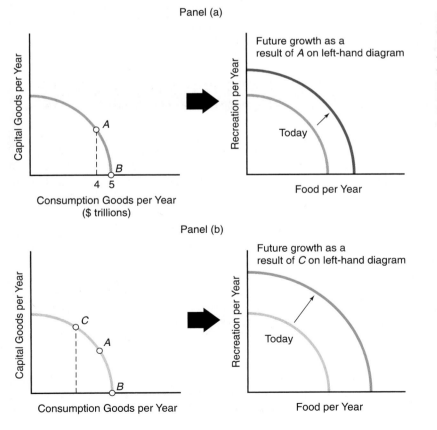

Panel (a)

FIGURE 2-5
Capital Goods and Growth
In panel (a), the nation chooses not to consume $1 trillion, so it invests that amount in capital goods. In panel (b), it chooses even more capital goods. The PPC moves even more to the right on the right-hand diagram in panel (b) as a result.

In panel (b), we show the results of our willingness to forgo more current consumption. We move to point *C,* where we have many fewer consumer goods today but produce a lot more capital goods. This leads to more future growth in this simplified model, and thus the production possibilities curve in the right-hand side of panel (b) shifts outward more than it did in the right-hand side of panel (a).

In other words, the more we give up today, the more we can have tomorrow, provided, of course, that the capital goods are productive in future periods.

CONCEPTS IN BRIEF

- The use of capital requires using productive resources to produce capital goods that will later be used to produce consumer goods.

- A trade-off is involved between current consumption and capital goods or, alternatively, between current consumption and future consumption because the more we invest in capital goods today, the greater the amount of consumer goods we can produce in the future and the smaller the amount of consumer goods we can produce today.

SPECIALIZATION AND GREATER PRODUCTIVITY

Specialization

The division of productive activities among persons and regions so that no one individual or one area is totally self-sufficient. An individual may specialize, for example, in law or medicine. A nation may specialize in the production of coffee, computers, or cameras.

Specialization involves working at a relatively well-defined, limited endeavor, such as accounting or teaching. It involves a division of labor among different individuals and regions. Most individuals do specialize. For example, you could change the oil in your car if you wanted to. Typically, though, you take your car to a garage and let the mechanic change the oil. You benefit by letting the garage mechanic specialize in changing the oil and in doing other repairs on your car. The specialist will get the job finished sooner than you could and has the proper equipment to make the job go more smoothly. Specialization usually leads to greater productivity, not only for each individual but also for the nation.

Specialization pays off for companies around the globe. This often has proved true in the automotive industry.

INTERNATIONAL POLICY EXAMPLE

Why the Light Turned Green Once the Trabi Was Parked

Among residents of eastern Germany, one of the best-recalled failures of communist rule was a little auto known as the "Trabi." Years after the reunification of Germany, people still joke about the car. For instance, "Why didn't the Trabi move when the light turned green? Because its tire got stuck on a piece of gum." Or "Why do deluxe Trabis have heated rear windows? To keep your hands warm as you push it." Another goes "How do you double a Trabi's value? Fill the gasoline tank."

Today the punch line is different, however. The company that once manufactured Trabis now has a booming business. The key to its success is that it no longer builds cars. Instead, it supplies auto parts to General Motors, Volkswagen, and DaimlerChrysler. What the company learned was that it was better off specializing in making auto parts—and leaving assembly of the parts to someone else.

For Critical Analysis
How do General Motors, Volkswagen, and Daimler-Chrysler gain from specialization?

Absolute Advantage

Specialization occurs because different individuals and different nations have different skills. Sometimes it seems that some individuals are better at doing everything than anyone else. A president of a large company might be able to type better than any of the typists, file better than any of the file clerks, and wash windows better than any of the window washers. The president has an **absolute advantage** in all of these endeavors—if he were to spend a given amount of time in one of these activities, he could produce more than anyone else in the company. The president does not, however, spend his time doing those other activities. Why not? Because he is being paid the most for undertaking the president's managerial duties. The president specializes in one particular task in spite of having an absolute advantage in all tasks. Indeed, absolute advantage is irrelevant in predicting how he uses his time; only *comparative advantage* matters.

Absolute advantage
The ability to produce more units of a good or service using a given quantity of labor or resource inputs. Equivalently, the ability to produce the same quantity of a good or service using fewer units of labor or resource inputs.

Comparative Advantage

Comparative advantage is the ability to perform an activity at a lower opportunity cost. You have a comparative advantage in one activity whenever you have a lower opportunity cost of performing that activity. Comparative advantage is always a *relative* concept. You may be able to change the oil in your car; you might even be able to change it faster than the local mechanic. But if the opportunity cost you face by changing the oil exceeds the mechanic's opportunity cost, the mechanic has a comparative advantage in changing the oil. The mechanic faces a lower opportunity cost for that activity.

Comparative advantage
The ability to produce a good or service at a lower opportunity cost compared to other producers.

You may be convinced that everybody can do everything better than you. In this extreme situation, do you still have a comparative advantage? The answer is yes. What you need to do to discover your comparative advantage is to find a job in which your *disadvantage* relative to others is smaller. You do not have to be a mathematical genius to figure this out. The market tells you very clearly by offering you the highest income for the job for which you have a smaller disadvantage compared to others. Stated differently, to find your comparative advantage no matter how much better everybody else can do the jobs that you want to do, you simply find which job maximizes your income.

The coaches of sports teams are constantly faced with determining each player's comparative advantage. Babe Ruth was originally one of the best pitchers in professional baseball when he played for the Boston Red Sox. After he was traded to the New York Yankees, the owner and the coach decided to make him an outfielder, even though he was a better pitcher than anyone else on the team roster. They wanted "The Babe" to concentrate on his hitting. Good pitchers do not bring in as many fans as home-run kings. Babe Ruth's comparative advantage was clearly in hitting homers rather than practicing and developing his pitching game.

Scarcity, Self-Interest, and Specialization

In Chapter 1, you learned about the assumption of rational self-interest. To repeat, for the purposes of our analyses we assume that individuals are rational in that they will do what is in their own self-interest. They will not consciously carry out actions that will make them worse off. In this chapter, you learned that scarcity requires people to make choices. We assume that they make choices based on their self-interest. When they make these choices, they attempt to maximize benefits net of opportunity cost. In so doing, individuals choose their comparative advantage and end up specializing. Ultimately, when people specialize, they increase the money income they make and therefore become richer. When all individuals and businesses specialize simultaneously, the gains are seen in greater material well-being. With any given set of resources, specialization will result in higher output.

INTERNATIONAL EXAMPLE

Why Foreign Graduate Students Specialize When Studying in the United States

Specialization is evident in the fields of endeavor that foreign students choose when they come to the United States for graduate studies. Consider the following statistics: More than 60 percent of U.S. doctorates in engineering and 55 percent of those in mathematics, computer science, and the physical sciences are earned by foreign-born students. Yet foreign nationals are awarded relatively few advanced degrees in business, law, or medicine. The reason has nothing to do with intelligence or giftedness; it is simply that many more of the best American students choose schools in these professional fields rather than ones offering science and engineering programs.

Why does this specialization occur? For American students, the greatest returns for about the same effort come from business, law, and medicine. In contrast, foreign-born graduate students face fewer language and cultural obstacles (and hence better job prospects) if they choose technical subjects.

When students from foreign countries come to American graduate schools to obtain their Ph.D. degrees, more than 70 percent of them remain in the United States after graduation, thereby augmenting America's supply of engineers and scientists. Such specialization has helped the United States maintain its leadership in both the technoscientific and sociocultural areas.

For Critical Analysis

What type of capital do foreign-born students bring with them to the United States?

THE DIVISION OF LABOR

Division of labor
The segregation of a resource into different specific tasks; for example, one automobile worker puts on bumpers, another doors, and so on.

In any firm that includes specialized human and nonhuman resources, there is a **division of labor** among those resources. The best-known example comes from Adam Smith, who in *The Wealth of Nations* illustrated the benefits of a division of labor in the making of pins, as depicted in the following example:

> One man draws out the wire, another straightens it, a third cuts it, a fourth points it, a fifth grinds it at the top for receiving the head; to make the head requires two or three distinct operations; to put it on is a peculiar business, to whiten the pins is another; it is even a trade by itself to put them into the paper.

Making pins this way allowed 10 workers without very much skill to make almost 48,000 pins "of a middling size" in a day. One worker, toiling alone, could have made perhaps 20 pins a day; therefore, 10 workers could have produced 200. Division of labor allowed for an increase in the daily output of the pin factory from 200 to 48,000! (Smith did not attribute all of the gain to the division of labor according to talent but credited also the use of machinery and the fact that less time was spent shifting from task to task.)

What we are discussing here involves a division of the resource called labor into different kinds of labor. The different kinds of labor are organized in such a way as to increase the amount of output possible from the fixed resources available. We can therefore talk about an organized division of labor within a firm leading to increased output.

COMPARATIVE ADVANTAGE AND TRADE AMONG NATIONS

To find out about how much international trade takes place, go to **www.wto.org**, and click on "Statistics" in the left margin.

Though most of our analysis of absolute advantage, comparative advantage, and specialization has dealt with individuals, it is equally applicable to nations. First consider the United States. The Plains states have a comparative advantage in the production of grains and other agricultural goods. The states to the north and east tend to specialize in industrialized production, such as automobiles. Not surprisingly, grains are shipped from the Plains states to the northern states, and automobiles are shipped in the reverse direction. Such specialization and trade allow for higher incomes and standards of living. If both the Plains states and the northern states were politically defined as separate nations, the same analysis would still hold, but we would call it international trade. Indeed, Europe is comparable to the United States in area and population, but instead of one nation, Europe has 15. What in America we call *interstate* trade, in Europe they call *international* trade. There is no difference, however, in the economic results—both yield greater economic efficiency and higher average incomes.

Political problems that do not normally arise within a particular nation often do between nations. For example, if California avocado growers develop a cheaper method than growers in southern Florida to produce a tastier avocado, the Florida growers will lose out. They cannot do much about the situation except try to lower their own costs of production or improve their product. If avocado growers in Mexico, however, develop a cheaper method to produce better-tasting avocados, both California and Florida growers can (and likely will) try to raise political barriers that will prevent Mexican avocado growers from freely selling their product in America. U.S. avocado growers will use such arguments as "unfair" competition and loss of American jobs. In so doing, they are only partly right: Avocado-growing jobs may decline in America, but jobs will not necessarily decline overall. If the argument of U.S. avocado growers had any validity, every time a region in the United States developed a better way to produce a product manufactured somewhere else in the country, employment in America would decline. That has never happened and never will.

> **FAQ**
>
> ### Isn't too much international trade bad for the U.S. economy?
>
> No, despite what you may read or hear, international trade is just like any other economic activity. Indeed, you can think of international trade as a production process that transforms goods that we sell to other countries (exports) into goods that we buy from other countries (imports). This process is a mutually beneficial exchange that takes place across political borders. Because international trade occurs only because it is in the interests of both buyers and sellers, people in both nations gain from trade.

When nations specialize where they have a comparative advantage and then trade with the rest of the world, the average standard of living in the world rises. In effect, international trade allows the world to move from inside the global production possibilities curve toward the curve itself, thereby improving worldwide economic efficiency.

CONCEPTS IN BRIEF

- With a given set of resources, specialization results in higher output; in other words, there are gains to specialization in terms of greater material well-being.

- Individuals and nations specialize in their areas of comparative advantage in order to reap the gains of specialization.

- Comparative advantages are found by determining which activities have the lowest opportunity cost—that is, which activities yield the highest return for the time and resources used.

- A division of labor occurs when different workers are assigned different tasks. Together, the workers produce a desired product.

NETNOMICS

Allocating Scarce Space on the Web

Nearly half of all users of the World Wide Web visit fewer than 10 Internet sites per month. Companies that want to sell their products on the Internet know this. They also know that when individuals access the Internet, their homepage is typically that of their Internet service provider (Netscape, Explorer) or a search engine such as Yahoo! Consequently, many companies advertise on those Web pages.

This is why each time you access the Net, you see advertising—banners, buttons, keywords, hot links, and other promotions. Some of the biggest advertisers on the Web are Microsoft, Toyota, General Motors, Disney, IBM, AT&T, and American Express. Internet-based companies such as Amazon.com also are major Web advertisers. It is estimated that by 2005, advertisers will be spending more than $25 billion a year on the Web.

The owner of any Web page that carries advertising faces an opportunity cost. For example, advertisers widely consider the opening page of the Yahoo! search engine "prime real estate" because so many people see it each day. But there is relatively little space on the screen. Thus when Yahoo! allocates space to promote its own services and products, it gives up space it could sell. But if it fills up too much of the screen with ads, some users will switch to a less cluttered search engine. That fact makes Web page design a crucial business concern.

The Costs of Raising a Child Are Not the Same for Everyone

The U.S. Department of Agriculture (USDA) has estimated the costs of raising a child. These include explicit expenses parents incur in providing the child with housing, food, clothing, day care, education, health care, and transportation. Panel (a) of Figure 2-6 shows the USDA's estimates of these expenses that typical American parents in upper-, middle-, and lower-income families with only one child born in 1997 will incur during each of the first 17 years of the child's life. (These estimates take into account projected inflation. Also, note that a wife often reduces or halts her income-earning activities before a child is born, so there is also an "age 0" in the chart.) As you might expect, higher-income parents incur greater direct expenses; they are more likely to buy high-tech toys and trendy clothing.

"Quality Time" with Kids Has a Market Value

Another key component of the cost of raising a child, however, is the wages that parents forgo when they spend time taking kids to school, the doctor, soccer games, and so on. In some families, one spouse stays home most of the time to provide these services. In others, both parents work but take turns allocating some of their time each day to these duties. No matter how they choose to balance the time, parents forgo wages they

FIGURE 2-6

The Full Cost of Raising a Child

As shown in panel (a), the dollar cost of raising a child increases with the child's age and is more for higher-income parents. The same is true of opportunity cost, as shown in panel (b). Panel (c) reveals that forgone wages (opportunity cost) make up the largest part of total child-rearing expenses.

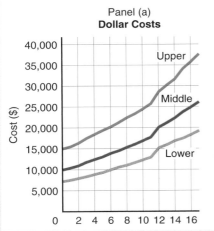

Panel (a)
Dollar Costs

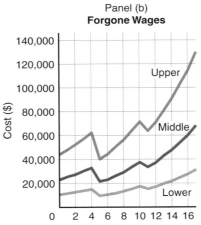

Panel (b)
Forgone Wages

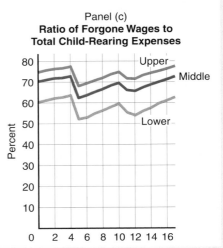

Panel (c)
Ratio of Forgone Wages to Total Child-Rearing Expenses

FOR CRITICAL ANALYSIS

1. Note in panel (b) that the forgone-wage component of the opportunity cost of child raising drops when a child reaches the age of 5 and then dips again slightly around age 11. What institutional factors do you suppose might account for this pattern?

2. In recent decades, population growth in lower-income countries has exceeded population growth in higher-income countries. Based on our discussion, can you provide a hypothesis explaining why?

otherwise could have earned if they had allocated their time to income-generating activities.

Panel (b) shows the USDA's estimates of forgone wages for parents in a typical one-child family. Not surprisingly, the forgone wages are much higher for upper-income parents than for parents in middle- and lower-income families.

Forgone Wages and the Opportunity Cost of Raising a Child

The sum of explicit expenses and forgone wages constitutes the total opportunity cost of raising a child. Thus adding together the costs at each age in panels (a) and (b) would give the amounts that couples forgo by engaging in the activity of parenting rather than earning the highest possible wages and allocating their incomes to other activities. If you compare the dollar amounts in panels (a) and (b), however, it is clear that forgone wages are the key component of the total opportunity cost of child raising. Panel (c) verifies this fact. It shows the ratio of forgone wages to total child-raising expenses for each parental income category. Within each income group, and at each age of the child, forgone wages consistently exceed half the total opportunity cost of raising a child. For higher-income parents, forgone wages are consistently in excess of two-thirds of the total opportunity cost.

We can infer an important fact from Figure 2-6. When people acquire more training and education and move into higher-wage occupations, the opportunity cost of raising a child rises significantly. Other things being equal—for instance, if we assume that parents derive roughly the same satisfaction from raising children irrespective of their income—this is likely to induce higher-income people to have fewer children.

SUMMARY DISCUSSION OF LEARNING OBJECTIVES

1. **The Problem of Scarcity, Even for the Affluent:** Scarcity is very different from poverty. No one can obtain all one desires from nature without sacrifice. Thus even the richest people face scarcity, because they have to make choices among alternatives. Despite their high levels of income or wealth, affluent people, like everyone else, typically want more than they can have (in terms of goods, power, prestige, and so on).

2. **Why Economists Consider Individuals' Wants but Not Their "Needs":** Goods are all things from which individuals derive satisfaction. Economic goods are those for which the desired quantity exceeds that amount that is directly available from nature at a zero price. The goods that we want are not necessarily those that we need. To economists, the term *need* is undefinable, whereas humans have unlimited *wants,* which are defined as the goods and services on which we place a positive value.

3. **Why Scarcity Leads People to Evaluate Opportunity Costs:** We measure the opportunity cost of anything by the highest-valued alternative that one must give up to obtain it. The trade-offs that we face as individuals and as a society can be represented by a production possibilities curve (PPC), and moving from one point on a PPC to another entails incurring an opportunity cost. The reason is that along a PPC, all currently available resources and technology are being used, so obtaining more of one good requires shifting resources to production of that good and away from production of another. That is, there is an opportunity cost of allocating scarce resource toward producing one good instead of another good.

4. **Why Obtaining Increasing Increments of a Good Requires Giving Up More and More Units of Other Goods:** Typically, resources are specialized. Thus when society allocates additional resources to producing more and more of a single good, it must increasingly employ resources that would be better suited for producing other goods. As a result, the law of increasing relative cost holds. Each additional unit of a good can be obtained only by giving up more and more of other goods, which means that the production possibilities curve that society faces is bowed outward.

5. **The Trade-Off Between Consumption Goods and Capital Goods:** If we allocate more resources to producing capital goods today, then, other things being equal, the economy will grow by a larger amount. Thus the production possibilities curve will shift outward by a larger amount in the future, which means that we can have more consumption goods in the future. The trade-off, however, is that producing more capital goods today entails giving up consumption goods today.

6. **Absolute Advantage Versus Comparative Advantage:** A person has an absolute advantage if she can produce more of a specific good than someone else who uses the same amount of resources. This also means that she can produce the same amount of that good using fewer resources. Nevertheless, the individual may be better off producing a different good if she has a comparative advantage in producing the other good, meaning that she can produce the other good at lower opportunity cost than someone else. By specializing in producing the good for which she has a comparative advantage, she assures herself of reaping gains from specialization in the form of a higher income.

Key Terms and Concepts

Absolute advantage (39)	Human capital (28)	Production (27)
Comparative advantage (39)	Inefficient point (34)	Production possibilities curve
Consumption (36)	Labor (28)	(PPC) (31)
Division of labor (40)	Land (28)	Scarcity (27)
Economic goods (28)	Law of increasing relative cost (35)	Services (28)
Efficiency (34)	Opportunity cost (30)	Specialization (38)
Entrepreneurship (28)	Physical capital (28)	Technology (33)
Goods (28)		

Problems

Answers to the odd-numbered problems appear at the back of the book.

2-1. The following table illustrates the points a student can earn on examinations in economics and biology if the student uses all available hours for study.

Economics	Biology
100	40
90	50
80	60
70	70
60	80
50	90
40	100

Plot this student's production possibilities curve. Does the PPC illustrate increasing or decreasing opportunity costs?

2-2. Based on the information provided in Problem 2-1, what is the opportunity cost to this student of allocating sufficient additional study time on economics to move her grade up from a 90 to a 100?

2-3. Consider the following costs that a student incurs by attending a public university for one semester: $3,000 for tuition, $1,000 for room and board, $500 for books, $3,000 in wages lost that the student could have earned working, and 3 percent interest lost on the $4,500 paid for tuition, room and board, and books. Calculate the total opportunity cost that the student incurs by attending college for one semester.

2-4. Consider a change in the table in Problem 2-2. The student's set of opportunities is now as follows:

Economics	Biology
100	40
90	60
80	75
70	85
60	93
50	98
40	100

Plot this student's production possibilities curve. Does the PPC illustrate increasing or decreasing opportunity costs? What is the opportunity cost to this student for the additional amount of study time on economics required to move his grade from 60 to 70? From 90 to 100?

2-5. Construct a production possibilities curve for a nation facing increasing opportunity costs for producing food and video games. Show how the PPC changes given the following events.

   a. A new and better fertilizer is invented.

   b. There is a surge in labor, which can be employed in both the agricultural sector and the video game sector.

   c. A new programming language is invented that is less costly to code and is more memory-efficient, enabling the use of smaller games cartridges.

   d. A heat wave and drought results in a 10 percent decrease in usable farmland.

2-6. The president of a university announces to the local media that the university was able to construct its sports complex at a lower cost than it had previously projected. The president argues that the university can now purchase a yacht for the president at no additional cost. Explain why this statement is false by considering opportunity cost.

2-7. You can wash, fold, and iron a basket of laundry in two hours and prepare a meal in one hour. Your roommate can wash, fold, and iron a basket of laundry in three hours and prepare a meal in one hour. Who has the absolute advantage in laundry, and who has an absolute advantage in meal preparation? Who has the comparative advantage in laundry, and who has a comparative advantage in meal preparation?

2-8. Based on the information in Problem 2-7, should you and your roommate specialize in a particular task? Why? And if so, who should specialize in which task? Show how much labor time you save if you choose to "trade" an appropriate task with your roommate as opposed to doing it yourself.

2-9. On the one hand, Canada goes to considerable lengths to protect its television program and magazine producers from U.S. competitors. The United States, on the other hand, often seeks protection from food imports from Canada. Construct an argument showing that from an economywide viewpoint, these efforts are misguided.

2-10. Using only the concept of comparative advantage, evaluate this statement: "A professor with a Ph.D. in economics should never mow his or her own lawn, because this would fail to take into account the professor's comparative advantage."

2-11. Country A and country B produce the same consumption goods and capital goods and currently have *identical* production possibilities curves. They also have the same resources at present, and they have access to the same technology.

   a. At present, does either country have a comparative advantage in producing capital goods? Consumption goods?

   b. Currently, country A has chosen to produce more consumption goods, compared with country B. Other things being equal, which will experience the larger outward shift of its PPC during the next year?

   c. Suppose that a year passes with no changes in technology or in factors other than the capital goods and consumption goods choices the countries initially made. Both countries' PPCs have shifted outward from their initial positions, but not in a parallel fashion. Country B's opportunity cost of producing consumption goods is now higher than in country A. Does either country have a comparative advantage in producing capital goods? Consumption goods?

Economics on the Net

Opportunity Cost and Labor Force Participation
Many students choose to forgo full-time employment to concentrate on their studies, thereby incurring a sizable opportunity cost. This application explores the nature of this opportunity cost.

Internet URL:
http://stats.bls.gov/news.release/hsgec.news.htm

Title: College Enrollment and Work Activity of High School Graduates

Navigation: Start at the Bureau of Labor Statistics (BLS) homepage (stats.bls.gov). Click on Data Home (stats.bls.gov/datahome.htm), and then click on News Releases (stats.bls.gov/newsrels.htm). Next, click on Employment and Unemployment (stats.bls.gov/newsrels.htm#OEUS), and then click on College Enrollment and Work Activity of High School Graduates (stats.bls.gov/newsrels.htm/hsgec.toc.htm). Finally, click on College Enrollment and Work Activity of High School Graduates.

Application Read the abbreviated report on college enrollment and work activity of high school graduates. Then answer the following questions.

1. Based on the article, explain who the BLS considers to be in the labor force and who it does not view as part of the labor force.

2. What is the difference in labor force participation rates between high school students entering four-year universities and those entering two-year universities? Using the concept of opportunity cost, explain the difference.

3. What is the difference in labor force participation rates between part-time college students and full-time college students? Using the concept of opportunity cost, explain the difference.

For Group Study and Analysis Read the last paragraph of the article, and then divide the class into two groups. The first group should explain, based on the concept of opportunity cost, the difference in labor force participation rates between youths not in school but with a high school diploma and youths not in school and without a high school diploma. The second half should explain, based on opportunity cost, the difference in labor force participation rates between men and women not in school but with a high school diploma and between men and women not in school and without a high school diploma.

DEMAND AND SUPPLY

This farm worker near Shaanxi, China, obtains water the old-fashioned way. Chinese officals claim to have a "water problem." Should water be analyzed differently than other resources?

Signs of water stress appear throughout China. Of China's 600 largest cities, half are "running short" of water. Some cities turn on water for general use by their residents only two hours per day. Each day, hundreds of farmers are finding their wells pumped dry. Nevertheless, annual rainfall levels in most of China have hovered within normal ranges. Indeed, in some locales in recent years, above-normal rainfalls have caused flooding.

Can residents of China do nothing but hope for more rain? In this chapter, you will learn about one important factor contributing to China's water stress. You will also learn how to reason out one important part of the solution to this problem—a solution that China's leaders have slowly moved toward adopting. To do this, you will need the tools of demand and supply analysis.

Did You Know That... more than 75 million people currently own portable cellular phones? This is a huge jump from the mere 200,000 who owned them in 1985. Since 1992, two out of every three new telephone numbers have been assigned to cellular phones. There are several reasons for the growth of cellular phones, not the least being the dramatic reduction in both price and size due to improved and cheaper computer chips that go into making them. There is something else at work, though. It has to do with crime. In a recent survey, 46 percent of new cellular phone users said that personal safety was the main reason they bought a portable phone. In Florida, for example, most cellular phone companies allow users simply to dial *FHP to reach the Florida Highway Patrol. The rush to cellular phones is worldwide. Over the past decade, sales have grown by nearly 50 percent every year outside the United States.

We could attempt to explain the phenomenon by saying that more people like to use portable phones. But that explanation is neither satisfying nor entirely accurate. If we use the economist's primary set of tools, *demand and supply,* we will have a better understanding of the cellular phone explosion, as well as many other phenomena in our world. Demand and supply are two ways of categorizing the influences on the price of goods that you buy and the quantities available. As such, demand and supply form the basis of virtually all economic analysis of the world around us.

As you will see throughout this text, the operation of the forces of demand and supply take place in *markets.* A **market** is an abstract concept referring to all the arrangements individuals have for exchanging with one another. Goods and services are sold in markets, such as the automobile market, the health market, and the compact disc market. Workers offer their services in the labor market. Companies, or firms, buy workers' labor services in the labor market. Firms also buy other inputs in order to produce the goods and services that you buy as a consumer. Firms purchase machines, buildings, and land. These markets are in operation at all times. One of the most important activities in these markets is the setting of the prices of all of the inputs and outputs that are bought and sold in our complicated economy. To understand the determination of prices, you first need to look at the law of demand.

Chapter Outline

- The Law of Demand
- The Demand Schedule
- Shifts in Demand
- The Law of Supply
- The Supply Schedule
- Shifts in Supply
- Putting Demand and Supply Together

Market
All of the arrangements that individuals have for exchanging with one another. Thus we can speak of the labor market, the automobile market, and the credit market.

THE LAW OF DEMAND

Demand has a special meaning in economics. It refers to the quantities of specific goods or services that individuals, taken singly or as a group, will purchase at various possible prices, other things being constant. We can therefore talk about the demand for microprocessor chips, French fries, compact disc players, children, and criminal activities.

Associated with the concept of demand is the **law of demand,** which can be stated as follows:

When the price of a good goes up, people buy less of it, other things being equal.
When the price of a good goes down, people buy more of it, other things being equal.

The law of demand tells us that the quantity demanded of any commodity is inversely related to its price, other things being equal. In an inverse relationship, one variable moves up in value when the other moves down. The law of demand states that a change in price causes a change in the quantity demanded in the *opposite* direction.

Notice that we tacked on to the end of the law of demand the statement "other things being equal." We referred to this in Chapter 1 as the *ceteris paribus* assumption. It means, for example, that when we predict that people will buy fewer DVD (digital videodisk)

Demand
A schedule of how much of a good or service people will purchase at any price during a specified time period, other things being constant.

Law of demand
The observation that there is a negative, or inverse, relationship between the price of any good or service and the quantity demanded, holding other factors constant.

players if their price goes up, we are holding constant the price of all other goods in the economy as well as people's incomes. Implicitly, therefore, if we are assuming that no other prices change when we examine the price behavior of DVD players, we are looking at the *relative* price of DVD players.

The law of demand is supported by millions of observations of people's behavior in the marketplace. Theoretically, it can be derived from an economic model based on rational behavior, as was discussed in Chapter 1. Basically, if nothing else changes and the price of a good falls, the lower price induces us to buy more over a certain period of time because we can enjoy additional net gains that were unavailable at the higher price. For the most part, if you examine your own behavior, you will see that it generally follows the law of demand.

Relative Prices Versus Money Prices

Relative price
The price of one commodity divided by the price of another commodity; the number of units of one commodity that must be sacrificed to purchase one unit of another commodity.

Money price
The price that we observe today, expressed in today's dollars. Also called the *absolute* or *nominal price.*

The **relative price** of any commodity is its price in terms of another commodity. The price that you pay in dollars and cents for any good or service at any point in time is called its **money price.** Consider an example that you might hear quite often around parents and grandparents. "When I bought my first new car, it cost only fifteen hundred dollars." The implication, of course, is that the price of cars today is outrageously high because the average new car might cost $25,000. But that is not an accurate comparison. What was the price of the average house during that same year? Perhaps it was only $12,000. By comparison, then, given that houses today average about $175,000, the price of a new car today doesn't sound so far out of line, does it?

The point is that money prices during different time periods don't tell you much. You have to find out relative prices. Consider an example of the price of CDs versus cassettes from last year and this year. In Table 3-1, we show the money price of CDs and cassettes for two years during which they have both gone up. That means that we have to pay out in today's dollars and cents more for CDs and more for cassettes. If we look, though, at the relative prices of CDs and cassettes, we find that last year, CDs were twice as expensive as cassettes, whereas this year they are only $1\frac{3}{4}$ times as expensive. Conversely, if we compare cassettes to CDs, last year they cost only half

FAQ

Isn't postage a lot more expensive than it used to be?

No, in reality, the *relative price* of postage in the United States has fallen steadily over the years. The absolute dollar price of a first-class stamp rose from 3 cents in 1940 to 33 cents at the beginning of the twenty-first century. Nevertheless, the price of postage relative to the average of all other prices has declined since reaching a peak in 1975.

TABLE 3-1
Money Price Versus Relative Price
The money price of both compact disks (CDs) and cassettes has risen. But the relative price of CDs has fallen (or conversely, the relative price of cassettes has risen).

	Money Price		Relative Price	
	Price Last Year	Price This Year	Price Last Year	Price This Year
CDs	$12	$14	$\frac{\$12}{\$6} = 2.0$	$\frac{\$14}{\$8} = 1.75$
Cassettes	$ 6	$ 8	$\frac{\$6}{\$12} = 0.5$	$\frac{\$8}{\$14} = 0.57$

as much as CDs, but today they cost about 57 percent as much. In the one-year period, though both prices have gone up in money terms, the relative price of CDs has fallen (and equivalently, the relative price of cassettes has risen).

INTERNATIONAL EXAMPLE

The High Relative Price of a U.S. Education

In 1993, about 40 percent of all college students classified as "international students"—students working toward degrees outside their home countries—were enrolled in U.S. colleges and universities. This figure has shrunk to just over 30 percent today, and it gradually continues to decline.

Have foreign students decided that the quality of American higher education is diminishing? Some may have made this judgment, but a more likely explanation for the falling U.S. share of international students is the higher relative price of a U.S. college education. Throughout the 1990s, tuition and other fees that U.S. colleges and universities charged for their services rose much faster than the average price

of other goods and services. They also rose faster than tuition and fees at foreign universities. For instance, even before the sharp 1997–1998 economic contraction in Southeast Asia, increasing numbers of students from this region had begun studying at Australian universities. Colleges in Australia are not only closer to home but also less expensive.

For Critical Analysis

If the relative price of education at U.S. universities continues to increase, what other means could these universities use to try to regain their lost share of international students?

CONCEPTS IN BRIEF

- The law of demand posits an inverse relationship between the quantity demanded of a good and its price, other things being equal.
- The law of demand applies when other things, such as income and the prices of all other goods and services, are held constant.

THE DEMAND SCHEDULE

Let's take a hypothetical demand situation to see how the inverse relationship between the price and the quantity demanded looks (holding other things equal). We will consider the quantity of minidisks demanded *per year.* Without stating the *time dimension,* we could not make sense out of this demand relationship because the numbers would be different if we were talking about the quantity demanded per month or the quantity demanded per decade.

In addition to implicitly or explicitly stating a time dimension for a demand relationship, we are also implicitly referring to *constant-quality units* of the good or service in question. Prices are always expressed in constant-quality units in order to avoid the problem of comparing commodities that are in fact not truly comparable.

In panel (a) of Figure 3-1 on page 52, we see that if the price were $1 per minidisk, 50 disks would be bought each year by our representative individual, but if the price were $5 per disk, only 10 minidisks would be bought each year. This reflects the law of demand. Panel (a) is also called simply demand, or a *demand schedule,* because it gives a schedule of alternative quantities demanded per year at different possible prices.

FIGURE 3-1
The Individual Demand Schedule and the Individual Demand Curve

In panel (a), we show combinations A through E of the quantities of minidisks demanded, measured in constant-quality units at prices ranging from $5 down to $1 per disk. In panel (b), we plot combinations A through E on a grid. The result is the individual demand curve for minidisks.

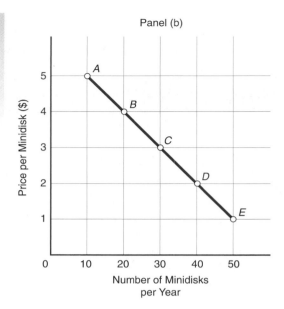

Panel (b)

Panel (a)

Combination	Price per Constant-Quality Minidisks	Quantity of Constant-Quality Minidisks per Year
A	$5	10
B	4	20
C	3	30
D	2	40
E	1	50

The Demand Curve

Tables expressing relationships between two variables can be represented in graphical terms. To do this, we need only construct a graph that has the price per constant-quality minidisk on the vertical axis and the quantity measured in constant-quality minidisks per year on the horizontal axis. All we have to do is take combinations A through E from panel (a) of Figure 3-1 and plot those points in panel (b). Now we connect the points with a smooth line, and *voilà,* we have a **demand curve.*** It is downward-sloping (from left to right) to indicate the inverse relationship between the price of minidisks and the quantity demanded per year. Our presentation of demand schedules and curves applies equally well to all commodities, including toothpicks, hamburgers, textbooks, credit, and labor services. Remember, the demand curve is simply a graphical representation of the law of demand.

Demand curve
A graphical representation of the demand schedule; a negatively sloped line showing the inverse relationship between the price and the quantity demanded (other things being equal).

Individual Versus Market Demand Curves

The demand schedule shown in panel (a) of Figure 3-1 and the resulting demand curve shown in panel (b) are both given for an individual. As we shall see, the determination of price in the marketplace depends on, among other things, the **market demand** for a particular commodity. The way in which we measure a market demand schedule and derive a market demand curve for minidisks or any other commodity is by summing (at each price) the individual demand for all buyers in the market. Suppose that the market demand for minidisks consists of only two buyers: buyer 1, for whom we've already shown the demand schedule, and buyer 2, whose demand schedule is displayed in column 3 of panel (a) of

Market demand
The demand of all consumers in the marketplace for a particular good or service. The summing at each price of the quantity demanded by each individual.

*Even though we call them "curves," for the purposes of exposition we often draw straight lines. In many real-world situations, demand and supply curves will in fact be lines that do curve. To connect the points in panel (b) with a line, we assume that for all prices in between the ones shown, the quantities demanded will be found along that line.

FIGURE 3-2
The Horizontal Summation of Two Demand Schedules

Panel (a) shows how to sum the demand schedule for one buyer with that of another buyer. In column 2 is the quantity demanded by buyer 1, taken from panel (a) of Figure 3-1. Column 4 is the sum of columns 2 and 3. We plot the demand curve for buyer 1 in panel (b) and the demand curve for buyer 2 in panel (c). When we add those two demand curves horizontally, we get the market demand curve for two buyers, shown in panel (d).

Panel (a)

(1) Price per Minidisk	(2) Buyer 1's Quantity Demanded	(3) Buyer 2's Quantity Demanded	(4) = (2) + (3) Combined Quantity Demanded per Year
$5	10	10	20
4	20	20	40
3	30	40	70
2	40	50	90
1	50	60	110

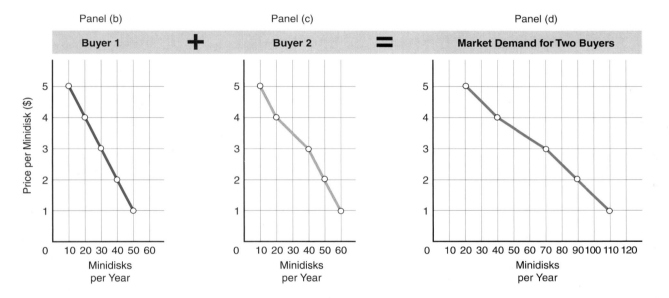

Figure 3-2. Column 1 shows the price, and column 2 shows the quantity demanded by buyer 1 at each price. These data are taken directly from Figure 3-1. In column 3, we show the quantity demanded by buyer 2. Column 4 shows the total quantity demanded at each price, which is obtained by simply adding columns 2 and 3. Graphically, in panel (d) of Figure 3-2, we add the demand curves of buyer 1 [panel (b)] and buyer 2 [panel (c)] to derive the market demand curve.

There are, of course, numerous potential consumers of minidisks. We'll simply assume that the summation of all of the consumers in the market results in a demand schedule, given in panel (a) of Figure 3-3 on page 54, and a demand curve, given in panel (b). The quantity demanded is now measured in millions of units per year. Remember, panel (b) in Figure 3-3 shows the market demand curve for the millions of users of minidisks. The "market" demand curve that we derived in Figure 3-2 was undertaken assuming that there were only two buyers in the entire market. That's why the "market" demand curve for two buyers in panel (d) of Figure 3-2 is not a smooth line, whereas the true market demand curve in panel (b) of Figure 3-3 is a smooth line with no kinks.

Now consider some special aspects of the market demand curve for compact disks.

Putting
Economics in Action
to Work

For practice working with demand schedules, start the *EIA* CD and click on "Demand and Supply." Then click on "The Demand for Walkmans."

FIGURE 3-3

The Market Demand Schedule for Minidisks
In panel (a), we add up the existing demand schedules for minidisks. In panel (b), we plot the quantities from panel (a) on a grid; connecting them produces the market demand curve for minidisks.

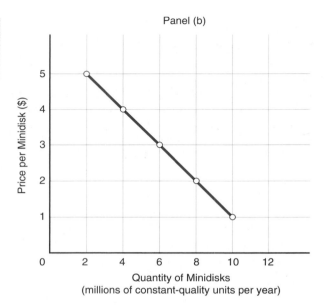

Panel (b)

Panel (a)

Price per Constant-Quality Minidisk	Total Quantity Demanded of Constant-Quality Minidisks per Year (millions)
$5	2
4	4
3	6
2	8
1	10

EXAMPLE

Garth Brooks, Used CDs, and the Law of Demand

A few years ago, country singer Garth Brooks tried to prevent his latest album from being sold to any chain or store that also sells used CDs. His argument was that the used-CD market deprived labels and artists of earnings. His announcement came after Wherehouse Entertainment, Inc., a 339-store retailer based in Torrance, California, started selling used CDs side by side with new releases, at half the price. Brooks, along with the distribution arms of Sony, Warner Music, Capitol-EMI, and MCA, was trying to quash the used-CD market. By so doing, it appears that none of these parties understands the law of demand.

Let's say the price of a new CD is $15. The existence of a secondary used-CD market means that to people who choose to resell their CDs for $5, the cost of a new CD is in fact only $10. Because we know that quantity demanded is inversely related to price, we know that more of a new CD will be sold at a price of $10 than of the same CD at a price of $15. Taking only this force into account, eliminating the used-CD market tends to reduce sales of new CDs.

But there is another force at work here, too. Used CDs are substitutes for new CDs. If used CDs are not available, some people who would have purchased them will instead purchase new CDs. If this second effect outweighs the incentive to buy less because of the higher effective price, then Brooks is behaving correctly in trying to suppress the used CD market.

For Critical Analysis
Can you apply this argument to the used-book market, in which both authors and publishers have long argued that used books are "killing them"?

CONCEPTS IN BRIEF

- We measure the demand schedule in terms of a time dimension and in constant-quality units.

- The market demand curve is derived by summing the quantity demanded by individuals at each price. Graphically, we add the individual demand curves horizontally to derive the total, or market, demand curve.

SHIFTS IN DEMAND

Assume that the federal government gives every student registered in a college, university, or technical school in the United States a minidisk player-recorder. The demand curve presented in panel (b) of Figure 3-3 would no longer be an accurate representation of total market demand for minidisks. What we have to do is shift the curve outward, or to the right, to represent the rise in demand. There will now be an increase in the number of minidisks demanded at *each and every possible price*. The demand curve shown in Figure 3-4 will shift from D_1 to D_2. Take any price, say, $3 per minidisk. Originally, before the federal government giveaway of player-recorders, the amount demanded at $3 was 6 million minidisks per year. After the government giveaway, however, the new amount demanded at $3 is 10 million minidisks per year. What we have seen is a shift in the demand for minidisks.

The shift can also go in the opposite direction. What if colleges uniformly outlawed the use of minidisk players by any of their students? Such a regulation would cause a shift inward—to the left—of the demand curve for minidisks. In Figure 3-4, the demand curve would shift to D_3; the amount demanded would now be less at each and every possible price.

The Other Determinants of Demand

The demand curve in panel (b) of Figure 3-3 is drawn with other things held constant, specifically all of the other factors that determine how much will be bought. There are many such determinants. The major other determinants are income; tastes and preferences; the prices of related goods; expectations regarding future prices, future incomes, and future product availability; and market size (number of buyers). Let's examine each determinant more closely.

Income. For most goods, an increase in income will lead to an increase in demand. The expression *increase in demand* always refers to a comparison between two different demand curves. Thus for most goods, an increase in income will lead to a rightward shift in the position of the demand curve from, say, D_1 to D_2 in Figure 3-4. You can avoid confusion about shifts in curves by always relating a rise in demand to a rightward shift in the

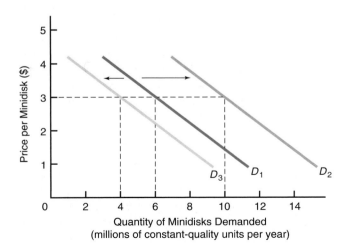

Price per Minidisk ($)

Quantity of Minidisks Demanded
(millions of constant-quality units per year)

FIGURE 3-4
A Shift in the Demand Curve
If some factor other than price changes, the only way we can show its effect is by moving the entire demand curve, say, from D_1 to D_2. We have assumed in our example that the move was precipitated by the government's giving a free minidisk player-recorder to every registered college student in America. That meant that at *all* prices, a larger number of minidisks would be demanded than before. Curve D_3 represents reduced demand compared to curve D_1, caused by a law prohibiting computers on campus.

Normal goods
Goods for which demand rises as income rises. Most goods are considered normal.

Inferior goods
Goods for which demand falls as income rises.

demand curve and a fall in demand to a leftward shift in the demand curve. Goods for which the demand rises when income rises are called **normal goods.** Most goods, such as shoes, computers, and CDs, are "normal goods." For some goods, however, demand *falls* as income rises. These are called **inferior goods.** Beans might be an example. As households get richer, they tend to spend less and less on beans and more and more on meat. (The terms *normal* and *inferior* are merely part of the economist's lexicon; no value judgments are associated with them.)

Remember, a shift to the left in the demand curve represents a fall in demand, and a shift to the right represents a rise, or increase, in demand.

EXAMPLE

Is Dental Care Becoming an Inferior Good?

A British health minister once claimed that the demand for health care is infinite because in the end everyone is in a losing battle against death. This is not so for American dentistry, however. As aggregate U.S. income levels have risen during the past 25 years, overall spending on dental care services has declined.

It isn't that fewer Americans are seeing dentists each year. They just do not require as many fillings or extractions. As incomes rose across the land, people purchased more expensive and effective toothpastes. More towns, cities, and counties began to fluoridate their water as the relative price of this anticavity agent declined, so changing relative prices have also played a role. And higher incomes of their residents have per-

mitted more municipalities to purchase fluoridation systems.

At every age, the average American now has about two more teeth than 25 years ago. Unfortunately for dentists who specialize in treating decaying and diseased teeth, Americans' teeth are healthier than ever before.

For Critical Analysis
Many fledgling dentists have begun specializing in "cosmetic dentistry" desired by clients with healthy but less than beautiful teeth. Compared to traditional dental care services, is cosmetic dentistry more or less likely to be a normal good?

Tastes and Preferences.   A change in consumer tastes in favor of a good can shift its demand curve outward to the right. When Frisbees® became the rage, the demand curve for them shifted outward to the right; when the rage died out, the demand curve shifted inward to the left. Fashions depend to a large extent on people's tastes and preferences. Economists have little to say about the determination of tastes; that is, they don't have any "good" theories of taste determination or why people buy one brand of product rather than others. Advertisers, however, have various theories that they use to try to make consumers prefer their products over those of competitors.

Prices of Related Goods: Substitutes and Complements.   Demand schedules are always drawn with the prices of all other commodities held constant. That is to say, when deriving a given demand curve, we assume that only the price of the good under study changes. For example, when we draw the demand curve for butter, we assume that the price of margarine is held constant. When we draw the demand curve for stereo speakers, we assume that the price of stereo amplifiers is held constant. When we refer to *related goods,* we are talking about goods for which demand is interdependent. If a change in the price of one good shifts the demand for another good, those two goods are related. There are two types of related goods: *substitutes* and *complements.* We can define and distinguish between substitutes and complements in terms of how the change in price of one commodity affects the demand for its related commodity.

Butter and margarine are **substitutes.** Either can be consumed to satisfy the same basic want. Let's assume that both products originally cost $2 per pound. If the price of butter remains the same and the price of margarine falls from $2 per pound to $1 per pound, people will buy more margarine and less butter. The demand curve for butter will shift inward to the left. If, conversely, the price of margarine rises from $2 per pound to $3 per pound, people will buy more butter and less margarine. The demand curve for butter will shift outward to the right. In other words, an increase in the price of margarine will lead to an increase in the demand for butter, and an increase in the price of butter will lead to an increase in the demand for margarine. For substitutes, a price change in the substitute will cause a change in demand *in the same direction.*

For **complements,** goods typically consumed together, the situation is reversed. Consider stereo speakers and stereo amplifiers. We draw the demand curve for speakers with the price of amplifiers held constant. If the price per constant-quality unit of stereo amplifiers decreases from, say, $500 to $200, that will encourage more people to purchase component stereo systems. They will now buy more speakers, at any given speaker price, than before. The demand curve for speakers will shift outward to the right. If, by contrast, the price of amplifiers increases from $200 to $500, fewer people will purchase component stereo systems. The demand curve for speakers will shift inward to the left. To summarize, a decrease in the price of amplifiers leads to an increase in the demand for speakers. An increase in the price of amplifiers leads to a decrease in the demand for speakers. Thus for complements, a price change in a product will cause a change in demand *in the opposite direction.*

Are new learning technologies complements or substitutes for college instructors? Read on.

Substitutes

Two goods are substitutes when either one can be used for consumption to satisfy a similar want—for example, coffee and tea. The more you buy of one, the less you buy of the other. For substitutes, the change in the price of one causes a shift in demand for the other in the same direction as the price change.

Complements

Two goods are complements if both are used together for consumption or enjoyment—for example, coffee and cream. The more you buy of one, the more you buy of the other. For complements, a change in the price of one causes an opposite shift in the demand for the other.

EXAMPLE

Getting Your Degree via the Internet

In this class and in others, you have most likely been exposed to such instructional technologies as films, videos, and interactive CD-ROM learning systems. The future for some of you, or at least the next few generations, may be quite different. All of the instructional technology that your professor provides may be packaged in the form of on-line courses. Many institutions of higher learning are now using the Internet to provide full instruction. It is called *distance learning* or *distributive learning.* And it is worldwide. For example, the University of Michigan, in conjunction with companies in Hong Kong, South Korea, and Europe, offers a global M.B.A. through the Internet. A professor teaches a course "live" via video and uses the software program Lotus Notes, which allows course information to be sent via the Internet. Students submit their homework assignments the same way. Duke University runs the

Global Executive M.B.A. program, in which students "attend" CD-ROM video lectures, download additional video and audio materials, and receive interactive study aids, all via the Internet.

Virtually all major college publishers now have projects to develop distance learning via the Internet. In addition, a consortium of over 100 universities has put in place what is called Internet II. Internet II permits full-motion video and virtually instantaneous interactivity for participating universities. The age of fully interactive distance learning with full-motion video is not far off. Certainly, even better technology, as yet undeveloped, will speed up this process.

For Critical Analysis

What do you predict will happen to the demand curve for college professors in the future?

Expectations.   Consumers' expectations regarding future prices, future incomes, and future availability may prompt them to buy more or less of a particular good without a change in its current money price. For example, consumers getting wind of a scheduled 100 percent price increase in minidisks next month may buy more of them today at today's prices. Today's demand curve for minidisks will shift from D_1 to D_2 in Figure 3-4. The opposite would occur if a decrease in the price of minidisks were scheduled for next month.

Expectations of a rise in income may cause consumers to want to purchase more of everything today at today's prices. Again, such a change in expectations of higher future income will cause a shift in the demand curve from D_1 to D_2 in Figure 3-4.

Finally, expectations that goods will not be available at any price will induce consumers to stock up now, increasing current demand.

Market Size (Number of Buyers).   An increase in the number of buyers (holding per capita income constant) shifts the market demand curve outward. Conversely, a reduction in the number of buyers shifts the market demand curve inward.

Changes in Demand Versus Changes in Quantity Demanded

We have made repeated references to demand and to quantity demanded. It is important to realize that there is a difference between a *change in demand* and a *change in quantity demanded.*

Demand refers to a schedule of planned rates of purchase and depends on a great many nonprice determinants. Whenever there is a change in a nonprice determinant, there will be a change in demand—a shift in the entire demand curve to the right or to the left.

A quantity demanded is a specific quantity at a specific price, represented by a single point on a demand curve. When price changes, quantity demanded changes according to the law of demand, and there will be a movement from one point to another along the same demand curve. Look at Figure 3-5. At a price of $3 per minidisk, 6 million disks per year are demanded. If the price falls to $1, quantity demanded increases to 10 million per year. This movement occurs because the current market price for the product changes. In Figure 3-5, you can see the arrow pointing down the given demand curve D.

FIGURE 3-5
Movement Along a Given Demand Curve
A change in price changes the quantity of a good demanded. This can be represented as movement along a given demand schedule. If, in our example, the price of minidisks falls from $3 to $1 apiece, the quantity demanded will increase from 6 million to 10 million units per year.

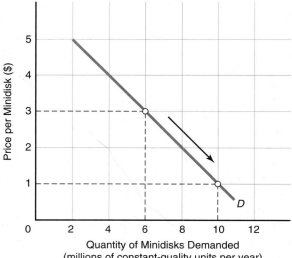

When you think of demand, think of the entire curve. Quantity demanded, in contrast, is represented by a single point on the demand curve.

A change or shift in demand causes the *entire* curve to move. The *only* thing that can cause the entire curve to move is a change in a determinant *other than its own price.*

In economic analysis, we cannot emphasize too much the following distinction that must constantly be made:

A change in a good's own price leads to a change in quantity demanded, for any given demand curve, other things held constant. This is a movement *on* the curve.

A change in any other determinant of demand leads to a change in demand. This causes a movement *of* the curve.

● Demand curves are drawn with determinants other than the price of the good held constant. These other determinants are (1) income; (2) tastes and preferences; (3) prices of related goods; (4) expectations about future prices, future incomes, and future availability of goods; and (5) market size (the number of buyers in the market). If any one of these determinants changes, the demand schedule will shift to the right or to the left.

● A change in demand comes about only because of a change in the other determinants of demand. This change in demand shifts the demand curve to the left or to the right.

● A change in the quantity demanded comes about when there is a change in the price of the good (other things held constant). Such a change in quantity demanded involves a movement along a given demand curve.

CONCEPTS IN BRIEF

THE LAW OF SUPPLY

The other side of the basic model in economics involves the quantities of goods and services that firms will offer for sale to the market. The **supply** of any good or service is the amount that firms will produce and offer for sale under certain conditions during a specified time period. The relationship between price and quantity supplied, called the **law of supply,** can be summarized as follows:

At higher prices, a larger quantity will generally be supplied than at lower prices, all other things held constant. At lower prices, a smaller quantity will generally be supplied than at higher prices, all other things held constant.

There is generally a direct relationship between quantity supplied and price. For supply, as the price rises, the quantity supplied rises; as price falls, the quantity supplied also falls. Producers are normally willing to produce and sell more of their product at a higher price than at a lower price, other things being constant. At $5 per minidisk, manufacturers would almost certainly be willing to supply a larger quantity than at $1 per unit, assuming, of course, that no other prices in the economy had changed.

As with the law of demand, millions of instances in the real world have given us confidence in the law of supply. On a theoretical level, the law of supply is based on a model in which producers and sellers seek to make the most gain possible from their activities. For example, as a minidisk manufacturer attempts to produce more and more minidisks over the same time period, it will eventually have to hire more workers, pay overtime wages (which are higher), and overutilize its machines. Only if offered a higher price per minidisk will the minidisk manufacturer be willing to incur these higher costs. That is why the law of supply implies a direct relationship between price and quantity supplied.

Supply
A schedule showing the relationship between price and quantity supplied for a specified period of time, other things being equal.

Law of supply
The observation that the higher the price of a good, the more of that good sellers will make available over a specified time period, other things being equal.

Putting
Economics in Action
to Work

To gain more experience with the concept of the law of supply, go to the *EIA* CD's table of contents and click on "Demand and Supply." Then click on "The Law of Supply."

THE SUPPLY SCHEDULE

Just as we were able to construct a demand schedule, we can construct a *supply schedule,* which is a table relating prices to the quantity supplied at each price. A supply schedule can also be referred to simply as *supply.* It is a set of planned production rates that depends on the price of the product. We show the individual supply schedule for a hypothetical producer in panel (a) of Figure 3-6. At $1 per minidisk, for example, this producer will supply 20,000 minidisks per year; at $5, this producer will supply 55,000 minidisks per year.

The Supply Curve

Supply curve
The graphical representation of the supply schedule; a line (curve) showing the supply schedule, which generally slopes upward (has a positive slope), other things being equal.

We can convert the supply schedule in panel (a) of Figure 3-6 into a **supply curve,** just as we earlier created a demand curve in Figure 3-1. All we do is take the price-quantity combinations from panel (a) of Figure 3-6 and plot them in panel (b). We have labeled these combinations *F* through *J.* Connecting these points, we obtain an upward-sloping curve that shows the typically direct relationship between price and quantity supplied. Again, we have to remember that we are talking about quantity supplied *per year,* measured in constant-quality units.

The Market Supply Curve

Just as we had to sum the individual demand curves to get the market demand curve, we need to sum the individual producers' supply curves to get the market supply curve. Look at Figure 3-7, in which we horizontally sum two typical minidisk manufacturers' supply curves. Supplier 1's data are taken from Figure 3-6; supplier 2 is added. The numbers are presented in panel (a). The graphical representation of supplier 1 is in panel (b), of supplier 2 in panel (c), and of the summation in panel (d). The result, then, is the supply curve for minidisks for suppliers 1 and 2. We assume that there are more suppliers of minidisks, however. The total market supply schedule and total market demand curve for minidisks are represented in Figure 3-8, with the curve in panel (b) obtained by adding all of the supply

---

FIGURE 3-6

The Individual Producer's Supply Schedule and Supply Curve for Minidisks

Panel (a) shows that at higher prices, a hypothetical supplier will be willing to provide a greater quantity of minidisks. We plot the various price-quantity combinations in panel (a) on the grid in panel (b). When we connect these points, we find the individual supply curve for diskettes. It is positively sloped.

Panel (a)

Combination	Price per Constant-Quality Minidisk	Quantity of Minidisks Supplied (thousands of constant-quality units per year)
F	$5	55
G	4	40
H	3	35
I	2	25
J	1	20

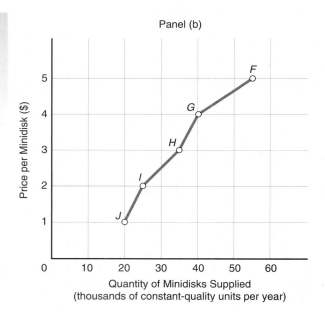

Panel (b)

Panel (a)

(1) Price per Minidisk	(2) Supplier 1's Quantity Supplied (thousands)	(3) Supplier 2's Quantity Supplied (thousands)	(4) = (2) + (3) Combined Quantity Supplied per Year (thousands)
$5	55	35	90
4	40	30	70
3	35	20	55
2	25	15	40
1	20	10	30

FIGURE 3-7
Horizontal Summation of Supply Curves

In panel (a), we show the data for two individual suppliers of minidisks. Adding how much each is willing to supply at different prices, we come up with the combined quantities supplied in column 4. When we plot the values in columns 2 and 3 on grids in panels (b) and (c) and add them horizontally, we obtain the combined supply curve for the two suppliers in question, shown in panel (d).

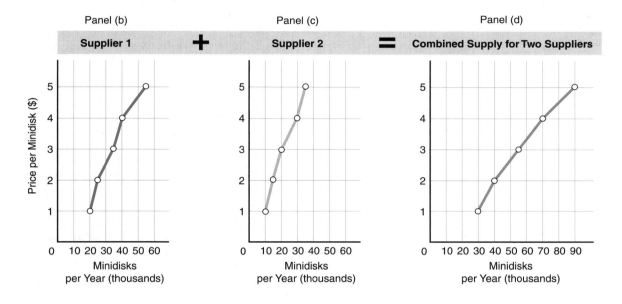

FIGURE 3-8
The Market Supply Schedule and the Market Supply Curve for Minidisks

In panel (a), we show the summation of all the individual producers' supply schedules; in panel (b), we graph the resulting supply curve. It represents the market supply curve for diskettes and is upward-sloping.

Panel (a)

Price per Constant-Quality Minidisk	Quantity of Minidisks Supplied (millions of constant-quality units per year)
$5	10
4	8
3	6
2	4
1	2

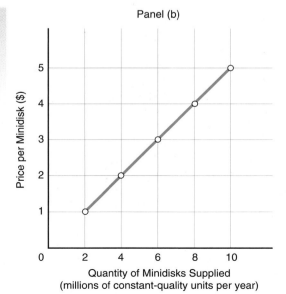

curves such as those shown in panels (b) and (c) of Figure 3-7. Notice the difference between the market supply curve with only two suppliers in Figure 3-7 and the one with a large number of suppliers—the entire true market—in panel (b) of Figure 3-8. We assume that the true total market supply curve is a straight line.

Notice what happens at the market level when price changes. If the price is $3, the quantity supplied is 6 million. If the price goes up to $4, the quantity supplied increases to 8 million per year. If the price falls to $2, the quantity supplied decreases to 4 million per year. Changes in quantity supplied are represented by movements along the supply curve in panel (b) of Figure 3-8.

CONCEPTS IN BRIEF

- ◉ There is normally a direct, or positive, relationship between price and quantity of a good supplied, other things held constant.

- ◉ The supply curve normally shows a direct relationship between price and quantity supplied. The market supply curve is obtained by horizontally adding individual supply curves in the market.

SHIFTS IN SUPPLY

When we looked at demand, we found out that any change in anything relevant besides the price of the good or service caused the demand curve to shift inward or outward. The same is true for the supply curve. If something besides price changes and alters the willingness of suppliers to produce a good or service, then we will see the entire supply curve shift.

Consider an example. A new method of coating minidisks has been invented. It reduces the cost of production by 50 percent. In this situation, minidisk producers will supply more product at *all* prices because their cost of so doing has fallen dramatically. Competition among manufacturers to produce more at each and every price will shift the supply schedule outward to the right from S_1 to S_2 in Figure 3-9. At a price of $3, the quantity supplied was originally 6 million per year, but now the quantity supplied (after the reduction in the costs of production) at $3 a minidisk will be 9 million a year. (This is similar to what has happened to the supply curve of personal computers and fax machines in recent years as computer memory chip prices have fallen.)

Consider the opposite case. If the cost of making minidisks doubles, the supply curve in Figure 3-9 will shift from S_1 to S_3. At each and every price, the number of minidisks supplied will fall due to the increase in the price of raw materials.

FIGURE 3-9
A Shift in the Supply Schedule
If the cost of producing minidisks were to fall dramatically, the supply schedule would shift rightward from S_1 to S_2 such that at all prices, a larger quantity would be forthcoming from suppliers. Conversely, if the cost of production rose, the supply curve would shift leftward to S_3.

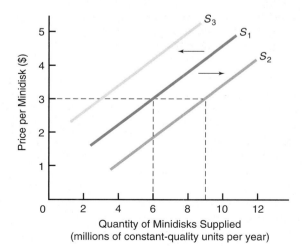

The Other Determinants of Supply

When supply curves are drawn, only the price of the good in question changes, and it is assumed that other things remain constant. The other things assumed constant are the costs of resources (inputs) used to produce the product, technology and productivity, taxes and subsidies, producers' price expectations, and the number of firms in the industry. These are the major nonprice determinants of supply. If *any* of them changes, there will be a shift in the supply curve.

Cost of Inputs Used to Produce the Product.   If one or more input prices fall, the supply curve will shift outward to the right; that is, more will be supplied at each and every price. The opposite will be true if one or more inputs become more expensive. For example, when we draw the supply curve of new cars, we are holding the cost of steel (and other inputs) constant. When we draw the supply curve of blue jeans, we are holding the cost of cotton fabric fixed. Likewise, when we draw a supply curve for caviar, we are holding constant the cost of obtaining a fundamental input—a particular kind of fish.

INTERNATIONAL EXAMPLE

Caviar Poaching Is Making a Pricey Delicacy Even Pricier

You've probably heard that caviar is nothing but fish eggs. That is true, but the best caviar comes from a fish called the sturgeon, which thrives in the waters of the Volga River in Russia and the Caspian Sea. Caviar is a big but dwindling business. The reason is that in years past, poachers have removed so many sturgeon from their watery home that their population today is lower than in prior years.

The immediate effect? A leftward shift in the market supply curve. The market outcome? A big increase in the market price of caviar. In 1998, an ounce of prized caviar from a particular sturgeon, the beluga, sold for $55 in New York caviar boutiques. Since then, the market price has steadily risen, and within a few years it is expected to top $100 per ounce.

For Critical Analysis

The Russian government is trying to beef up its fisheries police force that patrols the Volga River, and nations bordering the Caspian Sea are working on a way to enforce the ban on poaching. If successful, how are these policies likely to affect the market price of caviar?

Technology and Productivity.   Supply curves are drawn by assuming a given technology, or "state of the art." When the available production techniques change, the supply curve will shift. For example, when a better production technique for minidisks becomes available, the supply curve will shift to the right. A larger quantity will be forthcoming at each and every price because the cost of production is lower.

Taxes and Subsidies.   Certain taxes, such as a per-unit tax, are effectively an addition to production costs and therefore reduce the supply. If the supply curve were S_1 in Figure 3-9, a per-unit tax increase would shift it to S_3. A **subsidy** would do the opposite; it would shift the curve to S_2. Every producer would get a "gift" from the government of a few cents for each unit produced.

Subsidy
A negative tax; a payment to a producer from the government, usually in the form of a cash grant.

Price Expectations.   A change in the expectation of a future relative price of a product can affect a producer's current willingness to supply, just as price expectations affect a consumer's current willingness to purchase. For example, minidisk suppliers may withhold from the market part of their current supply if they anticipate higher prices in the future. The current amount supplied at each and every price will decrease.

Number of Firms in the Industry.   In the short run, when firms can only change the number of employees they use, we hold the number of firms in the industry constant. In the long run, the number of firms (or the size of some existing firms) may change. If the number of firms increases, the supply curve will shift outward to the right. If the number of firms decreases, it will shift inward to the left.

Changes in Supply Versus Changes in Quantity Supplied

We cannot overstress the importance of distinguishing between a movement along the supply curve—which occurs only when the price changes for a given supply curve—and a shift in the supply curve—which occurs only with changes in other nonprice factors. A change in price always brings about a change in quantity supplied along a given supply curve. We move to a different coordinate on the existing supply curve. This is specifically called a *change in quantity supplied.* When price changes, quantity supplied changes, and there will be a movement from one point to another along the same supply curve.

When you think of *supply,* think of the entire curve. Quantity supplied is represented by a single point on the supply curve.

A change or shift in supply causes the entire curve to move. The *only* thing that can cause the entire curve to move is a change in a determinant *other than price.*

Consequently,

A change in the price leads to a change in the quantity supplied, other things being constant. This is a movement *on* the curve.

A change in any other determinant of supply leads to a change in supply. This causes a movement *of* the curve.

<table>
<tr><td rowspan="3">CONCEPTS
IN BRIEF</td></tr>
</table>

- ◉ If the price changes, we *move along* a curve—there is a change in quantity demanded or supplied. If some other determinant changes, we *shift* a curve—there is a change in demand or supply.
- ◉ The supply curve is drawn with other things held constant. If other determinants of supply change, the supply curve will shift. The other major determinants are (1) input costs, (2) technology and productivity, (3) taxes and subsidies, (4) expectations of future relative prices, and (5) the number of firms in the industry.

PUTTING DEMAND AND SUPPLY TOGETHER

In the sections on supply and demand, we tried to confine each discussion to supply or demand only. But you have probably already realized that we can't view the world just from the supply side or just from the demand side. There is an interaction between the two. In this section, we will discuss how they interact and how that interaction determines the prices that prevail in our economy. Understanding how demand and supply interact is essential to understanding how prices are determined in our economy and other economies in which the forces of supply and demand are allowed to work.

Let's first combine the demand and supply schedules and then combine the curves.

Demand and Supply Schedules Combined

Let's place panel (a) from Figure 3-3 (the market demand schedule) and panel (a) from Figure 3-8 (the market supply schedule) together in panel (a) of Figure 3-10. Column 1 shows the price; column 2, the quantity supplied per year at any given price; and column 3,

See how the U.S. Department of Agriculture seeks to estimate demand and supply conditions for major agricultural products at **http://usda.mannlib. cornell.edu/reports/ waobr/wasde-bb.**

FIGURE 3-10

Putting Demand and Supply Together

In panel (a), we see that at the price of $3, the quantity supplied and the quantity demanded are equal, resulting in neither an excess in the quantity demanded nor an excess in the quantity supplied. We call this price the equilibrium, or market clearing, price. In panel (b), the intersection of the supply and demand curves is at *E,* at a price of $3 and a quantity of 6 million per year. At point *E,* there is neither an excess in the quantity demanded nor an excess in the quantity supplied. At a price of $1, the quantity supplied will be only 2 million per year, but the quantity demanded will be 10 million. The difference is excess quantity demanded at a price of $1. The price will rise, so we will move from point *A* up the supply curve and point *B* up the demand curve to point *E.* At the other extreme, $5 elicits a quantity supplied of 10 million but a quantity demanded of only 2 million. The difference is excess quantity supplied at a price of $5. The price will fall, so we will move down the demand curve and the supply curve to the equilibrium price, $3 per minidisk.

Panel (a)

(1) Price per Constant-Quality Minidisk	(2) Quantity Supplied (minidisks per year)	(3) Quantity Demanded (minidisks per year)	(4) Difference (2) − (3) (minidisks per year)	(5) Condition
$5	10 million	2 million	8 million	Excess quantity supplied (surplus)
4	8 million	4 million	4 million	Excess quantity supplied (surplus)
3	6 million	6 million	0	Market clearing price—equilibrium (no surplus, no shortage)
2	4 million	8 million	−4 million	Excess quantity demanded (shortage)
1	2 million	10 million	−8 million	Excess quantity demanded (shortage)

Panel (b)

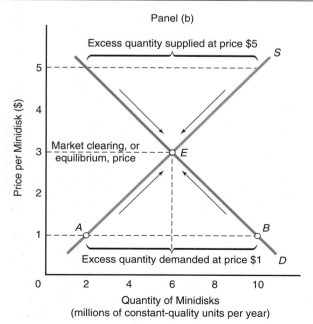

the quantity demanded. Column 4 is merely the difference between columns 2 and 3, or the difference between the quantity supplied and the quantity demanded. In column 5, we label those differences as either excess quantity supplied (called a *surplus,* which we shall discuss shortly) or excess quantity demanded (a commonly known as a *shortage,* discussed shortly). For example, at a price of $1, only 2 million minidisks would be supplied, but the quantity demanded would be 10 million. The difference would be -8 million, which we label excess quantity demanded (a shortage). At the other end of the scale, a price of $5 would elicit 10 million in quantity supplied, but quantity demanded would drop to 2 million, leaving a difference of +8 million units, which we call excess quantity supplied (a surplus).

Now, do you notice something special about the price of $3? At that price, both the quantity supplied and the quantity demanded per year are 6 million. The difference then is zero. There is neither excess quantity demanded (shortage) nor excess quantity supplied (surplus). Hence the price of $3 is very special. It is called the **market clearing price**—it clears the market of all excess supply or excess demand. There are no willing consumers who want to pay $3 per minidisk but are turned away by sellers, and there are no willing suppliers who want to sell minidisks at $3 who cannot sell all they want at that price. Another term for the market clearing price is the **equilibrium price,** the price at which there is no tendency for change. Consumers are able to get all they want at that price, and suppliers are able to sell the amount that they want at that price.

Market clearing, or equilibrium, price
The price that clears the market, at which quantity demanded equals quantity supplied; the price where the demand curve intersects the supply curve.

Equilibrium

Equilibrium
The situation when quantity supplied equals quantity demanded at a particular price.

We can define **equilibrium** in general as a point at which quantity demanded equals quantity supplied at a particular price. There tends to be no movement away from this point unless demand or supply changes. Any movement away from this point will set into motion certain forces that will cause movement back to it. Therefore, equilibrium is a stable point. Any point that is not at equilibrium is unstable and cannot be maintained.

The equilibrium point occurs where the supply and demand curves intersect. The equilibrium price is given on the vertical axis directly to the left of where the supply and demand curves cross. The equilibrium quantity demanded and supplied is given on the horizontal axis directly underneath the intersection of the demand and supply curves. Equilibrium can change whenever there is a *shock.*

A shock to the supply-and-demand system can be represented by a shift in the supply curve, a shift in the demand curve, or a shift in both curves. Any shock to the system will result in a new set of supply-and-demand relationships and a new equilibrium; forces will come into play to move the system from the old price-quantity equilibrium (now a disequilibrium situation) to the new equilibrium, where the new demand and supply curves intersect.

Panel (b) in Figure 3-3 and panel (b) in Figure 3-8 are combined as panel (b) in Figure 3-10. The only difference now is that the horizontal axis measures both the quantity supplied and the quantity demanded per year. Everything else is the same. The demand curve is labeled *D,* the supply curve *S.* We have labeled the intersection of the supply curve with the demand curve as point *E,* for equilibrium. That corresponds to a market clearing price of $3, at which both the quantity supplied and the quantity demanded are 6 million units per year. There is neither excess quantity supplied nor excess quantity demanded. Point *E,* the equilibrium point, always occurs at the intersection of the supply and demand curves. This is the price toward which the market price will automatically tend to gravitate.

Putting Economics in Action to Work

To study market equilibrium in more detail, start the *EIA* CD, and click on "Demand and Supply." Then click on "Putting Demand and Supply Together."

EXAMPLE

Why Babysitters Are Earning More

Though good data are hard to come by, parents today agree that the market price of babysitting is way up. Two factors have worked together to bring this about. To see how, take a look at Figure 3-11. There you see the original supply and demand curves for babysitting services in the early 1980s, labeled S_1 and D_1. The market price is P_1, and the equilibrium quantity is Q_1. Now let's think about two events that occurred in the 1990s and early 2000s.

First, there was a population shift. In 1980, there were about 39 million Americans aged 10 to 19, the typical age of babysitters. By the early 2000s, there were about 5 percent fewer people in this age group. Thus the number of suppliers of babysitting services declined at any given price; the market supply schedule shifted leftward, from S_1 to S_2.

At the same time, the number of children younger than 10 rose from 33 million in 1980 to nearly 40 million in the early 2000s. Furthermore, U.S. incomes rose, so more parents desired to eat out and be entertained without their children in tow. These two factors together increased the demand for babysitting services in the 2000s. That is, at any given price, the quantity of babysitting services demanded rose. The demand curve shifted from D_1 to D_2.

As you can see in Figure 3-11, the net effect of these two shifts is an unambiguous rise in the market price of babysitting services, from P_1 to P_2. The equilibrium quantity of babysitting services may increase or decrease. We have illustrated a situation in which it does not change. That is, it is entirely possible that parents in the 2000s are paying a lot more for exactly the same amount of babysitting services that parents purchased at a lower price in the 1980s.

For Critical Analysis

Suppose that in a few years, retiring baby boomers decide to earn extra income by offering to spend some of their time babysitting. What would happen to the equilibrium price of babysitting services? Why?

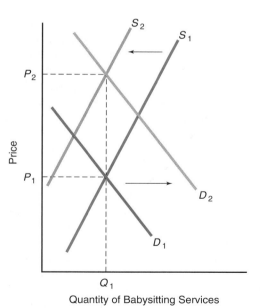

FIGURE 3-11

The Changing Price of Babysitting Services
Simultaneous shifts in the demand curve for babysitting services from D_1 to D_2 and in the supply curve for babysitting services from S_1 to S_2 will cause the equilibrium price of babysitting services to rise from P_1 to P_2. The equilibrium quantity may increase, decrease, or, as illustrated, remain unchanged.

Shortages

The demand and supply curves depicted in Figure 3-10 represent a situation of equilibrium. But a non-market-clearing, or disequilibrium, price will put into play forces that cause the price to change toward the market clearing price at which equilibrium will again be sustained. Look again at panel (b) in Figure 3-10 on page 65. Suppose that instead of being at the market clearing price of $3, for some reason the market price is $1. At this price, the quantity demanded exceeds the quantity supplied, the former being 10 million per year and the latter, 2 million per year. We have a situation of excess quantity demanded at the price of $1. This is usually called a **shortage.** Consumers of minidisks would find that they could not buy all that they wished at $1 apiece. But forces will cause the price to rise: Competing consumers will bid up the price, and suppliers will raise the price and increase output, whether explicitly or implicitly. (Remember, some buyers would pay $5 or more rather than do without minidisks. They do not want to be left out.) We would move from points *A* and *B* toward point *E*. The process would stop when the price again reached $3 per minidisk.

Shortage
A situation in which quantity demanded is greater than quantity supplied at a price below the market clearing price.

At this point, it is important to recall a distinction made in Chapter 2:

Shortages and scarcity are not the same thing.

A shortage is a situation in which the quantity demanded exceeds the quantity supplied at a price *below* the market clearing price. Our definition of scarcity was much more general and all-encompassing: a situation in which the resources available for producing output are insufficient to satisfy all wants. Any choice necessarily costs an opportunity, and the opportunity is lost. Hence we will always live in a world of scarcity because we must constantly make choices, but we do not necessarily have to live in a world of shortages.

Surpluses

Now let's repeat the experiment with the market price at $5 rather than at the market clearing price of $3. Clearly, the quantity supplied will exceed the quantity demanded at that price. The result will be an excess quantity supplied at $5 per unit. This excess quantity supplied is often called a **surplus.** Given the curves in panel (b) in Figure 3-10, however, there will be forces pushing the price back down toward $3 per minidisk: Competing suppliers will attempt to reduce their inventories by cutting prices and reducing output, and consumers will offer to purchase more at lower prices. Suppliers will want to reduce inventories, which will be above their optimal level; that is, there will be an excess over what each seller believes to be the most profitable stock of minidisks. After all, inventories are costly to hold. But consumers may find out about such excess inventories and see the possibility of obtaining increased quantities of minidisks at a decreased price. It behooves consumers to attempt to obtain a good at a lower price, and they will therefore try to do so. If the two forces of supply and demand are unrestricted, they will bring the price back to $3 per minidisk.

Surplus
A situation in which quantity supplied is greater than quantity demanded at a price above the market clearing price.

Shortages and surpluses are resolved in unfettered markets—markets in which price changes are free to occur. The forces that resolve them are those of competition: In the case of shortages, consumers competing for a limited quantity supplied drive up the price; in the case of surpluses, sellers compete for the limited quantity demanded, thus driving prices down to equilibrium. The equilibrium price is the only stable price, and all (unrestricted) market prices tend to gravitate toward it.

What happens when the price is set below the equilibrium price? Here come the scalpers.

POLICY EXAMPLE

Should Shortages in the Ticket Market Be Solved by Scalpers?

If you have ever tried to get tickets to a playoff game in sports, a popular Broadway play, or a superstar's rock concert, you know about "shortages." The standard ticket situation for a Super Bowl is shown in Figure 3-12. At the face-value price of Super Bowl tickets (P_1), the quantity demanded (Q_2) greatly exceeds the quantity supplied (Q_1). Because shortages last only so long as prices and quantities do not change, markets tend to exhibit a movement out of this disequilibrium toward equilibrium. Obviously, the quantity of Super Bowl tickets cannot change, but the price can go as high as P_2.

Enter the scalper. This colorful term is used because when you purchase a ticket that is being resold at a price that is higher than face value, the seller is skimming an extra profit off the top. If an event sells out, ticket prices by definition have been lower than market clearing prices. People without tickets may be willing to buy high-priced tickets because they place a greater value on the entertain-

ment event than the face value of the ticket. Without scalpers, those individuals would not be able to attend the event. In the case of the Super Bowl, various forms of scalping occur nationwide. Tickets for a seat on the 50-yard line have been sold for more than $2,000 a piece. In front of every Super Bowl arena, you can find ticket scalpers hawking their wares.

In most states, scalping is illegal. In Pennsylvania, convicted scalpers are either fined $5,000 or sentenced to two years behind bars. For an economist, such legislation seems strange. As one New York ticket broker said, "I look at scalping like working as a stockbroker, buying low and selling high. If people are willing to pay me the money, what kind of problem is that?"

For Critical Analysis

What happens to ticket scalpers who are still holding tickets after an event has started?

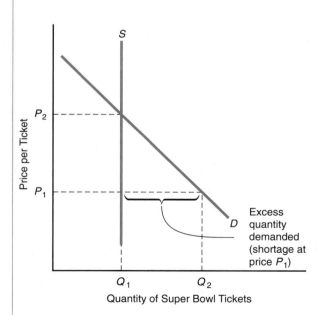

FIGURE 3-12

Shortages of Super Bowl Tickets
The quantity of tickets for any one Super Bowl is fixed at Q_1. At the price per ticket of P_1, the quantity demanded is Q_2, which is greater than Q_1. Consequently, there is an excess quantity demanded at the below-market-clearing price. Prices can go as high as P_2 in the scalpers' market.

CONCEPTS IN BRIEF

● The market clearing price occurs at the intersection of the market demand curve and the market supply curve. It is also called the equilibrium price, the price from which there is no tendency to change unless there is a change in demand or supply.

● Whenever the price is greater than the equilibrium price, there is an excess quantity supplied (a surplus).

● Whenever the price is less than the equilibrium price, there is an excess quantity demanded (a shortage).

NETNOMICS

Stealth Attacks by New Technologies

Successful new products often get off to a slow start. Eventually, however, consumers substitute away from the old products to the point at which demand for the old products effectively disappears. Consider handwritten versus printed manuscripts. For several years in the mid-fifteenth century, printed books were a rarity, and manuscript-copying monks and scribes continued to turn out the bulk of written forms of communication. By the 1470s, however, printed books were more common than handwritten manuscripts. By the end of the fifteenth century, manuscripts had become the rare commodity.

A more recent example involves train engines. Just before 1940, after the diesel-electric engine for train locomotives was invented, an executive of a steam-engine company declared, "They'll never replace the steam locomotive." In fact, it only took 20 years to prove the executive wrong. By 1960, steam engines were regarded as mechanical dinosaurs.

To generate the bulk of its profits, the U.S. Postal Service relies on revenues from first-class mail. To keep its first-class customers satisfied, it recently deployed a $5 billion automation system that reads nine addresses per second and paints envelopes with bar codes to speed sorting. Yet the postal service has lost about $4 billion in first-class mail business since 1994. Around that time, people began to compare the 25-cent cost of a one-minute phone call with the 32-cent cost of first-class postage. Then they began to substitute away from first-class letters to faxes. Other people got access to the Internet and began to send messages by electronic mail, at no additional charge. First-class mail increasingly looks like a steam-engine dinosaur.

Some observers of the software industry think the same sort of thing could happen to a powerhouse of the present: Microsoft Windows. Today the code for this program is on most personal computers on the planet. Competing operating system applications offered by Sun Microsystems's Java software and others currently run more slowly than Windows. But they consume many fewer lines of computer code and hence promise swift accessibility via the Internet. It is conceivable that someday people may log on to the Internet and pay by the minute to use such software to run their computers, thereby freeing up their hard drives for other uses. Thus today's dominant operating system may someday look a lot like a handwritten manuscript does to generations accustomed to reading printed books instead of handwritten manuscripts.

China's Water Shortage: Too Little Rain or Not Enough Pricing?

In China, lack of water has been a big problem. In some towns, people have to wait in long lines at water distribution points set up by local governments. Farmers have lost entire crops. Lacking water to cool machinery, factories have had to cut back on production. Problems are acute in areas where the land is nearly flat, as in large portions of the northern half of China. A recent geophysical analysis indicates that water tables are falling rapidly in these regions. Satellite images show springs, lakes, and rivers drying up.

One Approach: Brute Force

China's government decided in the late 1990s to spare no expense in fighting the water shortage. It began planning vast projects for building tunnels for water to pass through, to expend large amounts of electricity to pump water uphill thousands of feet, to construct huge dams, and to displace hundreds of thousands of people from their homes to make it all possible. Many of these projects are being funded by loans from the World Bank.

The main idea behind these projects, of course, is to move water from the countryside to the cities. But many observers point out that even if all these massive efforts succeed, China's cities will still be living on borrowed time. Among the most water-short is the Chinese capital city of Beijing, which has already exhausted groundwater reserves and now takes irrigation water away from farmers.

The Missing Element: Pricing

To this point, an important element has been missing from the story. Until recently, most water in China could be consumed at no charge. Government pumping stations provided it at a zero price to all takers. In 1998, the government finally enacted a water-pricing policy, but Chinese farmers continue to pay only one-tenth of the opportunity cost of obtaining the water they use to irrigate their crops.

Think about what you have learned in this chapter. Whenever the price of a good, such as water, is below its market clearing price, the quantity demanded exceeds the quantity supplied, and a shortage occurs. To an economist, China's problem is a classic example of a shortage induced by well-intended efforts to set the price of a good below its market price. Naturally, if city-dwellers, farmers, and companies in China can obtain water at very close to a zero price, they will desire to consume water in excess of the amount of water available at that price. That is, the quantity of water demanded will exceed the quantity of water supplied. An economist could have predicted the outcomes before they occurred: overpumped wells, dry fields, and water rationing in cities.

What solution does a typical economist propose? It is for China to let the price system work. Even minor increases in water prices would do wonders to induce people to conserve water. It also would induce Chinese residents to shift water from low-value uses to high-value uses. Pricing water might also eliminate the perceived "need" to think big and build huge dams, tunnels, pumping stations, and the like. By instead thinking smaller and simply permitting the price of water rise toward free-market levels, China could end its water shortage.

Concepts Applied

Demand

Supply

Market Price

Opportunity Cost

Shortage

FOR CRITICAL ANALYSIS

1. Even at a posted price of zero, was Chinese water really "free"?

2. A common argument against letting the market determine the prices of "necessity goods" such as water is that having to pay for water is hard on the average citizen. In most countries, who ultimately pays for government-funded dam projects, tunnels through mountains, and machinery to pump water uphill?

SUMMARY DISCUSSION OF LEARNING OBJECTIVES

1. **The Law of Demand:** According to the law of demand, other things being equal, individuals will purchase fewer units of a commodity at a higher price, and they will purchase more units of the commodity at a lower price.

2. **Relative Prices Versus Money Prices:** When determining the quantity of a commodity to purchase, people respond to changes in its relative price, the price of the commodities in terms of other commodities, rather than a change in the commodity's money price expressed in today's dollars. If the price of a CD rises by 50 percent next year while at the same time all other prices, including your wages, also increase by 50 percent, then the relative price of the CD has not changed. Thus in a world of generally rising prices, you have to compare the price of one good with the general level of prices of other goods in order to decide whether the relative price of that one good has gone up, gone down, or stayed the same.

3. **A Change in Quantity Demanded Versus a Change in Demand:** The demand schedule shows the relationship between various possible prices and respective quantities purchased per unit of time. Graphically, the demand schedule is a downward-sloping demand curve. A change in the price of the good generates a change in the quantity demanded, which is a movement along the demand curve. The determinants of the demand for a good other than the price of the good are (a) income, (b) tastes and preferences, (c) the prices of related goods, (d) expectations, and (e) market size (the number of buyers). Whenever any of these determinants of demand changes, there is a change in the demand for the good, and the demand curve shifts to a new position.

4. **The Law of Supply:** According to the law of supply, sellers will produce and offer for sale more units of a commodity at a higher price, and they will produce and offer for sale fewer units of the commodity at a lower price.

5. **A Change in Quantity Supplied Versus a Change in Supply:** The supply schedule shows the relationship between various possible prices and respective quantities produced and sold per unit of time. On a graph, the supply schedule is a supply curve that slopes upward. A change in the price of the good generates a change in the quantity supplied, which is a movement along the supply curve. The determinants of the supply of a good other than the price of the good are (a) input costs, (b) technology and productivity, (c) taxes and subsidies, (d) price expectations, and (e) the number of sellers. Whenever any of these determinants of supply changes, there is a change in the supply of the good, and the supply curve shifts to a new position

6. **Determining the Market Price and the Equilibrium Quantity:** The market price of a commodity and equilibrium quantity of the commodity that is produced and sold are determined by the intersection of the demand and supply curves. At this intersection point, the quantity demanded by buyers of the commodity just equals the quantity supplied by sellers. At the market price at this point of intersection, the plans of buyers and sellers mesh exactly. Hence there is neither an excess quantity of the commodity supplied (surplus) nor an excess quantity of the commodity demanded (shortage) at this equilibrium point.

Key Terms and Concepts

Complements (57)

Demand (49)

Demand curve (52)

Equilibrium (66)

Inferior goods (56)

Law of demand (49)

Law of supply (59)

Market (49)

Market clearing, or equilibrium, price (66)

Market demand (52)

Money price (50)

Normal goods (56)

Relative price (50)

Shortage (68)

Subsidy (63)

Substitutes (57)

Supply (59)

Supply curve (60)

Surplus (68)

Problems

Answers to the odd-numbered problems appear at the back of the book.

3-1. Suppose that in a recent market period, an industrywide survey determined the following relationship between the price of rock music CDs and the quantity supplied and quantity demanded.

Price	Quantity Demanded	Quantity Supplied
$9	100 million	40 million
$10	90 million	60 million
$11	80 million	80 million
$12	70 million	100 million
$13	60 million	120 million

Illustrate the supply and demand curves for rock CDs given the information in the table. What are the equilibrium price and quantity? If the industry price is $10, is there a shortage or surplus of CDs? How much is the shortage or surplus?

3-2. Suppose that a survey for a later market period indicates that the quantities supplied in the table in Problem 3-1 are unchanged. The quantity demanded, however, has increased by 30 million at each price. Construct the resulting demand curve in the illustration you made for Problem 3-1. Is this an increase or a decrease in demand? What are the new equilibrium quantity and the new market price? Give two examples that might cause such a change.

3-3. In the market for rock music CDs, explain whether the following event would cause an increase or a decrease in demand or an increase or a decrease in the quantity demanded. Also explain what happens to the equilibrium quantity and the market price.

    a. The price of CD packaging material declines.
    b. The price of CD players declines.
    c. The price of cassette tapes increases dramatically.
    d. A booming economy increases the income of the typical CD buyer.
    e. Many rock fans suddenly develop a fondness for country music.

3-4. Give an example of a complement and a substitute in consumption for each of the following items.

    a. Bacon
    b. Tennis racquets
    c. Coffee
    d. Automobiles

3-5. At the end of the 1990s, the United States imposed high taxes on a number of European goods due to a trade dispute. One of these goods was Roquefort cheese. Show how this tax affects the market for Roquefort cheese, shifting the appropriate curve and indicating a new equilibrium quantity and market price.

3-6. Problem 3-5 described a tax imposed on Roquefort cheese. Illustrate the effect of the tax on Roquefort cheese on other types of blue cheese, shifting the appropriate curve and indicating a new equilibrium quantity and market price.

3-7. Consider the market for laptop computers. Explain whether the following events would cause an increase or a decrease in supply or an increase or a decrease in the quantity supplied. Illustrate each, and show what would happen to the equilibrium quantity and the market price.

    a. The price of memory chips used in laptop computers declines.
    b. The price of memory chips used in desktop personal computers declines.
    c. The number of manufactures of laptop computers increases.
    d. The price of computer peripherals, printers, fax-modems, and scanners decreases.

3-8. The United States offers significant subsidy payments to U.S. sugar growers. Describe the effects of the introduction of such subsidies on the market for sugar and the market for artificial sweeteners. Explain whether the demand curve or supply curve shifts in each market, and if so, in which direction. Also explain what happens to the equilibrium quantity and the market price in each market.

3-9. The supply curve for season tickets for basketball games for your school's team is vertical because there are a fixed number of seats in the school's gymnasium. Before preseason practice sessions begin, your school's administration commits itself to selling season tickets the day before the first basketball game at a predetermined price that it believes to be equal to the market price. The school will not change that price at any time prior to and including the day tickets go on sale. Illustrate, within a supply and demand framework, the effect of each of the following events on the market for season tickets on the day the school opens ticket sales, and indicate whether a surplus or a shortage would result.

a. The school's star player breaks a leg during preseason practice.

b. During preseason practice, a published newspaper poll of coaches of teams in your school's conference surprises everyone by indicating that your school's team is in the running to win the conference championship.

c. At a preseason practice session that is open to the public, the school president announces that all refreshments served during games will be free of charge throughout the season.

d. Most of your school's basketball fans enjoy an up-tempo, "run and gun" approach to basketball, but after the team's coach quits following the first preseason practice, the school's administration immediately hires a new coach who believes in a deliberate style of play that relies heavily on slow-tempo, four-corners offense.

3-10. Advances in computer technology allow individuals to purchase and download music from the Internet. Buyers may download single songs or complete tracks of songs that are also sold on CDs. Explain the impact of this technological advance on the market for CDs sold in retail stores.

Economics on the Net

Canadian Taxes and Energy Markets The Canadian government follows the example set by the U.S. government and governments of other countries by imposing taxes on some sources of energy and subsidizing other energy sources. This application helps you apply concepts you learned in this chapter to evaluate the effects of taxes and subsidies.

Internet URL:
www.eia.doe.gov/emeu/env/canada.html

Title: Canada Environment Review

Navigation: Begin at the Energy Information Agency homepage (www.eia.doe.gov). Click on International (www.eia.doe.gov/emeu/international/contents.html). Select Canada from the list of nations (http://www.eia.doe.gov/emeu/canada.html). Scroll down to, and click on Environmental Review.

Application Read the first three sections of this article ("General Background," "Energy and Environmental Policy," and "Energy Taxes and Subsidies"). Then answer the following questions.

1. Draw a diagram of possible demand and supply curves for the market for gasoline. The tax described in the third section of the article is paid by sellers of gasoline. Thus to induce each gasoline seller to supply the same quantity as it would have supplied before the tax, the price that the seller receives must be higher by the amount of the tax. Given this information, illustrate the effect of this tax on the market supply curve. Illustrate and explain how the tax reduces consumption of transportation gas.

2. Draw a diagram of the market for vehicles powered by natural gas. Illustrate the effect of a subsidy on the supply of natural-gas-powered vehicles, and explain how the subsidy encourages the use of these vehicles.

For Group Study and Analysis The final paragraph under "Energy Taxes and Subsidies" describes a study of tax incentives for conservation and renewable energy technologies. Discuss how a tax incentive affects the supply of renewable energy technologies. Discuss how a tax that "encourages" energy conservation might affect a firm engaged in manufacturing. Debate whether one approach is preferred over the other.

EXTENSIONS OF DEMAND AND SUPPLY ANALYSIS

A basic principle in economics is that people respond to incentives. Why might this young person quit school to become a systems programmer?

A few years ago, after a top-flight college athlete turned professional following his sophomore season, a television news commentator called for a law prohibiting college stars from becoming pros "too soon." "He's too young to know what's in his own best interest," the commentator said, without noting that the athlete's salary would dwarf his own.

Other student stars, this time in the academic sphere, have also been responding to market incentives. In the face of soaring entry-level salaries, hordes of computer science students have been dropping their studies in favor of high-paying jobs. College deans and presidents have decried this trend, arguing that ultimately market salaries will fall. The students, they say, are grabbing near-term gains, but lacking degrees, they eventually face the prospect of lower future earnings. Do these academic naysayers have a point? To answer this question, you must learn more about how markets work.

Did You Know That... according to the U.S. Customs Service, the second most serious smuggling problem along the Mexican border, just behind drugs, involves the refrigerant Freon? Selling Freon is more profitable than dealing in cocaine, and illegal Freon smuggling is a bigger business than gunrunning. Freon is used in many air conditioners in cars and homes. Its use is already illegal in the United States, but residents of developing countries may legally use it until the year 2005. When an older U.S. air conditioner needs fixing, it is often cheaper to pay a relatively high price for illegally smuggled Freon than to modify the unit to use a replacement coolant. You can analyze illegal markets, such as the one for Freon, using the supply and demand analysis you learned in Chapter 3. Similarly, you can use this analysis to examine legal markets and the "shortage" of skilled information technology specialists, the "shortage" of apartments in certain cities, and many other phenomena. All of these examples are part of our economy, which we characterize as a *price system*.

THE PRICE SYSTEM

A **price system,** otherwise known as a *market system,* is one in which relative prices are constantly changing to reflect changes in supply and demand for different commodities. The prices of those commodities are the signals to everyone within the system as to what is relatively scarce and what is relatively abundant. Indeed, it is the *signaling* aspect of the price system that provides the information to buyers and sellers about what should be bought and what should be produced. In a price system, there is a clear-cut chain of events in which any changes in demand and supply cause changes in prices that in turn affect the opportunities that businesses and individuals have for profit and personal gain. Such changes influence our use of resources.

EXCHANGE AND MARKETS

The price system features **voluntary exchange,** acts of trading between individuals that make both parties to the trade subjectively better off. The **terms of exchange**—the prices we pay for the desired items—are determined by the interaction of the forces underlying supply and demand. In our economy, the majority of exchanges take place voluntarily in markets. A market encompasses the exchange arrangements of both buyers and sellers that underlie the forces of supply and demand. Indeed, one definition of a market is a low-cost institution for facilitating exchange. A market increases incomes by helping resources move to their highest-valued uses by means of prices. Prices are the providers of information.

Transaction Costs

Individuals turn to markets because markets reduce the cost of exchanges. These costs are sometimes referred to as **transaction costs,** which are broadly defined as the costs associated with finding out exactly what is being transacted as well as the cost of enforcing contracts. If you were Robinson Crusoe and lived alone on an island, you would never incur a transaction cost. For everyone else, transaction costs are just as real as the costs of production. High-speed large-scale computers have allowed us to reduce transaction costs by increasing our ability to process information and keep records.

Price system
An economic system in which relative prices are constantly changing to reflect changes in supply and demand for different commodities. The prices of those commodities are signals to everyone within the system as to what is relatively scarce and what is relatively abundant.

Voluntary exchange
An act of trading, done on a voluntary basis, in which both parties to the trade are subjectively better off after the exchange.

Terms of exchange
The terms under which trading takes place. Usually the terms of exchange are equal to the price at which a good is traded.

Consider some simple examples of transaction costs. The supermarket reduces transaction costs relative to your having to go to numerous specialty stores to obtain the items you desire. Organized stock exchanges, such as the New York Stock Exchange, have reduced transaction costs of buying and selling stocks and bonds. In general, the more organized the market, the lower the transaction costs. One group of individuals who constantly attempt to lower transaction costs are the much maligned middlemen.

Transaction costs
All of the costs associated with exchanging, including the informational costs of finding out price and quality, service record, and durability of a product, plus the cost of contracting and enforcing that contract.

The Role of Middlemen

As long as there are costs to bringing together buyers and sellers, there will be an incentive for intermediaries, normally called middlemen, to lower those costs. This means that middlemen specialize in lowering transaction costs. Whenever producers do not sell their products directly to the final consumer, there are, by definition, one or more middlemen involved. Farmers typically sell their output to distributors, who are usually called wholesalers, who then sell those products to supermarkets.

Recently, technology has changed the way middlemen work.

EXAMPLE

Middlemen Flourish on the Internet

At one time, people speculated that the Internet would be bad news for middlemen. People would just click their mouse to head to a Web site where they could deal directly with a company. In fact, every day there are new companies establishing middleman sites all over the Web. For instance, one Web site, Kelley Blue Book (www.kbb.com), allows you to get exact dealer invoice prices and destination charges for automobiles so that you can learn what wholesale prices car dealers pay for the cars. You can even find out the prices of optional equipment.

To help consumers locate harder-to-find items, software companies have developed *intelligent shopping*

agents, sometimes called "shopbots," which are programs that search the Web to find specific items. Even though human beings are not the middlemen in this instance, the software companies provide middleman services by offering to sell or lease these programs.

For Critical Analysis

Any of us connected to the Internet can find the same information that an Internet middleman (or shopbot, for that matter) can find. Why, then, would someone pay for the services of an Internet middleman?

CHANGES IN DEMAND AND SUPPLY

It is in markets that we see the results of changes in demand and supply. In certain situations, it is possible to predict what will happen to equilibrium price and equilibrium quantity when a change occurs in demand or supply. Specifically, whenever one curve is stable while the other curve shifts, we can tell what will happen to price and quantity. Consider the four possibilities in Figure 4-1 (p. 78). In panel (a), the supply curve remains stable but demand increases from D_1 to D_2. Note that the result is both an increase in the market clearing price from P_1 to P_2 and an increase in the equilibrium quantity from Q_1 to Q_2.

In panel (b), there is a decrease in demand from D_1 to D_3. This results in a decrease in both the relative price of the good and the equilibrium quantity. Panels (c) and (d) show the effects of a shift in the supply curve while the demand curve is stable. In panel (c), the supply

FIGURE 4-1

Shifts in Demand and in Supply: Determinate Results
In panel (a), the supply curve is stable at S. The demand curve shifts outward from D_1 to D_2. The equilibrium price and quantity rise from P_1, Q_1 to P_2, Q_2, respectively. In panel (b), again the supply curve remains stable at S. The demand curve, however, shifts inward to the left, showing a decrease in demand from D_1 to D_3. Both equilibrium price and equilibrium quantity fall. In panel (c), the demand curve now remains stable at D. The supply curve shifts from S_1 to S_2. The equilibrium price falls from P_1 to P_2. The equilibrium quantity increases, however, from Q_1 to Q_2. In panel (d), the demand curve is stable at D. Supply decreases as shown by a leftward shift of the supply curve from S_1 to S_3. The market clearing price increases from P_1 to P_3. The equilibrium quantity falls from Q_1 to Q_3.

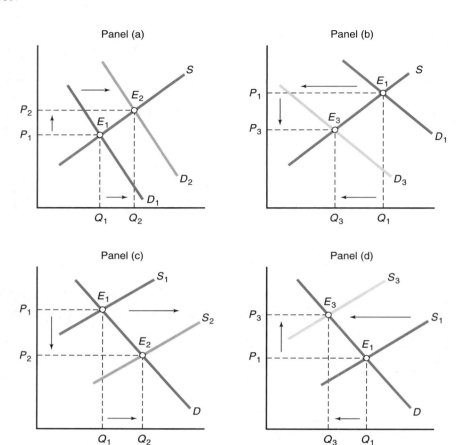

curve has shifted rightward. The relative price of the product falls; the equilibrium quantity increases. In panel (d), supply has shifted leftward—there has been a supply decrease. The product's relative price increases; the equilibrium quantity decreases.

EXAMPLE

The Upside of the Yo-Yo Cycle

Toymaking is a big business. It is also a volatile business. Consider the simple yo-yo. For years, kids couldn't get enough yo-yos, and the industry boomed. Then it fell on hard times—how could pieces of wood or plastic attached to a string compete with action figures and video games? But after years of dormant sales, yo-yos suddenly are hot again in places such as Australia, Japan, and the United Kingdom. Companies that manufacture yo-yos have found that they cannot keep up with this increasing worldwide demand at prevailing prices. Toy retailers can't keep yo-yos in stock. One San Francisco store maintains a yo-yo waiting list that runs to 200 names.

We can turn to demand and supply to see why this situation has arisen in the market for yo-yos. As you can see in Figure 4-2, when the demand schedule for yo-yos shifts rightward, the quantity of yo-yos demanded exceeds the quantity supplied, so at the initial market price, a shortage of yo-yos results. Adjustment to market equilibrium will entail a rise in the market price of yo-yos, which will raise the quantity of yo-yos supplied toward equality with the quantity demanded. Consistent

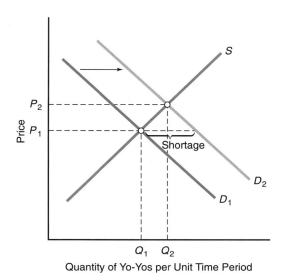

FIGURE 4-2
Responses to a Shift in Yo-Yo Demand
When demand shifts to D_2 but supply stays the same, there will be shortages at the prevailing price P. Eventually, price will rise to P_2 and equilibrium will occur at Q_2.

with this prediction, some yo-yo manufacturers report that their existing plants now run 24 hours a day, seven days a week. Many producers are opening new production lines. In the meantime, yo-yo prices have risen considerably at toy stores around the globe.

For Critical Analysis
The current yo-yo craze is unlikely to last. When it ends, what kinds of adjustments are likely to occur in the market for yo-yos?

When Both Demand and Supply Shift

The examples given in Figure 4-1 each showed a theoretically determinate outcome of a shift in either the demand curve holding the supply curve constant or the supply curve holding the demand curve constant. When both supply and demand curves change, the outcome is indeterminate for either equilibrium price or equilibrium quantity.

When both demand and supply increase, all we can be certain of is that equilibrium quantity will increase. We do not know what will happen to equilibrium price until we determine whether demand increased relative to supply (equilibrium price will rise) or supply increased relative to demand (equilibrium price will fall). The same analysis applies to decreases in both demand and supply, except that in this case equilibrium quantity falls.

We can be certain that when demand decreases and supply increases, the equilibrium price will fall, but we do not know what will happen to the equilibrium quantity unless we actually draw the new curves. If supply decreases and demand increases, we can be sure that equilibrium price will rise, but again we do not know what happens to equilibrium quantity without drawing the curves. In every situation in which both supply and demand change, you should always draw graphs to determine the resulting change in equilibrium price and quantity.

*Putting
Economics in Action
to Work*

To improve your ability to reason through the effects of shifts in demand and supply, start the *EIA* CD, and click on "Demand and Supply." Then click on "Predicting Changes in Prices and Quantities."

PRICE FLEXIBILITY AND ADJUSTMENT SPEED

We have used as an illustration for our analysis a market in which prices are quite flexible. Some markets are indeed like that. In others, however, price flexibility may take the form of indirect adjustments such as hidden payments or quality changes. For example, although the published price of bouquets of flowers may stay the same, the freshness of the flowers may change, meaning that the price per constant-quality unit changes. The published price of French bread might stay the same, but the quality could go up or down, thereby changing the price per constant-quality unit. There are many ways to change prices without actually changing the published price for a *nominal* unit of a product or service.

We must also consider the fact that markets do not return to equilibrium immediately. There must be an adjustment time. A shock to the economy in the form of an oil embargo, a drought, or a long strike will not be absorbed overnight. This means that even in unfettered market situations, in which there are no restrictions on changes in prices and quantities, temporary excess quantities supplied and excess quantities demanded may appear. Our analysis simply indicates what the market clearing price ultimately will be, given a demand curve and a supply curve. Nowhere in the analysis is there any indication of the speed with which a market will get to a new equilibrium if there has been a shock. The price may overshoot the equilibrium level. Remember this warning when we examine changes in demand and in supply due to changes in their nonprice determinants.

CONCEPTS IN BRIEF

● The terms of exchange in a voluntary exchange are determined by the interaction of the forces underlying demand and supply. These forces take place in markets, which tend to minimize transaction costs.

● When the demand curve shifts outward or inward with a stable supply curve, equilibrium price and quantity increase or decrease, respectively. When the supply curve shifts outward or inward given a stable demand curve, equilibrium price moves in the direction opposite of equilibrium quantity.

● When there is a shift in demand or supply, the new equilibrium price is not obtained instantaneously. Adjustment takes time.

THE RATIONING FUNCTION OF PRICES

A shortage creates a situation that forces price to rise toward a market clearing, or equilibrium, level. A surplus brings into play forces that cause price to fall toward its market clearing level. The synchronization of decisions by buyers and sellers that creates a situation of equilibrium is called the *rationing function of prices*. Prices are indicators of relative scarcity. An equilibrium price clears the market. The plans of buyers and sellers, given the price, are not frustrated.* It is the free interaction of buyers and sellers that sets the price that eventually clears the market. Price, in effect, rations a commodity to demanders who are willing and able to pay the highest price. Whenever the rationing function of prices is frustrated by government-enforced price ceilings that set prices below the market clearing level, a prolonged shortage situation is not allowed to be corrected by the upward adjustment of the price.

---

*There is a difference between frustration and unhappiness. You may be unhappy because you can't buy a Rolls Royce, but if you had sufficient income, you would not be frustrated in your attempt to purchase one at the current market price. By contrast, you would be frustrated if you went to your local supermarket and could get only two cans of your favorite soft drink when you had wanted to purchase a dozen and had the necessary funds.

There are other ways to ration goods. *First come, first served* is one method. *Political power* is another. *Physical force* is yet another. Cultural, religious, and physical differences have been and are used as rationing devices throughout the world.

Consider first come, first served as a rationing device. In countries that do not allow prices to reflect true relative scarcity, first come, first served has become a way of life. We call this *rationing by queues,* where *queue* means "line," as in Britain. Whoever is willing to wait in line the longest obtains meat that is being sold at less than the market clearing price. All who wait in line are paying a higher *total* price than the money price paid for the meat. Personal time has an opportunity cost. To calculate the total price of the meat, we must add up the money price plus the opportunity cost of the time spent waiting.

Lotteries are another way to ration goods. You may have been involved in a rationing-by-lottery scheme during your first year in college when you were assigned a university-provided housing unit. Sometimes for popular classes, rationing by lottery is used to fill the available number of slots.

Rationing by *coupons* has also been used, particularly during wartime. In the United States during World War II, families were allotted coupons that allowed them to purchase specified quantities of rationed goods, such as meat and gasoline. To purchase such goods, you had to pay a specified price *and* give up a coupon.

Rationing by waiting may occur in situations in which entrepreneurs are free to change prices to equate quantity demanded with quantity supplied but choose not to do so. This results in queues of potential buyers. The most obvious conclusion seems to be that the price in the market is being held below equilibrium by some noncompetitive force. That is not true, however.

The reason is that queuing may also arise when the demand characteristics of a market are subject to large or unpredictable fluctuations, and the additional costs to firms (and ultimately to consumers) of constantly changing prices or of holding sufficient inventories or providing sufficient excess capacity to cover these peak demands are greater than the costs to consumers of waiting for the good. This is the usual case of waiting in line to purchase a fast-food lunch or to purchase a movie ticket a few minutes before the next show.

The Essential Role of Rationing

In a world of scarcity, there is, by definition, competition for what is scarce. After all, any resources that are not scarce can be had by everyone at a zero price in as large a quantity as everyone wants, such as air to burn in internal combustion engines. Once scarcity arises, there has to be some method to ration the available resources, goods, and services. The price system is one form of rationing; the others that we mentioned are alternatives. Economists cannot say which system of rationing is best. They can, however, say that rationing via the price system leads to the most efficient use of available resources. This means that generally in a price system, further trades could not occur without making somebody worse off. In other words, in a freely functioning price system, all of the gains from mutually beneficial trade will be exhausted.

CONCEPTS IN BRIEF

◉ Prices in a market economy perform a rationing function because they reflect relative scarcity, allowing the market to clear. Other ways to ration goods include first come, first served; political power; physical force; lotteries; and coupons.

◉ Even when businesspeople can change prices, some rationing by waiting will occur. Such queuing arises when there are large unexpected changes in demand coupled with high costs of satisfying those changes immediately.

THE POLICY OF GOVERNMENT-IMPOSED PRICE CONTROLS

Price controls
Government-mandated minimum or maximum prices that may be charged for goods and services.

Price ceiling
A legal maximum price that may be charged for a particular good or service.

Price floor
A legal minimum price below which a good or service may not be sold. Legal minimum wages are an example.

Nonprice rationing devices
All methods used to ration scarce goods that are price-controlled. Whenever the price system is not allowed to work, nonprice rationing devices will evolve to ration the affected goods and services.

Black market
A market in which goods are traded at prices above their legal maximum prices or in which illegal goods are sold.

The rationing function of prices is often not allowed to operate when governments impose price controls. **Price controls** typically involve setting a **price ceiling**—the maximum price that may be allowed in an exchange. The world has had a long history of price ceilings applied to some goods, wages, rents, and interest rates, among other things. Occasionally a government will set a **price floor**—a minimum price below which a good or service may not be sold. These have most often been applied to wages and agricultural products. Let's consider price controls in terms of price ceilings.

Price Ceilings and Black Markets

As long as a price ceiling is below the market clearing price, imposing a price ceiling creates a shortage, as can be seen in Figure 4-3. At any price below the market clearing, or equilibrium, price of P_e, there will always be a larger quantity demanded than quantity supplied—a shortage, as you will recall from Chapter 3. Normally, whenever a shortage exists, there is a tendency for price and output to rise to equilibrium levels. This is exactly what we pointed out when discussing shortages in the labor market. But with a price ceiling, this tendency cannot be fully realized because everyone is forbidden to trade at the equilibrium price.

The result is fewer exchanges and **nonprice rationing devices.** In Figure 4-3, at an equilibrium price of P_e, the equilibrium quantity demanded and supplied (or traded) is Q_e. But at the price ceiling of P_1, the equilibrium quantity offered is only Q_s. What happens if there is a shortage? The most obvious nonprice rationing device to help clear the market is queuing, or long lines, which we have already discussed.

Typically, an effective price ceiling leads to a **black market.** A black market is a market in which the price-controlled good is sold at an illegally high price through various methods. For example, if the price of gasoline is controlled at lower than the market clearing price, a gas station attendant may take a cash payment on the side in order to fill up a driver's car (as happened in the 1970s in the United States during price controls on gasoline). If the price of beef is controlled at below its market clearing price, the butcher may give special service to a customer who offers the butcher great seats at an upcoming foot-

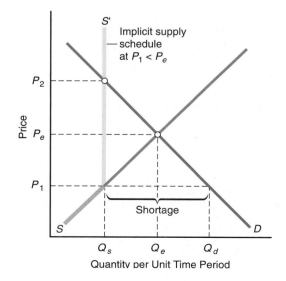

FIGURE 4-3
Black Markets
The demand curve is *D*. The supply curve is *S*. The equilibrium price is P_e. The government, however, steps in and imposes a maximum price of P_1. At that lower price, the quantity demanded will be Q_d, but the quantity supplied will only be Q_s. There is a "shortage." The implicit price (including time costs) tends to rise to P_2. If black markets arise, as they generally will, the equilibrium black market price will end up somewhere between P_1 and P_2.

ball game. Indeed, the number of ways in which the true implicit price of a price-controlled good or service can be increased is infinite, limited only by the imagination. (Black markets also occur when goods are made illegal—their legal price is set at zero.)

Whenever a nation attempts to freeze all prices, a variety of problems arise. Many of them occurred a few years ago in one African country, Sierra Leone.

INTERNATIONAL EXAMPLE

Price Controls in Sierra Leone

Lisa Walker spent a year as a Peace Corps volunteer in Sierra Leone, West Africa, and she kept a diary of her experiences. One thing she wrote about was what happened when the government imposed price controls on many common items: "For the last five days," she wrote, "nobody has sold cigarettes, kerosene, Maggi [bouillon] cubes, or rice here . . . . This is the result of the government's new order. The government says that Maggi cubes have to be sold for 30 cents, but sellers bought them for 50 cents, so when military men enter the village to enforce the government price, those with Maggis hide them. Same story for cigarettes and kerosene. The rice supplies are now hidden because of government prices. Unless one is willing to pay an outrageous price, it is impossible to buy rice in the marketplace. The only way to get rice legally is to buy it from the government. This means standing in long lines for many hours to get a rationed amount. I don't know how Sierra Leoneans are managing or how long this artificial rice shortage will last."

For Critical Analysis

How would you graphically illustrate the market for rice in Sierra Leone in the presence of price controls?

CONCEPTS IN BRIEF

● Government policy can impose price controls in the form of price ceilings and price floors.

● An effective price ceiling is one that sets the legal price below the market clearing price and is enforced. Effective price ceilings lead to nonprice rationing devices and black markets.

THE POLICY OF CONTROLLING RENTS

Over 200 American cities and towns, including Berkeley and New York City, operate under some kind of rent control. **Rent control** is a system under which the local government tells building owners how much they can charge their tenants in rent. In the United States, rent controls date back to at least World War II. The objective of rent control is to keep rents below levels that would be observed in a freely competitive market.

Rent control
The placement of price ceilings on rents in particular cities.

The Functions of Rental Prices

In any housing market, rental prices serve three functions: (1) to promote the efficient maintenance of existing housing and stimulate the construction of new housing, (2) to allocate existing scarce housing among competing claimants, and (3) to ration the use of existing housing by current demanders.

Rent Controls and Construction. Rent controls have discouraged the construction of new rental units. Rents are the most important long-term determinant of profitability, and rent controls have artificially depressed them. Consider some examples. In a recent year in

Putting
Economics in Action
to Work

To get practice examining the effects of rent controls, start the *EIA* CD, and click on "Markets in Action." Then click on "Competitive Housing Market."

Dallas, Texas, with a 16 percent rental vacancy rate but no rent control laws, 11,000 new rental housing units were built. In the same year in San Francisco, California, only 2,000 units were built. The major difference? San Francisco has only a 1.6 percent vacancy rate but stringent rent control laws. In New York City, until a change in the law in 1997, the only rental units being built were luxury units, which were exempt from controls.

Effects on the Existing Supply of Housing.   When rental rates are held below equilibrium levels, property owners cannot recover the cost of maintenance, repairs, and capital improvements through higher rents. Hence they curtail these activities. In the extreme situation, taxes, utilities, and the expenses of basic repairs exceed rental receipts. The result is abandoned buildings. Numerous buildings have been abandoned in New York City. Some owners have resorted to arson, hoping to collect the insurance on their empty buildings before the city claims them for back taxes.

Rationing the Current Use of Housing.   Rent controls also affect the current use of housing because they restrict tenant mobility. Consider the family whose children have gone off to college. That family might want to live in a smaller apartment. But in a rent-controlled environment, there can be a substantial cost to giving up a rent-controlled unit. In most rent-controlled cities, rents can be adjusted only when a tenant leaves. That means that a move from a long-occupied rent-controlled apartment to a smaller apartment can involve a hefty rent hike. This artificial preservation of the status quo became known in New York as "housing gridlock."

Attempts at Evading Rent Controls

The distortions produced by rent controls lead to efforts by both property owners and tenants to evade the rules. This leads to the growth of expensive government bureaucracies whose job it is to make sure that rent controls aren't evaded. In New York City, property owners have had an incentive to make life unpleasant for tenants to drive them out or to evict them on the slightest pretense as the only way to raise the rent. The city has responded by making evictions extremely costly for property owners. Eviction requires a tedious and expensive judicial proceeding. Tenants, for their part, routinely try to sublet all or part of their rent-controlled apartments at fees substantially above the rent they pay to the owner. Both the city and the property owners try to prohibit subletting and typically end up in the city's housing courts—an entire judicial system developed to deal with disputes involving rent-controlled apartments. The overflow and appeals from the city's housing courts is now clogging the rest of New York's judicial system.

Who Gains and Who Loses from Rent Controls?

The big losers from rent controls are clearly property owners. But there is another group of losers—low-income individuals, especially single mothers, trying to find their first apartment. Some observers now believe that rent controls have worsened the problem of homelessness in such cities as New York.

Typically, owners of rent-controlled apartments often charge "key money" before a new tenant is allowed to move in. This is a large up-front cash payment, usually illegal but demanded nonetheless—just one aspect of the black market in rent-controlled apartments. Poor individuals cannot afford a hefty key money payment, nor can they assure the owner that their rent will be on time or even paid each month. Because controlled rents are usually below market clearing levels, there is little incentive for apartment owners to take any risk on low-income-earning individuals as tenants. This is particularly true when a prospective tenant's chief source of income is a welfare check. Indeed, a large number of the litigants in the New York housing courts are welfare mothers who have missed their rent payments due to emergency expenses or delayed welfare checks. Often their appeals end in evictions and a new home in a temporary public shelter—or on the streets.

Who benefits from rent control? Ample evidence indicates that upper-income professionals benefit the most. These are the people who can use their mastery of the bureaucracy and their large network of friends and connections to exploit the rent control system. Consider that in New York, actresses Mia Farrow and Cicely Tyson live in rent-controlled apartments, paying well below market rates. So do State Senate Democratic leader Manfred Ohrenstein, the director of the Metropolitan Museum of Art, the chairman of Pathmark Stores, and writer Alistair Cooke.

INTERNATIONAL EXAMPLE

The End of Rent Controls in Egypt

Since Gamal Abdel Nasser's efforts to recast Egypt along socialist lines in the 1950s, farmland in this nation was subject to strict rent controls. Consequently, for more than 40 years, rents paid by tenant farmers—roughly 10 percent of the Egyptian populace—were frozen. Due to the considerable inflation that took place in Egypt during this period, the relative rental price of land was rapidly approaching zero. Tenants effectively took over lands they did not own, practically free of charge. A consequence was that the value of the land was very low to its owners, and this discouraged the adoption of modern cultivation techniques. Many tenant farmers in Egypt continued to plant only subsistence crops using their hands, hoes, and water buffaloes.

In 1992, Egypt adopted a law that reversed its rent controls. It phased in the law very gradually, however. Only recently has it permitted landowners to charge their tenants market prices. In some cases, landowners have evicted tenants to make way for more modern, less labor-intensive farming techniques. This has made the subject of rent control one of the most potent political issues in this Middle Eastern nation.

For Critical Analysis
What market-based policies might the Egyptian government adopt to reduce the impact of the removal of rent controls on tenant farmers?

CONCEPTS IN BRIEF

● Rental prices perform three functions: (1) allocating existing scarce housing among competing claimants, (2) promoting efficient maintenance of existing houses and stimulating new housing construction, and (3) rationing the use of existing houses by current demanders.

● Effective rent controls reduce or alter the three functions of rental prices. Construction of new rental units is discouraged. Rent controls decrease spending on maintenance of existing ones and also lead to "housing gridlock."

● There are numerous ways to evade rent controls; key money is one.

PRICE FLOORS IN AGRICULTURE

Another way that government can affect markets is by imposing price floors or price supports. In the United States, price supports are most often associated with agricultural products.

Price Supports

During the Great Depression, the federal government swung into action to help farmers. In 1933, it established a system of price supports for many agricultural products. Until recently, there were price supports for wheat, feed grains, cotton, rice, soybeans, sorghum, and

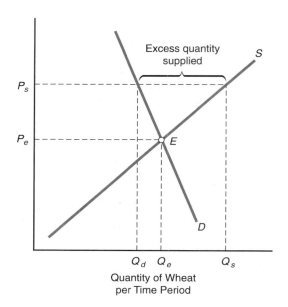

FIGURE 4-4

Agricultural Price Supports
Free market equilibrium occurs at E, with an equilibrium price of P_e and an equilibrium quantity of Q_e. When the government set a support price at P_s, the quantity demanded was Q_d, and the quantity supplied was Q_s. The difference was the surplus, which the government bought. Note that farmers' total income was from consumers ($P_s \times Q_d$) plus taxpayers [($Q_s - Q_d$) × P_s].

dairy products. The nature of the supports was quite simple: The government simply chose a *support price* for an agricultural product and then acted to ensure that the price of the product never fell below the support level. Figure 4-4 shows the market demand and supply of wheat. Without a price support program, competitive forces would yield an equilibrium price of P_e and an equilibrium quantity of Q_e. Clearly, if the government were to set the support price at P_e or below, the quantity of wheat demanded would equal the quantity of wheat supplied at point E because farmers can sell all they want at the market clearing price of P_e, above the price floor.

Until 1996, however, the government set the support price *above* P_e, at P_s. At a support price of P_s, the quantity demanded is only Q_d, but the quantity supplied is Q_s. The difference between them is called the *excess quantity supplied,* or *surplus.* As simple as this program seems, two questions arise: How did the government decide on the level of the support price P_s? And how did it prevent market forces from pushing the actual price down to P_e?

If production exceeded the amount consumers wanted to buy at the support price, what happened to the surplus? Quite simply, the government had to buy the surplus—the difference between Q_s and Q_d—if the price support program was to work. As a practical matter, the government acquired the quantity $Q_s - Q_d$ indirectly through a government agency. The government either stored the surplus or sold it to foreign countries at a greatly reduced price (or gave it away free of charge) under the Food for Peace program.

Who Benefited from Agricultural Price Supports?

Traditionally advocated as a way to guarantee a decent wage for low-income farmers, most of the benefits of agricultural price supports were skewed toward owners of very large farms. Price supports were made on a per-bushel basis, not on a per-farm basis. Thus traditionally, the larger the farm, the bigger the benefit from agricultural price supports. In addition, *all* of the benefits from price supports ultimately accrued to *landowners* on whose land price-supported crops could grow. Except for peanuts, tobacco, and sugar, the price support program was eliminated in 1996.

PRICE FLOORS IN THE LABOR MARKET

The **minimum wage** is the lowest hourly wage rate that firms may legally pay their workers. Proponents want higher minimum wages to ensure low-income workers a "decent" standard of living. Opponents claim that higher minimum wages cause increased unemployment, particularly among unskilled minority teenagers.

The federal minimum wage started in 1938 at 25 cents an hour, about 40 percent of the average manufacturing wage at the time. Typically, its level has stayed at about 40 to 50 percent of average manufacturing wages. It was increased to $5.15 in 1995 and may be higher by the time you read this. Many states and cities have their own minimum wage laws that sometimes exceed the federal minimum.

What happens when the government passes a floor on wages? The effects can be seen in Figure 4-5. We start off in equilibrium with the equilibrium wage rate of W_e and the equilibrium quantity of labor demanded and supplied equal to Q_e. A minimum wage, W_m, higher than W_e, is imposed. At W_m, the quantity demanded for labor is reduced to Q_d, and some workers now become unemployed. Note that the reduction in employment from Q_e to Q_d, or the distance from B to A, is less than the excess quantity of labor supplied at wage rate W_m. This excess quantity supplied is the distance between A and C, or the distance between Q_d and Q_s. The reason the reduction in employment is smaller than the excess supply of labor at the minimum wage is that the latter also includes a second component that consists of the additional workers who would like to work more hours at the new, higher minimum wage. Some workers may become

Minimum wage
A wage floor, legislated by government, setting the lowest hourly rate that firms may legally pay workers.

Can imposing price floors help keep industries from going out of business and worsening a nation's unemployment problem?

Yes, certain price floor arrangements can induce companies to keep producing unsold output, at least for a while. The social cost of such a policy can be very high, however. China's government, for instance, recently became concerned when a number of industries were unable to sell all their output at government-mandated price floors. The industries were threatening to downsize and lay off millions of Chinese workers. The government began purchasing unsold goods and storing them in warehouses. Of course, China's taxpayers must foot the bill for all this overproduction.

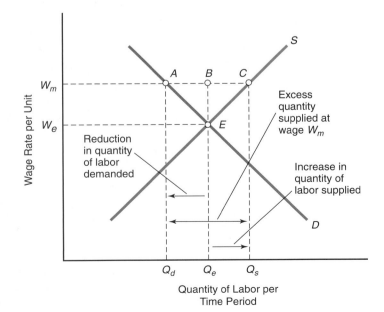

FIGURE 4-5
The Effect of Minimum Wages
The market clearing wage rate is W_e. The market clearing quantity of employment is Q_e, determined by the intersection of supply and demand at point E. A minimum wage equal to W_m is established. The quantity of labor demanded is reduced to Q_d; the reduction in employment from Q_e to Q_d is equal to the distance between B and A. That distance is smaller than the excess quantity of labor supplied at wage rate W_m. The distance between B and C is the increase in the quantity of labor supplied that results from the higher minimum wage rate.

To keep up to date on recent federal and state developments concerning minimum wages, go to **www.epfnet.org**, and click on "Minimum wage/living wage."

Putting Economics in Action to Work

To gain further understanding of the effects of the minimum wage, start the *EIA* CD, and click on "Markets in Action." Then click on "A Market for Low-Skilled Labor."

unemployed as a result of the minimum wage, but others will move to sectors where minimum wage laws do not apply; wages will be pushed down in these uncovered sectors.

In the long run (a time period that is long enough to allow for adjustment by workers and firms), some of the reduction in labor demanded will result from a reduction in the number of firms, and some will result from changes in the number of workers employed by each firm. Economists estimate that a 10 percent increase in the real minimum wage decreases total employment of those affected by 1 to 2 percent.*

QUANTITY RESTRICTIONS

Governments can impose quantity restrictions on a market. The most obvious restriction is an outright ban on the ownership or trading of a good. It is presently illegal to buy and sell human organs. It is also currently illegal to buy and sell certain psychoactive drugs such as cocaine, heroin, and marijuana. In some states, it is illegal to start a new hospital without obtaining a license for a particular number of beds to be offered to patients. This licensing requirement effectively limits the quantity of hospital beds in some states. From 1933 to 1973, it was illegal for U.S. citizens to own gold except for manufacturing, medicinal, or jewelry purposes.

POLICY EXAMPLE

Should the Legal Quantity of Cigarettes Supplied Be Set at Zero?

Nicotine has been used as a psychoactive drug by the native peoples of the Americas for approximately 8,000 years. Five hundred years ago, Christopher Columbus introduced tobacco to the Europeans, who discovered that once they overcame the nausea and dizziness produced by chewing, snorting, or smoking the tobacco, they simply could not get along without it. Nicotine quickly joined alcohol and caffeine as one of the world's most popular psychoactive drugs.

In the century after Columbus returned from the Americas with tobacco, consumption of and addiction to nicotine spread rapidly around the world. There followed numerous efforts to quash what had become known as the "evil weed." In 1603, the Japanese prohibited the use of tobacco and repeatedly increased the penalties for violating the ban, which wasn't lifted until 1625. By the middle of the seventeenth century, similar bans on tobacco were in place in Bavaria, Saxony, Zurich, Turkey, and Russia, with punishments ranging from confiscation of property to execution. Even in the early twentieth century, several state governments in the United States attempted to ban the use of tobacco.

A proposed quantity restriction—outright prohibition—was in the news again a few years ago when the head of the Food and Drug Administration announced that his agency had concluded that nicotine is addictive. He even argued that it should be classified with marijuana, heroin, and cocaine.

What can we predict if tobacco were ever completely prohibited today? Because tobacco is legal, the supply of illegal tobacco is zero. If the use of tobacco were restricted, the supply of illegal tobacco would not remain zero for long. Even if U.S. tobacco growers were forced out of business, the production of tobacco in other countries would increase to meet the demand. Consequently, the supply curve of illegal tobacco products would shift outward to the right as more foreign sources determined they wanted to enter the illegal U.S. tobacco market. The demand curve for illegal tobacco products would emerge almost immediately after the quantity restriction. The price people pay to satisfy their nicotine addiction would go up.

For Critical Analysis
What other goods or services follow the same analysis as the one presented here?

---

*Because we are referring to a long-run analysis here, the reduction in labor demanded would be demonstrated by an eventual shift inward to the left of the short-run demand curve, *D,* in Figure 4-5.

Some of the most common quantity restrictions exist in the area of international trade. The U.S. government, as well as many foreign governments, imposes import quotas on a variety of goods. An **import quota** is a supply restriction that prohibits the importation of more than a specified quantity of a particular good in a one-year period. The United States has had import quotas on tobacco, sugar, and immigrant labor. For many years, there were import quotas on oil coming into the United States. There are also "voluntary" import quotas on certain goods. Japanese automakers have agreed since 1981 "voluntarily" to restrict the amount of Japanese cars they send to the United States.

Import quota
A physical supply restriction on imports of a particular good, such as sugar. Foreign exporters are unable to sell in the United States more than the quantity specified in the import quota.

CONCEPTS IN BRIEF

● With a price support system, the government sets a minimum price at which, say, qualifying farm products can be sold. Any farmers who cannot sell at that price can "sell" their surplus to the government. The only way a price support system can survive is for the government or some other entity to buy up the excess quantity supplied at the support price.

● When a floor is placed on wages at a rate that is above market equilibrium, the result is an excess quantity of labor supplied at that minimum wage.

● Quantity restrictions may take the form of import quotas, which are limits on the quantity of specific foreign goods that can be brought into the United States for resale purposes.

NETNOMICS

On-Line Ticket Scalpers Literally "Buy Out the House."

Recently, a large group of fans of a popular band from the 1970s, the Eagles, waited through the wee hours of the morning for the first tickets to go on sale for an upcoming concert at a Los Angeles arena. They had already waited so long that they were not overly concerned when the cashier opened the window to the ticket booth a couple of minutes late. They were a little more upset, however, when after making repeated attempts to place the ticket order of the first person in line, the cashier announced that only the highest-price seats to the show were still available—all the lower-priced seats had been completely sold out. It turned out that during the cashier's slight delay in opening the ticket booth, buyers on the Internet had, with a few clicks of a mouse, drained the pool of lower-priced tickets.

Although more people still buy tickets in person or over the phone, Internet buyers are purchasing tickets on-line in the largest permitted quantities. A number of buyers purchase additional lots using different names and credit cards. Once they have snapped up all the tickets they can, these on-line purchasers become scalpers, selling their tickets at on-line auctions. As noted in Chapter 3, scalping tickets is illegal in most states, but enforcement of these laws with respect to Internet sales is all but impossible. Auction sites such as eBay.com, Ubid.com, and BuyandSell.com provide forums that electronically bring together buyers and sellers of most anything, including tickets to entertainment and sporting events. For instance, when the movie *Star Wars: The Phantom Menace* was first released, tickets with a face value of $8.50 could be sold on eBay.com for as high as $40, a markup of 370 percent.

ISSUES & APPLICATIONS

Computer Science Students Respond to Incentives, Just Like Everyone Else

The past several years have witnessed an upsurge of interest in computer courses. Across the nation, enrollments in computer courses rose by more than 40 percent in just four years.

A Shrinkage of Computer Science Students: Does It Compute?

Concepts Applied

Shift in Supply

Shift in Demand

Equilibrium

At the same time, however, fewer students who begin training for graduate degrees in computer science are finishing their studies. This trend has filtered down to undergraduates as well. Increasingly, computer science majors are following the example set by college dropout Bill Gates, the Microsoft co-founder.

What is luring these students from their studies is high entry-level wages. The starting salary for a promising computer specialist without a college degree can be as high as $60,000. For students who already have undergraduate degrees and have completed some graduate-level training, far higher salaries beckon.

Will Dropping Out Pay Off in the End?

Computer science professors and college officials think many of these students are making a big mistake. They point, for instance, to the boom-and-bust cycles that have been so common in information technology (IT) professions. As shown in panel (a) of Figure 4-6, employment growth for computer programmers and systems analysts has seesawed from year to year before leveling off somewhat recently. Academics in computer science warn students that as so many of them leave their studies to enter the marketplace, a rise in the market supply of IT specialists will ultimately drive salaries below today's levels.

It is of course in the best interest of professors and university officials to try to stem the tide of student defectors from academia to the private marketplace. Could they have a point nonetheless? Take a look at panel (b) of Figure 4-6, in which the initial demand for and supply of IT specialists are D_1 and S_1, respectively. Now suppose that there is a big jump in the demand for people with training in this area, as shown by the shift from D_1 to D_2. The result is a rise in the equilibrium wage. This encourages more people who currently possess IT skills to provide their services, resulting in an increase in the quantity of employed IT specialists. Now consider what happens when additional people—such as today's undergraduate and graduate students who leave school early—expect to receive higher wages in the near future and enter this market. Recall that when the sellers of any service, including labor services, anticipate earning a higher price, the result is a rise in market supply. The supply schedule therefore shifts from S_1 to S_2 in panel (b), pushing the equilibrium wage back down somewhat.

Thus academic naysayers are correct that other things being equal, the entry of students without degrees into the market for IT specialists should ultimately tend to depress wages. Nevertheless, this argument is based on the *ceteris paribus* assumption (see Chapter 1) that the demand schedule will not shift any farther to the right. As more and more consumers move on-line, the demand for IT specialists may in fact continue to increase. If so, the academic field of computer science may continue to shrink.

FOR CRITICAL ANALYSIS

1. As noted, a key factor determining what happens to future earnings of IT specialists will be changes in the demand for their services. What other factors will matter?

2. If wages for IT specialists do eventually fall back to or below their previous levels, what is likely to happen to college enrollments?

FIGURE 4-6
The Market for Computer Science Specialists
Employment opportunities for computer science specialists have experienced booms and busts over the past decade, as seen in panel (a). Leaving school before getting a degree may still make sense nonetheless. As panel (b) shows, demand has increased sufficiently that even with an increase in supply, wage rates will remain higher than they are today for information technology workers.

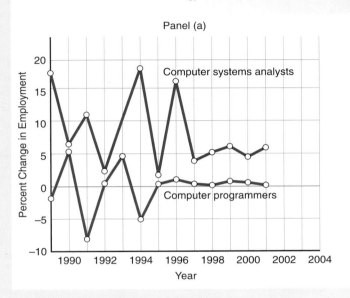

Panel (a)

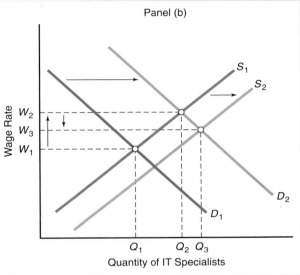

Panel (b)

SUMMARY DISCUSSION OF LEARNING OBJECTIVES

1. **Essential Features of the Price System:** The price system, otherwise called the market system, allows prices to respond to changes in supply and demand for different commodities. Consumers' and business managers' decisions on resource use depend on what happens to prices. In the price system, exchange takes place in markets. The terms of exchange are communicated by prices in the marketplace, where individuals strive to minimize transaction costs, sometimes through the use of middlemen who bring buyers and sellers together.

2. **How Changes in Demand and Supply Affect the Market Price and Equilibrium Quantity:** With a stable supply curve, an increase in demand causes an increase in the market price and an increase in the equilibrium quantity, and a decrease in demand induces a fall in the market price and a decline in

the equilibrium quantity. With a stable demand curve, an increase in supply causes a decrease in the market price and an increase in the equilibrium quantity, and a decrease in supply causes a rise in the market price and a decline in the equilibrium quantity. When both demand and supply shift at the same time, indeterminate results occur. We must know the direction and degree of each shift in order to predict the change in the market price and the equilibrium quantity.

3. **The Rationing Function of Prices:** In the market system, prices perform a rationing function—they ration scarce goods and services. Other ways of rationing include first come, first served; political power; physical force; lotteries; and coupons.

4. **The Effects of Price Ceilings:** Government-imposed price controls that require prices to be no

higher than a certain level are price ceilings. If a government sets a price ceiling below the market price, then at the ceiling price the quantity of the good demanded will exceed the quantity supplied. There will be a shortage of the good at the ceiling price. This can lead to nonprice rationing devices and black markets.

5. **The Effects of Price Floors:** Government-mandated price controls that require prices to be no lower than a certain level are price floors. If a government sets a price floor above the market price, then at the floor price the quantity of the good supplied will exceed the quantity demanded. There will be a surplus of the good at the floor price.

6. **Government-Imposed Restrictions on Market Quantities:** Quantity restrictions can take the form of outright government bans on the sale of certain goods, such as human organs or various psychoactive drugs. They can also arise from licensing requirements that limit the number of producers and thereby restrict the amount supplied of a good or service. Another example is an import quota, which limits the number of units of a foreign-produced good that can be legally sold domestically.

Key Terms and Concepts

Black market (82)

Import quota (89)

Minimum wage (87)

Nonprice rationing devices (82)

Price ceiling (82)

Price controls (82)

Price floor (82)

Price system (76)

Rent control (83)

Terms of exchange (76)

Transaction costs (77)

Voluntary exchange (76)

Problems

Answers to the odd-numbered problems appear at the back of the book.

4-1. Suppose that a rock band called the Raging Economists has released its first CD with Polyrock Records at a list price of $14.99. Explain how price serves as a purveyor of information to the band, the producer, and the consumer of rock CDs.

4-2. The pharmaceutical industry has benefited from advances in research and development that enable manufacturers to identify potential cures more quickly and therefore at lower cost. At the same time, our aging society has increased the demand for new drugs. Construct a supply and demand diagram of the market for pharmaceutical drugs. Illustrate the impact of these developments, and evaluate the effects on the market price and the equilibrium quantity.

4-3. The following table depicts the quantity demanded and quantity supplied of one-bedroom apartments in a small college town.

Monthly Rent	Quantity Demanded	Quantity Supplied
$400	3,000	1,600
$450	2,500	1,800
$500	2,000	2,000
$550	1,500	2,200
$600	1,000	2,400

What are the market price and equilibrium quantity of one-bedroom apartments in this town? Suppose that the mayor of this town decides to make housing more affordable for the local college students by imposing a rent control that holds the price of one-bedroom apartments to $450 a month. Explain the impact of this action on students desiring to live off campus and on owners of one-bedroom apartments. How many apartments are rented at the rate of $450 per month?

4-4. The United States provides considerable protection from foreign competition for its sugar industry. Suppose that one way it does this is by imposing a price floor that is above the market clearing price. Illustrate the U.S. sugar market with the price floor in place. Discuss the effects of the subsidy on conditions in the market for sugar in the United States.

4-5. The Canadian government and Canadian sugar industry have often complained that U.S. sugar manufacturers "dump" their sugar surpluses in the Canadian market. U.S. chocolate manufacturers and other U.S. businesses that use sugar as an input in their products have often complained that the high U.S. price of sugar hurts them in domestic and international markets. Explain how the imposition of a price floor for U.S. sugar, as described in Problem 4-4, affects these two markets. What are the changes in equilibrium quantities and market prices?

4-6. Suppose that the U.S. government places a ceiling on the price of Internet access. As a result, a black market for Internet providers arises, in which Internet service providers develop hidden means of connecting U.S. consumers. Illustrate the black market for Internet access, including the implicit supply schedule, the legal price, the black market supply and demand, and the black market equilibrium price and quantity. Also show why there is a shortage of Internet access at the legal price.

4-7. Airline routes are typically controlled by imposing a quota on the number of airline companies that may use the route and the number of flights on the route. Suppose that the following table illustrates the demand and supply schedules for seats on round-trip flights between Toronto and Chicago:

Price	Quantity Demanded	Quantity Supplied
$200	2,000	1,200
$300	1,800	1,400
$400	1,600	1,600
$500	1,400	1,800
$600	1,200	2,000

What are the market price and equilibrium quantity in this market? Now suppose that federal authorities limit the number of round-trip flights between the two cities to ensure that no more than 1,200 passengers can be flown. Explain the effects of this quota on the market price, quantity demanded, and quantity supplied.

4-8. The consequences of legalizing or decriminalizing illegal drugs have long been debated. Some individuals claim that legalization will lower the price of these drugs and therefore reduce related crime. Others claim that more people will use these drugs and the nation will face a health problem. Suppose that some of these drugs are legalized so that anyone may sell them and use them. Now consider the two claims—that price will fall and quantity will increase. Based on positive economic analysis, are these claims sound?

4-9. Look back at Figure 4-4. Suppose that the equilibrium price, P_e, is $1.00 per bushel of wheat and the support price is $1.25. In addition, suppose that the equilibrium quantity, Q_e, is 5 million bushels and the quantity supplied, Q_s, and quantity demanded, Q_d, with the price support are 8 million and 4 million, respectively. What was the total revenue of farmers before the price support program? What was the total revenue after the price support program? What is the cost of this program to taxpayers?

4-10. Using the information in Problem 4-9, calculate the total expenditures of wheat consumers before and after the price support program. Explain why these answers make sense.

Economics on the Net

The Floor on Milk Prices　The U.S. government maintains a price floor for milk. This application explains more about how the government implements the floor price and gives you an opportunity to apply what you have learned in this chapter to a real-world issue.

Internet URL:

www.dismal.com/thoughts/th_ct_082499.stm

Title: Even the Logic Is Milky

Navigation:　Start at the Dismal Economist homepage (www.dismal.com). Select Thoughts (www.dismal.com/thoughts/archive/archives.asp). Under Farmer's Market, click on Even the Logic Is Milky.

Application　Read the short commentary by Craig Thomas, and answer the following questions.

1. Based on the government-set price control concepts discussed in this chapter, explain the federal milk market and the Northeast Dairy Compact in place in the United States.

2. Reread paragraphs 6 through 8. Based on this information, draw a diagram illustrating the supply and demand of milk in the Northeast Dairy Compact and the supply and demand of milk outside of the Northeast Dairy Compact. Illustrate how the compact affects the quantities demanded and supplied for participants in the compact. In addition, show how this affects the market for milk produced by nonparticipants.

3. Thomas notes that Midwest dairy farmers have lost their market dominance. In light of your answer to question 2, explain how this occurred.

For Group Discussion and Analysis　Discuss the impact of the Northeast Dairy Compact on farmers inside and outside the compact. Discuss the impact of the Northeast Dairy Compact on consumers inside and outside the compact. Debate the impact of eliminating the compact based on your earlier discussions. Identify in your debate which arguments are based on positive economic analysis and which on normative arguments.

THE PUBLIC SECTOR AND PUBLIC CHOICE

The average American reaches "tax freedom day" in early May. But the opportunity cost of filling out income tax forms is not considered in this calculation. On-line tax filing may reduce this cost but will never eliminate it.

In July 1776, John Adams wrote that Independence Day would be an occasion for "games, sports, guns, bells, bonfires, and illuminations, from one end of the continent to the other, from this time forevermore." For the average American, however, April 11 might also be a day to rejoice each year. This is touted as "tax freedom day"—the day when the average taxpayer has earned enough to pay all *federal* taxes for the current year. But don't overdo the celebrating. Almost another month's work will be required before the true tax freedom day arrives, on May 10. This is when the average American has earned enough to pay all federal, state, and local taxes *combined*. After nearly four and a half months of labor, U.S. taxpayers begin to earn income that they can keep for themselves.

Why does the U.S. government tax so much of its citizens' earnings for its own use? Before you can consider this question, you must learn some details about the public sector in America.

LEARNING OBJECTIVES

After reading this chapter, you should be able to:

1. Explain how market failures such as externalities might justify economic functions of government

2. Distinguish between private goods and public goods and explain the nature of the free-rider problem

3. Describe political functions of government that entail its involvement in the economy

4. Distinguish between average tax rates and marginal tax rates

5. Explain the structure of the U.S. income tax system

6. Discuss the central elements of the theory of public choice

Market failure
A situation in which an unrestrained market economy leads to too few or too many resources going to a specific economic activity.

Externality
A consequence of an economic activity that spills over to affect third parties. Pollution is an externality.

Third parties
Parties who are not directly involved in a given activity or transaction.

Did You Know That... the U.S. government's total "take" from income taxes now exceeds $1 trillion each year? What is a trillion dollars? It is a million times a million. People earning an annual income of $200,000 or more typically pay just over 40 percent of these income taxes, and folks earning between $100,000 and $200,000 per year pay about 22 percent. Thus people earning more than $100,000 per year annually pay more than $620 billion in income taxes. People also pay miscellaneous other taxes, including sales and excise taxes. These also total to more than $1 trillion each year. So we cannot ignore the presence of government in our society. One of the reasons the government exists is to take care of what some people argue the price system does not do well.

WHAT A PRICE SYSTEM CAN AND CANNOT DO

Throughout the book so far, we have alluded to the benefits of a price system. High on the list is economic efficiency. In its most ideal form, a price system allows resources to move from lower-valued uses to higher-valued uses through voluntary exchange. The supreme point of economic efficiency occurs when all mutually advantageous trades have taken place. In a price system, consumers are sovereign; that is to say, they have the individual freedom to decide what they wish to purchase. Politicians and even business managers do not ultimately decide what is produced; consumers decide. Some proponents of the price system argue that this is its most important characteristic. A market organization of economic activity generally prevents one person from interfering with another in respect to most of his or her activities. Competition among sellers protects consumers from coercion by one seller, and sellers are protected from coercion by one consumer because other consumers are available.

Sometimes the price system does not generate these results, with too few or too many resources going to specific economic activities. Such situations are called **market failures.** Market failures prevent the price system from attaining economic efficiency and individual freedom, as well as other social goals. Market failures offer one of the strongest arguments in favor of certain economic functions of government, which we now examine.

CORRECTING FOR EXTERNALITIES

In a pure market system, competition generates economic efficiency only when individuals know the true opportunity cost of their actions. In some circumstances, the price that someone actually pays for a resource, good, or service is higher or lower than the opportunity cost that all of society pays for that same resource, good, or service.

Consider a hypothetical world in which there is no government regulation against pollution. You are living in a town that until now has had clean air. A steel mill moves into town. It produces steel and has paid for the inputs—land, labor, capital, and entrepreneurship. The price it charges for the steel reflects, in this example, only the costs that the steel mill incurred. In the course of production, however, the mill gets one input—clean air—by simply taking it. This is indeed an input because in the making of steel, the furnaces emit smoke. The steel mill doesn't have to pay the cost of using the clean air; rather, it is the people in the community who pay that cost in the form of dirtier clothes, dirtier cars and houses, and more respiratory illnesses. The effect is similar to what would happen if the steel mill could take coal or oil or workers' services free. There has been an **externality,** an external cost. Some of the costs associated with the production of the steel have "spilled over" to affect **third parties,** parties other than the buyer and the seller of the steel.

External Costs in Graphical Form

Look at panel (a) in Figure 5-1 on page 98. Here we show the demand curve for steel as D. The supply curve is S_1. The supply curve includes only the costs that the firms have to pay. The equilibrium, or market clearing, situation will occur at quantity Q_1. Let us take into account the fact that there are externalities—the external costs that you and your neighbors pay in the form of dirtier clothes, cars, and houses and increased respiratory disease due to the air pollution emitted from the steel mill; we also assume that all other suppliers of steel use clean air without having to pay for it. Let's include these external costs in our graph to find out what the full cost of steel production really is. This is equivalent to saying that the price of an input used in steel production increased. Recall from Chapter 3 that an increase in input prices shifts the supply curve. Thus in panel (a) of the figure, the supply curve shifts from S_1 to S_2; the external costs equal the vertical distance between A and E_1. If the external costs were somehow taken into account, the equilibrium quantity would fall to Q_2 and the price would rise to P_2. Equilibrium would shift from E to E_1. If the price does not account for external costs, third parties bear those costs—represented by the distance between A and E_1—in the form of dirtier clothes, houses, and cars and increased respiratory illnesses.

External Benefits in Graphical Form

Externalities can also be positive. To demonstrate external benefits in graphical form, we will use the example of inoculations against communicable disease. In panel (b) of Figure 5-1, we show the demand curve as D_1 (without taking account of any external benefits) and the supply curve as S. The equilibrium price is P_1, and the equilibrium quantity is Q_1. We assume, however, that inoculations against communicable diseases generate external benefits to individuals who may not be inoculated but will benefit nevertheless because epidemics will not break out. If such external benefits were taken into account, the demand curve would shift from D_1 to D_2. The new equilibrium quantity would be Q_2, and the new equilibrium price would be P_2. With no corrective action, this society is not devoting enough resources to inoculations against communicable diseases.

When there are external costs, the market will tend to *overallocate* resources to the production of the good or service in question, for those goods or services will be deceptively low-priced. With the example of steel, too much will be produced because the steel mill owners and managers are not required to take account of the external cost that steel production is imposing on the rest of society. In essence, the full cost of production is unknown to the owners and managers, so the price they charge the public for steel is lower than it would be otherwise. And of course, the lower price means that buyers are willing and able to buy more. More steel is produced and consumed than is socially optimal.

When there are external benefits, the market *underallocates* resources to the production of that good or service because the good or service is relatively too expensive (because the demand is relatively too low). In a market system, too many of the goods that generate external costs are produced and too few of the goods that generate external benefits are produced.

How the Government Corrects Negative Externalities

The government can in theory correct externality situations in a variety of ways in all cases that warrant such action. In the case of negative externalities, at least two avenues are open to the government: special taxes and legislative regulation or prohibition.

Putting Economics in Action to Work

Get practice thinking about external costs and external benefits. Start the *EIA* CD, click on "Externalities and Public Goods," and then click on "Externalities."

FIGURE 5-1

External Costs and Benefits

In panel (a), we show a situation in which the production of steel generates external costs. If the steel mills ignore pollution, at equilibrium the quantity of steel will be Q_1. If the mills had to pay for the additional cost borne by nearby residents that is caused by the steel mill's production, the supply curve would shift the vertical distance $A-E_1$, to S_2. If consumers were forced to pay a price that reflected the spillover costs, the quantity demanded would fall to Q_2. In panel (b), we show the situation in which inoculations against communicable diseases generate external benefits to those individuals who may not be inoculated but who will benefit because epidemics will not occur. If each individual ignores the external benefit of inoculations, the market clearing quantity will be Q_1. If external benefits are taken into account by purchasers of inoculations, however, the demand curve would shift to D_2. The new equilibrium quantity would be Q_2 and the price would be higher, P_2.

Panel (a)

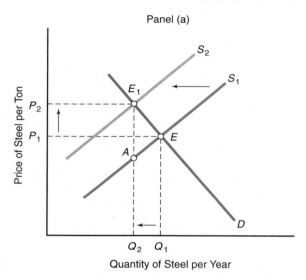

Panel (b)

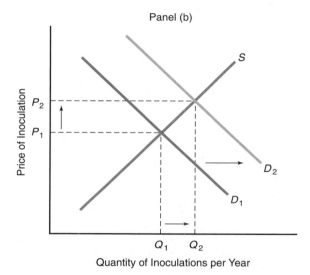

Quantity of Steel per Year

Quantity of Inoculations per Year

Special Taxes.   In our example of the steel mill, the externality problem originates from the fact that the air as a waste disposal place is costless to the firm but not to society. The government could make the steel mill pay a tax for dumping its pollutants into the air. The government could attempt to tax the steel mill commensurate with the cost to third parties from smoke in the air. This, in effect, would be a pollution tax or an **effluent fee.** The ultimate effect would be to reduce the supply of steel and raise the price to consumers, ideally making the price equal to the full cost of production to society.

Regulation.   To correct a negative externality arising from steel production, the government could specify a maximum allowable rate of pollution. This action would require that the steel mill install pollution abatement equipment at its facilities, that it reduce its rate of output, or some combination of the two. Note that the government's job would not be that simple, for it still would have to determine the level of pollution and then actually measure its output from steel production in order to enforce such regulation.

How the Government Corrects Positive Externalities

What can the government do when the production of one good spills *benefits* over to third parties? It has several policy options: financing the production of the good or producing the good itself, subsidies (negative taxes), and regulation.

Effluent fee
A charge to a polluter that gives the right to discharge into the air or water a certain amount of pollution. Also called a *pollution tax.*

Learn more about how the U.S. government uses regulations to try to protect the environment at **http://es.epa.gov/oeca**

Government Financing and Production. If the positive externalities seem extremely large, the government has the option of financing the desired additional production facilities so that the "right" amount of the good will be produced. Again consider inoculations against communicable diseases. The government could—and often does—finance campaigns to inoculate the population. It could (and does) even produce and operate centers for inoculation in which such inoculations would be given at no charge.

Subsidies. A subsidy is a negative tax; it is a payment made either to a business or to a consumer when the business produces or the consumer buys a good or a service. In the case of inoculations against communicable diseases, the government could subsidize everyone who obtains an inoculation by directly reimbursing those inoculated or by making payments to private firms that provide inoculations. If you are attending a state university, taxpayers are defraying part of the cost of providing your education; you are being subsidized by as much as 80 percent of the total cost. Subsidies reduce the net price to consumers, thereby causing a larger quantity to be demanded.

Regulation. In some cases involving positive externalities, the government can require by law that a certain action be undertaken by individuals in the society. For example, regulations require that all school-age children be inoculated before entering public and private schools. Some people believe that a basic school education itself generates positive externalities. Perhaps as a result of this belief, we have regulations—laws—that require all school-age children to be enrolled in a public or private school.

● External costs lead to an overallocation of resources to the specific economic activity. Two possible ways of correcting these spillovers are taxation and regulation.

● External benefits result in an underallocation of resources to the specific activity. Three possible government corrections are financing the production of the activity, subsidizing private firms or consumers to engage in the activity, and regulation.

CONCEPTS IN BRIEF

THE OTHER ECONOMIC FUNCTIONS OF GOVERNMENT

Besides correcting for externalities, the government performs many other economic functions that affect the way exchange is carried out. In contrast, the political functions of government have to do with deciding how income should be redistributed among households and selecting which goods and services have special merits and should therefore be treated differently. The economic and political functions of government can and do overlap.

Let's look at four more economic functions of government.

Providing a Legal System

The courts and the police may not at first seem like economic functions of government (although judges and police personnel must be paid). Their activities nonetheless have important consequences on economic activities in any country. You and I enter into contracts constantly, whether they be oral or written, expressed or implied. When we believe that we have been wronged, we seek redress of our grievances within our legal institutions. Moreover, consider the legal system that is necessary for the smooth functioning of our system. Our system has defined quite explicitly the legal status of businesses, the rights of private ownership, and a method for the enforcement of contracts. All relationships among consumers and businesses are governed by the legal rules of the game. We might consider the government in its judicial function, then, as the referee when there are disputes in the economic arena.

Much of our legal system is involved with defining and protecting *property rights*. **Property rights** are the rights of an owner to use and to exchange his or her property. One might say that property rights are really the rules of our economic game. When property rights are well defined, owners of property have an incentive to use that property efficiently. Any mistakes in their decision about the use of property have negative consequences that the owners suffer. Furthermore, when property rights are well defined, owners of property have an incentive to maintain that property so that if those owners ever desire to sell it, it will fetch a better price.

Establishing and maintaining an independent constitutional judiciary, a familiar activity in the United States, is relatively new to Central and Eastern European countries.

Property rights
The rights of an owner to use and to exchange property.

INTERNATIONAL EXAMPLE

Post-Communist Rule of Law

Prior to the collapse of the Soviet empire, Central and Eastern European nations did not have an independent constitutional judiciary. Today that has changed. As a result, the institutional climate in these nations is more favorable for both domestic and foreign businesses.

The new constitutional frameworks in Central and Eastern European countries are based in large part on the U.S. Constitution. They emphasize the doctrines of separation of powers and checks and balances. They even give the courts the power of judicial review. (In the United States, this power allows the courts to declare laws unconstitutional.) A case in point is Hungary. There, legislators passed laws providing for restitution of nationalized land to pre-Communist owners. The court ruled that such laws were retroactive and thus invalid. The Hungarian court further stated that the only basis for returning land to former owners was through the transition to a market economy.

Bulgaria's constitutional court has consistently angered politicians. The court curbed government efforts to control radio and television. In Poland, the constitutional court voided a law passed by Parliament that would have lowered pensions of former state employees. This legal decision alone created a government obligation to pay almost $3 billion in compensation to almost 10 million Poles. This forced the government to sell bonds to pay for those pensions.

The trend toward highly independent court systems continues throughout Central and Eastern Europe.

For Critical Analysis
Why would an independent constitutional judiciary be important to someone who wished to invest in a new business in a Central or Eastern European country?

Promoting Competition

Antitrust legislation
Laws that restrict the formation of monopolies and regulate certain anticompetitive business practices.

Monopoly
A firm that has great control over the price of a good. In the extreme case, a monopoly is the only seller of a good or service.

Many people believe that the only way to attain economic efficiency is through competition. One of the roles of government is to serve as the protector of a competitive economic system. Congress and the various state governments have passed **antitrust legislation.** Such legislation makes illegal certain (but not all) economic activities that might restrain trade—that is, prevent free competition among actual and potential rival firms in the marketplace. The avowed aim of antitrust legislation is to reduce the power of **monopolies**—firms that have great control over the price of the goods they sell. A large number of antitrust laws have been passed that prohibit specific anticompetitive actions. Both the Antitrust Division of the Department of Justice and the Federal Trade Commission attempt to enforce these antitrust laws. Various state judicial agencies also expend efforts at maintaining competition.

Providing Public Goods

The goods used in our examples up to this point have been **private goods.** When I eat a cheeseburger, you cannot eat the same one. So you and I are rivals for that cheeseburger, just as much as rivals for the title of world champion are. When I use a CD-ROM player, you cannot use the same player. When I use the services of an auto mechanic, that person cannot work at the same time for you. That is the distinguishing feature of private goods—their use is exclusive to the people who purchase or rent them. The **principle of rival consumption** applies to all private goods by definition. Rival consumption is easy to understand. With private goods, either you use them or I use them.

There is an entire class of goods that are not private goods. These are called **public goods.** The principle of rival consumption does not apply to them. That is, they can be consumed *jointly* by many individuals simultaneously. National defense, police protection, and the legal system, for example, are public goods. If you partake of them, you do not necessarily take away from anyone else's share of those goods.

Characteristics of Public Goods.   Several distinguishing characteristics of public goods set them apart from all other goods.*

1. *Public goods are often indivisible.* You can't buy or sell $5 worth of our ability to annihilate the world with bombs. Public goods cannot usually be produced or sold very easily in small units.

2. *Public goods can be used by more and more people at no additional cost.* Once money has been spent on national defense, the defense protection you receive does not reduce the amount of protection bestowed on anyone else. The opportunity cost of your receiving national defense once it is in place is zero.

3. *Additional users of public goods do not deprive others of any of the services of the goods.* If you turn on your television set, your neighbors don't get weaker reception because of your action.

4. *It is difficult to design a collection system for a public good on the basis of how much individuals use it.* It is nearly impossible to determine how much any person uses or values national defense. No one can be denied the benefits of national defense for failing to pay for that public good. This is often called the **exclusion principle.**

One of the problems of public goods is that the private sector has a difficult, if not impossible, time providing them. There is little or no incentive for individuals in the private sector to offer public goods because it is so difficult to make a profit so doing. Consequently, true public goods must necessarily be provided by government.

Private goods
Goods that can be consumed by only one individual at a time. Private goods are subject to the principle of rival consumption.

Principle of rival consumption
The recognition that individuals are rivals in consuming private goods because one person's consumption reduces the amount available for others to consume.

Public goods
Goods to which the principle of rival consumption does not apply; they can be jointly consumed by many individuals simultaneously at no additional cost and with no reduction in quality or quantity.

Exclusion principle
The principle that no one can be excluded from the benefits of a public good, even if that person hasn't paid for it.

INTERNATIONAL EXAMPLE

Is a Lighthouse a Public Good?

One of the most common examples of a public good is asserted to be a lighthouse. Arguably, it satisfies all the criteria listed in points 1 through 4. One historical example suggests, however, that a lighthouse was not a public good, in that a collection system was devised and enforced on the basis of how much individuals used it.
(cont.)

---

*Sometimes the distinction is made between pure public goods, which have all the characteristics we have described here, and quasi- or near-public goods, which do not. The major feature of near-public goods is that they are jointly consumed, even though nonpaying customers can be, and often are, excluded—for example, movies, football games, and concerts.

In the thirteenth century, the city of Aigues-Mortes, a French southern port, erected a tower, called the King's Tower, designed to assert the will and power of Louis IX (Saint Louis). The 105-foot tower served as a lighthouse for ships. More important, it served as a lookout so that ships sailing on the open sea, but in its view, did not escape paying for use of the lighthouse.

Those payments were then used for the construction of the city walls.

For Critical Analysis

Explain how a lighthouse satisfies the characteristics of public goods described in points 1, 2, and 3.

Free-rider problem

A problem that arises when individuals presume that others will pay for public goods so that, individually, they can escape paying for their portion without causing a reduction in production.

Free Riders.   The nature of public goods leads to the **free-rider problem,** a situation in which some individuals take advantage of the fact that others will take on the burden of paying for public goods such as national defense. Free riders will argue that they receive no value from such government services as national defense and therefore really should not pay for it. Suppose that citizens were taxed directly in proportion to how much they tell an interviewer that they value national defense. Some people will probably tell interviewers that they are unwilling to pay for national defense because they don't want any of it—it is of no value to them. We may all want to be free riders if we believe that someone else will provide the commodity in question that we actually value.

The free-rider problem arises with respect to the international burden of defense and how it should be shared. A country may choose to belong to a multilateral defense organization, such as the North Atlantic Treaty Organization (NATO), but then consistently attempt to avoid contributing funds to the organization. The nation knows it would be defended by others in NATO if it were attacked but would rather not pay for such defense. In short, it seeks a "free ride."

Ensuring Economywide Stability

The government attempts to stabilize the economy by smoothing out the ups and downs in overall business activity. Our economy sometimes faces the problems of unemployment and rising prices. The government, especially the federal government, has made an attempt to solve these problems by trying to stabilize the economy. The notion that the federal government should undertake actions to stabilize business activity is a relatively new idea in the United States, encouraged by high unemployment rates during the Great Depression of the 1930s and subsequent theories about possible ways by which government could reduce unemployment. In 1946, the government passed the Employment Act, a landmark law concerning government responsibility for economic performance. It established three goals for government accountability: full employment, price stability, and economic growth. These goals have provided the justification for many government economic programs during the post–World War II period.

CONCEPTS IN BRIEF

- ● The economic activities of government include (1) correcting for externalities, (2) providing a judicial system, (3) promoting competition, (4) producing public goods, and (5) ensuring economywide stability.

- ● Public goods can be consumed jointly. The principle of rival consumption does not apply as it does with private goods.

- ● Public goods have the following characteristics: (1) They are indivisible; (2) once they are produced, there is no opportunity cost when additional consumers use them; (3) your use of a public good does not deprive others of its simultaneous use; and (4) consumers cannot conveniently be charged on the basis of use.

THE POLITICAL FUNCTIONS OF GOVERNMENT

At least two areas of government are in the realm of political, or normative, functions rather than that of the economic ones discussed in the first part of this chapter. These two areas are (1) the regulation and provision of merit and demerit goods and (2) income redistribution.

Merit and Demerit Goods

Certain goods are considered to have special merit. A **merit good** is defined as any good that the political process has deemed socially desirable. (Note that nothing inherent in any particular good makes it a merit good. The designation is entirely subjective.) Some examples of merit goods in our society are sports stadiums, museums, ballets, plays, and concerts. In these areas, the government's role is the provision of merit goods to the people in society who would not otherwise purchase them at market clearing prices or who would not purchase an amount of them judged to be sufficient. This provision may take the form of government production and distribution of merit goods. It can also take the form of reimbursement for payment on merit goods or subsidies to producers or consumers for part of the cost of merit goods. Governments do indeed subsidize such merit goods as professional sports, concerts, ballets, museums, and plays. In most cases, such merit goods would rarely be so numerous without subsidization.

Merit good
A good that has been deemed socially desirable through the political process. Museums are an example.

Demerit good
A good that has been deemed socially undesirable through the political process. Heroin is an example.

Demerit goods are the opposite of merit goods. They are goods that, through the political process, are deemed socially undesirable. Heroin, cigarettes, gambling, and cocaine are examples. The government exercises its role in the area of demerit goods by taxing, regulating, or prohibiting their manufacture, sale, and use. Governments justify the relatively high taxes on alcohol and tobacco by declaring them demerit goods. The best-known example of governmental exercise of power in this area is the stance against certain psychoactive drugs. Most psychoactives (except nicotine, caffeine, and alcohol) are either expressly prohibited, as is the case for heroin, cocaine, and opium, or heavily regulated, as in the case of prescription psychoactives.

Do government-funded sports stadiums have a positive effect on local economies?

Probably not, even though in recent years many cities have decided that new football and baseball stadiums are merit goods worthy of public funding. Their rationale is that there is no collective mechanism besides government to ensure the construction of the stadiums that will draw big crowds. A local government, goes the argument, can regard a stadium as an investment because the crowds it draws benefit the local economy. Spending by the crowds can also generate tax revenues that help the government recoup its expenses. According to economist Andrew Zimbalist, however, "There has not been an independent study by an economist over the last 30 years that suggests you can anticipate a positive economic impact" from government investments in sports facilities.

Income Redistribution

Another relatively recent political function of government has been the explicit redistribution of income. This redistribution uses two systems: the progressive income tax (described later in this chapter) and transfer payments. **Transfer payments** are payments made to individuals for which no services or goods are rendered in return. The three key money transfer payments in our system are welfare, Social Security, and unemployment insurance benefits. Income redistribution also includes a large amount of income **transfers in kind,** as opposed to money transfers. Some income transfers in kind are food stamps, Medicare and Medicaid, government health care services, and subsidized public housing.

Transfer payments
Money payments made by governments to individuals for which in return no services or goods are concurrently rendered. Examples are welfare, Social Security, and unemployment insurance benefits.

Transfers in kind
Payments that are in the form of actual goods and services, such as food stamps, subsidized public housing, and medical care, and for which in return no goods or services are rendered concurrently.

The government has also engaged in other activities as a form of redistribution of income. For example, the provision of public education is at least in part an attempt to redistribute income by making sure that the poor have access to education.

- Political, or normative, activities of the government include the provision and regulation of merit and demerit goods and income redistribution.
- Merit and demerit goods do not have any inherent characteristics that qualify them as such; rather, collectively, through the political process, we make judgments about which goods and services are "good" for society and which are "bad."
- Income redistribution can be carried out by a system of progressive taxation, coupled with transfer payments, which can be made in money or in kind, such as food stamps and Medicare.

PAYING FOR THE PUBLIC SECTOR

Jean-Baptiste Colbert, the seventeenth-century French finance minister, said the art of taxation was in "plucking the goose so as to obtain the largest amount of feathers with the least possible amount of hissing." In the United States, governments have designed a variety of methods of plucking the private-sector goose. To analyze any tax system, we must first understand the distinction between marginal tax rates and average tax rates.

Marginal and Average Tax Rates

If somebody says, "I pay 28 percent in taxes," you cannot really tell what that person means unless you know if he or she is referring to average taxes paid or the tax rate on the last dollars earned. The latter concept refers to the **marginal tax rate.***

The marginal tax rate is expressed as follows:

Marginal tax rate
The change in the tax payment divided by the change in income, or the percentage of additional dollars that must be paid in taxes. The marginal tax rate is applied to the highest tax bracket of taxable income reached.

$$\text{Marginal tax rate} = \frac{\text{change in taxes due}}{\text{change in taxable income}}$$

It is important to understand that the marginal tax rate applies only to the income in the highest **tax bracket** reached, where a tax bracket is defined as a specified level of taxable income to which a specific and unique marginal tax rate is applied.

The marginal tax rate is not the same thing as the **average tax rate,** which is defined as follows:

Tax bracket
A specified interval of income to which a specific and unique marginal tax rate is applied.

$$\text{Average tax rate} = \frac{\text{total taxes due}}{\text{total taxable income}}$$

Average tax rate
The total tax payment divided by total income. It is the proportion of total income paid in taxes.

Taxation Systems

No matter how governments raise revenues—from income taxes, sales taxes, or other taxes—all of those taxes fit into one of three types of taxation systems: proportional, progressive, and regressive, according to the relationship between the percentage of tax, or tax rate, paid and income. To determine whether a tax system is proportional, progressive, or regressive, we simply ask, What is the relationship between the average tax rate and the marginal tax rate?

*The word *marginal* means "incremental" (or "decremental") here.

Proportional Taxation.   **Proportional taxation** means that regardless of an individual's income, taxes comprise exactly the same proportion. In terms of marginal versus average tax rates, in a proportional taxation system, the marginal tax rate is always equal to the average tax rate. If every dollar is taxed at 20 percent, then the average tax rate is 20 percent, as is the marginal tax rate.

A proportional tax system is also called a *flat-rate tax.* Taxpayers at all income levels end up paying the same *percentage* of their income in taxes. If the proportional tax rate were 20 percent, an individual with an income of $10,000 would pay $2,000 in taxes, while an individual making $100,000 would pay $20,000, the identical 20 percent rate being levied on both.

Proportional taxation
A tax system in which regardless of an individual's income, the tax bill comprises exactly the same proportion. Also called a *flat-rate tax.*

Progressive Taxation.   Under **progressive taxation,** as a person's taxable income increases, the percentage of income paid in taxes increases. In terms of marginal versus average tax rates, in a progressive system, the marginal tax rate is above the average tax rate. If you are taxed 5 percent on the first $10,000 you make, 10 percent on the next $10,000 you make, and 30 percent on the last $10,000 you make, you face a progressive income tax system. Your marginal tax rate is always above your average tax rate.

Progressive taxation
A tax system in which as income increases, a higher percentage of the additional income is taxed. The marginal tax rate exceeds the average tax rate as income rises.

Regressive Taxation.   With **regressive taxation,** a smaller percentage of taxable income is taken in taxes as taxable income increases. The marginal rate is *below* the average rate. As income increases, the marginal tax rate falls, and so does the average tax rate. The U.S. Social Security tax is regressive. Once the legislative maximum taxable wage base is reached, no further Social Security taxes are paid. Consider a simplified hypothetical example: Every dollar up to $50,000 is taxed at 10 percent. After $50,000 there is no Social Security tax. Someone making $100,000 still pays only $5,000 in Social Security taxes. That person's average Social Security tax is 5 percent. The person making $50,000, by contrast, effectively pays 10 percent. The person making $1 million faces an average Social Security tax rate of only 0.5 percent in our simplified example.

Regressive taxation
A tax system in which as more dollars are earned, the percentage of tax paid on them falls. The marginal tax rate is less than the average tax rate as income rises.

● Marginal tax rates are applied to marginal tax brackets, defined as spreads of income over which the tax rate is constant.

● Tax systems can be proportional, progressive, or regressive, depending on whether the marginal tax rate is the same as, greater than, or less than the average tax rate as income rises.

**CONCEPTS
IN BRIEF**

THE MOST IMPORTANT FEDERAL TAXES

The federal government imposes income taxes on both individuals and corporations and collects Social Security taxes and a variety of other taxes.

The Federal Personal Income Tax

The most important tax in the U.S. economy is the federal personal income tax, which accounts for about 49 percent of all federal revenues. All American citizens, resident aliens, and most others who earn income in the United States are required to pay federal income taxes on all taxable income. The rates that are paid rise as income increases, as can be seen in Table 5-1. Marginal income tax rates at the federal level have varied from as

To learn about what distinguishes recent so-called "flat-tax" proposals from a truly proportional income tax system, go to **www.ncpa.org/pi/taxes/tax7. html** and click on "Flat Tax Proposals."

	Single Persons		Married Couples	
Marginal Tax Bracket		Marginal Tax Rate	Marginal Tax Bracket	Marginal Tax Rate
$0–$25,750		15%	$0–$43,050	15%
$25,751–$62,450		28%	$43,051–$104,050	28%
$62,451–$130,250		31%	$104,051–$158,550	31%
$130,251–$283,150		36%	$158,551–$283,150	36%
$283,151 and up		39.6%	$283,151 and up	39.6%

Source: U.S. Department of the Treasury.

low as 1 percent after the passage of the Sixteenth Amendment to as high as 94 percent (reached in 1944). There were 14 separate tax brackets prior to the Tax Reform Act of 1986, which reduced the number to three. Advocates of a more progressive income tax system in the United States argue that such a system redistributes income from the rich to the poor, taxes people according to their ability to pay, and taxes people according to the benefits they receive from government. Although there is much controversy over the redistributional nature of our progressive tax system, there is no strong evidence that in fact the tax system has ever done much income redistribution in this country. Currently, about 85 percent of all Americans, rich or poor, pay roughly the same proportion of their total income in federal taxes.

POLICY EXAMPLE

The Federal Income Tax, Then and Now

The United States first used an income tax during the Civil War. Congress ended the federal income tax in 1872. Adoption of the Sixteenth Amendment to the U.S. Constitution in 1913 brought back the income tax, however. Debate over the constitutional amendment was heated. One lawmaker argued passionately that ultimately "a hand from Washington will stretch out to every man's house." Many proponents of the amendment ridiculed him. After all, exempted from paying any taxes were single people with incomes below $3,000 (about $46,300 today) and married couples with incomes less than $4,000 (about $61,800 today). Thus initially, only U.S. citizens with relatively high incomes would be assessed income taxes of any significance.

Take a look at Table 5-2. It shows the tax rates imposed on various income brackets in 1913 and those same brackets expressed in 2000 dollars. A 1 percent tax rate would be in effect on incomes up to around $309,000. The highest rate, 7 percent, would apply to incomes over $7.7 million measured in 2000 dollars. Obviously, that is not the present situation—take a look at Table 5-1. Clearly, the federal income tax system as initiated in 1913 was a quite different animal from our current system. Looking back at Table 5-1, you can see that current tax rates are considerably higher than rates in 1913, and they affect virtually all Americans. A hand from Washington may not have stretched out to every house in 1913, but it certainly does today.

For Critical Analysis
The first income tax form was the size of a postcard. Why are tax forms so much thicker and more complicated today?

Tax Rate	Income Level in 1913	Equivalent Income Level in 2000 Dollars
1%	Up to $20,000	Up to $308,955
2%	$20,000–$50,000	$308,956–$772,388
3%	$50,000–$75,000	$772,389–$1,158,582
4%	$75,000–$100,000	$1,158,583–$1,544,776
5%	$100,000–$250,000	$1,544,777–$3,861,940
6%	$250,000–$500,000	$3,861,941–$7,723,881
7%	Over $500,000	Over $7,723,881

TABLE 5-2
1913 U. S. Income Tax Rates and Brackets

Source: U.S. Department of the Treasury.

The Treatment of Capital Gains

The difference between the buying and selling price of an asset, such as a share of stock or a plot of land, is called a **capital gain** if it is a profit and a **capital loss** if it is not. As of 2000, there were several capital gains tax rates.

Capital gains are not always real. If you pay $100,000 for a house in one year and sell it for 50 percent more 10 years later, your nominal capital gain is $50,000. But what if, during those 10 years, there has been inflation such that average prices also went up by 50 percent? Your *real* capital gain would be zero. But you still have to pay taxes on that $50,000. To counter this problem, many economists have argued that capital gains should be indexed to the rate of inflation. This is exactly what is done with the marginal tax brackets in the federal income tax code. Tax brackets for the purposes of calculating marginal tax rates each year are expanded at the rate of inflation, or the rate at which the average of all prices is rising. So if the rate of inflation is 10 percent, each tax bracket is moved up by 10 percent. The same concept could be applied to capital gains. So far, Congress has refused to enact such a measure.

Capital gain
The positive difference between the purchase price and the sale price of an asset. If a share of stock is bought for $5 and then sold for $15, the capital gain is $10.

Capital loss
The negative difference between the purchase price and the sale price of an asset.

The Corporate Income Tax

Corporate income taxes account for about 12 percent of all federal taxes collected and almost 8 percent of all state and local taxes collected. Corporations are generally taxed on the difference between their total revenues (or receipts) and their expenses. The federal corporate income tax structure is given in Table 5-3.

Double Taxation.   Because individual stockholders must pay taxes on the dividends they receive, paid out of *after-tax* profits by the corporation, corporate profits are taxed twice.

Corporate Taxable Income	Corporate Tax Rate
$0–$50,000	15%
$50,001–$75,000	25%
$75,001–$10,000,000	34%
$10,000,000 and up	35%

TABLE 5-3
Federal Corporate Income Tax Schedule
The use rates were in effect through 2001.

Source: Internal Revenue Service.

If you receive $1,000 in dividends, you have to declare them as income, and you must pay taxes at your marginal tax rate. Before the corporation was able to pay you those dividends, it had to pay taxes on all its profits, including any that it put back into the company or did not distribute in the form of dividends. Eventually the new investment made possible by those **retained earnings**—profits not given out to stockholders—along with borrowed funds will be reflected in the increased value of the stock in that company. When you sell your stock in that company, you will have to pay taxes on the difference between what you paid for the stock and what you sold it for. In both cases, dividends and retained earnings (corporate profits) are taxed twice.

Retained earnings
Earnings that a corporation saves, or retains, for investment in other productive activities; earnings that are not distributed to stockholders.

Tax incidence
The distribution of tax burdens among various groups in society.

Who Really Pays the Corporate Income Tax?   Corporations can exist only as long as consumers buy their products, employees make their goods, stockholders (owners) buy their shares, and bondholders buy their bonds. Corporations per se do not do anything. We must ask, then, who really pays the tax on corporate income. This is a question of **tax incidence.** (The question of tax incidence applies to all taxes, including sales taxes and Social Security taxes.) There remains considerable debate about the incidence of corporate taxation. Some economists say that corporations pass their tax burdens on to consumers by charging higher prices. Other economists believe that it is the stockholders who bear most of the tax. Still others believe that employees pay at least part of the tax by receiving lower wages than they would otherwise. Because the debate is not yet settled, we will not hazard a guess here as to what the correct conclusion may be. Suffice it to say that you should be cautious when you advocate increasing corporation income taxes. You may be the one who ultimately ends up paying the increase, at least in part, if you own shares in a corporation, buy its products, or work for it.

CONCEPTS IN BRIEF

● Because corporations must first pay an income tax on most earnings, the personal income tax shareholders pay on dividends received (or realized capital gains) constitutes double taxation.

● The corporate income tax is paid by one or more of the following groups: stockholder-owners, consumers of corporate-produced products, and employees in corporations.

Social Security and Unemployment Taxes

An increasing percentage of federal tax receipts is accounted for each year by taxes (other than income taxes) levied on payrolls. These taxes are for Social Security, retirement, survivors' disability, and old-age medical benefits (Medicare). As of 2000, the Social Security tax was imposed on earnings up to $72,600 at a rate of 6.2 percent on employers and 6.2 percent on employees. That is, the employer matches your "contribution" to Social Security. (The employer's contribution is really paid, at least in part, in the form of a reduced wage rate paid to employees.) A Medicare tax is imposed on all wage earnings at a combined rate of 2.9 percent. These taxes and the base on which they are levied are slated to rise in the next decade. Social Security taxes came into existence when the Federal Insurance Contributions Act (FICA) was passed in 1935. The future of Social Security is the subject of Chapter 6.

There is also a federal unemployment tax, which obviously has something to do with unemployment insurance. This tax rate is 0.8 percent on the first $7,000 of annual wages of each employee who earns more than $1,500. Only the employer makes the tax payment. This tax covers the costs of the unemployment insurance system and the costs of employment services. In addition to this federal tax, some states with an unemployment system impose an additional tax of up to about 3 percent, depending on the past record of the particular employer. An employer who frequently lays off workers will have a slightly higher state unemployment tax rate than an employer who never lays off workers.

SPENDING, GOVERNMENT SIZE, AND TAX RECEIPTS

The size of the public sector can be measured in many different ways. One way is to count the number of public employees. Another is to look at total government outlays. Government outlays include all government expenditures on employees, rent, electricity, and the like. In addition, total government outlays include transfer payments, such as welfare and Social Security. In Figure 5-2, you see that government outlays prior to World War I did not exceed 10 percent of annual national income. There was a spike during World War I, a general increase during the Great Depression, and then a huge spike during World War II. Contrary to previous postwar periods, after World War II government outlays as a percentage of total national income rose steadily before leveling off in the 1990s and 2000s.

Government Receipts

The main revenue raiser for all levels of government is taxes. We show in the two pie diagrams in Figure 5-3 on page 110 the percentage of receipts from various taxes obtained by the federal government and by state and local governments.

The Federal Government. The largest source of receipts for the federal government is the individual income tax. It accounts for 48.6 percent of all federal revenues. After that come social insurance taxes and contributions (Social Security), which account for 33.2 percent of total revenues. Next come corporate income taxes and then a number of other items, such as taxes on imported goods and excise taxes on such things as gasoline and alcoholic beverages.

State and Local Governments. As can be seen in Figure 5-3, there is quite a bit of difference in the origin of receipts for state and local governments and for the federal government. Personal and corporate income taxes account for only 20.4 percent of total state and

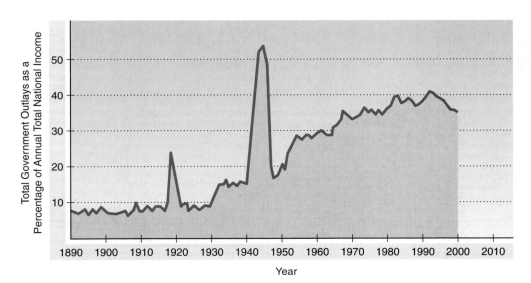

FIGURE 5-2
Total Government Outlays over Time
Here you see that total government outlays (federal, state, and local combined) remained small until the 1930s, except during World War I. Since World War II, government outlays have not fallen back to their historical average.

Sources: Facts and Figures on Government Finance and *Economic Indicators,* various issues.

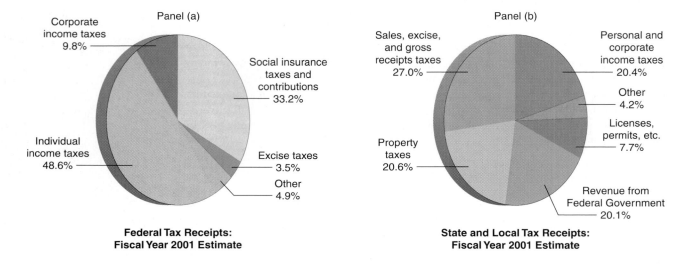

FIGURE 5-3
Sources of Government Tax Receipts
Over 82 percent of federal revenues come from income and Social Security taxes (a), whereas state government revenues are spread more evenly across sources (b), with less emphasis on taxes based on individual income.
Source: U.S. Department of Commerce, Bureau of Economic Analysis.

Panel (a)

Corporate income taxes 9.8%

Social insurance taxes and contributions 33.2%

Individual income taxes 48.6%

Excise taxes 3.5%

Other 4.9%

Federal Tax Receipts: Fiscal Year 2001 Estimate

Panel (b)

Sales, excise, and gross receipts taxes 27.0%

Personal and corporate income taxes 20.4%

Other 4.2%

Licenses, permits, etc. 7.7%

Property taxes 20.6%

Revenue from Federal Government 20.1%

State and Local Tax Receipts: Fiscal Year 2001 Estimate

To consider whether Internet sales should be taxed, go to
www.ecommercetax.com

local revenues. There are even a number of states that collect no personal income tax. The largest sources of state and local receipts (other than from the federal government) are personal and corporate income taxes, sales taxes, and property taxes.

Comparing Federal with State and Local Spending.   A typical federal government budget is given in panel (a) of Figure 5-4. The largest three categories are defense, income security, and Social Security, which together constitute 52.9 percent of the total federal budget.

The makeup of state and local expenditures is quite different. As panel (b) shows, education is the biggest category, accounting for 35.1 percent of all expenditures.

CONCEPTS IN BRIEF

● Total government outlays including transfers have continued to grow since World War II and now account for about 35 percent of yearly total national output.

● Government spending at the federal level is different from that at the state and local levels. At the federal level, defense, income security, and Social Security account for about 53 percent of the federal budget. At the state and local levels, education comprises 35 percent of all expenditures.

COLLECTIVE DECISION MAKING: THE THEORY OF PUBLIC CHOICE

Governments consist of individuals. No government actually thinks and acts; rather, government actions are the result of decision making by individuals in their roles as elected representatives, appointed officials, and salaried bureaucrats. Therefore, to understand how government works, we must examine the incentives for the people in government as well

FIGURE 5-4
Federal Government Spending Compared to State and Local Spending
The federal government's spending habits are quite different from those of the states and cities in panel (a), you can see that the categories of most importance in the federal budget are defense, income security, and Social Security, which make up 52.9 percent. In panel (b), the most important category at the state and local level is education, which makes up 35.1 percent. "Other" includes expenditures in such areas as waste treatment, garbage collection, mosquito abatement, and the judicial system.
Sources: Budget of the United States Government; Government Finances.

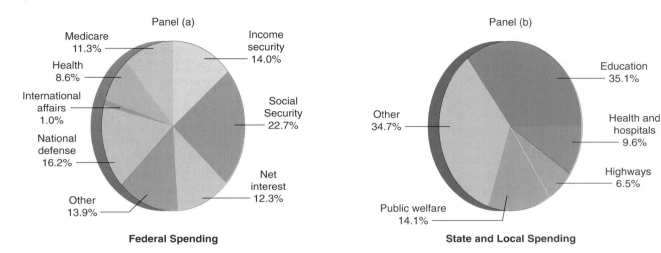

Panel (a)

Medicare 11.3%
Health 8.6%
International affairs 1.0%
National defense 16.2%
Other 13.9%
Income security 14.0%
Social Security 22.7%
Net interest 12.3%

Federal Spending

Panel (b)

Education 35.1%
Health and hospitals 9.6%
Highways 6.5%
Public welfare 14.1%
Other 34.7%

State and Local Spending

as those who would like to be in government—avowed or would-be candidates for elective or appointed positions—and special-interest lobbyists attempting to get government to do something. At issue is the analysis of **collective decision making.** Collective decision making involves the actions of voters, politicians, political parties, interest groups, and many other groups and individuals. The analysis of collective decision making is usually called the **theory of public choice.** It has been given this name because it involves hypotheses about how choices are made in the public sector, as opposed to the private sector. The foundation of public-choice theory is the assumption that individuals will act within the political process to maximize their *individual* (not collective) well-being. In that sense, the theory is similar to our analysis of the market economy, in which we also assume that individuals are motivated by self-interest.

To understand public-choice theory, it is necessary to point out other similarities between the private market sector and the public, or government, sector; then we will look at the differences.

Collective decision making
How voters, politicians, and other interested parties act and how these actions influence nonmarket decisions.

Theory of public choice
The study of collective decision making.

Similarities in Market and Public-Sector Decision Making

In addition to the similar assumption of self-interest being the motivating force in both sectors, there are other similarities.

Scarcity. At any given moment, the amount of resources is fixed. This means that for the private and the public sectors combined, there is a scarcity constraint. Everything that is spent by all levels of government, plus everything that is spent by the private sector, must add up to the total income available at any point in time. Hence every government action has an opportunity cost, just as in the market sector.

Competition.   Although we typically think of competition as a private-market phenomenon, it is also present in collective action. Given the scarcity constraint government also faces, bureaucrats, appointed officials, and elected representatives will always be in competition for available government funds. Furthermore, the individuals within any government agency or institution will act as individuals do in the private sector: They will try to obtain higher wages, better working conditions, and higher job-level classifications. We assume that they will compete and act in their own, not society's, interest.

Similarity of Individuals.   Contrary to popular belief, there are not two types of individuals, those who work in the private sector and those who work in the public sector; rather, individuals working in similar positions can be considered similar. The difference, as we shall see, is that the individuals in government face a different **incentive structure** than those in the private sector. For example, the costs and benefits of being efficient or inefficient differ when one goes from the private to the public sector.

Incentive structure
The system of rewards and punishments individuals face with respect to their own actions.

One approach to predicting government bureaucratic behavior is to ask what incentives bureaucrats face. Take the United States Postal Service (USPS) as an example. The bureaucrats running that government corporation are human beings with IQs not dissimilar to those possessed by workers in similar positions at Microsoft or American Airlines. Yet the USPS does not function like either of these companies. The difference can be explained, at least in part, in terms of the incentives provided for managers in the two types of institutions. When the bureaucratic managers and workers at Microsoft make incorrect decisions, work slowly, produce shoddy products, and are generally "inefficient," the profitability of the company declines. The owners—millions of shareholders—express their displeasure by selling some of their shares of company stock. The market value, as tracked on the stock exchange, falls. But what about the USPS? If a manager, a worker, or a bureaucrat in the USPS gives shoddy service, there is no straightforward mechanism by which the organization's owners—the taxpayers—can express their dissatisfaction. Despite the postal service's status as a "government corporation," taxpayers as shareholders do not really own shares of stock in the organization that they can sell.

The key, then, to understanding purported inefficiency in the government bureaucracy is not found in an examination of people and personalities but rather in an examination of incentives and institutional arrangements.

POLICY EXAMPLE

The U.S. Postal Service: Little Changed After More than Two Centuries

Like many private businesses, the federal government often desires to send urgent overnight mail. So to whom does it turn for delivery of the more than 8 million express letters and packages leaving federal offices for points around the nation and the world? Federal Express. Why not the U.S. Postal Service? The answer is that the USPS cannot legally reduce its prices to bid for competitive contracts. Even though the postal service now must make its own way without drawing on taxpayers, it still operates under a two-century-old mandate to serve every address, from backwoods farmhouses to crime-ridden urban apartments. It must do this while charging the same price to send a letter—whether regular first class or overnight delivery—from one point in New York City to another as it does from New York City to Anchorage, Alaska. This has made the postal service the provider of choice for transmitting items such as Pampers rebate coupons or proof-of-purchase seals from cereal boxes. But it has cost the USPS big revenues in the express-mail business. Its share of the overnight delivery pie is less than 10 percent. In recent years, supporters and critics of the postal service have both agreed that Congress must ultimately loosen the restraints that keep the USPS from competing with private firms in the marketplace. In the words of one member of Congress, if the postal service does not escape the bureaucratic shackles that bind it and compete in the private market-place, it may "slowly strangle itself."

For Critical Analysis

If the U.S. Postal Service cannot reduce its prices, in what other ways can it try to compete for big overnight delivery contracts?

Differences Between Market and Collective Decision Making

There are probably more dissimilarities between the market sector and the public sector than there are similarities.

Government Goods at Zero Price.   The majority of goods that governments produce are furnished to the ultimate consumers without direct money charge. **Government, or political, goods** can be either private or public goods. The fact that they are furnished to the ultimate consumer free of charge does *not* mean that the cost to society of those goods is zero, however; it only means that the price *charged* is zero. The full opportunity cost to society is the value of the resources used in the production of goods produced and provided by the government.

For example, none of us pays directly for each unit of consumption of defense or police protection. Rather, we pay for all these things indirectly through the taxes that support our governments—federal, state, and local. This special feature of government can be looked at in a different way. There is no longer a one-to-one relationship between consumption of a government-provided good and payment for that good. Consumers who pay taxes collectively pay for every political good, but the individual consumer may not be able to see the relationship between the taxes that he or she pays and the consumption of the good. Indeed, most taxpayers will find that their tax bill is the same whether or not they consume, or even like, government-provided goods.

Use of Force.   All governments are able to engage in the legal use of force in their regulation of economic affairs. For example, governments can exercise the use of *expropriation,* which means that if you refuse to pay your taxes, your bank account and other assets may be seized by the Internal Revenue Service. In fact, you have no choice in the matter of paying taxes to governments. Collectively, we decide the total size of government through the political process, but individually, we cannot determine how much service we pay for just for ourselves during any one year.

Voting Versus Spending.   In the private market sector, a dollar voting system is in effect. This dollar voting system is not equivalent to the voting system in the public sector. There are at least three differences:

1. In a political system, one person gets one vote, whereas in the market system, each dollar one spends counts separately.
2. The political system is run by **majority rule,** whereas the market system is run by **proportional rule.**
3. The spending of dollars can indicate intensity of want, whereas because of the all-or-nothing nature of political voting, a vote cannot.

Ultimately, the main distinction between political votes and dollar votes here is that political outcomes may differ from economic outcomes. Remember that economic efficiency is a situation in which, given the prevailing distribution of income, consumers get the economic goods they want. There is no corresponding situation using political voting. Thus we can never assume that a political voting process will lead to the same decisions that a dollar voting process will lead to in the marketplace.

Government, or political, goods
Goods (and services) provided by the public sector; they can be either private or public goods.

Majority rule
A collective decision-making system in which group decisions are made on the basis of more than 50 percent of the vote. In other words, whatever more than half of the electorate votes for, the entire electorate has to accept.

Proportional rule
A decision-making system in which actions are based on the proportion of the "votes" cast and are in proportion to them. In a market system, if 10 percent of the "dollar votes" are cast for blue cars, 10 percent of the output will be blue cars.

Indeed, consider the dilemma every voter faces. Usually a voter is not asked to decide on a single issue (although this happens); rather, a voter is asked to choose among candidates who present a large number of issues and state a position on each of them. Just consider the average U.S. senator, who has to vote on several thousand different issues during a six-year term. When you vote for that senator, you are voting for a person who must make thousands of decisions during the next six years.

NETNOMICS

Protecting Private Property on the Internet: The Problem of Cyberpiracy

The U.S. Constitution grants Congress the power "to promote the Progress of Science and useful Arts, by securing for limited Times to Authors and Inventors the exclusive Rights to their respective Writings and Discoveries." Today, copyright laws are governed by the Copyright Act of 1976, as amended. This act has not been particularly effective, however, in preventing the theft of *intellectual property*. In contrast to physical property, intellectual property is any creation whose source is a person's mind or creativity.

Recent technological developments have greatly simplified the pirating of films, tapes, and CDs. Within days after the initial release of *Star Wars: The Phantom Menace*, people in China were selling tapes of the film that U.S. moviegoers had made by smuggling hand-held videocassette recorders into theaters. The pirating of recorded music is also widespread. The International Federation of the Phonographic Industry (IFPI) estimates that one-fifth of all sales of recorded music are of pirated copies. The group estimates that one in three sales of CDs is pirated.

The IFPI's estimates are problematic, however. When estimating what legitimate CD sales would be in the absence of pirating, the IFPI assumes that pirated copies displace legitimate copies one for one, even though the pirated copies have much lower prices than legitimate copies. This assumption is a clear violation of the law of demand. In fact, there will be a larger quantity demanded at a lower price. Thus the lower-priced pirated copies of recorded music induce purchasers to buy more of them. If pirated copies did not exist, we could predict that legal sales of CDs would not simply replace them one for one.

This same analysis can apply to pirated copies of software. A person with a little computer background can develop relatively straightforward ways to transfer files from certain software programs for use by others who have not paid to use them. The Business Software Alliance estimates that a least half the global market for software is pirated products (remember the law of demand, however—this does not mean that if no pirating took place, legitimate sales of software would double).

There has been a significant change in pirating with the advent of the Internet: Not all pirates do so to profit. Some people, meaning to be kindhearted, offer downloadable copies of software and recorded music at no charge. Without ways to reduce this kind of unauthorized bootlegging, regardless of the motives of the bootleggers, people will reduce the time, effort, and creative energy they put into the development of software, recorded music, and other intellectual property.

This has led to calls from the film, recording, and software industries for stepped-up government efforts to protect their products under the copyright laws. Nonetheless, it is not clear how much the government can do when confronted with millions of Web sites to police. Many observers think that the solution will ultimately come from the private sector.

ISSUES & APPLICATIONS

A Global Comparison of Income Tax Systems

Britain adopted the first national income tax in 1799 as a "temporary measure." Today residents of most developed nations pay income taxes every year. These nations typically strive to achieve progressivity of their tax structures.

Marginal Tax Rates in Other Nations

As you can see in panel (a) of Figure 5-5, Japan and several European nations have the highest marginal tax rates for the highest-income residents. By contrast, Hong Kong and Singapore stand out with much lower tax rates for the "rich." Residents with the lowest incomes also face lower marginal tax rates in these latter two nations.

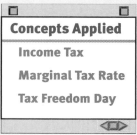

Concepts Applied

Income Tax

Marginal Tax Rate

Tax Freedom Day

FIGURE 5-5: Worldwide Income Tax Comparisons

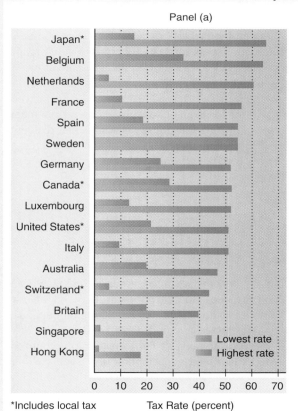

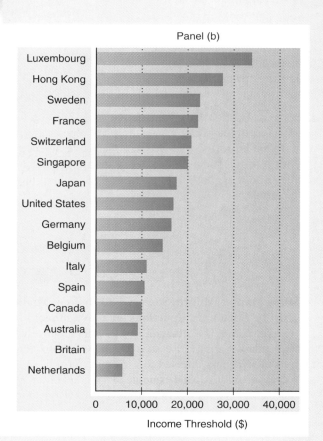

*Includes local tax

TABLE 5-4

Tax Freedom Day in Selected Nations
These figures exclude state, province, and local taxes.

Singapore	March 4	**Canada**	May 12
United States	April 11	**Germany**	May 23
Japan	April 12	**Italy**	June 2
Australia	April 25	**France**	June 12
Spain	May 5	**Netherlands**	June 12
Switzerland	May 6	**Belgium**	June 17
Britain	May 9	**Sweden**	July 3

Source: Organization for Economic Cooperation and Development.

FOR CRITICAL ANALYSIS

1. Some observers have attributed the strong employment and economic performance of Hong Kong and Singapore (despite the recession that affected Asian economies in 1997 and 1998) to the relatively small tax bite that they impose on income earners. Do you see any merit to this argument?

2. Does tax freedom day tell us anything about marginal tax rates? Does it tell us something about average tax rates?

Panel (b) of Figure 5-5 shows that some countries impose greater income tax burdens on lower-income residents than others do. A person can earn the equivalent of over $20,000 per year before owing any income taxes in Luxembourg, Hong Kong, Sweden, France, Switzerland, and Singapore. In contrast, in the United Kingdom and the Netherlands, a person earning less than the equivalent of $10,000 annually may owe income taxes to the government.

Tax Freedom Day—Anywhere Between March and July, Depending on Where You Live

Some governments rely more than others on the income tax as a significant source of tax revenues. For this reason, some international tax analysts like to look at a broader measure of tax assessments—the tax freedom day for a nation's average resident, which is the day each year when sufficient income has been earned to meet the nation's total tax bills.

Table 5-4 reports the "tax freedom day" for fourteen nations, based on tax payments to national governments. Based on this overall measure of tax assessments, residents of Sweden are the most tax-burdened people among developed nations: An average Swede begins to earn income on her or his own behalf only after the midpoint of each year!

SUMMARY DISCUSSION OF LEARNING OBJECTIVES

1. **How Market Failures Such as Externalities Might Justify Economic Functions of Government:** A market failure is a situation in which an unhindered free market gives rise to too many or too few resources' being directed to a specific form of economic activity. A good example of a market failure is an externality, which is a spillover effect on third parties not directly involved in producing or purchasing a good or service. In the case of a negative externality, firms do not pay for the costs arising from spillover effects that their production of a good

imposes on others, so they produce too much of the good in question. Government may be able to improve on the situation by restricting production or by imposing fees on producers. In the case of a positive externality, buyers fail to take into account the benefits that their consumption of a good yields to others, so they purchase too little of the good. Government may be able to induce more consumption of the good by regulating the market or subsidizing consumption. It can also provide a legal system to adjudicate disagreements about property rights, conduct antitrust policies to discourage monopoly and promote competition, provide public goods, and engage in policies designed to promote economic stability.

2. **Private Goods Versus Public Goods and the Free-Rider Problem:** Private goods are subject to the principle of rival consumption, meaning that one person's consumption of such a good reduces the amount available for another person to consume. This is not so for public goods, which can be consumed by many people simultaneously at no additional cost and with no reduction in quality or quantity of the good. Indeed, public goods are subject to the exclusion principle: No individual can be excluded from the benefits of a public good even if that person fails to help pay for it. This leads to the free-rider problem, which is that a person who thinks that others will pay for a public good will seek to avoid contributing to financing production of the good.

3. **Political Functions of Government That Lead to Its Involvement in the Economy:** Through the political process, people may decide that certain goods are merit goods, which they deem socially desirable, or demerit goods, which they feel are socially undesirable. They may call on government to promote the production of merit goods but to restrict or even ban the production and sale of demerit goods. In addition, the political process may determine that income redistribution is socially desirable, and governments may become involved in supervising transfer payments or in-kind transfers in the form of nonmoney payments.

4. **Average Tax Rates Versus Marginal Tax Rates:** The average tax rate is the ratio of total tax payments to total income. By contrast, the marginal tax rate is the change in tax payments induced by a change in total taxable income. Thus the marginal tax rate applies to the last dollar that a person earns.

5. **The U.S. Income Tax System:** The United States' income tax system assesses taxes against both personal and business incomes. It is designed to be a progressive tax system, in which the marginal tax rate increases as income rises, so that the marginal tax rate exceeds the average tax rate. This contrasts with a regressive tax system, in which higher-income people pay lower marginal tax rates, resulting in a marginal tax rate that is less than the average tax rate. The marginal tax rate equals the average tax rate only under proportional taxation, in which the marginal tax rate does not vary with income.

6. **Central Elements of the Theory of Public Choice:** The theory of public choice is the study of collective decision making, or the process through which voters, politicians, and other interested parties interact to influence nonmarket choices. Public choice theory emphasizes the incentive structures, or system of rewards or punishments, that affect the provision of government goods by the public sector of the economy. This theory points out that certain aspects of public-sector decision making, such as scarcity and competition, are similar to those that affect private-sector choices. Others, however, such as legal coercion and majority-rule decision making, differ from those involved in the market system.

Key Terms and Concepts

Antitrust legislation (100)

Average tax rate (104)

Capital gain (107)

Capital loss (107)

Collective decision making (111)

Demerit good (103)

Effluent fee (98)

Exclusion principle (101)

Externality (96)

Free-rider problem (102)

Government, or political, goods (113)

Incentive structure (112)

Majority rule (113)

Marginal tax rate (104)

Market failure (96)

Merit good (103)

Monopoly (100)

Principle of rival consumption (101)

Private goods (101)

Progressive taxation (105)

Property rights (100)

Proportional rule (113)

Proportional taxation (105)

Public goods (101)

Regressive taxation (105)

Retained earnings (107)

Tax bracket (104)

Tax incidence (107)

Theory of public choice (111)

Third parties (96)

Transfer payments (103)

Transfers in kind (103)

Problems

Answers to the odd-numbered problems appear at the back of the book.

5-1. Suppose that studies reveal that repeated application of a particular type of pesticide used on orange trees eventually causes harmful contamination of groundwater. The pesticide is produced by a large number of chemical manufacturers and is applied annually in orange groves throughout the world. Most orange growers regard the pesticide as a key input in their production of oranges.

   a. Use a diagram of the market for the pesticides to illustrate the essential implications of a failure of pesticide manufacturers' costs to reflect the social costs associated with groundwater contamination.

   b. Use your diagram from part (a) to explain a government policy that might be effective in achieving the socially optimal amount of pesticide production.

5-2. Now draw a diagram of the market for oranges. Explain how the government policy you discussed in part (b) of Problem 5-1 is likely to affect the market price and equilibrium quantity in the orange market. In what sense do consumers of oranges "pay" for dealing with the spillover costs of pesticide production?

5-3. The government of a major city in the United States has determined that mass transit, such as bus lines, helps alleviate traffic congestion, thereby benefiting both individual auto commuters and companies who desire to move workers, products, and factors of production speedily along streets and highways. Nevertheless, even though several private bus lines are in service, commuters in the city are failing to take the social benefits of the use of mass transit into account.

   a. Use a diagram of the market for the bus service to illustrate the essential implications of a failure of commuters to take into account the social benefits associated with bus ridership.

   b. Use your diagram from part (a) to explain a government policy that might be effective in achieving the socially optimal use of bus services.

5-4. Draw a diagram of the market for automobiles, which are a substitute means of transit. Explain how the government policy you discussed in part (b) of Problem 5-3 is likely to affect the market price and equilibrium quantity in the auto market. How are auto consumers affected by this policy to attain the spillover benefits of bus transit?

5-5. To promote increased use of port facilities in a major coastal city, a state government has decided to construct a state-of-the-art lighthouse at a projected cost of $10 million. The state proposes to pay half this cost and asks the city to raise the additional funds. Rather than raise its $5 million in funds via an increase in city taxes and fees, however, the city's government asks major businesses in and near the port area to contribute voluntarily to the project. Discuss key problems that the city is likely to face in raising the funds.

5-6. A senior citizen gets a part-time job at a fast-food restaurant. She earns $8 per hour for each hour she works, and she works exactly 25 hours per week. Thus her total pretax weekly income is $200. Her total income tax assessment each week is $40, but she has determined that she is assessed $3 in taxes for the final hour she works each week.

   a. What is this individual's average tax rate each week?

   b. What is the marginal tax rate for the last hour she works each week?

5-7. For purposes of assessing income taxes, there are three official income levels for workers in a small country: high, medium, and low. For the last hour on the job during a 40-hour workweek, a high-income worker pays a marginal income tax rate of 15 percent, a medium-income worker pays a marginal tax rate of 20 percent, and a low-income worker is assessed a 25 percent marginal income tax rate. Based only on this information, does this nation's income tax system appear to be progressive, proportional, or regressive?

5-8. Governments of country A and country B spend the same amount each year. In country A, the government allocates 25 percent of its spending to functions relating to dealing with market externalities and public goods, and it allocates the rest of its expenditures to funding the provision of merit goods and efforts to restrict the production of demerit goods. In country B, however, these relative spending allocations are reversed. Given this information, which country's government is more heavily involved in the economy through economic functions of government as opposed to political functions of government? Explain.

5-9. A government agency is contemplating launching an effort to expand the scope of its activities. One rationale for doing so is that another government agency could make the same effort and, if successful, receive larger budget allocations in future years. Another rationale for expanding the agency's activities is that this will make the jobs of its workers more interesting, which may help the agency attract better-qualified employees. Nevertheless, to broaden its legal mandate, the agency will have to convince more than half of the House of Representatives and the Senate to approve a formal proposal to expand its activities. In addition, to expand its activities, the agency must have the authority to force private companies it does not currently regulate to be officially licensed by agency personnel. Identify which aspects of this problem are similar to those faced by firms that operate in private markets and which aspects are specific to the public sector.

Economics on the Net

Putting Tax Dollars to Work In this application, you will learn about how the U.S. government allocates its expenditures. This will enable you to conduct your own evaluation of the current functions of the federal government within the U.S. economy.

Internet URL:
www.access.gpo.gov/usbudget/fy2000/pdf/hist.pdf

Title: Historical Tables: Budget of the United States Government

Navigation: Begin at the home page of the U.S. Government Printing Office (w2w.access.gpo.gov). Under Executive Office of the President, select Office of Management and Budget, and click on Budget Documents. Then click on Historical Tables.

Application After the document downloads, examine Section 3, Federal Government Outlays by Function, and in particular Table 3.1, Outlays by Superfunction and Function. Then answer the following questions:

1. What government functions have been capturing growing shares of government spending in recent years? Which of these do you believe to be related to the problem of addressing externalities, providing public goods, or dealing with other market failures? Which appear to be related to political functions instead of economic functions?

2. Which government functions are receiving declining shares of total spending? Are any of these related to the problem of addressing externalities, providing public goods, or dealing with other market failures? Are any related to political functions instead of economic functions?

For Group Study and Analysis Assign groups to the following overall categories of government functions: national defense, health, income security, and Social Security. Have each group prepare a brief report concerning long-term and recent trends in government spending on each category. Each group should take a stand on whether specific spending on items in its category are likely to relate to resolving market failures, public funding of merit goods, regulating the sale of demerit goods, and so on.

YOUR FUTURE WITH SOCIAL SECURITY

Of the three generations of this American family hiking in Vermont, the oldest will benefit the most from the Social Security system. Does that mean that the youngest may not benefit at all?

You've probably heard of chain letters. The basic notion is this: If you send, say, a dollar to each of several people on a list and then add your name to the list and mail it to your friends, you'll supposedly soon receive thousands of dollars from other people all over the world. There is a government program that has at times operated very much like a chain letter. The name of this program? Social Security.

The government retirement system that started 65 years ago was a good deal for your grandparents and probably will be a break-even proposition for your parents. But Social Security and a related program, Medicare, pose an enormous challenge for the economy.

Why have Social Security and Medicare become such problems? To find out, you need to learn more about how Social Security operates and what it will look like in your future.

After reading this chapter, you should be able to:

1. Identify the fundamental goals of Social Security and Medicare and the problems these programs pose for today's students

2. Analyze how Medicare affects the incentives to consume medical services

3. Explain why the Social Security Trust Fund is not a stock of savings we can draw on

4. Identify the key forces that caused the tremendous rise in Social Security spending

5. Explain how Social Security could be reformed

Did You Know That... America is getting old? The 78 million baby boomers born between 1946 and 1964 are entering middle age. Indeed, the future of America is now on display in Florida, where one person in five is over age 65. In 30 years, almost 20 percent of *all* Americans will be 65 or older.

Two principal forces are behind America's "senior boom." First, people are living longer. Average life expectancy in 1900 was 47. Today it is 77, and is likely to reach 80 within the next decade. Second, the birthrate is near record low levels. Today's mothers are having *half* the number of children that their mothers had. In short, the elderly are living longer, and the ranks of the young are growing too slowly to offset the added pressure of large numbers of retirees on the economy. Together, these forces are pushing the average age of the population higher and higher; in fact, the number of seniors is growing at *twice* the rate of the rest of the population. In 1970, the **median age** in the United States—the age that divides the older half of the population from the younger half—was 28; by 2000, the median age was over 35 and rising rapidly. Compounding these factors, the average age at retirement has been declining as well, from 65 in 1963 to 62 currently. Only 30 percent of the people age 55 and over hold jobs today, compared with 45 percent in 1930.

In this chapter, you will find out how the aging of America has caused an explosion of government spending, and you will learn about the potential impact of this increased spending on your future tax bills and retirement plans.

Chapter Outline

- **The Medicare and Social Security Problem**
- **Medicare**
- **Social Security**
- **The Trust Fund That Isn't**
- **How Did We Get from There to Here?**
- **Reform**

Median age
The age that divides the older half of the population from the younger half.

THE MEDICARE AND SOCIAL SECURITY PROBLEM

Why should you be concerned with government programs designed to assist the elderly portion of the population? The main reason is that the elderly are expensive. In fact, people over 65 now consume over one-third of the federal government's budget. Social Security payments to retirees are the biggest item, now running over $300 billion a year. Medicare, the federal program that pays hospital and doctors' bills for the elderly, costs over $200 billion a year and is growing rapidly. Moreover, fully a third of the $150 billion-a-year budget for Medicaid, the government-sponsored program that helps pay medical bills for the poor of all ages, goes to people over the age of 65.

If current laws are maintained, the elderly will consume 40 percent of all federal spending within 10 years: Medicare's share of gross domestic product (GDP) will double, as will the number of "very old" people—those over 85, who are most in need of care. Within 25 years, probably *one-half* of the federal budget will go to caring for the elderly. In a nutshell, senior citizens are the beneficiaries of an expensive and rapidly growing share of all federal spending.

Responsibility for paying the growing bills for Social Security and Medicare falls squarely on current and future workers, because both programs are financed by taxes on payrolls. Thirty years ago, these programs were adequately financed with a payroll levy of less than 10 percent of the typical worker's earnings. Today, the tax rate exceeds 15 percent of median wages, and it is expected to grow rapidly.

Consider what will happen if there is no change in the current structure of the Social Security system. By the year 2020, early baby boomers, born in the late 1940s and early 1950s, will have retired. Late baby boomers, born in the 1960s, will be nearing retirement. Both groups will leave today's college students, and their children, with a potentially staggering bill to pay. For Social Security and Medicare to be maintained, the payroll tax rate may have to rise to 25 percent of wages over the next 20 years. And a payroll tax rate of 40 percent is not unlikely by the middle of the twenty-first century.

For alternative perspectives on the problems of Social Security and Medicare, go to **www.epfnet.org**, and click on "Social Security/Medicare."

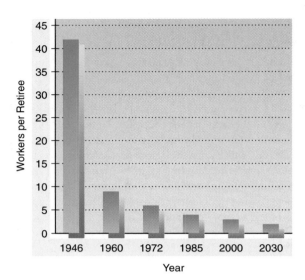

FIGURE 6-1
Workers Per Retiree
The average number of workers per Social Security retiree has declined dramatically since the program's inception.
Sources: Social Security Administration and author's estimates.

Why is the retirement age falling?

Part of the exodus of the elderly from the workplace is due simply to their prosperity. Older people have higher disposable incomes than any other age group in the population, and they are using their wealth to consume more leisure. But early retirement is also being prompted by American businesses. Career advancement often slows after age 40; over 60 percent of American corporations offer early retirement plans, while only about 5 percent offer inducements to delay retirement. Even more important is the federal government's tax treatment of the elderly. Individuals age 70 and over, especially those in middle-income brackets, can be subject to a crushing array of taxes. They must pay taxes on up to 85 percent of their Social Security benefits, contribute payroll taxes if they keep working, and bear the loss of $1 in Social Security benefits for every $3 of wage income over about $10,000. Because these taxes can "piggyback" on each other, effective marginal tax rates can become astronomical for the elderly. In fact, for a fairly typical couple trying to supplement their retirement checks, income from work can be subject to a tax rate in excess of 80 percent, so little take-home pay remains after taxes. No wonder so many seniors are saying "no thanks" to seemingly attractive jobs.

One way to think about the future bill that could face today's college students and their successors in the absence of fundamental changes in Social Security is to consider the number of retirees each worker must support. In 1946, payroll taxes from 42 workers supported one Social Security recipient. By 1960, nine workers funded each retiree's Social Security benefits. Today, as shown in Figure 6-1, roughly three workers provide for each retiree's Social Security *and* Medicare benefits. Unless the current system is changed, by 2030 only two workers will be available to pay the Social Security and Medicare benefits due each recipient. In that event, a working couple would find itself responsible for supporting not only itself and its family but also someone outside the family who is receiving Social Security and Medicare benefits.

These figures illustrate why efforts to reform these programs have begun to dominate the nation's public agenda. Fortunately, the fact that Social Security and Medicare are your problems means that they are also your government's problems. What remains to be seen is how the government will ultimately resolve them.

CONCEPTS IN BRIEF

◉ Social Security and Medicare payments are using up a large and growing portion of the federal budget.

● Because of a shrinking number of workers available to support each retiree, the expense for future workers to fund these programs will grow rapidly unless reforms are implemented.

MEDICARE

Not surprisingly, medical expenses are a major concern for many elderly Americans. Since 1965, that concern has been reflected in the existence of the Medicare program, which heavily subsidizes the medical expenses of persons over the age of 65. In return for paying a tax on their earnings while in the workforce (currently set at 2.9 percent of wages and salaries), retirees are ensured that the majority of their hospital and doctor's bills will be paid for with public monies.

Visit the U. S. Government's official Medicare Web site at **www.medicare.gov**

The United States Compared to Other Nations

As we shall see, the design of the Medicare system encourages the consumption of medical services and drives up total spending on such services—spending that is paid for out of current taxes. Reflecting those facts, each person under the age of 65 in America currently pays an average of around $1,500 *per year* in federal taxes to subsidize medical care for the elderly. Some 30 percent of Medicare's budget goes to patients in their last year of life. Coronary bypass operations—costing over $30,000 apiece—are routinely performed on Americans in their sixties and even seventies. And for those over 65, Medicare picks up the tab. Even heart transplants are now performed on people in their sixties, paid for by Medicare for those over 65. Britain's National Health Service generally will not provide kidney dialysis for people over 55. Yet Medicare subsidizes dialysis for more than 200,000 people, whose average age is 63. The cost: more than $8 billion a year. Overall, the elderly receive Medicare benefits worth 5 to 20 times the payroll taxes (plus interest) they paid for this program.

The Simple Economics of Medicare

To understand how, in only 35 years, Medicare became the second-biggest domestic spending program in existence, a bit of economics is in order. Consider Figure 6-2 on page 124, which shows the demand and supply of medical care.

The initial equilibrium price is P_0, and equilibrium quantity is Q_0. Perhaps because the government believes that Q_0 is not enough medical care for these consumers, suppose that the government begins paying a subsidy that eventually is set at M for each unit of medical care consumed. This will simultaneously tend to raise the price per unit of care received by providers (doctors, hospitals, and so on) and lower the perceived price per unit that consumers see when they make decisions about how much medical care to consume. As presented in the figure, the price received by providers rises to P_s, while the price paid by demanders falls to P_d. As a result, demanders of medical care want to consume Q_m units, and suppliers are quite happy to provide it for them.

Medicare Incentives at Work

We can now understand the problems that plague the Medicare system today. First, one of the things that people observed during the 20 years after the founding of Medicare was a huge upsurge in physicians' incomes and medical school applications, the spread of private

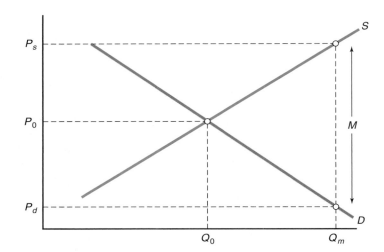

FIGURE 6-2:

The Economic Effects of Medicare Subsidies
When the government pays a per-unit subsidy M for medical care, consumers pay the price P_d for the quantity of services Q_m. Providers receive the price P_s for supplying this quantity.

for-profit hospitals, and the rapid proliferation of new medical tests and procedures. All of this was being encouraged by the rise in the price of medical services from P_0 to P_s, which encouraged entry into this market.

Second, government expenditures on Medicare have routinely turned out to be far in excess of the expenditures forecast at the time the program was put in place or each time it was expanded. The reasons for this are easy to see. Bureaucratic planners often fail to recognize the incentive effects of government programs. On the demand side, they fail to account for the huge increase in consumption (from Q_0 to Q_m) that will result from a subsidy like Medicare. On the supply side, they fail to recognize that the larger amount of services can only be extracted from suppliers at a higher price, P_s. Consequently, original projected spending on Medicare was an area like $Q_0 \times (P_0 - P_d)$, because original plans for the program only allowed for consumption of Q_0 and assumed that the subsidy would have to be only $P_0 - P_d$ per unit. In fact, consumption rises to Q_m and marginal cost per unit of service rise to P_s, necessitating an increase in the per-unit subsidy to M. Hence actual expenditures turn out to be the far larger number $Q_m \times M$. The introduction of Medicare thus turned out to be more expensive than predicted, and every expansion of the program has followed the same pattern.

Third, total spending on medical services soars, consuming far more income than initially expected. Originally, total spending on medical services was $P_0 \times Q_0$. In the presence of Medicare, spending rises to $P_s \times Q_m$. This helps explain why current health care spending in the United States is 14 percent of GDP—the largest percentage spent anywhere in the world.

Finally, note that with the subsidy in place, consumers end up consuming many relatively low-value services that are nevertheless extremely costly to provide. For example, the value to consumers of the last few units of service consumed is only P_d per unit, but the cost of providing each of these units is P_s per unit. Hence the economic waste of having these last units provided—that is, the excess of cost over value received—is exactly equal to the subsidy per unit, M. This makes it clear why the United States spends so much money on high-cost procedures that have very low expected benefits for recipients: In America, the elderly are allowed to choose what they wish to consume at subsidized prices; in other countries, they often are not given the choice.

Spending and More Spending

Given these features of the Medicare system, it is little wonder that current health outlays per older person (over the age of 65) now average about $10,000 per year, a figure that has been rising at an inflation-adjusted rate of about 4 percent per year. At this sort of growth rate, real expenditures on each senior will average $25,000 per year by 2020. Moreover, the 65-and-older population will expand from 13 percent of the population today to 16.5 percent over that period. The combination of more elderly and more spending on each of them implies that medical spending is likely to rise to 20 percent of GDP over this period. As Victor Fuchs of Stanford University has observed, "Although people justifiably worry about Social Security, paying for old folks' health care is the real 800-pound gorilla facing the economy."

Public Versus Private Incentives

So far, the federal government's response to soaring Medicare costs has been to impose arbitrary reimbursement caps on specific procedures. Medicare's Prospective Payment System gives doctors and hospitals a flat fee for each of a wide variety of treatments and procedures. In principle, this should cap Medicare payments and give providers an incentive to cut costs by allowing them to pocket the difference. But as a practical matter, each of the caps is set in isolation from the others and without regard to the other incentives the caps give providers. Thus to avoid going over Medicare's reimbursement cap, hospitals often discharge patients too soon or in an unstable condition, making them more likely to end up back in the hospital or in a nursing home. For example, many hospitals fail to send elderly patients to rehabilitation centers after hip surgery. Six to 18 months later, the patients are back in the hospital with hip problems. Similarly, less than one-half of all Medicare heart patients receive anticlotting drugs after heart surgery, even though such drugs reduce the risk of a second heart attack by 50 percent. The result is elderly individuals who are sicker than they otherwise would be and Medicare costs that are actually higher *overall* because of the reimbursement caps on specific treatments and procedures.

Of course, even private health insurance companies and health maintenance organizations (HMOs)—organizations that are responsible for delivering, or arranging for the delivery of, and paying for their members' medical care—put limits on reimbursement levels. But they do so with a sharp eye to the reasonably predictable ways that physicians and patients are likely to respond to these caps. Hence insurers and HMOs go to great lengths to bundle services and reimbursement levels in ways that minimize the cost of achieving a given health outcome. Medicare administrators appear to pay far less attention to this issue.

CONCEPTS IN BRIEF

- Medicare subsidizes the consumption of medical care by the elderly, thus increasing the amount of such care consumed.

- Expenditures on programs such as Medicare almost invariably turn out to be more than forecasted because of a rise in consumption and a rise in the per-unit cost of providing the services.

- People tend to purchase large amounts of low-value, high-cost services in programs like Medicare because they do not directly bear the full cost of their decisions.

- Medicare managers do a poorer job of accounting for the incentive effects of their decisions than private sector managers because they have fewer incentives to do so.

SOCIAL SECURITY

The Social Security system was founded in 1935, as America was beginning to recover from the Great Depression. The financial resources of many people had been demolished during the previous six years: Jobs had been lost, stock prices had tumbled, and thousands of banks had failed, wiping out the accounts of their depositors. It was widely feared that recent retirees and workers soon to retire faced destitution. Moreover, many people argued that the elderly should be protected from any similar disasters in the future. Hence the decision was made to establish Social Security as a means of guaranteeing a minimum level of pension benefits to all persons. Today, many people regard Social Security as a kind of "social compact"—a national promise to successive generations that they will receive support in their old age.

Good Times for the First Retirees

The first Social Security taxes (called "contributions") were collected in 1937, but it was not until 1940 that retirement benefits were first paid. Ida May Fuller was the first person to receive a regular Social Security pension. She had paid a total of $25 in **Social Security contributions** before she retired. By the time she died in 1975 at age 100, she had received benefits totaling $23,000. Although Fuller did perhaps better than most, for the average retiree of 1940, the Social Security system was still more generous than any private investment plan anyone is likely to devise: After adjusting for inflation, the **rate of return** on their contributions was an astounding 135 percent. (Roughly speaking, every $100 of combined employer and employee contributions yielded $135 *per year* during each and every year of that person's retirement. This is also called the **inflation-adjusted return.**) Ever since then, however, the rate of return has decreased. Nonetheless, Social Security was an excellent deal for most retirees during the twentieth century. Figure 6-3 shows the rate of return for people retiring in different years.

Given that the inflation-adjusted long-term rate of return on the stock market is about 10 percent, it is clear that for retirees, Social Security was a good deal until at least 1970. In fact, because Social Security benefits are a lot less risky than stocks, Social Security actually remained a pretty good investment for many people until around 1990.

Social Security has managed to pay such high returns because at each point in time, current retirees are paid benefits out of the contributions of those who are currently working.

Social Security contributions
The mandatory taxes paid out of workers' wages and salaries. Although half are supposedly paid by employers, in fact the net wages of employees are lower by the full amount.

Rate of return
The interest rate necessary to make the present values of the costs and benefits of an action equal. For a situation in which a cost is incurred today and a benefit received one year from now, it is the percentage excess of the future benefit over the present cost.

Inflation-adjusted return
A rate of return that is measured in terms of real goods and services, that is, after the effects of inflation have been factored out.

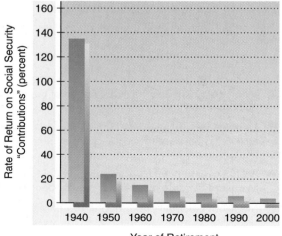

FIGURE 6-3
Private Rates of Return on Social Security Contributions, by Year of Retirement
The rate of return on Social Security contributions has steadily declined.
Sources: Social Security Administration and author's estimates.

(The contributions of today's retirees were long ago used to pay the benefits of previous retirees.) As long as Social Security was pulling in growing numbers of workers, either through a burgeoning workforce or by expanding its coverage of individuals in the work-force, the impressive rates of return during the early years of the program were possible. But as membership growth slowed as the post–World War II baby boom generation began to reach retirement age, the rate of return fell. Moreover, because the early participants received more than they contributed, it follows that later participants must receive less— and that ultimately means a *negative* rate of return. And for today's college students— indeed, for most people now under the age of 30 or so—that negative rate of return is what lies ahead, unless reforms are implemented.

Lesser Benefits for Some

Another aspect of today's low Social Security rate of return is worth noting. The system was originally designed to assist those most likely to be in need of assistance in their retirement years, and even today, low-income individuals do earn a higher rate of return on their contributions than higher-income people. But blacks do much worse than whites under the current system, because their life expectancy is significantly lower: Many collect nothing because they die before becoming eligible for their pensions. In addition, although women were generally net beneficiaries of the system in its early years, mainly through their spouses' contributions, that pattern has been changing as women entered the workforce in greater numbers: They are paying more in contribu-tions but will receive proportionately less in benefits. In fact, families with two income earners now receive a substantially lower rate of return on their contributions than fam-ilies with only one earner.

CONCEPTS IN BRIEF

- During the early years of the Social Security system, taxes were low and benefits were relatively robust, resulting in a high rate of return for retirees.
- As taxes have risen relative to benefits, the rate of return has fallen steadily.
- Blacks have often fared poorly under Social Security, as have two-earner families in recent years.

THE TRUST FUND THAT ISN'T

During the early years of Social Security's existence, payroll taxes were collected, but no benefits were paid. The monies collected over this period were used to purchase bonds issued by the U.S. Treasury, and this accumulation of bonds was called the Social Security Trust Fund. (Medicare has a similar trust fund; because the basic principles apply to both funds, only Social Security's is discussed here in detail.) Even today, Social Security tax collections continue to exceed benefits, and so the trust fund has continued to grow. As the baby boomers move into retirement in a few years, benefit payments each year will exceed tax receipts, and the Social Security system will begin to sell the bonds in the trust fund to finance the difference. Eventually—current estimates are that in the absence of actions to alter the current system, it will be around the year 2030—all of the bonds in the trust fund will have been sold. Any further benefits will have to be explicitly financed out of current-day taxes.

To learn more about Social Security, go to **http://tap.epn.org/ ideacentral/economic/**, and click on "Understanding Social Security."

The Prefunding Myth

Many supporters of the current system argue that the "prefunding" of Social Security that has taken place so far is advantageous, because it has enabled the system to build up assets. This, these supporters contend, is much like a private pension fund that builds up assets for its members during their working years or the process by which individuals build up assets in their own individual retirement accounts to draw on during their retirement years. According to this line of reasoning, the Social Security Trust Fund represents net assets that society can use to finance future benefit payments. Nothing could be further from the truth.

The obligations of the Social Security system consist of the benefits that the system promises to pay. It is equally true that the financing for those obligations consists of the taxes on the public that will be levied over time. The question is this: Given the promised level of benefits, does it matter whether the taxes it will take to pay those benefits are levied before, during, or after the benefits are paid? The answer is no. A given stream of benefits can be paid for with smaller taxes now or larger taxes later, but the economic value of those taxes now or later must be exactly equivalent, given the stream of benefits that has been promised.

Congressional Meddling

Whenever current Social Security taxes exceed current benefits (as they have for the past 60 years), Congress has been unable to resist the temptation to spend the difference on other programs. For instance, in 1999, President Clinton and Congress quibbled over who should receive credit for the government budget surplus of nearly $123 billion. In fact, $124 billion of this "budget surplus" was the Social Security Trust Fund, which the president and Congress had borrowed to fund current spending. Thus the federal government actually operated at a *deficit* of about $1 billion that year.

But to maintain the fiction that the Social Security system is an insurance plan, Congress gives Social Security IOUs for the money that it spends. These IOUs are simply Treasury bonds, which of course are redeemable only for future taxes to be levied on the American people. Thus the "assets" owned by Social Security are nothing more than promises of the Treasury to make payments based on taxes collected from Americans.

Essentially, by borrowing from the Social Security Trust Fund and issuing IOUs, Congress transforms what looks like a prefunded system into a pay-as-you-go operation. After all, when it is time for the trust fund to redeem those IOUs, Congress must increase taxes, cut other spending, or borrow more money to raise the cash. But this would be true even if there were *no* Treasury bonds in the trust fund: All benefits must ultimately be paid for out of taxes. So although the design of the system's funding may originally have been well intentioned, the accounting fiction of the trust fund is nothing more than that: a fiction designed to disguise the true system.

POLICY EXAMPLE

Smoothing Taxes over Time

If the trust fund is a fiction, why would prefunding ever be the preferred means of financing the system? Tax smoothing is one possible explanation.

Whenever the government imposes taxes, the people who are expected to pay those taxes have a natural incentive to try to avoid or evade them. These efforts to avoid taxes (and the corresponding effort by the government to prevent such avoidance) use up ("waste") scarce resources. Moreover, as taxes rise relative to income in any given period, the efforts devoted to avoiding (and collecting) taxes tend to rise disproportionately, implying that so do the resources that are wasted in such activities.

Hence for any given level of taxes to be collected over time, the amount of resources that are wasted in avoiding and collecting those taxes can be minimized by following this rule: Keep the ratio of taxes to income constant over time; that is, smooth taxes over time. Suppose (as has been true) that Social Security benefits rise over time faster than income, implying that the ratio of benefits to income is expected to rise.

Ideally, we want to keep the ratio of taxes to income constant, which implies that taxes will initially have to be high relative to benefits, eventually becoming low relative to the more rapidly growing benefits. The result is "prefunding" of benefits, much as we had during the early years of the Social Security system.

For Critical Analysis

What incentive does prefunding give to members of Congress who might be looking for additional funds to be used to pay for other programs?

CONCEPTS IN BRIEF

● Social Security is paid for out of taxes, regardless of when those taxes are imposed. Prefunding does not create any additional wealth that can be used to pay benefits.

● Congress has consistently reappropriated much or all of the excess of Social Security taxes over benefits that have been collected.

HOW DID WE GET FROM THERE TO HERE?

If Social Security started as a system designed to relieve the misery of the destitute elderly in the aftermath of the Great Depression, it has certainly become something much different. There is no doubt that it has helped raise the standard of living of the 65-and-older age group to the highest of all the age groups. But it has also become the single largest drain on the U.S. taxpayer and the most important domestic policy problem facing politicians and public alike. What happened? There are many facets to the story, but we shall focus here on just two of them, both a mixture of economics and politics.

For a more detailed history of the Social Security system, go to **www.ssa.gov/history**

A Tale of Two Generations

The first of the forces that transformed Social Security is what we shall call the confluence of the generations. Until the 1960s, Social Security looked little different from when it had been founded three decades before. Tax collections still exceeded benefits, which had remained modest. And despite expansions of the system to cover industries and occupations not originally eligible, the political and economic scope of the system were relatively unobtrusive. Things began to change with the entry of the baby boom generation into the labor market: Taxes began flowing into the system at an unprecedented rate. And because the number of people then collecting benefits was small relative to the burgeoning labor force, and the boomers themselves were 40 years from collecting benefits themselves, the Social Security Trust Fund soon became a rich prize in the political arena.

In the early 1970s, the first members of the generation that had suffered through the Great Depression and then fought World War II began retiring. Most had private savings that were modest at best and strong memories of having endured much on behalf of their nation. Thus we had the confluence of a large source of cash (the taxes paid by the boomers) and a worthy cause on which to spend it (the retirement benefits of the generation that had fought to keep the world free in World War II). The result was enormous political pressure to expand Social Security benefits.

Inflation

At the same time, America was going through a period of inflation that was, by the standards of the day, quite significant, running as high as 4 percent per year. At the time, the dollar value of Social Security benefits was set by Congress and thus could be changed only by explicit congressional action. But a 4 percent rise in the price level in such circumstances meant a 4 percent decline in the real value of benefits that were fixed in dollar terms. This was not the sort of thing any member of Congress wanted to have happen to the deserving World War II generation who was collecting those benefits. And this was particularly true because the elderly were already well known for voting more regularly than any other age group. So Congress looked for a way to protect retirees from inflation, without at the same time having to vote on the level of Social Security benefits every year. With the aid of President Richard Nixon, who was himself facing reelection in 1972, Congress found what appeared to be the ideal answer: Benefits were indexed, or linked, to the Consumer Price Index (CPI), a measure of the dollar cost of consuming a fixed market basket of goods that we shall discuss in greater detail in Chapter 7. Once a year, the percentage increase in the CPI was computed, and nominal Social Security benefits were then automatically increased by the same percentage amount.

Bias in the CPI

There was one significant hitch in this process. The CPI is biased upward; that is, it tends to overstate the actual rate of inflation, by an amount estimated to be about 1.1 percent per year. Thus if the true inflation rate is 3 percent, the CPI will measure it at, say, 4.1 percent; if the true rate is 4.5 percent, the CPI will say 5.6 percent. What this meant was that every year, Social Security recipients were getting their benefits increased not just by enough to protect them from inflation but also by what amounted to an automatic raise in real benefits of about 1.1 percent per year. This may not sound like much, but over the next 30 years or so, the power of compounding translated this into a 50 percent increase in real benefits. Thus a simple device introduced to protect the elderly from the ravages of inflation became a powerful tool for increasing benefits well above the levels ever contemplated at the system's founding—and all without the necessity for any overt action by Congress.

CONCEPTS IN BRIEF

- ◎ The combination of a politically powerful older generation and a larger younger generation capable of paying payroll taxes into the system created the incentives for the huge increase in Social Security benefits over the past 30 years.

- ◎ The cost-of-living adjustment, calculated using the Consumer Price Index, was the means by which much of this increase in real benefits occurred because it did not compensate for the upward bias in the CPI.

REFORM

America now finds itself with a social compact—the Social Security system—that entails a flow of promised benefits that will exceed the inflow of taxes by about 2010. What, if anything, might be done about this? There have been several proposals, each of which will be discussed. But the point to keep in mind throughout is this: The entire burden of Social Security consists of the benefits that it promises to pay. Under the system currently in place, all of these benefits must be paid out of taxes levied on the American people. So unless we

Year	1935	1955	1975	2000
Payroll tax rate	2%	4%	11.7%	15.3%
Wage base to which tax is applied	$3,000	$4,200	$14,100	$72,600

TABLE 6-1
The Rise of Payroll Taxes
Both the payroll tax rate and the wage base are rising.

Source: Social Security Administration and author's estimates.

fundamentally alter the nature of the system, there are only four options—or combinations of these four options—for preserving the current social compact: (1) raise taxes, (2) reduce the number of people eligible for benefits, (3) cut the amount of benefits each person is eligible to receive, or (4) find a way to make the funding base of the system grow at a more robust rate.

Raising Taxes

The history of Social Security has been one of steadily increasing tax rates, applied to an ever-increasing wage base. Table 6-1 shows the tax rate (which includes Medicare taxes since 1965) for selected years, and the wage base to which that tax rate is applied.

The combination of a rising tax rate and a taxable base that in recent years has grown faster than the inflation rate means that payroll taxes are becoming an increasingly important source of revenue for the federal government. Indeed, as revealed in Figure 6-4, payroll taxes are now almost 40 times as important to the federal government as they were 65 years ago.

Given the steady rise in both the tax rate and the wage base to which it applies, it is perhaps not surprising that many of the proposals for "reforming" Social Security advocate more of the same: Raise the tax rate or increase the wage base. For example, one prominent proposal calls for increasing the payroll tax rate by 2.2 percentage points, lifting the overall rate to 17.5 percent. Such a move would generate additional tax collections of about $80 billion per year initially, an amount equivalent to a 10 percent increase in everyone's personal taxes. This is a huge tax hike, amounting to $880 per year for a worker earning $40,000; indeed, this would be the largest tax increase of any type in our nation's history. Even so, it will *at best* keep current taxes above current benefits until 2020, after which the system will again be in deficit. Although the long-run tax hike that it will take to keep

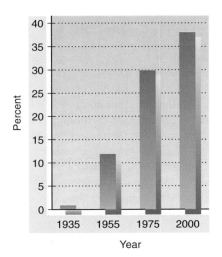

FIGURE 6-4

Payroll Taxes as a Share of Total Federal Tax Receipts, 1935–2000
Payroll taxes account for an increasing share of total federal tax revenues.

Sources: Social Security Administration, Council of Economic Advisers, and author's estimates.

Social Security solvent is subject to considerable uncertainty, best estimates now put that tax increase at around *seven* percentage points, not 2.2. Just to cover Social Security's projected deficits, the payroll tax will have to be increased to more than 22 percent.

Eliminating the Wage Cap

Another proposal is to eliminate the cap on the level of wages to which the payroll tax is applied. (This cap was lifted several years ago for the 2.9 percent Medicare component of payroll taxes.) All wage and salaries payments to workers would then be subject to the full brunt of payroll taxes. Although this proposal would not alter the tax obligations of workers earning less than $72,600 per year, it would result in a big hike in the marginal tax rate paid by millions of American workers. Indeed, the top rate paid would become 54.9 percent, the highest since the 1970s. Moreover, although this too would generate about $80 billion per year in additional tax revenues, it is not a long-term solution: Given projected benefit levels, the tax rate will eventually have to be increased. In fact, even the combination of eliminating the wage cap and a 2.2 percentage point tax increase is not enough to keep tax collections above benefit payments over the long run.

Cutting Benefits

The alternative to an increase in taxes is a cut in benefits. A small step in this direction has actually been taken, although not for the express purpose of reducing Social Security obligations. During the late 1990s, the Bureau of Labor Statistics revised the CPI to take better account of quality improvements in goods. One of the side effects of these revisions was to reduce slightly the upward bias in the CPI and thus reduce slightly the amount by which real benefits will be increased due to future cost-of-living adjustments.

No one has proposed cutting statutory benefits for existing retirees; future retirees are the target. One possibility is to raise the age of full eligibility. The eligibility age rose to 67 in 1999, but it could be increased further, perhaps to as high as 70. Another option is to cut benefits that are paid to nonworking spouses. A third proposal is to impose "means testing" on some or all Social Security benefits. As things stand now, all individuals covered by the system collect benefits when they retire, regardless of their assets or other sources of retirement income. Under a system of means testing, individuals with substantial alternative sources of retirement income would receive reduced Social Security benefits.

Immigration

Many experts believe that significant changes in America's immigration laws could offer the best hope for dealing with the tax burdens and workforce shrinkage of the future. About a million immigrants come to America each year, the largest number in our nation's history. Yet more than 90 percent of new immigrants are admitted on the basis of a selection system unchanged since 1952, under which the right of immigration is tied to family relationships. As a result, most people are admitted to the United States because they happen to be the spouses, children, or siblings of earlier immigrants, rather than because they have skills or training highly valued in the American workplace. Both Canada and Australia have modified their immigration laws to expand opportunities for immigrants who possess skills in short supply, with results that are generally regarded quite favorably in both nations. Unless Congress manages to overhaul America's immigration preference system, the taxes paid by new immigrants are unlikely to relieve much of the pressure building due to our aging population.

Investing in the Stock Market

Historically high returns were earned on most stock market investments during the 1990s. It is thus not surprising that some observers, including members of the Clinton administration, advocated that the Social Security system purchase stocks rather than Treasury bonds with the current excess of payroll taxes over current benefit payments. (Because this would necessitate that the Treasury borrow more from the public, this amounts to having the government borrow money from the public for the purpose of investing in the stock market.)

Although the added returns on stock investments could help stave off tax increases or benefit cuts, there are a few potential problems with this proposal. First, the rate of return on stocks during the 1990s was high by historical standards; we cannot expect such returns routinely in the future.

Second, the extra returns on stock market investments are not a sure thing; after all, during the early 1930s, the stock market dropped in value by nearly 90 percent. Despite the stock market's higher long-term returns, the inherent uncertainty of those returns is not entirely consistent with the function of Social Security as a source of *guaranteed* retirement income.

Finally, and most important, there is the issue of what stocks to invest in. There would surely be political pressure to invest in companies that happened to be politically popular and to refrain from investing in those that were unpopular, regardless of their returns. This sort of politically motivated investing would definitely reduce the expected returns from the government's stock portfolio—possibly even below the returns on Treasury bonds. This is exactly what has happened in Singapore: Workers there are required to pay 20 percent of their salary into the government-run Provident Fund, which has earned returns substantially below the market average.

INTERNATIONAL EXAMPLE

Privatizing Pensions in Chile

In 1981, Chile's state-run pension system was effectively bankrupt. So the government set up a mandatory system that was privately operated and funded. Workers were required to pay a minimum of 10 percent of their income each year into a private retirement account that the workers owned and controlled. To compensate workers for the public pensions they were giving up, the government issued "recognition bonds" that reflected the value of prior contributions to the old system. The government promised to redeem these bonds upon worker retirement, with the funding to come from a mixture of selling off state-owned enterprises and taxes on future workers and businesses.

The system is generally popular and well regarded by participants, perhaps in part because returns have averaged 13 percent per year. Annual retirement benefits are expected to be 50 percent to 70 percent above those payable under the old system. Nevertheless, the system is not flawless. Management charges on the retirement accounts have averaged nearly 3 percent per year, more than double the average charge on similar voluntary funds in the United States. Just as important, funds were initially restricted to investing only in Chile, a fact that depressed returns during the early years. Fund managers can now invest overseas, but 99 percent of fund assets remain invested in Chile, due to a peculiar incentive system imposed by the government. If a fund's return in any 12-month period is over two percentage points below the average for all funds, the firm managing that fund must make good the shortfall from its own capital. But there is no reward for outperforming the other funds. Not surprisingly, all of the funds have similar portfolios, and these portfolios are less risky—and yield lower average returns—than would be the case without this government-imposed reimbursement scheme.

For Critical Analysis

If the United States were to contemplate privatizing Social Security, what lessons might it learn from Chile's experience?

Growing the Economy

One way for the current Social Security problem to "go away" would be for the U.S. economy to grow at a faster pace. This would cause wages and salaries, which typically comprise more than 70 percent of total U.S. income, to increase, thereby expanding the tax base of the Social Security system. Additional funds would then flow into the Social Security system each year, thereby helping preserve the program's solvency.

As you learned in Chapter 2, expanding the economy's technological capabilities and producing more capital goods can help increase the nation's overall ability to produce and consume. Certainly, the U.S. economy has maintained steady growth in its productive capabilities. From the perspective of the Social Security system, however, the pace of growth has not been sufficient. As you will learn in Chapter 9, there are certain things that we could try to do to speed the pace of the nation's economic growth. Nevertheless, so far we have been unable to push the growth rate of national income much beyond 2 to 3 percent per year for more than a few years at a stretch. Saving the Social Security system without reforming it would require pushing long-term annual income growth up by at least 1 percentage point. In the absence of such a sustained increase in economic growth, the nation cannot postpone reforming its social compact.

CONCEPTS IN BRIEF

- One way or another, Social Security benefits will have to be cut, or taxes increased, or both.
- Although proposed tax increases will reduce the long-run Social Security deficit, no politicians have yet proposed raising them high enough to eliminate that deficit.
- Immigration would help the U.S. situation somewhat by increasing the workforce relative to the stock of retirees.
- Investing trust fund monies in the stock market might help, but there is a danger that political maneuvering with the funds would drastically reduce the returns.

ISSUES & APPLICATIONS

The Social Security Con Game

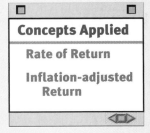

As we discussed in this chapter, Social Security offered retirees a rate of return in excess of 10 percent until around 1970. Given that the inflation-adjusted long-term rate of return on the stock market is about 10 percent, it is clear that for retirees, as noted, Social Security was an excellent deal for all beneficiaries until at least 1970 and for many until around 1990. But if investments on the stock market yielded only a 10 percent average real rate of return, how was Social Security able to offer such astonishingly high returns for so long? Moreover, why is it no longer able to do so?

The answer is that Social Security has been operated exactly like a Ponzi scheme, named after Charles Ponzi, a con artist operating in Boston during the early 1920s. Ponzi offered potential investors returns much like those paid to early Social Security retirees and actually managed to pay them for a while, in the same manner Social Security paid them—out of the funds contributed by new entrants into the plan. Because nothing was actually being invested or even produced in the plan, Ponzi's scheme, to stay afloat, required increasing numbers of participants to make ever-larger contributions, used to pay off the promises made to earlier contributors. As soon as people realized what was going on, the scheme collapsed, and Ponzi was prosecuted for fraud and sent to jail—but not before 10,000 investors had been bilked.

Concepts Applied

Rate of Return

Inflation-adjusted Return

Ponzi's Scheme

It is arguable that Social Security has operated in much the same manner since its inception, although its operation is legally sanctioned and it is not in danger of immediate collapse. At each point in time, current retirees are paid benefits out of the contributions of people who are currently working and paying in. (The contributions of today's retirees were long ago used to pay the benefits of previous retirees.) As membership growth slows, the rate of return falls. And as noted, because the early participants received more than they contributed, later participants must necessarily receive less—and that ultimately means a *negative* rate of return.

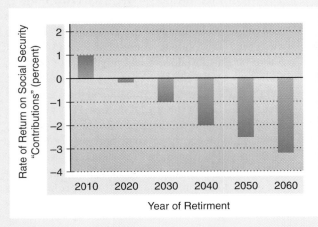

FIGURE 6-5

Projected Social Security Rates of Return for Future Retirees

While those who paid into Social Security in earlier years got a good deal, those who are now paying in and those who will pay in the future are facing low or negative rates of return.

Sources: Social Security Administration and author's estimates.

1. Based on what you have learned in this chapter, how might society find a way to avoid the negative projected rates of return displayed in Figure 6-5?

2. If the U.S. economy had grown at a much faster pace than it actually did between its inception and the present, would Social Security now look so much like a Ponzi scheme?

Parallels?

Indeed, as Figure 6-5 on the previous page shows, under any plausible assumptions about the future, unless the current Social Security system is changed, negative rates of returns will be the norm for retirees in the twenty-first century. In fact, for today's college students, who will begin retiring—if they can afford it—around 2040, in the absence of reform the situation looks particularly grim. As one economist has put it, "Today's students could get a better deal if they put their cash in a mattress—and then started smoking in bed." So unless you are not planning to retire, you'd better start saving now—or convincing your representatives in Congress to continue efforts to find a way to change the current system. Fortunately, there is every indication that the government is aware of the magnitude of the problem. It remains to be seen what proposed solution may ultimately be adopted.

SUMMARY DISCUSSION OF LEARNING OBJECTIVES

1. **The Fundamental Problem That Social Security and Medicare Pose for Today's Students:** Both programs have promised (and paid) benefits far in excess of the amounts that can be sustained, given the taxes levied to finance the programs. In the future, taxes will have to be higher and benefits lower, and it is today's students who will suffer on both counts. In fact, the rate of return on both programs will almost surely be negative for anyone who is today under the age of 30. It is not surprising that Americans who are currently retired and those who are about to retire are very much in favor of keeping Social Security just the way it has always been. They have realized a very high rate of return on their "contributions" to the Social Security System.

2. **The Effect of Medicare on the Incentives to Consume Medical Services:** Medicare subsidizes the consumption of medical services by the elderly. As a result, the quantity consumed is higher, and so is the price per unit of those services. Thus Americans spend a larger proportion of GDP on medical care than any other nation in the world. Medicare also encourages people to consume medical services that are very low

in value relative to the cost of providing them and places a substantial tax burden on other sectors of the economy. As Medicare has increasingly taken over the medical costs of the elderly, they have responded rationally by demanding more and better services. When the government foots the bill, decisions about what health services to purchase are not the same as in the private sector, where individuals pay the full opportunity cost of the products or services they use.

3. **The Myth That the Social Security Trust Fund Is a Stock of Savings:** Social Security benefits must be paid out of taxes. Because the Treasury bonds in the trust fund are nothing more than claims against future taxes, they do not add anything to society's ability to pay for Social Security benefits. Nonetheless, both the federal government and the media continue to talk about the Social Security Trust Fund as if it were the same as, say, a private pension fund into which individuals make contributions during their working years. The formal existence of something called a trust fund has allowed the government and the media to ignore the fact that our current Social Security system is a pay-as-you-go system.

4. **The Key Forces That Caused the Tremendous Rise in Social Security Spending:** The first force was the emergence of a politically powerful generation of elderly, who felt deserving of a retirement subsidized by younger persons. The second force was the entry of the huge baby boom generation into the workforce, which greatly increased the amount of money available to pay retirement benefits to the elderly. An important mechanism for creating higher real benefits has been the cost-of-living adjustment. Because of an upward bias in the index used to calculate this adjustment, real Social Security benefits have increased by 50 percent over the past several decades. This upward bias, however, is less today than in the past. The federal government has made some small corrections in how it calculates the price index in order to reduce the upward bias.

5. **How Social Security Could Be Reformed:** Because future benefits vastly exceed future scheduled taxes, some combination of higher taxes and lower benefits will have to be implemented. The situation could also be eased a bit if more immigration into the country were permitted. But an even better long-term reform would be to begin phasing out the current system and replacing it with one that is entirely privately run. Many possible replacement programs have been proposed by politicians and economists alike. Some have pointed to the apparent success of the privatization of the social security system in Chile. However, changing from a public system to a private system faces enormous political roadblocks in the United States.

Key Terms and Concepts

Inflation-adjusted return (126)

Rate of return (126)

Social Security contributions (126)

Median age (121)

Problems

Answers to the odd-numbered problems appear at the back of the book.

6-1. Suppose you invest $100 today and receive in return $150 exactly one year from now. What is the rate of return on this investment? (Hint: What is the percentage by which next year's benefit exceeds—or falls short of—this year's cost?)

6-2. Suppose you invest $100 today and receive in return $80 exactly one year from now. What is the rate of return on this investment? (Hint: What is the percentage by which next year's benefit exceeds—or falls short of—this year's cost?)

6-3. Suppose your employer is paying you a wage of $10 per hour, and you are working 40 hours per week. Now the government imposes a $2 per hour tax on your employment: $1 is collected from your employer and $1 is collected from you. The proceeds of the tax are used by the government to buy for you groceries that are valued by you at exactly $80 per week. You are eligible for the grocery program only as long as you continue to work. Once the plan is in place, what hourly wage will the employer pay you?

6-4. Suppose that the current price of a CD-ROM drive is $100 and that people are buying 1 million drives per year. In order to improve computer literacy, the government decides to begin subsidizing the purchase of new CD-ROM drives. The government believes that the appropriate price is $60 per drive, so the program offers to send people cash for the difference between $60 and whatever the people pay for each drive they buy.
   a. If no one changes his or her drive-buying behavior, how much will this program cost the taxpayers?
   b. Will the subsidy cause people to buy more, less, or the same number of drives? Explain.
   c. Suppose people end up buying 1.5 million drives once the program is in place. If the market price of drives does not change, how much will this program cost the taxpayers?

d. Under the assumption that the program causes people to buy 1.5 million drives and also causes the market price of drives to rise to $120, how much will this program cost the taxpayers?

6-5. Scans of internal organs using magnetic resonance imaging (MRI) devices are often covered by subsidized health insurance programs such as Medicare. Consider the following table illustrating hypothetical quantities of individual MRI testing procedures demanded and supplied at various prices, and then answer the questions that follow.

Price	Quantity Demanded	Quantity Supplied
$100	100,000	40,000
$300	90,000	60,000
$500	80,000	80,000
$700	70,000	100,000
$900	60,000	120,000

a. In the absence of a government-subsidized health plan, what is the equilibrium price of a battery of MRI tests? What is the amount of society's total expense on MRI tests?

b. Suppose that the government establishes a health plan guaranteeing that all qualified participants can purchase MRI tests at an effective price (that is, out-of-pocket cost) to the individual of $100 per set of tests. How many batteries of MRI tests will people consume?

c. What is the per-unit cost incurred by producers to provide the amount of MRI tests demanded at the government-guaranteed price of $100? What is society's total expense on MRI tests?

d. Under the government's coverage of MRI tests, what is the per-unit subsidy it provides? What is the total subsidy that the government pays to support MRI testing at its guaranteed price?

6-6. Suppose that the following Social Security reform became law: All current Social Security recipients will continue to receive their benefits, but no increase will be made other than cost-of-living adjustments; Americans between age 40 and retirement not yet on Social Security can opt to continue with the current system; those who opt out can place what they would have "contributed" to Social Security into one or more government-approved mutual funds; and those under 40 must place their "contributions" into one or more government-approved mutual funds.

Now answer the following questions:
a. Who will be in favor of this reform and why?
b. Who will be against this reform and why?
c. What might happen to stock market indexes?
d. What additional risk is involved for those who end up in the private system?
e. What additional benefits are possible for the people in the private system?
f. Which firms in the mutual fund industry might not be approved by the federal government and why?

Economics on the Net

Social Security Privatization There are many proposals for reforming Social Security, but only one fundamentally alters the nature of the current system: privatization. The purpose of this exercise is to learn more about what would happen if Social Security were privatized.

Internet URL: www.socialsecurity.org

Title: Social Security Privatization

Navigation: The entries you'll want to use are in the left-hand column.

Application For each of the entries noted, read the entry and answer the question.

1. Click on *African Americans and Social Security.* What are the likely consequences of Social Security privatization for African Americans? Why?

2. Click on *Women and Social Security.* What are the likely consequences of Social Security privatization for women? Why?

3. Click on *Low-Wage Workers and Social Security.* What are the likely consequences of Social Security privatization for low-wage workers? Why?

For Group Study and Analysis Taking into account the mix of gender, ethnic background, and other factors, is your group as a whole likely to be made better off or worse off if Social Security is privatized? Should your decision to support or oppose privatization be based solely on how it affects you personally? Or should your decision take into account how it might affect others in your group?

It will be worthwhile for those not nearing retirement age to examine what the "older" generation thinks about the idea of privatizing the Social Security system in the United States. So create two groups—one for and one against privatization. Each group will examine the following Web site and come up with arguments in favor or against the ideas expressed on it.

Go to http://www.x-pac.org. Make sure that each side in this debate carefully reads the page on the stance of the organization. Accept or rebut each statement, depending on the side to which you have been assigned. Be prepared to defend your reasons with more than just your feelings. At a minimum, be prepared to present arguments that are logical, if not entirely backed by facts.

Case Background

Cyber Dynamics International Corporation (CDI) is engaged in both business-to-consumer and business-to-business Internet applications as well as the production and distribution of new software programs. CDI is based in Singapore, but it sells its products and services throughout the world, including the United States.

The management of CDI is well aware of the fact that in the Internet world, everything happens at, well, Internet speed. New competitors are getting stronger every day. One of them appears to be Global Online, Inc. Indeed, in a recent planning meeting at CDI, the chief executive officer asked her management team to look into expanding into new areas on the Internet, new software applications, and new countries.

A week later, the various officers and managers of the company came forth with the following recommendations:

1. Lower the price of Internet access to compete more aggressively with Global Online and America Online.

2. Add numerous new features to the company's existing popular business accounting program and raise its price.

3. Break up the existing advertising and sales division into two separate divisions.

4. Open a major software manufacturing plant somewhere in the United States.

5. Enter into a partnership with a software company in the People's Republic of China.

6. Create a new employee benefit in the form of a pension plan that will pay loyal workers a certain sum of money every month after they retire.

Points to Analyze

1. Do you think it matters that CDI's headquarters are in Singapore? To whom might it matter and why?

2. In recommendation 1, a manager suggested that the company lower its price of Internet access. If it does, will the number of Internet access subscribers increase or decrease? Under what circumstances will total revenues increase? Decrease?

3. If the company's accounting program is enhanced, under what circumstances might it be able to raise the price and actually sell more copies?

4. Recommendation 3 argues in favor of splitting a division into two separate parts. What famous economist might applaud this action and why?

5. If you were in charge of deciding whether to support the recommendation that a software manufacturing plant be located in the United States, what are some of the factors that you might want to analyze to reach your

conclusion? One might be the going wage rate that would have to be paid to new workers. But there is another key cost for companies doing business in the United States. What is it?

6. Even if you are convinced that entering the marketplace in the People's Republic of China is an exciting prospect ("everybody's doing it"), you might encounter some problems pairing up with an existing Chinese company. Think about the economic functions of government that you learned in Chapter 5. Which function (or lack thereof) might create the biggest problem for your company's new partnership in China?

7. Although the suggestion to create a new employee benefit involving a retirement system might seem appealing because it would attract more and better workers, would you want to offer the same retirement plan to your workers in all countries? What government-funded institution should you examine first in each country before you make such a decision?

1. Go to the Web site of Global Online, Inc., at **www.GlobalOnline.com**. Once there, navigate through some of the sections.
   a. Why do you think there are different ads that appear on different pages?
   b. Who pays for those ads?
   c. How do you think they work?
   d. If you wanted to sell your used car, do you think this would be a good place to advertise? Why or why not?
   e. Even if it were a good place to advertise, what would probably prevent you from placing your ad?

2. Now go to the Web site for Global Online Services at **www.GlobalOnline.com**.

   a. Do you think this is part of Global Online, Inc.? Why or why not?
   b. To what audience is this Web site addressing itself?
   c. Under what circumstances would you want to hire the services of Global Online Services?

3. Go to any popular search engine, such as Yahoo.com, Profusion.com, Mama.com, or Lycos.com.
   a. Type in the word *global*, and see what happens. Why do you think so many companies include the word *global* in their names today?
   b. Type in the word *online*, and see what happens. Why do so many companies what to include the word online in their names today?

Casing the Internet

Part 2

Introduction to Macroeconomics and Economic Growth

THE MACROECONOMY: UNEMPLOYMENT, INFLATION, AND DEFLATION

These signs in front of a shop in Bandung, the capital of West Java province in Indonesia, tell a tale of falling prices. Who is hurt by deflation?

For years, people have complained about rising prices for pretty much everything except electronics. Indeed, most Americans alive today have never experienced a time when the average of all prices did not go up, year in and year out. That has been true for people everywhere else in the world, too. So it came as a shock to learn that at the end of the 1990s, the average of all prices was no longer rising much in many parts of the world. Some countries, such as Japan, were even experiencing *falling* prices. Could falling prices cause serious problems in Asia? Could they spill over to Europe? Might there be repercussions in the United States? Before you can answer these questions, you need to learn more about unemployment, inflation, and deflation.

LEARNING OBJECTIVES

After reading this chapter, you should be able to:

1. Explain how the U.S. government calculates the official unemployment rate

2. Discuss the types of unemployment

3. Describe how price indexes are calculated and review the key types of price indexes

4. Distinguish between nominal and real interest rates

5. Evaluate who loses and who gains from inflation

6. Understand key features of business fluctuations

Chapter Outline

- ◉ **Unemployment**

- ◉ **Inflation and Deflation**

- ◉ **Changing Inflation and Unemployment: Business Fluctuations**

Did You Know That... although the United States is considered a highly advanced industrialized nation, less and less of its employment is involved in manufacturing? The same is true of Japan, Germany, France, Italy, and the United Kingdom, where the number of manufacturing workers has been dropping steadily since 1970, despite significant increases in total adult population. Yet the result has *not* been workers permanently out of jobs. Even so, work is a major policy issue facing many countries today. At the core of macroeconomics—the study of the performance and structure of the national economy—are the issues of employment and, more importantly, unemployment.

UNEMPLOYMENT

Unemployment
The total number of adults (aged 16 years or older) who are willing and able to work and who are actively looking for work but have not found a job.

Unemployment is normally defined as adults actively looking for work, but without a job. Unemployment creates a cost to the entire economy in terms of lost output. One researcher estimated that at the beginning of the 1990s when unemployment was about 7 percent and factories were running at 80 percent of their capacity, the amount of output that the economy lost due to idle resources was almost 4 percent of the total production throughout the United States. (In other words, we were somewhere inside the production possibilities curve that we talked about in Chapter 2.) That was the equivalent of almost $275 billion of schools, houses, restaurant meals, cars, and movies that *could have been* produced. It is no wonder that policymakers closely watch the unemployment figures published by the Department of Labor's Bureau of Labor Statistics.

On a more personal level, the state of being unemployed often results in hardship and failed opportunities as well as a lack of self-respect. Psychological researchers believe that being fired creates at least as much stress as the death of a close friend. The numbers that we present about unemployment can never fully convey its true cost to this or any other nation.

Historical Unemployment Rates

Labor force
Individuals aged 16 years or older who either have jobs or are looking and available for jobs; the number of employed plus the number of unemployed.

The unemployment rate, defined as a proportion of the measured **labor force** that is unemployed, reached a low of 1.2 percent of the labor force at the end of World War II, after having reached 25 percent during the Great Depression in the 1930s. You can see in Figure 7-1 what happened to unemployment in the United States over the past century. The highest level ever was reached in the Great Depression, but unemployment was also very high during the Panic of 1893.

Employment, Unemployment, and the Labor Force

Figure 7-2 presents the population of individuals 16 years of age or older broken into three segments: (1) employed, (2) unemployed, and (3) not in the civilian labor force (a category that includes homemakers, full-time students, children, military personnel, persons in institutions, and retired persons). The employed and the unemployed, added together, make up the labor force. In 2000, the labor force amounted to 135.4 million + 5.8 million = 141.2 million Americans. To calculate the unemployment rate, we simply divide the number of unemployed by the number of people in the labor force and multiply by 100: 5.8 million/141.2 million × 100 = 4.1 percent.

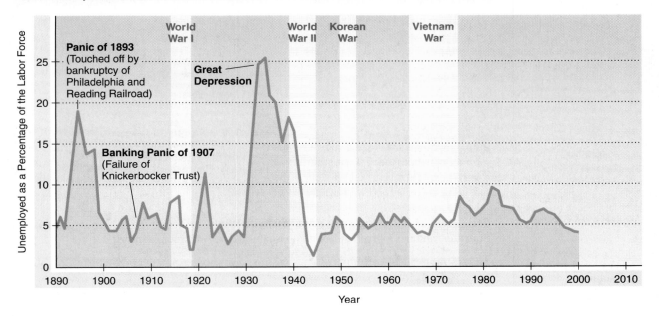

FIGURE 7-1

More than a Century of Unemployment

Unemployment reached lows during World Wars I and II of less than 2 percent and highs during the Great Depression of more than 25 percent.

Source: U.S. Department of Labor, Bureau of Labor Statistics.

The Arithmetic Determination of Unemployment

Because there is a transition between employment and unemployment at any point in time—people are leaving jobs and others are finding jobs—there is a simple relationship between the employed and the unemployed, as can be seen in Figure 7-3 on page 148. People departing jobs are shown at the top of the diagram, and people taking new jobs are shown at the bottom. If job leavers and job finders are equal, the unemployment rate stays the same. If departures exceed new hires, the unemployment rate rises.

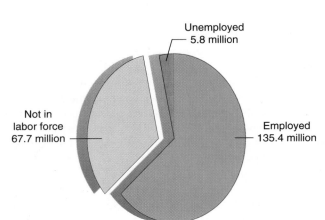

FIGURE 7-2

Adult Population

The population aged 16 and older can be broken down into three groups: people who are employed, those who are unemployed, and those not in the labor force.

Source: U.S. Department of Labor, Bureau of Labor Statistics.

FIGURE 7-3
The Logic of the Unemployment Rate

Individuals who leave jobs but remain in the labor force are subtracted from the employed and added to the unemployed. When the unemployed find jobs, they are subtracted from the unemployed and added to the employed. In an unchanged labor force, if both flows are equal, the unemployment rate is stable. If more people leave jobs than find them, the unemployment rate increases, and vice versa.

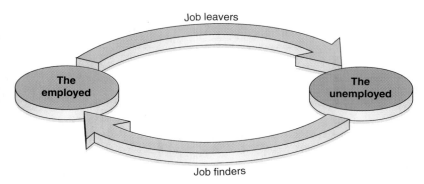

Stock

The quantity of something, measured at a given point in time—for example, an inventory of goods or a bank account. Stocks are defined independently of time, although they are assessed at a point in time.

Flow

A quantity measured per unit of time; something that occurs over time, such as the income you make per week or per year or the number of individuals who are fired every month.

Job loser

An individual in the labor force whose employment was involuntarily terminated.

Reentrant

An individual who used to work full time but left the labor force and has now reentered it looking for a job.

Job leaver

An individual in the labor force who quits voluntarily.

New entrant

An individual who has never held a full-time job lasting two weeks or longer but is now seeking employment.

Discouraged workers

Individuals who have stopped looking for a job because they are convinced that they will not find a suitable one.

The number of unemployed is some number at any point in time. It is a **stock** of individuals who do not have a job but are actively looking for one. The same is true for the number of employed. The number of people departing jobs, whether voluntarily or involuntarily, is a **flow,** as is the number of people finding jobs. Picturing a bathtub like the one in Figure 7-4 is a good way of remembering how stocks and flows work.

Categories of Individuals Who Are Without Work.   According to the Bureau of Labor Statistics, an unemployed individual may fall into any of four categories:

1. A **job loser,** whose employment was involuntarily terminated or who was laid off (40 to 60 percent of the unemployed)
2. A **reentrant,** having worked a full-time job before but having been out of the labor force (20 to 30 percent of the unemployed)
3. A **job leaver,** who voluntarily ended employment (less than 10 to around 15 percent of the unemployed)
4. A **new entrant,** who has never worked a full-time job for two weeks or longer (10 to 13 percent of the unemployed)

Duration of Unemployment.   If you are out of a job for a week, your situation is typically much less serious than if you are out of a job for 14 weeks. An increase in the duration of unemployment can increase the unemployment rate because workers stay unemployed longer, thereby creating a greater number of them at any given time. The most recent information on duration of unemployment paints the following picture: 37.1 percent of those who become unemployed find a new job by the end of one month, an additional 31.8 percent find a job by the end of two months, and only 16.3 percent are still unemployed after six months. The average duration of unemployment for all unemployed has been 15.2 weeks over the past decade.

When overall business activity goes into a downturn, the duration of unemployment tends to rise, thereby causing much of the increase in the estimated unemployment rate. In a sense, then, it is the increase in the *duration* of unemployment during a downturn in national economic activity that generates the bad news that concerns policymakers in Washington, D.C. Furthermore, the individuals who stay unemployed longer than six months are the ones who create the pressure on Congress to "do something." What Congress does typically is extend and supplement unemployment benefits.

The Discouraged Worker Phenomenon.   Critics of the published unemployment rate calculated by the federal government believe that it fails to reflect the true numbers of **discouraged workers** and "hidden unemployed." Though there is no exact definition or way

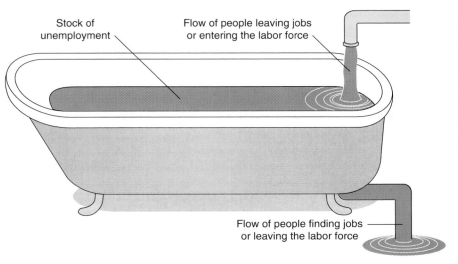

FIGURE 7-4
Visualizing Stocks and Flows
Unemployment at any point in time is some number that represents a stock, such as the amount of water in a bathtub. People who lose their jobs or enter the labor force constitute a new flow into the bathtub. Those who find jobs or leave the labor force can be thought of as the water that flows out by the drain.

to measure discouraged workers, the Department of Labor defines them as people who have dropped out of the labor force and are no longer looking for a job because they believe that the job market has little to offer them. To what extent do we want to include in the measured labor force individuals who voluntarily choose not to look for work or those who take only a few minutes a day to scan the want ads and then decide that there are no jobs?

Some economists argue that people who work part time but are willing to work full time should be classified as "semihidden" unemployed. Estimates range as high as 6 million workers at any one time. Offsetting this factor, though, is *overemployment.* An individual working 50 or 60 hours a week is still counted as only one full-time worker.

Labor Force Participation.   The way in which we define unemployment and membership in the labor force will affect what is known as the **labor force participation rate.** It is defined as the proportion of working-age individuals who are employed or seeking employment.

Figure 7-5 illustrates the labor force participation rates since 1950. The major change has been the increase in female labor force participation. If we take into account only

Labor force participation rate
The percentage of noninstitutionalized working-age individuals who are employed or seeking employment.

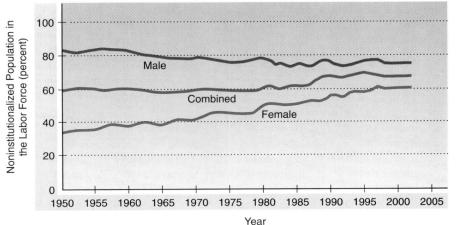

FIGURE 7-5
Labor Force Participation Rates by Sex
The combined labor force participation rate has increased in recent years. However, over the same period, the male participation rate has fallen, and the female rate has risen markedly.
Source: U.S. Department of Labor, Bureau of Labor Statistics, including projections.

married women aged 25 to 34, this increase is even more striking because it occurred over a shorter period of time. In 1960, about 29 percent of such women participated in the labor force outside of the home, compared with nearly 75 percent today.

● Unemployed persons are adults who are willing and able to work and are actively looking for a job but have not found one. The unemployment rate is computed by dividing the number of unemployed by the total labor force, which is equal to those who are employed plus those who are unemployed.

● The unemployed are job losers, reentrants, job leavers, and new entrants to the labor force. The flow of people leaving jobs and people finding jobs determines the stock of unemployed as well as the stock of employed.

● The duration of unemployment affects the unemployment rate. The number of unemployed workers can remain the same, but if the duration of unemployment increases, the measured unemployment rate will go up.

● Whereas overall labor force participation has risen only a bit since World War II, there has been a major increase in female labor force participation, particularly among married women between the ages of 25 and 34.

The Major Types of Unemployment

Unemployment has been categorized into four basic types: frictional, structural, cyclical, and seasonal.

Frictional Unemployment.   Of the more than 135 million Americans in the labor force, more than 13 million will have either changed jobs or taken new jobs during the year; every single month, about one worker in 20 will have quit, been laid off (told to expect to be rehired later), or been permanently fired; another 6 percent will have gone to new jobs or returned to old ones. In the process, more than 20 million persons will have reported themselves unemployed at one time or another. What we call **frictional unemployment** is the continuous flow of individuals from job to job and in and out of employment. There will always be some frictional unemployment as resources are redirected in the market because transaction costs are never zero. To eliminate frictional unemployment, we would have to prevent workers from leaving their present jobs until they had already lined up other jobs at which they would start working immediately, and we would have to guarantee first-time job seekers a job *before* they started looking.

Frictional unemployment
Unemployment due to the fact that workers must search for appropriate job offers. This takes time, and so they remain temporarily unemployed.

Structural Unemployment.   Structural changes in our economy cause some workers to become unemployed permanently or for very long periods of time because they cannot find jobs that use their particular skills. This is called **structural unemployment.** Structural unemployment is not caused by general business fluctuations, although business fluctuations may affect it. And unlike frictional unemployment, structural unemployment is not related to the movement of workers from low-paying to high-paying jobs.

Structural unemployment
Unemployment resulting from a poor match of workers' abilities and skills with current requirements of employers.

At one time, economists thought about structural unemployment only from the perspective of workers. The concept applied to workers who did not have the ability, training, and skills necessary to obtain available jobs. Today, it still encompasses these workers. In addition, however, economists increasingly look at structural unemployment from the viewpoint of employers, many of which face government mandates to provide funds for social insurance programs for their employees, to announce plant closings months or even years in advance, and so on. There is now considerable evidence that government labor market policies influence how many positions businesses wish to fill, thereby affecting structural unemployment. In the United States, many businesses appear to have adjusted by hiring more "temporary workers" or establishing short-term contracts with "private consultants," which may have reduced the extent of U.S. structural unemployment in recent years. A similar adjustment to government labor market mandates may be taking place in Europe.

INTERNATIONAL EXAMPLE

Structural Unemployment in Europe Never Seems to Go Away

From 1980 to 2000, about 33 million jobs were created in the United States, mostly in the private sector. Yet in the European Union (EU), virtually no private-sector jobs were created during the same period. As U.S. unemployment dropped to a 30-year low of 4.1 percent, EU unemployment stayed well above 10 percent. Any modestly trained outside observer understands why the EU is in such trouble: high taxes paid by employers on all employees and rigid labor markets. Employers pay their governments an amount equal to 50 to 200 percent of employees' wages as "social charges." Moreover, government-mandated minimum wages often far exceed the value low-skilled workers might contribute to potential employers. Consequently, many low-skilled unemployed are unable to find jobs. Firing workers is legally difficult and always costly because obligatory severance pay is high. Even so, many fired European workers take their

employers to court to try to regain their jobs or obtain even higher payments.

One result of this situation is that temporary employment is booming throughout Europe. One researcher estimated that 30 percent of the world's temporary labor market resides in France alone. Almost 90 percent of new hires in France, for example, are on short-term contracts.

Hardest hit is the portion of the labor force under age 25. In the EU, the average unemployment rate for that group is about 20 percent, and in France it exceeds 25 percent.

For Critical Analysis

If the reasons for the EU's high structural unemployment rate are so obvious, why aren't governments relaxing strict labor laws and reducing "social charges" levied on employers?

Cyclical Unemployment. **Cyclical unemployment** is related to business fluctuations. It is defined as unemployment associated with changes in business conditions—primarily recessions and depressions. The way to lessen cyclical unemployment would be to reduce the intensity, duration, and frequency of ups and downs of business activity. Economic policymakers attempt, through their policies, to reduce cyclical unemployment by keeping business activity on an even keel.

Cyclical unemployment
Unemployment resulting from business recessions that occur when aggregate (total) demand is insufficient to create full employment.

Seasonal Unemployment. **Seasonal unemployment** comes and goes with seasons of the year in which the demand for particular jobs rises and falls. In northern states, construction workers can often work only during the warmer months; they are seasonally unemployed during the winter. Summer resort workers can usually get jobs in resorts only during the summer season. They, too, become seasonally unemployed during the winter; the opposite is true for ski resort workers.

The unemployment rate that the Bureau of Labor Statistics releases each month is "seasonally adjusted." This means that the reported unemployment rate has been adjusted to remove the effects of variations in seasonal unemployment. Thus the unemployment rate that the media dutifully announce reflects only the sum of frictional unemployment, structural unemployment, and cyclical unemployment.

Seasonal unemployment
Unemployment resulting from the seasonal pattern of work in specific industries. It is usually due to seasonal fluctuations in demand or to changing weather conditions, rendering work difficult, if not impossible, as in the agriculture, construction, and tourist industries.

Full Employment

Does full employment mean that everybody has a job? Certainly not, for not everyone is looking for a job—full-time students and full-time homemakers, for example, are not. Is it possible for everyone who is looking for a job always to find one? No, because transaction costs in the labor market are not zero. Transaction costs include any activity whose goal is to enter into, carry out, or terminate contracts. In the labor market, these costs involve time spent looking for a job, being interviewed, negotiating the pay, and so on.

Isn't it true that much of today's employment consists of part-time jobs, contrary to the way it used to be?

That's the picture that seems to be written in the popular media, but it is inaccurate. Former Harvard Professor Lawrence Katz examined the data and discovered that despite minor ups and downs, there has not been a significant change in part-time employment in a decade and a half. Indeed, it is not much different from what it was 25 years ago. Moreover, surveys of part-time workers show that almost 80 percent of those interviewed say they do not want full-time jobs. These individuals include students, seniors, and parents with young children.

We will always have some frictional unemployment as individuals move in and out of the labor force, seek higher-paying jobs, and move to different parts of the country. **Full employment** is therefore a vague concept implying some sort of balance or equilibrium in an ever-shifting labor market. Of course, this general notion of full employment must somehow be put into numbers so that economists and others can determine whether the economy has reached the full-employment point.

Economists do this by estimating the **natural rate of unemployment,** the rate that is expected to prevail in the long run once all workers and employers have fully adjusted to any changes in the economy. If correctly estimated, the natural rate of unemployment should not reflect cyclical unemployment. When seasonally adjusted, the natural unemployment rate should take into account only frictional and structural unemployment.

A long-standing difficulty, however, has been a lack of agreement about how to estimate the natural unemployment rate. From the mid-1980s to the early 1990s, the President's Council of Economic Advisers (CEA) consistently estimated that the natural unemployment rate in the United States was about 6.5 percent. Even into the early 2000s, the approach to estimating the natural rate of unemployment that Federal Reserve staff economists have employed—which was intended to improve on the CEA's traditional method—yielded a natural rate just over 6 percent. Of course, when the measured unemployment rate fell below 5 percent in 1997 and hit 4.1 percent in 2000, economists began to rethink their approach to estimating the natural unemployment rate. This led some to alter their estimation methods to take into account such factors as greater rivalry among domestic businesses and increased international competition, which leads to an estimated natural rate of unemployment of roughly 5 percent. We shall return to the concept of the natural unemployment rate in Chapter 10.

Part of this reduction in the natural rate of unemployment in the United States may be due to a change in the age and sex composition of the labor force.

Full employment
An arbitrary level of unemployment that corresponds to "normal" friction in the labor market. In 1986, a 6.5 percent rate of unemployment was considered full employment. Today, it is assumed to be 5 percent or possibly even less.

Natural rate of unemployment
The rate of unemployment that is estimated to prevail in long-run macroeconomic equilibrium, when all workers and employers have fully adjusted to any changes in the economy.

EXAMPLE

Why Is the Average Unemployment Rate Falling?

Of course, a booming economy for a decade has a lot to do with falling unemployment rates in the United States, which have become the envy of the world. But economists Robert Horn and Phillip Heap of James Madison University believe that much of the change in the average unemployment rate has had to do with the change in the age and gender composition of the labor force. They point out that unemployment rates vary by age and to a lesser extent by gender. Thus any decreases in the relative importance of groups with historically high unemployment rates will reduce the overall unemployment rate. Specifically, they argue that the percentage of the labor force made up of teenage workers has dropped from 8.8 percent in 1970 to less than 6 percent today—thus reducing the overall unemployment rate. They further point out that the share of the labor force accounted for by women aged 25 to 44 rose from about 14 percent to almost 25 percent over the past three decades. This has tended also to reduce the employ-

ment rate, because women of this age bracket historically have lower unemployment rates than other groups. Their conclusion? If the age and gender composition of the labor force remains as it is today, the average rate of unemployment will also remain relatively low.

For Critical Analysis
Why do you think teenage unemployment rates are relatively high in general?

CONCEPTS IN BRIEF

● Frictional unemployment occurs because of transaction costs in the labor market. For example, workers do not have all the information necessary about vacancies. Structural unemployment occurs when the demand for a commodity permanently decreases so that workers find that the jobs that they are used to doing are no longer available.

● The level of frictional unemployment is used in part to determine our (somewhat arbitrary) definition of full employment.

INFLATION AND DEFLATION

During World War II, you could buy bread for 8 to 10 cents a loaf and have milk delivered fresh to your door for about 25 cents a half gallon. The average price of a new car was less than $700, and the average house cost less than $3,000. Today bread, milk, cars, and houses all cost more—a lot more. Prices are more than 10 times what they were in 1940. Clearly, this country has experienced quite a bit of *inflation* since then. We define **inflation** as an upward movement in the average level of prices. The opposite of inflation is **deflation,** defined as a downward movement in the average level of prices. Notice that these definitions depend on the *average* level of prices. This means that even during a period of inflation, some prices can be falling if other prices are rising at a faster rate. The prices of electronic equipment have dropped dramatically since the 1960s, even though there has been general inflation.

Inflation
The situation in which the average of all prices of goods and services in an economy is rising.

Deflation
The situation in which the average of all prices of goods and services in an economy is falling.

To discuss what has happened to prices here and in other countries, we have to know how to measure inflation.

Inflation and the Purchasing Power of Money

A rose is a rose is a rose, Gertrude Stein contended, but a dollar is not always a dollar. The value of a dollar does not stay constant when there is inflation. The value of money is usually talked about in terms of **purchasing power.** A dollar's purchasing power is the real goods and services that it can buy. Consequently, another way of defining inflation is as a decline in the purchasing power of money. The faster the rate of inflation, the greater the rate of decline in the purchasing power of money.

Purchasing power
The value of money for buying goods and services. If your money income stays the same but the price of one good that you are buying goes up, your effective purchasing power falls, and vice versa.

One way to think about inflation and the purchasing power of money is to discuss dollar values in terms of *nominal* versus *real* values. The nominal value of anything is simply its price expressed in today's dollars. In contrast, the real value of anything is its value expressed in purchasing power, which varies with the overall price level. Let's say that you received a $100 bill from your grandparents this year. One year from now, the nominal value of that bill will still be $100. The real value will depend on what the purchasing power of money is after one year's worth of inflation. Obviously, if there has been a lot of inflation in one year, the real value of that $100 bill will have diminished.

To find out about inflation and unemployment in other countries, go to **www.imf.org/external/**, and click on "Publications." Then click on "World Economic Outlook."

Measuring the Rate of Inflation

How can we measure the rate of inflation? This is a thorny problem for government statisticians. It is easy to determine how much the price of an individual commodity has risen: If last year a light bulb cost 50 cents and this year it costs 75 cents, there has been a 50 percent rise in the price of that light bulb over a one-year period. We can express the change in the individual light bulb price in one of several ways: The price has gone up 25 cents; the price is one and a half (1.5) times as high; the price has risen by 50 percent. An *index number* of this price rise is simply the second way (1.5) multiplied by 100, meaning that the index today would stand at 150. We multiply by 100 to eliminate decimals because it is easier to think in terms of percentage changes using integers. This is the standard convention adopted for convenience in dealing with index numbers or price levels.

Computing a Price Index.   The measurement problem becomes more complicated when it involves a large number of goods, especially if some prices have risen faster than others and some have even fallen. What we have to do is pick a representative bundle, a so-called market basket, of goods and compare the cost of that market basket of goods over time. When we do this, we obtain a **price index,** which is defined as the cost of a market basket of goods today, expressed as a percentage of the cost of that identical market basket of goods in some starting year, known as the **base year.**

Price index
The cost of today's market basket of goods expressed as a percentage of the cost of the same market basket during a base year.

Base year
The year that is chosen as the point of reference for comparison of prices in other years.

$$\text{Price index} = \frac{\text{cost today of market basket}}{\text{cost of market basket in base year}} \times 100$$

In the base year, the price index will always be 100, because the year in the numerator and in the denominator of the fraction is the same; therefore, the fraction equals 1, and when we multiply it by 100, we get 100. A simple numerical example is given in Table 7-1. In the table, there are only two goods in the market basket—corn and computers. The *quantities* in the basket remain the same between the base year, 1992, and the current year, 2002; only the *prices* change. Such a *fixed-quantity* price index is the easiest to compute because the statistician need only look at prices of goods and services sold every year rather than actually observing how much of these goods and services consumers actually purchase each year.

Consumer Price Index (CPI)
A statistical measure of a weighted average of prices of a specified set of goods and services purchased by wage earners in urban areas.

Producer Price Index (PPI)
A statistical measure of a weighted average of prices of commodities that firms produce and sell.

GDP deflator
A price index measuring the changes in prices of all new goods and services produced in the economy.

Real-World Price Indexes.   Government statisticians calculate a number of price indexes. The most often quoted are the **Consumer Price Index (CPI),** the **Producer Price Index (PPI),** and the **GDP deflator.** The CPI attempts to measure changes only in the level of prices of goods and services purchased by wage earners. The PPI attempts to show what has happened to average price of goods and services produced and sold by a typical firm. There are also *wholesale price indexes* that track the price level for commodities that firms purchase from other firms. The GDP deflator attempts to show changes in the level of prices of all new goods and services produced in the economy. The most general indicator of inflation is the GDP deflator because it measures the changes in the prices of everything produced in the economy.

(1) Commodity	(2) Market Basket Quantity	(3) 1992 Price per Unit	(4) Cost of Market Basket in 1992	(5) 2002 Price per Unit	(6) Cost of Market Basket at 2002 Prices
Corn	100 bushels	$ 4	$ 400	$ 8	$ 800
Computers	2	500	1,000	425	850
Totals			$1,400		$1,650

$$\text{Price index} = \frac{\text{cost of market basket in 2002}}{\text{cost of market basket in base year 1992}} \times 100 = \frac{\$1,650}{\$1,400} \times 100 = 117.86$$

TABLE 7-1

Calculating a Price Index for a Two-Good Market Basket
In this simplified example, there are only two goods—corn and computers. The quantities and base-year prices are given in columns 2 and 3. The cost of the 1992 market basket, calculated in column 4, comes to $1,400. The 2002 prices are given in column 5. The cost of the market basket in 2002, calculated in column 6, is $1,650. The price index for 2002 compared with 1992 is 117.86.

The CPI. The Bureau of Labor Statistics (BLS) has the task of identifying a market basket of goods and services of the typical consumer. Today, the BLS uses as its base the time period 1982–1984. It intended to change the base to 1993–1995 but has yet to do so. It has, though, updated its market basket of goods to reflect consumer spending patterns for 1993–1995. All CPI numbers since February 1998 reflect the new expenditure weights.

Economists have known for years that the way the BLS measures changes in the Consumer Price Index is flawed. Specifically, the BLS has been unable to account for the way consumers substitute less expensive items for higher-priced items. The reason is that the CPI is a fixed-quantity price index, meaning that each month the BLS samples only prices, rather than relative quantities purchased by consumers. In addition, until recently, the BLS has been unable to take quality changes into account as they occur. Currently, though, the BLS is subtracting from certain list prices estimated effects of qualitative improvements and adding to other list prices for a deterioration in quality. A remaining flaw is that the CPI usually ignores successful new products until long after they have been introduced.

EXAMPLE

New Product Bias in the CPI: The Case of Cellular Phones

Any new product that is successful, by definition, makes the people who choose to purchase it better off. Successful new products should therefore reduce the cost of maintaining a given standard of living, and so successful new product introductions should reduce the CPI or at least lessen increases in it. Nevertheless, the government is often slow to recognize this fact when it calculates the CPI. Consider the research done by economist Jerry Hausman of MIT. He looked at cellular phones. Since the late 1980s, cell phone prices have dropped by 90 percent and quality has improved great-

ly. As of 1998, however, the price of cellular phones was still not included in the government's CPI calculations. Hausman estimated that Americans are $24 billion to $50 billion better off because cellular phones exist. That is about 0.5 percent of the nation's annual national output.

For Critical Analysis
"When people don't know about a new product, they don't miss it, and therefore they are not worse off." Analyze this statement.

The PPI. There are a number of Producer Price Indexes, including one for foodstuffs, another for intermediate goods (goods used in the production of other goods), and one for finished goods. Most of the producer prices included are in mining, manufacturing, and agriculture. The PPIs can be considered general-purpose indexes for nonretail markets.

Although in the long run the various PPIs and the CPI generally show the same rate of inflation, such is not the case in the short run. Most often the PPIs increase before the CPI because it takes time for producer price increases to show up in the prices that consumers pay for final products. Often changes in the PPIs are watched closely as a hint that inflation is going to increase or decrease.

The GDP Deflator.   The broadest price index reported in the United States is the GDP deflator, where GDP stands for gross domestic product, or annual total national income. Unlike the CPI and the PPIs, the GDP deflator is not based on a fixed market basket of goods and services. The basket is allowed to change with people's consumption and investment patterns. In this sense, the changes in the GDP deflator reflect both price changes and the public's market responses to those price changes. Why? Because new expenditure patterns are allowed to show up in the GDP deflator as people respond to changing prices.

Historical Changes in the CPI.   Until the mid-1990s, the Consumer Price Index showed a fairly dramatic trend upward since about World War II. Figure 7-6 shows the annual rate of change in the Consumer Price Index since 1860. Prior to World War II, there were numerous periods of deflation along with periods of inflation. Persistent year-in and year-out inflation seems to be a post–World War II phenomenon, at least in this country. As far back as before the American Revolution, prices used to rise during war periods but then would fall back to more normal levels afterward. This occurred after the Revolutionary War, the War of 1812, the Civil War, and to a lesser extent World War I. Consequently, the overall price level in 1940 wasn't much different from 150 years earlier.

POLICY EXAMPLE

The Labor Department Quietly Reduces Its Inflation Statistics

The Consumer Price Index has been inaccurate because it ignores many changes in quality, increased discount shopping at club warehouses, and other developments in the consumer market. The statisticians responsible for computing the CPI each month know this. As a result, they have made changes in the index. Without much fanfare, the Labor Department has modified the way it calculates the CPI. It altered its sampling procedure for food and nonfood items, and it made its treatment of rent, hospital prices, and generic drugs more accurate. After those adjustments, government-estimated inflation rates dropped by 0.2 to 0.3 percent. Further calculation changes in 1998 and 1999 reduced estimated inflation by another 0.75 percent.

For Critical Analysis
The government has not changed past published data on the CPI. Why is this fact important to a policymaker today?

CONCEPTS IN BRIEF

- Once we pick a market basket of goods, we can construct a price index that compares the cost of that market basket today with the cost of the same market basket in a base year.
- The Consumer Price Index (CPI) is the most often used price index in the United States. The Producer Price Index (PPI) is the second most mentioned.
- The GDP deflator measures what is happening to the average price level of *all* new, domestically produced final goods and services in our economy.

FIGURE 7-6

Inflation and Deflation in U.S. History

Since the Civil War, the United States has experienced alternating inflation and deflation. Here we show them as reflected by changes in the Consumer Price Index. Since World War II, the periods of inflation have not been followed by periods of deflation; that is, even during peacetime, the price index has continued to rise. The yellow areas represent wartime.

Source: U.S. Department of Labor, Bureau of Labor Statistics.

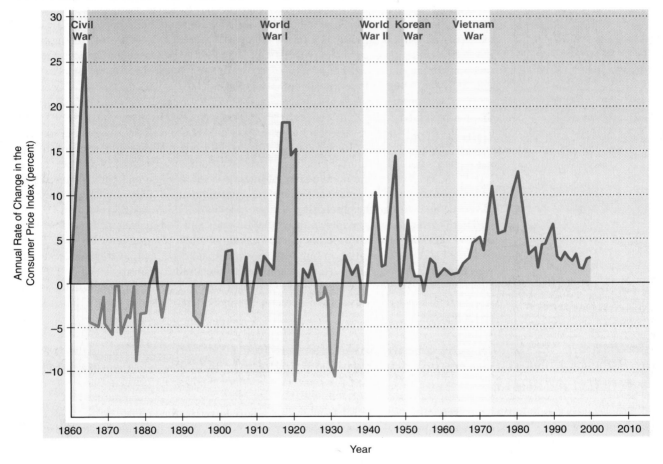

Anticipated Versus Unanticipated Inflation

To determine who is hurt by inflation and what the effects of inflation are in general, we have to distinguish between anticipated and unanticipated inflation. We will see that the effects on individuals and the economy are vastly different, depending on which type of inflation exists.

Anticipated inflation is the rate of inflation that the majority of individuals believe will occur. If the rate of inflation this year turns out to be 10 percent, and that's about what most people thought it was going to be, we are in a situation of fully anticipated inflation.

Unanticipated inflation is inflation that comes as a surprise to individuals in the economy. For example, if the inflation rate in a particular year turns out to be 10 percent when on average people thought it was going to be 5 percent, there will have been unanticipated inflation—inflation greater than anticipated.

Anticipated inflation
The inflation rate that we believe will occur; when it does, we are in a situation of fully anticipated inflation.

Unanticipated inflation
Inflation at a rate that comes as a surprise, either higher or lower than the rate anticipated.

Some of the problems caused by inflation arise when it is unanticipated, for when it is anticipated, many people are able to protect themselves from its ravages. Keeping the distinction between anticipated and unanticipated inflation in mind, we can easily see the relationship between inflation and interest rates.

Inflation and Interest Rates

Nominal rate of interest
The market rate of interest expressed in today's dollars.

Let's start in a hypothetical world in which there is no inflation and anticipated inflation is zero. In that world, you may be able to borrow money—to buy a computer or a car, for example—at a **nominal rate of interest** of, say, 10 percent. If you borrow the money to purchase a computer or a car and your anticipation of inflation turns out to be accurate, neither you nor the lender will have been fooled. The dollars you pay back in the years to come will be just as valuable in terms of purchasing power as the dollars that you borrowed.

Real rate of interest
The nominal rate of interest minus the anticipated rate of inflation.

What you ordinarily need to know when you borrow money is the *real rate of interest* that you will have to pay. The **real rate of interest** is defined as the nominal rate of interest minus the anticipated rate of inflation. If you are able to borrow money at 10 percent and you anticipated an inflation rate of 10 percent, your real rate of interest would be zero—lucky you, particularly if the actual rate of inflation turned out to be 10 percent. In effect, we can say that the nominal rate of interest is equal to the real rate of interest plus an *inflationary premium* to take account of anticipated inflation. That inflationary premium covers depreciation in the purchasing power of the dollars repaid by borrowers.*

There is fairly strong evidence that inflation rates and nominal interest rates move in parallel. Periods of rapid inflation create periods of high nominal interest rates. In the early 1970s, when the inflation rate was between 4 and 5 percent, average interest rates were around 8 to 10 percent. At the beginning of the 1980s, when the inflation rate was near 9 percent, interest rates had risen to between 12 and 14 percent. By the early 1990s, when the inflation rate was about 3 percent, nominal interest rates had fallen to between 4 and 8 percent.

INTERNATIONAL EXAMPLE

Deflation and Real Interest Rates in Japan

Wholesale prices in Japan have been falling for several years. In the past few years, consumer prices also have been falling, which means that Japan has been experiencing deflation. What does this have to do with real interest rates in Japan? Real interest rates are roughly equivalent to nominal, or market, rates minus the expected rate of inflation. Market interest rates are rarely negative. If the nominal interest rate a Japanese resident has to pay for a mortgage is 4 percent and the expected rate of *deflation* is 3 percent, then the expected real rate of interest is 7 percent, which is extremely high by historical standards. (In the United States, for example, real interest rates have hovered around 3 percent for most of its history.) The point is that in the United States, where we have learned to expect some inflation, we subtract that anticipated inflation from nominal interest rates to obtain real interest rates. In Japan, with expectations of deflation, the Japanese end up *adding* the expected deflationary rate to the nominal rate of interest to get real rates of interest.

For Critical Analysis
Why can't nominal interest rates be negative?

---

*Whenever there are relatively high rates of anticipated inflation, we must add an additional factor to the inflationary premium—the product of the real rate of interest times the anticipated rate of inflation. Usually this last term is omitted because the anticipated rate of inflation is not high enough to make much of a difference.

Does Inflation Necessarily Hurt Everyone?

Most people think that inflation is bad. After all, inflation means higher prices, and when we have to pay higher prices, are we not necessarily worse off? The truth is that inflation affects different people differently. Its effects also depend on whether it is anticipated or unanticipated.

Unanticipated Positive Inflation: Creditors Lose and Debtors Gain. In most situations, unanticipated inflation benefits borrowers because the nominal interest rate they are being charged does not fully compensate for the inflation that actually occurred. In other words, the lender did not anticipate inflation correctly. Whenever inflation rates are underestimated for the life of a loan, creditors lose and debtors gain. Periods of considerable unanticipated (higher than anticipated) inflation occurred in the late 1960s, the early 1970s, and the late 1970s. During those years, creditors lost and debtors gained.

Protecting Against Inflation. Banks attempt to protect themselves against inflation by raising nominal interest rates to reflect anticipated inflation. Adjustable-rate mortgages in fact do just that: The interest rate varies according to what happens to interest rates in the economy. Workers can protect themselves by **cost-of-living adjustments (COLAs),** which are automatic increases in wage rates to take account of increases in the price level.

To the extent that you hold non-interest-bearing cash, you will lose because of inflation. If you have put $100 in a mattress and the inflation rate is 10 percent for the year, you will have lost 10 percent of the purchasing power of that $100. If you have your funds in a non-interest-bearing checking account, you will suffer the same fate. Individuals attempt to reduce the cost of holding cash by putting it into interest-bearing accounts, a wide variety of which often pay nominal rates of interest that reflect anticipated inflation.

The Resource Cost of Inflation. Some economists believe that the main cost of unanticipated inflation is the opportunity cost of resources used to protect against inflation and the distortions introduced as firms attempt to plan for the long run. Individuals have to spend time and resources to figure out ways to cover themselves in case inflation is different from what it has been in the past. That may mean spending a longer time working out more complicated contracts for employment, for purchases of goods in the future, and for purchases of raw materials.

Inflation requires that price lists be changed. This is called the **repricing,** or **menu, cost of inflation.** The higher the rate of inflation, the higher the repricing cost of inflation.

Another major problem with inflation is that usually it does not proceed perfectly evenly. Consequently, the rate of inflation is not exactly what people anticipate. When this is so, the purchasing power of money changes in unanticipated ways. Because money is what we use as the measuring rod of the value of transactions we undertake, we have a more difficult time figuring out what we have really paid for things. As a result, resources tend to be misallocated in such situations because people have not really valued them accurately.

Think of any period during which you have to pay a higher price for something that was cheaper before. You are annoyed. But every time you pay a higher price, that represents the receipt of higher income for someone else. Therefore, it is impossible for all of us to be worse off because of rising prices. (Of course, we all become poorer if great variations in the rate of inflation cause us to incur the cost of resource misallocations.) There are numerous costs to inflation, but they aren't the ones commonly associated with inflation. One way to think of inflation is that it is simply a *change in the accounting system.* One year the price of fast-food hamburgers averages $1; 10 years later the price of fast-food

Cost-of-living adjustments (COLAs)
Clauses in contracts that allow for increases in specified nominal values to take account of changes in the cost of living.

Repricing, or **menu, cost of inflation**
The cost associated with recalculating prices and printing new price lists when there is inflation.

hamburgers averages $2. Clearly, $1 doesn't mean the same thing 10 years later. If we changed the name of our unit of accounting each year so that one year we paid $1 for fast-food hamburgers and 10 years later we paid, say, 1 peso, this lesson would be driven home.

● Whenever inflation is greater than anticipated, creditors lose and debtors gain. Whenever the rate of inflation is less than anticipated, creditors gain and debtors lose.

● Holders of cash lose during periods of inflation because the purchasing power of their cash depreciates at the rate of inflation.

● Households and businesses spend resources in attempting to protect themselves against unanticipated inflation, thus imposing a resource cost on the economy whenever there is unanticipated inflation.

CHANGING INFLATION AND UNEMPLOYMENT: BUSINESS FLUCTUATIONS

Business fluctuations
The ups and downs in overall business activity, as evidenced by changes in national income, employment, and the price level.

Expansion
A business fluctuation in which overall business activity is rising at a more rapid rate than previously or at a more rapid rate than the overall historical trend for the nation.

Contraction
A business fluctuation during which the pace of national economic activity is slowing down.

Recession
A period of time during which the rate of growth of business activity is consistently less than its long-term trend or is negative.

Depression
An extremely severe recession.

Some years unemployment goes up, and some years it goes down. Some years there is a lot of inflation, and other years there isn't. We have fluctuations in all aspects of our macroeconomy. The ups and downs in economywide economic activity are sometimes called **business fluctuations.** When business fluctuations are positive, they are called **expansions** —speedups in the pace of national economic activity. The opposite of an expansion is a **contraction,** which is a slowdown in the pace of national economic activity. The top of an expansion is usually called its *peak,* and the bottom of a contraction is usually called its *trough.* Business fluctuations used to be called *business cycles,* but that term no longer seems appropriate because *cycle* implies regular or automatic recurrence, and we have never had automatic recurrent fluctuations in general business and economic activity. What we have had are contractions and expansions that vary greatly in length. For example, nine post–World War II expansions averaged 48 months, but three of those exceeded 55 months, and two lasted less than 25 months.

If the contractionary phase of business fluctuations becomes severe enough, we call it a **recession.** An extremely severe recession is called a **depression.** Typically, at the beginning of a recession, interest rates rise, and as the recession gets worse, they fall. At the same

FIGURE 7-7
The Typical Course of Business Fluctuations
An idealized business cycle would go from peak to trough and back again in a regular cycle.

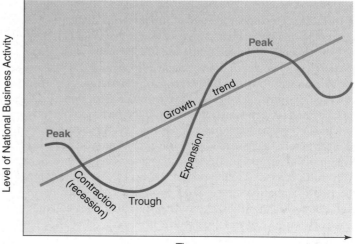

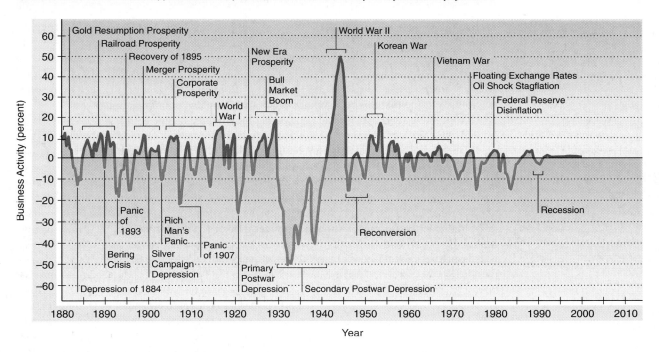

FIGURE 7-8

National Business Activity, 1880 to the Present

Variations around the trend of U.S. business activity have been frequent since 1880.

Sources: American Business Activity from 1790 to Today, 67th ed., AmeriTrust Co., January 1996, plus author's projections.

time, people's income starts to fall and the duration of unemployment increases so that the unemployment rate increases. In times of expansion, the opposite occurs.

In Figure 7-7, you see that typical business fluctuations occur around a growth trend in overall national business activity shown as a straight upward-sloping line. Starting out at a peak, the economy goes into a contraction (recession). Then an expansion starts that moves up to its peak, higher than the last one, and the sequence starts over again.

The official dating of business recessions is done by the National Bureau of Economic Research in New York City; Cambridge, Massachusetts; and Palo Alto, California.

A Historical Picture of Business Activity in the United States

Figure 7-8 traces U.S. business activity from 1880 to the present. Note that the long-term trend line is shown as horizontal, so all changes in business activity focus around that trend line. Major changes in business activity in the United States occurred during the Great Depression and World War II. Note that none of the business fluctuations that you see in Figure 7-8 exactly mirror the idealized typical course of a business fluctuation shown in Figure 7-7.

Explaining Business Fluctuations: External Shocks

As you might imagine, because changes in national business activity affect everyone, economists for decades have attempted to understand and explain business fluctuations. For years, one of the most obvious explanations has been external events that tend to disrupt

Learn about how economists formally determine when a recession is under way by going to **www.nber.org** and clicking on "Data"

the economy. In many of the graphs in this chapter, you have seen that World War II was a critical point in this nation's economic history. A war is certainly an external shock—something that originates outside of our economy.

Other examples of external shocks, particularly for an agrarian nation, have to do with abrupt changes in the weather. Long-term drought tended to create downturns in national business activity when the majority of Americans worked on farms. Today, major droughts or floods usually affect specific regions of the U.S. economy. Even a hurricane or an earthquake that dramatically affects one area rarely causes a national economic downturn.

In the 1970s, due to actions on the part of certain countries in the Middle East, the United States received an "oil shock." The price of oil increased dramatically then, and some economists argue that this had a major effect on national economic activity.

Leading indicators
Factors that economists find to exhibit changes before changes in business activity.

To try to help identify external shocks that may induce business fluctuations and thereby make fluctuations easier to predict, the U.S. Department of Commerce tabulates a composite index (a weighted average) of **leading indicators.** These are factors that economists at the Commerce Department have found typically occur *before* changes in business activity. Economic downturns often follow reductions in the average workweek and a higher number of unemployment insurance claims, drops in orders that consumers place for new goods or that businesses place for new plants and equipment, an improvement in the ability of the sellers of inputs or supplies to meet new orders, a decrease in the prices of raw materials, a drop in the quantity of money in circulation, a fall in the number of new permits issued for new residential and business construction, a decline in average stock prices, or a drop in consumer confidence as revealed by a regular survey conducted at the University of Michigan.

The reason that the Commerce Department reports a composite index of leading indicators, however, is that external shocks sometimes cause these indicators to move in different directions. For instance, a fall in the average workweek and a rise in unemployment insurance claims may reflect a slight tapering off in the pace of a business expansion that businesspeople could regard as *good* news because it signals no inflationary pressures on the horizon—and hence little reason for the Federal Reserve to seek a rise in market interest rates. This could, for example, induce businesses to increase their orders for new plants and equipment, and it could encourage individuals to borrow to finance new home construction. It could even cause stock prices to rise.

Thus it is not enough for us to say simply that business downturns are caused by external shocks. In the first place, if that were the only determinant of recessions, there would be little reason to study macroeconomics. Second, we know that historically we have had business recessions in the absence of any external shocks. We therefore need a theory of why national economic activity changes. The remainder of the macro chapters in this book develop a series of models that will help you understand the ups and downs of our business fluctuations.

CONCEPTS IN BRIEF

● The ups and downs in economywide business activity are called business fluctuations, which consist of expansions and contractions in overall business activity.

● The lowest point of a contraction is called the trough; the highest point of an expansion is called the peak.

● A recession is a downturn in business activity for some length of time.

● One possible explanation for business fluctuations relates to external shocks, such as wars, dramatic increases in the prices of raw materials, and earthquakes, floods, and droughts.

NETNOMICS

Is Frictional Unemployment on Its Way Out?

Even in tight labor markets, frictional unemployment still exists because of the transaction costs required in changing jobs. The advent of the Internet, however, may be reducing frictional unemployment more than anticipated. Of course, some will always exist, but perhaps less than prior to the Internet.

The standard way of looking for another job is some combination of asking friends for contacts, looking at the "help wanted" ads, submitting résumés, using an employment agency, and even knocking on businesses' doors.

Now there's an Internet job market that is growing at lightning speed. Newspaper employment ads have started to instruct job seekers to send their résumés to a particular e-mail address. One reason is convenience, but an even more important reason is that electronic résumés allow prospective employers to scan for keywords and in that way rapidly locate qualified candidates for unfilled jobs. A big company like Intel, the chip maker for most of the world's computers, receives thousands of résumés electronically each year via the Internet. Those that it receives by conventional means it scans into a database using optical character recognition (OCR) technology. The company can then search both types electronically for key candidate qualifications.

Employment agencies on the Net are taking off. CareerPaths was cofounded by six major newspapers. It contains almost 500,000 job openings. Monster.com carries almost 300,000. CareerMosaic allows you to post your résumé, search for a job, and visit job fairs. Big-time power executives can go to Exec-U-Net and pay a fee to go job-searching on-line.

The Professional Job Network lets you select from over 1 million openings each month on-line, 24 hours a day. Some of these are jobs advertised in more than 1,000 newspapers and 500 trade journals; others are unadvertised opportunities with an additional 200,000 employers. There is also a listing from 200 professional job banks worldwide.

Job hunting will never be the same.

Is the World Facing the Danger of Deflation?

In 1989, the number of newspaper articles around the world mentioning deflation was less than 50. Ten years later, more than 1,000 such articles appeared. What accounts for this new focus on falling prices?

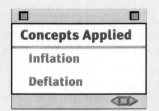

Concepts Applied

Inflation

Deflation

Inflation Trending Downward Worldwide

With a few exceptions, such as Russia, the rate of inflation in most of the world has declined. Indeed, by the year 2000, the rate of change of the Consumer Price Index in Europe was less than 1 percent. The rate of change of the Producer Price Index was negative. By 1999, Japan was already experiencing consistent deflation. The People's Republic of China had started to experience a similar deflation.

Causes for Concern

Commentators on the increase in deflation around the world contend that there are a number of causes for concern. First, they note that lower commodity prices cause real incomes in rich countries to go up but devastate producers in many economically troubled emerging economies.

They further argue that an even bigger risk is the failure of policymakers, workers, companies, and investors to adjust to the new reality. Nearly everyone in the post–World War II world has become used to high or even modest inflation and has no experience with deflation. The commentators point out that back in the nineteenth century, when deflation was a more common occurrence in the United States and elsewere, everyone was used to compensating for falling prices.

Few people alive today have had any such experience on any economywide level. Workers, particularly in unions, may need time to adapt to the notion of deflation. In the interim, they will demand higher nominal wage increases than are justified, because out of habit they will include an inflationary premium in their wage requests. Employers will resist, perhaps knowing better than employees that the inflationary premium should be zero or negative.

Deflation Versus Falling Relative Prices

Even during a period of low or nonexistent inflation, some prices rise and some prices fall. Some of the popular press has focused on price decreases in the goods sector, particularly in computers, telecommunications, and imported items. But at the same time, in the services sector, many prices have been rising—this is simple arithmetic, for if the Consumer Price Index is still going up, even at a relatively slow rate, some prices have to be rising. Remember that deflation is defined as a *consistent* decline in the average of *all* prices.

FOR CRITICAL ANALYSIS

1. When inflation occurs, most people complain about rising prices. If deflation occurs, why shouldn't everyone be happier?

2. How would you personally find it difficult to adjust to deflation?

3. How might you benefit from deflation?

SUMMARY DISCUSSION OF LEARNING OBJECTIVES

1. **How the U.S. Government Calculates the Official Unemployment Rate:** The total number of workers who are officially unemployed are those people aged 16 or older who are willing and able to work and who are actively looking for work but have not found a job. To calculate the unemployment rate, the government determines what percentage this quantity is of the labor force, which consists of all people aged 16 years or older who either have jobs or are available for and actively seeking employment. Thus the official unemployment rate does not include discouraged workers who have stopped looking for work because they are convinced that they will not find suitable employment; these individuals are not included in the labor force.

2. **The Types of Unemployment:** Workers who are temporarily unemployed because they are searching for appropriate job offers are frictionally unemployed. The structurally unemployed lack the skills currently required by prospective employers. Unemployment resulting from business contractions are cyclically unemployed. And certain workers can find themselves seasonally unemployed because of the seasonal patterns of occupations within specific industries. The natural unemployment rate includes the portion of workers who are frictionally, structurally, and seasonally unemployed during a given interval. The overall rate of unemployment adds the portion of the labor force that is cyclically unemployed.

3. **How Price Indexes Are Calculated and Key Price Indexes:** To calculate any price index, economists multiply 100 times the ratio of the cost of a market basket of goods and services in the current year to the cost of the same market basket in a base year. The market basket used to compute the Consumer Price Index (CPI) is a weighted set of goods and services purchased by a typical consumer in urban areas. The Producer Price Index (PPI) is a weighted average of prices of goods sold by a typical firm. The GDP deflator measures changes in the overall level of prices of all goods produced in the economy during a given interval.

4. **Nominal Interest Rate Versus Real Interest Rate:** The nominal interest rate is the market rate of interest expressed in terms of current dollars. The real interest rate takes into account inflation that borrowers and lenders anticipate will erode the value of nominal interest payments during the period that a loan is repaid. Hence the real interest rate equals the nominal interest rate minus the expected inflation rate.

5. **Losers and Gainers from Inflation:** Creditors lose as a result of unanticipated inflation, or inflation that comes as a surprise after they have made a loan, because the real value of the interest payments they receive will turn out to be lower than they had expected. Borrowers gain when unanticipated inflation occurs, because the real value of their interest payments declines. Key costs of inflation are the expenses that individuals and businesses incur to protect themselves against inflation, costs of altering business plans because of unexpected changes in prices, and menu costs arising from expenses incurred in repricing goods and services.

6. **Key Features of Business Fluctuations:** Business fluctuations are increases and decreases in business activity. A positive fluctuation is an expansion, which is an upward movement in business activity from a trough, or low point, to a peak, or high point. A negative fluctuation is a contraction, which is a drop in the pace of business activity from a previous peak to a new trough.

Key Terms and Concepts

Anticipated inflation (157)

Base year (154)

Business fluctuations (160)

Consumer Price Index (CPI) (154)

Contraction (160)

Cost-of-living adjustments (COLAs) (159)

Cyclical unemployment (151)

Deflation (153)

Depression (160)

Discouraged workers (148)

Expansion (160)

Flow (148)

Frictional unemployment (150)

Full employment (152)

Problems

Answers to the odd-numbered problems appear at the back of the book.

7-1. Suppose that you receive two offers to begin employment after you complete your studies, which will be one year from now. You wish to take one of the two positions. You are indifferent between the jobs and their locations, however, and both job offers include the same benefits package. Job A will entail an annual salary of $24,000 beginning a year from now, and job B will pay an annual salary of $25,000. Neither salary will be adjusted until you complete a year of employment. After you study the regions where the firms are located, you determine that there is likely to be no inflation over the two years where employer A is located. By way of contrast, employer B is in an area where the annual inflation rate over the next two years is likely to be 5 percent. Which job should you accept?

7-2. Suppose that an elderly woman is retired, but she has become bored with retirement and is considering going back to work. She receives $3,000 in Social Security payments each month, and this is her only source of income. If she accepts other employment, her Social Security payment drops by $1 for every $2 in pretax earnings from that source of employment. She has been offered a job as an assistant manager of a fast-food restaurant at a pretax salary of $2,500 per month. Out of these earnings, she would have to pay a 7 percent Social Security tax and a 15 percent income tax. What would be her effective monthly earnings from working at the fast-food job, taking into account both the resulting change in her Social Security payment and the taxes that she would have to pay on her earned income?

7-3. During the course of a year, the labor force consists of the same 1,000 people. Of these, there are 20 who lack skills that employers desire and hence remain unemployed throughout the year. At the same time, every month during the year, 30 different people become unemployed and 30 other different people who were unemployed find jobs. There are no seasonal employment patterns.
   a. What is the frictional unemployment rate?
   b. What is the unemployment rate?
   c. Suppose that a system of unemployment compensation is established. Each month, 30 new people (not including the 20 lacking required skills) continue to become unemployed, but each monthly group of newly unemployed now takes two months to find a job. After this change, what is the frictional unemployment rate?
   d. After the change discussed in part (c), what is the unemployment rate?

7-4. Suppose that a nation has a labor force of 100 people. In January, Amy, Barbara, Carine, and Denise are unemployed; in February, those four find jobs, but Evan, Franceso, George, and Horatio become unemployed. Suppose further that every month, the previous four who were unemployed find jobs and four different people become unemployed. Throughout the year, however, the same three people—Ito, Jack, and Kelley—continually remain unemployed because they lack sufficient skills to obtain open jobs.
   a. What is this nation's frictional unemployment rate?
   b. What is its structural unemployment rate?
   c. What is its unemployment rate?

7-5. In a country with a labor force of 200, a different group of 10 people becomes unemployed each month. Each group, however, becomes employed once again a month later. No others outside these groups are unemployed.
   a. What is this country's unemployment rate?
   b. What is the average duration of unemployment?
   c. Suppose that institution of a system of unemployment compensation increases to two months the interval that it takes each group of job losers to become employed each month. Nevertheless, a different group of 10 people still becomes unemployed each month. Now what is the average duration of unemployment?
   d. Following the change discussed in part (c), what is the country's unemployment rate?

7-6. A nation's frictional unemployment rate is 1 percent. Seasonal unemployment does not exist in this country. Its cyclical rate of unemployment is 3 percent, and its structural unemployment rate is 4 percent. What is this nation's overall rate of unemployment? What is its natural rate of unemployment?

7-7. In 1999, the cost of a market basket of goods was $2,000. In 2001, the cost of the same market basket of goods was $2,100. Use the price index formula to calculate the price index for 2001 if 1999 is the base year.

7-8. The real interest rate is 4 percent, and the nominal interest rate is 6 percent. What is the anticipated rate of inflation?

7-9. Suppose that in 2003 there is a sudden, unanticipated burst of inflation. Consider the situations faced by the following individuals. Who gains and who loses?
   a. A homeowner whose wages will keep pace with inflation in 2003 but whose monthly mortgage interest payments to a savings bank will remain fixed
   b. An apartment landlord who has guaranteed to his tenants that their monthly rent payments during 2003 will be the same as they were during 2002
   c. A banker who made an auto loan that the auto buyer will repay at a fixed rate of interest during 2003
   d. A retired individual who earns a pension with fixed monthly payments from her past employer during 2003

7-10. In January 2000, a nation's economic activity reached a peak, and a trough occurred in July 2000. The next peak occurs in August 2001, and another trough occurs in November 2002. Finally, there is another peak in October 2003. Identify the intervals of expansions and contractions (recessions).

Economics on the Net

Looking at the Unemployment and Inflation Data This chapter reviewed key concepts relating to unemployment and inflation. In this application, you get a chance to examine U.S. unemployment and inflation data on your own.

Internet URL: http://stats.bls.gov/top20.html

Title: Bureau of Labor Statistics: Most Requested Series

Navigation: Begin at the homepage of the Bureau of Labor Statistics (http://stats.bls.gov). Then click on Most Requested Series, followed by Overall BLS Most Requested Series.

Application Perform the indicated operations, and answer the following questions:

1. Click checkmarks in the boxes for Civilian Labor Force, Employment, and Unemployment. Select the All Years box, and choose to report in the form of Tables. Can you identify periods of sharp cyclical swings? Do they show up in data for the labor force, employment, or unemployment?

2. Are cyclical factors important?

For Group Study and Analysis Divide the class into groups, and assign a price index to each group. Ask each group to take a look at the index for All Years and to identify periods during which their index accelerated or decelerated (or even fell). Do the indexes ever provide opposing implications about inflation and deflation?

MEASURING THE ECONOMY'S PERFORMANCE

Mulitnational consulting firms often use large-scale economic models to predict economy wide chages. Why do such firms employ economists from all over the world??

If you watch the evening news, read newspapers and newsmagazines, or listen to news on the radio, you cannot miss hearing about the economy. One of the most eagerly awaited statistics, often touted in the media, concerns the federal government's quarterly estimate of how fast the economy is growing. Much is at stake here. Federal government policy aimed at stabilizing the economy hinges on these numbers. If the economy appears to be slowing down, that may indicate one policy; if the economy appears to be "overheating," that may lead to a different policy. A whole industry has developed to predict what will happen to the overall economy— and hence what the next policy change will be. How successful are those economic soothsayers? Before we can address this issue, you need to learn how the government derives its estimates of national economic performance.

LEARNING OBJECTIVES

After reading this chapter, you should be able to:

1. Describe the circular flow of income and output

2. Define gross domestic product (GDP)

3. Understand the limitations of using GDP as a measure of national welfare

4. Explain the expenditure approach to tabulating GDP

5. Explain the income approach to computing GDP

6. Distinguish between nominal GDP and real GDP

Did You Know That... whenever a single person who is currently paying a housekeeper marries that housekeeper, government statistics show that the economy's performance has declined? The reason for this seeming anomaly is that government statisticians do not yet consider unpaid housework as contributing to the total annual national income of the country (even though the same services would have to be purchased if not provided free of charge). In spite of such measurement problems, the statistics about the nation's economic performance are watched closely throughout the year by investors, bankers, businesspeople, and macroeconomic policymakers. After all, most people like to know where they stand financially at the end of each month or year. Why shouldn't we have similar information about the economy as a whole? The way we do this is by using what has become known as **national income accounting,** the main focus of this chapter.

But first we need to look at the flow of income within an economy, for it is the flow of goods and services from businesses to consumers and payments from consumers to businesses that constitutes economic activity.

Chapter Outline

- The Simple Circular Flow
- National Income Accounting
- Two Main Methods of Measuring GDP
- Other Components of National Income Accounting
- Distinguishing Between Nominal and Real Values
- Comparing GDP Throughout the World

THE SIMPLE CIRCULAR FLOW

The concept of a circular flow of income (ignoring taxes) involves two principles:

1. In every economic exchange, the seller receives exactly the same amount that the buyer spends.
2. Goods and services flow in one direction and money payments flow in the other.

In the simple economy shown in Figure 8-1 on page 170, there are only businesses and households. It is assumed that businesses sell their *entire* output *immediately* to households and that households spend their *entire* income *immediately* on consumer products. Households receive their income by selling the use of whatever factors of production they own, such as labor services.

Profits Explained

We have indicated in Figure 8-1 that profit is a cost of production. You might be under the impression that profits are not part of the cost of producing goods and services, but profits are indeed a part of this cost because entrepreneurs must be rewarded for providing their services or they won't provide them. Their reward, if any, is profit. The reward—the profit—is included in the cost of the factors of production. If there were no expectations of profit, entrepreneurs would not incur the risk associated with the organization of productive activities. That is why we consider profits a cost of doing business.

Total Income or Total Output

The arrow that goes from businesses to households at the bottom of Figure 8-1 is labeled "Total income." What would be a good definition of **total income**? If you answered "the total of all individuals' income," you would be right. But all income is actually a payment for something, whether it be wages paid for labor services, rent paid for the use of land, interest paid for the use of capital, or profits paid to entrepreneurs. It is the amount paid to the resource suppliers. Therefore, total income is also defined as the annual *cost* of producing the entire output of **final goods and services.**

The arrow going from households to businesses at the top of the figure represents the dollar value of output in the economy. This is equal to the total monetary value of all final goods

National income accounting
A measurement system used to estimate national income and its components; one approach to measuring an economy's aggregate performance.

Total income
The yearly amount earned by the nation's resources (factors of production). Total income therefore includes wages, rent, interest payments, and profits that are received, respectively, by workers, landowners, capital owners, and entrepreneurs.

Final goods and services
Goods and services that are at their final stage of production and will not be transformed into yet other goods or services. For example, wheat is not ordinarily considered a final good because it is usually used to make a final good, bread.

FIGURE 8-1

The Circular Flow of Income and Product

Businesses provide final goods and services to households (upper clockwise loop), who in turn pay for them with money (upper counterclockwise loop). Money flows in a counterclockwise direction and can be thought of as a circular flow. The dollar value of output is identical to total income because profits are defined as being equal to total business receipts minus business outlays for wages, rents, and interest.

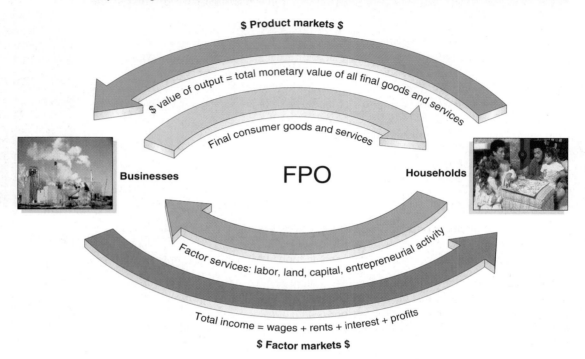

$ Product markets $

$ value of output = total monetary value of all final goods and services

Final consumer goods and services

FPO

Businesses   **Households**

Factor services: labor, land, capital, entrepreneurial activity

Total income = wages + rents + interest + profits

$ Factor markets $

and services for this simple economy. In essence, it represents the total business receipts from the sale of all final goods and services produced by businesses and consumed by households. Business receipts are the opposite side of household expenditures. When households purchase goods and services with money, that money becomes a *business receipt*. Every transaction, therefore, simultaneously involves an expenditure as well as a receipt.

Product Markets.   Transactions in which households buy goods take place in the product markets—that's where households are the buyers and businesses are the sellers of consumer goods. *Product market* transactions are represented in the upper loops in Figure 8-1. Note that consumer goods and services flow to household demanders, while money flows in the opposite direction to business suppliers.

Factor Markets.   *Factor market* transactions are represented by the lower loops in Figure 8-1. In the factor market, households are the sellers; they sell resources such as labor, land, capital, and entrepreneurial ability. Businesses are the buyers in factor markets; business expenditures represent receipts or, more simply, income for households. Also, in the lower loops of Figure 8-1, factor services flow from households to businesses, while the money paid for these services flows in the opposite direction from businesses to households. Observe also the flow of money (counterclockwise) from households to businesses and back again from businesses to households: It is an endless circular flow.

Why the Dollar Value of Total Output Must Equal Total Income

Total income represents the income received by households in payment for the production of goods and services. Why must total income be identical to the dollar value of total output? First, as Figure 8-1 shows, spending by one group is income to another. Second, it is a matter of simple accounting and the economic definition of profit as a cost of production. Profit is defined as what is *left over* from total business receipts after all other costs—wages, rents, interest—have been paid. If the dollar value of total output is $1,000 and the total of wages, rent, and interest for producing that output is $900, profit is $100. Profit is always the *residual* item that makes total income equal to the dollar value of total output.

CONCEPTS
IN BRIEF

● In the circular flow model of income and output, households sell factor services to businesses that pay for those factor services. The receipt of payments is total income. Businesses sell goods and services to households that pay for them.

● The dollar value of total output is equal to the total monetary value of all final goods and services produced.

● The dollar value of final output must always equal total income; the variable that makes this so is known as profit.

NATIONAL INCOME ACCOUNTING

We have already mentioned that policymakers need information about the state of the national economy. Historical statistical records on the performance of the national economy aid economists in testing their theories about how the economy really works. National income accounting is therefore important. Let's start with the most commonly presented statistic on the national economy.

Gross Domestic Product (GDP)

Gross domestic product (GDP) represents the total market value of the nation's annual final product, or output, produced per year by factors of production located within national borders. We therefore formally define GDP as the total market value of all final goods and services produced in an economy during a year. We are referring here to a *flow of production*. A nation produces at a certain rate, just as you receive income at a certain rate. Your income flow might be at a rate of $5,000 per year or $50,000 per year. Suppose you are told that someone earns $500. Would you consider this a good salary? There is no way to answer that question unless you know whether the person is earning $500 per month or per week or per day. Thus you have to specify a time period for all flows. Income received is a flow. You must contrast this with, for example, your total accumulated savings, which are a stock measured at a point in time, not over time. Implicit in just about everything we deal with in this chapter is a time period—usually one year. All the measures of domestic product and income are specified as *rates* measured in dollars per year.

Gross domestic product (GDP)
The total market value of all final goods and services produced by factors of production located within a nation's borders.

Stress on Final Output

Intermediate goods
Goods used up entirely in the production of final goods.

Value added
The dollar value of an industry's sales minus the value of intermediate goods (for example, raw materials and parts) used in production.

GDP does not count **intermediate goods** (goods used up entirely in the production of final goods) because to do so would be to count them twice. For example, even though grain that a farmer produces may be that farmer's final product, it is not the final product for the nation. It is sold to make bread. Bread is the final product.

We can use a numerical example to clarify this point further. Our example will involve determining the value added at each stage of production. **Value added** is the amount of dollar value contributed to a product at each stage of its production. In Table 8-1, we see the difference between total value of all sales and value added in the production of a donut. We also see that the sum of the values added is equal to the sale price to the final consumer. It is the 45 cents that is used to measure GDP, not the 96 cents. If we used the 96 cents, we would be double-counting from stages 2 through 5, for each intermediate good would be counted at least twice—once when it was produced and again when the good it was used in making was sold. Such double counting would grossly exaggerate GDP.

TABLE 8-1

Sales Value and Value Added at Each Stage of Donut Production

(1) Stage of Production	(2) Dollar Value of Sales	(3) Value Added
Stage 1: Fertilizer and seed	$.03	$.03
Stage 2: Growing	.06	.03
Stage 3: Milling	.12	.06
Stage 4: Baking	.30	.18
Stage 5: Retailing	.45	.15
Total dollar value of all sales	$.96	Total value added $.45

Stage 1:   A farmer purchases 3 cents' worth of fertilizer and seed, which are used as factors of production in growing wheat.

Stage 2:   The farmer grows the wheat, harvests it, and sells it to a miller for 6 cents. Thus we see that the farmer has added 3 cents' worth of value. Those 3 cents represent income paid to the farmer.

Stage 3:   The miller purchases the wheat for 6 cents and adds 6 cents as the value added; that is, there is 6 cents for the miller as income. The miller sells the ground wheat flour to a donut-baking company.

Stage 4:   The donut-baking company buys the flour for 12 cents and adds 18 cents as the value added. It then sells the donut to the final retailer.

Stage 5:   The donut retailer sells fresh hot donuts at 45 cents apiece, thus creating an additional value of 15 cents.

We see that the total value of transactions involved in the production of one donut was 96 cents, but the total value added was 45 cents, which is exactly equal to the retail price. The total value added is equal to the sum of all income payments.

Exclusion of Financial Transactions, Transfer Payments, and Secondhand Goods

Remember that GDP is the measure of the value of all final goods and services produced in one year. Many more transactions occur that have nothing to do with final goods and services produced. There are financial transactions, transfers of the ownership of preexisting goods, and other transactions that should not and do not get included in our measure of GDP.

Financial Transactions.   There are three general categories of purely financial transactions: (1) the buying and selling of securities, (2) government transfer payments, and (3) private transfer payments.

Securities.   When you purchase a share of existing stock in Microsoft Corporation, someone else has sold it to you. In essence, there was merely a *transfer* of ownership rights. You paid $100 to obtain the stock certificate. Someone else received the $100 and gave up the stock certificate. No producing activity was consummated at that time. Hence the $100 transaction is not included when we measure gross domestic product.

Government Transfer Payments.   Transfer payments are payments for which no productive services are concurrently provided in exchange. The most obvious government transfer payments are Social Security benefits, veterans' payments, and unemployment compensation. The recipients make no contribution to current production in return for such transfer payments (although they may have made contributions in the past to receive them). Government transfer payments are not included in GDP.

Private Transfer Payments.   Are you receiving money from your parents in order to live at school? Has a wealthy relative ever given you a gift of money? If so, you have been the recipient of a private transfer payment. This is merely a transfer of funds from one individual to another. As such, it does not constitute productive activity and is not included in gross domestic product.

Transfer of Secondhand Goods.   If I sell you my two-year-old stereo, no current production is involved. I transfer to you the ownership of a sound system that was produced years ago; in exchange, you transfer to me $550. The original purchase price of the stereo was included in GDP in the year I purchased it. To include it again when I sell it to you would be counting the value of the stereo a second time.

Other Excluded Transactions.   Many other transactions are not included in GDP for practical reasons:

- Household production—home cleaning, child care, and other tasks performed by people in their *own* households and for which they are not paid through the marketplace
- Otherwise legal underground transactions—those that are legal but not reported and hence not taxed, such as paying housekeepers in cash that is not declared as income
- Illegal underground activities—these include prostitution, illegal gambling, and the sale of illicit drugs

Many economists criticize measured GDP statistics because the underground economy is not included.

For the most up-to-date U. S. economic data, visit the Web site of the Bureau of Economic Analysis, **www.bea.doc.gov**

INTERNATIONAL EXAMPLE

The Underground Economy Is Alive and Thriving

To be sure, much of the underground economy has to do with illegal activities, particularly illegal drug sales. But in many countries outside the United States, the underground economy is a way of life for virtually all activities. This is true today in such countries as Russia, where even the use of money in many transactions has more or less disappeared. Professor Avi Shama of the University of Mexico believes that 90 percent of all private-sector production, sales, and profits are never reported to the tax authorities in Russia. But look at Figure 8-2. There you see the size of the underground economy in Europe, Canada, Australia, Japan, and the United States. Italy's underground economy is the most prominent. Why? Because the difference between an Italian worker's net take-home pay and his or her employer's cost for that worker—which includes taxes and other government-mandated employee costs—is 200 percent (the figure in the United States is 79 percent). It is not surprising that at least 25 percent of Italian economic activity takes place without the government's knowing it. But the Italian government does know what is happening. Consequently, Italian tax policemen stand outside of restaurants, beauty salons, and shops. They can ask for the legally required receipt. A customer without such a receipt can be fined on the spot.

For Critical Analysis
How can a country reduce the size of its underground economy?

FIGURE 8-2

The Size of the Underground Economy, by Country.
These estimates indicate that Italy has the largest underground economy, relative to those of other nations.
Source: Friedrich Schneider, Linz University.

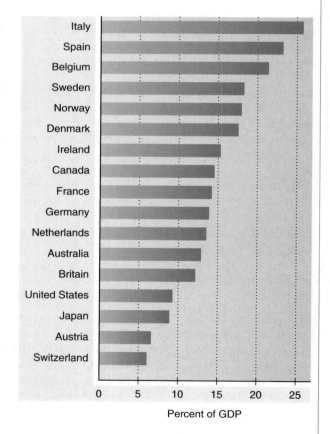

Percent of GDP

Recognizing GDP's Limitations

Like any statistical measure, gross domestic product is a concept that can be both well used and misused. Economists find it especially valuable as an overall indicator of a nation's economic performance. But it is important to realize that GDP has important weaknesses. Because it includes only the value of goods and services traded in markets, it excludes *non-market* production, such as the household services of homemakers discussed earlier. This can cause some problems in comparing the GDP of an industrialized country with the GDP of a highly agrarian nation in which nonmarket production is relatively more important. It also causes problems if nations have different definitions of legal versus illegal activities. For instance, a nation with legalized gambling will count the value of gambling services, which has a reported market value as a legal activity. But in a country in which gambling is illegal, individuals who provide such services will not report the market value of gambling activities, and so they will not be counted in that country's GDP. This can complicate comparing GDP in the nation where gambling is legal with GDP in the country that prohibits gambling.

Furthermore, although GDP is often used as a benchmark measure for standard-of-living calculations, it is not necessarily a good measure of the well-being of a nation. No measured figure of total national annual income can take account of changes in the degree of labor market discrimination, declines or improvements in personal safety, or the quantity or quality of leisure time. Measured GDP also says little about our environmental quality of life. As the now-defunct Soviet Union illustrated to the world, the large-scale production of such goods as minerals, electricity, and irrigation for farming can have negative effects on the environment: deforestation from strip mining, air and soil pollution from particulate emissions or nuclear accidents at power plants, and erosion of the natural balance between water and salt in bodies of water such as the Aral Sea. Hence it is important to recognize the following point:

> GDP is a measure of production and an indicator of economic activity. It is not a measure of a nation's overall welfare.

Nonetheless, GDP is a relatively accurate and useful measure to map changes in the economy's domestic economic performance. Understanding GDP is thus important for recognizing changes in economic performance over time.

CONCEPTS IN BRIEF

- GDP is the total market value of final goods and services produced in an economy during a one-year period by factors of production within the nation's borders. It represents the dollar value of the flow of production over a one-year period.

- To avoid double counting, we look only at final goods and services produced or, alternatively, at value added.

- In measuring GDP, we must exclude (1) purely financial transactions, such as the buying and selling of securities; (2) government transfer payments and private transfer payments; and (3) the transfer of secondhand goods.

- Many other transactions are excluded from GDP, among them household services rendered by homemakers, underground economy transactions, and illegal economic activities.

- GDP is a useful measure for tracking changes in overall economic activity over time, but it is not a measure of the well-being of a nation's residents, because it fails to account for nonmarket transactions, the amount and quality of leisure time, environmental or safety issues, discrimination, and other factors that influence general welfare.

TWO MAIN METHODS OF MEASURING GDP

If the definition of GDP is the total value of all final goods and services produced during a year, then to measure GDP we could add up the prices times the quantities of every individual commodity produced. But this would involve a monumental, if not impossible, task for government statisticians.

The circular flow diagram presented in Figure 8-1 gives us a shortcut method for calculating GDP. We can look at the *flow of expenditures,* which consists of consumption, investment, government purchases of goods and services, and net expenditures in the foreign sector (net exports). This is called the **expenditure approach** to measuring GDP, in which we add the dollar value of all final goods and services. We could also use the *flow of income,* looking at the income received by everybody producing goods and services. This is called the **income approach,** in which we add the income received by all factors of production.

Deriving GDP by the Expenditure Approach

To derive GDP using the expenditure approach, we must look at each of the separate components of expenditures and then add them together. These components are consumption expenditures, investment, government expenditures, and net exports.

Consumption Expenditures.   How do we spend our income? As households or as individuals, we spend our income through consumption expenditure (*C*), which falls into three categories: **durable consumer goods, nondurable consumer goods,** and **services.** Durable goods are *arbitrarily* defined as items that last more than three years; they include automobiles, furniture, and household appliances. Nondurable goods are all the rest, such as food and gasoline. Services are intangible commodities: medical care, education, and so on.

Housing expenditures constitute a major proportion of anybody's annual expenditures. Rental payments on apartments are automatically included in consumption expenditure estimates. People who own their homes, however, do not make rental payments. Consequently, government statisticians estimate what is called the *implicit rental value* of owner-occupied homes. It is equal to the amount of rent you would have to pay if you did not own the home but were renting it from someone else.

Gross Private Domestic Investment.   We now turn our attention to **gross private domestic investment** (*I*) undertaken by businesses. When economists refer to investment, they are referring to additions to productive capacity. **Investment** may be thought of as an activity that uses resources today in such a way that they allow for greater production in the future and hence greater consumption in the future. When a business buys new equipment or puts up a new factory, it is investing; it is increasing its capacity to produce in the future.

The layperson's notion of investment often relates to the purchase of stocks and bonds. For our purposes, such transactions simply represent the *transfer of ownership* of assets called stocks and bonds. Thus you must keep in mind the fact that in economics, investment refers *only* to *additions* to productive capacity, not to transfers of assets.

In our analysis, we will consider the basic components of investment. We have already mentioned the first one, which involves a firm's buying equipment or putting up a new factory. These are called **producer durables,** or **capital goods.** A producer durable, or a

Expenditure approach
A way of computing national income by adding up the dollar value at current market prices of all final goods and services.

Income approach
A way of measuring national income by adding up all components of national income, including wages, interest, rent, and profits.

Durable consumer goods
Consumer goods that have a life span of more than three years.

Nondurable consumer goods
Consumer goods that are used up within three years.

Services
Mental or physical labor or help purchased by consumers. Examples are the assistance of doctors, lawyers, dentists, repair personnel, housecleaners, educators, retailers, and wholesalers; things purchased or used by consumers that do not have physical characteristics.

Gross private domestic investment
The creation of capital goods, such as factories and machines, that can yield production and hence consumption in the future. Also included in this definition are changes in business inventories and repairs made to machines or buildings.

Investment
Any use of today's resources to expand tomorrow's production or consumption.

Producer durables, or capital goods
Durable goods having an expected service life of more than three years that are used by businesses to produce other goods and services.

capital good, is simply a good that is purchased not to be consumed in its current form but to be used to make other goods and services. The purchase of equipment and factories—capital goods—is called **fixed investment.**

The other type of investment has to do with the change in inventories of raw materials and finished goods. Firms do not immediately sell off all their products to consumers. Some of this final product is usually held in inventory waiting to be sold. Firms hold inventories to meet future expected orders for their products. When a firm increases its inventories of finished products, it is engaging in **inventory investment.** Inventories consist of all finished goods on hand, goods in process, and raw materials.

The reason that we can think of a change in inventories as being a type of investment is that an increase in such inventories provides for future increased consumption possibilities. When inventory investment is zero, the firm is neither adding to nor subtracting from the total stock of goods or raw materials on hand. Thus if the firm keeps the same amount of inventories throughout the year, inventory *investment* has been zero.

In estimating gross private domestic investment, government statisticians also add consumer expenditures on *new* residential structures because new housing represents an addition to our future productive capacity in the sense that a new house can generate housing services in the future.

Fixed investment
Purchases by businesses of newly produced producer durables, or capital goods, such as production machinery and office equipment.

Inventory investment
Changes in the stocks of finished goods and goods in process, as well as changes in the raw materials that businesses keep on hand. Whenever inventories are decreasing, inventory investment is negative; whenever they are increasing, inventory investment is positive.

POLICY EXAMPLE

Can the Government Catch Up with the Real-Life Economy?

For years, government statisticians have been classifying the industries in the United States according to the Standard Industrial Classification, or SIC. This system was developed in the 1930s. With so many complaints about how out outdated the SIC categories were, the government finally did start changing how it classifies industries. It has developed the North American Industry Classification System (NAICS). Three hundred new industries have been added, including satellite communications. It has also regrouped new and existing industries together. There is a grouping called "information," which includes publishing, software, broadcasting, telecommunications, and motion pictures. Unfortunately, the new NAICS data will not be fully integrated into federal statistics until around 2005.

For Critical Analysis
Does it matter whether we have accurate information on the growth or decline of industries that reflect the economy? Why or why not?

Government Expenditures.   In addition to personal consumption expenditures, there are government purchases of goods and services (*G*). The government buys goods and services from private firms and pays wages and salaries to government employees. Generally, we value goods and services at the prices at which they are sold. But many government goods and services are not sold in the market. Therefore, we cannot use their market value when computing GDP. The value of these goods is considered equal to their *cost*. For example, the value of a newly built road is considered equal to its construction cost and is included in the GDP for the year it was built.

Net Exports (Foreign Expenditures).   To get an accurate representation of gross domestic product, we must include the foreign sector. As Americans, we purchase foreign goods called *imports*. The goods that foreigners purchase from us are our *exports*. To get an idea of the *net* expenditures from the foreign sector, we subtract the value of imports from the value of exports to get net exports (*X*) for a year:

Net exports (X) = total exports − total imports

To understand why we subtract imports rather than ignoring them altogether, consider that we are using the expenditures approach. If we want to estimate *domestic* output, we have to subtract U.S. expenditures on the goods of other nations.

INTERNATIONAL EXAMPLE

What the GDP Figures in China Really Mean

For years, the Western world has been regaled by impressive figures on the growth in the Chinese economy. While the United States has been happy with growth rates of 3 and 4 percent per year, the Chinese economy has been growing at 7, 8, even 9 percent per year. But what do such statistics really mean? One Chinese economist in Beijing, Lu Feng, compared China's official production rate of meat, eggs, and fish products with what people actually consumed. He concluded that real output in these sectors had been exaggerated by over 40 percent. The reason is that local officials want to show good output performance, so they overstate agricultural output. The same problem plagues the industrial sector. The reality is that so long as China does not correct its reported output figures by doing many sampling surveys, it is bound to exaggerate its real GDP and thus its economic growth.

For Critical Analysis

Why do government statisticians in the United States not face a similar problem?

Mathematical Representation Using the Expenditure Approach

We have just defined the components of GDP using the expenditure approach. When we add them all together, we get a definition for GDP, which is as follows:

$$GDP = C + I + G + X$$

where

C = consumption expenditures

I = investment expenditures

G = government expenditures

X = net exports

The Historical Picture.   To get an idea of the relationship among $C, I, G,$ and $X,$ look at Figure 8-3, which shows gross domestic product, personal consumption expenditures, government purchases, and gross private domestic investment plus net exports since 1929. When we add up the expenditures of the household, business, government, and foreign sectors, we get GDP.

Depreciation
Reduction in the value of capital goods over a one-year period due to physical wear and tear and also to obsolescence; also called *capital consumption allowance*.

Net domestic product (NDP)
GDP minus depreciation.

Depreciation and Net Domestic Product.   We have used the terms *gross domestic product* and *gross private domestic investment* without really indicating what *gross* means. The dictionary defines it as "without deductions," the opposite of *net*. Deductions for what? you might ask. The deductions are for something we call **depreciation.** In the course of a year, machines and structures wear out or are used up in the production of domestic product. For example, houses deteriorate as they are occupied, and machines need repairs or they will fall apart and stop working. Most capital, or durable, goods depreciate. An estimate of this is subtracted from gross domestic product to arrive at a figure called **net domestic product (NDP),** which we define as follows:

FIGURE 8-3
GDP and Its Components
Here we see a display of gross domestic product, personal consumption expenditures, government purchases, and gross private domestic investment plus net exports for the years since 1929. Actually, during the Great Depression of the 1930s, gross private domestic investment *plus* net exports was negative because we were investing very little at that time.

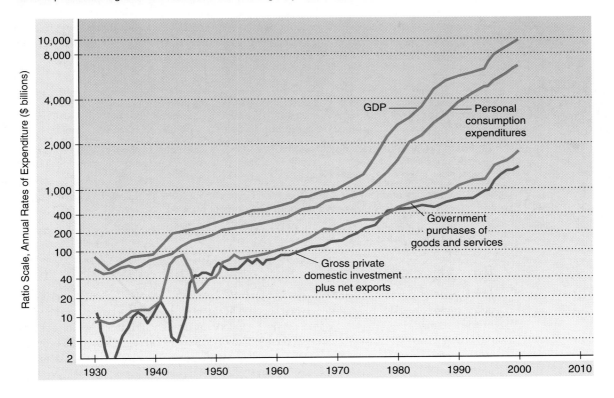

$$NDP = GDP - depreciation$$

Depreciation is also called **capital consumption allowance** because it is the amount of the capital stock that has been consumed over a one-year period. In essence, it equals the amount a business would have to put aside to repair and replace deteriorating machines. Because we know that

$$GDP = C + I + G + X$$

we know that the formula for NDP is

$$NDP = C + I + G + X - depreciation$$

Alternatively, because net $I = I - $ depreciation,

$$NDP = C + net\ I + G + X$$

Net investment measures *changes* in our capital stock over time and is positive nearly every year. Because depreciation does not vary greatly from year to year as a percentage of GDP, we get a similar picture of what is happening to our national economy by looking at either NDP or GDP data.

Capital consumption allowance
Another name for depreciation, the amount that businesses would have to save in order to take care of the deterioration of machines and other equipment.

Net investment
Gross private domestic investment minus an estimate of the wear and tear on the existing capital stock. Net investment therefore measures the change in capital stock over a one-year period.

Net investment is an important variable to observe over time nonetheless. If everything else remains the same in an economy, changes in net investment can have dramatic consequences for future economic growth (a topic we cover in more detail in Chapter 9). Positive net investment by definition expands the productive capacity of our economy. This means that there is increased capital, which will generate even more income in the future. When net investment is zero, we are investing just enough to take account of depreciation. Our economy's productive capacity remains unchanged. Finally, when net investment is negative, we can expect negative economic growth prospects in the future. Negative net investment means that our productive capacity is actually declining—we are disinvesting. This actually occurred during the Great Depression.

CONCEPTS IN BRIEF

◉ The expenditure approach to measuring GDP requires that we add up consumption expenditures, gross private investment, government purchases, and net exports. Consumption expenditures include consumer durables, consumer nondurables, and services.

◉ Gross private domestic investment *excludes* transfers of asset ownership. It includes only additions to the productive capacity of a nation, repairs on existing capital goods, and changes in business inventories.

◉ We value government expenditures at their cost because we do not usually have market prices at which to value government goods and services.

◉ To obtain net domestic product (NDP), we subtract from GDP the year's depreciation of the existing capital stock.

Deriving GDP by the Income Approach

If you go back to the circular flow diagram in Figure 8-1, you see that product markets are at the top of the diagram and factor markets are at the bottom. We can calculate the value of the circular flow of income and product by looking at expenditures—which we just did—or by looking at total factor payments. Factor payments are called income. We calculate **gross domestic income (GDI),** which we will see is identical to gross domestic product (GDP). Using the income approach, we have four categories of payments to individuals: wages, interest, rent, and profits.

Gross domestic income (GDI)
The sum of all income—wages, interest, rent, and profits—paid to the four factors of production.

To examine recent trends in U. S. GDP and its components, go to **www.stls.frb.org/fred** and click on "Gross Domestic Product and Components."

1. *Wages.* The most important category is, of course, wages, including salaries and other forms of labor income, such as income in kind and incentive payments. We also count Social Security taxes (both the employees' and the employers' contributions).
2. *Interest.* Here interest payments do not equal the sum of all payments for the use of funds in a year. Instead, interest is expressed in *net* rather than in gross terms. The interest component of total income is only net interest received by households plus net interest paid to us by foreigners. Net interest received by households is the difference between the interest they receive (from savings accounts, certificates of deposit, and the like) and the interest they pay (to banks for mortgages, credit cards, and other loans).
3. *Rent.* Rent is all income earned by individuals for the use of their real (nonmonetary) assets, such as farms, houses, and stores. As stated previously, we have to include here the implicit rental value of owner-occupied houses. Also included in this category are royalties received from copyrights, patents, and assets such as oil wells.
4. *Profits.* Our last category includes total gross corporate profits plus *proprietors' income.* Proprietors' income is income earned from the operation of unincorporated businesses, which include sole proprietorships, partnerships, and producers' cooperatives. It is unincorporated business profit.

All of the payments listed are *actual* factor payments made to owners of the factors of production. When we add them together, though, we do not yet have gross domestic income. We have to take account of two other components: **indirect business taxes,** such as sales and business property taxes, and depreciation, which we have already discussed.

Indirect Business Taxes. Indirect taxes are the (nonincome) taxes paid by consumers when they buy goods and services. When you buy a book, you pay the price of the book plus any state and local sales tax. The business is actually acting as the government's agent

Indirect business taxes
All business taxes except the tax on corporate profits. Indirect business taxes include sales and business property taxes.

FIGURE 8-4
Gross Domestic Product and Gross Domestic Income, 2000 (in billions of 2000 dollars per year)
By using the two different methods of computing the output of the economy, we come up with gross domestic product and gross domestic income, which are by definition equal. One approach focuses on expenditures, or the flow of product; the other approach concentrates on income, or the flow of costs.

Source: U.S. Department of Commerce. First quarter preliminary data annualized.

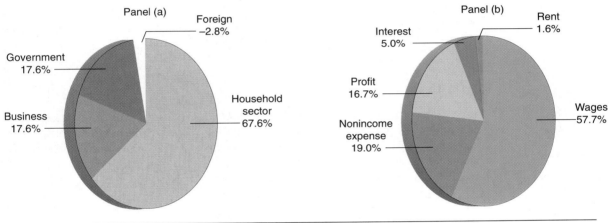

Expenditure Point of View—Product Flow		Income Point of View—Cost Flow	
Expenditures by Different Sectors:		Domestic Income (at Factor Cost):	
Household sector		*Wages*	
Personal consumption expenses	$6,661.5	All wages, salaries, and supplemental employee compensation	$5,678.4
Government sector		*Rent*	
Purchase of goods and services	1,734.6	All rental income of individuals plus implicit rent on owner-occupied dwellings	155.4
Business sector		*Interest*	
Gross private domestic investment (including depreciation)	1,727.0	Net interest paid by business	490.2
Foreign sector		*Profit*	
Net exports of goods and services	−273.6	Proprietorial income	701.3
		Corporate profits before taxes deducted	952.0
		Nonincome expense items	
		Indirect business taxes and other adjustments	762.1
		Depreciation	1,215.4
		Statistical discrepancy	−105.3
Gross domestic product	$9,849.5	Gross domestic income	$9,849.5

in collecting the sales tax, which it in turn passes on to the government. Such taxes therefore represent a business expense and are included in gross domestic income.

Depreciation.   Just as we had to deduct depreciation to get from GDP to NDP, so we must *add* depreciation to go from net domestic income to gross domestic income. Depreciation can be thought of as the portion of the current year's GDP that is used to replace physical capital consumed in the process of production. Because somebody has paid for the replacement, depreciation must be added as a component of gross domestic income.

The last two components of GDP—indirect business taxes and depreciation—are called **nonincome expense items.**

Figure 8-4 on the previous page shows a comparison between gross domestic product and gross domestic income for 2000. Whether you decide to use the expenditure approach or the income approach, you will come out with the same number. There are sometimes statistical discrepancies, but they are usually relatively small.

> **Nonincome expense items**
> The total of indirect business taxes and depreciation.

CONCEPTS IN BRIEF

- To derive GDP using the income approach, we add up all factor payments, including wages, interest, rent, and profits.

- To get an accurate estimate of GDP with this method, we must also add indirect business taxes and depreciation to those total factor payments.

OTHER COMPONENTS OF NATIONAL INCOME ACCOUNTING

Gross domestic income or product does not really tell how much income people have access to for spending purposes. To get to those kinds of data, we must make some adjustments, which we now do.

National Income (NI)

We know that net domestic product (NDP) represents the total market value of goods and services available for both consumption, used in a broader sense here to mean "resource exhaustion," and net additions to the economy's stock of capital. NDP does not, however, represent the income available to individuals within that economy because it includes indirect business taxes, such as sales taxes. We therefore deduct these indirect business taxes from NDP to arrive at the figure for all factor income of resource owners. The result is what we define as **national income (NI)**—income *earned* by the factors of production.

> **National income (NI)**
> The total of all factor payments to resource owners. It can be obtained by subtracting indirect business taxes from NDP.

Personal Income (PI)

National income does not actually represent what is available to individuals to spend because some people obtain income for which they have provided no concurrent good or service and others earn income but do not receive it. In the former category are mainly recipients of transfer payments from the government, such as Social Security, welfare, and food stamps. These payments represent shifts of funds within the economy by way of the government, where no good or service is concurrently rendered in exchange. For the other category, income earned but not received, the most obvious examples are corporate retained earnings that are plowed back into the business, contributions to social insurance,

	Billions of Dollars
Gross domestic product (GDP)	9,849.5
Minus depreciation	−1,215.4
Net domestic product (NDP)	8,634.1
Minus indirect business taxes and other adjustments	−762.1
National income (NI)	7,872.0
Minus corporate taxes, Social Security contributions, corporate retained earnings	−1,236.5
Plus government and business transfer payments	+1,606.8
Personal income (PI)	8,242.3
Minus personal income tax and nontax payments	−1,253.2
Disposable personal income (DPI)	6,989.1

TABLE 8-2
Going from GDP to Disposable Income, 2000

Source: U.S. Department of Commerce.

and corporate income taxes. When transfer payments are added and when income earned but not received is subtracted, we end up with **personal income (PI)**—income *received* by the factors of production prior to the payment of personal income taxes.

Disposable Personal Income (DPI)

Everybody knows that you do not get to take home all your salary. To get **disposable personal income (DPI),** we subtract all personal income taxes from personal income. This is the income that individuals have left for consumption and saving.

Deriving the Components of GDP

Table 8-2 takes you through the steps necessary to derive the various components of GDP. It shows how you go from gross domestic product to net domestic product to national income to personal income and then to disposable personal income. On the endpapers of your book, you can see the historical record for GDP, NDP, NI, PI, and DPI for selected years since 1929.

We have completed our rundown of the different ways that GDP can be computed and of the different variants of national income and product. What we have not yet touched on is the difference between national income measured in this year's dollars and national income representing real goods and services.

Personal income (PI)
The amount of income that households actually receive before they pay personal income taxes.

Disposable personal income (DPI)
Personal income after personal income taxes have been paid.

CONCEPTS IN BRIEF

● To obtain national income, we subtract indirect business taxes from net domestic product. National income gives us a measure of all factor payments to resource owners.

● To obtain personal income, we must add government transfer payments, such as Social Security benefits and food stamps. We must subtract income earned but not received by factor owners, such as corporate retained earnings, Social Security contributions, and corporate income taxes.

● To obtain disposable personal income, we subtract all personal income taxes from personal income. Disposable personal income is income that individuals actually have for consumption or saving.

DISTINGUISHING BETWEEN NOMINAL AND REAL VALUES

Nominal values
The values of variables such as GDP and investment expressed in current dollars, also called *money values*; measurement in terms of the actual market prices at which goods are sold.

Real values
Measurement of economic values after adjustments have been made for changes in the average of prices between years.

So far we have shown how to measure *nominal* income and product. When we say "nominal," we are referring to income and product expressed in the current "face value" of today's dollar. Given the existence of inflation or deflation in the economy, we must also be able to distinguish between the **nominal values** that we will be looking at and the **real values** underlying them. Nominal values are expressed in current dollars. Real income involves our command over goods and services—purchasing power—and therefore depends on money income and a set of prices. Thus real income refers to nominal income corrected for changes in the weighted average of all prices. In other words, we must make an adjustment for changes in the price level. Consider an example. Nominal income *per person* in 1960 was only about $2,800 per year. In 2000, nominal income per person was close to $36,000. Were people really that bad off in 1960? No, for nominal income in 1960 is expressed in 1960 prices, not in the prices of today. In today's dollars, the per-person income of 1960 would be closer to $10,000, or about 28 percent of today's income per person. This is a meaningful comparison between income in 1960 and income today. Next we will show how we can translate nominal measures of income into real measures by using an appropriate price index, such as the CPI or the GDP deflator discussed in Chapter 7.

Correcting GDP for Price Changes

If a compact disk (CD) costs $15 this year, 10 CDs will have a market value of $150. If next year they cost $20 each, the same 10 CDs will have a market value of $200. In this case, there is no increase in the total quantity of CDs, but the market value will have increased by one-third. Apply this to every single good and service produced and sold in the United States and you realize that changes in GDP, measured in *current* dollars, may not be a very useful indication of economic activity. If we are really interested in variations in the *real* output of the economy, we must correct GDP (and just about everything else we look at) for changes in the average of overall prices from year to year. Basically, we need to generate an index that approximates the changes in average prices and then divide that estimate into the value of output in current dollars to adjust the value of output to what is called **constant dollars,** or dollars corrected for general price level changes. This price-corrected GDP is called *real GDP.*

Constant dollars
Dollars expressed in terms of real purchasing power using a particular year as the base or standard of comparison, in contrast to current dollars.

EXAMPLE

Correcting GDP for Price Index Changes, 1990–2000

Let's take a numerical example to see how we can adjust GDP for changes in the price index. We must pick an appropriate price index in order to adjust for these price level changes. We mentioned the Consumer Price Index, the Producer Price Index, and the GDP deflator in Chapter 7. Let's use the GDP deflator to adjust our figures. Table 8-3 gives 13 years of GDP figures. Nominal GDP figures are shown in column 2. The price index (GDP deflator) is in column 3, with base year of 1996 when the GDP deflator equals 100. Column 4 shows real (inflation-adjusted) GDP in 1996 dollars.

The formula for real GDP is

$$\text{Real GDP} = \frac{\text{nominal GDP}}{\text{price level}} \times 100$$

The step-by-step derivation of real (constant-dollar) GDP is as follows: The base year is 1996, so the price index for that year must equal 100. In 1996, nominal GDP was $7,813.2 billion, and so too was real GDP expressed in 1996 dollars. In 1997, the price level increased to 101.7. Thus to correct 1997's nominal GDP for inflation, we divide the price index, 101.7, into the nominal GDP figure of $8,300.9 billion and

(1) Year	(2) Nominal GDP (billions of dollars per year)	(3) Price Level Index base year 1996 = 100)	(4) = [(2) ÷ (3)] × 100 Real GDP (billions of dollars per year (in constant 1996 dollars)
1990	5,803.2	86.8	6,683.5
1991	5,986.2	89.8	6,669.2
1992	6,318.9	91.7	6,891.1
1993	6,642.3	94.2	7,054.1
1994	7,054.3	96.1	7,337.8
1995	7,400.5	98.2	7,537.1
1996	7,813.2	100.0	7,813.2
1997	8,300.9	101.7	8,165.1
1998	8,759.9	102.9	8,516.3
1999	9,254.6	104.4	8,867.0
2000	9,849.5	106.4	9,256.2

Source: U.S. Department of Commerce, Bureau of Economic Analysis.

TABLE 8-3
Correcting GDP for Price Index Changes
To correct GDP for price index changes, we first have to pick a price index (the GDP deflator) with a specific year as its base. In our example, the base level is 1996 prices; the price index for that year is 100. To obtain 1996 constant-dollar GDP, we divide the price index into nominal GDP and multiply by 100. In other words, we divide column 3 into column 2 and multiply by 100. This gives us column 4, which is a measure of real GDP expressed in 1996 purchasing power.

then multiply it by 100. The result is $8,165.1 billion, which is 1997 GDP expressed in terms of the purchasing power of dollars in 1996. What about a situation when the price index is lower than in 1996? Look at 1990. Here the price index shown in column 3 is only 86.8. That means that in 1990, the average of all prices was about 87 percent of prices in 1996. To obtain 1990 GDP expressed in terms of 1996 purchasing power, we divide nominal GDP, $5,803.2 billion, by 86.8 and then

multiply by 100. The result is a larger number— $6,683.5 billion. Column 4 in Table 8-3 is a better measure of how the economy has performed than column 2, which shows nominal GDP changes.

For Critical Analysis
A few years ago, the base year for the GDP deflator was 1992. What does a change in the base year for the price index affect?

Plotting Nominal and Real GDP

Nominal GDP and real GDP since 1970 are plotted in Figure 8-5 on page 186. Notice that there is quite a big gap between the two GDP figures, reflecting the amount of inflation that has occurred. Note, further, that the choice of a base year is arbitrary. We have chosen 1996 as the base year in our example. This happens to be the base year that is currently used by the government.

Per Capita GDP

Looking at changes in real gross domestic product may be deceiving, particularly if the population size has changed significantly. If real GDP over a 10-year period went up 100 percent, you might jump to the conclusion that the real income of a typical person in

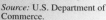

FIGURE 8-5
Nominal and Real GDP
Here we plot both nominal and real GDP. Real GDP is expressed in the purchasing power of 1996 dollars. The gap between the two represents price level changes.
Source: U.S. Department of Commerce.

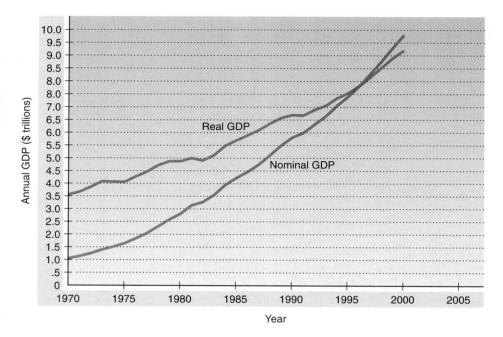

the economy had increased by that amount. But what if during the same period population increased by 200 percent? Then what would you say? Certainly, the amount of real GDP per person, or *per capita real GDP,* would have fallen, even though *total* real GDP had risen. What we must do to account not only for price changes but also for population changes is first deflate GDP and then divide by the total population, doing this for each year. If we were to look at certain less developed countries, we would find that in many cases, even though real GDP has risen over the past several decades, per capita real GDP has remained constant or fallen because the population has grown just as rapidly or more quickly.

The Chain-Weighted Measure of the Growth in Real GDP

In December 1995, the Commerce Department's Bureau of Economic Analysis (BEA) made a fundamental change in the way it computes real gross domestic product. Remember that real GDP consists of consumer spending, business investment, government expenditures on goods and services, and net foreign trade. To calculate real GDP, the BEA had used a weighted sum of 1,100 components of these four categories. Until 1996, these 1,100 components were fixed in weight, and their relative importance changed only periodically. For example, the last revision was made in 1987. Otherwise stated, the BEA had been using a *fixed-weight* measure of changes in real GDP.

Now the BEA changes the weights of the different components of real GDP to reflect changes in their relative prices and in their relative shares in the overall economy's output. The new measure is called *chain-weighted real GDP.* Rather than a specific number, an index is used. Thus to calculate a year's *change* in real GDP, it is necessary to compare one year's index with the previous year's index. The BEA publishes both the chain-weighted real GDP index and its dollar equivalent. You can find chain-weighted real GDP statistics on the endpapers of this book, which show our national income accounts.

- To correct nominal GDP for price changes, we first use a base year for our price index and assign it the number 100. Then we construct an index based on how a weighted average of the price level has changed relative to that base year. For example, if in the next year a weighted average of the price level indicates that prices have increased by 10 percent, we would assign it the number 110. We then divide each year's price index, so constructed, into its respective nominal GDP figure (and multiply by 100).

- We can divide the population into real GDP to obtain per capita real GDP.

COMPARING GDP THROUGHOUT THE WORLD

It is relatively easy to compare the standard of living of a family in Los Angeles with that of one living in Boston. Both families get paid in dollars and can buy the same goods and services at Kmart, McDonald's, and Costco. It is not so easy, however, to make a similar comparison between a family living in the United States and one in, say, India. The first problem concerns money. Indians get paid in rupees, their national currency, and buy goods and services with those rupees. But how do we compare the average standard of living measured in rupees with that measured in dollars?

Foreign Exchange Rates

In earlier chapters, you have encountered international examples that involved local currencies, but the dollar equivalent always has been given. The dollar equivalent is calculated by looking up the **foreign exchange rate** that is published daily in major newspapers throughout the world. If you know that you can exchange $1 for 5 francs, the exchange rate is 5 to 1 (or otherwise stated, a franc is worth 20 cents). So if French incomes per capita are, say, 100,000 francs, that translates at an exchange rate of 5 francs to $1, to $20,000. For years, statisticians calculated relative GDP by simply adding up each country's GDP in its local currency and dividing by each respective dollar exchange rate.

Foreign exchange rate
The price of one currency in terms of another.

True Purchasing Power

The problem with simply using foreign exchange rates to convert other countries' GDP and per capita GDP into dollars is that not all goods and services are bought and sold in a world market. Restaurant food, housecleaning services, and home repairs do not get exchanged across countries. In countries that have very low wages, those kinds of services are much cheaper than foreign exchange rate computations would imply. Government statistics claiming that per capita income in some poor country is only $300 a year seem shocking. But such a statistic does not tell you the true standard of living of people in that country. Only by looking at what is called **purchasing power parity** can you determine other countries' true standards of living compared to ours.

Purchasing power parity
Adjustment in exchange rate conversions that takes into account differences in the true cost of living across countries.

INTERNATIONAL EXAMPLE

Purchasing Power Parity Comparisons of World Incomes

A few years ago, the International Monetary Fund accepted the purchasing power parity approach as the correct one. It started presenting international statistics on each country's GDP relative to every other's based on purchasing power parity. The results were surprising. As you can see from Table 8-4, India has a higher per capita GDP compared to what was measured at market foreign exchange rates.

For Critical Analysis

What percentage increase is there in per capita GDP in India when one switches from foreign exchange rates to purchasing power parity?

TABLE 8-4
Comparing GDP Internationally

Country	Annual GDP Based on Purchasing Power Parity (billions of U.S. dollars)	Per Capita GDP Based on Purchasing Power Parity (U.S. dollars)	Per Capita GDP Based on Foreign Exchange Rates (U.S. dollars)
United States	6,897.2	26,528	26,528
Japan	2,493.8	19,399	26,424
China	2,490.1	1,692	375
Germany	2,007.4	19,870	24,421
France	1,421.6	18,450	23,489
Russia	1,101.8	6,903	2,640
India	1,100.4	1,155	379
Italy	1,099.0	17,050	17,990
United Kingdom	1,088.0	16,352	16,804
Brazil	980.4	5,251	2,794

Sources: International Monetary Fund; World Bank; Organization for Economic Cooperation and Development.

CONCEPTS IN BRIEF

- The foreign exchange rate is the price of one currency in terms of another.
- Statisticians often calculate relative GDP by adding up each country's GDP in its local currency and dividing by the dollar exchange rate.
- Because not all goods and services are bought and sold in the world market, we must correct exchange rate conversions of other countries' GDP figures to take into account differences in the true cost of living across countries.

NETNOMICS

Has Real GDP Measurement Kept Pace with the Internet?

A key ingredient in the measurement of real GDP is of course the price index. Changes in the prices of things you buy eventually show up as changes in the measured price index. The price you pay for many items, however, consist really of two prices: the nominal price you pay in dollars plus the price of your time involved in the transaction, measured by its opportunity cost. If a good was sold at an artificially low price, thereby creating lines of people waiting to buy it, the measured price of the good would not reflect its true price.

Slowly but surely, the Internet is reducing the time spent engaging in many transactions. For example, people who trade stocks and bonds on-line do not have to spend any time dealing with securities brokers. Individuals who use the Internet for on-line banking spend considerably less time per transaction than they did only a few years ago. On-line purchasing of airline tickets also often saves time for each transaction.

There is a time saving on the seller's side also. But this time saving translates into lower costs for the sellers. These lower costs are generally picked up by government statisticians. In contrast, the other half of the equation—the consumer's reduced time spent per each transaction—is apparently not picked up by official government statistics.

The point is that in a world of increasing Internet use and consequent reductions in time spent per transaction, the level and rate of growth of real GDP may be greater than measured. Why? Because the price level may not be accurately reflecting the changes in true prices by including the opportunity cost of time.

How Well Do Economists Predict GDP?

A joke among economists is that they have been able to forecast nine of the last seven recessions. Underlying this joke is a reality: The people who make their living forecasting changes in real GDP do not have a stellar track record. Actually, this assessment is a little too harsh. Forecasting economists have done a pretty good job predicting *long-run* trends in real GDP. Where they go wrong is in predicting downturns, otherwise known as recessions. In Table 8-5, you can see that forecasters missed four of the five past downturns in our economy since the 1960s. The best that can be said about typical economic forecasts of downturns is that they are usually late. In other words, downturns seemed to be recognized only after they have begun.

How the Forecasters Do It

Most forecasters use large-scale computer models to develop their estimates of changes in real GDP. These computer models attempt to make sense of how our multitrillion-dollar economy works. Sometimes these models involve hundreds of sectors. A sector, such as automobiles, may be shown to depend on a wide range of variables—interest rates, price changes, and so on. Some experts argue that even the largest-scale computer models of our economy can no longer handle its changing nature. Furthermore, the U.S. economy is increasingly part of an interconnected world. Little long-term research has been done to discover how changes in the rest of the world's economies ultimately affect the U.S. economy.

Concepts Applied

National Income Accounting

GDP

Real GDP

TABLE 8-5

Economic Forecasts: Missing the Mark

The forecasts given in the table are taken from *Business Week* surveys through the years. Only the recession that started at the beginning of 1980 was correctly anticipated by the economic forecasters surveyed. They missed the other four downturns completely.

Start of Recession	Date of Forecast	Forecasted Growth over the Next Year (%)	Actual Growth in Real GDP (%)
December 1969	December 1969	1.5	−.6
November 1973	December 1973	1.5	−1.8
January 1980	December 1979	−.7	−.3
July 1990	December 1989	2.1	−.1
July 1991	December 1990	2.2	.7

Source: Business Week, September 30, 1996, p. 92.

Other Difficulties in Predicting Downturns

The globalization of the American economy cannot be used as an excuse for missing the downturn that started in December 1969. The 1960s was a decade of sustained economic growth (similar to the 1990s). A year before the downturn started, economic forecasters as a group pegged the probability of recession in the coming year at less than 15 percent. Their excuse for missing this downturn was that they did not foresee federal government defense spending cuts and rising interest rates caused by contractionary government policies.

The forecasters' reasons for missing the 1973 downturn was that they could not predict the embargo imposed by oil-producing countries at that time. The recession of 1990 arrived without much warning at all. Indeed, virtually no economic model predicted that recession.

Economic forecasters defend themselves by stating that recessions that happen quickly are virtually impossible to predict. Those that commence slowly are countered by government policy and presumably do not actually occur. So, according to these forecasters, only when policymakers are caught by surprise do we have recessions.

FOR CRITICAL ANALYSIS

1. Explain how a business could be hurt by relying on an inaccurate forecast of changes in real GDP.

2. Computing power is relatively cheap and incredibly massive today compared to the 1960s. Nonetheless, large-scale computer economic models have done no better in predicting economic downturns? Why?

SUMMARY DISCUSSION OF LEARNING OBJECTIVES

1. **The Circular Flow of Income and Output:** The circular flow of income and output captures two fundamental principles: (a) In every economic transaction, the seller receives exactly the same amount that the buyer spends; and (b) goods and services flow in one direction and money payments flow in the other direction. In the circular flow, households ultimately purchase the nation's total output of final goods and services. They make these purchases from income—wages, rents, interest, and profits—earned from selling labor, land, capital, and entrepreneurial services. Hence the values of total income and total output must be the same in the circular flow.

2. **Gross Domestic Product (GDP):** A nation's gross domestic product is the total market value of its final output of goods and services produced within a given year using factors of production located within the nation's borders. Because GDP measures a flow of production during a year, it is not a measure of a nation's wealth, which is a stock at a given point in time.

3. **The Limitations of Using GDP as a Measure of National Welfare:** Gross domestic product is a useful measure for tracking year-to-year changes in a nation's overall economic activity. Nevertheless, it excludes nonmarket transactions that may contribute to or detract from general welfare. It also fails to account for factors such as labor market discrimination, personal safety, environmental quality, and the amount of and quality of leisure time available to a nation's residents. Thus GDP is not a measure of national well-being.

4. **The Expenditure Approach to Tabulating GDP:** To calculate GDP using the expenditure approach, we sum consumption spending, investment expenditures, government spending, and net export expenditures. Thus we add the total amount spent on newly produced goods and services during the year to obtain the dollar value of the output produced and purchased during the year.

5. **The Income Approach to Computing GDP:** To tabulate GDP using the income approach, we first add total wages and salaries, rental income, interest income, profits, and nonincome expense items—indirect business taxes and depreciation—to obtain gross domestic income, which is equivalent to gross domestic product. Thus the total value of all income earnings (equivalent to total factor costs) equals GDP.

6. **Distinguishing Between Nominal GDP and Real GDP:** Nominal GDP is the value of newly produced output during the current year measured at current market prices. Real GDP adjusts the value of current output into constant dollars by correcting for changes in the overall level of prices from year to year. To calculate real GDP, we divide nominal GDP by the price level (the GDP deflator) and multiply by 100.

Key Terms and Concepts

Capital consumption allowance (179)

Constant dollars (184)

Depreciation (178)

Disposable personal income (DPI) (183)

Durable consumer goods (176)

Expenditure approach (176)

Final goods and services (169)

Fixed investment (177)

Foreign exchange rate (187)

Gross domestic income (GDI) (180)

Gross domestic product (GDP) (171)

Gross private domestic investment (176)

Income approach (176)

Indirect business taxes (181)

Intermediate goods (172)

Inventory investment (177)

Investment (176)

National income (NI) (182)

National income accounting (169)

Net domestic product (NDP) (178)

Net investment (179)

Nominal values (184)

Nondurable consumer goods (176)

Nonincome expense items (182)

Personal income (PI) (183)

Producer durables, or capital goods (176)

Purchasing power parity (187)

Real values (184)

Services (176)

Total income (169)

Value added (172)

Problems

Answers to the odd numbered problems appear at the back of the book.

8-1. Consider the following hypothetical data for the U.S. economy in 2005, where all amounts are in trillions of dollars.

Consumption	11.0
Indirect business taxes	.8
Depreciation	1.3
Government spending	1.8
Imports	1.7
Gross private domestic investment	2.0
Exports	1.5

  a. Based on the data, what is GDP? NDP? NI?

  b. Suppose that in 2006, exports fall to $1.3 trillion, imports rise to $1.85 trillion, and gross private domestic investment falls to $1.25 trillion. What will GDP be in 2006, assuming that other values do not change between 2005 and 2006?

  c. Note that according to the fictitious data, depreciation (capital consumption allowance) exceeds gross private domestic investment in 2006. How would this affect future U.S. productivity, particularly if it were to continue beyond 2006?

8-2. Look back at Table 8-3, which explains how to calculate real GDP in terms of 1996 constant dollars. Change the base year to 1998. Recalculate the price index, and then recalculate real GDP—that is, express column 4 of Table 8-3 in terms of 1998 dollars instead of 1996 dollars.

8-3. Consider the following hypothetical data for the U.S. economy in 2005, and assume that there are no statistical discrepancies or other adjustments.

Profit	2.8
Indirect business taxes	.8
Rent	.7
Interest	.8
Wages	8.2

Depreciation	1.3
Consumption	11.0
Exports	1.5
Government and business transfer payments	2.0
Personal income taxes and nontax payments	1.7
Imports	1.7
Corporate taxes and retained earnings	.5
Social Security contributions	2.0
Government spending	1.8

a. What is gross domestic income? GDP?

b. What is gross private domestic investment?

c. What is personal income? Personal disposable income?

8-4. Which of the following are production activities that are included in GDP? Which are not?

a. Mr. King paints his own house.

b. Mr. King paints houses for a living.

c. Mrs. King earns income by taking baby photos in her home photography studio.

d. Mrs. King takes photos of planets and stars as part of her astronomy hobby.

e. E*Trade charges fees to process Internet orders for stock trades.

f. Mr. Ho purchases 300 shares of America Online stock via an Internet trade order.

g. Mrs. Ho receives a Social Security payment.

h. Ms. Chavez makes a $300 payment for an Internet-based course on stock trading.

i. Mr. Langham sells a used laptop computer to his neighbor.

8-5. Explain what happens to the official measure of GDP in each of the following situations.

a. A woman who makes a living charging for investment advice on her Internet Web site marries one of her clients, to whom she now provides advice at no charge.

b. A tennis player who recently had won two top professional tournaments earlier this year as an amateur turns professional and continues his streak by winning two more before the year is out.

c. A company that had been selling used firearms illegally finally gets around to obtaining an operating license and performing background checks as specified by law prior to each gun sale.

8-6. Which one of the following activities of a computer manufacturer during the current year are included in this year's measure of GDP?

a. The manufacturer purchases a chip in June, uses it as a component in a computer in August, and sells the computer to a customer in November.

b. A retail outlet of the company sells a computer manufactured during the current year.

c. A marketing arm of the company receives fee income during the current year when a buyer of a one of its computers elects to use the computer manufacturer as her Internet service provider.

8-7. Consider the following table for the economy of a nation whose residents produce five goods.

	1997		2002	
Good	Price	Quantity	Price	Quantity
Shampoo	$ 2	15	$ 4	20
DVD drives	200	10	250	10
Books	40	5	50	4
Milk	3	10	4	3
Candy	1	40	2	20

Assuming a 1997 baseyear:

a. What is nominal GDP for 1997 and 2002?

b. What is real GDP for 1997 and 2002?

8-8. In the table for Problem 8-7, if 1997 is the base year, what is the price index for 1997? For 2002? (Round decimal fractions to the nearest tenth.)

8-9. Suppose that early in a year, a hurricane hits a town in Florida and destroys a sizable amount of residential housing. A portion of this stock of housing, which had a market value of $100 million (not including the market value of the land), was uninsured. The owners of the houses spent a total of $5 million during the rest of the year to pay salvage companies to help them save remaining belongings. A small percentage of uninsured owners had sufficient resources to spend a total of $15 million during the year to pay construction companies to rebuild their homes. Some were able to devote their own time, the opportunity cost of which was valued at $3 million, to work on rebuilding their homes. The remaining people, however, chose to sell their land at its market value and abandon the remains of their houses. What was the combined effect of these transactions on GDP for this year? In what ways, if any, does the effect on GDP reflect a loss in welfare for these individuals?

8-10. Suppose that in 2004, geologists discover large reserves of oil under a barren tundra in Alaska. These reserves have a market value estimated at $50 billion at current oil prices. Oil companies spend $1 billion to hire workers and move and position equipment to begin exploratory pumping during that same year. In the process of loading some of the oil onto tankers at a port, one company accidentally creates a spill into a bay and ultimately pays more than $1 billion to other companies to clean it up. Nevertheless, the oil spill kills thousands of birds, seals, and other wildlife. What was the combined effect of these events on GDP for this year? In what ways, if any, does the effect on GDP reflect a loss in national welfare?

Economics on the Net

Tracking the Components of Gross Domestic Product One way to keep tabs on the components of GDP is via the FRED database at the Web site of the Federal Reserve Bank of St. Louis.

Internet URL: www.stls.frb.org/fred/data/gdp.html

Title: Gross Domestic Product and Components

Navigation: Begin at the homepage of the Federal Reserve Bank of St. Louis (www.stls.frb.org). Click on FRED (www.stls.frb.org/fred). Then click on Data Files and click on Gross Domestic Product and Components.

Application

1. Click on Gross Domestic Product. Write down nominal GDP data for the past 10 quarters.

2. Back up to Real Gross Domestic Product in Fixed 1992 Dollars. Write down the amounts for the past 10 quarters. Use the formula on page 184 to calculate the price level for each quarter. Has the price level decreased or increased in recent quarters?

For Group Study and Analysis Divide the class into "consumption," "investment," "government sector," and "foreign sector" groups. Have each group evaluate the contribution of each category of spending to GDP and to its quarter-to-quarter volatility. Reconvene the class, and discuss the factors that appear to create the most variability in GDP.

GLOBAL ECONOMIC GROWTH AND DEVELOPMENT

This type of logging operation at Mount Adams, Washington, may soon be a thing of the past. In today's modern facilities, newly felled trees slide onto platforms guided by computers. The logs then go into computer-automated sawing systems. How does such improved technology add to our economic growth?

In Portland, Oregon, a newly felled tree slides onto a platform. A spinning saw approaches the timber to start cutting 2-inch by 4-inch boards. Then it hesitates. Data received by a computer guiding the saw have indicated a rise in the market price of 4-inch by 4-inch boards. The computer has readjusted the saw's position to cut the timber into the larger boards. The saw begins to cut into the timber.

American companies have spent the past several years making huge investments in computers. As you will learn in this chapter, economists differ in their assessments of exactly how much computerization has contributed to growth of the American economy.

To understand why economists reach different conclusions about this issue, you need to know how to measure a nation's economic growth. You also need to understand the key determinants of economic growth. Both are central topics of this chapter.

LEARNING OBJECTIVES

After reading this chapter, you should be able to:

1. Define economic growth

2. Recognize the importance of economic growth rates

3. Describe the fundamental determinants of economic growth

4. Explain why productivity increases are crucial for maintaining economic growth

5. Understand the basis of new growth theory

6. Discuss the fundamental factors that contribute to a nation's economic development

195

Did You Know That... at the turn of the twentieth century, Argentina had the sixth highest per capita income in the world, whereas it is now around fortieth, somewhat below Iran? Consider also that 100 years ago, Hong Kong was basically a barren rock, whereas today its per capita income exceeds that of France and the United Kingdom. How can we explain such dramatic changes in relative living standards? From an arithmetic point of view, the answer is simple: Argentina experienced little and in some cases negative economic growth over the past century, whereas Hong Kong had significant economic growth. That answer, though, does not tell us why economic growth rates differed in these two countries. That is the task of this chapter. Should you care about the rate of economic growth in the United States? The answer is yes, if you care about your future standard of living and that of your children and grandchildren. You have already demonstrated that you care about your future standard of living; otherwise, you would not be bothering to obtain a higher education. Obviously, you want to make sure that you experience economic growth as an individual. Now it is time to consider the nation as a whole.

HOW DO WE DEFINE ECONOMIC GROWTH?

Remember from Chapter 2 that we can show economic growth graphically as an outward shift of a production possibilities curve, as is seen in Figure 9-1. If there is economic growth between 2000 and 2025, the production possibilities curve will shift outward toward the red curve. The distance that it shifts represents the amount of economic growth, defined as the increase in the productive capacity of a nation. Although it is possible to come up with a measure of a nation's increased productive capacity, it would not be easy. Therefore, we turn to a more readily obtainable definition of economic growth.

Most people have a general idea of what economic growth means. When a nation grows economically, its citizens must be better off in at least some ways, usually in terms of their material well-being. Typically, though, we do not measure the well-being of any nation solely in terms of its total output of real goods and services or in terms of real GDP without making some adjustments. After all, India has a GDP about three times as large as that of Switzerland. The population in India, though, is about 125 times greater than that of Switzerland. Consequently, we view India as a relatively poor country and Switzerland as a relatively rich country. That means that to measure how much a country is growing in terms of annual increases in real GDP, we have to adjust for population growth. Our formal definition becomes this: **Economic growth** occurs when there are increases in *per capita* real GDP; it is measured by the rate of change in per capita real GDP per year.

Economic growth
Increases in per capita real GDP measured by its rate of change per year.

FIGURE 9-1
Economic Growth
If there is growth between 2000 and 2025, the production possibilities curve for the entire economy will shift outward from the blue line labeled 2000 to the red line labeled 2025. The distance that it shifts represents an increase in the productive capacity of the nation.

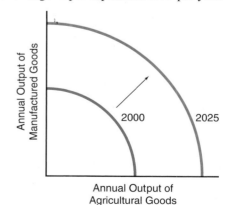

Annual Output of
Manufactured Goods

2000   2025

Annual Output of
Agricultural Goods

FIGURE 9-2

The Historical Record of U.S. Economic Growth

The graph traces per capita real GDP in the United States since 1900. Data are given in 1996 dollars.

Source: U.S. Department of Commerce.

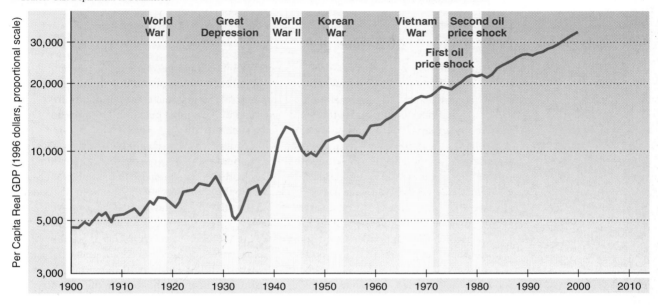

Figure 9-2 presents the historical record of real GDP per person in the United States.

INTERNATIONAL EXAMPLE

Growth Rates Around the World

Table 9-1 shows the annual average rate of growth of income per person in selected countries. Notice that the United States during the time period under study is positioned about midway in the pack. Even though we are one of the world's richest countries, our rate of economic growth through the 1990s was not particularly

TABLE 9-1

Per Capita Growth Rates in Various Countries

Country	Average Annual Rate of Growth of Income Per Capita, 1970–2000 (%)	Country	Average Annual Rate of Growth of Income Per Capita, 1970–2000 (%)
Switzerland	1.9	Italy	2.8
Sweden	2.0	United States	2.9
Germany	2.2	Spain	3.0
United Kingdom	2.3	Japan	3.9
Netherlands	2.4	Turkey	5.6
Canada	2.6	China	7.0
France	2.7		

Sources: World Bank; International Monetary Fund.

high. The reason that U.S. per capita income has remained higher than per capita incomes in most other nations is that the United States has been able to sustain growth over many decades. This is something that most other countries have so far been unable to accomplish.

Problems in Definition

Our definition of economic growth says nothing about the *distribution* of output and income. A nation might grow very rapidly in terms of increases in per capita real output, while at the same time its poor people remain poor or become even poorer. Therefore, in assessing the economic growth record of any nation, we must be careful to pinpoint which income groups have benefited the most from such growth.

Real standards of living can go up without any positive economic growth. This can occur if individuals are, on average, enjoying more leisure by working fewer hours but producing as much as they did before. For example, if per capita real GDP in the United States remained at $30,000 a year for a decade, we could not automatically jump to the conclusion that Americans were, on average, no better off. What if, during that same 10-year period, average hours worked fell from 37 per week to 33 per week? That would mean that during the 10 years under study, individuals in the labor force were "earning" four hours more leisure a week. Actually, nothing so extreme has occurred in this country, but something similar has. Average hours worked per week fell steadily until the 1960s, at which time they leveled off. That means that during much of the history of this country, the increase in per capita real GDP *understated* the actual economic growth that we were experiencing because we were enjoying more and more leisure as time passed.

Is Economic Growth Bad?

Some commentators on our current economic situation believe that the definition of economic growth ignores its negative effects. Some psychologists even contend that we are made worse off because of economic growth. They say that the more we grow, the more "needs" are created so that we feel worse off as we become richer. Our expectations are rising faster than reality, so we presumably always suffer from a sense of disappointment. Clearly, the economist's measurement of economic growth does not take into account the spiritual and cultural aspects of the good life. As with all activities, there are costs and benefits. You can see some of those listed in Table 9-2.

In any event, any measure of economic growth that we use will be imperfect. Nonetheless, the measures that we do have allow us to make comparisons across countries and over time and, if used judiciously, can enable us to gain important insights. Per capita real GDP,

To get the latest figures and estimates on economic growth throughout the world, go to **www.imf.org/external** and click on "Publications." Then click on "World Economic Outlook."

TABLE 9-2
Costs and Benefits of Economic Growth

Benefits	Costs
Reduction in illiteracy	Environmental pollution
Reduction in poverty	Breakdown of the family
Improved health	Isolation and alienation
Longer lives	Urban congestion
Political stability	

used so often, is not always an accurate measure of economic well-being, but it is a serviceable measure of productive activity.

The Importance of Growth Rates

Notice back in Table 9-1 that the growth rates in real per capita income for most countries differ by very little—generally only a few percentage points. You might want to know why such small differences in growth rates are important. What would it matter if we grew at 3 percent rather than at 4 percent per year?

It matters a lot—not for next year or the year after but for the more distant future. The power of *compounding* is impressive. Let's see what happens with three different annual rates of growth: 3 percent, 4 percent, and 5 percent. We start with $1 trillion per year of gross domestic product of the United States at some time in the past. We then compound this $1 trillion, or allow it to grow, into the future at these three different growth rates. The difference is huge. In 50 years, $1 trillion per year becomes $4.38 trillion per year if compounded at 3 percent per year. Just one percentage point more in the growth rate, 4 percent, results in a real GDP of $7.11 trillion per year in 50 years, almost double the previous amount. Two percentage points difference in the growth rate—5 percent per year—results in a real GDP of $11.5 trillion per year in 50 years, or nearly three times as much. Obviously, there is a great difference in the results of economic growth for very small differences in annual growth rates. That is why nations are concerned if the growth rate falls even a little in absolute percentage terms.

Thus when we talk about growth rates, we are basically talking about compounding. In Table 9-3, we show how $1 compounded annually grows at different interest rates. We see in the 3 percent column that $1 in 50 years grows to $4.38. We merely multiplied $1 trillion times 4.38 to get the growth figure in our earlier example. In the 5 percent column, $1 grows to $11.50 after 50 years. Again, we multiplied $1 trillion times 11.50 to get the growth figure for 5 percent in the preceding example.

	Interest Rate						
Number of Years	3%	4%	5%	6%	8%	10%	20%
1	1.03	1.04	1.05	1.06	1.08	1.10	1.20
2	1.06	1.08	1.10	1.12	1.17	1.21	1.44
3	1.09	1.12	1.16	1.19	1.26	1.33	1.73
4	1.13	1.17	1.22	1.26	1.36	1.46	2.07
5	1.16	1.22	1.28	1.34	1.47	1.61	2.49
6	1.19	1.27	1.34	1.41	1.59	1.77	2.99
7	1.23	1.32	1.41	1.50	1.71	1.94	3.58
8	1.27	1.37	1.48	1.59	1.85	2.14	4.30
9	1.30	1.42	1.55	1.68	2.00	2.35	5.16
10	1.34	1.48	1.63	1.79	2.16	2.59	6.19
20	1.81	2.19	2.65	3.20	4.66	6.72	38.30
30	2.43	3.24	4.32	5.74	10.00	17.40	237.00
40	3.26	4.80	7.04	10.30	21.70	45.30	1,470.00
50	4.38	7.11	11.50	18.40	46.90	117.00	9,100.00

TABLE 9-3
One Dollar Compounded Annually at Different Interest Rates
Here we show the value of a dollar at the end of a specified period during which it has been compounded annually at a specified interest rate. For example, if you took $1 today and invested it at 5 percent per year, it would yield $1.05 at the end of one year. At the end of 10 years, it would equal $1.63, and at the end of 50 years, it would equal $11.50.

EXAMPLE

What If the United States Had Grown a Little Bit Less or More Each Year?

In 1870, the per-person real GDP expressed in 2000 dollars was $3,485. That figure had grown to $32,250 by the beginning of 2000. The average economic growth rate was therefore about 1.75 percent per year. What if the U.S. growth rate over the same century and a quarter had been simply 1 percent less—only 0.75 percent per year? Per capita real GDP in 2000 would have been only 30 percent of what it actually was. The United States would have ranked somewhere around thirty-fifth on the scale of per capita income throughout the world. We would have been poorer than Greece or Portugal.

Consider a rosier scenario: What if the U.S. economic rate of growth had been one point higher, or 2.75 percent per year? Today's per capita real GDP would be more than three times its actual value, or about $118,500!

For Critical Analysis

Can you relate this example to anything in your own life? (Hint: Use the compound interest rates in Table 9-3 to make various predictions about your future standard of living.)

CONCEPTS IN BRIEF

- Economic growth can be defined as the increase in real per capita output measured by its rate of change per year.

- The benefits of economic growth are reductions in illiteracy, poverty, and illness and increases in life spans and political stability. The costs of economic growth may include environmental pollution, alienation, and urban congestion.

- Small percentage-point differences in growth rates lead to large differences in real GDP over time. These differences can be seen by examining a compound interest table such as the one in Table 9-3.

PRODUCTIVITY INCREASES: THE HEART OF ECONOMIC GROWTH

Let's say that you are required to type 10 term papers and homework assignments a year. You have a computer; but you do not know how to touch-type. You end up spending an average of two hours per typing job. The next summer, you buy a touch-typing tutorial to use on your computer and spend a few minutes a day improving your typing speed. The following term, you spend only one hour per typing assignment, thereby saving 10 hours a semester. You have become more productive. This concept of productivity relates to your ability (and everyone else's) to produce the same output with fewer labor hours. Thus **labor productivity** is normally measured by dividing the total real domestic output (real GDP) by the number of workers or the number of labor hours. Labor productivity increases whenever average output produced per worker during a specified time period increases. Clearly, there is a relationship between economic growth and increases in labor productivity. If you divide all resources into just capital and labor, economic growth can be defined simply as the cumulative contribution to per capita GDP growth of three components: the rate of growth of capital, the rate of growth of labor, and the rate of growth of capital and labor productivity. If everything else remains constant, improvements in labor productivity ultimately lead to economic growth and higher living standards.

Figure 9-3 traces measured U.S. productivity growth since 1970. Productivity in the manufacturing sector has grown at a steady pace. As we discuss later in this chapter, one

Labor productivity
Total real domestic output (real GDP) divided by the number of workers (output per worker).

For information about the latest trends in U.S. labor productivity, go to **http://stats.bls.gov/ mprhome.htm**, and click on "Multifactor Productivity Trends."

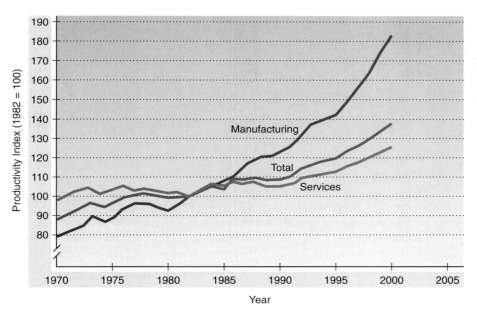

FIGURE 9-3

Nonfarm U.S. Productivity Growth

Whereas productivity in the services sector started increasing only in the early 1980s, productivity in the manufacturing sector has been increasing almost consistently since 1970.

Sources: U.S. Department of Commerce; U.S. Department of Labor, Bureau of Labor Statistics.

by-product of increased productivity in manufacturing has been a relative decline in employment in manufacturing industries. Greater productivity has led to reduced job growth in the manufacturing sector relative to other parts of the economy.

Growth of total productivity, however, has been slowed by stagnant growth in measured productivity in the service sector of the American economy.

Isn't growth in a nation's manufacturing industries the key to growth in jobs and incomes?

No, this is not the case. In fact, information technology (IT) industries are now the biggest creators of jobs in the United States. Key IT employers produce such goods as software, computers, semiconductors, and telecommunications equipment. In recent years, more than one-third of all new American jobs have been in such industries.

EXAMPLE

The Productivity Paradox

In the course of a book review he wrote in 1987, Nobel economist Robert Solow made the offhand comment, "You can seen the computer age everywhere but in the productivity statistics." This comment summed up what has become known as the *productivity paradox*: the seeming lack of productivity gains from information technologies.

The service-sector productivity trend shown in Figure 9-3 illustrates the paradox. Widespread adoption of information technologies in service industries were supposed to allow these industries to reap big efficiency gains. Bar-coding of merchandise was supposed to allow salesclerks at retailers to do their work more efficiently. Financial electronic data interchange was supposed to provide big productivity enhancements in financial services. These productivity gains were slow to emerge—either that, or the data are wrong.

For Critical Analysis

Higher education is a good example of a service industry. College campuses are now full of computers. How would you propose to measure the effect of computers on productivity in higher education?

SAVING: A FUNDAMENTAL DETERMINANT OF ECONOMIC GROWTH

Economic growth does not occur in a vacuum. It is not some predetermined fate of a nation. Rather, economic growth depends on certain fundamental factors. One of the most important factors that affect the rate of economic growth and hence long-term living standards is the rate of saving.

A basic proposition in economics is that if you want more tomorrow, you have to take less today.

To have more consumption in the future, you have to consume less today and save the difference between your consumption and your income.

On a national basis, this implies that higher saving rates eventually mean higher living standards in the long run, all other things held constant. Concern has been growing in America that we are not saving enough, which means that our rate of saving may be too low. Saving is important for economic growth because without saving, we cannot have investment. If all income is consumed each year, there is nothing left over for saving, which could be used by business for investment. If there is no investment in our capital stock, there could be little hope of much economic growth.

The relationship between the rate of savings and per capita real GDP is shown in Figure 9-4. Among the nations with the highest rates of saving are Japan and Germany.

INTERNATIONAL EXAMPLE

Japan and Germany Save and Invest More than the United States, but Does it Matter?

Japan and Germany have saving rates that are more than twice the U.S. rate. As a result, they have accumulated more capital. On a per capita basis, Japan has 22 percent more invested capital than the United States, and Germany has 13 percent more. Nevertheless, the United States creates more wealth per capita than Germany and Japan do. In 2000 dollars, the United States created an estimated $29,950 of new wealth per capita, compared with $23,600 for Japan and $24,750 for Germany.

At least part of the difference results from more efficient use of capital in the United States. Economists estimate that a unit of capital in Germany or Japan generates final output that is about a third lower than that in the United States. In other words, if a $1 million factory produces 1 million units of output per year in the United States, a comparable factory would produce about 670,000 units of output per year in Germany or Japan.

For Critical Analysis
"Americans overconsume, undersave, and underinvest." How do the figures presented here counter this statement?

CONCEPTS IN BRIEF

- ◉ Economic growth is numerically equal to the rate of growth of capital plus the rate of growth of labor plus the rate of growth in the productivity of capital and of labor. Improvements in labor productivity, all other things being equal, lead to greater economic growth and higher living standards.

- ◉ One fundamental determinant of the rate of growth is the rate of saving. To have more consumption in the future, we have to save rather than consume. In general, countries that have had higher rates of saving have had higher rates of growth in real GDP.

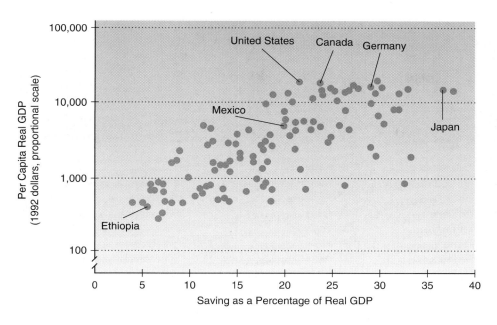

FIGURE 9-4

Relationship Between Rate of Saving and Per Capita Real GDP

This diagram shows the relationship between per capita real GDP and the rate of saving expressed as the average share of annual real GDP saved. The data cover several dozen nations since 1960. Centrally planned economies and major oil-producing countries are not shown.

Source: After Robert Summers and Alan Heston, "A New Set of International Comparisons of Real Product and Price Level," *Review of Income and Wealth,* March 1988.

NEW GROWTH THEORY AND THE DETERMINANTS OF GROWTH

A simple arithmetic definition of economic growth has already been given. The growth rates of capital and labor plus the growth rate of their productivity constitute the rate of economic growth. Economists have had good data on the growth of the physical capital stock in the United States as well as on the labor force. But when you add those two growth rates together, you still do not get the total economic growth rate in the United States. The difference has to be due to improvements in productivity. Economists typically labeled this "improvements in technology," and that was that. More recently, proponents of what is now called the **new growth theory** argue that technology cannot simply be looked at as an outside factor without explanation. Technology must be understood in terms of what drives it. What are the forces that make productivity grow in America and elsewhere?

New growth theory
A theory of economic growth that examines the factors that determine why technology, research, innovation, and the like are undertaken and how they interact.

Growth in Technology

Consider some startling statistics about the growth in technology. Microprocessor speeds may increase from 1,000 megahertz to 5,000 megahertz by the year 2011. By that same year, the size of the thinnest circuit line within a transistor will decrease by 77 percent. The

FAQ *Don't new technologies destroy jobs?*

No, even though numerous "experts" in the media like to paint a gloomy picture of a future in which ordinary working people lose their livelihood to computers. Such claims have been popular since the weaving machine with a single operator replaced the work that 10 people did previously. But of course, the other nine were not unemployed forever. They and their offspring ultimately found new ways to earn a living. Theoretically, there is no limit on labor employment, which depends on the supply of and demand for labor. The demand for labor is not fixed. Workers released from industries that are more productive find work elsewhere, typically in other industries that can expand because of the freed-up resources made available by technological progress. In the end, technological change often *expands* employment opportunities for the nation's workforce.

typical memory capacity (RAM) of computers will jump from 128 megabytes, or about twice the equivalent text in the *Encyclopaedia Britannica,* to 128 gigabytes—a thousand-fold increase.

By 2005, new microchip plants will produce 1,000 transistors a week for every person on earth. Predictions are that computers may become as powerful as the human brain by 2020.

EXAMPLE

Our High-Tech Economy

Four decades ago, one in six American businesses was automotive-related. Today, autos and light trucks account for about 3.5 percent of GDP. So does spending on computers and related equipment. Yet despite the fact that high technology's share has doubled in the past decade, government statisticians still refuse to use chip inventories and personal computer sales as economic indicators. The reason is that the economic welfare created by high-tech industries is much harder to measure than, say, tons of steel or bushels of corn.

For Critical Analysis

When software is distributed at no charge on the Internet, does that contribute to the economy?

Technology: A Separate Factor of Production

We now recognize that technology must be viewed as a separate factor of production that is sensitive to rewards. Otherwise stated, one of the major foundations of new growth theory is this:

The greater the rewards, the more technological advances we will get.

Let's consider several aspects of technology here, the first one being research and development.

Research and Development

A certain amount of technological advance results from research and development (R&D) activities that have as their goal the development of specific new materials, new products, and new machines. How much spending a nation devotes to R&D can have an impact on its long-term economic growth. Part of how much a nation spends depends on what businesses decide is worth spending. That in turn depends on their expected rewards from successful R&D. If your company develops a new way to produce computer memory chips, how much will it be rewarded? The answer depends on whether others can freely copy the new technique.

Patent
A government protection that gives an inventor the exclusive right to make, use, or sell an invention for a limited period of time (currently, 20 years).

Patents.   To protect new techniques developed through R&D, we have a system of **patents,** protections whereby the federal government gives the patent holder the exclusive right to make, use, and sell an invention for a period of 20 years. One can argue that this special position given owners of patents increases expenditures on R&D and therefore adds to long-term economic growth.

Positive Externalities and R&D.   As we discussed in Chapter 5, positive externalities are benefits from an activity that are not enjoyed by the instigator of the activity. In the case of R&D spending, a certain amount of the benefits go to other companies that do not have to pay for them. In particular, according to economists David Coe of the International Monetary Fund and Elhanan Helpman of Tel Aviv University, about a quarter of the global productivity gains of R&D investment in the top seven industrialized countries goes to foreigners. For every 1 percent rise in the stock of research and development in America alone, for example, productivity in the rest of the world increases by about 0.25 percent. One country's R&D expenditures benefit foreigners because foreigners are able to import goods from technologically advanced countries and then use them as inputs in making their own industries more efficient. In addition, countries that import high-tech goods are able to imitate the technology.

The Open Economy and Economic Growth

People who study economic growth today tend to emphasize the importance of the openness of the economy. Free trade encourages a more rapid spread of technology and industrial ideas. Moreover, open economies may experience higher rates of economic growth because their own industries have access to a bigger market. When trade barriers are erected in the form of tariffs and the like, domestic industries become isolated from global technological progress. This occurred for many years in former communist countries and in many developing countries in Latin America and elsewhere. Figure 9-5 shows the relationship between economic growth and the openness as measured by the level of protectionism of a given economy.

Innovation and Knowledge

We tend to think of technological progress as, say, the invention of the transistor. But invention means nothing by itself; **innovation** is required. Innovation involves the transformation of something new, such as an invention, into something that benefits the economy either by lowering production costs or providing new goods and services. Indeed, the new growth theorists believe that real wealth creation comes from innovation and that invention is but a facet of innovation.

Innovation
Transforming an invention into something that is useful to humans.

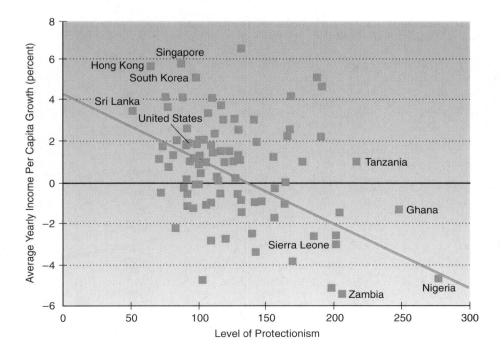

FIGURE 9-5
The Relationship Between Protectionism and Economic Growth
Closed economies are ones in which the government prevents imports from entering the country and sometimes exports from leaving the country. Such protectionism closes off the economy to new technologies. Here you see the relationship between the level of protectionism and economic growth rates measured on a per capita basis. The data seem to indicate that the more closed an economy, the lower its rate of growth, all other things held constant.
Source: Economic Review, Fourth Quarter 1993, p. 3.

Historically, technologies have moved relatively slowly from invention to innovation to widespread use, and the dispersion of new technology remains for the most part slow and uncertain. The inventor of the transistor thought it might be used to make better hearing aids. At the time it was invented, the *New York Times*'s sole reference to it was in a small weekly column called "News of Radio." When the laser was invented, no one really knew what it could be used for. It was initially used to help in navigation, measurement, and chemical research. Today, it is used in the reproduction of music, printing, surgery, and telecommunications. Tomorrow, who knows?

Figure 9-6 shows the process by which raw ideas turn into written ideas that are submitted for study in typical research and development laboratories. Businesses select a few of these for initial study and choose fewer still to evaluate in large research projects. Out of these full-scale research efforts, a few significant developments emerge and are launched as new products. If businesses are lucky, one or two of these product launches may ultimately pay off.

The Importance of Ideas and Knowledge

Economist Paul Romer has added at least one important factor that determines the rate of economic growth. He contends that production and manufacturing knowledge is just as important as the other determinants and perhaps even more so. He considers knowledge a factor of production that, like capital, has to be paid for by forgoing current consumption. Economies must therefore invest in knowledge just as they invest in machines. Because past investment in capital may make it more profitable to acquire more knowledge, there exists the possibility of an investment-knowledge cycle in which investment spurs knowl-

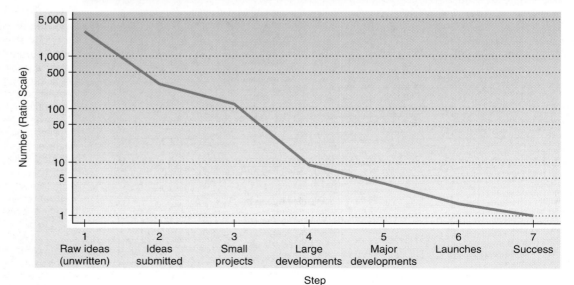

FIGURE 9-6

The Winnowing Process of Research and Development
Only a portion of new ideas are actually submitted for formal study, and just a fraction of these become subjects of research projects. Very few ideas actually lead to the development of new products.

edge and knowledge spurs investment. A once-and-for-all increase in a country's rate of investment may permanently raise that country's growth rate. (According to traditional theory, a once-and-for-all increase in the rate of saving and therefore in the rate of investment simply leads to a new steady-state standard of living but not one that continues to increase.)

Another way of looking at knowledge is that it is a store of ideas. According to Romer, ideas are what drive economic growth. We have become, in fact, an idea economy. Consider Microsoft Corporation. A relatively small percentage of that company's labor force is involved in actually building products. Rather, a majority of Microsoft employees are attempting to discover new ideas that can be translated into computer code that can then be turned into products. The major conclusion that Romer and other new growth theorists draw is this:

Economic growth can continue as long as we keep coming up with new ideas.

EXAMPLE

Catch the Wave—It May Be the Shortest Yet

A major twentieth-century Austrian economist, Joseph Schumpeter, proposed the idea of "creative destruction." Schumpeter argued that a normal, healthy economy was not one that grew along a steady path. It was one that was constantly in a state of disruption because of a dizzying pace of technological innovations.

Inspired by the work of a Russian economist named Nikolai Kondratieff, Schumpeter concluded that industrial revolutions occur in cycles of about 50 to 60 years. Figure 9-7 illustrates the cycles that he had in mind, which are sometimes known as *Kondratieff waves*. In Schumpeter's view, each cycle is fueled by entirely different clusters of industries. Each cluster emerges following a period of fermentation of new technological discoveries and innovations. For instance, a first industrial wave was driven by new technologies for using water power, manufacturing textiles, and building with iron. A second wave developed from innovations in steam power, rail transportation, and the fabrication of steel. The adoption of technologies driven by electricity, chemicals, and the internal-combustion engine started a third wave. By the time Schumpeter died in 1950, a fourth industrial cycle, fueled by innovations in oil and natural gas, electronics, and air travel, had begun.

FIGURE 9-7

Waves of Industrial Revolution

Based on the ideas of Nikolai Kondratieff, the Austrian economist Joseph Schumpeter argued that industrial revolutions occur in waves. Schumpeter argued that four waves have taken place since the 1700s, and the advent of the new information technologies based on digital communications may represent the early years of a fifth wave.

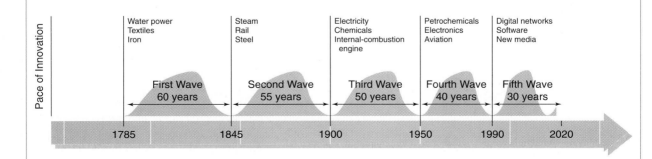

The figure depicts a fifth wave, driven by developments in digital networks, computer software, and new telecommunications technologies that may have begun in the early 1990s.

Economists who subscribe to Schumpeter's views argue that the tools of this new wave—computer analyzers, gene sequencers, Internet shopbots, patent searchers, text parsers, and the like—are getting better all the time. This, they argue, is likely to speed the pace of innovation. Thus the fifth wave could well be even shorter than the 40-year one that preceded it.

For Critical Analysis

New growth theorists like to stake a claim to developing a really "new" idea? Did Schumpeter beat them to the punch?

The Importance of Human Capital

Knowledge, ideas, and productivity are all tied together. One of the threads is the quality of the labor force. Increases in the productivity of the labor force are a function of increases in human capital, the fourth factor of production discussed in Chapter 2. Recall that human capital is the knowledge and skills that people in the workforce acquire through education, on-the-job training, and self-teaching. To increase your own human capital, you have to invest by forgoing income-earning activities while you attend school. Society also has to invest in the form of libraries and teachers. According to the new growth theorists, human capital is at least as important as physical capital, particularly when trying to explain international differences in living standards.

It is therefore not surprising that one of the most effective ways that developing countries can become developed is by investing in secondary schooling.

One can argue that policy changes that increase human capital will lead to more technological improvements. One of the reasons why concerned citizens, policymakers, and politicians are looking for a change in America's schooling system is that our educational system seems to be falling behind that of other countries. This lag is greatest in science and mathematics—precisely the areas that are required for developing better technology.

CONCEPTS IN BRIEF

- ◉ New growth theory argues that the greater the rewards, the more rapid the pace of technology. And greater rewards spur research and development.

- ◉ The openness of a nation's economy seems to correlate with its rate of economic growth.

- ◉ Invention and innovation are not the same thing. Inventions are useless until innovation transforms them into things that people find valuable.

- ◉ According to the new growth economists, economic growth can continue as long as we keep coming up with new ideas.

- ◉ Increases in human capital can lead to greater rates of economic growth. These come about by increased education, on-the-job training, and self-teaching.

POPULATION AND IMMIGRATION AS THEY AFFECT ECONOMIC GROWTH

There are several ways to view population growth as it affects economic growth. On the one hand, population growth means an increase in the amount of labor, which is one component of economic growth. On the other hand, population growth can be seen as a drain on the economy because for any given amount of GDP, more population means lower per capita GDP. According to MIT economist Michael Kremer, the first view is historically correct. His conclusion is that population growth drives technological progress, which then increases economic growth. The theory is simple: If there are 50 percent more people in the United States, there will be 50 percent more geniuses. And with 50 percent more people, the rewards for creativity are commensurately greater. Otherwise stated, the larger the potential market, the greater the incentive to become ingenious.

Does the same argument apply to immigration? Yes, according to the late economist Julian Simon, who pointed out that "every time our system allows in one more immigrant, on average, the economic welfare of American citizens goes up. . . . Additional immigrants, both the legal and the illegal, raise the standard of living of U.S. natives and have little or no negative impact on any occupational or income class." He further argued that immigrants do not displace natives from jobs but rather create jobs through their purchases and by starting new businesses. Immigrants' earning and spending simply expand the economy.

Not all researchers agree with Simon, and few studies exist to test the theories advanced here. The area is currently the focus of much research.

PROPERTY RIGHTS AND ENTREPRENEURSHIP

If you were in a country where bank accounts and businesses were periodically expropriated by the government, how willing would you be to leave your money in a savings account or to invest in a business? Certainly you would be less willing than if such things never occurred. In general, the more certain private property rights are, the more capital accumulation there will be. People will be willing to invest their savings in endeavors that will increase their wealth in future years. They have property rights in their wealth that are sanctioned and enforced by the government. In fact, some economic historians have attempted to show that it was the development of well-defined private property rights that allowed Western Europe to increase its growth rate after many centuries of stagnation. The ability and certainty with which they can reap the gains from investing also determine the extent to which business owners in other countries will invest capital in developing countries. The threat of nationalization that hangs over some developing nations probably prevents the massive amount of foreign investment that might be necessary to allow these nations to develop more rapidly.

The property rights, or legal structure, in a nation are closely tied to the degree with which individuals use their own entrepreneurial skills. In Chapter 2, we identified entrepreneurship as the fifth factor of production. Entrepreneurs are the risk takers who seek out new ways to do things and create new products. To the extent that entrepreneurs are allowed to capture the rewards from their entrepreneurial activities, they will seek to engage in those activities. In countries where such rewards cannot be captured because of a lack of property rights, there will be less entrepreneurship. Typically, this results in fewer investments and a lower rate of growth.

CONCEPTS IN BRIEF

● While some economists argue that population growth stifles economic growth, others contend that the opposite is true. The latter economists consequently believe that immigration should be encouraged rather than discouraged.

● Well-defined and protected property rights are important for fostering entrepreneurship. In the absence of well-defined property rights, individuals have less incentive to take risks, and economic growth rates suffer.

ECONOMIC DEVELOPMENT

Development economics
The study of factors that contribute to the economic development of a country.

How did developed countries travel paths of growth from extreme poverty to relative riches? That is the essential issue of **development economics,** which is the study of why some countries grow and develop and others do not and of policies that might help developing economies get richer. It is not enough simply to say that people in different countries are different and therefore that is why some countries are rich and some countries are poor. Economists do not deny that different cultures create different work ethics, but they are unwilling to accept such a pat and fatalistic answer.

Look at any world map. About four-fifths of the countries you will see on the map are considered relatively poor. The goal of economists who study development is to help the more than 4 billion today with low living standards join the 2 billion people who have at least moderately high living standards.

Putting World Poverty into Perspective

Most Americans cannot even begin to understand the reality of poverty in the world today. At least one-half, if not two-thirds, of the world's population lives at subsistence level, with just enough to eat for survival. Indeed, the World Bank estimates that nearly 30 percent of the world's people live on less than $1 per day. The official poverty line in the United States is set beyond the average income of at least half the human beings on the planet. This is not to say that we should ignore domestic problems with the poor and homeless simply because they are living better than many people elsewhere in the world. Rather, it is necessary for Americans to maintain an appropriate perspective on what are considered problems for this country relative to what are considered problems elsewhere.

The Relationship Between Population Growth and Economic Development

World population is growing at the rate of 2.8 people a second. That amounts to 242,000 a day or 88.3 million a year. Today, there are just over 6 billion people on earth. By 2030, according to the United Nations, there will be 8.5 billion. Panel (a) of Figure 9-8 shows which countries are growing the most. Panel (b) emphasizes an implication of panel (a), which is that virtually all the growth in population is occurring in developing nations. Some countries, such as Germany, are expected to lose population over the next several decades.

Ever since the Reverend Thomas Robert Malthus wrote his essay *An Essay on the Principle of Population* in 1798, excessive population growth has been a concern. Modern-day Malthusians are able to generate just as much enthusiasm for the concept that population growth is bad. Over and over, media pundits and a number of scientists tell us that rapid population growth threatens economic development and the quality of life.

Nevertheless, Malthus's prediction that population would outstrip food supplies has never held true, according to economist Nicholas Eberstadt of the Harvard Center for Population Studies. As the world's population has grown, so has the world's food supply, measured by calories per person. Furthermore, the price of food, corrected for inflation, has been falling steadily for more than a century. That means that the supply of food has been expanding faster than the rise in demand caused by increased population.

Furthermore, economists have found that as nations become richer, average family size declines. Otherwise stated, the more economic development occurs, the slower the population growth rate becomes. Predictions of birthrates in developing countries have often turned out to be overstated if those countries experience rapid economic growth. This was

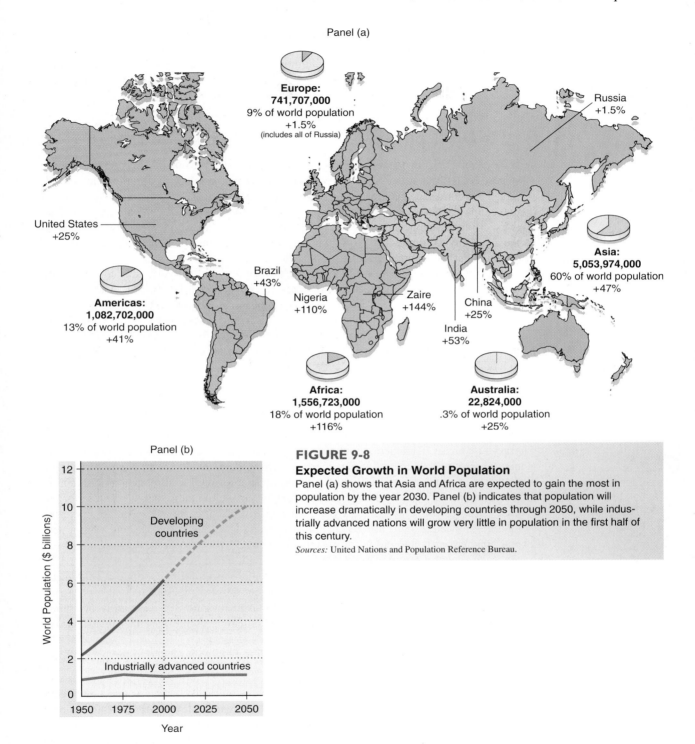

Panel (a)

Europe:
741,707,000
9% of world population
+1.5%
(includes all of Russia)

Russia
+1.5%

United States
+25%

Asia:
5,053,974,000
60% of world population
+47%

Brazil
+43%

Nigeria
+110%

Zaire
+144%

China
+25%

India
+53%

Americas:
1,082,702,000
13% of world population
+41%

Africa:
1,556,723,000
18% of world population
+116%

Australia:
22,824,000
.3% of world population
+25%

Panel (b)

Developing
countries

Industrially advanced countries

World Population ($ billions)

Year

FIGURE 9-8

Expected Growth in World Population

Panel (a) shows that Asia and Africa are expected to gain the most in population by the year 2030. Panel (b) indicates that population will increase dramatically in developing countries through 2050, while industrially advanced nations will grow very little in population in the first half of this century.

Sources: United Nations and Population Reference Bureau.

the case in Hong Kong, Mexico, Taiwan, and Colombia. Recent research on population and economic development has revealed that social and economic modernization has been accompanied by what might be called a fertility revolution—the spread of deliberate family size limitation within marriage and a decline in childbearing. Modernization reduces infant mortality, which in turn reduces the incentive for couples to have many children to make sure that a certain number survive to adulthood. Modernization also lowers the demand for children for a variety of reasons, not the least being that couples in more developed countries do not need to rely on their children to take care of them in old age.

The Stages of Development: Agriculture to Industry to Services

If we analyze the development of modern rich nations, we find that they went through three stages. First is the agricultural stage, when most of the population is involved in agriculture. Then comes the manufacturing stage, when much of the population becomes involved in the industrialized sector of the economy. And finally there is a shift toward services. That is exactly what happened in the United States: The so-called tertiary, or service, sector of the economy continues to grow, whereas the manufacturing sector (and its share of employment) is declining in relative importance.

It is important to understand, however, the requirement for early specialization in a nation's comparative advantage (see Chapter 2). The doctrine of comparative advantage is particularly appropriate for the developing countries of the world. If trading is allowed among nations, a country is normally best off if it produces what it has a comparative advantage in producing and imports the rest (for more details, see Chapter 32). This means that many developing countries should continue to specialize in agricultural production or in labor-intensive manufactured goods.

Keys to Economic Development

One theory of development states that for a country to develop, it must have a large natural resource base. This theory continues to assert that much of the world is running out of natural resources, thereby limiting economic growth and development. We must point out that only the narrowest definition of a natural resource could lead to such an opinion. In broader terms, a natural resource is something occurring in nature that we can use for our own purposes. As emphasized by the new growth theory, natural resources therefore include knowledge of the use of something. The natural resources that we could define several hundred years ago did not, for example, include hydroelectric power—no one knew that such a natural resource existed or how to bring it into existence.

Natural resources by themselves are not particularly useful for economic development, as demonstrated by Japan's extensive development despite a lack of naturally occurring crude oil and by Brazil's slow pace of development in spite of a vast array of natural resources. Resources must be transformed into something usable for either investment or consumption.

Economists have found that four factors seem to be highly related to the pace of economic development:

1. *An educated population.* Both theoretically and empirically, we know that a more educated workforce aids economic development because it allows individuals to build on the ideas of others. According to economists David Gould and Roy Ruffin, increasing the rate of enrollment in secondary schools by only 2 percentage points, from 8 percent to 10 percent, raises the average rate of economic growth by half a percent per year. Thus we must conclude that developing countries can advance more rapidly if they

To contemplate whether there may be a relationship between inequality and a nation's growth, visit the home page of the World Bank's Thematic Group on Inequality, Poverty, and Socioeconomic Performance at **www.worldbank.org/poverty/inequal/tgindex.htm**.

invest more heavily in secondary education. Or stated in the negative, economic development cannot be sustained if a nation allows a sizable portion of its population to avoid education. After all, education allows young people who grew up poor to acquire skills that enable them to avoid poverty as adults.

2. *Establishing a system of property rights.* As noted, if you were in a country in which bank accounts and businesses were periodically expropriated by the government, you would be reluctant to leave your money in a savings account or to invest in a business. Expropriation of private property rarely takes place in developed countries. It has occurred in numerous developing countries, however. For example, private property was once nationalized in Chile and largely still is in Cuba. Economists have found that, other things being equal, the more certain private property rights are, the more private capital accumulation and economic growth there will be.

3. *Letting "creative destruction" run its course.* As discussed earlier, Harvard economist Joseph Schumpeter championed the concept of "creative destruction," through which new businesses ultimately create new jobs and economic growth after first destroying old jobs, old companies, and old industries. Such change is painful and costly, but it is necessary for economic advancement. Nowhere is this more important than in developing countries, where the principle is often ignored. Many developing nations have had a history of supporting current companies and industries by discouraging new technologies and new companies from entering the marketplace. The process of creative destruction has not been allowed to work its magic in these countries.

4. *Limiting protectionism.* Open economies experience faster economic development than economies closed to international trade. Trade encourages individuals and businesses to discover ways to specialize so that they can become more productive and earn higher incomes. Increased productivity and subsequent increases in economic growth are the results. Thus the less government protects the domestic economy by imposing trade barriers, the faster that economy will experience economic development. According to a study by economists Nouriel Roubini and Xavier Sala-i-Martin, when a country goes from being relatively open to relatively closed via government-enacted trade barriers, it will have a 2.5 percentage-point decrease in its annual rate of economic growth.

CONCEPTS IN BRIEF

- Although many people believe that population growth hinders economic development, there is little evidence to support that notion. What is clear is that economic development tends to lead to a reduction in the rate of population growth.

- Historically, there are three stages of economic development: the agricultural stage, the manufacturing stage, and the service-sector stage, when a large part of the workforce is employed in providing services.

- Although one theory of economic development holds that a sizable natural resource base is the key to a nation's development, this fails to account for the importance of the human element: The labor force must be capable of using a country's natural resources.

- Fundamental factors contributing to the pace of economic development are training and education, a well-defined system of property rights, allowing new generations of companies and industries to replace older generations, and promoting an open economy by allowing international trade.

NETNOMICS

Direct Effects of Information Technology on Growth of Real Output: Computer Production

Some economists think that the solution to the "productivity paradox"—the seemingly slow response of productivity growth to computerization—is that we do a poor job of measuring the contribution of information technology to the economy's overall productivity. There is one growth effect of the computerization revolution that is relatively straightforward to measure, however. That is the direct impact of computer production on economic growth.

Fairly widespread use of the Internet for electronic mail began in 1993, and initial forays by companies into Internet commerce started shortly thereafter. As people started to learn about how much they could do on the Internet, they rapidly began to acquire computers. As you can see in the last line of Table 9-4, computer production then increased dramatically thereafter.

The Bureau of Economic Analysis (BEA), a unit of the Department of Commerce, has developed a way to track the effect of computers on the growth of aggregate real production in the U.S. economy. You can see how they do this in Table 9-4. The first line of the table shows annual growth rates for real GDP. The second line displays growth rates for real GDP *excluding* the production of computer components in all the various aspects of computing real GDP—for instance, in calculations of producers' durable equipment, personal consumption expenditures, and government spending.

The third line of the table gives the difference between the first and second lines. This difference is the BEA's estimate of the contribution of computer production to the growth of real GDP. As you can see, before Internet use became widespread in the mid-1990s, computers added no more than one- to two-tenths to the measured growth of real GDP. Now, however, computers have a direct growth effect—not taking into account indirect effects through changes in productivity of labor and capital—of close to one-half percentage point per year.

TABLE 9-4

Real GDP, Final Sales of Computers, and GDP less Final Sales of Computers: Percent Change from Preceding Year

	1989	1990	1991	1992	1993	1994	1995	1996	1997	1998	1999	2000*
Real GDP growth	3.5	1.8	−0.5	3.0	2.7	4.0	2.7	3.6	4.2	4.3	4.2	4.0
Real GDP growth less growth in final sales of computers	3.4	1.7	−0.6	2.9	2.5	3.9	2.3	3.2	3.9	3.9	3.8	3.5
Difference in growth rates	.1	.1	.1	.1	.2	.1	.4	.4	.3	.4	.4	.5
Growth in real final sales of computers, total	56.8	52.3	52.6	54.8	54.8	57.6	70.4	78.2	83.2	92.1	97.9	99.8

Sources: U.S. Department of Commerce, Bureau of Economic Analysis; author's estimates.

ISSUES & APPLICATIONS

What Explains the Productivity Paradox?

For several years running, the acquisition of computers, telecommunications equipment, and other information technologies has been the main type of capital investment undertaken by U.S. businesses. Owners and managers anticipated big cost savings and revenue enhancements to result. Economists also anticipated higher productivity of labor and capital—and thus increased economic growth.

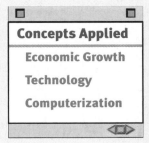

Concepts Applied

Economic Growth

Technology

Computerization

Looking at the Past

Take a look, however, at panel (a) of Figure 9-9 (p. 216). This chart traces movements in an overall index of the productivity of labor and capital since 1870. Two features of this chart are striking. One is the big upswing in the growth of overall productivity between the early 1930s and the mid-1970s. Another is the apparent lack of productivity growth since the late 1970s. This is the productivity paradox we noted earlier: So far, the widespread adoption of information technologies has not measurably increased productivity growth.

Accounting for the Productivity Paradox

What happened to the big productivity enhancements that the computer revolution was supposed to deliver? One possibility is that they are not there because computers have failed to provide the benefits that nearly everyone had expected. Some economists, for example, argue that in spite of all the recent investment in computers, they are still such a small portion of the aggregate capital stock that they are unlikely ever to be an important source of economic growth.

Another possibility is that other factors—perhaps weaker American public schools and diminished growth of human capital, as some analysts have argued—have tended to reduce overall productivity even as computers have added to it. Overall productivity therefore has remained flat.

A third possibility is that measures of overall productivity are wrong. Many economists have contended for years that current measures of the output of service industries understate the actual output rates of these industries, which include banks, insurance companies, brokerage firms, and other heavy users of new computer technologies. In spite of efforts to better measure service productivity in 1999, economists find that the U.S. banking industry is roughly half as productive as it was in the 1970s—yet no economist really believes this is so. As you can see in panel (b), the relative importance of service industries as employers has increased steadily since the 1960s. This means that the importance of productivity measurement difficulties in service industries are increasingly affecting aggregate productivity numbers. Look back at Figure 9-3. There you see that much slower measured growth of service productivity has pulled down the measure of total productivity in recent years.

There is a fourth possibility. Note in panel (a) of the figure that overall productivity in the U.S. economy remained relatively flat for some time after telephones, typewriters, electric lights, and automobiles came into use. Paul David of Stanford University suggests that we may have been witnessing a similar lag in the response of productivity to the inventions and innovations we have recently experienced. If he is right, U.S. productivity may jump to significantly higher levels in the future.

FIGURE 9-9

Productivity Growth and the Increasing Importance of Services

Panel (a) shows that following a period of heightened productivity growth from the 1930s through the early 1970s, overall productivity leveled off before increasing again in recent years. One possible explanation for the flattening of overall productivity growth is the upsurge in the production of services relative to total U.S. output depicted in panel (b). Measured service productivity growth has been weak relative to growth of manufacturing productivity.

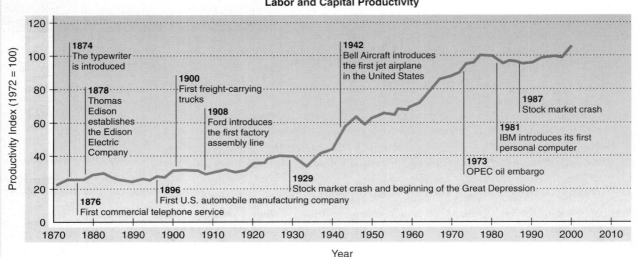

Panel (a)
Labor and Capital Productivity

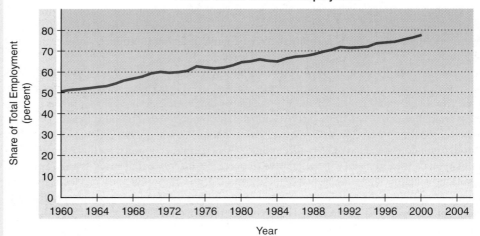

Panel (b)
Private-Sector Services Employment

FOR CRITICAL ANALYSIS

1. What might account for a lagged response of productivity growth to new innovations?

2. A good example of a service industry is higher education. How would you propose to measure the output and productivity of higher education?

SUMMARY DISCUSSION OF LEARNING OBJECTIVES

1. **Economic growth:** The rate of economic growth is the annual rate of change in per capita real GDP. This measure of the growth of a nation's economy takes into account both its growth in overall production of goods and services and its population. It is an average measure that does not account for possible changes in the distribution of income or various welfare costs or benefits that may accompany growth of the economy.

2. **Why Economic Growth Rates Are Important:** Over long intervals, relatively small differences in the rate of economic growth can accumulate to produce large disparities in per capita incomes. The reason is that, like accumulations of interest, economic growth compounds over time. Thus a nation that experiences per capita income growth of 3 percent per year has a level of per capita income that is more than four times higher after 50 years, but a country with a per capita income growth rate of 4 percent per year ends up with a per capita income level more than seven times higher.

3. **The Key Determinants of Economic Growth:** The fundamental factors contributing to economic growth are growth in a nation's pool of labor, growth of its capital stock, and growth in the productivity of its capital and labor. A key determinant of capital accumulation is a nation's saving rate. Higher saving rates contribute to greater investment and hence increased capital accumulation and economic growth.

4. **Why Productivity Increases Are Crucial for Maintaining Economic Growth:** For a nation with a relatively stable population and a steady rate of capital accumulation, productivity growth emerges as the main factor influencing near-term changes in economic growth. Relatively slow measured growth of productivity in U.S. service industries during the past couple of decades appears to have contributed to relatively slow growth in overall U.S. productivity.

5. **New Growth Theory:** This is a relatively recent theory that examines why individuals and businesses conduct research into inventing and developing new technologies and how this process interacts with the rate of economic growth. This theory emphasizes how rewards to technological innovation contribute to higher economic growth rates. A key implication of the theory is that ideas and knowledge are crucial elements of the growth process.

6. **Fundamental Factors That Contribute to a Nation's Economic Development:** The key characteristics shared by nations that succeed in attaining higher levels of economic development are significant opportunities for their residents to obtain training and education, protection of property rights, policies that permit new companies and industries to replace older ones, and avoiding protectionist barriers that hinder international trade.

Key Terms and Concepts

Development economics (210)	Innovation (205)	New growth theory (203)
Economic growth (196)	Labor productivity (200)	Patent (204)

Problems

Answers to the odd-numbered problems appear at the back of the book.

9-1. The graph shows a production possibilities curve for 2003 and two potential production possibilities curves for 2004, denoted 2004_A and 2004_B.

    a. Which of the labeled points corresponds to maximum feasible 2003 production that is more likely to be associated with the curve denoted 2004_A?

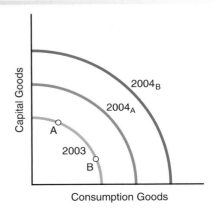

b. Which of the labeled points corresponds to maximum feasible 2003 production that is more likely to be associated with the curve denoted 2004$_B$?

9-2. Consider the following table displaying annual growth rates for nations X, Y, and Z, each of which entered 1999 with real per capita GDP equal to $20,000:

	Annual Growth Rate (%)			
Country	1999	2000	2001	2002
X	7	3	3	4
Y	4	5	7	9
Z	5	4	3	2

a. Which nation was most likely to have suffered a sizable 1999 earthquake that destroyed a significant portion of its stock of capital goods? What is this nation's per capita real GDP at the end of 2002, rounded to the nearest dollar?

b. Which nation was most likely to have adopted policies in 1999 that encouraged a gradual shift in production from capital goods to consumption goods? What is this nation's per capita real GDP at the end of 2002, rounded to the nearest dollar?

c. Which nation was most likely to have adopted policies in 1999 that encouraged a gradual shift in production from consumption goods to capital goods? What is this nation's per capita real GDP at the end of 2002, rounded to the nearest dollar?

9-3. Per capita real GDP in country F grows at a rate of 3 percent and in country G at a rate of 6 percent. Both begin with equal levels of per capita real GDP. Use Table 9-3 to determine how much higher per capita real GDP will be in country G after 20 years. How much higher will real GDP be in country G after 40 years?

9-4. Per capita real GDP in country L is three times as high as in country M. The economic growth rate in country M, however, is 8 percent, while country L's economy grows at a rate of 5 percent. Use Table 9-3 to determine approximately how many years it will be before per capita real GDP in country M surpasses per capita real GDP in country L?

9-5. Per capita real GDP in country S is only half as great as per capita real GDP in country T. Country T's rate of economic growth is 4 percent. The government of country S, however, enacts policies that achieve a growth rate of 20 percent. Use Table 9-3 to determine how long country S must maintain this growth rate before its per capita real GDP surpasses that of country T.

9-6. In 2001, a nation's population was 10 million. Its nominal GDP was $40 billion, and its price index was 100. In 2002, its population had increased to 12 million. Its nominal GDP had risen to $57.6 billion, and its price index had increased to 120. What was this nation's economic growth rate during the year?

9-7. Between the start of 2001 and the start of 2002, a country's economic growth rate was 4 percent. Its population did not change during the year, nor did its price level. What was the rate of increase of the country's nominal GDP during this one-year interval?

9-8. A nation's government determines that a 5 percent increase in its human capital generates a 3 percent increase in per capita real GDP in the same year. Initially, per capital real GDP in this nation was $10,000. The government launches an "education initiative" that causes its human capital level to rise by 5 percent per year for three years. Other things being equal, what is per capita real GDP in this nation three years hence, rounded to the nearest hundred dollars?

Economics on the Net

Multifactor Productivity and Its Growth Growth in productivity is a key factor determining a nation's overall economic growth. This application helps you perform your own evaluation of the factors contributing to U.S. growth.

Internet URL:
http://stats.bls.gov/news.release/prod3.toc.htm

Title: Bureau of Labor Statistics: Multifactor Productivity Trends

Navigation: Begin at the multifactor productivity homepage of the Bureau of Labor Statistics (http://stats.bls.gov/mprhome.htm). Then click on Multifactor Productivity Trends.

Application Read the summary and answer following questions.

1. What does multifactor productivity measure? Based on your reading of this chapter, how does multifactor productivity relate to the determination of economic growth?

2. Click on Manufacturing Industries: Multifactor Productivity Trends. According to these data, which industries have exhibited the greatest productivity growth in recent years? Which industries have shown the least productivity growth?

For Group Study and Analysis Divide the class into three groups to examine multifactor productivity data for the private business sector, the private nonfarm business sector, and the manufacturing sector. (Be sure to tell the groups to read the Sources and Footnotes discussion following the multifactor productivity tables so that they will know how the sectors are defined.) Have each group identify periods when multifactor productivity growth was particularly fast or slow. Then compare notes. Does it appear to make a big difference which sector one looks at when evaluating periods of largest and smallest growth in multifactor productivity?

Case Background

Web Capital, Inc., is an Internet service provider (ISP). Its owners and managers have launched an effort to develop a worldwide clientele. Currently, Web Capital's managers are focusing their attention on the People's Republic of China.

Evaluating the Chinese Environment As early as 1981, reformers within the Chinese government had pushed for expanding the nation's telecommunications network as part of an overall effort to modernize the national economy. Nevertheless, during the following decade, the nation's investment in its information technology infrastructure was meager by the standards of developing nations. Furthermore, the nation experienced rising inflation that by 1994 was in excess of 24 percent per year. The central government began to worry that it had no effective means for controlling an overheating economy that it perceived as prone to rapid booms followed by hard-to-predict busts.

By late 1994, both reformers and hard-liners in the Chinese leadership had reached a consensus that creation of a modern information technology infrastructure was a desirable objective. In 1998, China launched a major effort to develop an Internet of its own, and it sought to link businesses and, ultimately, consumers within a centralized telecommunications network. Current estimates indicate that as many as 75 million Chinese people could have access to Web-connected computers by 2003.

The Management Issue at Web Capital Web Capital is exploring the potential for the company to negotiate a contract to become one of two or three primary providers of Internet service for this emerging Chinese network.

Following a meeting with top government telecommunications officials, a review committee comprised of mid-level managers identified the following key factors that senior officers should contemplate before making a final decision about whether the company should enter into the contract:

1. In the current working draft of the contract, the Chinese government requires Web Capital to commit to a specific, sizable investment measured in current-year quantities of yuan, the Chinese currency. It cannot invest more or less.

2. Initially, the contract grants Web Capital the right to market its services to up to 2 million households in a specific geographic region. How quickly the potential for new ISP subscribers in this region might grow during the following years will largely depend on the economy's growth.

3. Actual company sales of Internet access services will depend on a number of factors, including the hours of employment and the average hourly wages earned by Chinese households during the term of the contract.

4. There is some evidence that structural, seasonal, and frictional unemployment have trended downward throughout China in recent years.

5. There is considerable evidence that per capita income growth in China is far from equally spread across Chinese households.

1. What are the near-term risks that Web Capital is likely to face if it makes a significant investment in China?

2. Looking into the longer term, are there reasons to be optimistic about China's overall growth and, by implication, growth in the market for ISP services in China? Are there reasons to be pessimistic? Be as specific as you can.

3. Web Capital has determined that successful market penetration in China will require a minimal real capital investment that is very close to the amount the contract specifies. Although China's annual inflation rate has been below 3 percent since 1997, the average rate of increase in consumer prices was 16 percent per year between 1993 and 1996, and inflation has picked up in recent quarters. Given the current terms of the contract, is this a legitimate area of concern for Web Capital's management?

4. In what ways does the recent experience with high growth rates in per capita incomes make the terms of the contract look more advantageous for Web Capital? In what ways do the terms look less advantageous? Why?

5. Based on experiences in North America, Europe, and South America, Web Capital has learned that high- and middle-income individuals are most likely to be willing to include ISP fees in their monthly household budgets. Should this raise any management concerns with respect to a potential investment in China?

1. Is there really evidence of a boom-and-bust cycle in China? To investigate this issue, go to the International Monetary Fund's home page at **www.imf.org,** and click on "Publications." In the right-hand column, click on "World Economic Outlook." At this site, you can download the final file of this report.
   a. Look at Table 6, titled "Developing Countries—by Country: Real GDP." Has China's economy experienced a recession during the past decade?
   b. Now examine Table 12, titled "Developing Countries—by Country: Consumer Prices." Has China's inflation rate been volatile during the past decade?
   c. Based on your answers to parts (a) and (b), has nominal GDP been volatile during the past decade?

2. The World Bank has funded projects intended to support increased economic growth in rural parts of China. You can read about one of these projects at **www.worldbank.org/html/ extdr/extme/1349.htm.**
   a. Based on this article, in what ways might World Bank loans assist in improving China's economic growth?
   b. Can you see any way that World Bank loans to China could, under some circumstances, actually hinder China's growth prospects?

Part 3
National Income Determination and Fiscal Policy

REAL GDP AND THE PRICE LEVEL IN THE LONG RUN

What goes on inside the Federal Reserve building is a mystery to many. But the policymakers inside can and do influence various aspects of our economy. Why should the Fed be concerned about such things as the long-run equilibrium price level?

In January 1989, a *New York Times* feature article focused on a "new theory" that Federal Reserve economists had developed, known as the *P** model. The theory's aim was to identify a price level consistent with the economy's long-run growth path. The idea was that if the Fed could identify this price level, called *P**, it could adjust the quantity of money in circulation appropriately to achieve long-run price stability and essentially eliminate inflation. Other economists chuckled when they read about this so-called new theory because they knew something the article's author apparently didn't—that the thinking behind the *P** model had been around for a long, long time. Nevertheless, research to identify *P** continues. By the time you complete your study of this chapter, you will understand the basis of the *P** model. It will also be clear why economists today remain interested in its implications.

LEARNING OBJECTIVES

After reading this chapter, you should be able to:

1. Understand the concept of long-run aggregate supply

2. Describe the effect of economic growth on the long-run aggregate supply curve

3. Explain why the aggregate demand curve slopes downward and list key factors that cause this curve to shift

4. Discuss the meaning of long-run equilibrium for the economy as a whole

5. Evaluate why economic growth can cause deflation

6. Evaluate likely reasons for persistent inflation in recent decades

Did You Know That... the children's classic *The Wonderful Wizard of Oz,* written in 1900 by L. Frank Baum, was also an allegory about how a nation should achieve long-run price stability? According to economist Hugh Rockoff of Rutgers University, Baum's book was intended to support the populist political movement that arose in the 1890s. The economic issue of central concern to the populists was widespread *deflation*. The U.S. price level had generally declined since the end of the Civil War, and from time to time unexpected drops in prices greatly disrupted the lives of farmers, shopkeepers, and workers in the Midwest and West. According to Rockoff, the small-minded Munchkins that Dorothy meets after a tornado transports her to the Land of Oz probably symbolize inhabitants of eastern states whom Baum perceived as insensitive to the plight of informally educated but commonsensical western farmers (symbolized by the Scarecrow) and urban workers in danger of losing their hearts and souls (symbolized by the Tin Man). The city inhabited by the Wizard of Oz, the Emerald City (symbolic of Washington, D.C.) is green—the color of money. The same is true of the Wizard's home, the Emerald Palace (representing the White House). Before Dorothy and her friends enter the Emerald City, however, they must put on green-colored glasses held together with gold buckles, symbolizing the U.S. government's forcing westerners to use money supported only by gold. The populists believed that the way to halt the nation's persistent and variable deflation was to expand the quantity of money in circulation by basing money's value on silver as well as gold. For this reason, in Baum's book the slippers that help Dorothy get back to Kansas are made of silver (the writers of the 1939 movie version of the book changed these to ruby slippers). Rockoff speculates that the Cowardly Lion represents William Jennings Bryan, the "roaring orator" and presidential candidate who decried gold but then retreated—in a way that Baum evidently found cowardly—for political reasons. Oz, of course, is the abbreviation for ounces, in which gold is measured, and the yellow brick road is paved with bars of gold.

Why did the United States experience persistent deflation during the latter part of the nineteenth century? Did the populists and their literary supporter, L. Frank Baum, have a legitimate point in arguing that the United States ought to expand the quantity of money in circulation to halt deflation? To answer these questions, you must learn about the factors that influence the long-run stability of the price level.

OUTPUT GROWTH AND THE LONG-RUN AGGREGATE SUPPLY CURVE

In Chapter 2, we showed the derivation of the production possibilities curve. At any point in time, the economy can be inside or on the PPC but never outside it. Along the PPC, a country's resources are fully employed in the production of goods and services, and the sum total of all goods and services produced is the nation's real output, or real GDP. Economists refer to the total of all planned production for the entire economy as the **aggregate supply** of real output.

Aggregate supply
The total of all planned production for the economy.

The Long-Run Aggregate Supply Curve

Put yourself in a world in which nothing has been changing, year in and year out. The price level has not changed. Technology has not changed. The prices of inputs that firms must purchase have not changed. Labor productivity has not changed. All resources are fully employed, so the economy operates on its production possibilities curve, such as the one

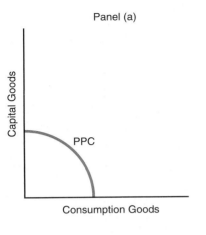

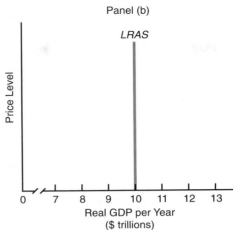

FIGURE 10-1

The Production Possibilities and the Economy's Long-Run Aggregate Supply Curve

At a point in time, a nation's base of resources and its technological capabilities define the position of its production possibilities curve, as shown in panel (a). This defines the real GDP that the nation can produce when resources are fully employed, which determines the position of the long-run aggregate supply curve (*LRAS*) displayed in panel (b). Because people have complete information and input prices adjust fully to changes in output prices in the long run, the *LRAS* is vertical.

depicted in panel (a) of Figure 10-1. This is a world that is fully adjusted and in which people have all the information they are ever going to get about that world. The **long-run aggregate supply curve** (*LRAS*) in this world is some amount of output of real goods and services—say, $10 trillion of real GDP. We can show long-run aggregate supply simply by a vertical line at $10 trillion of real GDP. This is what you see in panel (b) of the figure. That curve, labeled *LRAS,* is a vertical line determined by technology and **endowments,** or resources that exist in our economy. It is the full-information and full-adjustment level of real output of goods and services. It is the level of real output that will continue being produced year after year, forever, if nothing changes.

Another way of viewing the *LRAS* is to think of it as the full-employment level of real GDP. When the economy reaches full employment along its production possibilities curve, no further adjustments will occur unless a change occurs in the other variables that we are assuming constant and stable. Some economists like to think of the *LRAS* as occurring at the level of real GDP consistent with the natural rate of unemployment, the unemployment rate that occurs in an economy with full adjustment in the long run. As we discussed in Chapter 7, many economists like to think of the natural rate of unemployment as consisting of frictional and structural unemployment.

To understand why the long-run aggregate supply curve is vertical, think about the long run, which is a sufficiently long period that all factors of production and prices, including wages and other input prices, can change. A change in the level of prices of goods and services has no effect on real output (real GDP per year) in the long run, because higher output prices will be accompanied by comparable changes in input prices. Suppliers will therefore have no incentive to increase or decrease output. Remember that in the long run, everybody has full information, and there is full adjustment to price level changes.

Long-run aggregate supply curve
A vertical line representing real output of goods and services after full adjustment has occurred. Can also be viewed as representing the real output of the economy under conditions of full employment—the full-employment level of real GDP.

Endowments
The various resources in an economy, including both physical resources and such human resources as ingenuity and management skills.

To find out how fast one key input price—wages—are adjusting, go to **http://stats.bls.gov**, and then click on "Data," followed by "Most Requested Series" and then "Employment Cost Index."

Economic Growth and Long-Run Aggregate Supply

In Chapter 9, you learned about the factors that determine growth in per capita output: the annual growth rate of labor, the rate of year-to-year capital accumulation, and the rate of growth of the productivity of labor and capital. As time goes by, population gradually

FIGURE 10-2

The Long-Run Aggregate Supply Curve and Shifts in It
In panel (a), we repeat a diagram that we used in Chapter 2 to show the meaning of economic growth. Over time, the production possibilities curve shifts outward. In panel (b), we demonstrate the same principle by showing the long-run aggregate supply curve as initially a vertical line at *LRAS* at $10 trillion of real GDP per year. As our endowments increase, the *LRAS* moves outward to *LRAS*₂₀₀₄.

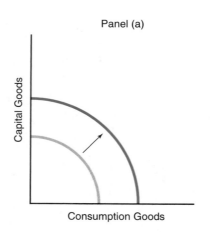

Panel (a)

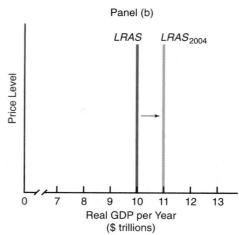

Panel (b)

increases, and labor force participation rates change. The capital stock typically grows as businesses add such capital equipment as new information technology hardware. Furthermore, technology improves. Thus the economy's production possibilities increase, and the production possibilities curve shifts outward, as shown in panel (a) of Figure 10-2.

The result is economic growth: Aggregate real GDP and real GDP per capita increase. This means that at least in a growing economy such as ours, *LRAS* will shift outward to the right, as in panel (b). We have drawn *LRAS* for the year 2004 to the right of our original *LRAS* of $10 trillion of real GDP. The number we have attached to *LRAS*₂₀₀₄ is $11 trillion of real GDP, but that is only a guess. The point is that it is to the right of today's *LRAS* curve.

We may conclude that in a growing economy, the *LRAS* shifts ever farther to the right over time. If it were the case that the pace at which *LRAS* shifts rightward were constant, real GDP would increase at a steady annual rate. As shown in Figure 10-3, this means that real GDP would increase along a long-run, or *trend*, path that is an upward-sloping line. Thus if the *LRAS* shifts rightward from $10 trillion to $11 trillion between now and 2004 and then increases at a steady pace of $500 billion per year every year thereafter, in 2006 long-run real GDP will equal $12 trillion, in 2008 it will equal $13 trillion, and so on.

Does the government include business software when tracking investment and growth?

Yes, but it only began doing so in late 1999. Now the Bureau of Economic Analysis (BEA), a unit of the U.S. Department of Commerce, treats business software purchases as a type of capital accumulation. Estimates are that this change will add 0.15 to 0.30 percentage point to estimates of GDP growth in the 1990s and 2000s. Furthermore, the BEA's revisions have for some periods boosted measured private-sector capital accumulation by as much as a third. This isn't surprising, perhaps, given that in recent years about half the approximately $8,000 in annual per-employee capital spending by businesses was allocated to expenditures on information technology—much of which went to purchases of new and updated software.

CONCEPTS IN BRIEF

● The long-run aggregate supply curve, *LRAS*, is a vertical line determined by amounts of available resources such as labor and capital and by technology and resource productivity. The position of the *LRAS* gives the full-information and full-adjustment level of real output of goods and services.

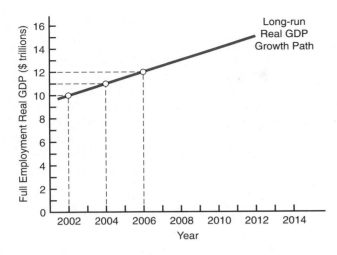

FIGURE 10-3

A Sample Long-Run Growth Path for Real GDP

Year-to-year shifts in the long-run aggregate supply curve yield a long-run trend path for real GDP growth. In this example, real GDP grows by a steady amount of $500 billion each year.

The natural rate of unemployment occurs at the long-run level of real GDP given by the position of the *LRAS*.

● If labor or capital increases from year to year or if the productivity of either of these resources rises from one year to the next, the *LRAS* shifts rightward. In a growing economy, therefore, real GDP gradually rises over time.

SPENDING AND TOTAL EXPENDITURES

In equilibrium, individuals, businesses, and governments purchase all the goods and services produced, valued in trillions of real dollars. As explained in Chapters 7 and 8, GDP is the dollar value of total expenditures on domestically produced final goods and services. Because all expenditures are made by individuals, firms, or governments, the total value of these expenditures must be what each of these market participants decides it shall be. The decisions of individuals, managers of firms, and government officials determine the annual dollar value of total expenditures. You can certainly see this in your role as an individual. You decide what the total dollar amount of your expenditures will be in a year. You decide how much you want to spend and how much you want to save. Thus if we want to know what determines the total value of GDP, the answer would be clear: the spending decisions of individuals like you; firms; and local, state, and national governments. In an open economy, we must also include foreign individuals, firms, and governments (foreigners, for short) that decide to spend their money income in the United States.

Simply stating that the dollar value of total expenditures in this country depends on what individuals, firms, governments, and foreigners decide to do really doesn't tell us much, though. Two important issues remain:

1. What determines the total amount that individuals, firms, governments, and foreigners want to spend?
2. What determines the equilibrium price level and the rate of inflation (or deflation)?

The *LRAS* tells us only about the economy's long-run, or trend, real GDP. To answer these additional questions, we must consider another important concept. This is **aggregate demand,** which is the total of all planned real expenditures in the economy.

Aggregrate demand
The total of all planned expenditures for the entire economy.

AGGREGATE DEMAND

Aggregate demand curve
A curve showing planned purchase rates for all final goods and services in the economy at various price levels, all other things held constant.

The **aggregate demand curve,** *AD,* gives the various quantities of all final commodities demanded at various price levels, all other things held constant. Recall the components of GDP that you studied in Chapter 8: consumption spending, investment expenditures, government purchases, and net foreign demand for domestic production. They are all components of aggregate demand. Throughout this chapter and the next, whenever you see the aggregate demand curve, realize that it is a shorthand way of talking about the components of GDP that are measured by government statisticians when they calculate total economic activity each year. In Chapter 12, you will look more closely at the relationship between these components and in particular how consumption spending depends on income.

The Aggregate Demand Curve

The aggregate demand curve gives the total amount of *real* domestic output that will be purchased at each price level. This consists of the output of final goods and services in the economy—everything produced for final use by households, businesses, the government, and foreign residents. It includes stereos, socks, shoes, medical and legal services, computers, and millions of other goods and services that people buy each year. A graphical representation of the aggregate demand curve is seen in Figure 10-4. On the horizontal axis is measured real gross domestic output, or real GDP. For our measure of the price level, we use the GDP price deflator on the vertical axis. The aggregate demand curve is labeled *AD.* If the GDP deflator is 100, aggregate quantity demanded is $10 trillion per year (point *A*). At price level 120, it is $9 trillion per year (point *B*). At price level 140, it is $8 trillion per year (point *C*). The higher the price level, the lower the total real output demanded by the economy, everything else remaining constant, as shown by the arrow along *AD* in Figure 10-4. Conversely, the lower the price level, the higher the total real output demanded by the economy, everything else staying constant.

Let's take the year 2000. Looking at U.S. Department of Commerce preliminary statistics reveals the following information:

FIGURE 10-4

The Aggregate Demand Curve
Because of the real-balance, interest rate, and open economy effects, the aggregate demand curve, *AD*, slopes downward. If the price level is 100, we will be at point *A* with $10 trillion of real GDP demanded per year. As the price level increases to 120 and 140, we will move up the aggregate demand curve to points *B* and *C*.

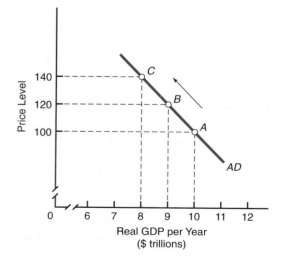

- GDP was $9,849.5 billion.
- The price level as measured by GDP deflator was 106.41 (base year is 1996, for which the index equals 100).
- Real GDP (output) was $9,256.2 billion in 1996 dollars.

What can we say about 2000? Given the dollar cost of buying goods and services and all of the other factors that go into spending decisions by individuals, firms, governments, and foreigners, the total amount of real domestic output demanded by firms, individuals, governments, and foreigners was $9,256.2 billion in 2000 (in terms of 1996 dollars).

What Happens When the Price Level Rises?

What if the price level in the economy rose to 160 tomorrow? What would happen to the amount of real goods and services that individuals, firms, governments, and foreigners wish to purchase in the United States? We know from Chapter 3 that when the price of one good or service rises, the quantity of it demanded will fall. But here we are talking about the *price level*—the average price of *all* goods and services in the economy. The answer is still that the total quantities of real goods and services demanded would fall, but the reasons are different. When the price of one good or service goes up, the consumer substitutes other goods and services. For the entire economy, when the price level goes up, the consumer doesn't simply substitute one good for another, for now we are dealing with the demand for *all* goods and services in the nation. There are *economywide* reasons that cause the aggregate demand curve to slope downward. They involve at least three distinct forces: the *real-balance effect,* the *interest rate effect,* and the *open economy effect.*

The Real-Balance Effect.   A rise in the price level will have an effect on spending. Individuals, firms, governments, and foreigners carry out transactions using money, a portion of which consists of currency and coins that you have in your pocket (or stashed away) right now. Because people use money to purchase goods and services, the amount of money that people have influences the amount of goods and services they want to buy. For example, if you found a $10 bill on the sidewalk, the amount of money you had would rise. Given your now greater level of money balances—currency in this case— you would almost surely increase your spending on goods and services. Similarly, if while on a trip downtown you had your pocket picked, there would be an effect on your desired spending. For example, if your wallet had $30 in it when it was stolen, the reduction in your cash balances—in this case currency—would no doubt cause you to reduce your planned expenditures. You would ultimately buy fewer goods and services. This response is sometimes called the **real-balance effect** (or *wealth effect*) because it relates to the real value of your cash balances. While your *nominal* cash balances may remain the same, any change in the price level will cause a change in the *real* value of those cash balances—hence the real-balance effect on the quantity of aggregate goods and services demanded.

   When you think of the real-balance effect, just think of what happens to your real wealth if you have, say, a $100 bill hidden under your mattress. If the price level increases by 10 percent, the purchasing power of that $100 bill drops by 10 percent, so you have become less wealthy. That will reduce your spending on all goods and services by some small amount.

The Interest Rate Effect.   There is a more subtle but equally important effect on your desire to spend. As the price level rises, interest rates increase. This raises borrowing costs

Real-balance effect
The change in expenditures resulting from the real value of money balances when the price level changes, all other things held constant. Also called the *wealth effect.*

Interest rate effect
One of the reasons that the aggregate demand curve slopes downward is that higher price levels increase the interest rate, which in turn causes businesses and consumers to reduce desired spending due to the higher price of borrowing.

for consumers and businesses. They will borrow less and consequently spend less. The fact that a higher price level pushes up interest rates and thereby reduces borrowing and spending is known as the **interest rate effect.**

Higher interest rates make it more costly for people to buy houses and cars. Higher interest rates also make it less profitable for firms to install new equipment and to erect new office buildings. Whether we are talking about individuals or firms, the effect of a rise in the price level will cause higher interest rates, which in turn reduces the amount of goods and services that people are willing to purchase. Therefore, an increase in the price level will tend to reduce the aggregate quantity of goods and services demanded. (The opposite occurs if the price level declines.)

The Open Economy Effect: The Substitution of Foreign Goods.   Recall from Chapter 8 that GDP includes net exports—the difference between exports and imports. In an open economy, we buy imports from other countries and ultimately pay for them through the foreign exchange market. The same is true for foreigners who purchase our goods (exports). Given any set of exchange rates between the U.S. dollar and other currencies, an increase in the price level in the United States makes American goods more expensive relative to foreign goods. Foreigners have downward-sloping demand curves for American goods. When the relative price of American goods goes up, foreigners buy fewer American goods and more of their own. At home, relatively cheaper prices for foreign goods cause Americans to want to buy more foreign goods instead of American goods. The result is a fall in exports and a rise in imports when the domestic price level rises. That means that a price level increase tends to reduce net exports, thereby reducing the amount of real goods and services purchased in the United States. This is known as the **open economy effect.**

Open economy effect
One of the reasons that the aggregate demand curve slopes downward is that higher price levels result in foreigners' desiring to buy fewer American-made goods while Americans now desire more foreign-made goods, thereby reducing net exports. This is equivalent to a reduction in the amount of real goods and services purchased in the United States.

What Happens When the Price Level Falls?

What about the reverse? Suppose now that the GDP deflator falls to 100 from an initial level of 120. You should be able to trace the three effects on desired purchases of goods and services. Specifically, how do the real-balance, interest rate, and open economy effects cause people to want to buy more? You should come to the conclusion that the lower the price level, the greater the quantity of output of goods and services demanded.

The aggregate demand curve, *AD,* shows the quantity of aggregate output that will be demanded at alternative price levels. It is downward-sloping, just like the demand curve for individual goods. The higher the price level, the lower the quantity of aggregate output demanded, and vice versa.

Demand for All Goods and Services Versus Demand for a Single Good or Serivce

Even though the aggregate demand curve, *AD,* in Figure 10-4 on page 230 looks similar to the one for individual demand, *D,* for a single good or service that you encountered in Chapters 3 and 4, the two are not the same. When we derive the aggregate demand curve, we are looking at the entire economic system. The aggregate demand curve, *AD,* differs from an individual demand curve, *D,* because we are looking at the *entire* circular flow of income and product when we construct *AD.*

SHIFTS IN THE AGGREGATE DEMAND CURVE

In Chapter 3, you learned that any time a nonprice determinant of demand changed, the demand curve shifted inward to the left or outward to the right. The same analysis holds for the aggregate demand curve, except we are now talking about the non-price-level determinants of aggregate demand. So when we ask the question, "What determines the position of the aggregate demand curve?" the fundamental proposition is as follows:

> Any non-price-level change that increases aggregate spending (on domestic goods) shifts *AD* to the right. Any non-price-level change that decreases aggregate spending (on domestic goods) shifts *AD* to the left.

The list of potential determinants of the position of the aggregate demand curve is long. Some of the most important "curve shifters" for aggregate demand are presented in Table 10-1.

Putting *Economics in Action* to Work

Use *EIA* to gain further understanding of the effects of aggregate demand and aggregate supply shocks. Click on "Aggregate Demand and Supply." Then click on "Aggregate Demand Shocks" or "Aggregate Supply Shocks."

Changes That Cause an Increase in Aggregate Demand	Changes That Cause a Decrease in Aggregate Demand
A drop in the foreign exchange value of the dollar	A rise in the foreign exchange value of the dollar
Increased security about jobs and future income	Decreased security about jobs and future income
Improvements in economic conditions in other countries	Declines in economic conditions in other countries
A reduction in real interest rates (nominal interest rates corrected for inflation) not due to price level changes	A rise in real interest rates (nominal interest rates corrected for inflation) not due to price level changes
Tax decreases	Tax increases
An increase in the amount of money in circulation	A decrease in the amount of money in circulation

TABLE 10-1

Determinants of Aggregate Demand
Aggregate demand consists of the demand for domestically produced consumption goods, investment goods, government purchases, and net exports. Consequently, any change in the demand for any one of these components of real GDP will cause a change in aggregate demand. Some possibilities are listed here.

CONCEPTS IN BRIEF

● Aggregate demand is the total of all planned expenditures in the economy, and aggregate supply is the total of all planned production in the economy. The aggregate demand curve shows the various quantities of all commodities demanded at various price levels; it is downward-sloping.

● There are three reasons why the aggregate demand curve is downward-sloping: the real-balance effect, the interest rate effect, and the open economy effect.

● The real-balance effect occurs because price level changes alter the real value of cash balances, thereby causing people to desire to spend more or less, depending on whether the price level decreases or increases.

● The interest rate effect is caused via interest rate changes that mimic price level changes. At higher interest rates, people desire to buy fewer houses and cars, and vice versa.

● The open economy effect occurs because of a shift toward foreign goods when the domestic price level increases and a shift away from foreign goods when the domestic price level decreases.

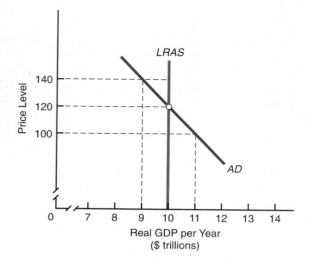

FIGURE 10-5

Long-Run Economywide Equilibrium

For the economy as a whole, long-run equilibrium occurs at the price level where the aggregate demand curve crosses the long-run aggregate supply curve. At this long-run equilibrium price level, which is 120 in the diagram, total planned real expenditures equal total planned production at full employment, which in our example is a real GDP of $10 trillion.

LONG-RUN EQUILIBRIUM AND THE PRICE LEVEL

As noted in Chapter 3, equilibrium occurs where the demand and supply curves intersect. The same is true for the economy as a whole, as shown in Figure 10-5: The equilibrium price level occurs at the point where the aggregate demand curve *(AD)* crosses the long-run aggregate supply curve *(LRAS)*. At this equilibrium price level of 120, the total of all planned real expenditures for the entire economy is equal to total planned production along the economy's trend growth path for real GDP. Thus the equilibrium depicted in Figure 10-5 is the economy's *long-run equilibrium.*

Note that if the price level were to increase to 140, total planned production would exceed total planned real expenditures. Inventories of unsold goods would begin to accumulate, and firms would stand ready to offer services that people would not wish to purchase. As a result, the price level would tend to fall. If the price level were 100, then total planned real expenditures by individuals, businesses, and the government would exceed total planned production by firms, and the price level would move toward 120.

THE EFFECTS OF ECONOMIC GROWTH ON THE PRICE LEVEL

We now have a basic theory of how real output and the price level are determined in the long run when all of a nation's resources can change over time and all input prices can adjust fully to changes in the overall level of prices of goods and services that firms produce. Let's begin by evaluating the effects of economic growth on the nation's price level.

Take a look at panel (a) of Figure 10-6, which shows what happens, other things being equal, when the *LRAS* shifts rightward over time. If the economy were to grow steadily during, say, a 10-year interval, the long-run aggregate supply schedule would shift to the right, from $LRAS_1$ to $LRAS_2$. In the example illustrated in the figure, this results in a downward movement along the aggregate demand schedule. The equilibrium price level falls, from 120 to 60. Thus if all factors that affect total planned real expenditures are unchanged, so that the aggregate demand curve does not noticeably move during the 10-year period of real GDP growth, the growing economy in the example would experience deflation. This is

FIGURE 10-6
Secular Deflation Versus Long-Run Price Stability in a Growing Economy

Panel (a) illustrates what happens when economic growth occurs without a corresponding increase in aggregate demand. The result is a decline in the price level over time, known as *secular deflation.* Panel (b) shows that in principle, secular deflation can be avoided if the aggregate demand curve shifts rightward at the same pace that the long-run aggregate supply curve shifts to the right.

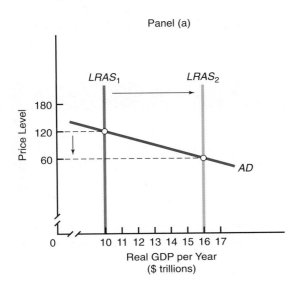
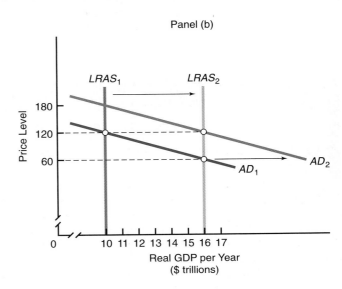

known as **secular deflation,** or a persistently declining price level resulting from economic growth in the presence of relatively unchanged aggregate demand.

L. Frank Baum and his contemporaries experienced secular deflation during the three decades preceding publication of *The Wonderful Wizard of Oz.* For instance, compared with 1872 levels, by 1894 the price of bricks had fallen by 50 percent, the price of sugar by 67 percent, the price of wheat by 69 percent, the price of nails by 70 percent, and the price of copper by nearly 75 percent. Baum and other populists at the turn of the twentieth century offered a proposal for ending deflation and achieving long-run price stability: They wanted the government to expand the quantity of money in circulation by issuing new money backed by silver. As we discussed earlier, an increase in the quantity of money in circulation raises total planned real expenditures at any given price level and thereby causes the aggregate demand curve to shift to the right. Although economic historians have been divided about how effectively silver-backed money would have maintained long-run price stability, it is clear from panel (b) of Figure 10-6 that the increase in the quantity of money surely would have pushed the price level back upward. As you can see in panel (b), in principle just the right increase in aggregate demand could indeed stabilize the equilibrium price level at its initial value of 120.

In fact, in 1890 Congress passed the Treasury Note Act, otherwise known as the Silver Purchase Act, which required the U.S. Treasury to purchase silver and issue currency known as silver certificates. This effort to expand the quantity of money barely got off the ground, however, before stock market panics hit in the spring and summer of 1893. People began to hoard gold, and the price of silver fell. To limit the government's losses on its silver holdings, Congress, at the urging of President Grover Cleveland, repealed the Silver

Secular deflation
A persistent decline in prices resulting from economic growth in the presence of stable aggregate demand.

To learn about how the price level has changed during recent years, go to **www.stls.frb.org/fred** and click on "Gross Domestic Product and Components" (for GDP deflators) or "Monthly Consumer Prices" (for consumer price indexes).

Purchase Act. William Jennings Bryan sought the Democratic presidential nomination to oppose Republican William McKinley in 1896, and in an emotional speech, he decried the repeal of the Silver Purchase Act, saying, "You shall not press down upon the brow of labor this crown of thorns, you shall not crucify mankind upon a cross of gold." Although Bryan's speechmaking abilities made him a public sensation, he nonetheless lost the election, which sounded the death knell of the populist effort to increase the quantity of money in circulation via silver certificates. According to Rutgers economist Hugh Rockoff, Baum represented the twin enemies of silver, Presidents Cleveland (of New York) and McKinley (of Ohio), as the Wicked Witch of the East and the Wicked Witch of the West.

INTERNATIONAL EXAMPLE

Corporations Adjust to Potential and True Deflation

For decades, conventional wisdom among corporate financial officers was that they can lower their companies' costs by financing purchases of capital by borrowing—taking out loans from banks, selling commercial paper, issuing new bonds, and the like. The reason is that debt has traditionally been less expensive to a firm than the issuing of new shares. Corporate managers could count on inflation to erode the value of the firm's debts even as the selling price of the company's output increased.

In a deflationary environment, however, these dynamics are reversed. Deflation *increases* the real value of outstanding debts. At the same time, companies find that to repay their loans, they must dip into profits that are declining because of falling output prices. In 1997 and 1998, companies based in Southeast Asia learned this lesson with a vengeance. From Russia to Thailand to Indonesia, companies faced lower selling prices and mounting real values of indebtedness. Of course, they were hit by a double whammy: The relative values of local currencies also fell during 1997 and 1998, and many debts of these

companies were denominated in dollars. Thus companies found themselves having to give up more of their profits denominated in domestic currencies to obtain the dollars they required to make their debt payments.

Closer to home, however, even some U.S. corporate managers are getting nervous. A few have openly called for changing their long-term fundraising philosophies now in anticipation of future deflation, even though the overall rate of inflation remains positive. For some industries, however, the deflationary future has already arrived. Companies specializing in manufacturing, chemicals, oil, and natural gas products already are seeing their selling prices decline year in and year out. Corporate treasurers in these industries are now talking about a "new balance sheet paradigm" in which companies will rely much more heavily on issuing stock instead of borrowing.

For Critical Analysis

In what ways might deflation affect the average individual's financial well-being?

CAUSES OF INFLATION

Of course, so far during your lifetime, deflation has not been a problem in the United States. Figure 10-7 shows annual U.S. inflation rates for the past few decades. Clearly, inflation rates have been variable. The other obvious fact, however, is that inflation rates have consistently been *positive*. The price level in the United States has *risen* almost every year. For today's United States, secular deflation has not been a big political issue. If anything, it is a secular *inflation* that has plagued the nation.

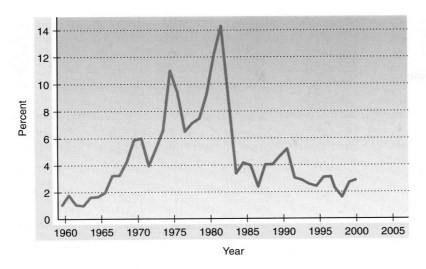

FIGURE 10-7
Inflation Rates in the United States
U.S. inflation rates rose considerably during the 1970s but declined to lower levels since the 1980s. Nevertheless, the United States has experienced inflation every year since 1959.

Sources: Economic Report of the President; Economic Indicators, various issues.

Supply-Side Inflation?

What causes such persistent inflation? The classical model provides two possible explanations for inflation. One potential rationale is depicted in panel (a) of Figure 10-8. This panel shows a rise in the price level caused by a *decline in long-run aggregate supply.* Hence one possible reason for persistent inflation would be continual reductions in the production of real output.

FIGURE 10-8
Explaining Persistent Inflation
As shown in panel (a), it is possible for a decline in long-run aggregate supply to cause a rise in the price level. Long-run aggregate supply *increases,* however, in a growing economy, so this cannot explain the observation of persistent U.S. inflation. Panel (b) provides the true explanation of persistent inflation, which is that increases in aggregate demand push up the long-run equilibrium price level. Thus it is possible to explain persistent inflation in a growing economy if the aggregate demand curve shifts rightward at a faster pace than the long-run aggregate supply curve.

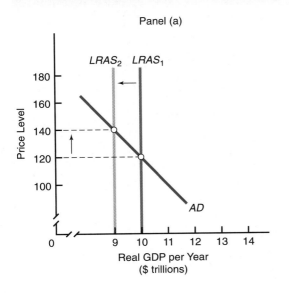

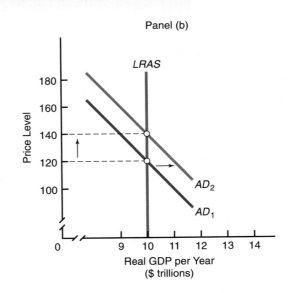

Recall now the factors that would cause the aggregate supply schedule to shift leftward. One might be reductions in labor force participation, induced perhaps by a population decline, higher marginal tax rates on wages, or the provision of government benefits that give households incentives not to supply labor services to firms. Although tax rates and government benefits have definitely increased during recent decades, so has the U.S. population. Nevertheless, the significant overall rise in real GDP that has taken place during the past few decades tells us that population growth and productivity gains have dominated other factors. In fact, the aggregate supply schedule has actually shifted *rightward,* not leftward, over time. Consequently, this supply-side explanation for persistent inflation *cannot* be the true explanation.

Demand-Side Inflation

This leaves only one other explanation for the persistent inflation that the United States has experienced in recent decades. This explanation is depicted in panel (b) of Figure 10-8. If aggregate demand increases for a given level of long-run aggregate supply, the price level must increase. The reason is that at an initial price level such as 120, people desire to purchase more goods and services than firms are willing and able to produce given currently available resources and technology. As a result, the rise in aggregate demand leads only to a general rise in the price level, such as the increase to a value of 140 depicted in the figure.

From a long-run perspective, we are left with only one possibility: Persistent inflation in a growing economy is possible only if the aggregate demand curve shifts rightward over time at a faster pace than rightward progression of the long-run aggregate supply curve. Thus in contrast to the experience of people who lived in the latter portion of the nineteenth century, in which aggregate demand grew too slowly relative to aggregate supply to maintain price stability, your grandparents, parents, and you have lived in times during which

FIGURE 10-9

Economic Growth and Inflation in the United States, 1970 to the Present

This figure shows the points where aggregate demand and aggregate supply have intersected each year from 1970 to the present. The United States has experienced economic growth over this period, but not without inflation.

Sources: Economic Report of the President; Economic Indicators, various issues.

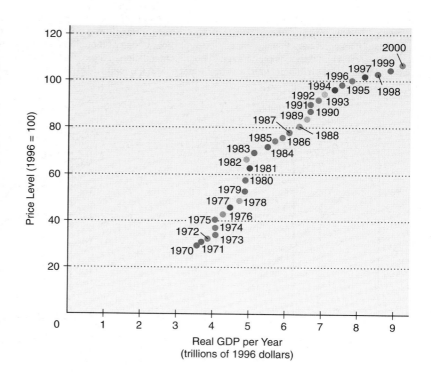

aggregate demand grew too *speedily*. The result has been a continual upward drift in the price level, or long-term inflation.

Take a look at Figure 10-9, which shows that real output has grown in most years since 1970. Apparently, however, the U.S. economy has been unable to experience economic growth without higher prices every single year.

POLICY EXAMPLE

Is There a Simple Explanation for the Price Level's Upward Drift?

As you will learn in more detail in Chapter 17, a group of economists known as *monetarists* have been given this name because they believe that changes in the quantity of money in circulation are the predominant cause of changes in the position of the aggregate demand curve. Consequently, they also believe that changes in the quantity of money are the fundamental determinant of movements in the price level.

Take a look at panel (a) of Figure 10-10. There you can see that two key measures of the price level—the GDP deflator and the Consumer Price Index (CPI)—have persistently drifted upward over recent decades, though at a somewhat reduced pace in recent years. Now look at panel (b) of the figure. This panel plots the Federal Reserve's primary measure of the total quantity of money in circulation, M2, which among other things includes the total amount of currency and coins, checking accounts, and savings accounts in the United States. As you can see, the amount of money circulating in the U.S. economy has also drifted persistently upward in recent decades, although its pace of growth has also tapered off in recent years. To monetarists, the correspondence of these trends is not coincidence. Money growth, they conclude, is the predominant factor explaining the rate of inflation.

For Critical Analysis
If the monetarists are correct, what U.S. policymaker is most responsible for attaining, or failing to attain, stability of the long-run equilibrium price level?

FIGURE 10-10
The GDP Deflator and Consumer Price Index and the Quantity of Money in Circulation

Panel (a) shows that both the GDP deflator and the CPI have risen during recent decades. As indicated in panel (b), so has the quantity of money in circulation.

Sources: Economic Report of the President; Economic Indicators, various issues.

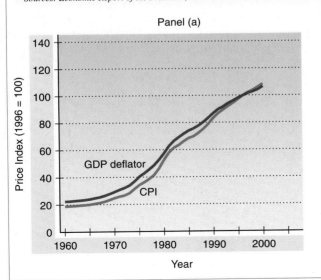

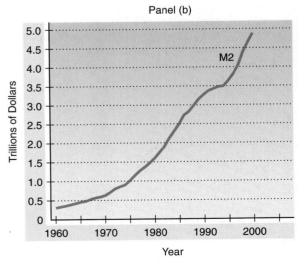

CONCEPTS IN BRIEF

● When the economy is in long-run equilibrium, the price level adjusts to equate total planned real expenditures by individuals, businesses, and the government with total planned production by firms.

● Economic growth causes the long-run aggregate supply schedule to shift rightward over time. If the position of the aggregate demand curve does not change, therefore, the long-run equilibrium price level tends to decline, and there is secular deflation.

● Because the U.S. economy has generally grown in recent decades, the persistent inflation during those years has been caused by the aggregate demand curve shifting rightward at a faster pace than the long-run aggregate supply curve.

NETNOMICS

The "New" Economy, the Long-Run Aggregate Supply Curve, and Inflation

Call it what you may, the Internet economy, the new economy, the network economy, or even the information economy. The most promising technologies today are chiefly due to communications among computers—connections rather than computations. We are currently enhancing and extending the relationships between all businesses and all people.

Sometimes it may seem that economists do not seem to agree about much. Nevertheless, one thing they do agree about is a likely high rate of growth in the portion of GDP marketed and sold on the Internet. The value of electronic-commerce transactions, including those among businesses, grew from almost zero in 1996 to $43 billion, or 0.5 percent of U.S. GDP, in 1998. Current forecasts call for commerce over the Internet to more than double every year and reach as much as $1.3 trillion by 2003, which likely would be more than 10 percent of GDP.

Furthermore, the growth of the Internet has allowed for the creation of more entrepreneurial talent among people whose creative lives have become enmeshed in the Web. Recall from Chapter 2 that entrepreneurship is an important factor of production. If in fact the new economy creates more entrepreneurship, then the long-run aggregate supply curve *(LRAS)* may be moving out to the right faster than previously thought possible. This could well help temper rises in the long-run equilibrium price level and help keep a lid on the inflation rate.

ISSUES & APPLICATIONS

What Is P^*, and Why Should We Care?

In 1991, the *American Economic Review* published a study by Federal Reserve economists Jeffrey Hallman, Richard Porter, and David Small. This study proposed the so-called P^* model. This was a theory of what the price level ought to be in long-run equilibrium for the U.S. economy. By the time of its formal publication, however, many economists were already well aware of the study, because the *New York Times* and the *Washington Post* had previously published feature articles about the study's "new theory" and its implications for Federal Reserve policymaking.

There Is Nothing Novel About the Theory of P^*

After the newspaper stories appeared, a few economists poked some good-natured fun at the three Fed economists. On bulletin boards around the country, a mock front-page story purported to be from a well-known "tabloid" (actually computer-generated) appeared. Above second-level headlines shouting that "Elvis Found Alive" and "Boy Shaves Head to Rent as Advertising Space" was a giant headline saying "Three Fed Economists Think of P^* at the Same Time!!!" Below the headline was a *New York Times* photo of the three economists that had been spliced into the mock front page.

The reason this was a joke among economists was that the theory of P^* was news to no one with an even rudimentary background in macroeconomics. Indeed, it should not be news to you now that you have nearly completed your study of this chapter. The reason is that P^* is nothing other than the equilibrium price level that emerges in the economy's long-run equilibrium. Poorly informed news reporters had not realized this fact, even though the economists who did the study had probably done their best to make this fact clear in interviews—or perhaps news editors realized that a headline about a new application of an old theory might not attract their readers' attention.

What Is New Is the Fed's Interest

What Hallman, Porter, and Small had successfully accomplished, however, was to refocus economists' attention on thinking about what the price level ought to be in long-run equilibrium. Prior to their study, most economists concentrated on trying to understand short-term movements in the price level. The study highlighted how it might be possible to estimate the price level that ought to emerge in the absence of variations in short-term factors that can often cause the price level to deviate from its long-run equilibrium value. (This is a key subject of Chapter 11.) More important, the Federal Reserve itself seemed narrowly focused on short-term factors as well. Evidence for this was the phenomenon of *base drift,* which is a tendency for the quantity of money in circulation to vary over time without necessarily returning to a level consistent with a single long-run average growth rate.

To see how base drift occurs, consider point *A* in Figure 10-11, where we assume that in the fourth quarter of a given year, Fed announces a desired growth rate for the quantity of money in circulation of no less than 4 percent and no greater than 8 percent. The midrange of these two growth rates is its announced *target* growth rate of 6 percent. During the weeks that follow, however, the Fed permits money growth to drift toward the upper part of its target growth range. Then, at the time indicated by point *B,* Fed officials reaffirm their commitment to the same target growth rate and range of permitted deviations from this target.

FIGURE 10-11
Base Drift

If the Federal Reserve permits the quantity of money in circulation to drift toward the upper part of its target growth range during one year and then resets its target growth ranges at the beginning of a second year, the result is base drift. This can cause the price level to fail to settle at a single long-run average level.

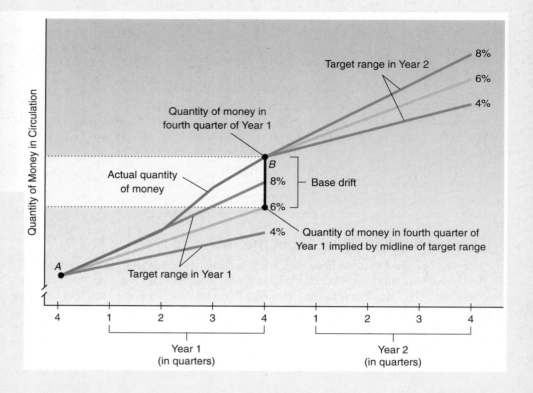

1. Why is a stable price level desirable?

2. How might random meanderings of the price level affect creditors and debtors, and under what circumstances might one of these groups be pleased with upward drift of the price level?

The result, however, is *upward drift* of the quantity of money. As a result, there is no stable rate of money growth, and the Fed contributes to intermittent outward shifts of the aggregate demand curve.

A result of base drift is that the price level never settles down to a long-run average level. Instead, the price level meanders with no clear long-run trend. Consistent with the general upward drift in the quantity of money in circulation, the general pattern of price level drift has been upward.

Since the Hallman-Porter-Small study, economists have endeavored to determine the best way to estimate the long-run equilibrium price level. The hope is that if a foolproof way of estimating this price level can be determined, it might serve as a guide for monetary policy. This would allow the Fed to ignore short-run movements in the price level and aim directly at a long-run objective of price stability.

SUMMARY DISCUSSION OF LEARNING OBJECTIVES

1. **Long-Run Aggregate Supply:** The long-run aggregate supply curve is vertical at the amount of real GDP that firms plan to produce when they have full information and when complete adjustment of input prices to any changes in output prices has taken place. This is the full-employment level of real output, or the output level at which the natural rate of unemployment—the sum of frictional and structural unemployment as a percentage of the labor force—arises.

2. **Economic Growth and the Long-Run Aggregate Supply Curve:** Economic growth is an expansion of a country's production possibilities. Thus the production possibilities curve shifts rightward when the economy grows, and so does the nation's long-run aggregate supply curve. In a growing economy, the changes in full-employment output defined by the shifting long-run aggregate supply curve define the nation's long-run, or trend, growth path.

3. **Why the Aggregate Demand Curve Slopes Downward and Factors That Cause It to Shift:** A rise in the price level reduces the real value of cash balances in the hands of the public, which induces people to cut back on spending. This is the real-balance effect. In addition, higher interest rates typically accompany increases in the price level, and this interest rate effect induces people to cut back on borrowing and, consequently, spending. Finally, a rise in the price level at home causes domestic goods to be relatively more expensive relative to foreign goods, so that there is a fall in exports and a rise in imports, both of which cause domestic planned expenditures to fall. These three factors together account for the downward slope of the aggregate demand curve. A shift in the aggregate demand curve results from a change in total planned real expenditures at any given price level and may be caused by a number of factors, including changes in security about jobs and future income, tax changes, variations in the quantity of money in circulation, changes in real interest rates, movements in exchange rates, and changes in economic conditions in other countries.

4. **Long-Run Equilibrium for the Economy:** In a long-run economywide equilibrium, the price level adjusts until total planned real expenditures equal total planned production. Thus the long-run equilibrium price level is determined at the point where the aggregate demand curve intersects the long-run aggregate supply curve. If the price level is below its long-run equilibrium value, total planned real expenditures exceed total planned production, and the level of prices of goods and services tends to rise back toward the long-run equilibrium price level. By contrast, if the price level is above its long-run equilibrium value, total planned production is greater than total planned real expenditures, and the price level declines in the direction of the long-run equilibrium price level.

5. **Why Economic Growth Can Cause Deflation:** If the aggregate demand curve is relatively stable during a period of economic growth, the long-run aggregate supply curve shifts rightward along the aggregate demand curve. The long-run equilibrium price level falls, so there is deflation. Historically, economic growth has in this way generated secular deflation, or relatively long periods of decline prices.

6. **Likely Reasons for Recent Persistent Inflation:** One event that can induce inflation is a decline in long-run aggregate supply, because this causes the long-run aggregate supply curve to shift leftward along the aggregate demand curve. In a growing economy, however, the long-run aggregate supply curve generally shifts rightward. This indicates that a much more likely cause of persistent inflation is a pace of aggregate demand growth that exceeds the pace at which long-run aggregate supply increases.

Key Terms and Concepts

Aggregate demand (229)	Endowments (227)	Open economy effect (232)
Aggregate demand curve (230)	Interest rate effect (232)	Real-balance effect (231)
Aggregate supply (226)	Long-run aggregate supply curve (227)	Secular deflation (235)

Problems

Answers to the odd-numbered problems appear at the back of the book.

10-1. Many economists view the natural rate of unemployment as arising when the economy is producing a level of real GDP consistent with the position of its long-run aggregate supply curve. How can there be positive unemployment in this situation?

10-2. Suppose that the long-run aggregate supply curve is positioned at a real GDP level of $12 trillion, and the long-run equilibrium price level (in index number form) is 120. What is the full-employment level of *nominal* GDP?

10-3. Continuing from Problem 10-2, suppose that the full-employment level of *nominal* GDP in the following year rises to $16.8 trillion. The long-run equilibrium price level, however, remains unchanged. By how much (in real dollars) has the long-run aggregate supply curve shifted to the right in the following year?

10-4. The position of a nation's long-run aggregate supply curve has not changed, but its long-run equilibrium price level has increased. Which of the following factors might account for this event?
   a. A rise in the value of the domestic currency relative to other world currencies
   b. An increase in the quantity of money in circulation
   c. An increase in the real interest rate
   d. A decrease in taxes
   e. A rise in real incomes of countries that are key trading partners of this nation
   f. Increased long-run economic growth

10-5. Suppose that there is a sudden rise in the price level. What happens to economywide spending on purchases of goods and services? Why?

10-6. Suppose that the economy is a long-run situation with complete information and speedy adjustment of input prices to changes in the prices of goods and services. If there is a sudden rise in the price level, what happens to economywide production of goods and services?

10-7. Consider the accompanying diagram when answering the questions that follow.

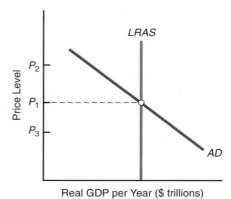

a. Suppose that the current price level is P_2. Explain why the price level will decline toward P_1.
b. Suppose that the current price level is P_3. Explain why the price level will rise toward P_1.

10-8. A country's long-run equilibrium price level has increased, but the position of its aggregate demand schedule has not changed. What has happened? What specific factors might have accounted for this event?

10-9. Most economists argue that the main reason that price level nonstationarity is undesirable is that it is often unpredictable. Explain the rationale behind this argument.

10-10. Is predictable deflation necessarily undesirable? Support your position.

Economics on the Net

Wages, Productivity, and Aggregate Supply How much firms pay their employees and the productivity of those employees influence firms' total planned production, so changes in these factors affect the position of the aggregate supply curve. This application gives you the opportunity to examine recent trends in measures of the overall wages and productivity of workers.

Internet URL: http://stats.bls.gov/eag.table.html
Title: Bureau of Labor Statistics: Economy at a Glance

Navigation: Begin at the home page of the Bureau of Labor Statistics (http://stats.bls.gov). Then click on U.S. Economy at a Glance.

Application Perform the indicated operations, and answer the following questions.

1. Click on Economy at a Glance. Then scan down to "Hours, Earnings, and Productivity," and click on the graph box next to Employee Cost Index. What are

the recent trends in wages and salaries and in benefits? In the long run, how should these trends be related to movements in the overall price level?

2. Back up to U.S. Economy at a Glance, and now click on the graph box next to Productivity. How has labor productivity behaved recently? What does this imply for the long-run aggregate supply curve?

3. Back up to U.S. Economy at a Glance, and now click on the graph box next to "Change in Payroll Employment." Does it appear that the U.S. economy is currently in a long-run growth equilibrium?

For Group Study and Analysis

1. Divide the class into aggregate demand and long-run aggregate supply groups. Have each group search the Internet for data on factors that influence their assigned curve. For which factors do data appear to be most readily available? For which factors are data more sparse or more subject to measurement problems?

2. The opening page of Economy at a Glance displays a map of the United States. Assign regions of the nations to different groups, and have each group develop a short report about current and future prospects for economic growth within its assigned region. In what ways are there similarities across regions? In what ways are there regional differences?

CLASSICAL AND KEYNESIAN MACRO ANALYSES

These veiled Afghan women are attending a clandestine school. Afghanistan's Taliban government bars women from working or acquiring a formal education. What is the cost to Afghan society of such restrictions?

In the United States, there are over 135 million people in the measured labor force. Approximately 54 percent are males, and the remaining 46 percent are females. Try to imagine what would happen if Congress passed a law forbidding all females from working outside the home. The active labor force would fall sharply. To be sure, the economy would be much worse off, not to speak of the female members of the labor force. This hypothetical scenario actually happened a few years ago when the Muslim clerics who ruled Afghanistan issued a decree forbidding women to work. To analyze what happened to the labor market and the economy in Afghanistan, you need to understand where the labor market fits into the classical and Keynesian views of macroeconomics.

Did You Know That... in spite of continuing general inflation, magazine publishers tend to keep the same magazine prices for more than a year? According to one study by economist Stephen G. Cecchetti, the typical magazine publisher lets inflation eat away at a fourth of the magazine's price before a new price is printed on the magazine. This common example of "sticky" prices gives just a hint that our economy may not instantaneously adapt itself to changes in macroeconomic variables such as an increase in the overall price level. Economists want to know what causes fluctuations in employment, output, and the price level. The fact that magazine prices are sticky is just one empirical observation that would lead researchers to develop macroeconomic models that somehow reflect the less flexible nature of certain prices. Such was not the case with the classical economists, who had a different view of how the macroeconomy operated. We will start this chapter with a look at the classical model of the economy and then examine a model developed in the twentieth century.

THE CLASSICAL MODEL

The classical model, which traces its origins to the 1770s, was the first systematic attempt to explain the determinants of the price level and the national levels of output, income, employment, consumption, saving, and investment. The term *classical model* was coined by John Maynard Keynes (pronounced "kainz"), a Cambridge University economist, who used the term to refer to the way in which earlier economists had analyzed economic aggregates. Classical economists—Adam Smith, J. B. Say, David Ricardo, John Stuart Mill, Thomas Malthus, A. C. Pigou, and others—wrote from the 1770s to the 1930s. They assumed, among other things, that all wages and prices were flexible and that competitive markets existed throughout the economy.

Say's Law

Every time you produce something for which you receive income, you generate the income necessary to make expenditures on other goods and services. That means that an economy producing $10 trillion of GDP (final goods and services) simultaneously produces the income with which these goods and services can be purchased. As an accounting identity, *actual* aggregate output always equals *actual* aggregate income. Classical economists took this accounting identity one step further by arguing that total national supply creates its own national demand. They asserted what has become known as **Say's law:**

> Supply creates its own demand; hence it follows that *desired* expenditures will equal *actual* expenditures.

What does Say's law really mean? It states that the very process of producing specific goods (supply) is proof that other goods are desired (demand). People produce more goods than they want for their own use only if they seek to trade them for other goods. Someone offers to supply something only because he or she has a demand for something else. The implication of this, according to Say, is that no general glut, or overproduction, is possible in a market economy. From this reasoning, it seems to follow that full employment of labor and other resources would be the normal state of affairs in such an economy.

Say's law
A dictum of economist J. B. Say that supply creates its own demand; producing goods and services generates the means and the willingness to purchase other goods and services.

Say acknowledged that an oversupply of some goods might occur in particular markets. He argued that such surpluses would simply cause prices to fall, thereby decreasing production as the economy adjusted. The opposite would occur in markets in which shortages temporarily appeared.

All this seems reasonable enough in a simple barter economy in which households produce most of the goods they want and trade for the rest. This is shown in Figure 11-1, where there is a simple circular flow. But what about a more sophisticated economy in which people work for others and there is no barter but rather the use of money? Can these complications create the possibility of unemployment? And does the fact that laborers receive money income, some of which can be saved, lead to unemployment? No, said the classical economists to these last two questions. They based their reasoning on a number of key assumptions.

Assumptions of the Classical Model

The classical model makes four major assumptions:

1. *Pure competition exists.* No single buyer or seller of a commodity or an input can affect its price.
2. *Wages and prices are flexible.* The assumption of pure competition leads to the notion that prices, wages, interest rates, and the like are free to move to whatever level supply and demand dictate (as the economy adjusts). Although no *individual* buyer can set a price, the community of buyers or sellers can cause prices to rise or to fall to an equilibrium level.
3. *People are motivated by self-interest.* Businesses want to maximize their profits, and households want to maximize their economic well-being.
4. *People cannot be fooled by money illusion.* Buyers and sellers react to changes in relative prices. That is to say, they do not suffer from **money illusion.** For example, a worker will not be fooled into thinking that he or she is better off by a doubling of wages if the price level has also doubled during the same time period.

Money illusion
Reacting to changes in money prices rather than relative prices. If a worker whose wages double when the price level also doubles thinks he or she is better off, the worker is suffering from money illusion.

The classical economists concluded, after taking account of the four major assumptions, that the role of government in the economy should be minimal. If all prices and wages are flexible, any problems in the macroeconomy will be temporary. The market will come to the rescue and correct itself.

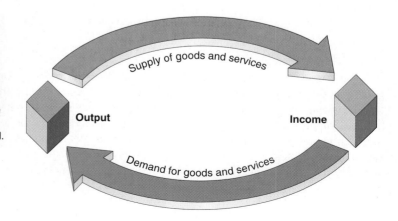

FIGURE 11-1

Say's Law and the Circular Flow

Here we show the circular flow of income and output. The very act of supplying a certain level of goods and services necessarily equals the level of goods and services demanded, in Say's simplified world.

Supply of goods and services

Output   Income

Demand for goods and services

Equilibrium in the Credit Market

When income is saved, it is not reflected in product demand. It is a type of *leakage* from the circular flow of income and output because saving withdraws funds from the income stream. Therefore, consumption expenditures *can* fall short of total current output. In such a situation, it does not appear that supply necessarily creates its own demand.

The classical economists did not believe that the complicating factor of saving in the circular flow model of income and output was a problem. They contended that each dollar saved would be invested by businesses so that the leakage of saving would be matched by the injection of business investment. *Investment* here refers only to additions to the nation's capital stock. The classical economists believed that businesses as a group would intend to invest as much as households wanted to save.

Equilibrium between the saving plans of consumers and the investment plans of businesses comes about, in the classical economists' world, through the working of the credit market. In the credit market, the *price* of credit is the interest rate. At equilibrium, the price of credit—the interest rate—ensures that the amount of credit demanded equals the amount of credit supplied. Planned investment just equals planned saving, so there is no reason to be concerned about the leakage of saving. This is illustrated graphically in Figure 11-2.

In the figure, the vertical axis measures the rate of interest in percentage terms; on the horizontal axis are the amounts of desired saving and desired investment per unit time period. The desired saving curve is really a supply curve of saving. It shows that people wish to save more at higher interest rates than at lower interest rates.

By contrast, the higher the rate of interest, the more expensive it is to invest and the lower the level of desired investment. Thus the desired investment curve slopes downward. In this simplified model, the equilibrium rate of interest is 10 percent, and the equilibrium quantity of saving and investment is $700 billion per year.

Track U.S. interest rates by going to
www.federalreserve.gov/ releases
and clicking on "Selected Interest Rates."

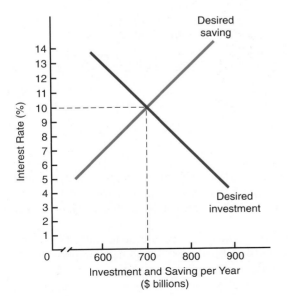

FIGURE 11-2
Equating Desired Saving and Investment in the Classical Model
The schedule showing planned investment is labeled "Desired investment." The supply of resources used for investment occurs when individuals do not consume but save instead. The desired saving curve is shown as an upward-sloping supply curve of saving. The equilibrating force here is, of course, the interest rate. At higher interest rates, people desire to save more. But at higher interest rates, businesses wish to engage in less investment because it is more expensive to invest. In this model, at an interest rate of 10 percent, the planned investment just equals planned saving, which is $700 billion per year.

POLICY EXAMPLE

Personal Saving Rates Are Nearly Zero

At various times in the past few years, the measured personal saving rate has fallen to 1 percent. Imagine what this means in terms of Figure 11-2. Because desired saving and investment are equal in equilibrium, it would seem that investment should be very low also. That hasn't happened, though. Nonetheless, government economists express concern. They argue that U.S. consumers have been borrowing heavily against future income gains.

But perhaps American consumers aren't so spending-crazy after all. Many Americans made large gains in the stock market and other personal investments in the latter part of the 1990s. Not surprisingly, they spent some of those gains. Because capital gains are excluded from U.S. government figures on disposable income, statistically the U.S. personal saving rate looks extemely low, but it really isn't.

In addition, we have not had to worry about funds for investment. For years, foreigners have poured hundreds of billions of dollars into the United States. Also, businesses have retained earnings and reinvested them—to the tune of over $1 trillion per year recently. Finally, governments at the state and federal levels have been running surpluses. Figure 11-3 shows the *gross* saving rate for the past decade. It includes personal, business, and government saving as a percentage of GDP. It has actually gone up since 1992, not down.

For Critical Analysis

Why should government policymakers care how much individuals spend or save?

FIGURE 11-3

Gross Saving and Personal Saving Rates in the United States, 1990–Present

As the U.S. personal saving rate has fallen, the gross saving rate has increased.

Source: U.S. Department of Commerce.

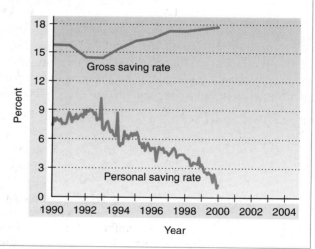

Equilibrium in the Labor Market

To find out the latest U.S. saving rate, go to **www.bea.doc.gov** and click on "GDP and related data" followed by "Personal saving as a percentage of disposable personal income."

Now consider the labor market. If an excess quantity of labor is supplied at a particular wage level, the wage level must be above equilibrium. By accepting lower wages, unemployed workers will quickly be put back to work. We show equilibrium in the labor market in Figure 11-4.

Assume that full-employment equilibrium exists at $12 per hour and 135 million workers employed. If the wage rate were $14 an hour, there would be unemployment— 145 million workers would want to work, but businesses would want to hire only 125 million. In the classical model, this unemployment is eliminated rather rapidly by wage rates dropping back to $12 per hour.

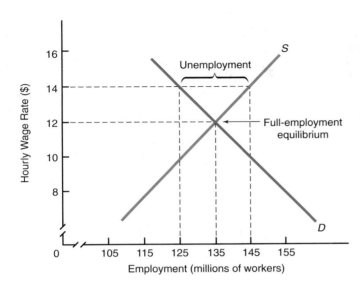

FIGURE 11-4
Equilibrium in the Labor Market
The demand for labor is downward sloping; at higher wage rates, firms will employ fewer workers. The supply of labor is upward sloping; at higher wage rates, more workers will work longer and more people will be willing to work. The equilibrium wage rate is $12 with an equilibrium employment per year of 135 million workers.

The Relationship Between Employment and Real GDP. Employment is not to be regarded simply as some isolated figure that government statisticians estimate. Rather, the level of employment in an economy determines its real GDP (output), other things held constant. A hypothetical relationship between input (number of employees) and output (rate of real GDP per year) is shown in Table 11-1. We have highlighted the row that has 135 million workers per year as the labor input. That might be considered a hypothetical level of full employment, and it is related to a rate of real GDP of $10 trillion per year.

Classical Theory, Vertical Aggregate Supply, and the Price Level

In the classical model, long-term unemployment is impossible. Say's law, coupled with flexible interest rates, prices, and wages, would always tend to keep workers fully employed so that the aggregate supply curve, as shown in Figure 11-5 on page 252, is vertical at Y_0. We have labeled the supply curve *LRAS*, consistent with the long-run aggregate supply curve introduced in Chapter 10. It was defined there as the quantity of output that would be produced in an economy with full information and full adjustment of wages and prices year in and year out. In the classical model, this happens to be the *only* aggregate supply curve that exists. *LRAS* is therefore at the full (natural) rate of unemployment. The classical economists made little distinction between the long run and the short run. Prices adjust so fast that the economy is essentially always on or quickly moving toward *LRAS*.

Labor Input per Year (millions of workers)	Real GDP per Year ($ trillions)
98	7
104	8
120	9
135	10
145	11
160	12

TABLE 11-1
The Relationship Between Employment and Real GDP

FIGURE 11-5

Classical Theory and Increases in Aggregate Demand

The classical theorists believed that Say's law, flexible interest rates, prices, and wages would always lead to full employment at Y_0 along the vertical aggregate supply curve, *LRAS*. With aggregate demand, AD_1, the price level is 100. An increase in aggregate demand shifts AD_1 to AD_2. At price level 100, the quantity of real GDP per year demanded is *A* on AD_2, or Y_1. But this is greater than full employment. Prices rise, and the economy quickly moves from E_1 to E_2 at the higher price level of 110. It will be at Point *A* for only a very brief interval.

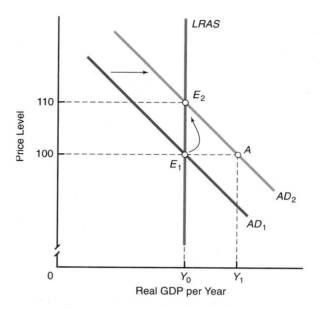

Furthermore, because the labor market adjusts rapidly, Y_0 is always at, or soon to be at, full employment. Full employment does not mean zero unemployment because there is always some frictional and structural unemployment (discussed in Chapter 7), even in the classical world. This is the natural rate of unemployment.

Effect of an Increase in Aggregate Demand in the Classical Model. In this model, any change in aggregate demand will quickly cause a change in the price level. Consider starting at E_1, at price level 100. If aggregate demand shifts to AD_2, the economy will tend toward point *A*, but because this is beyond full employment, prices will rise, and the economy will find itself back on the vertical *LRAS* at point E_2 at a higher price level, 110. The price level will increase as a result of the increase in *AD* because employers will end up bidding up wages for now more relatively scarce workers. In addition, factories will be bidding up the price of other inputs.

The level of real GDP per year clearly does not depend on the level of aggregate demand. Hence we say that in the classical model, the equilibrium level of real GDP per year is completely *supply determined*. Changes in aggregate demand affect only the price level, not the output of real goods and services.

Effect of a Decrease in Aggregate Demand in the Classical Model. The effect of a decrease in aggregate demand in the classical model is the converse of the analysis just presented for an increase in aggregate demand. You can simply reverse AD_2 and AD_1 in Figure 11-5. To help you see how this analysis works, consider the flowchart in Figure 11-6.

FIGURE 11-6

Effect of a Decrease in Aggregate Demand in the Classical Model

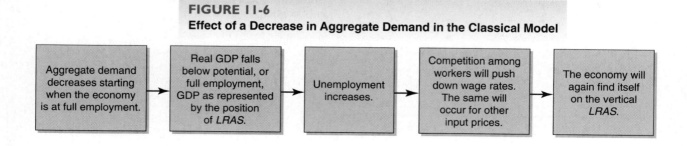

● Say's law states that supply creates its own demand and therefore *desired* expenditures will equal *actual* expenditures.

● The classical model assumes that (1) pure competition exists, (2) wages and prices are completely flexible, (3) individuals are motivated by self-interest, and (4) they cannot be fooled by money illusion.

● When saving is introduced into the model, equilibrium occurs in the credit market through changes in the interest rate such that desired saving equals desired investment at the equilibrium rate of interest.

● In the labor market, full employment occurs at a wage rate at which quantity demanded equals quantity supplied. That particular level of employment is associated with a full-employment value of real GDP per year.

● In the classical model, because the *LRAS* is vertical, the equilibrium level of real GDP is supply determined. Any changes in aggregate demand simply change the price level.

KEYNESIAN ECONOMICS AND THE KEYNESIAN SHORT-RUN AGGREGATE SUPPLY CURVE

The classical economists' world was one of fully utilized resources. There would be no unused capacity and no unemployment. But then post–World War I Europe entered a period of long-term economic decline that could not be explained by the classical model. John Maynard Keynes developed an explanation that has since become known as the Keynesian model. Keynes and his followers argued that prices, especially the price of labor (wages), were inflexible downward due to the existence of unions and of long-term contracts between businesses and workers. That meant that prices were "sticky." Keynes argued that in such a world, which has large amounts of excess capacity and unemployment, an increase in aggregate demand will not raise the price level, and a decrease in aggregate demand will not cause firms to lower prices. This situation is depicted in Figure 11-7. For simplicity, Figure 11-7 does not show the point where the economy reaches capacity, and that is why *SRAS* never starts to slope upward. Moreover, we don't show *LRAS* in Figure 11-7 either. It would be a vertical line at the level of real GDP per year that is consistent with full employment. The short-run aggregate supply curve is labeled as the horizontal line *SRAS*. If we start out in equilibrium with aggregate demand at AD_1, the equilibrium level of real GDP per year will be Y_1 and the equilibrium price level will be P_0. If there is a rise in aggregate demand, so that the aggregate demand curve

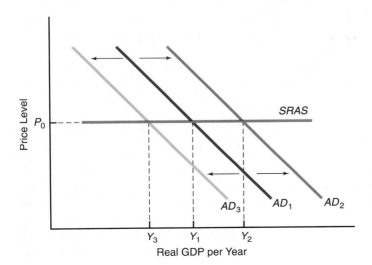

FIGURE 11-7

Demand-Determined Equilibrium Output at Less than Full Employment

Keynes assumed that prices will not fall when aggregate demand falls and that there is excess capacity so that prices will not rise when aggregate demand increases. Thus the short-run aggregate supply curve is simply a horizontal line at the given price level, P_0, represented by *SRAS*. An aggregate demand shock that increases aggregate demand to AD_2 will increase the equilibrium level of real output per year to Y_2. An aggregate demand shock that decreases aggregate demand to AD_3 will decrease the equilibrium level of real output to Y_3. The equilibrium price level will not change.

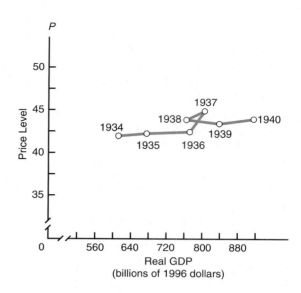

FIGURE 11-8
Real GDP and the Price Level, 1934–1940
In a depressed economy, increased aggregate spending can increase output without raising prices. This is what Keynes believed, and the data for the United States' recovery from the later years of the Great Depression seem to bear this out. In such circumstances, the level of real output is demand determined.

Putting Economics in Action to Work

For more practice with the aggregate demand curve, start the *EIA* CD and click on "Aggregate Demand and Supply." Then click on "Aggregate Demand."

Keynesian short-run aggregate supply curve
The horizontal portion of the aggregate supply curve in which there is unemployment and unused capacity in the economy.

shifts outward to the right to AD_2, the equilibrium price level will not change; only the equilibrium level of real GDP per year will increase, to Y_2. Conversely, if there is a fall in demand that shifts the aggregate demand curve to AD_3, the equilibrium price level will again remain at P_0, but the equilibrium level of real GDP per year will fall to Y_3.

Under such circumstances, the equilibrium level of real GDP per year is completely *demand determined*.

The horizontal short-run aggregate supply curve represented in Figure 11-7 is often called the **Keynesian short-run aggregate supply curve.** According to Keynes, unions and long-term contracts are real-world factors that explain the inflexibility of *nominal* wage rates. Such stickiness of wages makes *involuntary* unemployment of labor a distinct possibility. The classical assumption of everlasting full employment no longer holds.

A pretty good example of a horizontal short-run aggregate supply curve can be seen by examining data from the aftermath of the Great Depression of the 1930s. Look at Figure 11-8, where you see real GDP in billions of 1996 dollars on the horizontal axis and the price level index on the vertical axis. From the early days of recovery from the Great Depression to the outbreak of World War II, real GDP increased without much rise in the price level. During this period, the economy experienced neither supply constraints nor any dramatic changes in the price level. The most simplified Keynesian model in which prices do not change is essentially an immediate post-Depression model that fits the data very well during this period.

OUTPUT DETERMINATION USING AGGREGATE DEMAND AND AGGREGATE SUPPLY: FIXED VERSUS CHANGING PRICE LEVELS IN THE SHORT RUN

The underlying assumption of the simplified Keynesian model is that the relevant range of the short-run aggregate supply schedule (*SRAS*) is horizontal, as depicted in panel (a) of Figure 11-9. There you will see that short-run aggregate supply is fixed at price level 120. If aggregate demand is AD_1, then the equilibrium level of real GDP is $9 trillion per year. If aggregate demand increases to AD_2, then the equilibrium level of real GDP increases to $10 trillion per year.

As discussed in Chapter 10, the price level has clearly drifted upward during recent decades. Hence the assumption of totally sticky prices is an oversimplification. Modern

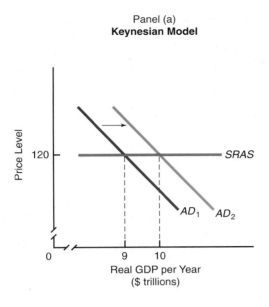

Panel (a)
Keynesian Model

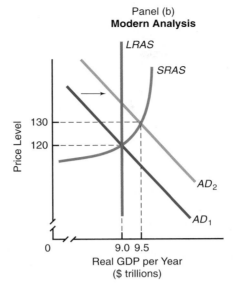

Panel (b)
Modern Analysis

FIGURE 11-9

Income Determination with Fixed Versus Flexible Prices
In panel (a), the price level index is fixed at 120. An increase in aggregate demand from AD_1 to AD_2 moves the equilibrium level of real GDP from $9 trillion per year to $10 trillion per year. In panel (b), *SRAS* is upward-sloping. The same shift in aggregate demand yields an equilibrium level of real GDP of only $9.5 trillion per year and a higher price level index at 130.

Keynesian analysis recognizes that *some*—but not complete—price adjustment takes place in the short run. Panel (b) of Figure 11-9 displays a more general **short-run aggregate supply curve** (*SRAS*). This curve represents the relationship between the price level and real output of goods and services in the economy with incomplete price adjustment and in the absence of complete information in the short run. Allowing for partial price adjustment implies that *SRAS* slopes upward, and its slope is steeper after it crosses long-run aggregate supply, *LRAS*. This is because higher and higher prices of output are required to induce firms to raise their output to levels temporarily exceed full-employment output. With gradual price adjustment in the short run, if aggregate demand is AD_1, then the equilibrium level of real GDP in panel (b) is also $9 trillion per year, also at a price level of 120. A similar increase in aggregate demand to AD_2 as occurred in panel (a) produces a different equilibrium, however. Equilibrium real GDP increases to $9.5 trillion per year, which is less than in panel (a) because part of the increase in *nominal* GDP has occurred through an increase in the price level to 130.

In the modern Keynesian short run, when the price level rises gradually, output can be expanded beyond the level consistent with its long-run growth path, discussed in Chapter 10, for a variety of reasons:

1. In the short run, most labor contracts implicitly or explicitly call for flexibility in hours of work at the given wage rate. Therefore, firms can use existing workers more intensively in a variety of ways: They can get them to work harder. They can get them to work more hours per day. And they can get them to work more days per week. Workers can also be switched from *uncounted* production, such as maintenance, to *counted* production, which generates counted output. The distinction between counted and uncounted is simply what is measured in the marketplace, particularly by government statisticians and accountants. If a worker cleans a machine, there is no measured output. But if that worker is put on the production line and helps increase the number of units produced each day, measured output will go up. That worker's production has then been counted.

2. Existing capital equipment can be used more intensively. Machines can be worked more hours per day. Some can be made to work at a faster speed. Maintenance can be delayed.

Short-run aggregate supply curve
The relationship between aggregate supply and the price level in the short run, all other things held constant. If prices adjust gradually in the short run, the curve is positively sloped.

3. Finally, and just as important, if wage rates are held constant, a higher price level means that profits go up, which induces firms to hire more workers. The duration of unemployment falls, and thus the unemployment rate falls. And people who were previously not in the labor force (homemakers and younger or older workers) can be induced to enter.

All these adjustments cause national output to rise as the price level increases.

SHIFTS IN THE AGGREGATE SUPPLY CURVE

Just as there were non-price-level factors that could cause a shift in the aggregate demand curve, there are non-price-level factors that can cause a shift in the aggregate supply curve. The analysis here is not quite so simple as the analysis for the non-price-level determinants for aggregate demand, for here we are dealing with both the short run and the long run—*SRAS* and *LRAS*. Still, anything other than the price level that affects output production will shift aggregate supply curves.

Shifts in Both Short- and Long-Run Aggregate Supply

There is a core class of events that causes a shift in both the short-run aggregate supply curve and the long-run aggregate supply curve. These include any change in our endowments of the factors of production.* Any change in a factor influencing economic growth—labor, capital, or technology—will shift *SRAS and LRAS*. Look at Figure 11-10. Initially, the two curves are $SRAS_1$ and $LRAS_1$. Now consider a big oil discovery in Tennessee in an area where no one thought oil existed. This shifts $LRAS_1$ to $LRAS_2$ at $10.5 trillion of real GDP. $SRAS_1$ also shifts outward horizontally to $SRAS_2$.

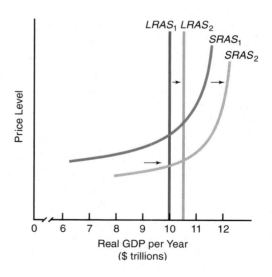

FIGURE 11-10
Shifts in Both Short- and Long-Run Aggregate Supply
Initially, the two supply curves are $SRAS_1$ and $LRAS_1$. Now consider a big oil find in Tennessee in an area where no one thought oil existed. This shifts $LRAS_1$ to $LRAS_2$ at $10.5 trillion of real GDP. $SRAS_1$ also shifts outward horizontally to $SRAS_2$.

*There is a complication here. A big enough increase in natural resources not only shifts aggregate supply outward but also affects aggregate demand. Aggregate demand is a function of people's wealth, among other things. A big oil discovery in America will make enough people richer that desired total spending will increase. For the sake of simplicity, we ignore this complication.

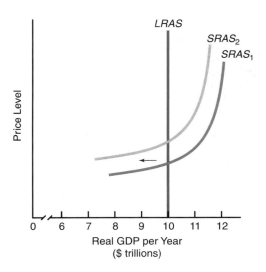

FIGURE 11-11
Shifts in *SRAS* Only
A temporary increase in an input price will shift the short-run aggregate supply curve from $SRAS_1$ to $SRAS_2$.

Shifts in *SRAS* Only

Some events, particularly those that are short-lived, will temporarily shift *SRAS* but not *LRAS*. One of the most obvious is a change in input prices, particularly those caused by external events that are not expected to last forever. Consider the possibility of an announced 90-day embargo of oil from the Middle East to the United States. Oil is an important input in many production activities. The 90-day oil embargo will cause at least a temporary increase in the price of this input. You can see what happens in Figure 11-11. *LRAS* remains fixed, but $SRAS_1$ shifts to $SRAS_2$, reflecting the increase in input prices—the higher price of oil. This is because the rise in the costs of production at each level of real GDP per year requires a higher price level to cover those increased costs.

We summarize the possible determinants of aggregate supply in Table 11-2. These determinants will cause a shift in either the short-run or the long-run aggregate supply curve, or both, depending on whether they are temporary or permanent.

Changes That Cause an Increase in Aggregate Supply	Changes That Cause a Decrease in Aggregate Supply
Discoveries of new raw materials	Depletion of raw materials
Increased competition	Decreased competition
A reduction in international trade barriers	An increase in international trade barriers
Fewer regulatory impediments to business	More regulatory impediments to business
An increase in labor supplied	A decrease in labor supplied
Increased training and education	Decreased training and education
A decrease in marginal tax rates	An increase in marginal tax rates
A reduction in input prices	An increase in input prices

TABLE 11-2
Determinants of Aggregate Supply
The determinants listed here can affect short-run or long-run aggregate supply (or both), depending on whether they are temporary or permanent.

● If we assume that we are operating on a horizontal short-run aggregate supply curve, the equilibrium level of real GDP per year is completely demand determined.

CONCEPTS
IN BRIEF

- The horizontal short-run aggregate supply curve has been called the Keynesian short-run aggregate supply curve because Keynes believed that many prices, especially wages, would not be reduced even when aggregate demand decreased.

- The modern Keynesian theory short-run aggregate supply curve, *SRAS*, shows the relationship between the price level and the real output of goods and services in the economy without full adjustment or full information. It is upward sloping because it allows only for partial price adjustment in the short run.

- Output can be expanded in the short run because firms can use existing workers and capital equipment more intensively. Also, in the short run, when input prices are fixed, a higher price level means higher profits, which induces firms to hire more workers.

- Any change in factors influencing long-run output growth, such as labor, capital, or technology, will shift both *SRAS* and *LRAS*. A temporary shift in input prices, however, will shift only *SRAS*.

CONSEQUENCES OF CHANGES IN AGGREGATE SHORT-RUN DEMAND

We now have a basic model to apply when evaluating short-run adjustments of the equilibrium price level and the equilibrium real GDP when there are shocks to the economy. Whenever there is a shift in our economy's curves, the equilibrium price level or real GDP level (or both) may change. These shifts are called **aggregate demand shocks** on the demand side and **aggregate supply shocks** on the supply side.

Aggregate demand shock
Any shock that causes the aggregate demand curve to shift inward or outward.

Aggregate supply shock
Any shock that causes the aggregate supply curve to shift inward or outward.

Effects When Aggregate Demand Falls While Aggregate Supply Is Stable

Now we can show what happens in the short run when aggregate supply remains stable but aggregate demand falls. The short-run outcome may be the possible cause of a recession and can under certain circumstances explain a rise in the unemployment rate.

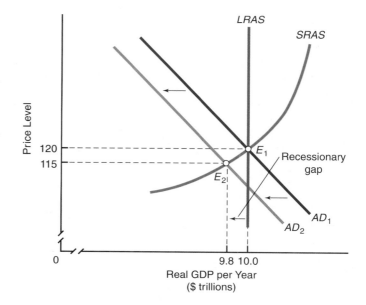

FIGURE 11-12

The Short-Run Effects of Stable Aggregate Supply and a Decrease in Aggregate Demand: The Recessionary Gap

If the economy is at equilibrium at E_1, with price level 120 and real GDP per year of $10 trillion, a shift inward of the aggregate demand curve to AD_2 will lead to a new short-run equilibrium at E_2. The equilibrium price level will fall to 115, and the short-run equilibrium level of real GDP per year will fall to $9.8 trillion. There will be a recessionary gap.

In Figure 11-12, you see that with AD_1, both long-run and short-run equilibrium are at $10 trillion of real GDP per year (because *SRAS* and *LRAS* also intersect AD_1 at that level of real GDP). The long-run equilibrium price level is 120. A reduction in aggregate demand shifts the aggregate demand curve to AD_2. The new intersection with *SRAS* is at $9.8 trillion per year, which is below the economy's long-run aggregate supply. The difference between $10 trillion and $9.8 trillion is called the **recessionary gap,** which is defined as the difference between the short-run equilibrium level of real GDP and how much the economy could be producing if it were operating at full employment on its *LRAS*.

In effect, at E_2, the economy is in short-run equilibrium at less than full employment. With too many unemployed inputs, input prices will begin to fall. Eventually, *SRAS* will have to shift down. Where will it intersect AD_2?

The Short-Run Effects When Aggregate Demand Increases

We can reverse the situation and have aggregate demand increase to AD_2, as is shown in Figure 11-13. The initial equilibrium conditions are exactly the same as in Figure 11-12. The move to AD_2 increases the short-run equilibrium from E_1 to E_2 such that the economy is operating at $10.2 trillion of real GDP per year, which exceeds *LRAS*. This is a condition of an overheated economy, typically called an **inflationary gap.**

At B_2 in Figure 11-13, the economy is at a short-run equilibrium that is beyond full employment. In the short run, more can be squeezed out of the economy than what occurs in the long run, full-information, full-adjustment situation. Firms would be operating beyond long-run capacity. Inputs would be working too hard. Input prices would begin to rise. That would eventually cause *SRAS* to shift upward. At what point on AD_2 in Figure 11-13 would the new *SRAS* stop shifting?

Recessionary gap
The gap that exists whenever the equilibrium level of real national income per year is less than the full-employment level as shown by the position of the long-run aggregate supply curve.

Inflationary gap
The gap that exists whenever the equilibrium level of real national income per year is greater than the full-employment level as shown by the position of the long-run aggregate supply curve.

Putting
Economics in Action
to Work

Get practice thinking about how real GDP and the price level are determined in the short run. Start the *EIA* CD, click on "Aggregate Demand and Supply," and then click on "Short-Run Macroeconomic Equilibrium."

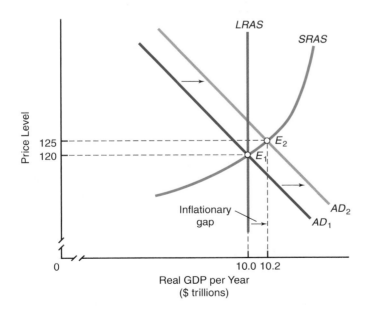

FIGURE 11-13
The Effects of Stable Aggregate Supply with an Increase in Aggregate Demand:
The Inflationary Gap
The economy is at equilibrium at E_1. An increase in aggregate demand of AD_2 leads to a new short-run equilibrium at E_2 with the price level rising from 120 to 125 and the equilibrium level of real GDP per year rising from $10 trillion to $10.2 trillion. The difference, $200 billion, is called the inflationary gap.

EXAMPLE

Effects on the Domestic Economy of a Short-Lived Foreign War

One way we can show what happens to the equilibrium price level and the equilibrium real GDP level with an aggregate demand shock is to consider a short-lived war (we actually had one in the Persian Gulf from August 1990 to early 1991). In Figure 11-14 you see the equilibrium price level of 110 and the equilibrium real GDP level of $10 trillion at the long-run aggregate supply curve. The quick war shifts aggregate demand from AD_{prewar} to $AD_{quick war}$. Equilibrium moves from E_1 to E_2, and the price level moves from 110 to 115. The short-run equilibrium real GDP increases to $10.2 trillion per year. The government's spending for the short-lived war caused AD to shift outward to the right. Also notice that the quick war temporarily pushed the economy above its long-run aggregate supply curve.

For Critical Analysis
What would happen if the short-lived war became permanent? How would you show it in Figure 11-14?

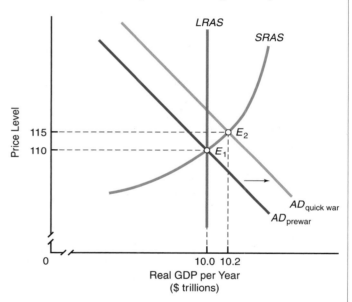

FIGURE 11-14
The Short-Run Effects of a War
A quick war will shift aggregate demand to $AD_{quick war}$. Equilibrium will move from E_1 to E_2 temporarily.

EXPLAINING SHORT-RUN VARIATIONS IN INFLATION: DEMAND-PULL OR COST-PUSH?

In Chapter 10, we noted that in a growing economy, the explanation for persistent inflation is that aggregate demand rises over time at a faster pace than the full-employment output level. Short-run variations in inflation, however, can arise as a result of both demand *and* supply factors. Figure 11-13 presents a demand-side theory explaining a short-run jump in inflation, sometimes called *demand-pull inflation*. Whenever the general level of prices rises in the short run because of increases in aggregate demand, we say that the economy is experiencing **demand-pull inflation**—inflation caused by increases in aggregate demand.

An alternative explanation for near-term increases in the price level comes from the supply side. Look at Figure 11-15. The initial equilibrium conditions are the same as in

Demand-pull inflation
Inflation caused by increases in aggregate demand not matched by increases in aggregate supply.

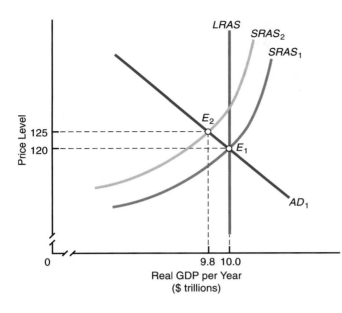

FIGURE 11-15

The Short-Run Effects of Stable Aggregate Demand and a Decrease in Aggregate Supply: Supply-Side Inflation

If aggregate demand remains stable but $SRAS_1$ shifts to $SRAS_2$, equilibrium changes from E_1 to E_2. The price level rises from 120 to 125. If there are continual decreases in aggregate supply of this nature, the situation is called cost-push inflation.

Figures 11-13 and 11-14. Now, however, there is a decrease in the aggregate supply curve, from $SRAS_1$ to $SRAS_2$. Equilibrium shifts from E_1 to E_2. The price level has increased from 120 to 125, too, while the equilibrium level of real GDP per year decreased from $10 trillion to $9.8 trillion. If there are continual decreases in aggregate supply, the situation is called **cost-push inflation.**

Cost-push inflation
Inflation caused by a continually decreasing short-run aggregate supply curve.

As the example of cost-push inflation shows, if the economy is initially in equilibrium on its *LRAS,* a decrease in *SRAS* will lead to a rise in the price level. Thus any abrupt change in one of the factors that determine aggregate supply will alter the equilibrium level of real GDP and the equilibrium price level. If the economy is for some reason operating to the left of its *LRAS,* an increase in *SRAS* will lead to a simultaneous *increase* in the equilibrium level of real GDP per year and a *decrease* in the price level. You should be able to show this in a graph similar to Figure 11-15.

My parents talk about paying only a quarter for a gallon of gas. Why was gas so cheap then?

You have to distinguish between the real and nominal price of a gallon of gas. Even if the nominal price of a gallon of gas in 1999 was around a dollar, or four times what it was in the 1950s, it still was actually cheaper in *real* terms. The price level had increased more than four times since then. At the beginning of the twenty-first, century, the real price of gas was probably the lowest it had ever been in the history of civilization.

EXAMPLE

The Oil Price Shock of the 1970s

One of the best examples of an aggregate supply shock occurred in the 1970s. Several times, the supply of crude oil to the United States was restricted. These restrictions were the result of actions taken by the Organization of Petroleum Exporting Countries (OPEC). The oil embargo had an almost immediate impact on the price of oil and petroleum products, mainly gasoline and heating oil. Higher oil prices raised the cost of production in many U.S. industries that relied on petroleum. The result was a shift in the aggregate supply curve as shown in Figure 11-16. The equilibrium shifted from E_1—$3 trillion of real GDP per year and a price level of 115—to E_2—equilibrium real GDP of $2.8 trillion and a price level of 120.

For Critical Analysis

If the price of oil had remained permanently high, what would have happened to *LRAS* in Figure 11-16?

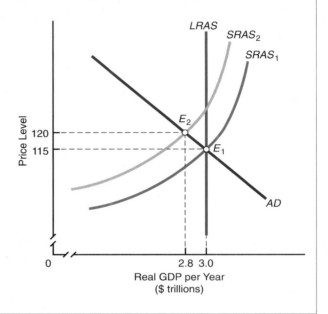

FIGURE 11-16

The Effects of Oil Price Shocks on the Economy

In the 1970s, the supply of crude oil to the United States was restricted. Higher oil prices raised the cost of production. $SRAS_1$ shifted to $SRAS_2$ and equilibrium went from E_1 to E_2 with a higher price level and a lower equilibrium real GDP per year.

AGGREGATE DEMAND AND SUPPLY IN AN OPEN ECONOMY

In many of the international examples in the preceding chapters, we had to translate foreign currencies into dollars when the open economy was discussed. We used the exchange rate, or the price of the dollar relative to other currencies. In Chapter 10, you also discovered that the open economy effect was one of the reasons why the aggregate demand curve slopes downward. When the domestic price level rises, Americans want to buy cheaper-priced foreign goods. The opposite occurs when the American domestic price level falls. Currently, the foreign sector of the American economy constitutes over 12 percent of all economic activities.

How a Stronger Dollar Affects Aggregate Supply

Assume that the dollar becomes stronger in international foreign exchange markets. If last week the dollar could buy 1 euro but this week it now buys 1.25 euros, it has become stronger. To the extent that American companies import raw and partially processed goods from abroad, a stronger dollar can lead to lower input prices. This will lead to a shift outward to the right in the short-run aggregate supply curve as shown in panel (a) of Figure 11-17. In that simplified model, equilibrium GDP would rise and the price level would fall. The result might involve increased employment and lower inflation.

FIGURE 11-17

The Effects of a Stronger Dollar

When the dollar increases in value in the international currency market, lower prices for imported inputs result, causing a shift outward to the right in the short-run aggregate supply schedule from $SRAS_1$ to $SRAS_2$ in panel (a). If nothing else changes, equilibrium shifts from E_1 to E_2 at a lower price level and a higher equilibrium real GDP per year. A stronger dollar can also affect the aggregate demand curve because it will lead to fewer net exports and cause AD_1 to fall to AD_2 in panel (b). Equilibrium would move from E_1 to E_2, a lower price level, and a lower equilibrium real GDP per year.

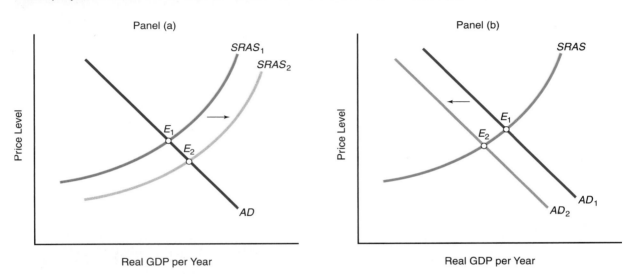

How a Stronger Dollar Affects Aggregate Demand

There is another effect of a stronger dollar that we must consider. Foreigners will find that American goods are now more expensive, expressed in their own currency. After all, a $10 compact disk before the stronger dollar cost a French person 10 euros when the exchange rate was 1 to 1. After the dollar became stronger and the exchange rate increased to 1.25 to 1, that same $10 CD would cost 12.5 euros. Conversely, Americans will find that the stronger dollar makes imported goods cheaper. The result for Americans is fewer exports and more imports, or lower net exports (exports minus imports). If net exports fall, employment in export industries will fall: This is represented in panel (b) of Figure 11-17. After the dollar becomes stronger, the aggregate demand curve shifts inward from AD_1 to AD_2. The result is a tendency for equilibrium real GDP and the price level to fall and for unemployment to rise.

To track how the dollar's value is changing relative to other currencies, go to **www.ny.frb.org/pihome/ statistics/forex10.shtml**

The Net Effect

We have learned, then, that a stronger dollar *simultaneously* leads to an increase in *SRAS* and a decrease in *AD*. Remember from Chapter 4 that in such situations, the effect on real output depends on which curve shifts more. If the aggregate demand curve shifts more than the short-run aggregate supply curve, equilibrium real GDP will fall. Conversely, if the aggregate supply curve shifts more than the aggregate demand curve, equilibrium real GDP will rise.

You should be able to redo this entire analysis for a weaker dollar.

● Short-run equilibrium occurs at the intersection of the aggregate demand curve, *AD*, and the short-run aggregate supply curve, *SRAS*. Long-run equilibrium occurs at the intersection of *AD* and the long-run aggregate supply curve, *LRAS*. Any unanticipated shifts in aggregate demand or supply are called aggregate demand shocks or aggregate supply shocks.

● When aggregate demand shifts while aggregate supply is stable, a recessionary gap can occur, defined as the difference between the equilibrium level of real GDP and how much the economy could be producing if it were operating on its *LRAS*. The reverse situation leads to an inflationary gap.

● With stable aggregate supply, an abrupt shift in *AD* may lead to what is called demand-pull inflation. With a stable aggregate demand, an abrupt shift inward in *SRAS* may lead to what is called cost-push inflation.

● A change in the international value of the dollar can affect both the *SRAS* and aggregate demand. A stronger dollar will reduce the cost of imported inputs, thereby causing the *SRAS* to shift outward to the right, leading to a lower price level and a higher equilibrium real GDP per year, given no change in aggregate demand. In contrast, a stronger dollar will lead to lower net exports, causing the aggregate demand curve to shift inward, leading to a lower price level and a lower equilibrium real GDP per year. The net effect depends on which shift is more important. The opposite analysis applies to a weakening dollar in international currency markets.

NETNOMICS

Are New Information Technologies Making the Short-Run Aggregate Supply Schedule Less Steeply Sloped?

Evidence has been increasing that the short-run aggregate supply curve (*SRAS*) has become less steeply sloped since the early 1990s. Some economists credit widespread deregulation in the 1970s and 1980s with laying the foundation for a more shallowly sloped *SRAS* curve. The increase in domestic and international rivalry among sellers of goods and services, they argue, has made consumers much more sensitive to price differences across products. In equilibrium, therefore, the general level of prices exhibits less change, relative to years past, in response to a given change in output—hence a less steeply sloped *SRAS* curve.

Now continuing developments in information technologies promise to take this trend a step further. For the first time ever, information technologies are the biggest job creators. Depending on whose statistics you look at, such industries are producing between 25 and 40 percent of all new jobs. An information economy is fundamentally different from an industrial economy. Software and databases, for example, can be scaled up to gigantic capacity at little cost. Indeed, because of the ease of communicating data over the Internet, they have unlimited capacity at the very beginning. In other words, capacity as previously defined may be an outdated concept.

Hence beyond the point at which the *SRAS* curve crosses the *LRAS* curve, there will likely be less of a tendency for the *SRAS* curve to bend upward as the United States becomes more of an information economy. Perhaps today's and especially tomorrow's *SRAS* will have to be represented by a curve that is more nearly horizontal.

ISSUES & APPLICATIONS

Banning Women from the Labor Force: Its Effect on Afghanistan's Economy

Afghanistan suffered through 18 years of war until the mid-1990s, when the Taliban militia took over and proclaimed a Muslim fundamentalist state. As part of the Muslim principles as interpreted by the ruling clerics, women's activities were severely restricted. Women and girls were forbidden to go to offices and schools. The restriction on gainful employment for women was particularly painful to those who were sole supporters of their families. After 18 years of war, there were many fewer men around to support families.

The New Equilibrium in the Labor Market

Let's re-create Figure 11-4 for the Afghan labor market as Figure 11-18. In panel (a) you see the demand curve for labor, D, intersecting the former supply curve, S, at E_0. Employment in Afghanistan was in equilibrium at 6.6 million workers. The equilibrium wage rate was estimated to be 7,150 afghani, the national currency. (Of course, we are ignoring a very large nonmarket economy in Afghanistan.)

It was estimated that women made up 10 percent of the labor force. So after the ban, the supply curve shifted to S_1 such that total employment was reduced to 5.9 million

Concepts Applied

Labor Force

Supply and Demand of Labor

Relationship Between Employment and Real GDP

FIGURE 11-18

The Effects of Curtailing Female Employment in Afghanistan

Panel (a) shows that forbidding women and girls to be gainfully employed reduces the supply of labor, thereby causing a reduction in equilibrium employment and an increase in the market wage rate. As shown in panel (b), this reduction in productive labor caused the short-run aggregate supply curve to shift upward, causing an increase in the equilibrium price level and a reduction in equilibrium real GDP.

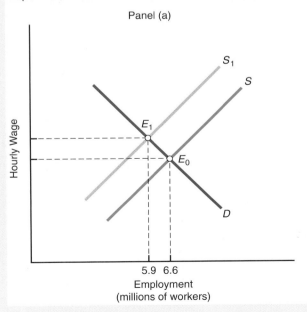

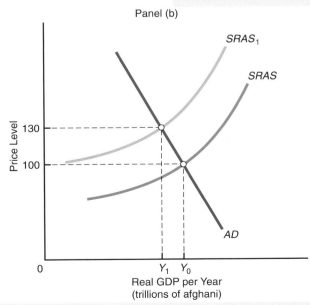

1. How would the analysis change, if at all, if we used a traditional Keynesian horizontal *SRAS* curve?

2. What would happen to the measured unemployment rate in Afghanistan after the ban on female work?

workers. The wage rate of those who continued to work—males—obviously had to go up. Those continuing to work were better off. But the economy as a whole had to have suffered from the ban on female work. Remember the relationship between employment and real GDP in Table 11-1. The smaller the labor input per year, the smaller the resulting real GDP per year.

The Reduction in Equilibrium Real GDP

Look at panel (b). The aggregate demand curve is labeled *AD*. The original short-run aggregate supply curve is labeled *SRAS*. After the ban on female work, Afghanistan had in essence lost a significant part of its productive inputs. The price of the remaining labor input did, of course, rise. The short-run aggregate supply curve shifted upward to $SRAS_1$. Equilibrium real GDP fell from Y_0 to Y_1. The price level rose from 100 to 130.

SUMMARY DISCUSSION OF LEARNING OBJECTIVES

1. **Central Assumptions of the Classical Model:** There are four fundamental assumptions of the classical model: (a) Pure competition prevails, so that no individual buyer or seller of a good or service or of a factor of production can affect its price; (b) wages and prices are completely flexible; (c) people are motivated by self-interest; and (d) buyers and sellers do not experience money illusion, meaning that they respond only to changes in relative prices.

2. **Short-Run Determination of Equilibrium Real GDP and the Price Level in the Classical Model:** Under the four assumptions of the classical model, the short-run aggregate supply curve is vertical at the full-employment output level and thus corresponds to the long-run aggregate supply curve. So even in the short run, real GDP cannot increase in the absence of changes in factors, such as labor, capital, and technology, which induce longer-term economic growth. Given the current position of the classical aggregate supply curve, short-run movements in the equilibrium price level are generated by variations in aggregate demand.

3. **Circumstances Under Which the Short-Run Aggregate Supply Curve May Be Horizontal or Upward-Sloping:** If output prices and wages and other input prices are "sticky," perhaps because of the unions or labor contracts, the short-run aggregate supply schedule can be horizontal over much of its range. This is the Keynesian short-run aggregate

supply curve. More generally, however, to the extent that there is gradual but incomplete adjustment of prices in the short run, the short-run aggregate supply curve slopes upward.

4. **Factors That Induce Shifts in the Short-Run and Long-Run Aggregate Supply Curves:** The long-run aggregate supply curve shifts in response to changes in the availability of labor or capital or to changes in technology and productivity, and changes in these factors also cause the short-run aggregate supply curve to shift. Because output prices may adjust only partially to changing input prices in the short run, however, a widespread change in the prices of factors of production, such as an economy-wide change in wages, can cause a shift in the short-run aggregate supply curve without affecting the long-run aggregate supply curve.

5. **Effects of Aggregate Demand and Supply Shocks on Equilibrium Real Output in the Short Run:** An aggregate demand shock that causes the aggregate demand curve to shift leftward pushes equilibrium real output below the full-employment output level in the short run, so that there is a recessionary gap. An aggregate demand shock that induces a rightward shift in the aggregate demand curve results in an inflationary gap in which the short-run equilibrium level of real GDP exceeds the full-employment GDP level.

6. **Causes of Short-Run Variations in the Inflation Rate:** In the short run, an upward movement in the

price level can occur in the form of demand-pull inflation when the aggregate demand curve shifts rightward along an upward-sloping short-run aggregate supply curve. Cost-push inflation can arise in the short run when the short-run aggregate supply curve shifts leftward along the aggregate demand curve.

Key Terms and Concepts

Aggregate demand shock (258)

Aggregate supply shock (258)

Cost-push inflation (261)

Demand-pull inflation (260)

Inflationary gap (259)

Keynesian short-run aggregate supply curve (254)

Money illusion (248)

Recessionary gap (259)

Say's law (247)

Short-run aggregate supply curve (255)

Problems

Answers to the odd-numbered problems appear at the back of the book.

11-1. Consider a country whose economic structure matches the assumptions of the classical model. After reading a recent best-seller documenting a growing population of low-income elderly people who were ill-prepared for retirement, most residents of this country decide to increase their saving at any given interest rate. Explain whether or how this could affect the following:
   a. The current equilibrium interest rate
   b. Current equilibrium national output
   c. Current equilibrium employment
   d. Current equilibrium investment
   e. Future equilibrium national output

11-2. "There is *absolutely no distinction* between the classical model and the model of long-run equilibrium discussed in Chapter 10." Is this statement true or false? Support your answer.

11-3. A nation in which the classical model applies experiences a decline in the quantity of money in circulation. Use an appropriate aggregate demand and aggregate supply diagram to explain what happens to equilibrium output and to the equilibrium price level.

11-4. The classical model is appropriate for a country that has suddenly experienced an influx of immigrants who possess a wide variety of employable skills and who have reputations for saving relatively large portions of their incomes, as compared with native-born residents, at any given

interest rate. Evaluate the effects of this event on the following:
   a. Current equilibrium employment
   b. Current equilibrium national output
   c. The current equilibrium interest rate
   d. Current equilibrium investment
   e. Future equilibrium national output

11-5. Suppose that the Keynesian short-run aggregate supply curve is applicable for a nation's economy. Use appropriate diagrams to assist in answering the following questions:
   a. What are two factors that can cause the nation's real GDP to increase in the short run?
   b. What are two factors that can cause the nation's real GDP to increase in the long run?

11-6. What determines how steeply the short-run aggregate supply curve is sloped?

11-7. At a point along the short-run aggregate supply curve that is to the right of the point where it crosses the long-run aggregate supply curve, what must be true of the unemployment rate relative to the natural rate of unemployment? Why?

11-8. The stock market crashes in an economy with an upward-sloping short-run aggregate supply curve, and consumer and business confidence plummets. What are the short-run effects on equilibrium real GDP and the equilibrium price level?

11-9. Consider an open economy in which the aggregate supply curve slopes upward in the short run and businesses buy a large portion of their nonhuman factors of production from abroad. In contrast, consumers import few foreign-made goods, and foreign residents purchase few domestically produced goods. What is the most likely short-run effect on this nation's economy if the value of its currency weakens sharply and for a prolonged period in foreign exchange markets?

11-10. Consider an open economy in which the aggregate supply curve slopes upward in the short run.

Firms in this nation do not import raw materials or any other productive inputs from abroad, but foreign residents purchase many of the nation's export goods. What is the most likely short-run effect on this nation's economy if there is a significant downturn in economic activity in other nations around the world?

Economics on the Net

Money, the Price Level, and Real GDP   The classical and Keynesian theories have differing predictions about how changes in the quantity of money in circulation should affect the equilibrium price level and equilibrium real GDP. Here you get a chance to take your own look at the data on growth in the money supply, the price level, and real GDP in the United States.

Internet URL:
www.stls.frb.org/docs/publications/mt/

Title: Federal Reserve Bank of St. Louis Monetary Trends

Navigation: Begin at the home page of the Federal Reserve Bank of St. Louis (www.stls.frb.org). Click on Economic Research, and then click on FRED. Then click on *Monetary Trends* Publication. Finally, click on Gross Domestic Product and M2.

Application Read the article; then answer the questions that follow.

1. Classical theory indicates that, *ceteris paribus*, changes in the price level should be closely related to

changes in aggregate demand induced by variations in the quantity of money. Take a look at the charts showing "Gross Domestic Product Price Index" and "M2." Are annual percentage changes in these variables closely related?

2. Keynesian theory predicts that, *ceteris paribus*, changes in GDP and the quantity of money should be directly related. Take a look at the charts showing "Real Gross Domestic Product" and "M2." Are annual percentage changes in these variables closely related?

For Group Study and Analysis Both classical and Keynesian theories of relationships among real GDP, the price level, and the quantity of money hinge on specific assumptions. Have class groups search through the FRED database to evaluate factors that provide support for either theory's predictions. Which approach appears to receive greater support from recent data? Does this necessarily imply that this is the "true theory"? Why or why not?

CONSUMPTION, INCOME, AND THE MULTIPLIER

Some countries are allocating a much larger percentage of GDP to net investment. The Czech Republic is one of them. Should the U.S. be worried about being "overtaken" by those countries that are investing so much?

During the 1990s and the early 2000s, the United States allocated about 17 percent of its GDP to net investment. This compares with an average of more than 20 percent in Western Europe and approximately 30 percent in Japan. Some commentators in the media have speculated that the lower measured investment rate in the United States will ultimately threaten the nation's long-term growth. A few go even further, arguing that because a relatively low investment rate depresses total spending, it serves as a drag on *current* U.S. output. How do changes in net investment spending affect economic activity? Is the U.S. investment rate really lagging so far behind the rest of the world? Studying this chapter will help you contemplate these and other questions about how total expenditures affect equilibrium U.S. national income.

LEARNING OBJECTIVES

After reading this chapter, you should be able to:

1. **Distinguish between saving and savings and explain how saving and consumption are related**

2. **Explain the key determinants of consumption and saving in the Keynesian model**

3. **Identify the primary determinants of planned investment**

4. **Describe how equilibrium national income is established in the Keynesian model**

5. **Evaluate why autonomous changes in total planned expenditures have a multiplier effect on equilibrium national income**

6. **Understand the relationship between total planned expenditures and the aggregate demand curve**

Did You Know That... personal consumption expenditures in the United States have averaged about two-thirds of gross domestic product for decades? Each year, Americans purchase millions of television sets, millions of pairs of shoes, millions of compact disks, and billions of stress-reducing pills, among other products and services. We are a nation of spenders, and our personal consumption expenditures keep the American economic machine moving day in and day out. As it turns out, John Maynard Keynes focused much of his research on what determines how much you and I decide to spend each year. Remember that total planned expenditures consist of consumption expenditures, plus expenditures for investment purposes, what the government spends, and what foreigners spend on domestically produced output, less what U.S. residents spend on foreign goods and services. Keynes focused on the relationship between how much people earn and their willingness to engage in personal consumption expenditures. In this chapter, you will learn about that relationship as well as the influence of investment, government, and the foreign sector on the economy's equilibrium level of real GDP—the values of both income and output in the circular flow—per year.

SOME SIMPLIFYING ASSUMPTIONS IN A KEYNESIAN MODEL

Continuing in the Keynesian tradition, we will assume that the short-run aggregate supply curve within the current range of real GDP is horizontal. That is to say, we assume that it is similar to Figure 11-7 on page 253, meaning that the equilibrium level of real GDP is demand determined. That is why Keynes wished to examine the elements of desired aggregate expenditures. Because of the Keynesian assumption of inflexible prices, inflation is not a concern. Hence real values are identical to nominal values.

To simplify the income determination model that follows, a number of assumptions are made:

1. Businesses pay no indirect taxes (for example, sales taxes).
2. Businesses distribute all of their profits to shareholders.
3. There is no depreciation (capital consumption allowance), so gross private domestic investment equals net investment.
4. The economy is closed—that is, there is no foreign trade.

Given all these simplifying assumptions, real disposable income will be equal to real national income minus taxes.*

Another Look at Definitions and Relationships

You can do only two things with a dollar of disposable income: consume it or save it. If you consume it, it is gone forever. If you save the entire dollar, however, you will be able to

---

*Strictly speaking, we are referring here to net taxes—the difference between taxes paid and transfer payments received. If taxes are $1 trillion but individuals receive transfer payments—Social Security, unemployment benefits, and so forth—of $300 billion, net taxes are equal to $700 billion.

consume it (and perhaps more if it earns interest) at some future time. That is the distinction between **consumption** and **saving.** Consumption is the act of using income for the purchase of consumption goods. **Consumption goods** are goods purchased by households for immediate satisfaction. Consumption goods are such things as food, clothing, and movies. By definition, whatever you do not consume you save and can consume at some time in the future.

Stocks and Flows: The Difference Between Saving and Savings. It is important to distinguish between *saving* and *savings. Saving* is an action that occurs at a particular rate—for example, $10 a week or $520 a year. This rate is a flow. It is expressed per unit of time, usually a year. Implicitly, then, when we talk about saving, we talk about a *flow* or rate of saving. *Savings,* by contrast, is a *stock* concept, measured at a certain point or instant in time. Your current *savings* are the result of past *saving.* You may presently have *savings* of $2,000 that are the result of four years' *saving* at a rate of $500 per year. Consumption is also a flow concept. You consume from after-tax income at a certain rate per week, per month, or per year.

Relating Income to Saving and Consumption. Obviously, a dollar of take-home income can be either consumed or not consumed. Realizing this, we can see the relationship among saving, consumption, and disposable income:

$$\text{Consumption} + \text{saving} \equiv \text{disposable income}$$

This is called an *accounting identity*. It has to hold true at every moment in time. From it we can derive the definition of saving:

$$\text{Saving} \equiv \text{disposable income} - \text{consumption}$$

Recall that disposable income is what you actually have left to spend after you pay taxes.

Investment

Investment is also a flow concept. As noted earlier, *investment* as used in economics differs from the common use of the term. In common speech, it is often used to describe putting money into the stock market or real estate. In economic analysis, investment is defined as expenditures by firms on new machines and buildings—**capital goods**—that are expected to yield a future stream of income. This is called *fixed investment.* We also include changes in business inventories in our definition. This we call *inventory investment.*

Consumption
Spending on new goods and services out of a household's current income. Whatever is not consumed is saved. Consumption includes such things as buying food and going to a concert.

Saving
The act of not consuming all of one's current income. Whatever is not consumed out of spendable income is, by definition, saved. *Saving* is an action measured over time (a flow), whereas *savings* are a stock, an accumulation resulting from the act of saving in the past.

Consumption goods
Goods bought by households to use up, such as food, clothing, and movies.

Investment
Spending by businesses on things such as machines and buildings, which can be used to produce goods and services in the future. The investment part of total output is the portion that will be used in the process of producing goods in the future.

Capital goods
Producer durables; nonconsumable goods that firms use to make other goods.

◉ If we assume that we are operating on a horizontal short-run aggregate supply curve, the equilibrium level of real GDP per year is completely demand determined.

◉ *Saving* is a flow, something that occurs over time. It equals disposable income minus consumption. *Savings* are a stock. They are the accumulation resulting from saving.

◉ Investment is also a flow. It includes expenditures on new machines, buildings, and equipment and changes in business inventories.

CONCEPTS IN BRIEF

DETERMINANTS OF PLANNED CONSUMPTION AND PLANNED SAVING

In the classical model, the supply of saving was determined by the rate of interest: The higher the rate of interest, the more people wanted to save and therefore the less people wanted to consume. According to Keynes, the interest rate is not the most important determinant of an individual's saving and consumption decisions.

Keynes argued that saving and consumption decisions depend primarily on an individual's current real disposable income.

The relationship between planned consumption expenditures of households and their current level of real disposable income has been called the **consumption function.** It shows how much all households plan to consume per year at each level of real disposable income per year. The first two columns of Table 12-1 illustrate a consumption function for a hypothetical household.

We see from Table 12-1 that as real disposable income rises, planned consumption also rises, but by a smaller amount, as Keynes suggested. Planned saving also increases with disposable income. Notice, however, that below an income of $10,000, the planned saving of this hypothetical family is actually negative. The further that income drops below that level, the more the family engages in **dissaving,** either by going into debt or by using up some of its existing wealth.

Consumption function
The relationship between amount consumed and disposable income. A consumption function tells us how much people plan to consume at various levels of disposable income.

Dissaving
Negative saving; a situation in which spending exceeds income. Dissaving can occur when a household is able to borrow or use up existing assets.

TABLE 12-1

Real Consumption and Saving Schedules: A Hypothetical Case
Column 1 presents real disposable income from zero up to $20,000 per year; column 2 indicates planned consumption per year; column 3 presents planned saving per year. At levels of disposable income below $10,000, planned saving is negative. In column 4, we see the average propensity to consume, which is merely planned consumption divided by disposable income. Column 5 lists average propensity to save, which is planned saving divided by disposable income. Column 6 is the marginal propensity to consume, which shows the proportion of *additional* income that will be consumed. Finally, column 7 shows the proportion of *additional* income that will be saved, or the marginal propensity to save.

Combination	(1) Real Disposable Income per Year (Y_d)	(2) Planned Real Consumption per Year (C)	(3) Planned Real Saving Per Year ($S \equiv Y_d - C$) (1) − (2)	(4) Average Propensity to Consume ($APC \equiv C/Y_d$) (2) ÷ (1)	(5) Average Propensity to Save ($APS \equiv S/Y_d$) (3) ÷ (1)	(6) Marginal Propensity to Consume ($MPC \equiv \Delta C/\Delta Y_d$)	(7) Marginal Propensity to Save ($MPS \equiv \Delta S/\Delta Y_d$)
A	$ 0	$ 2,000	$−2,000	—	—	—	—
B	2,000	3,600	−1,600	1.8	−.8	.8	.2
C	4,000	5,200	−1,200	1.3	−.3	.8	.2
D	6,000	6,800	− 800	1.133	−.133	.8	.2
E	8,000	8,400	− 400	1.05	−.05	.8	.2
F	10,000	10,000	0	1.0	.0	.8	.2
G	12,000	11,600	400	.967	.033	.8	.2
H	14,000	13,200	800	.943	.057	.8	.2
I	16,000	14,800	1,200	.925	.075	.8	.2
J	18,000	16,400	1,600	.911	.089	.8	.2
K	20,000	18,000	2,000	.9	.1	.8	.2

Graphing the Numbers

We now graph the consumption and saving relationships presented in Table 12-1. In the upper part of Figure 12-1, the vertical axis measures the level of planned real consumption per year, and the horizontal axis measures the level of real disposable income per year. In the lower part of the figure, the horizontal axis is again real disposable income per year, but now the vertical axis is planned real saving per year. All of these are on a dollars-per-year basis, which emphasizes the point that we are measuring flows, not stocks.

As you can see, we have taken income-consumption and income-saving combinations *A* through *K* and plotted them. In the upper part of Figure 12-1, the result is called the *consumption function*. In the lower part, the result is called the *saving function*. Mathematically, the saving function is the *complement* of the consumption function because consumption plus saving always equals disposable income. What is not consumed is, by definition, saved. The difference between actual disposable income and the planned rate of consumption per year *must* be the planned rate of saving per year.

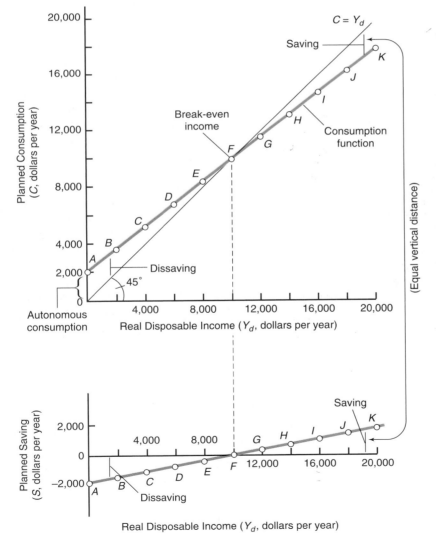

FIGURE 12-1

The Consumption and Saving Functions

If we plot the combinations of real disposable income and planned real consumption from columns 1 and 2 in Table 12-1, we get the consumption function. At every point on the 45-degree line, a vertical line drawn to the income axis is the same distance from the origin as a horizontal line drawn to the consumption axis. Where the consumption function crosses the 45-degree line at *F*, we know that planned real consumption equals real disposable income and there is zero saving. The vertical distance between the 45-degree line and the consumption function measures the rate of real saving or dissaving at any given income level. If we plot the relationship between column 1, real disposable income, and column 3, planned real saving, from Table 12-1, we arrive at the saving function shown in the lower part of this diagram. It is the complement of the consumption function presented above it.

45-degree reference line
The line along which planned real expenditures equal real national income per year.

How can we find the rate of saving or dissaving in the upper part of Figure 12-1? We draw a line that is equidistant from both the horizontal and the vertical axes. This line is 45 degrees from either axis and is often called the **45-degree reference line.** At every point on the 45-degree reference line, a vertical line drawn to the income axis is the same distance from the origin as a horizontal line drawn to the consumption axis. Thus at point *F,* where the consumption function intersects the 45-degree line, real disposable income equals planned real consumption. Point *F* is sometimes called the *break-even income point* because there is neither positive nor negative real saving. This can be seen in the lower part of Figure 12-1 as well. The planned annual rate of real saving at a real disposable income level of $10,000 is indeed zero.

Dissaving and Autonomous Consumption

To the left of point *F* in either part of Figure 12-1, this hypothetical family engages in dissaving, either by going into debt or by consuming existing assets, including savings. The rate of real saving or dissaving in the upper part of the figure can be found by measuring the vertical distance between the 45-degree line and the consumption function. This simply tells us that if our hypothetical family starts above $10,000 of real disposable income per year and then temporarily finds its real disposable income below $10,000, it will not cut back its real consumption by the full amount of the reduction. It will instead go into debt or consume existing assets in some way to compensate for part of the loss.

Autonomous consumption
The part of consumption that is independent of (does not depend on) the level of disposable income. Changes in autonomous consumption shift the consumption function.

Now look at the point on the diagram where real disposable income is zero but planned consumption per year is $2,000. This amount of real planned consumption, which does not depend at all on actual real disposable income, is called **autonomous consumption.** The autonomous consumption of $2,000 is *independent* of the level of disposable income. That means that no matter how low the level of real income of our hypothetical family falls, the family will always attempt to consume at least $2,000 per year. (We are, of course, assuming here that the family's real disposable income does not equal zero year in and year out. There is certainly a limit to how long our hypothetical family could finance autonomous consumption without any income.) That $2,000 of yearly consumption is determined by things other than the level of income. We don't need to specify what determines autonomous consumption; we merely state that it exists and that in our example it is $2,000 per year. Just remember that the word *autonomous* means "existing independently." In our model, autonomous consumption exists independently of the hypothetical family's level of real disposable income. (Later we will review some of the non-real-disposable-income determinants of consumption.) There are many possible types of autonomous expenditures. Hypothetically, we can consider that investment is autonomous—independent of income. We can assume that government expenditures are autonomous. We will do just that at various times in our discussions to simplify our analysis of income determination.

Average propensity to consume (APC)
Consumption divided by disposable income; for any given level of income, the proportion of total disposable income that is consumed.

Average Propensity to Consume and to Save

Let's now go back to Table 12-1, and this time let's look at columns 4 and 5: **average propensity to consume (APC)** and **average propensity to save (APS).** They are defined as follows:

Average propensity to save (APS)
Saving divided by disposable income; for any given level of income, the proportion of total disposable income that is saved.

$$APC \equiv \frac{consumption}{real\ disposable\ income}$$

$$APS \equiv \frac{savings}{real\ disposable\ income}$$

Notice from column 4 in Table 12-1 that for this hypothetical family, the average propensity to consume decreases as real disposable income increases. This decrease simply means that the fraction of the family's real disposable income going to consumption falls as income rises. The same fact can be found in column 5. The average propensity to save (APS), which at first is negative, finally hits zero at an income level of $10,000 and then becomes positive. In this example, the APS reaches a value of 0.1 at income level $20,000. This means that the household saves 10 percent of a $20,000 income.

It's quite easy for you to figure out your own average propensity to consume or to save. Just divide your total real disposable income for the year into what you consumed and what you saved. The result will be your personal APC and APS, respectively, at your current level of income. This gives the proportions of total income that are consumed and saved.

Marginal Propensity to Consume and to Save

Now we go to the last two columns in Table 12-1: **marginal propensity to consume (MPC)** and **marginal propensity to save (MPS).** The term *marginal* refers to a small incremental or decremental change (represented by the Greek letter delta, Δ, in Table 12-1). The marginal propensity to consume, then, is defined as

$$\text{MPC} \equiv \frac{\text{change in consumption}}{\text{change in real disposable income}}$$

The marginal propensity to save is defined similarly as

$$\text{MPS} \equiv \frac{\text{change in saving}}{\text{change in real disposable income}}$$

What do MPC and MPS tell you? They tell you what percentage of a given increase or decrease in income will go toward consumption and saving, respectively. The emphasis here is on the word *change*. The marginal propensity to consume indicates how much you will change your planned consumption if there is a change in your real disposable income. If your marginal propensity to consume is 0.8, that does not mean that you consume 80 percent of *all* disposable income. The percentage of your real disposable income that you consume is given by the average propensity to consume, or APC. As Table 12-1 indicates, the APC is not equal to 0.8. In contrast, an MPC of 0.8 means that you will consume 80 percent of any *increase* in your disposable income. Hence the MPC cannot be less than zero or greater than one. We assume that individuals increase their planned consumption by more than zero and less than 100 percent of any increase in real disposable income that they receive.

Consider a simple example in which we show the difference between the average propensity to consume and the marginal propensity to consume. Assume that your consumption behavior is exactly the same as our hypothetical family's behavior depicted in Table 12-1. You have an annual real disposable income of $18,000. Your planned consumption rate, then, from column 2 of Table 12-1 is $16,400. So your average propensity to consume is $16,400/$18,000 = 0.911. Now suppose that at the end of the year your boss gives you an after-tax bonus of $2,000. What would you do with that additional $2,000 in real disposable income? According to the table, you would consume $1,600 of it and save $400. In that case, your *marginal* propensity to consume would be $1,600/$2,000 = 0.8, and your marginal propensity to save would be $400/$2,000 = 0.2. What would happen to your *average* propensity to consume? To find out, we add $1,600 to $16,400 of planned consumption, which gives us a new consumption rate of $18,000. The average propensity to consume is then $18,000 divided by the new higher salary of $20,000. Your APC drops from 0.911 to 0.9. By contrast,

Marginal propensity to consume (MPC)
The ratio of the change in consumption to the change in disposable income. A marginal propensity to consume of 0.8 tells us that an additional $100 in take-home pay will lead to an additional $80 consumed.

Marginal propensity to save (MPS)
The ratio of the change in saving to the change in disposable income. A marginal propensity to save of 0.2 indicates that out of an additional $100 in take-home pay, $20 will be saved. Whatever is not saved is consumed. The marginal propensity to save plus the marginal propensity to consume must always equal 1, by definition.

your MPC remains, in our simplified example, 0.8 all the time. Look at column 6 in Table 12-1. The MPC is 0.8 at every level of income. (Therefore, the MPS is always equal to 0.2 at every level of income.) Underlying the constancy of MPC is the assumption that the amount that you are willing to consume out of additional income will remain the same in percentage terms no matter what level of real disposable income is your starting point.

Some Relationships

Consumption plus saving must equal income. Both your total real disposable income and the change in total real disposable income are either consumed or saved. The proportions of either measure must equal 1, or 100 percent. This allows us to make the following statements:

$$APC + APS = 1 \ (= 100 \text{ percent of total income})$$

$$MPC + MPS = 1 \ (= 100 \text{ percent of the } \textit{change} \text{ in income})$$

The average propensities as well as the marginal propensities to consume and save must total 1, or 100 percent. Check the two statements by adding the figures in columns 4 and 5 for each level of real disposable income in Table 12-1. Do the same for columns 6 and 7.

Causes of Shifts in the Consumption Function

A change in any other relevant economic variable besides real disposable income will cause the consumption function to shift. There is a virtually unlimited number of such nonincome determinants of the position of the consumption function. When population increases or decreases, for example, the consumption function will shift up or down, respectively. Real household **wealth** is also a determinant of the position of the consumption function. An increase in real wealth of the average household will cause the consumption function to shift upward. A decrease in real wealth will cause it to shift downward. So far we have been talking about the consumption function of an individual or a household. Now let's move on to the national economy. We'll consider the consumption function for the entire nation.

Wealth
The stock of assets owned by a person, household, firm, or nation. For a household, wealth can consist of a house, cars, personal belongings, stocks, bonds, bank accounts, and cash.

CONCEPTS IN BRIEF

● The consumption function shows the relationship between planned rates of consumption and real disposable income per year. The saving function is the complement of the consumption function because saving plus consumption must equal real disposable income.

● The average propensity to consume (APC) is equal to consumption divided by real disposable income. The average propensity to save (APS) is equal to saving divided by real disposable income.

● The marginal propensity to consume (MPC) is equal to the change in planned consumption divided by the change in real disposable income. The marginal propensity to save (MPS) is equal to the change in planned saving divided by the change in real disposable income.

● Any change in real disposable income will cause the planned rate of consumption to change; this is represented by a movement along the consumption function. Any change in a nonincome determinant of consumption will shift the consumption function.

DETERMINANTS OF INVESTMENT

Investment, you will remember, consists of expenditures on new buildings and equipment and changes in business inventories. Real gross private domestic investment in the United States has been extremely volatile over the years relative to real consumption. If we were to look at net private domestic investment (investment after depreciation has been deducted), we would see that in the depths of the Great Depression and at the peak of the World War II effort, the figure was negative. In other words, we were eating away at our capital stock—we weren't even maintaining it by completely replacing depreciated equipment.

If we compare real investment expenditures historically with real consumption expenditures, we find that the latter are less variable over time than the former. Why is this so? One possible reason is that the real investment decisions of businesspeople are based on highly variable, subjective estimates of how the economic future looks.

The Planned Investment Function

Consider that at all times, businesses perceive an array of investment opportunities. These investment opportunities have rates of return ranging from zero to very high, with the number (or dollar value) of all such projects inversely related to the rate of return. Because a project is profitable only if its rate of return exceeds the opportunity cost of the investment—the rate of interest—it follows that as the interest rate falls, planned investment spending increases, and vice versa. Even if firms use retained earnings (internal financing) to fund an investment, the higher the market rate of interest, the greater the *opportunity cost* of using those retained earnings. Thus it does not matter in our analysis whether the firm must seek financing from external sources or can obtain such financing by using retained earnings. Just consider that as the interest rate falls, more investment opportunities will be profitable, and planned investment will be higher.

It should be no surprise, therefore, that the investment function is represented as an inverse relationship between the rate of interest and the value of planned investment. A hypothetical investment schedule is given in panel (a) of Figure 12-2 and plotted in panel (b). We see from this schedule that if, for example, the rate of interest is 7 percent, the dollar value of planned investment will be $1.1 trillion per year. Notice, by the way, that planned investment is also given on a per-year basis, showing that it represents a flow, not a stock. (The stock counterpart of investment is the stock of capital in the economy measured in dollars at a point in time.)

What Causes the Investment Function to Shift?

Because planned investment is assumed to be a function of the rate of interest, any non-interest-rate variable that changes can have the potential of shifting the investment function. Expectations of businesspeople is one of those variables. If higher future sales are expected, more machines and bigger plants will be planned for the future. More investment will be undertaken because of the expectation of higher future profits. In this case, the investment schedule, *I,* would shift outward to the right, meaning that more investment would be desired at all rates of interest. Any change in productive technology can potentially shift the investment function. A positive change in productive technology would stimulate demand for additional capital goods and shift the *I* outward to the right. Changes in business taxes can also shift the investment schedule. If they increase, we predict a leftward shift in the planned investment function because higher taxes imply a lower (after-tax) rate of return.

See how U.S. real private investment has varied in recent years by going to **www.stls.frb.org/fred** and clicking on "Gross Domestic Product and Components" and then "Real Fixed Private Investment."

FIGURE 12-2

Planned Investment

In the hypothetical planned investment schedule in panel (a), the rate of planned investment is inversely related to the rate of interest. If we plot the data pairs from panel (a), we obtain the investment function, *I*, in panel (b). It is negatively sloped.

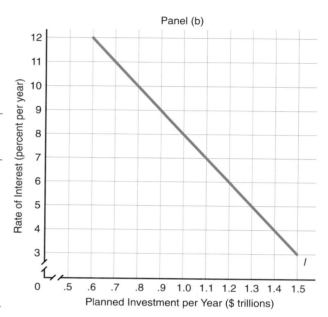

Panel (a)

Rate of Interest (percent per year)	Planned Investment per Year ($ trillions)
12	0.6
11	0.7
10	0.8
9	0.9
8	1.0
7	1.1
6	1.2
5	1.3
4	1.4
3	1.5

CONCEPTS IN BRIEF

- The planned investment schedule shows the relationship between investment and the rate of interest; it slopes downward.

- The non-interest-rate determinants of planned investment are expectations, innovation and technological changes, and business taxes.

- Any change in the non-interest-rate determinants of planned investment will cause the planned investment function to shift so that at each and every rate of interest a different amount of planned investment will be obtained.

CONSUMPTION AS A FUNCTION OF REAL NATIONAL INCOME

We are interested in determining the equilibrium level of real national income per year. But when we examined the consumption function earlier in this chapter, it related planned consumption expenditures to the level of real disposable income per year. We have already shown where adjustments must be made to GDP in order to get real disposable income (see Table 8-2 in Chapter 8). Real disposable income turns out to be less than real national income because net taxes (taxes minus government transfer payments) are usually about 11 to 18 percent of national income. A representative average is about 15 percent, so disposable income, on average, has in recent years been around 85 percent of national income.

If we are willing to assume that real disposable income, Y_d, differs from real national income by an amount T every year, we can relatively easily substitute real national income for real disposable income in the consumption function.

We can now plot any consumption function on a diagram in which the horizontal axis is no longer real disposable income but rather real national income, as in Figure 12-3. Notice that there is an autonomous part of consumption that is so labeled. The difference between this graph and the graphs presented earlier in this chapter is the change in the horizontal axis from real disposable income to real national income per year. For the rest of this chapter, assume that this calculation has been made, and the result is that the MPC out of real national income equals 0.8, suggesting that 20 percent of changes in real national income are either saved or paid in taxes: In other words, of an additional $100 earned, an additional $80 will be consumed.

The 45-Degree Reference Line

Like the earlier graphs, Figure 12-3 shows a 45-degree reference line. The 45-degree line bisects the quadrant into two equal spaces. Thus along the 45-degree reference line, planned consumption expenditures, *C,* equal real national income per year, *Y.* One can see, then, that at any point where the consumption function intersects the 45-degree reference line, planned consumption expenditures will be exactly equal to real national income per year, or $C = Y$. Note that in this graph, because we are looking only at planned consumption on the vertical axis, the 45-degree reference line is where planned consumption, *C,* is always equal to real national income per year, *Y.* Later, when we add investment, government spending, and net exports to the graph, the 45-degree reference line with respect to *all* planned expenditures will be labeled as such on the vertical axis. In any event, consumption and real national income are equal at $7.5 trillion per year. That is where the consumption curve, *C,* intersects the 45-degree reference line. At that income level, all income is consumed.

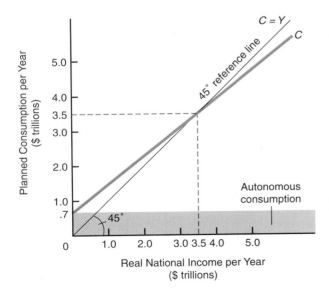

FIGURE 12-3

Consumption as a Function of Real National Income
This consumption function shows the rate of planned expenditures for each level of real national income per year. In this example, there is an autonomous component in consumption equal to $0.7 trillion ($700 billion). Along the 45-degree reference line, planned consumption expenditures per year, *C,* are identical to real national income per year, *Y.* The consumption curve intersects the 45-degree reference line at a value of $3.5 trillion per year.

Adding the Investment Function

Another component of private aggregate demand is, of course, investment spending, *I*. We have already looked at the planned investment function, which related investment to the rate of interest. You see that as the downward-sloping curve in panel (a) of Figure 12-4. Recall from Figure 11-2 that the equilibrium rate of interest is determined at the intersection of the desired savings schedule, which is labeled *S* and is upward-sloping. The equilibrium rate of interest is 7 percent, and the equilibrium rate of investment is $1.1 trillion per year. The $1.1 trillion of real investment per year is *autonomous* with respect to real national income—that is, it is independent of real national income. In other words, given that we have a determinant investment level of $1.1 trillion at a 7 percent rate of interest, we can treat this level of investment as constant, regardless of the level of national income. This is shown in panel (b) of Figure 12-4. The vertical distance of investment spending is $1.1 trillion. Businesses plan on investing a particular amount—$1.1 trillion per year—and will do so no matter what the level of real national income.

How do we add this amount of investment spending to our consumption function? We simply add a line above the *C* line that we drew in Figure 12-3 that is higher by the vertical distance equal to $1.1 trillion of autonomous investment spending. This is shown by the arrow in panel (c) of Figure 12-4. Our new line, now labeled *C* + *I*, is called the *consumption plus investment line*. In our simple economy without government expenditures and net exports, the *C* + *I* curve represents total planned expenditures as they relate to different levels of real national income per year. Because the 45-degree reference line shows all the points where planned expenditures (now *C* + *I*) equal real national income, we label it *C* + *I* = *Y*. Equilibrium *Y* equals $9 trillion per year. Equilibrium occurs when total planned expenditures equal total planned production (given that any amount of production in this model in the short run can occur without a change in the price level).

FIGURE 12-4

Combining Consumption and Investment

In panel (a), we show the determination of real investment in trillions of dollars per year. It occurs where the investment schedule intersects the saving schedule at an interest rate of 7 percent and is equal to $1.1 trillion per year. In panel (b), investment is a constant $1.1 trillion per year. When we add this amount to the consumption line, we obtain in panel (c) the *C* + *I* line, which is vertically higher than the *C* line by exactly $1.1 trillion. Real national income is equal to *C* + *I* at $9 trillion per year where total planned expenditure, *C* + *I*, is equal to actual real national income, for this is where the *C* + *I* line intersects the 45-degree reference line, on which *C* + *I* is equal to *Y* at every point.

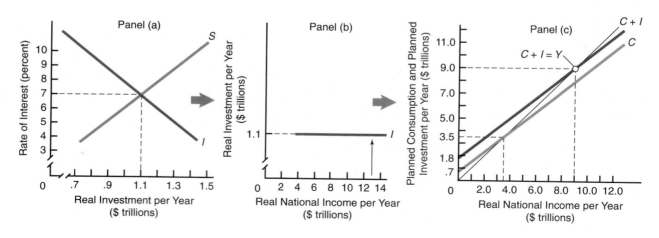

SAVING AND INVESTMENT: PLANNED VERSUS ACTUAL

Figure 12-5 shows the planned investment curve as a horizontal line at $1.1 trillion per year. Investment is completely autonomous in this simplified model—it does not depend on the level of income.

The planned saving curve is represented by *S*. Because in our model whatever is not consumed is, by definition, saved, the planned saving schedule is the complement of the planned consumption schedule, represented by the *C* line in Figure 12-3. For better exposition, we look at only a part of the saving and investment schedules—real national incomes between $7 and $11 trillion per year.

Why does equilibrium have to occur at the intersection of the planned saving and planned investment schedules? If we are at *E* in Figure 12-5, planned saving equals planned investment. All anticipations are validated by reality. There is no tendency for businesses to alter the rate of production or the level of employment because they are neither increasing nor decreasing their inventories in an unplanned way.

If we are producing at a real national income level of $11 trillion instead of $9 trillion, planned investment, as usual, is $1.1 trillion per year, but it is exceeded by planned saving, which is $1.5 trillion per year. This means that consumers will purchase less of total output than businesses had anticipated. Unplanned business inventories will now rise at the rate of $400 billion per year, bringing actual investment into line with actual saving because the $400 billion increase in inventories is included in actual investment. But this rate of output cannot continue for long. Businesses will respond to this unplanned increase in inventories by cutting back production and employment, and we will move toward a lower level of real national income.

Conversely, if the real national income is $7 trillion per year, planned investment continues annually at $1.1 trillion; but at that output rate, planned saving is only $700 billion. This means that households and businesses are purchasing more of real national income than businesses had planned. Businesses will find that they must draw down their inventories below the planned level by $400 billion (business inventories will fall now at the unplanned rate of $400 billion per year), bringing actual investment into equality with

---

FIGURE 12-5

Planned and Actual Rates of Saving and Investment

Only at the equilibrium level of real national income of $9 trillion per year will planned saving equal actual saving, planned investment equal actual investment, and hence planned saving equal planned investment.

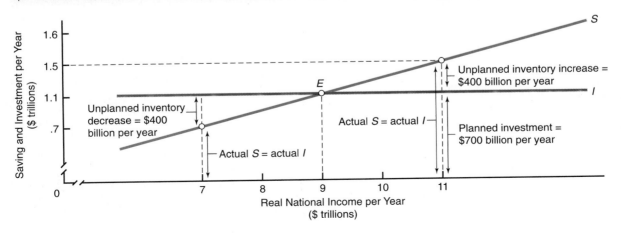

actual saving because the $400 billion decline in inventories is included in actual investment (thereby decreasing it). But this situation cannot last forever either. In their attempt to increase inventories to the desired previous level, businesses will increase output and employment, and real national income will rise toward its equilibrium value of $9 trillion per year. Figure 12-5 demonstrates the necessary equality between actual saving and actual investment. Inventories adjust so that saving and investment, after the fact, are *always* equal in this simplified model. (Remember that changes in inventories count as part of investment.)

Every time the saving rate planned by households differs from the investment rate planned by businesses, there will be a shrinkage or an expansion in the circular flow of income and output (introduced in Chapter 8) in the form of unplanned inventory changes. Real national income and employment will change until unplanned inventory changes are again zero—that is, until we have attained the equilibrium level of real national income.

CONCEPTS IN BRIEF

- ◉ We assume that the consumption function has an autonomous part that is independent of the level of real national income per year. It is labeled "autonomous consumption."

- ◉ For simplicity, we assume that investment is autonomous with respect to real national income and therefore unaffected by the level of real national income per year.

- ◉ The equilibrium level of real national income can be found where planned saving equals planned investment.

- ◉ Whenever planned saving exceeds planned investment, there will be unplanned inventory accumulation, and national income will fall as producers reduce output. Whenever planned saving is less than planned investment, there will be unplanned inventory depletion, and national income will rise as producers increase output.

KEYNESIAN EQUILIBRIUM WITH GOVERNMENT AND THE FOREIGN SECTOR ADDED

Government

We have to add government spending, *G,* to our macroeconomic model. We assume that the level of resource-using government purchases of goods and services (federal, state, and local), *not* including transfer payments, is determined by the political process. In other words, *G* will be considered autonomous, just like investment (and a certain component of consumption). In the United States, resource-using government expenditures are around 25 percent of real national income. The other side of the coin, of course, is that there are taxes, which are used to pay for much of government spending. We will simplify our model greatly by assuming that there is a constant **lump-sum tax** of $1.5 trillion a year to finance $1.5 trillion of government spending. This lump-sum tax will reduce disposable income and consumption by the same amount. We show this in Table 12-2 (column 2), where we give the numbers for a complete model.

Lump-sum tax
A tax that does not depend on income or the circumstances of the taxpayer. An example is a $1,000 tax that every family must pay, irrespective of its economic situation.

The Foreign Sector

Not a week goes by without a commentary in the media about the problem of our foreign trade deficit. For many years, we have been buying merchandise and services from foreign residents—imports—the value of which exceeds the value of the exports we have been selling to them. The difference between exports and imports is *net exports,* which we label *X* in our graphs.

TABLE 12-2
The Determination of Equilibrium Real National Income with Net Exports
Figures are trillions of dollars.

(1) Real National Income	(2) Taxes	(3) Real Disposable Income	(4) Planned Consumption	(5) Planned Saving	(6) Planned Investment	(7) Government Spending	(8) Net Exports (exports − imports)	(9) Total Planned Expenditures (4) + (6) + (7) + (8)	(10) Unplanned Inventory Changes	(11) Direction of Change in Real National Income
4.0	1.5	2.5	2.7	−.2	1.1	1.5	−.1	5.2	−1.2	Increase
5.0	1.5	3.5	3.5	0	1.1	1.5	−.1	6.0	−1.0	Increase
6.0	1.5	4.5	4.3	.2	1.1	1.5	−.1	6.8	−.8	Increase
7.0	1.5	5.5	5.1	.4	1.1	1.5	−.1	7.6	−.6	Increase
8.0	1.5	6.5	5.9	.6	1.1	1.5	−.1	8.4	−.4	Increase
9.0	1.5	7.5	6.7	.8	1.1	1.5	−.1	9.2	−.2	Increase
10.0	1.5	8.5	7.5	1.0	1.1	1.5	−.1	10.0	0	Neither (equilibrium)
11.0	1.5	9.5	8.3	1.2	1.1	1.5	−.1	10.8	+.2	Decrease
12.0	1.5	10.5	9.1	1.4	1.1	1.5	−.1	11.6	+.4	Decrease

The level of exports depends on international economic conditions, especially in the countries that buy our products. Imports depend on economic conditions here at home. For simplicity, let us assume that imports exceed exports (net exports, *X*, is negative) and furthermore that the level of net exports is autonomous—independent of national income. Assume a level of *X* of −$100 billion per year, as shown in column 8 of Table 12-2.

To find out how the North American Free Trade Agreement has affected U.S. imports and exports, go to **www.nafta.net**

Determining the Equilibrium Level of Real National Income per Year

We are now in a position to determine the equilibrium level of real national income per year under the continuing assumptions that the price level is unchanging; that investment, government, and the foreign sector are autonomous; and that planned consumption expenditures are determined by the level of real national income. As can be seen in Table 12-2, total planned expenditures of $10 trillion per year equal real national income of $10 trillion per year, and this is where we reach equilibrium.

Remember that equilibrium *always* occurs when total planned expenditures equal total production (given that any amount of production in this model in the short run can occur without a change in the price level).

Now look at Figure 12-6, which shows the equilibrium level of real national income. There are two curves, one showing the consumption function, which is the exact duplicate of the one shown in Figure 12-3, and the other being the $C + I + G + X$ curve, which intersects the 45-degree reference line (representing equilibrium) at $10 trillion per year.

Whenever total planned expenditures differ from real national income, there are unplanned inventory changes. When total planned expenditures are greater than real

FIGURE 12-6

The Equilibrium Level of Real National Income

The consumption function, with no government and thus no taxes, is shown as C. When we add autonomous investment, government, taxes, and net exports, we obtain $C + I + G + X$. We move from E_1 to E_2. The equilibrium level of real national income is $10 trillion per year.

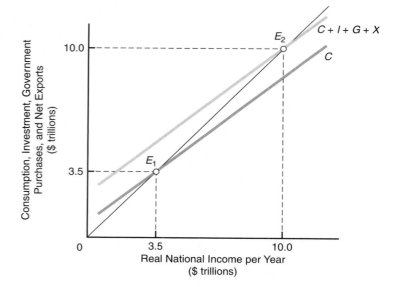

national income, inventory levels drop in an unplanned manner. To get them back up, firms seek to expand their production, which increases real national income. Real national income rises toward its equilibrium level. Whenever total planned expenditures are less than real national income, the opposite occurs. There are unplanned inventory increases, causing firms to cut back on their production. The result is a drop in real national income toward the equilibrium level.

CONCEPTS IN BRIEF

◉ When we add autonomous investment, I, and autonomous government spending, G, to the consumption function, we obtain the $C + I + G$ curve, which represents total planned expenditures for a closed economy. In an open economy, we add the foreign sector, which consists of exports minus imports, or net exports, X. Total planned expenditures are thus represented by the $C + I + G + X$ curve.

◉ The equilibrium level of real national income can be found by locating the intersection of the total planned expenditures curve with the 45-degree reference line. At that level of real national income per year, planned consumption plus planned investment plus government expenditures plus net exports will equal real national income.

◉ Whenever total planned expenditures exceed real national income, there will be unplanned decreases in inventories; the size of the circular flow of income will increase, and a higher level of equilibrium real national income will prevail. Whenever planned expenditures are less than real national income, there will be unplanned increases in inventories; the size of the circular flow will shrink, and a lower equilibrium level of real national income will prevail.

THE MULTIPLIER

Look again at panel (c) of Figure 12-4. Assume for the moment that the only expenditures included in real national income are consumption expenditures. Where would the equilibrium level of income be in this case? It would be where the consumption function (C) intersects the 45-degree reference line, which is at $3.5 trillion per year. Now we add the autonomous amount of planned investment, $1.1 trillion, and then determine what the new equilibrium level of income will be. It turns out to be $9 trillion per year. Adding $1.1 trillion per year of investment spending increased the equilibrium level of income by *five* times that amount, or by $5.5 trillion per year.

What is operating here is the multiplier effect of changes in autonomous spending. The **multiplier** is the number by which a permanent change in autonomous investment or autonomous consumption is multiplied to get the change in the equilibrium level of real national income. Any permanent increases in autonomous investment or in any autonomous component of consumption will cause an even larger increase in real national income. Any permanent decreases in autonomous spending will cause even larger decreases in the equilibrium level of real national income per year. To understand why this multiple expansion (or contraction) in the equilibrium level of real national income occurs, let's look at a simple numerical example.

We'll use the same figures we used for the marginal propensity to consume and to save. MPC will equal 0.8, or $\frac{4}{5}$, and MPS will equal 0.2, or $\frac{1}{5}$. Now let's run an experiment and say that businesses decide to increase planned investment permanently by $100 billion a year. We see in Table 12-3 that during what we'll call the first round in column 1, investment is increased by $100 billion; this also means an increase in real national income of $100 billion, because the spending by one group represents income for another, shown in column 2. Column 3 gives the resultant increase in consumption by households that received this additional $100 billion in real income. This is found by multiplying the MPC by the increase in real income. Because the MPC equals 0.8, consumption expenditures during the first round will increase by $80 billion.

Multiplier
The ratio of the change in the equilibrium level of real national income to the change in autonomous expenditures; the number by which a change in autonomous investment or autonomous consumption, for example, is multiplied to get the change in the equilibrium level of real national income.

TABLE 12-3
The Multiplier Process
We trace the effects of a permanent $100 billion increase in autonomous investment spending on the equilibrium level of real national income. If we assume a marginal propensity to consume of 0.8, such an increase will eventually elicit a $500 billion increase in the equilibrium level of real national income per year.

	Assumption: MPC = 0.8, or $\frac{4}{5}$		
(1) Round	(2) Annual Increase in Real National Income ($ billions per year)	(3) Annual Increase in Planned Consumption ($ billions per year)	(4) Annual Increase in Planned Saving ($ billions per year)
1 ($100 billion per year increase in *I*)	100.00	80.000	20.000
2	80.00	64.000	16.000
3	64.00	51.200	12.800
4	51.20	40.960	10.240
5	40.96	32.768	8.192
.	.	.	.
.	.	.	.
.	.	.	.
All later rounds	163.84	131.072	32.768
Totals (*C* + *I* + *G*)	500.00	400.000	100.000

But that's not the end of the story. This additional household consumption is also spending, and it will provide $80 billion of additional real income for other individuals. Thus during the second round, we see an increase in real income of $80 billion. Now, out of this increased real income, what will be the resultant increase in consumption expenditures? It will be 0.8 times $80 billion, or $64 billion. We continue these induced expenditure rounds and find that because of an initial increase in autonomous investment expenditures of $100 billion, the equilibrium level of real national income will eventually increase by $500 billion. A permanent $100 billion increase in autonomous investment spending has induced an additional $400 billion increase in consumption spending, for a total increase in real national income of $500 billion. In other words, the equilibrium level of real national income will change by an amount equal to five times the change in investment.

The Multiplier Formula

It turns out that the autonomous spending multiplier is equal to the reciprocal of the marginal propensity to save. In our example, the MPC was $\frac{4}{5}$; therefore, because MPC + MPS = 1, the MPS was equal to $\frac{1}{5}$. The reciprocal is 5. That was our multiplier. A $100 billion increase in planned investment led to a $500 billion increase in the equilibrium level of real income. Our multiplier will always be the following:

$$\text{Multiplier} \equiv \frac{1}{1 - \text{MPC}} \equiv \frac{1}{\text{MPS}}$$

You can always figure out the multiplier if you know either the MPC or the MPS. Let's consider some examples. If MPS $= \frac{1}{4}$,

$$\text{Multiplier} = \frac{1}{\frac{1}{4}} = 4$$

Repeating again that MPC + MPS = 1, then MPS = 1 − MPC. Hence we can always figure out the multiplier if we are given the marginal propensity to consume. In this example, if the marginal propensity to consume were given as $\frac{3}{4}$,

$$\text{Multiplier} = \frac{1}{1 - \frac{3}{4}} = \frac{1}{\frac{1}{4}} = 4$$

By taking a few numerical examples, you can demonstrate to yourself an important property of the multiplier:

The smaller the marginal propensity to save, the larger the multiplier.

Otherwise stated:

The larger the marginal propensity to consume, the larger the multiplier.

Demonstrate this to yourself by computing the multiplier when the marginal propensities to save equal $\frac{3}{4}$, $\frac{1}{2}$, and $\frac{1}{4}$. What happens to the multiplier as the MPS gets smaller?

When you have the multiplier, the following formula will then give you the change in the equilibrium level of real national income due to a permanent change in autonomous spending:

$$\text{Multiplier} \times \text{change in autonomous spending} = \text{change in equilibrium level of real national income}$$

The multiplier, as we have mentioned, works for a permanent increase or permanent decrease in autonomous spending. In our earlier example, if the autonomous component of consumption had fallen by $100 billion, the reduction in the equilibrium level of real national income per year would have been $500 billion per year.

Significance of the Multiplier

Depending on the size of the multiplier, it is possible that a relatively small change in planned investment or autonomous consumption can trigger a much larger change in the equilibrium level of real national income per year. In essence, the multiplier magnifies the fluctuations in the equilibrium level of real national income initiated by changes in autonomous spending.

As was just stated, the larger the marginal propensity to consume, the larger the multiplier. If the marginal propensity to consume is $\frac{1}{2}$, the multiplier is 2. In that case, a $1 billion decrease in (autonomous) investment will elicit a $2 billion decrease in the equilibrium level of real national income per year. Conversely, if the marginal propensity to consume is $\frac{9}{10}$, the multiplier will be 10. That same $1 billion decrease in planned investment expenditures with a multiplier of 10 will lead to a $10 billion decrease in the equilibrium level of real national income per year.

EXAMPLE

Changes in Investment and the Great Depression

Changes in autonomous spending lead to shifts in the total expenditures ($C + I + G + X$) curve and, as you have seen, cause a multiplier effect on the equilibrium level of real GDP per year. A classic example apparently occurred during the Great Depression. Indeed, some economists believe that it was an autonomous downward shift (collapse) in the investment function that provoked the Great Depression. Look at panel (a) of Figure 12-7. There you see the net investment (gross investment minus depreciation) in the United States from 1929 to 1941 (expressed in 1992 dollars). Clearly, during business contractions, decision makers in the

FIGURE 12-7

Net Private Domestic Investment and Real GDP During the Great Depression

In panel (a), you see how net private investment expressed in billions of 1992 dollars became negative starting in 1931 and stayed negative for several years. It became positive in 1936 and 1937, only to become negative again in 1938. Look at panel (b). There you see how changes in GDP seem to mirror changes in net private domestic investment.

Source: U.S. Bureau of the Census.

Panel (a)

Year	Net Private Domestic Investment (billions of 1992 dollars)
1929	85.96
1930	24.48
1931	−26.89
1932	−83.34
1933	−80.20
1934	−43.51
1935	− 6.13
1936	18.39
1937	54.20
1938	− 9.54
1939	24.27
1940	66.89
1941	107.71

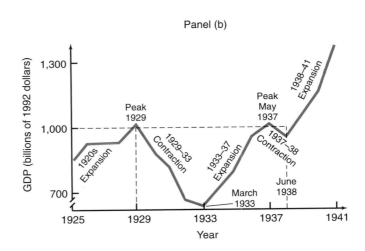

business world can and do decide to postpone long-range investment plans for buildings and equipment. This causes the business recovery to be weak unless those business plans are revised. If you examine real GDP in panel (b) of Figure 12-7, you see that the contraction that started in 1929 reached its trough in 1933. The expansion was relatively strong for the following four years, and then there was another contraction from 1937 to 1938. Some researchers argue that even though the 1937–1938 contraction initially was more severe than the one that started in 1929, it was short-lived because long-range investment plans were revised upward by the end of 1938.

For Critical Analysis

Why might businesses have revised their investment plans upward in 1938?

THE MULTIPLIER EFFECT WHEN THE PRICE LEVEL CAN CHANGE

Clearly, the multiplier effect on the equilibrium overall level of *real* national income will not be as great if part of the increase in *nominal* national income occurs because of increases in the price level. We show this in Figure 12-8. The intersection of AD_1 and *SRAS* is at a price level of 120 with equilibrium real national income of $10 trillion per year. An increase in autonomous spending shifts the aggregate demand curve outward to the right to AD_2. If price level remained at 120, the short-run equilibrium level of real GDP would increase to $10.5 trillion per year because, for the $100 billion increase in autonomous spending, the multiplier would be 5, as it was in Table 12-3. But the price level does not stay fixed because ordinarily the *SRAS* curve is positively sloped. In this diagram, the new short-run equilibrium level of real national income is hypothetically $10.3 trillion of real national income per year. Instead of the multiplier being 5, the multiplier with respect to equilibrium changes in the output of real goods and services—real national income—is only 3. The multiplier is smaller because part of the additional income is used to pay higher prices; not all is spent on increased output, as is the case when the price level is fixed.

If the economy is at an equilibrium level of real national income that is greater than *LRAS,* the implications for the multiplier are even more severe. Look again at Figure 12-8. The *SRAS* curve starts to slope upward more dramatically after $10 trillion of real national income per year. Therefore, any increase in aggregate demand will lead to a proportionally

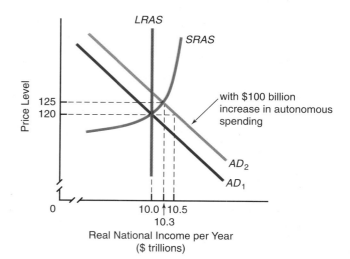

FIGURE 12-8

Multiplier Effect on Equilibrium of Real National Income

A $100 billion increase in autonomous spending (investment, government, or net exports), which moves AD_1 to AD_2, will yield a full multiplier effect only if prices are constant. If the price index increases from 120 to 125, the multiplier effect is less, and the equilibrium level of real national income goes up only to, say, $10.3 trillion per year instead of $10.5 trillion per year.

greater increase in the price level and a smaller increase in the equilibrium level of real national income per year. The multiplier effect of any increase in autonomous spending will be relatively small because most of the changes will be in the price level. Moreover, any increase in the short-run equilibrium level of real national income will tend to be temporary because the economy is temporarily above *LRAS*—the strain on its productive capacity will raise prices.

THE RELATIONSHIP BETWEEN AGGREGATE DEMAND AND THE $C + I + G + X$ CURVE

There is clearly a relationship between the aggregate demand curves that you studied in Chapters 10 and 11 and the $C + I + G + X$ curve developed in this chapter. After all, aggregate demand consists of consumption, investment, and government purchases, plus the foreign sector of our economy. There is a major difference, however, between the aggregate demand curve, *AD*, and the $C + I + G + X$ curve: The latter is drawn with the price level held constant, whereas the former is drawn, by definition, with the price level changing. In other words, the $C + I + G + X$ curve shown in Figure 12-6 is drawn with the price level fixed. To derive the aggregate demand curve, we must now allow the price level to change. Look at the upper part of Figure 12-9. Here we show the $C + I + G + X$

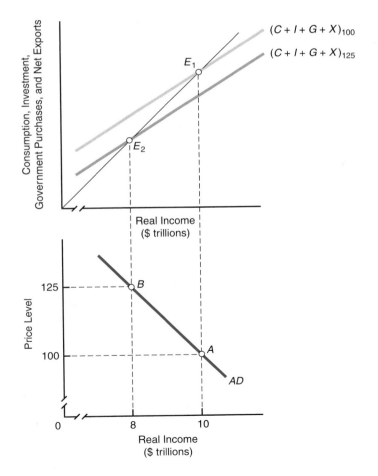

FIGURE 12-9

The Relationship Between *AD* and the $C + I + G + X$ Curve

In the upper graph, the $C + I + G + X$ curve at a price level equal to 100 intersects the 45-degree reference line at E_1, or $10 trillion of real income per year. That gives us point *A* (price level = 100; real income = $10 trillion) in the lower graph. When the price level increases to 125, the $C + I + G + X$ curve shifts downward, and the new equilibrium level of real income is at E_2 at $8 trillion per year. This gives us point *B* in the lower graph. Connecting points *A* and *B*, we obtain the aggregate demand curve.

curve at a price level equal to 100 and equilibrium at $10 trillion of income per year. This gives us point A in the lower graph, for it shows what real income would be at a price level of 100.

Now let's assume that in the upper graph, the price level increases to 125. What are the effects?

1. A higher price level can decrease the purchasing power of any cash that people hold (the real-balance effect). This is a decrease in real wealth, and it causes consumption expenditures, C, to fall, thereby putting downward pressure on the $C + I + G + X$ curve.

2. Because individuals attempt to borrow more to replenish their real cash balances, interest rates will rise, which will make it more costly for people to buy houses and cars (the interest rate effect). Higher interest rates make it more costly, for example, to install new equipment and to erect new buildings. Therefore, the rise in the price level indirectly causes a reduction in the quantity of aggregate goods and services demanded.

3. In an open economy, our higher price level causes the foreign demand for our goods to fall (the open economy effect). Simultaneously, it increases our demand for others' goods. If the foreign exchange price of the dollar stays constant for a while, there will be an increase in imports and a decrease in exports, thereby reducing the size of X, again putting downward pressure on the $C + I + G + X$ curve.

The result is that a new $C + I + G + X$ curve at a price level equal to 125 generates an equilibrium at E_2 at $8 trillion of real income per year. This gives us point B in the lower part of Figure 12-9. When we connect points A and B, we obtain the aggregate demand curve, AD.

CONCEPTS IN BRIEF

◉ Any change in autonomous spending shifts the expenditure curve and causes a multiplier effect on the equilibrium level of real national income per year.

◉ The multiplier is equal to the reciprocal of the marginal propensity to save.

◉ The smaller the marginal propensity to save, the larger the multiplier. Otherwise stated, the larger the marginal propensity to consume, the larger the multiplier.

◉ The $C + I + G + X$ curve is drawn with the price level held constant, whereas the AD curve allows the price level to change. Each different price level generates a new $C + I + G + X$ curve.

NETNOMICS

The Internet Is Making Investment a Fuzzier Concept

Before 1999, the government had treated spending on the software used to post Web pages, download programs, or transmit Internet orders the same as electricity that powered computers and equipment that linked people to the Internet: as a once-and-for-all cost of production. Of course, unlike electricity, software can last for a long time. This is why the government now counts business software expenditures as investment spending, classifying these expenditures as equivalent to spending on the computers and high-speed communications equipment that are the nuts and bolts of the Internet.

Many economists had pushed for this change for years, but now some are having second thoughts. Currently, most businesses purchase new or updated software for on-site installation on the hard drives of office computers. Sun Microsystems and other companies, however, are championing a new approach to computer software distribution that would fundamentally change how businesses use software. In this proposed model for computer operations, businesses would no longer store software on hard drives. Instead, companies would pay monthly or annual fees to software providers in exchange for real-time access to computer operating systems, word processing software, and computer spreadsheet programs directly from the Internet. The Internet-based providers of these new "software services" would automatically update the software as often as new versions became available.

Currently, fees that companies pay for services rendered are costs of doing business and are not counted as investment. Even though there is no *functional* distinction between software stored on a hard drive for months or years and software accessed in real time on the Internet for a fee, the new approach to measuring investment makes a distinction: Spending on software that businesses purchase and store on hard drives is investment, but fees paid for real-time computer operations using software downloaded from the Internet are a short-term cost of doing business. It remains to be seen how government statisticians will deal with this new wrinkle.

ISSUES & APPLICATIONS

Is the U.S. Rate of Net Investment Understated?

As tabulated in the national income accounts, net investment includes spending only on physical capital—plants and equipment, infrastructure, and housing—and adjustments in inventories of produced goods. Using this measure of net investment, the portion of real GDP that U.S. residents allocate to net investment tends to lag behind much of the rest of the developed world. Some observers have interpreted this lower rate of investment as a factor that tends to depress total planned expenditures and hence equilibrium U.S. national income. After all, they point out, any reduction in investment cuts into total planned spending and thereby pulls down equilibrium real income via the multiplier. These observers also worry about a longer-term effect of lower U.S. investment: a fall-off in capital accumulation and reduced growth.

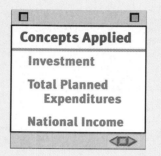

Concepts Applied

Investment

Total Planned Expenditures

National Income

A Measurement Problem?

Other economists are less concerned because they think that the current measure of net investment, which has remained more or less unchanged since national income accounting was developed more than 60 years ago, fails to capture the true meaning of the term. Recall that much investment is spending on capital, resources that may be used to produce output in the future. There are several types of expenditures that appear to fit economists' definition of investment but are not counted as investment:

Education: Spending on education yields returns over long periods of time, but only expenditures on schools and educational equipment are currently included in the official definition of investment spending. In recent years, the United States has allocated nearly 7 percent of its GDP to education. In Japan, this figure is less than 4 percent, and in most other countries it rarely exceeds 5.5 percent.

Research and development: As you learned in Chapter 9, some theories of economic growth view research and development as a fundamental aspect of the growth process. Nevertheless, in the national income accounts, government R&D expenses are counted as government consumption. Business R&D expenses are treated solely as a cost of production, so they are excluded from tabulations of private business investment. The United States spends close to 3 percent of its GDP on research and development, while in many other developed countries such expenses rarely top 2 percent of GDP.

Consumer durables: Only household spending on housing is counted as investment in the national income accounts. Yet U.S. households spend about 6 percent of GDP on durable goods such as automobiles, personal computers, and other relatively long-lived gadgets that yield service flows for years. The comparable figure in other industrialized countries is about 5 percent. All this spending shows up as consumption spending in the official statistics.

U.S. Investment Spending May Be a Bargain

Another neglected factor in comparing the U.S. investment rate with the rate of investment in other countries is that U.S. investment goods are less expensive. That is, a given dollar of spending on factories or computers provides more units of these goods in the United States relative to other countries.

What happens when all factors—relative differences in the prices of investment goods and spending on education, research and development, and consumer durables—are taken into account? The answer is a dramatic change in the international comparison: The adjusted measure of the U.S. investment rate exceeds 35 percent of GDP per year, while the average rate (adjusted in the same way) for other industrialized is about 30 percent. It is possible, therefore, that the United States actually leads the way in investment as broadly defined by economists.

FOR CRITICAL ANALYSIS

1. Some economists argue that military expenditures protect a nation's capital stock from seizure from other powers and thereby ensure returns on other forms of investment, so military spending should somehow count as "investment." What are pros and cons of this proposal?

2. Why is "investment" difficult to define?

SUMMARY DISCUSSION OF LEARNING OBJECTIVES

1. **The Difference Between Saving and Savings and the Relationship Between Saving and Consumption:** Saving is a flow over time, whereas savings is a stock of resources at a point in time. Thus, the portion of your disposable income you do not consume during a week, a month, or a year is an addition to your stock of savings. By definition, saving during a year plus consumption during that year must equal total disposable (after-tax) income earned that year.

2. **Key Determinants of Consumption and Saving in the Keynesian Model:** In the classical model, the interest rate is the fundamental determinant of saving, but in the Keynesian model, the primary determinant is disposable income. The reason is that as real disposable income increases, so do real consumption expenditures. Because consumption and saving equal disposable income, this means that saving must also vary with changes in disposable income. Of course, factors other than disposable income can affect consumption and saving. The portion of consumption that is not related to disposable income is called autonomous consumption. The ratio of saving to disposable income is the average propensity to save

(APS), and the ratio of consumption to disposable income is the average propensity to consume (APC). A change in saving divided by the corresponding change in disposable income is the marginal propensity to save (MPS), and a change in consumption divided by the corresponding change in disposable income is the marginal propensity to consume (MPC).

3. **The Primary Determinants of Planned Investment:** An increase in the interest rate raises the opportunity cost of retaining earnings for investment, so planned investment varies inversely with the interest rate. Hence the investment schedule slopes downward. Other factors that influence planned investment, such as business expectations, productive technology, or business taxes, can cause the investment schedule to shift. In the basic Keynesian model, changes in real national income do not affect planned investment, meaning that investment is autonomous with respect to national income.

4. **How Equilibrium National Income Is Established in the Keynesian Model:** In equilibrium, total planned consumption, investment, government, and net export expenditures equal total national income,

so that $C + I + G + X = Y$. This occurs at the point where the $C + I + G + X$ curve crosses the 45-degree reference line. In a world without government spending and taxes, equilibrium also occurs when planned saving is equal to planned investment. Furthermore, at the equilibrium level of national income, there is no tendency for business inventories to expand or contract.

5. **Why Autonomous Changes in Total Planned Expenditures Have a Multiplier Effect on Equilibrium National Income:** Any increase in autonomous expenditures, such as an increase in investment caused by a rise in business confidence, causes a direct rise in national income. This income increase in turn stimulates increased consumption, and the amount of this increase is the marginal propensity to consume multiplied by the rise in disposable income that results. As consumption increases, however, so does income, which induces a further increase in con-

sumption spending. The ultimate expansion of income is equal to the multiplier, $1/(1 - \text{MPC})$, times the increase in autonomous expenditures.

6. **The Relationship Between Total Planned Expenditures and the Aggregate Demand Curve:** An increase in the price level decreases the purchasing power of money holdings, which induces households and businesses to cut back on expenditures. In addition, as individuals and firms seek to borrow to replenish their cash balances, the interest rate tends to rise, which increases borrowing costs and further discourages spending. Furthermore, a higher price level reduces exports as foreign residents cut back on purchases of domestically produced goods. These effects combined shift the $C + I + G + X$ curve downward following a rise in the price level, so that equilibrium real national income falls. This yields the downward-sloping aggregate demand curve.

Key Terms and Concepts

Autonomous consumption (274)

Average propensity to consume (APC) (274)

Average propensity to save (APS) (274)

Capital goods (271)

Consumption (271)

Consumption function (272)

Consumption goods (271)

Dissaving (272)

45-degree reference line (274)

Investment (271)

Lump-sum tax (282)

Marginal propensity to consume (MPC) (275)

Marginal propensity to save (MPS) (275)

Multiplier (285)

Saving (271)

Wealth (276)

Problems

Answers to the odd-numbered problems appear at the back of the book.

12-1. Complete the accompanying table.
  a. Complete the table.
  b. Add two columns to the right of the table. Calculate the average propensity to save and the average propensity to consume at each level of disposable income. (Round to the nearest hundredth.)
  c. Determine the marginal propensity to save and the marginal propensity to consume.

Disposable Income	Saving	Consumption
$ 200	−$ 40	_____
400	0	_____
600	40	_____
800	80	_____
1,000	120	_____
1,200	160	_____

12-2. Classify each of the following as either a stock or a flow.
  a. Myung Park earns $850 per week.
  b. America Online purchases $100 million in new computer equipment this month.
  c. Sally Schmidt has $1,000 in a savings account at a credit union.
  d. XYZ, Inc., produces 200 units of output per week.
  e. Giorgio Giannelli owns three private jets.
  f. DaimlerChrysler's inventories decline by 750 autos per month.
  g. Russia owes $25 billion to the International Monetary Fund.

12-3. An Internet service provider (ISP) is contemplating an investment of $50,000 in new computer servers and related hardware. The ISP projects an annual rate of return on this investment of 6 percent.
  a. The current market interest rate is 5 percent per year. Will the ISP undertake the investment?
  b. Suddenly there is an economic downturn. Although the market interest rate does not change, the ISP anticipates will reduce the projected rate of return on the investment to 4 percent per year. Will the ISP now undertake the investment?

12-4. Consider the table when answering the following questions. For this hypothetical economy, the marginal propensity to save is constant at all levels of income, and investment spending is autonomous. There is no government.

Real National Income	Consumption	Saving	Investment
$ 2,000	$2,200	$____	$400
4,000	4,000	____	____
6,000	____	____	____
8,000	____	____	____
10,000	____	____	____
12,000	____	____	____

  a. Complete the table. What is the marginal propensity to save? What is the marginal propensity to consume?

b. Draw a graph of the consumption function. Then add the investment function to obtain $C + I$.

c. Under the graph of $C + I$, draw another graph showing the saving and investment curves. Note that the $C + I$ curve crosses the 45-degree reference line in the upper graph at the same level of real national income where the saving and investment curves cross in the lower graph. (If not, redraw your graphs.) What is this level of real national income?

d. What is the numerical value of the multiplier?

e. What is the equilibrium level of real national income without investment? What is the multiplier effect from the inclusion of investment?

f. What is the average propensity to consume at the equilibrium level of real national income?

g. If autonomous investment declines from $400 to $200, what happens to equilibrium real national income?

12-5. Consider the table when answering the following questions. For this hypothetical economy, the marginal propensity to consume is constant at all levels of income, and investment spending is autonomous. The equilibrium level of real national income is equal to $8,000. There is no government.

Real National Income	Consumption	Saving	Investment
$ 2,000	$ 2,000	____	____
4,000	3,600	____	____
6,000	5,200	____	____
8,000	6,800	____	____
10,000	8,400	____	____
12,000	10,000	____	____

  a. Complete the table. What is the marginal propensity to consume? What is the marginal propensity to save?
  b. Draw a graph of the consumption function. Then add the investment function to obtain $C + I$.
  c. Under the graph of $C + I$, draw another graph showing the saving and investment curves. Does the $C + I$ curve cross the 45-degree reference line in the upper graph at the same level of real national income where the saving

and investment curves cross in the lower graph, at the equilibrium real national income level of $8,000? (If not, redraw your graphs.)

d. What is the average propensity to save at the equilibrium level of real national income?

e. If autonomous consumption were to rise by $100, what would happen to equilibrium real national income?

12-6. Calculate the multiplier for the following cases.
   a. MPS = .25
   b. MPC = $\frac{5}{6}$
   c. MPS = .125
   d. MPC = $\frac{6}{7}$
   e. $C = \$200 + .85Y$

Economics on the Net

The Relationship Between Consumption and Real GDP   According to the basic consumption function we considered in this Chapter, comsumption rises at a fixed rate when both disposable income and real GDP increase. Your task here is to evaluate how reasonable this assumption is and to determine the relative extent to which variations in consumption appear to be related to variations in real GDP.

Internet URL: www.stls.frb.org/fred/data/gdp/gdpc92

Title: Gross Domestic Product and Components

Navigation: Begin at the homepage of the Federal Reserve Bank of St. Louis (www.stls.org). Click on FRED (www.stls.org/fred). Then click on Data Files and click on Gross Domestic Product and Components.

Application

1. Click on Personal Consumption Expenditures. Write down consumption expenditures for the past eight quarters. Now back up to Gross Domestic Product and Components, click on Gross Domestic Product, and write down GDP for the past eight quarters. Use these data to calculate implied values for the marginal propensity to consume, assuming that taxes do not vary with income. Is there any problem with this assumption?

2. Back up to Gross Domestic Product and Components. Now click on Gross Domestic Product in Chained (1992) Dollars. Scan through the data since the mid-1960s. In what years did the largest variations in GDP take place? What component or components of GDP appear to have accounted for these large movements?

For Group Study and Analysis Assign groups to use the FRED database to try to determine the best measure of aggregate U.S. disposable income for the past eight quarters. Reconvene the class, and discuss each group's approach to this issue.

THE KEYNESIAN CROSS AND THE MULTIPLIER

We can see the multiplier effect more clearly if we look at Figure B-1, in which we see only a small section of the graphs that we used in Chapter 12. We start with an equilibrium level of real national income of $9.5 trillion per year. This equilibrium occurs with total planned expenditures represented by $C + I + G + X$. The $C + I + G + X$ curve intersects the 45-degree reference line at $6.5 trillion per year. Now we increase investment, I, by $100 billion. This increase in investment shifts the entire $C + I + G + X$ curve vertically to $C + I' + G + X$. The vertical shift represents that $100 billion increase in autonomous investment. With the higher level of planned expenditures per year, we are no longer in equilibrium at E. Inventories are falling. Production will increase. Eventually, planned production will catch up with total planned expenditures. The new equilibrium level of real national income is established at E' at the intersection of the new $C + I' + G + X$ curve and the 45-degree reference line, along which $C + I + G + X = Y$ (total planned expenditures equal real national income). The new equilibrium level of real national income is $10 trillion per year. Thus the increase in equilibrium real national income is equal to five times the permanent increase in planned investment spending.

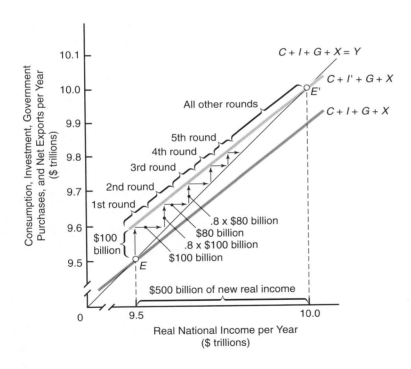

FIGURE B-1
Graphing the Multiplier
We can translate Table 12-3 in Chapter 12 into graphic form by looking at each successive round of additional spending induced by an autonomous increase in planned investment of $100 billion. The total planned expenditures curve shifts from $C + I + G + X$, with its associated equilibrium level of real national income of $9.5 trillion, to a new curve labeled $C + I' + G + X$. The new equilibrium level of real national income is $10 trillion. Equilibrium is again established.

FISCAL POLICY

After years of running deficits, the federal government started running surpluses at the end of the 1990s. How would this group of protesters suggest that the surpluses be eliminated?

In recent years, politicians across America have squabbled about whether the nation should "protect" current and expected future federal budget surpluses—government tax receipts in excess of government expenditures—and use them to pay off the government's debts. Others advocate spending the surpluses (in which case, of course, there would no longer be surpluses) on "crucial government programs." Still others argue that surpluses should be "returned to the American people" via tax cuts (in which case there would also no longer be surpluses). What kinds of budgetary policies, known as *fiscal policies,* should the government pursue? To contemplate this question, you must learn more about how changes in government spending and taxes affect the economy. Those effects are the subject of this chapter.

Did You Know That... the first type of income tax was probably established in the 1200s and 1300s during times of war in the Italian city-states? America's first income tax, enacted in 1861 to help pay for the Civil War, was 3 percent on incomes over $800 a year. Not until the Sixteenth Amendment to the Constitution was ratified in 1913 did most Americans come to know of the federal income tax, and even then very few had to pay it. Today, federal income taxes are taken for granted. More important for this chapter, the federal tax system is now viewed as being capable of affecting the equilibrium level of real GDP. On the spending side of the budget, changes in the federal government's expenditures are also viewed as potentially capable of changing the equilibrium level of real GDP.

DISCRECTIONARY FISCAL POLICY

Deliberate, discretionary changes in government expenditures or taxes (or both) to achieve certain national economic goals is the realm of **fiscal policy.** Some national goals are high employment (low unemployment), price stability, economic growth, and improvement in the nation's international payments balance. Fiscal policy can be thought of as a deliberate attempt to cause the economy to move to full employment and price stability more quickly than it otherwise might.

Fiscal policy has typically been associated with the economic theories of John Maynard Keynes and what is now called *traditional* Keynesian analysis. Recall from Chapter 11 that Keynes's explanation of the Great Depression was that there was insufficient aggregate demand. Because he believed that wages and prices were "sticky downward," he argued that the classical economists' picture of an economy moving automatically and quickly toward full employment was inaccurate. To Keynes and his followers, government had to step in to increase aggregate demand. In other words, expansionary fiscal policy initiated by the federal government was the way to ward off recessions and depressions.

Traditional Keynesian economics dominated academic discussion and government policymaking in the 1960s and 1970s. Perhaps the best-known policy action based on traditional Keynesian theory was the Kennedy-Johnson tax cut of 1964. When John F. Kennedy took office in 1961 promising to "get the country moving again," his advisers recommended a tax cut. The tax cut was not implemented until after Kennedy's death, but in 1964, federal taxes were slashed by $11 billion; within a year, the unemployment rate had fallen from 5.2 percent to 4.5 percent.

As you will see in Chapter 18, modern-day variants of Keynesian analysis are now taking center stage in policymaking discussions.

Changes in Government Spending

In Chapter 11, we looked at the recessionary gap and the inflationary gap (see Figures 11-12 and 11-13). The recessionary gap was defined as the amount by which the current level of real GDP fell short of the economy's potential production if it were operating on its *LRAS*. The inflationary gap was defined as the amount by which the equilibrium level of real GDP exceeds the long-run equilibrium level as given by *LRAS*. Let us examine fiscal policy first in the context of a recessionary gap.

When There Is a Recessionary Gap.   The government, along with firms, individuals, and foreigners, is one of the spending agents in the economy. When the government decides to spend more, all other things held constant, the dollar value of total spending must rise.

Fiscal policy
The discretionary changing of government expenditures or taxes to achieve national economic goals, such as high employment with price stability.

FIGURE 13-1

Expansionary and Contractionary Fiscal Policy: Changes in *G*

If there is a recessionary gap and short-run equilibrium is at E_1 in panel (a), fiscal policy can presumably increase aggregate demand to AD_2. The new equilibrium is at E_2 at higher real GDP per year and a higher price level. In panel (b), the economy is at short-run equilibrium at E_1, which is at a higher real income than the *LRAS*. To reduce this inflationary gap, fiscal policy can be used to decrease aggregate demand from AD_1 to AD_2. Eventually, equilibrium will fall to E_2, which is on the *LRAS*.

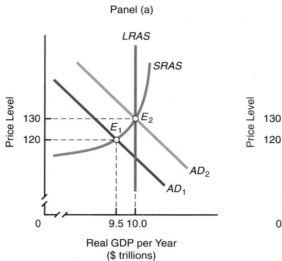

Panel (a)

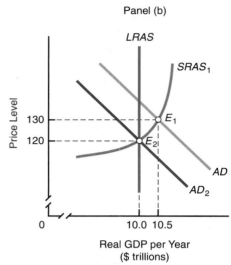

Panel (b)

Look at panel (a) of Figure 13-1. We start at short-run equilibrium with AD_1 intersecting *SRAS* at \$9.5 trillion of real GDP per year. There is a recessionary gap of \$500 billion of real GDP per year—the difference between *LRAS* (the economy's long-run potential) and the short-run equilibrium level of real GDP per year. When the government decides to spend more (expansionary fiscal policy), the aggregate demand curve shifts to the right to AD_2. Here we assume that the government knows exactly how much more to spend so that AD_2 intersects *SRAS* at \$10 trillion, or at *LRAS*. Because of the upward-sloping *SRAS,* the price level rises from 120 to 130 as real GDP goes to \$10 trillion per year.

When There Is an Inflationary Gap.   The entire process shown in panel (a) of Figure 13-1 can be reversed, as shown in panel (b). An inflationary gap occurs at the intersection of $SRAS_1$ and AD_1, at point E_1. The economy cannot be sustained at \$10.5 trillion indefinitely, because this exceeds long-run aggregate supply, which is in real terms \$10 trillion. If the government recognizes this and reduces its spending (pursues a contractionary fiscal policy), this action reduces aggregate demand from AD_1 to AD_2. Equilibrium will fall to E_2, where real GDP per year is \$10 trillion, which is on the *LRAS*. The price level will fall from 130 to 120.

To find out the fractions of GDP allocated to government spending and taxes in the most recent period, go to **www.stls.frb.org/fred/data/ gdp.html** and use the most recent data to calculate these ratios.

Changes in Taxes

The spending decisions of firms, individuals, and foreigners depend on the taxes levied on them. Individuals in their role as consumers look to their disposable (after-tax) income when determining their desired rates of consumption. Firms look at their after-tax profits when deciding on the levels of investment to undertake. Foreigners look at the tax-inclusive

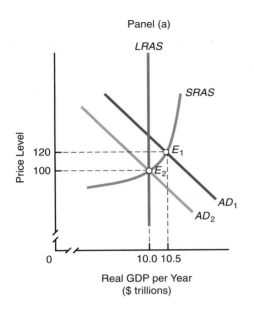

Panel (a)

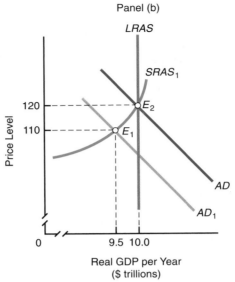

Panel (b)

FIGURE 13-2

Contractionary and Expansionary Fiscal Policy: Changes in *T*

In panel (a), the economy is initially at E_1, which exceeds *LRAS*. Contractionary fiscal policy can move aggregate demand to AD_2 so that the new equilibrium is at E_2 at a lower price level and now at *LRAS*. In panel (b), with a recessionary gap (in this case of $500 billion), taxes are cut. AD_1 moves to AD_2. The economy moves from E_1 to E_2, and real GDP is now at $10 trillion per year, the *LRAS* level.

cost of goods when deciding whether to buy in the United States or elsewhere. Therefore, holding all other things constant, a rise in taxes causes a reduction in aggregate demand because it reduces consumption, investment, or net exports. What actually happens depends, of course, on the parties on whom the taxes are levied.

When the Current Short-Run Equilibrium Is Greater than LRAS. Assume that aggregate demand is AD_1 in panel (a) of Figure 13-2. It intersects *SRAS* at E_1, which is at a level greater than *LRAS*. In this situation, an increase in taxes shifts the aggregate demand curve inward to the left. For argument's sake, assume that it intersects *SRAS* at E_2, or exactly where *LRAS* intersects AD_2. In this situation, the equilibrium level of real GDP falls from $10.5 trillion per year to $10 trillion per year. The price level falls from 120 to 100.

When the Current Short-Run Equilibrium Is Less than LRAS. Look at panel (b) in Figure 13-2. AD_1 intersects *SRAS* at E_1, with real GDP at $9.5 trillion, less than the *LRAS* of $10 trillion. In this situation, a decrease in taxes shifts the aggregate demand curve outward to the right. At AD_2, equilibrium is established at E_2, with the price level at 120 and equilibrium real GDP at $10 trillion per year.

FAQ

Don't cuts in income tax rates necessarily reduce the government's tax revenues by exactly the same percentage of income?

No, because cuts in income tax rates cause equilibrium national income to rise. Certainly, one effect of a cut in tax rates is a reduction in tax collections at the *current* level of national income. To jump to the conclusion implied by the question, however, assumes that the economy is static and unchanging in response to reduced tax rates. Lower income tax rates generate higher consumption, which pushes up equilibrium national income. This tends to push the government's tax receipts back up, because more income is taxed at the new lower rates. In theory, it is even possible that this "dynamic effect" of income tax rate cuts could lead to *higher* net tax revenues following cuts in income tax rates.

POLICY EXAMPLE

Did the New Deal Really Provide a Stimulus?

Many researchers have pointed out that Franklin Roosevelt's New Deal was influenced by Keynes's view that government had to increase "effective" aggregate demand. To be sure, the New Deal included what appeared on the surface to be large federal government expenditures and numerous government jobs programs. We have to look at the total picture, however. During the Great Depression, taxes were raised repeatedly. The Revenue Act of 1932, for example, passed during the depths of the Depression, brought the largest percentage increase in federal taxes in the history of the United States in peacetime—it almost doubled total federal tax revenues. Federal government deficits during the Depression years were small. In fact, in 1937 the total government budget—for federal, state, and local levels—was in surplus by $300 million. For many years during the period, at the same time that the federal government was increasing expenditures, local and state governments were decreasing them. If we measure the total of federal, state, and local fiscal policies, we find that they were truly expansive only in 1931 and 1936 compared to what the government was doing prior to the Great Depression. These two years were expansive only because of large payments to veterans, passed by Congress in both years over the vigorous opposition of the president.

For Critical Analysis
What other aspects of the New Deal might be studied to see if they had expansionary effects on the national economy?

CONCEPTS IN BRIEF

- Fiscal policy is defined as the discretionary change in government expenditures or taxes to achieve such national goals as high employment or reduced inflation.
- If there is a recessionary gap and the economy is operating at less than long-run average supply (LRAS), an increase in government spending can shift the aggregate demand curve to the right and perhaps lead to a higher equilibrium level of real GDP per year.
- If there is an inflationary gap, a decrease in government spending can shift the aggregate demand curve to the left, reducing the equilibrium level of real GDP per year to be consistent with LRAS.
- Changes in taxes can have similar effects on the equilibrium rate of real GDP and the price level. A decrease in taxes can lead to an increase in real GDP. In contrast, if there is an inflationary gap, an increase in taxes can decrease equilibrium real GDP.

POSSIBLE OFFSETS TO FISCAL POLICY

Fiscal policy does not operate in a vacuum. Important questions have to be answered: If government expenditures increase, how are those expenditures financed, and by whom? If taxes are increased, what does the government do with the taxes? What will happen if individuals worry about increases in *future* taxes because there is more government spending today with no increased taxes? All of these questions involve *offsets* to the effects of fiscal policy. We will look at each of them and others in detail.

Indirect Crowding Out

Let's take the first example of fiscal policy in this chapter, an increase in government expenditures. If government expenditures rise and taxes are held constant, something has to give. Our government does not simply take goods and services when it wants them. It has to pay for them. When it pays for them and does not simultaneously collect the same amount in taxes, it must borrow. That means that an increase in government spending without raising taxes creates additional government borrowing from the private sector (or from foreigners).

Induced Interest Rate Changes. Holding everything else constant, if the government attempts to borrow more from the private sector to pay for its increased budget deficit, it is not going to have an easy time selling its bonds. If the bond market is in equilibrium, when the government tries to sell more bonds, it is going to have to offer a better deal in order to get rid of them. A better deal means offering a higher interest rate. This is the interest rate effect of expansionary fiscal policy financed by borrowing from the public. In this sense, when the federal government finances increased spending by additional borrowing, it will push interest rates up. When interest rates go up, it is more expensive for firms to finance new construction, equipment, and inventories. It is also more expensive for individuals to finance their cars and homes. Thus a rise in government spending, holding taxes constant (in short, deficit spending), tends to crowd out private spending, dampening the positive effect of increased government spending on aggregate demand. This is called the **crowding-out effect.** In the extreme case, the crowding out may be complete, with the increased government spending having no net effect on aggregate demand. The final result is simply more government spending and less private investment and consumption. Figure 13-3 shows how the crowding-out effect occurs.

Crowding-out effect
The tendency of expansionary fiscal policy to cause a decrease in planned investment or planned consumption in the private sector; this decrease normally results from the rise in interest rates.

The Firm's Investment Decision. To understand the interest rate effect better, consider a firm that is contemplating borrowing $100,000 to expand its business. Suppose that the interest rate is 7 percent. The interest payments on the debt will be 7 percent times $100,000, or $7,000 per year ($583 per month). A rise in the interest rate to 10 percent will push the payments to 10 percent of $100,000, or $10,000 per year ($833 per month). The extra $250 per month in interest expenses will discourage some firms from making the investment. Consumers face similar decisions when they purchase houses and cars. An increase in the interest rate causes their monthly payments to go up, thereby discouraging some of them from purchasing cars and houses.

Graphical Analysis. You see in Figure 13-4 that the initial equilibrium, E_1, is below *LRAS*. But suppose that government expansionary fiscal policy in the form of increased government spending (without increasing current taxes) shifts aggregate demand from AD_1 to AD_2. In the absence of the crowding-out effect, the real output of goods and

FIGURE 13-3
The Crowding-Out Effect, Step-by-Step

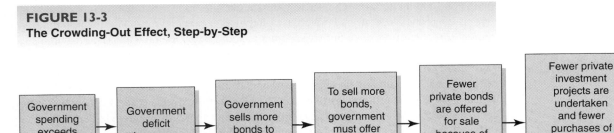

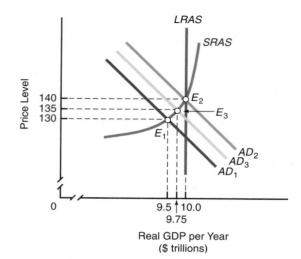

FIGURE 13-4

The Crowding-Out Effect
Expansionary fiscal policy that causes deficit financing initially shifts AD_1 to AD_2. Equilibrium initially moves toward E_2. But expansionary fiscal policy pushes up interest rates, which reduces interest-sensitive spending. This effect causes the aggregate demand curve to shift inward to AD_3, and the new short-run equilibrium is at E_3.

services would increase to $10 trillion per year, and the price level would rise to 140 (point E_2). With the (partial) crowding-out effect, however, as investment and consumption decline, partly offsetting the rise in government spending, the aggregate demand curve shifts inward to the left to AD_3. The new equilibrium is now at E_3, with real GDP of $9.75 trillion per year at a price level of 135. In other words, crowding out dilutes the effect of expansionary fiscal policy, and a recessionary gap remains.

Planning for the Future: The Ricardian Equivalence Theorem

Economists have implicitly assumed that people look at changes in taxes or changes in government spending only in the present. What if people actually think about the size of *future* tax payments? Does this have an effect on how they react to an increase in government spending with no tax increases? Some economists believe that the answer is yes. What if people's horizons extend beyond this year? Don't we then have to take into account the effects of today's government policies on the future?

Consider an example. The government wants to reduce taxes by $100 billion today. Assume that government spending remains constant. Assume further that the government initially has a balanced budget. Thus the only way for the government to pay for this $100 billion tax cut is to borrow $100 billion today. The public will owe $100 billion plus interest later. Realizing that a $100 billion tax cut today is mathematically equivalent to $100 billion plus interest later, people may wish to save the tax cut to meet future tax liabilities—payment of interest and repayment of debt.

Consequently, a tax cut may not affect total planned expenditures. A reduction in taxes without a reduction in government spending, according to the new classical economists, will therefore not necessarily have a large impact on aggregate demand.

Similarly, increased government spending without an increase in taxes will not necessarily have a large impact on aggregate demand. In terms of Figure 13-4, the aggregate demand curve will shift inward from AD_1 to AD_3. In the extreme case, if consumers fully compensate for a higher future tax liability by saving more, the aggregate demand curve shifts all the way back to AD_1 in Figure 13-4. This is the case of individuals fully discounting their increased tax liabilities. The result is that an increased budget deficit created entirely by a current tax cut has literally no effect on the economy. This is known as the **Ricardian equivalence theorem,** after the nineteenth-century economist David Ricardo, who first developed the argument publicly.

Ricardian equivalence theorem
The proposition that an increase in the government budget deficit has no effect on aggregate demand.

For economists who believe in the Ricardian equivalence theorem, it does not matter how government expenditures are financed—by taxes or by issuing debt. Is the Ricardian equivalence theorem correct? Research so far has not provided much compelling evidence either way.

Direct Expenditure Offsets

Government has a distinct comparative advantage over the private sector in certain activities such as diplomacy and national defense. Otherwise stated, certain resource-using activities in which the government engages do not compete with the private sector. In contrast, some of what government does competes directly with the private sector, such as education. When government competes with the private sector, **direct expenditure offsets** to fiscal policy may occur. For example, if the government starts providing milk at no charge to students who are already purchasing milk, there is a direct expenditure offset. Households spend less directly on milk, but government spends more.

The normal way to analyze the impact of an increase in government spending on aggregate demand is implicitly to assume that government spending is *not* a substitute for private spending. This is clearly the case for a cruise missile. Whenever government spending is a substitute for private spending, however, a rise in government spending causes a direct reduction in private spending to offset it.

Direct expenditure offsets
Actions on the part of the private sector in spending income that offset government fiscal policy actions. Any increase in government spending in an area that competes with the private sector will have some direct expenditure offset.

The Extreme Case. In the extreme case, the direct expenditure offset is dollar for dollar, so we merely end up with a relabeling of spending from private to public. Assume that you have decided to spend $100 on groceries. Upon your arrival at the checkout counter, you are met by a U.S. Department of Agriculture official. She announces that she will pay for your groceries—but only the ones in the cart. Here increased government spending is $100. You leave the store in bliss. But just as you are deciding how to spend the $100, an Internal Revenue Service agent meets you. He announces that as a result of the current budgetary crisis, your taxes are going to rise by $100. You have to pay right now. Increases in taxes have now been $100. We have a balanced-budget increase in government spending. In this scenario, there would be no change in total spending. We simply end up with higher government spending, which directly offsets exactly the same amount of consumption. Aggregate demand and GDP are unchanged. Otherwise stated, if there is a full direct expenditure offset, the government spending multiplier is zero.

The Less Extreme Case. Much government spending has a private-sector substitute. When government expenditures increase, there is a tendency for private spending to decline somewhat (but not in proportion), thereby mitigating the upward impact on total aggregate demand. To the extent that there are some direct expenditure offsets to expansionary fiscal policy, predicted changes in aggregate demand will be lessened. Consequently, real output and the price level will be less affected.

POLICY EXAMPLE

Crowding-Out Effects During World War II

Most American history books point to World War II as a clear-cut example of beneficial expansionary fiscal policy in action. The U.S. economy was pulled out of the Great Depression by enormous governmental out-lays for the war effort—or so the story goes. The actual situation was a little more complex, though. The U.S. economy's growth rate from 1933 to 1941 was already higher than that of any other recorded peacetime period of the same length. Moreover, the increase in military expenditures during World War II was not matched by a similar increase in total output. In fact, it looks as if the crowding-out effect was relatively large, at least much greater than the history books indicate. This can be readily observed in terms of what happened to per capita personal consumption expenditures. They dropped by 3.5 percent in real terms from 1941 and 1942 and did not rebound to 1941 levels until after 1944. In other words, the average American saw no real increase in living standards during the war, in spite of massive military expenditures.

For Critical Analysis

Given the information presented here, what could you say about the government's spending multiplier during World War II?

The Supply-Side Effects of Changes in Taxes

We have talked about changing taxes and changing government spending, the traditional tools of fiscal policy. We have not really talked about the possibility of changing marginal tax rates. Recall from Chapter 5 that the marginal tax rate is the rate applied to the last bracket of taxable income. In our federal tax system, higher marginal tax rates are applied as income rises. In that sense, the United States has a progressive federal individual income tax system. Expansionary fiscal policy might involve reducing marginal tax rates. Advocates of such changes argue that lower tax rates will lead to an increase in productivity because individuals will work harder and longer, save more, and invest more and that increased productivity will lead to more economic growth, which will lead to higher real GDP. The government, by applying lower marginal tax rates, will not necessarily lose tax revenues, for the lower marginal tax rates will be applied to a growing tax base because of economic growth—after all, tax revenues are the product of a tax rate times a tax base.

This relationship is sometimes called the Laffer curve, named after economist Arthur Laffer, who developed it in front of some journalists and politicians in 1974. It is reproduced in Figure 13-5. On the vertical axis are tax revenues, and on the horizontal axis is the marginal tax rate. As you can see, total tax revenues rise and then eventually fall as tax rates increase after some unspecified tax-revenue-maximizing rate.

People who support the notion that reducing taxes does not necessarily lead to reduced tax revenues are called supply-side economists. **Supply-side economics** involves changing the tax structure to create incentives to increase productivity. Due to a shift in the aggregate

Supply-side economics
The notion that creating incentives for individuals and firms to increase productivity will cause the aggregate supply curve to shift outward.

FIGURE 13-5
Laffer Curve
The Laffer Curve indicates that tax revenues initially rise with a higher tax rate. Eventually, however, tax revenues decline as the tax rate increases.

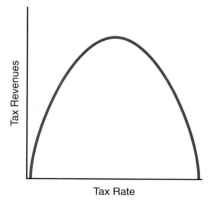

supply curve to the right, there can be greater output without upward pressure on the price level.

Consider the supply-side effects of changes in marginal tax rates on labor. An increase in tax rates reduces the opportunity cost of leisure, thereby inducing individuals (at least on the margin) to reduce their work effort and to consume more leisure. But an increase in tax rates will also reduce spendable income, thereby shifting the demand curve for leisure inward to the left. Here a reduction in real spendable income shifts the demand curve for all goods and services, including leisure, inward to the left. The outcome of these two effects on the choice of leisure (and thus work) depends on which of them is stronger. Supply-side economists argue that in the 1970s and 1980s, the first effect dominated: Increases in marginal tax rates caused workers to work less, and decreases in marginal tax rates caused workers to work more.

INTERNATIONAL EXAMPLE

Islam and Supply-Side Economics

Supply-side economics has a long history, dating back to at least the fourteenth century. The greatest of medieval Islamic historians, Abu Zayd Abd-ar-Rahman Ibn Khaldun (1332–1406), included an Islamic view of supply-side economics in his monumental book *The Muqaddimah* (1377). He pointed out that "when tax assessments . . . upon the subjects are low, the latter have the energy and desire to do things. Cultural enterprises grow and increase . . . . [Therefore] the number of individual imposts [taxes] and assessments mounts." If taxes are increased both in size and rates, "the result is that the interest of subjects in cultural enterprises dis-appears, because when they compare expenditures and taxes with their income and gain and see little profit they make, they lose all hope." Ibn Khaldun concluded that "at the beginning of a dynasty, taxation yields a large revenue from small assessments. At the end of a dynasty, taxation yields a small revenue from large assessments."

For Critical Analysis
How do this Islamic scholar's economic theories apply to the modern world?

CONCEPTS IN BRIEF

- Indirect crowding out occurs because of an interest rate effect in which the government's efforts to finance its deficit spending cause interest rates to rise, thereby crowding out private investment and spending, particularly on cars and houses. This is called the crowding-out effect.

- Direct expenditure offsets occur when government spending competes with the private sector and is increased. A direct crowding-out effect may occur.

- Many new classical economists believe in the Ricardian equivalence theorem, which holds that an increase in the government budget deficit has no effect on aggregate demand because individuals correctly perceive their increased future taxes and therefore save more today to pay for them.

- Changes in marginal tax rates may cause supply-side effects if a reduction in marginal tax rates induces enough additional work, saving, and investing. Government tax receipts can actually increase. This is called supply-side economics.

DISCRETIONARY FISCAL POLICY IN PRACTICE: COPING WITH TIME LAGS

We can discuss fiscal policy in a relatively precise way. We draw graphs with aggregate demand and supply curves to show what we are doing. We could even in principle estimate the offsets that we just discussed. However, even if we were able to measure all of these offsets exactly, would-be fiscal policymakers still face a problem: The conduct of fiscal policy involves a variety of time lags.

Policymakers must be concerned with time lags. Quite apart from the fact that it is difficult to measure economic variables, it takes time to collect and assimilate such data. Thus policymakers must contend with the **recognition time lag,** the months that may elapse before economic problems can be identified.*

After an economic problem is recognized, a solution must be formulated; thus there will be an **action time lag,** the period between the recognition of a problem and the implementation of policy to solve it. For fiscal policy, the action time lag is particularly long. Such policy must be approved by Congress and is subject to political wrangling and infighting. The action time lag can easily last a year or two. Then it takes time to put the policy into effect. After Congress enacts fiscal policy legislation, it takes time to decide such matters as who gets new federal construction contracts.

Finally, there is the **effect time lag:** After fiscal policy is enacted, it takes time for it to affect the economy. To demonstrate the effects, economists need only shift curves on a chalkboard, but in real time, multiplier effects take quite a while to work their way through the economy.

Because the various fiscal policy time lags are long, a policy designed to combat a recession might not produce results until the economy is already out of recession and perhaps experiencing inflation, in which case the fiscal policy would worsen the situation. Or a fiscal policy designed to eliminate inflation might not produce effects until the economy is in a recession; in that case, too, fiscal policy would make the economic problem worse rather than better.

Furthermore, because fiscal policy time lags tend to be *variable* (by anywhere from one to three years), policymakers have a difficult time fine-tuning the economy. Clearly, fiscal policy is more an art than a science.

Recognition time lag
The time required to gather information about the current state of the economy.

Action time lag
The time between recognizing an economic problem and implementing policy to solve it. The action time lag is quite long for fiscal policy, which requires congressional approval.

Effect time lag
The time that elapses between the onset of policy and the results of that policy.

INTERNATIONAL POLICY EXAMPLE

Keynesian Fiscal Policy Loses Its Luster

Some analysts argue that John Maynard Keynes was the most influential economist of the twentieth century, for he supposedly armed policymakers with fiscal weapons that allowed them to fight recession. Yet at the beginning of the twenty-first century, influential policymakers throughout the world are ignoring the concept of government spending as a way out of recessions.

Even though European governments have long favored welfare spending, the 11 that joined together to use the common currency called the euro also agreed to some specific anti-government-spending stipulations.

These countries, including France and Germany, are committed to keeping public deficits at 3 percent or less of gross domestic product. Whenever a country's public deficit exceeds this figure, the offending government can be fined up to 0.5 percent of its GDP. Deficit spending—a favorite Keynesian fiscal policy action—is tightly constrained in these countries.

In 1999, Brazil's president, Fernando Enrique Cardoso, stated that in the face of the then current recession, "we will need to put in place as rapidly as possible a fiscal austerity plan so that interest rates can fall and

---

*Final annual data for GDP, after various revisions, are not forthcoming for three to six months after the year's end.

Brazil can begin to grow again." He publicly announced that the country's government sector should shrink by 3 percent the following year even when his government economists predicted a probable 4 percent decrease in real GDP.

The International Monetary Fund did a study on fiscal policy a few years ago. It examined attempts by governments to reduce public spending and public debt. It looked at 62 attempts over two and a half decades. Its conclusion was that in the 14 cases for which the governments had aggressively reduced government spending, as in Denmark and Ireland, those economies had the fastest growth rates. The IMF contended that there may have been a "virtuous circle between economic growth and debt-reduction programs."

For Critical Analysis

How might Keynes have responded to this increase in anti-Keynesianism?

AUTOMATIC STABILIZERS

Not all changes in taxes (or in tax rates) or in government spending (including government transfers) constitute discretionary fiscal policy. There are several types of automatic (or nondiscretionary) fiscal policies. Such policies do not require new legislation on the part of Congress. Specific automatic fiscal policies—called **automatic, or built-in, stabilizers**—include the tax system itself and the government transfer system; the latter includes unemployment compensation and welfare spending.

Automatic, or built-in, stabilizers
Special provisions of certain federal programs that cause changes in desired aggregate expenditures without the action of Congress and the president. Examples are the federal tax system and unemployment compensation.

The Tax System as an Automatic Stabilizer

You know that if you work less, you are paid less, and therefore you pay fewer taxes. The amount of taxes that our government collects falls automatically during a recession. Basically, incomes and profits fall when business activity slows down, and the government's take drops too. Some economists consider this an automatic tax cut, which therefore stimulates aggregate demand. It reduces the extent of any negative economic fluctuation.

The progressive nature of both the federal personal and corporate income tax systems magnifies any automatic stabilization effect that might exist. If your hours of work are reduced because of a recession, you still pay federal personal income taxes. But because of our progressive system, you may drop into a lower tax bracket, thereby paying a lower marginal tax rate. As a result, your disposable income falls by a smaller percentage than your before-tax income falls.

Unemployment Compensation and Welfare Payments

Like our tax system unemployment compensation payments stabilize aggregate demand. Throughout the business cycle, unemployment compensation reduces *changes* in people's disposable income. When business activity drops, most laid-off workers automatically become eligible for unemployment compensation from their state governments. Their disposable income therefore remains positive, although certainly it is less than when they were employed. During boom periods there is less unemployment, and consequently fewer unemployment payments are made to the labor force. Less purchasing power is being added to the economy because fewer unemployment checks are paid out. Historically, the relationship between the unemployment rate and unemployment compensation payments has been strongly positive.

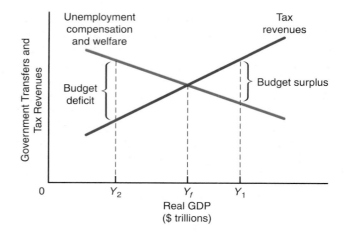

FIGURE 13-6
Automatic Stabilizers
Here we assume that as real national income rises, tax revenues rise and government transfers fall, other things remaining constant. Thus as the economy expands from Y_f to Y_1, a budget surplus automatically arises; as the economy contracts from Y_f to Y_2, a budget deficit automatically arises. Such automatic changes tend to drive the economy back toward its full-employment real national income.

Welfare payments act similarly as an automatic stabilizer. When a recession occurs, more people become eligible for welfare payments. Therefore, those people do not experience so dramatic a drop in disposable income as they would have otherwise.

Stabilizing Impact

The key stabilizing impact of our tax system, unemployment compensation, and welfare payments is their ability to mitigate undesirable changes in disposable income, consumption, and the equilibrium level of national income. If disposable income is prevented from falling as much as it would during a recession, the downturn will be moderated. In contrast, if disposable income is prevented from rising as rapidly as it would during a boom, the boom is less likely to get out of hand. The progressive income tax and unemployment compensation thus provide automatic stabilization to the economy. We present the argument graphically in Figure 13-6.

WHAT DO WE REALLY KNOW ABOUT FISCAL POLICY?

There are two ways of looking at fiscal policy, one that prevails during normal times and the other during abnormal times.

Fiscal Policy During Normal Times

To learn about the current outlook for the budget of the U.S. government, go to
www.cbo.gov

During normal times (without "excessive" unemployment, inflation, or problems in the national economy), we know that due to the recognition time lag and the modest size of any fiscal policy action that Congress will actually take, discretionary fiscal policy is probably not very effective. Congress ends up doing too little too late to help in a minor recession. Moreover, fiscal policy that generates repeated tax changes (as it has done) creates uncertainty, which may do more harm than good. To the extent that fiscal policy has any effect during normal times, it probably achieves this by way of automatic stabilizers rather than by way of discretionary policy.

Fiscal Policy During Abnormal Times

During abnormal times, fiscal policy may be effective. Consider some classic examples: the Great Depression and war periods.

The Great Depression.   When there is a catastrophic drop in real GDP, as there was during the Great Depression, fiscal policy may be able to stimulate aggregate demand. Because so many people are income-constrained during such periods, government spending is a way to get income into their hands.

Wartime.   Wars are in fact reserved for governments. War expenditures are not good substitutes for private expenditures—they have little or no direct expenditure offsets. Consequently, war spending as part of expansionary fiscal policy usually has noteworthy effects, such as occurred while we were waging World War II, during which real GDP increased dramatically.

The "Soothing" Effect of Keynesian Fiscal Policy

One view of traditional Keynesian fiscal policy does not relate to its being used on a regular basis. As you have learned in this chapter, there are many problems associated with attempting to use fiscal policy. But if we should encounter a severe downturn, fiscal policy is available. Knowing this may reassure consumers and investors. After all, the ability of the federal government to prevent another Great Depression—given what we know about how to use fiscal policy today—may take some of the large risk out of consumers' and investors' calculations. This may induce more buoyant and stable expectations of the future, thereby smoothing investment spending.

DEFICIT FINANCING AND THE PUBLIC DEBT

Discretionary fiscal policy has mostly resulted in the government's purposely spending more than it receives. This is often called *deficit financing* and creates a federal budget deficit. Sometimes it has even been called *Keynesian deficit financing,* for many economists consider increased government spending (without raising taxes) stimulative. Indeed, you have been reading about using discretionary fiscal policy to close a recessionary gap.

Flows Versus Stocks: Deficits and Debts

Each year that the government spends more than it collects in revenues, it runs a deficit. This is a flow, something that happens on a yearly basis or over time. The accumulation of deficits results in an increasing government debt. The debt is a stock, which is an accumulation of years' deficits.

For decades, federal budget deficits were common and indeed almost expected. That changed in 1998, when the federal government ran its first official surplus since 1969. Yet even though the government may not be running a budget deficit, the United States still has the stock of accumulated deficits: its net public debt.

The Federal Public Debt

All federal public debt, taken together, is called the **gross public debt.** Many government agencies own government securities. This interagency borrowing really has no effect on anything—it's like taking one IOU out of your left pocket and putting it into your right pocket. Therefore, when we subtract out the portion of the gross public debt held by government agencies, we arrive at the **net public debt.** The net public debt is currently about $2.6 trillion. You can see in Figure 13-7 on page 312 what has happened to the net U.S.

Gross Public Debt
All federal government debt irrespective of who owns it.

Net Public Debt
Gross public debt minus all government interagency borrowing.

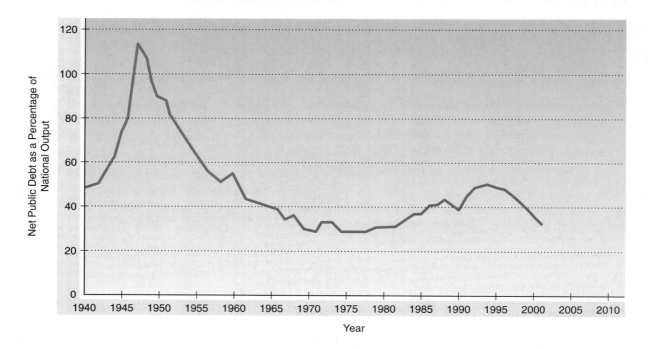

FIGURE 13-7

Net U.S. Public Debt as a Percentage of GDP

During World War II, the net public debt grew dramatically. It fell until the 1970s, rose again until the early 1990s, and has been declining ever since.

Source: U.S. Department of the Treasury.

public debt expressed as a percentage of GDP. It reached its peak right after World War II, fell until the 1970s, rose again until the early 1990s, and has been declining ever since.

CONCEPTS IN BRIEF

- Time lags of various sorts reduce the effectiveness of fiscal policy. These include the recognition time lag, the action time lag, and the effect time lag.

- Two automatic, or built-in, stabilizers are the tax system, unemployment compensation, and welfare payments.

- Built-in stabilizers tend automatically to moderate changes in disposable income resulting from changes in overall business activity.

- Though discretionary fiscal policy may not necessarily be a useful policy tool in normal times because of crowding out and time lags, it may work well during abnormal times, such as depressions and wartime. In addition, the existence of fiscal policy may have a soothing effect on consumers and investors.

- If the federal government's spending flow exceeds the taxes that it collects, the government runs a deficit. The gross public debt is the total accumulation of past years' deficits. The net public debt subtracts off the part of the gross public debt held by agencies of the government.

NETNOMICS

Deficit Financing: A Thing of the Past?

Governments throughout the world have often resorted to deficit financing when they have expanded government spending faster than tax collections. Most governments in Europe, for example, since World War II have gradually added more welfare programs. In addition, European governments have frequently argued that they can "create jobs" by expanding public-sector employment. Recently, for example, the French prime minister said that he would create 350,000 new jobs by hiring young people to engage in worthwhile public jobs. Such "job creation" requires funding nonetheless. The French government, like virtually all European governments, has been unable to match government spending with government revenues. It has consistently issued government securities to pay for increased government spending—debt financing.

Enter the Internet, and over goes the apple cart. Today, information about all aspects of governmental activities—spending, revenues, and the like—is available to everyone in the world on a second's notice via the Internet. Even more important, dealers in government securities can obtain this information at the speed of light. Because capital flows worldwide depend on perceived real rates of return—that is, rates of return corrected for inflation in whatever currency the securities are denominated—the owners of government securities anywhere in the world (pension plans, mutual funds, speculators, and the like) can instantaneously pull their capital out of a country when they get a sense that things aren't right. If the French government announces a new jobs program that must be financed by the sale of additional French government securities, the French government could be punished. How? By a quick net outflow of capital from France, thereby increasing its domestic interest rates.

The Internet helps spread information about government actions, the possibility of their positive or negative effects, and the economic growth outlook as a result. It also allows capital to be moved in and out of countries with the click of a mouse. Consequently, no government has the ability to engage in serious deficit financing anymore without being instantly punished.

Will the Government Allow the U.S. Economy to Drown in Black Ink?

During the 1970s, 1980s, and early 1990s, many economists strenuously argued that the federal government should end its deficit spending. Indeed, at one point in the 1990s, close to two-thirds of both houses of the U.S. Congress was swayed by arguments that the sea of red ink generated by spending on government consumption was crowding out private investment and slowing economic growth. The Senate, however, came up one vote short of passing a balanced-budget amendment to the U.S. Constitution.

Of course, many on the other side of the debate viewed private investment and government investment as equally productive and were unconcerned about any crowding-out effect. Ultimately, therefore, the *macroeconomic* argument about government deficits hinged on the amount of government spending on long-term capital investment and on the relative efficiency of government versus private investment.

A New Debate . . .

The terms of the debate have shifted as the government has taken in more taxes than it spends. Some forecasts indicate that in the absence of big tax cuts or increases in the rate of government expenditures, there may be federal budget surpluses for years into the future. During the latter years of the Clinton presidency, the U.S. Treasury used annual surpluses to pay off some of the government's accumulated debt from years past. The rosiest forecasts indicated the possibility of completely paying off the debt by 2015.

Nevertheless, a number of economists—many of whom had argued previously against large government deficits—now argue against running big federal surpluses. Their concern, once again, is the possibility of ill effects on economic growth.

. . . Or Just a Return to an Old Argument?

To understand why some might contend that budget surpluses can harm economic growth, note that when the government runs a surplus (meaning that it does not spend any excess of tax revenues over planned government expenditures), it adds to the total flow of saving in the economy. That is, the government becomes a net saver. So far, the government has saved by repurchasing some of its debt. In principle, it could save by buying privately placed debt, such as corporate bonds or stock.

If the government adds to national saving, then a likely result is an interest rate decline that stimulates private investment. Other things being equal, increased private investment tends to spur greater capital accumulation and push up the rate of economic growth. So why do some economists now grumble that government surpluses may *hinder* growth? Their argument hinges on the fact that when the government runs a surplus, it effectively saves *on behalf* of private individuals. It extracts taxes in excess of the amount required to cover the government's own expenses and then channels unspent taxes to financial markets. What critics of government surpluses question is the government's capability to channel this "forced saving" to the most productive uses. They worry that "too much" government saving may be directed to activities with low rates of return. If so, they argue, persistent government surpluses will lead to lower rates of economic growth than the nation could otherwise achieve.

This, of course, is the flip side of the argument against government deficits. In the case of deficits, a key issue is whether government investment is as productive as private investment. Likewise, in the case of surpluses, a fundamental issue is whether government saving is allocated as efficiently as private saving.

SUMMARY DISCUSSION OF LEARNING OBJECTIVES

1. **The Effects of Discretionary Fiscal Policies Using Traditional Keynesian Analysis:** Within the Keynesian short-run framework of analysis, a deliberate increase in government spending or reduction in taxes can raise aggregate demand. Thus, these fiscal policy actions can shift the aggregate demand curve outward along the short-run aggregate supply curve and thereby close a recessionary gap in which current real GDP is less than the long-run level of real GDP. Likewise, an intentional reduction in government spending or tax increase will reduce aggregate demand. These fiscal policy actions thereby shift the aggregate demand curve inward along the short-run aggregate supply curve and close an inflationary gap in which current real GDP exceeds the long-run level of real GDP.

2. **How Indirect Crowding Out and Direct Expenditure Offsets Can Reduce the Effectiveness of Fiscal Policy Actions:** Indirect crowding out occurs when the government engages in expansionary fiscal policy actions by running deficits, which it must finance by issuing bonds that compete with private bonds and thereby drive up market interest rates. This reduces, or crowds out, interest-sensitive private spending, thereby reduc-

ing the net effect of the fiscal expansion on aggregate demand. As a result, the aggregate demand curve shifts by a smaller amount than it would have in the absence of the crowding out effect, and fiscal policy has a somewhat lessened net effect on equilibrium national income. Increased government spending may also substitute directly for private expenditures, and the resulting decline in private spending directly offsets the increase in total planned expenditures that the government had intended to bring about. This also mutes the net change in aggregate demand brought about by a fiscal policy action.

3. **The Ricardian Equivalence Theorem:** According to this proposition, when the government cuts taxes and borrows to finance the tax reduction, people realize that eventually the government will have to repay the loan. Thus they anticipate that in the future there will have to be a tax increase. This induces them to save the proceeds of the tax cut to meet their future tax liabilities. Consequently, a tax cut fails to induce an increase in aggregate consumption spending. On net, therefore, a tax cut has no effect on total planned expenditures and aggregate demand if the Ricardian equivalence theorem is valid.

4. **Fiscal Policy Time Lags and the Effectiveness of Fiscal "Fine Tuning":** Efforts to engage in fiscal policy actions intended to bring about carefully planned changes in aggregate demand are often complicated by policy time lags. One of these is the recognition time lag, which is the time required to collect information about the economy's current situation. Another is the action time lag, the period between recognition of a problem and implementation of a policy intended to address it. Finally, there is the effect time lag, which is the interval that passes between policy implementation and the policy's effects on the economy. For fiscal policy, all of these lags can be very lengthy and variable, often lasting anywhere from one to three years. Hence, fiscal "fine tuning" may be a misnomer.

5. **Automatic Stabilizers:**   In our tax system, income taxes diminish automatically when economic activity drops, and unemployment compensation and welfare payments increase. Thus, when there is a decline in national income, the automatic reduction in income tax collections and increases in unemployment compensation and welfare payments tends to mute the reduction in total planned expenditures that otherwise would have resulted.   The existence of these government programs thereby tends to stabilize the economy automatically in the face of variations in autonomous expenditures that induce fluctuations in economic activity.

6. **Government Deficits Versus the Public Debt:** When governments run budget deficits, government spending during a given time interval exceeds tax collections during that period. Thus deficits are a flow over time. Governments finance deficits by issuing bonds, so deficit spending year after year leads to an accumulated public debt, which is a stock at a given point in time. The entire outstanding debt of the federal government is the gross public debt. Some of this debt is held by public agencies. When we subtract out their holdings of government debt, we tabulate the net public debt.   The net public debt increased from the end of the 1960s until 1998, when the federal government officially began to operate with budget surpluses again. Since 1998 the net public debt has declined somewhat.

Key Terms and Concepts

Action time lag (308)

Automatic, or built-in, stabilizers (309)

Crowding-out effect (303)

Direct expenditure offsets (305)

Effect time lag (308)

Fiscal policy (299)

Gross public debt (311)

Net public debt (311)

Recognition time lag (308)

Ricardian equivalence theorem (304)

Supply-side economics (306)

Problems

Answers to the odd-numbered problems appear at the back of the book.

13-1. Suppose that Congress and the president decide that economic performance is weakening and that the government should "do something" about the situation. They make no tax changes but do enact new laws increasing government spending on a variety of programs.

    a. Prior to congressional and presidential action, careful studies by government economists indicated that the direct multiplier effect of a rise in government expenditures on equilibri-um national income is equal to 6. Within the 12 months after the increase in government spending, however, it has become clear that the actual ultimate multiplier effect on real GDP will be unlikely to exceed half of that amount. What factors might account for this?

    b. Another year and a half elapses following passage of the government-spending boost. The government has undertaken no additional policy actions, nor have there been any other events of significance. Nevertheless, by the end of the second year, real national income has returned to its original level, and the price level has increased sharply. Provide a possible explanation for this outcome.

13-2. Suppose that Congress enacts a significant tax cut with the expectation that this action will stimulate aggregate demand and push up real GDP in the short run. In fact, however, neither real national income nor the price level changes significantly following the tax cut. What might account for this outcome?

13-3. Explain how time lags in discretionary fiscal policymaking could thwart the efforts of Congress and the president to stabilize real national income in the face of an economic downturn. Is it possible that these time lags could actually cause discretionary fiscal policy to *destabilize* real national income?

13-4. Under what circumstance might a tax reduction be associated with a long-run increase in real national income and a long-run reduction in the price level?

13-5. Which of the following is an example of a discretionary fiscal policy action?
   a. A recession occurs, and government-funded unemployment compensation payments are paid out to laid-off workers as a result.
   b. Congress votes to fund a new jobs program designed to put unemployed workers to work.
   c. The Federal Reserve decides to reduce the quantity of money in circulation in an effort to slow inflation.
   d. Under powers authorized by an act of Congress, the president decides to authorize an emergency release of funds for spending programs intended to head off economic crises.

13-6. Which of the following is an example of an automatic fiscal stabilizer?
   a. The Federal Reserve arranges to make loans to banks automatically whenever an economic downturn begins.
   b. As the economy heats up, the resulting increase in equilibrium income immediately results in higher income tax payments, which dampens consumption spending somewhat.
   c. As the economy starts to recover from a recession and more people go back to work, government-funded unemployment compensation payments begin to decline.
   d. To stem an overheated economy, the president, using special powers granted by Congress, authorizes emergency impoundment of funds that Congress had previously authorized for spending on government programs.

13-7. There is an inflationary gap. Discuss one discretionary fiscal policy action that might eliminate it.

13-8. There is a recessionary gap. Discuss one discretionary fiscal policy action that might eliminate it.

13-9. If the Ricardian equivalence theorem is not relevant, then a cut in the income tax rate should affect both the level of equilibrium real income and its stability. Explain why.

13-10. Suppose that Congress enacts a lump-sum tax cut of $750 billion. The marginal propensity to consume is equal to .75. If Ricardian equivalence holds true, what is the effect on equilibrium real income? On saving?

Economics on the Net

Federal Government Spending and Taxation A quick way to keep up with the federal government's spending and taxation is by examining federal budget data at the White House Internet address.

Internet URL: www.access.gpo.gov/usbudget/fy2000/pdf/hist.pdf

Title: Historical Tables: Budget of the United States Government

Navigation: Begin at the home page of the U.S. Government Printing Office (www.access.gpo.gov). Under Executive Office of the President, select

Office of Management and Budget, and click on Budget Documents. Then click on Historical Tables.

Application After the document downloads, perform the indicated operations and answer the questions.

1. Go to section 2, titled "Composition of Federal Government Receipts." Take a look at Table 2.2, "Percentage Composition of Receipts by Source." Before World War II, what was the key source of revenues of the federal government? What has been the key revenue source since World War II?

2. Now scan down the document to Table 2.3 "Receipts by Source as Percentages of GDP." Have any government revenue sources declined as a percentage of GDP? Which ones have noticeably risen in recent years?

3. In the Table of Contents in the left-hand margin of the Historical Tables, click on Table 7.1: Federal Debt at the End of the Year, 1940-2006. In light of the discussion in this chapter, which column shows the net public debt? What is the conceptual difference between the gross public debt and the net public debt? Last year, what was the dollar difference between these two amounts?

4. Table 7.1 includes estimates of the gross and net public debt through 2006. Suppose that these estimates turn out to be accurate. Calculate how much the net public debt should decline on average each year from 1997 to 2006. If the government managed to reduce its indebtedness by this amount every year indefinitely, how many years would it take to completely pay off the debt?

For Group Study and Analysis Split into four groups, and have each group examine section 3, "Federal Government Outlays by Function," and in particular Table 3.1, "Outlays by Superfunction and Function." Assign groups to the following functions: national defense, health, income security, and Social Security. Have each group prepare a brief report concerning long-term and recent trends in government spending on each function. Which functions are capturing growing shares of government spending in recent years? Which are receiving declining shares of total spending?

FISCAL POLICY: A KEYNESIAN PERSPECTIVE

The traditional Keynesian approach to fiscal policy differs in three ways from that presented in Chapter 13. First, it emphasizes the underpinnings of the components of aggregate demand. Second, it assumes that government expenditures are not substitutes for private expenditures and that current taxes are the only taxes taken into account by consumers and firms. Third, the traditional Keynesian approach focuses on the short run and so assumes that as a first approximation, the price level is constant.

CHANGES IN GOVERNMENT SPENDING

Figure C-1 measures real national income along the horizontal axis and total planned expenditures (aggregate demand) along the vertical axis. The components of aggregate demand are consumption (C), investment (I), government spending (G), and net exports (X). The height of the schedule labeled $C + I + G + X$ shows total planned expenditures (aggregate demand) as a function of income. This schedule slopes upward because consumption depends positively on income. Everywhere along the 45-degree reference line, planned spending equals income. At the point Y^*, where the $C + I + G + X$ line intersects the 45-degree line, planned spending is consistent with real national income. At any income less than Y^*, spending exceeds income, and so income and thus spending will tend to rise. At any level of income greater than Y^*, planned spending is less than income, and so income and thus spending will tend to decline. Given the determinants of C, I, G, and X, total spending (aggregate demand) will be Y^*.

The Keynesian approach assumes that changes in government spending cause no direct offsets in either consumption or investment spending because G is not a substitute for C, I, or X. Hence a rise in government spending from G to G' causes the $C + I + G + X$ line to shift upward by the full amount of the rise in government spending, yielding the line $C + I + G' + X$. The rise in government spending causes income to rise, which in turn causes consumption spending to rise, which further increases income. Ultimately, aggregate demand rises to Y^{**}, where spending again equals income. A key conclusion of the Keynesian analysis is that total spending rises by *more* than the original rise in government spending because consumption spending depends positively on income.

FIGURE C-1

The Impact of Higher Government Spending on Aggregate Demand
Government spending increases, causing $C + I + G + X$ to move to $C + I + G' + X$. Equilibrium increases to Y^{**}.

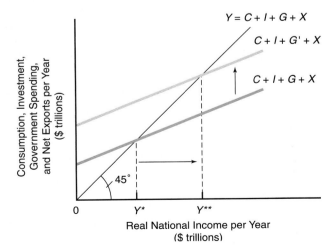

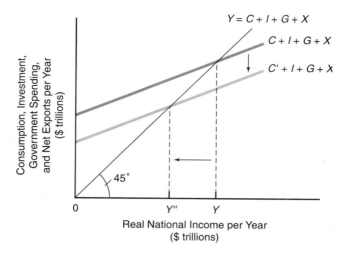

FIGURE C-2
The Impact of Higher Taxes on Aggregate Demand
Higher taxes cause consumption to fall to C'. Equilibrium decreases to Y''.

CHANGES IN TAXES

According to the Keynesian approach, changes in current taxes affect aggregate demand by changing the amount of disposable (after-tax) income available to consumers. A rise in taxes reduces disposable income and thus reduces consumption; conversely, a tax cut raises disposable income and thus causes a rise in consumption spending. The effects of a tax increase are shown in Figure C-2. Higher taxes cause consumption spending to decline from C to C', causing total spending to shift downward to $C' + I + G + X$. In general, the decline in consumption will be less than the increase in taxes because people will also reduce their saving to help pay the higher taxes.

THE BALANCED-BUDGET MULTIPLIER

One interesting implication of the Keynesian approach concerns the impact of a balanced-budget change in government spending. Suppose that the government increases spending by $1 billion and pays for it by raising current taxes by $1 billion. Such a policy is called a *balanced-budget increase in spending.* Because the higher spending tends to push aggregate demand *up* by *more* than $1 billion while the higher taxes tend to push aggregate demand *down* by *less* than $1 billion, a most remarkable thing happens: A balanced-budget increase in G causes total spending to rise by *exactly* the amount of the rise in G—in this case, $1 billion. We say that the *balanced-budget multiplier* is equal to 1. Similarly, a balanced-budget reduction in spending will cause total spending to fall by exactly the amount of the spending cut.

THE FIXED PRICE LEVEL ASSUMPTION

The final key feature of the Keynesian approach is that it typically assumes that as a first approximation, the price level is fixed. Recall that nominal income equals the price level multiplied by real output. If the price level is fixed, an increase in government spending that causes nominal income to rise will show up exclusively as a rise in *real* output. This will in turn be accompanied by a decline in the unemployment rate because the additional output can be produced only if additional factors of production, such as labor, are utilized.

Problems

Answers to the odd-numbered problems appear at the back of the book.

C-1. Assume that equilibrium income is $10.20 trillion and full-employment equilibrium is $10.55 trillion. The marginal propensity to save is $\frac{1}{7}$. Answer the questions using the data in the following graph.

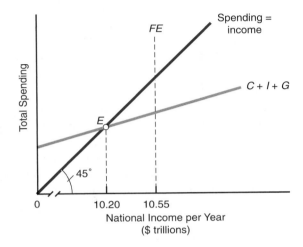

a. What is the marginal propensity to consume?

b. By how much must new investment or government spending increase to bring the economy up to full employment?

c. By how much must government cut personal taxes to stimulate the economy to the full-employment equilibrium?

C-2. Assume that MPC $=\frac{4}{5}$; then answer the following questions.

a. If government expenditures rise by $2 billion, by how much will the aggregate expenditure curve shift upward? By how much will equilibrium income change?

b. If taxes increase by $2 billion, by how much will the aggregate expenditure curve shift downward? By how much will equilibrium income change?

C-3. Assume that MPC $= \frac{4}{5}$; then answer the following questions.

a. If government expenditures rise by $1 billion, by how much will the aggregate expenditure curve shift upward?

b. If taxes rise by $1 billion, by how much will the aggregate expenditure curve shift downward?

c. If both taxes and government expenditures rise by $1 billion, by how much will the aggregate expenditure curve shift? What will happen to the equilibrium level of income?

d. How does our conclusion in the second part of (c) change if MPC $=\frac{3}{4}$? If MPC $=\frac{1}{2}$?

Part 3 Case Problem

Case Background

The year is 2013. It wasn't supposed to turn out this way. After successive years of federal surpluses that have paid down much of the U.S. government's debt and added to the Social Security trust fund, the nation is now mired in a severe recession.

The Current Situation Before leaving the Oval Office for the East Wing meeting, the president clicks the mouse on his computer and sees that this year real investment spending has declined by 3.6 percent, and export spending is down by 5 percent. Inflation is quite low, at an annual rate of 0.5 percent, which is near its average for the preceding three years. Nominal government spending actually fell by 2 percent last year and was down by an annualized rate of 3 percent in the most recent quarter.

The Fed's primary measure of the quantity of money in circulation has declined at an average rate of 1 percent during the past year. A broader measure of money has barely changed. Market interest rates have declined, however, by an average of about 1 percentage point, during the past 12 months. The value of the dollar relative to the currencies of the euro and the yen has risen by 12 percent during the same period.

Labor productivity is stagnant. Claims for unemployment compensation are up by 3.2 percent from last year. This understates the scope of the unemployment problem, however, because such a large portion of the labor force, relative to 10 years earlier, is now composed of temporary workers and consultants who are struggling to find steady employment. The overall unemployment rate last month was 7.5 percent, and the CEA estimates that it may increase to as much as 7.8 percent next month. Even so, information technology companies complain that they cannot find enough well-trained workers for many of the jobs that they would like to fill because job seekers lack the requisite technical training.

Trying to Reach a Consensus The president convenes the meeting, and key cabinet officials and the Fed chair each suggest a course of action.

- *Secretary of the Treasury:* In keeping with the president's commitment to paying off the national debt, the Treasury proposes no fundamental change in the stance of fiscal policy. The Treasury secretary does propose, however, selling dollars in foreign exchange markets in an effort to drive down the dollar's value.

- *Secretary of State:* The secretary of state proposes quick passage of legislation lowering barriers to entry by the most highly qualified immigrants in an effort to boost U.S. labor productivity.

- *Secretary of Labor:* The secretary recommends holding fast to the president's budgetary promises but cutting back on spending in some areas so that available public funds may be redirected toward job training programs targeted at preparing young people for high-tech jobs.

- *Federal Reserve Chair:* The Fed chair argues that its number one job is to contain inflation, and she notes that the Fed has done its job well for the past 3 1/2 years.

- *Chair of the Council of Economic Advisers:* The CEA favors abandoning the pledge to pay off the national debt, at least until the recession is over. The CEA majority recommends both a hike in government spending and across-the-board cuts in tax rates. It also strongly recommends a more expansionary monetary policy.

Points to Analyze

1. Which viewpoints are consistent with potential short-run efforts to stem the downturn in U.S. business activity? Which are directed at longer-term solutions?

2. Which perspective is most consistent with Keynesian economic analysis?

3. Which perspective is most consistent with classical economic analysis?

4. If the president takes the politically easy way out in light of the Fed chair's stance, how might this action help raise equilibrium real GDP?

5. If you were the president, what broad economic plan would you pull together from these suggestions? Why?

Casing the Internet

1. Go the homepage of the Bureau of Economic Analysis at www.bea.doc.gov. Click on "GDP and related data." Next to "Gross domestic product and other major NIPA series," click on "PDF" to download the latest data from the national income product accounts.
   a. Look at Table 1. Exports and imports made up what percentages of GDP in 1960? In 1980? In the most recent full year for which data are available? By these measures, does the United States appear to be a more open economy than in years past?
   b. In Table 1, what was government spending as a percentage of GDP in 1960? In 1980? In the most recent full year for which data are available? Is the government consuming a larger or smaller share of U.S. GDP than in earlier years?

2. Visit the homepage of the International Monetary Fund at www.imf.org. Click on "Publications" and then on "World Economic Outlook" (most recent issue). Download the last file, which contains statistical data.
   a. Look at Table 3, "Advanced Economies: Components of Real GDP." Across countries, which component of GDP tends to grow at the most stable pace over time?
   b. Again looking across countries, which component of GDP tends to exhibit the greatest stability over time?

Part 4
Money, Monetary Policy, and Stabilization

MONEY AND BANKING SYSTEMS

This advertising billboard in Buenos Aires, Argentina, may someday be displaying prices in dollars instead of the local currency. If Argentina used dollars instead of pesos, would Argentineans necessarily be better off?

A couple of years ago, Argentina's government made a startling announcement. It was, it said, thinking about scrapping the nation's currency, the peso. Furthermore, it might not even replace the peso with a new national money. Instead, the government might declare U.S. dollars to be the legal money of Argentina. Since then, a few other Latin American nations have contemplated the same plan. A similar idea has even emerged in Canada, where some economists floated a plan for dropping the Canadian dollar in favor of the dollar issued by their big neighbor to the south. Why would these countries think about giving up their own national currencies and using U.S. dollars instead? Before you can consider this question, you must learn about the functions of money. You must also understand how economists measure the total quantity of money in circulation. These are key topics in this chapter.

LEARNING OBJECTIVES

After reading this chapter, you should be able to:

1. Define the fundamental functions of money

2. Identify key properties that any good that functions as money must possess

3. Explain official definitions of the quantity of money in circulation

4. Understand why financial intermediaries such as banks exist

5. Describe the basic structure of the Federal Reserve System

6. Discuss the major functions of the Federal Reserve

Money
Any medium that is universally accepted in an economy both by sellers of goods and services as payment for those goods and services and by creditors as payment for debts.

Medium of exchange
Any asset that sellers will accept as payment.

Barter
The direct exchange of goods and services for other goods and services without the use of money.

Putting
Economics in Action
to Work

To gain further understanding of the concept of money, start the *EIA* CD and click on "Money and Banking." Then click on "The Functions of Money."

Did You Know That... the typical dollar bill changes hands 50 times a year? Paper bills and coins are not the only things we use as money, however. As you will see in this chapter, *money* is a much broader concept.

Money has been important to society for thousands of years. In 300 B.C., Aristotle claimed that everything had to "be accessed in money, for this enables men always to exchange their services, and so makes society possible." Money is indeed a part of our everyday existence. Nevertheless, we have to be careful when we talk about money. Often a person may say, "I wish I had more money," instead of "I wish I had a higher income," thereby confusing the concepts of money and income. Economists use the term ***money*** to mean anything that people generally accept in exchange for goods and services. Table 14-1 provides a list of some items that various civilizations have used as money. The best way to understand how these items served this purpose is to examine the functions of money.

THE FUNCTIONS OF MONEY

Money traditionally has four functions. The one that most people are familiar with is money's function as a *medium of exchange.* Money also serves as a *unit of accounting,* a *store of value* or *purchasing power,* and a *standard of deferred payment.* Anything that serves these four functions is money. Anything that could serve these four functions could be considered money.

Money as a Medium of Exchange

When we say that money serves as a **medium of exchange,** what we mean is that sellers will accept it as payment in market transactions. Without some generally accepted medium of exchange, we would have to resort to *barter.* In fact, before money was used, transactions took place by means of barter. **Barter** is simply a direct exchange—people do not use money as an intermediate item in conducting exchanges. In a barter economy, the shoemaker who wants to obtain a dozen water glasses must seek out a glassmaker who at exactly the same time is interested in obtaining a pair of shoes. For this to occur, there has to be a *double coincidence of wants* for each specific item to be exchanged. If there isn't, the shoemaker must go through several trades in order to obtain the desired dozen glasses—perhaps first trading shoes for jewelry, then jewelry for some pots and pans, and then the pots and pans for the desired glasses.

Money facilitates exchange by reducing the transaction costs associated with means-of-payment uncertainty—that is, with regard to goods that the partners in any exchange are willing to accept, the existence of money means that individuals no longer have to hold a diverse collection of goods as an exchange inventory. As a medium of exchange, money allows individuals to specialize in any area in which they have a comparative advantage and to receive money payments for their labor. Money payments can then be exchanged for the fruits of other people's labor. The use of money as a medium of exchange permits more specialization and the inherent economic efficiencies that come with it (and hence greater economic growth). Money is even more important when used for large amounts of trade.

			TABLE 14-1
Iron	Boar tusk	Playing cards	**Types of Money**
Copper	Red woodpecker scalps	Leather	This is a partial list of
Brass	Feathers	Gold	things that have been used
Wine	Glass	Silver	as money. Native
Corn	Polished beads (wampum)	Knives	Americans used *wampum*,
Salt	Rum	Pots	beads made from shells.
Horses	Molasses	Boats	Fijians used whale teeth.
Sheep	Tobacco	Pitch	The early colonists in North
Goats	Agricultural implements	Rice	America used tobacco.
Tortoise shells	Round stones with centers removed	Cows	And cigarettes were used
Porpoise teeth	Crystal salt bars	Paper	in prisoner-of-war camps
Whale teeth	Snail shells	Cigarettes	during World War II and in post–World War II Germany.

Source: Roger LeRoy Miller and David D. VanHoose, *Money, Banking, and Financial Markets with Their International and Cyber Nexus* (Cincinnati: Southwestern, 2001), p. 6.

Money as a Unit of Accounting

A **unit of accounting** is a way of placing a specific price on economic goods and services. It is the common denominator, the commonly recognized measure of value. The dollar is the monetary unit in the United States. It is the yardstick that allows individuals easily to compare the relative value of goods and services. Accountants at the U.S. Department of Commerce use dollar prices to measure national income and domestic product, a business uses dollar prices to calculate profits and losses, and a typical household budgets regularly anticipated expenses using dollar prices as its unit of accounting.

Another way of describing money as a unit of accounting is to say that it serves as a *standard of value* that allows economic actors to compare the relative worth of various goods and services. This allows for comparison shopping, for example.

Unit of accounting
A measure by which prices are expressed; the common denominator of the price system; a central property of money.

Must debts be specified in terms of the local currency?

FAQ

Not all countries, or the firms and individuals in those countries, will specify that debts owed must be paid in their own national monetary unit. For example, individuals, private corporations, and governments in other countries incur debts in terms of the U.S. dollar, even though the dollar is neither the medium of exchange nor the monetary unit in those countries. In the late 1990s, this became a significant problem for firms in Thailand, Malaysia, Indonesia, and South Korea when the values of the currencies in which they earned revenues—the Thai baht, the Malaysian ringgit, the Indonesian rupiah, and the South Korean won—all declined significantly in value relative to their dollar-denominated debts.

Money as a Store of Value

One of the most important functions of money is that it serves as a **store of value** or purchasing power. The money you have today can be set aside to purchase things later on. In the meantime, money retains its nominal value, which you can apply to those future purchases. If you have $1,000 in your checking account, you can choose to spend it today on goods and services, spend it tomorrow, or spend it a month from now. In this way, money provides a way to transfer value (wealth) into the future.

Store of value
The ability to hold value over time; a necessary property of money.

Money as a Standard of Deferred Payment

Standard of deferred payment
A property of an asset that makes it desirable for use as a means of settling debts maturing in the future; an essential property of money.

The fourth function of the monetary unit is as a **standard of deferred payment.** This function involves the use of money both as a medium of exchange and as a unit of accounting. Debts are typically stated in terms of a unit of accounting; they are paid with a monetary medium of exchange. That is to say, a debt is specified in a dollar amount and paid in currency (or by check). A corporate bond, for example, has a face value—the dollar value stated on it, which is to be paid upon maturity. The periodic interest payments on that corporate bond are specified and paid in dollars, and when the bond comes due (at maturity), the corporation pays the face value in dollars to the holder of the bond.

LIQUIDITY

Liquidity
The degree to which an asset can be acquired or disposed of without much danger of any intervening loss in *nominal* value and with small transaction costs. Money is the most liquid asset.

Money is an asset—something of value—that accounts for part of personal wealth. Wealth in the form of money can be exchanged later for other assets, goods, or services. Although it is not the only form of wealth that can be exchanged for goods and services, it is the most widely and most readily accepted one. This attribute of money is called **liquidity.** We say that an asset is *liquid* when it can easily be acquired or disposed of without high transaction costs and with relative certainty as to its value. Money is by definition the most liquid asset. Compare it, for example, with a share of stock listed on the New York Stock Exchange. To sell that stock, you usually call a stockbroker, who will place the sell order for you. This generally must be done during normal business hours. You have to pay a commission to the broker. Moreover, there is a distinct probability that you will get more or less for the stock than you originally paid for it. This is not the case with money. People can easily convert money to other asset forms. Therefore, most individuals hold at least a part of their wealth in the form of the most liquid of assets, money. You can see how assets rank in liquidity relative to one another in Figure 14-1.

When we hold money, however, we pay a price for this advantage of liquidity. Because cash in your pocket and many checking account balances do not earn interest, that price is the interest yield that could have been obtained had the asset been held in another form—for example, in the form of stocks and bonds.

> The cost of holding money (its opportunity cost) is measured by the alternative interest yield obtainable by holding some other asset.

MONETARY STANDARDS, OR WHAT BACKS MONEY

In the past, many different monetary standards have existed. For example, commodity money, which is a physical good that may be valued for other uses it provides, has been used (see Table 14-1). The main forms of commodity money were gold and silver. Today,

FIGURE 14-1
Degrees of Liquidity
The most liquid asset is cash. Liquidity decreases as you move from right to left.

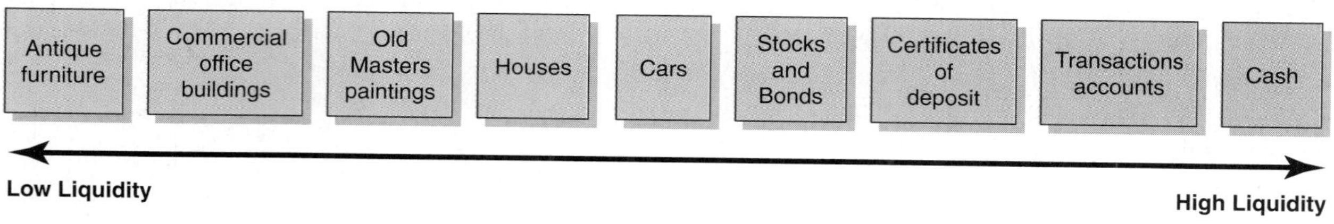

| Antique furniture | Commercial office buildings | Old Masters paintings | Houses | Cars | Stocks and Bonds | Certificates of deposit | Transactions accounts | Cash |

Low Liquidity ←————————————————————————————→ **High Liquidity**

though, most people throughout the world accept coins, paper currency, and balances in **transactions accounts** (checking accounts with banks and other financial institutions; also called checkable deposits) in exchange for items sold, including labor services. The question remains, why are we willing to accept as payment something that has no intrinsic value? After all, you could not sell checks to anybody for use as a raw material in manufacturing. The reason is that payments in the modern world arise from a **fiduciary monetary system.** This means that the value of the payments rests on the public's confidence that such payments can be exchanged for goods and services. *Fiduciary* comes from the Latin *fiducia,* which means "trust" or "confidence." In our fiduciary monetary system, money, in the form of currency or transactions accounts, is not convertible to a fixed quantity of gold, silver, or some other precious commodity. The bills are just pieces of paper. Coins have a value stamped on them that today is much greater than the market value of the metal in them. Nevertheless, currency and transactions accounts are money because of their acceptability and predictability of value.

Transactions accounts

Checking account balances in commercial banks and other types of financial institutions, such as credit unions and mutual savings banks; any accounts in financial institutions on which you can easily write checks without many restrictions.

Fiduciary monetary system

A system in which currency is issued by the government and its value is based uniquely on the public's faith that the currency represents command over goods and services.

INTERNATIONAL EXAMPLE

Is Gold Worth Its Weight?

For centuries, gold has been precious because it has been scarce. Today, however, this glittering metal may be overabundant, especially for international agencies, governments, and central banks. Gold accounts for more than a third of the official international reserves of a number of developed nations. Combined gold holdings of the International Monetary Fund (IMF) and the world's central banks exceed 30,000 tons, or the equivalent of about a dozen years of global mining output. All this gold is very expensive to move around. For this reason, it typically just sits unused, in sturdy vaults surrounded by armed guards. This is an expensive use for a metal. Moreover, over the past 25 years, gold has turned out to be a poor store of value. Returns on relatively low-risk bonds have been much higher than the rate of return from holding gold. Switzerland, for instance, determined that the cost of interest forgone by holding gold rather than U.S. Treasury bonds is about $400 a year per Swiss household.

Recently, the Swiss government began selling off half its 2,600 tons of gold reserves, third-largest in the world behind the United States and the European Mon-

etary Union. More recently, the IMF has auctioned off some of its gold holdings to finance debt relief for poor countries. The European System of Central Banks, which began the new century with 30 percent of its reserves in the form of gold, decided to reduce this fraction to 15 percent.

Official gold sales until late 1999 contributed to a decline in the world price of gold, thereby worsening the return to holding gold. This led companies operating gold mines in United States to lobby their representatives and senators, who successfully pushed through a law threatening a reduction of U.S. funding of the IMF unless it agreed to scale back gold sales it had planned for the early 2000s. It did so, and central banks also agreed to stop selling gold.

For Critical Analysis

It appears that today central banks' portfolios are weighted too heavily in favor of gold. Under what circumstances might central banks again determine that huge stocks of gold are worth holding?

Acceptability

Transactions accounts and currency are money because they are accepted in exchange for goods and services. They are accepted because people have confidence that these items can later be exchanged for other goods and services. This confidence is based on the knowledge that such exchanges have occurred in the past without problems. Even during a period of inflation, we might still be inclined to accept money in exchange for goods and services because it is so useful. Barter is a costly and time-consuming alternative.

Realize always that money is socially defined. Acceptability is not something that you can necessarily predict. For example, the U.S. government has tried to circulate types of money, such as the $2 bill, that were socially unacceptable. How many $2 bills have you seen lately? The answer is probably none. No one wanted to make room for $2 bills in register tills or billfolds.

Predictability of Value

The purchasing power of the dollar (its real value) varies inversely with the price level. The more rapid the rate of increase of some price level index, such as the Consumer Price Index, the more rapid the decrease in the real value, or purchasing power, of a dollar. Money still retains its usefulness even if its purchasing power is declining year in and year out, as in periods of inflation, if it still retains the characteristic of predictability of value. If you anticipate that the inflation rate is going to be around 10 percent during the next year, you know that any dollar you receive a year from now will have a purchasing power equal to 10 percent less than that same dollar today. Thus you will not necessarily refuse to accept money in exchange simply because you know that its value will decline by the rate of inflation during next year. You may, however, wish to be compensated for that expected decline in money's real value.

CONCEPTS IN BRIEF

- Money is defined by its functions, which are as a medium of exchange, a unit of accounting or standard of value, a store of value or purchasing power, and a standard of deferred payment.

- Because money is a highly liquid asset, it can be disposed of with low transaction costs and with relative certainty as to its value.

- Today's nations have fiduciary monetary systems—national currencies are not convertible into a fixed quantity of a commodity such as gold or silver.

- Money is accepted in exchange for goods and services because people have confidence that it can later be exchanged for other goods and services. Another reason for this is that it has predictable value.

DEFINING MONEY

Money is important. Changes in the total **money supply**—the amount of money in circulation—and changes in the rate at which the money supply increases or decreases affect important economic variables (at least in the short run), such as the rate of inflation, interest rates, employment, and the equilibrium level of real national income. Although there is widespread agreement among economists that money is indeed important, they have struggled to reach agreement about defining and measuring it. There are two basic approaches: the **transactions approach,** which stresses the role of money as a medium of exchange, and the **liquidity approach,** which stresses the role of money as a temporary store of value.

The Transactions Approach to Measuring Money: M1

Using the transactions approach to measuring money, the money supply consists of currency, checkable deposits, and traveler's checks.

Money supply
The amount of money in circulation.

Transactions approach
A method of measuring the money supply by looking at money as a medium of exchange.

Liquidity approach
A method of measuring the money supply by looking at money as a temporary store of value.

Putting Economics in Action to Work

For additional practice thinking about how to measure the money supply, start the *EIA* CD and click on "Money and Banking." Then click on "The Money Supply."

FIGURE 14-2
Composition of the U.S. M1 and M2 Money Supply, 2000

Panel (a) shows the M1 money supply, of which the greatest component is checkable deposits (over 65 percent). M2 consists of M1 plus three other components, the most important of which is small time deposits at all depository institutions (over 50 percent).

Sources: Federal Reserve Bulletin, Economic Indicators, various issues.

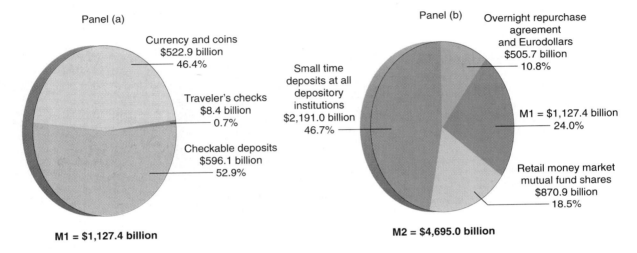

M1 = $1,127.4 billion

M2 = $4,695.0 billion

The official designation of the money supply, including currency, checkable deposits, and traveler's checks not issued by banks, is **M1.** The various elements of M1 for a typical year are presented in panel (a) of Figure 14-2.

Currency.　In the United States, currency includes coins minted by the U.S. Treasury and paper currency in the form of Federal Reserve notes issued by the Federal Reserve banks (to be discussed shortly). In other nations, currency also consists of coins and paper bills. The typical resident of another nation uses currency denominated in local money terms, but in many countries the U.S. dollar is the preferred currency for many transactions. For this reason, the bulk of U.S. currency "in circulation" actually does not circulate within the borders of the United States. Figure 14-3 on page 334 displays the estimated value of U.S. currency in circulation elsewhere in the world. In any given year, at least two-thirds of the dollars in existence circulate outside the United States!

Checkable Deposits.　Most major transactions today are done with checks. The convenience and safety of using checks and debit cards has made checkable deposit accounts the most important component of the money supply. For example, it is estimated that in 2000, currency transactions accounted for only 0.5 percent of the dollar amount of all transactions. The rest, excluding barter, involved checks. Checks are a way of transferring the ownership of deposits in financial institutions. They are normally acceptable as a medium of exchange. The financial institutions that offer checkable deposits are numerous and include commercial banks and virtually all **thrift institutions**—savings banks, savings and loan associations (S&Ls), and credit unions.

Traveler's Checks.　**Traveler's checks** are paid for by the purchaser at the time of transfer. The total quantity of traveler's checks outstanding issued by institutions other than

MI
The money supply, taken as the total value of currency plus checkable deposits plus traveler's checks not issued by banks.

Checkable Deposits
Any deposits in a thrift institution or a commercial bank on which a check may be written.

Thrift institutions
Financial institutions that receive most of their funds from the savings of the public; they include mutual savings banks, savings and loan associations, and credit unions.

Traveler's checks
Financial instruments purchased from a bank or a nonbanking organization and signed during purchase that can be used as cash upon a second signature by the purchaser.

FIGURE 14-3

The Value of American Currency in Circulation Outside the United States

The amount of U.S. dollars circulating beyond American borders has grown steadily in recent years.

Source: Board of Governors of the Federal Reserve System.

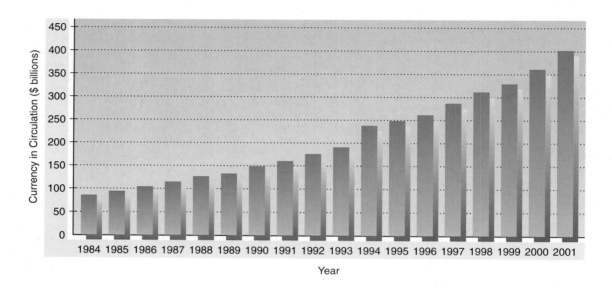

Year

Why aren't credit cards part of the money supply?

Even though a large percentage of U.S. transactions are accomplished using plastic credit cards, the credit card itself cannot be considered money. Remember the functions of money: a unit of accounting, a store of value, a standard of deferred payment—a credit card is none of these things. The use of your credit card in fact constitutes a *loan* to you by the issuer of the card, be it a bank, a retail store, a gas company, or American Express. The proceeds of the loan are paid to the business that sold you something. You must pay back the loan to the issuer of the credit card, either in full when you get your statement or with interest over time. Thus credit cards *defer* rather than complete transactions that ultimately involve the use of money.

Near moneys

Assets that are almost money. They have a high degree of liquidity; they can be easily converted into money without loss in value. Time deposits and short-term U.S. government securities are examples.

banks is part of the M1 money supply.* American Express, Citibank, Cook's, and other institutions issue traveler's checks.

The Liquidity Approach to Measuring Money: M2

The liquidity approach to defining and measuring the U.S. money supply involves taking into account not only the most liquid assets that people use as money, which are already included in the definition of M1, but also other assets that are highly liquid—that is, that can be converted into money quickly without loss of nominal dollar value and without much cost. Any (non-M1) assets that come under this definition have been called **near moneys.** Thus the liquidity approach to the definition of the money supply views money as a temporary store of value and so includes all of M1 *plus* all near moneys. Panel (b) of Figure 14-2 shows the components of **M2**—money as a temporary store of value. We examine each of these components in turn.

---

*Banks place the funds that are to be used to redeem traveler's checks in a special deposit account, and they are therefore already counted as checkable accounts. Nonbank issuers, however, do not place these funds in checkable accounts. Improvements in data collection have made it possible to estimate the total amount of nonbank traveler's checks, and since June 1981 they have been included in M1.

Savings Deposits. Total **savings deposits** in all **depository institutions** (such as commercial banks, savings banks, savings and loan associations, and credit unions) are part of the M2 money supply. A savings deposit has no set maturity.

Small-Denomination Time Deposits. A basic distinction has always been made between a checkable deposit, which is a checking account, and a **time deposit,** which theoretically requires notice of withdrawal and on which the financial institution pays the depositor interest. The name indicates that there is an agreed period during which the funds must be left in the financial institution. If the deposit holder withdraws funds before the end of that period, the institution issuing the deposit may apply a penalty. Time deposits include savings certificates and small **certificates of deposit (CDs).** The owner of a savings certificate is given a receipt indicating the amount deposited, the interest rate to be paid, and the maturity date. A CD is an actual certificate that indicates the date of issue, its maturity date, and other relevant contractual matters.

The distinction between checkable deposits and time deposits has blurred over time, but it is still used in the official definition of the money supply. To be included in the M2 definition of the money supply, however, time deposits must be less than $100,000—hence the name *small-denomination time deposits*. A variety of small-denomination time deposits are available from depository institutions, ranging in maturities from one month to 10 years.

Money Market Deposit Accounts (MMDAs). Since 1982, banks and thrift institutions have offered **money market deposit accounts (MMDAs),** which usually require a minimum balance and set limits on the number of monthly transactions (deposits and withdrawals by check).

Overnight Repurchase Agreements at Commercial Banks (REPOs, or RPs). A **repurchase agreement (REPO, or RP)** is made by a bank to sell Treasury or federal agency securities to its customers, coupled with an agreement to repurchase them at a price that includes accumulated interest. REPOs fill a gap in that depository institutions are not yet allowed to offer to businesses interest-bearing commercial checking accounts. Therefore, REPOs can be thought of as a financial innovation that bypasses regulations because businesses can deposit their excess cash in REPOs instead of leaving it in non-interest-bearing commercial checking accounts.

Overnight Eurodollars. **Eurodollar deposits** are dollar-denominated deposits in foreign commercial banks and in foreign branches of U.S. banks. *Dollar-denominated* simply means that although the deposit might be held at, say, a Caribbean commercial bank, its value is stated in terms of U.S. dollars rather than in terms of the local currency. The term *Eurodollar* is not completely accurate because banks outside continental Europe participate in the Eurodollar market and also because banks in some countries issue deposits denominated in German marks, Swiss francs, British pounds sterling, and Dutch guilders. This has led to wide use of the broader term *Eurocurrency deposits,* even though this is also not fully accurate given that banks in some countries also issue deposits denominated in non-European currencies such as the Japanese yen. (Note that Eurodollars and other Eurocurrencies are not the same as the *euro,* the monetary unit used by 11 European nations.)

M2
M1 plus (1) savings and small-denomination time deposits at all depository institutions, (2) overnight repurchase agreements at commercial banks, (3) overnight Eurodollars held by U.S. residents other than banks at Caribbean branches of member banks, (4) balances in retail money market mutual funds, and (5) money market deposit accounts (MMDAs).

Savings deposits
Interest-earning funds that can be withdrawn at any time without payment of a penalty.

Depository institutions
Financial institutions that accept deposits from savers and lend those deposits out at interest.

Time deposit
A deposit in a financial institution that requires notice of intent to withdraw or must be left for an agreed period. Withdrawal of funds prior to the end of the agreed period may result in a penalty.

Certificate of deposit (CD)
A time deposit with a fixed maturity date offered by banks and other financial institutions.

Money market deposit accounts (MMDAs)
Accounts issued by banks yielding a market rate of interest with a minimum balance requirement and a limit on transactions. They have no minimum maturity.

Repurchase agreement (REPO, or RP)
An agreement made by a bank to sell Treasury or federal agency securities to its customers, coupled with an agreement to repurchase them at a price that includes accumulated interest.

Eurodollar deposits
Deposits denominated in U.S. dollars but held in banks outside the United States, often in overseas branches of U.S. banks.

Money market mutual funds
Funds of investment companies that obtain funds from the public that are held in common and used to acquire short-maturity credit instruments, such as certificates of deposit and securities sold by the U.S. government.

Money Market Mutual Fund Balances.   Many individuals keep part of their assets in the form of shares in **money market mutual funds.** These retail mutual funds invest only in short-term credit instruments. The majority of these money market funds allow check-writing privileges, provided that the size of the check exceeds some minimum amount, usually $250. All money market mutual fund balances except those held by large institutions (which typically use them more like large time deposits) are included in M2.

M2 and Other Money Supply Definitions.   When all of these assets are added together, the result is M2. The composition of M2 is given in panel (b) of Figure 14-2.

Economists and researchers have come up with even broader definitions of money than M2.* More assets are simply added to the definition. Just remember that there is no best definition of the money supply. For different purposes and under varying institutional circumstances, different definitions are appropriate. The definition that seems to correlate best with economic activity on an economywide basis for most countries is probably M2.

CONCEPTS IN BRIEF

Find out about the latest trends in the monetary aggregates at **www.federalreserve.gov/ releases/**

● The money supply can be defined in a variety of ways, depending on whether we use the transactions approach or the liquidity approach. Using the transactions approach, the money supply consists of currency, checkable deposits, and traveler's checks. This is called M1.

● Checkable deposits (transactions accounts) are any deposits in financial institutions on which the deposit owner can write checks.

● Credit cards are not part of the money supply, for they simply defer transactions that ultimately involve the use of money.

● When we add savings deposits, small-denomination time deposits (certificates of deposit), money market deposit accounts, overnight REPOs, overnight Eurodollars, and retail money market mutual fund balances to M1, we obtain the measure known as M2, which comes close to reflecting economywide economic activity.

FINANCIAL INTERMEDIATION AND BANKS

Most nations, including the United States, have a banking system that consists of two types of institutions. One type consists of private banking institutions. These include commercial banks, which are privately owned profit-seeking institutions, and savings institutions, such as savings banks, savings and loan associations, and credit unions. Savings institutions may be profit-seeking institutions, or they may be *mutual* institutions that are owned by their depositors. The other type of institution is a **central bank,** which typically serves as a banker's bank and as a bank for the national treasury or finance ministry.

Central bank
A banker's bank, usually an official institution that also serves as a country's treasury's bank. Central banks normally regulate commercial banks.

Direct Versus Indirect Financing

When individuals choose to hold some of their savings in new bonds issued by a corporation, their purchases of the bonds are in effect direct loans to the business. This is an example of *direct finance,* in which people lend funds directly to a business. Business financing

*They include M3, which is equal to M2 plus large-denomination time deposits and REPOs (in amounts over $100,000) issued by commercial banks and thrift institutions, Eurodollars held by U.S residents and foreign branches of U.S. banks worldwide and all banking offices in the United Kingdom and Canada, and balances in both taxable and tax-exempt institution-only money market mutual funds. An even broader definition is called L, for *liquidity.* It is defined as M3 plus nonbank public holdings of U.S. savings bonds, Treasury bills, and other short-term securities.

is not always so direct. Individuals might choose instead to hold a time deposit at a bank. The bank may then lend to the same company. In this way, the same people can provide *indirect finance* to a business. The bank makes this possible by *intermediating* the financing of the company.

Financial Intermediation

Banks and other financial institutions are all in the same business—transferring funds from savers to investors. This process is known as **financial intermediation,** and its participants, such as banks and savings institutions, are **financial intermediaries.** The process of financial intermediation is illustrated in Figure 14-4.

Asymmetric Information, Adverse Selection, and Moral Hazard.   Why might people wish to direct their funds through a bank instead of lending them directly to a business? One important reason is **asymmetric information,** the fact that the business may have better knowledge of its own current and future prospects than potential lenders do. For instance, the business may know that it intends to use borrowed funds for projects with a high risk of failure that would make repaying the loan difficult. This potential for those who wish to borrow funds to use in unworthy projects is known as **adverse selection.** Alternatively, a business that had intended to undertake low-risk projects may change management after receiving a loan, and the new managers may use borrowed funds in riskier ways. The possibility that a borrower might engage in behavior that increases risk after borrowing funds is called **moral hazard.**

To minimize the possibility that a business might fail to repay on a loan, people thinking about lending funds directly to the business must study the business carefully before making the loan, and they must continue to monitor its performance afterward. Alternatively, they can choose to avoid the trouble by holding deposits with financial intermediaries,

Financial intermediation
The process by which financial institutions accept savings from businesses, households, and governments and lend the savings to other businesses, households, and governments.

Financial intermediaries
Institutions that transfer funds between ultimate lenders (savers) and ultimate borrowers.

Asymmetric information
Possession of information by one party in a financial transaction but not by the other party.

Adverse selection
The likelihood that individuals who seek to borrow money may use the funds that they receive for unworthy, high-risk projects.

Moral hazard
The possibility that a borrower might engage in riskier behavior after a loan has been obtained.

FIGURE 14-4
The Process of Financial Intermediation
The process of financial intermediation is depicted here. Note that ultimate lenders and ultimate borrowers are the same economic units—households, businesses, and governments—but not necessarily the same individuals. Whereas individual households can be net lenders or borrowers, households as an economic unit are net lenders. Specific businesses or governments similarly can be net lenders or borrowers; as economic units, both are net borrowers.

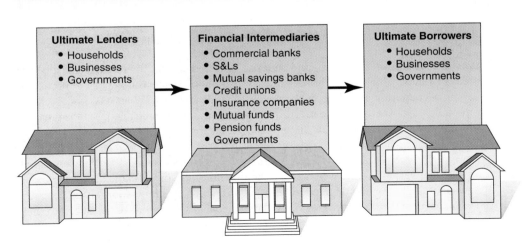

which then specialize in evaluating the creditworthiness of business borrowers and in keeping tabs on their progress until loans are repaid. Thus asymmetric information helps explain why people use financial intermediaries. Moral hazard can be involved when billions of dollars are lent to foreign governments. This is exactly what happened in Russia.

INTERNATIONAL EXAMPLE

Russia and Moral Hazard

Whenever funds are borrowed from a lender, the potential for moral hazard exists. On an international level, this is exactly what happened with the International Monetary Fund (which is financed in large part by U.S. taxpayers). Soon after the Soviet Union collapsed at the end of 1989, the largest new republic, Russia, asked Western nations to help it out. The IMF did just that with a $15 billion "bailout" loan. In order to get the loan, the Russian government agreed to undertake extensive market reforms, cut back on its military spending, and do whatever was necessary to change its economy and make sure it could pay back the money borrowed. Lo and behold, as soon as the billions were lent to Russia, government officials changed their behavior. Moral hazard slipped in as the Russian gov-

ernment suddenly found new uses for the funds that had more to do with encouraging people to vote for current leaders than to enact true reforms. The loan became more risky as a result. Not surprisingly, a few years later, the Russian government asked for even more funds from the IMF. But of course the inevitable was to happen again—no matter what the Russian government agreed to do to get the additional IMF loans, it started to renege as soon as the funds were received.

For Critical Analysis
Once the IMF makes a loan to a country "in trouble," what, if anything, can be done to reduce the moral hazard problem?

Larger Scale and Lower Management Costs.   Another important reason that financial intermediaries exist is that they make it possible for many people to pool their funds, thereby increasing the size, or *scale,* of the total amount of savings managed by an intermediary. This centralization of management reduces fund management costs and risks below the levels savers would incur if all were to manage their savings alone. *Pension fund companies,* which are institutions that specialize in managing funds that individuals save for retirement, owe their existence largely to their abilities to provide such cost savings to individual savers. Likewise, *investment companies,* which are institutions that manage portfolios of financial instruments called mutual funds on behalf of shareholders, also exist largely because of cost savings from their greater scale of operations.

Financial Institution Liabilities and Assets.   Every financial intermediary has its own sources of funds, which are **liabilities** of that institution. When you deposit $100 in your checking account in a bank, the bank creates a liability—it owes you $100—in exchange for the funds deposited. A commercial bank gets its funds from checking and savings accounts; an insurance company gets its funds from insurance policy premiums.

Each financial intermediary has a different primary use of its **assets.** For example, a credit union usually makes small consumer loans, whereas a savings bank makes mainly mortgage loans. Table 14-2 lists the assets and liabilities of typical financial intermediaries. Be aware, though, that the distinction between different financial institutions is becoming more and more blurred. As laws and regulations change, there will be less need to make any distinction. All may ultimately be treated simply as financial intermediaries.

Liabilities
Amounts owed; the legal claims against a business or household by nonowners.

Assets
Amounts owned; all items to which a business or household holds legal claim.

Financial Intermediary	Assets	Liabilities
Commercial banks	Car loans and other consumer debt, business loans, government securities, home mortgages	Transactions accounts, savings deposits, various other time deposits, money market deposit accounts
Savings and loan associations	Home mortgages, some consumer and business debt	Savings and loan shares, transactions accounts, various time deposits, money market deposit accounts
Mutual savings banks	Home mortgages, some consumer and business debt	Transactions accounts, savings accounts, various time deposits, money market deposit accounts
Credit unions	Consumer debt, long-term mortgage loans	Credit union shares, transactions accounts
Insurance companies	Mortgages, stocks, bonds, real estate	Insurance contracts, annuities, pension plans
Pension and retirement funds	Stocks, bonds, mortgages, time deposits	Pension plans
Money market mutual funds	Short-term credit instruments such as large-bank CDs, Treasury bills, and high-grade commercial paper	Fund shares with limited checking privileges

TABLE 14-2
Financial Intermediaries and Their Assets and Liabilities

Financial Intermediation Across National Boundaries

Some countries' governments restrict the financial intermediation process to within their national boundaries. They do so by imposing legal restraints called **capital controls** that bar certain flows of funds across their borders. Nevertheless, today many nations have reduced or even eliminated capital controls. This permits their residents to strive for **international financial diversification** by engaging in the direct or indirect financing of companies located in various nations.

Because business conditions may be good in one country, as they were in the United States in the late 1990s, at the same time that they are poor in another, such as Japan in the late 1990s, people can limit their overall lending risks through international financial diversification. One way to do this is to hold a portion of one's savings with an investment company that offers a **world index fund.** This is carefully designed set of globally issued bonds yielding returns that historically tend to move in offsetting directions. By holding world index funds, individuals can earn the average return on bonds from a number of nations while keeping overall risk of loss to a minimum.

Holding shares in a world index fund is an example of indirect finance across national borders through financial intermediaries. Banks located in various countries take part in the process of international financial intermediation by using some of the funds of depositors in their home nations to finance loans to companies based in other nations. Today, bank financing of U.S. business activities increasingly stems from loans by non-U.S. banks.

Capital controls
Legal restrictions on the ability of a nation's residents to hold and trade assets denominated in foreign currencies.

International financial diversification
Financing investment projects in more than one country.

World index fund
A portfolio of bonds issued in various nations whose yields generally move in offsetting directions, thereby reducing the overall risk of losses.

Bank	Country	Assets ($ Billions)
Fuji Industrial Bank	Japan	1,380
Asahi Sanwa Bank	Japan	1,044
Sumitomo Bank	Japan	1,002
Deutsche Bank	Germany	765
Bank of Tokyo-Mitsubishi	Japan	721
Citigroup Inc.	United States	717
BNP Paribas Group	France	702
Bank of America Corp.	United States	633
UBS AG	Switzerland	615
HSBC Holdings PLC	United Kingdom	569

Source: *American Banker*, March 31, 2000.

Indeed, as Table 14-3 indicates, the world's largest banks are not based in the United States. Today, most of the largest banking institutions, sometimes called *megabanks,* are based in Europe and Japan. These megabanks typically take in deposits and lend throughout the world. Although they report their profits and pay taxes in their home nations, these megabanks are in all other ways international banking institutions.

BANKING STRUCTURES THROUGHOUT THE WORLD

Multinational businesses have relationships with megabanks based in many nations. Individuals and companies increasingly retain the services of banks based outside their home countries. The business of banking varies from nation to nation, however. Each country has its own distinctive banking history, and this fact helps explain unique features of the world's banking systems. Countries' banking systems differ in a number of ways. In some nations, banks are the crucial component of the financial intermediation process, but in others, banking is only part of a varied financial system. In addition, some countries have only a few large banks, while others, such as the United States, have relatively large numbers of banks of various sizes. The legal environments regulating bank dealings with individual and business customers also differ considerably across nations.

A World of National Banking Structures

The extent to which banks are the predominant means by which businesses finance their operations is a key way that national banking systems differ. For instance, in Britain, nearly 70 percent of funds raised by businesses typically stem from bank borrowings, and the proportions for Germany and Japan are on the order of 50 percent and 65 percent, respectively. By way of contrast, U.S. businesses normally raise less than 30 percent of their funds through bank loans.

The relative sizes of banks also differ from one country to another. The five largest banks in Belgium, Denmark, France, Italy, Luxembourg, Portugal, Spain, and the United Kingdom have over 30 percent of the deposits of their nations' residents. In Greece and the Netherlands, this figure is over 80 percent. In contrast, the top five U.S. banks account for less than 15 percent of the deposit holdings of U.S. residents. In Germany, Japan, and Britain, about two-thirds of total bank assets are held by the largest 10 banks. In the United States, this figure is less than one-third.

Traditionally, another feature that has distinguished national banking systems has been the extent to which they have permitted **universal banking.** Under this form of banking, there are few, if any, limits on the ability of banks to offer a full range of financial services and to own shares of corporate stock. In Germany, Britain, and other European nations, banks have had the right to sell insurance and to own stock for many years. Japanese banks face greater restrictions on their activities than European banks, but many Japanese banks have long had the authority to buy stocks. Until very recently, U.S. banks could not hold *any* shares of stock, even for brief periods and were subject to limitations on their ability to offer insurance policies to their customers. This state of affairs changed, however, with passage of the Gramm-Leach-Bliley Act of 1999. This legislation authorized U.S. commercial banks to market insurance and to own stock. Consequently, national differences in banking powers are much narrower than they were just a few years ago.

Universal banking
Environment in which banks face few or no restrictions on their power to offer a full range of financial services and to own shares of stock in corporations.

Central Banks and Their Roles

The first central bank, which began operations in 1668, was Sweden's Sveriges Riksbank (called the Risens Standers Bank until 1867). In 1694, the British Parliament established the most historically famous of central banks, the Bank of England. It authorized the Bank of England to issue currency notes redeemable in silver, and initially the Bank of England's notes circulated alongside currency notes issued by the government and private finance companies. Until 1800, the Riksbank and the Bank of England were the only central banks. The number of central banks worldwide remained less than 10 as late as 1873. The number expanded considerably toward the end of the nineteenth century and again during the second half of the twentieth century, as shown in Figure 14-5.

FIGURE 14-5
The Number of Central Banking Institutions, 1670 to the Present
The twentieth century witnessed considerable growth in the number of central banks.

Source: Data from Forrest Capie, Charles Goodhart, and Norbert Schnadt, "The Development of Central Banking," in Forrest Capie et al., *The Future of Central Banking: The Tercentenary Symposium of the Bank of England* (Cambridge: Cambridge University Press, 1994.)

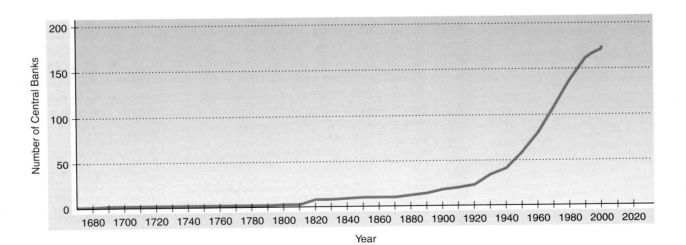

The duties of central banks fall into three broad categories:

1. Central banks perform banking functions for their nations' governments.
2. Central banks provide financial services for private banks.
3. Central banks conduct their nations' monetary policies.

The third is the area of central banking that receives most media attention, even though most central banks devote the bulk of their resources to the other two tasks.

THE FEDERAL RESERVE SYSTEM

The Fed
The Federal Reserve System; the central bank of the United States.

Putting *Economics in Action* to Work

To reinforce your understanding of the Federal Reserve's structure and functions, start the *EIA* CD, click on "Money and Banking," and then click on "The Federal Reserve System."

The Federal Reserve System, also known simply as **the Fed,** is the most important regulatory agency in the United States' monetary system and is usually considered the monetary authority. The Fed was established by the Federal Reserve Act, signed on December 23, 1913, by President Woodrow Wilson. The act was the outgrowth of recommendations from the National Monetary Commission, which had been authorized by the Aldridge-Vreeland Act of 1908. Basically, the commission had attempted to find a way to counter the periodic financial panics that had occurred in our country. Based on the commission's recommendations, which were developed after considerable study of the Bank of England and other central banks, Congress established the Federal Reserve System to aid and supervise banks and also to provide banking services for the U.S. Treasury.

Organization of the Federal Reserve System

Figure 14-6 shows how the Federal Reserve System is organized. It is managed by the Board of Governors, composed of seven full-time members appointed by the U.S. president with the approval of the Senate. The 12 Federal Reserve district banks have a total of 25 branches. The boundaries of the 12 Federal Reserve districts and the cities in which Federal Reserve banks are located are shown in Figure 14-7. The Federal Open Market Committee (FOMC) determines the future growth of the money supply and other important variables. This committee is composed of the members of the Board of Governors, the president of the New York Federal Reserve Bank, and presidents of four other Reserve banks, rotated periodically.

Depository Institutions

Depository institutions—all financial institutions that accept deposits—that comprise our monetary system consist of just over 8,500 commercial banks, about 1,100 savings and loan associations and savings banks, and 12,000 credit unions. All depository institutions may purchase services from the Federal Reserve System on an equal basis. Also, almost all depository institutions are required to keep a certain percentage of their deposits in reserve at the Federal Reserve district banks or as vault cash. This percentage depends on the bank's volume of business. (For further discussion, see Chapter 15.)

Functions of the Federal Reserve System

Here we will present in detail what the Federal Reserve does.

1. *The Fed supplies the economy with fiduciary currency.* The Federal Reserve banks supply the economy with paper currency called Federal Reserve notes. For example,

FIGURE 14-6

Organization of the Federal Reserve System

The 12 Federal Reserve district banks are headed by 12 separate presidents. The main authority of the Fed resides with the Board of Governors of the Federal Reserve System, whose seven members are appointed for 14-year terms by the president of the United States and confirmed by the Senate. Open market operations are carried out through the Federal Open Market Committee (FOMC), consisting of the seven members of the Board of Governors plus five presidents of the district banks (always including the president of the New York bank, with the others rotating).

Source: Board of Governors of the Federal Reserve System, *The Federal Reserve System: Purposes and Functions,* 7th ed. (Washington, D.C., 1984), p. 5.

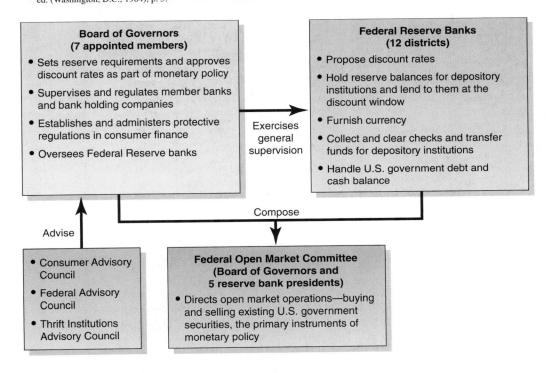

during holiday seasons, when there is an abnormally large number of currency transactions, more paper currency is desired. Commercial banks find this out as deposit holders withdraw large amounts of cash from their accounts. Commercial banks turn to the Federal Reserve banks to replenish vault cash. Hence the Federal Reserve banks must have on hand a sufficient amount of cash to accommodate the demands for paper currency at different times of the year. Note that even though all Federal Reserve notes are printed at the Bureau of Printing and Engraving in Washington, D.C., each note is assigned a code indicating from which of the 12 Federal Reserve banks it "originated." Moreover, each of these notes is an obligation (liability) of the Federal Reserve System, *not* the U.S. Treasury.

2. *The Fed provides a system for check collection and clearing.* The Federal Reserve System has established a clearing mechanism for checks. Suppose that John Smith in Chicago writes a check to Jill Jones, who lives in San Francisco. When Jill receives the check in the mail, she deposits it at her commercial bank. Her bank then deposits the check in the Federal Reserve Bank of San Francisco. In turn, the Federal Reserve Bank of San Francisco sends the check to the Federal Reserve Bank of Chicago. The Chicago Fed

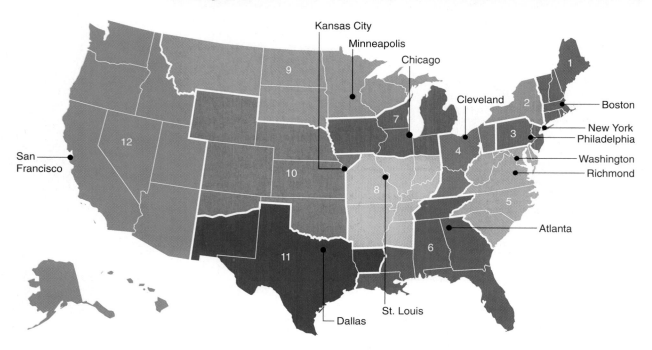

FIGURE 14-7
The Federal Reserve System
The Federal Reserve System is divided into 12 districts, each served by one of the Federal Reserve district banks, located in the cities indicated. The Board of Governors meets in Washington, D.C.

then sends the check to John Smith's commercial bank, where the amount of the check is deducted from John's account. The schematic diagram in Figure 14-8 illustrates this check-clearing process.

The Fed's check collection and clearing operations compete with private clearinghouses. Since the Fed began charging for these services, a considerable volume of this business has shifted back to the private sector. At present, the Federal Reserve processes about one-third of all checks in the United States.

3. *The Fed holds depository institutions' reserves.* The 12 Federal Reserve district banks hold the reserves (other than vault cash) of depository institutions. As you will see in Chapter 15, depository institutions are required by law to keep a certain percentage of their deposits as reserves. Even if they weren't required to do so by law, they would still wish to keep some reserves. Depository institutions act just like other businesses. A firm would not try to operate with a zero balance in its checking account. It would keep a positive balance on hand from which it could draw for expected and unexpected transactions. So, too, would a depository institution desire to have reserves in its banker's bank (the Federal Reserve) on which it could draw funds needed for expected and unexpected transactions.

4. *The Fed acts as the government's fiscal agent.* The Federal Reserve is the banker and fiscal agent for the federal government. The government, as we are all aware, collects large sums of money through taxation. The government also spends and distributes equally large sums. Consequently, the U.S. Treasury has a checking account with the Federal Reserve. Thus the Fed acts as the government's banker, along with commer-

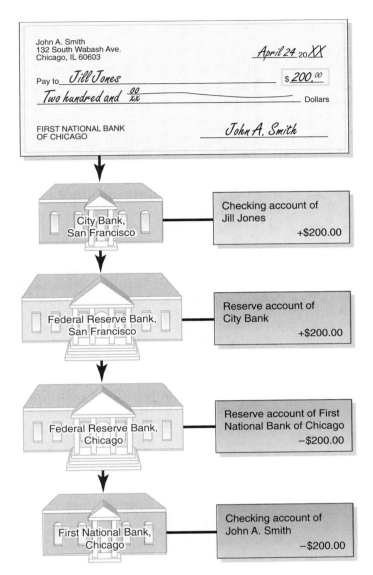

FIGURE 14-8
How a Check Clears
The check-clearing process for an out-of-town check normally involves four steps, including two with Federal Reserve district banks.

cial banks that hold government deposits. The Fed also helps the government collect certain tax revenues and aids in the purchase and sale of government securities.

5. *The Fed supervises depository institutions.* The Fed (along with the comptroller of the currency, the Federal Deposit Insurance Corporation, the Office of Thrift Supervision in the Treasury Department, and the National Credit Union Administration) is a supervisor and regulator of depository institutions. The Fed and other regulators periodically and without warning examine depository institutions to see what kinds of loans have been made, what has been used to back the loans, and who has received them. Whenever such an examination indicates that a bank is not conforming to current banking rules and standards, the Fed can exert pressure on the bank to alter its banking practices.

6. *The Fed acts as the "lender of last resort."* As a central bank, the Fed stands ready to assist, temporarily, any part of the banking system that is in trouble. In this sense, it

acts as a lender of last resort to depository institutions that it has decided should not fail.

7. *The Fed regulates the money supply.* Perhaps the Fed's most important task is its ability to regulate the nation's money supply. To understand how the Fed manages the money supply, we must examine more closely its reserve-holding function and the way in which depository institutions aid in expansion and contraction of the money supply. We will do this in Chapter 15.

8. *The Fed intervenes in foreign currency markets.* Sometimes the Fed attempts to keep the value of the dollar from changing. It does this by buying and selling U.S. dollars in foreign exchange markets. You will read more about this important topic in Chapter 33.

CONCEPTS IN BRIEF

- Financial intermediaries transfer funds from ultimate lenders (savers) to ultimate borrowers. This process of financial intermediation is undertaken by depository institutions such as commercial banks, savings and loan associations, savings banks, and credit unions, as well as by insurance companies, mutual funds, pension funds, and governments.

- Financial intermediaries specialize in tackling problems of asymmetric information. They address the adverse selection problem by carefully reviewing the creditworthiness of loan applicants, and they deal with the moral hazard problem by monitoring borrowers after they receive loans. Many financial intermediaries also take advantage of cost reductions arising from the centralized management of funds pooled from the savings of many individuals.

- In the absence of capital controls that inhibit flows of funds across national borders, many financial intermediaries also take advantage of overall risk reductions made possible by international financial diversification. This has led to the development of megabanks, which operate in many countries.

- A central bank is a banker's bank that typically acts as the fiscal agent for its nation's government as well. The central bank in the United States is the Federal Reserve System, which was established on December 13, 1913.

- There are 12 Federal Reserve district banks, with 25 branches. The Federal Reserve is managed by the Board of Governors in Washington, D.C. The Fed interacts with virtually all depository institutions in the United States, most of which must keep a certain percentage of deposits on reserve with the Fed. The Fed serves as chief regulatory agency for all depository institutions that have Federal Reserve System membership.

- The functions of the Federal Reserve System are to supply fiduciary currency, provide for check collection and clearing, hold depository institution reserves, act as the government's fiscal agent, supervise depository institutions, act as lender of last resort, regulate the supply of money, and intervene in foreign currency markets.

NETNOMICS

Electronic Check Processing

The typical U.S. resident writes nearly three times as many checks as a typical resident of Canada, France, or the United Kingdom. In 2000, the Federal Reserve banks and private clearinghouses processed over 70 billion checks. For a 365-day year, which contains 31,536,000 seconds, this implies that on an average day, these institutions processed well over 2,000 checks per second!

Most of the Federal Reserve's annual $2 billion budget, 25,000 employees (only about 1,600 of whom have job functions related to monetary policy), and small air force of 47 jets and cargo planes are devoted to check-clearing services. To clear checks, the Fed uses automated clearing mechanisms. Since the 1970s, checks have been encrypted with magnetic ink that machines can read directly, which permits automatic sorting, computer crediting, and machine-assisted distribution of checks.

At the time of its introduction, this magnetic encryption system increased the cost efficiency of check collection considerably. Today, however, the technology that the Fed and private clearinghouses use to clear checks looks increasingly antiquated. Current estimates are that alternative electronic payment technologies cost between one-third and one-half as much to use. In an effort to make the check-clearing process more efficient, therefore, the Fed is moving toward full implementation of *electronic check processing* (ECP). Once ECP is in place—which will require large initial setup costs for new hardware and software—magnetic encryption information will be fully scannable for processing by electronic transfer systems already in place. Under ECP, therefore, once a check is turned in to a bank, clearinghouses will essentially convert it to an electronic impulse.

The Dollarization Movement: Is the Fed Destined to Be a Multinational Central Bank?

In 1998, Brazil faced an economic crisis, and Brazilian interest rates shot up considerably. So did interest rates in Argentina, Brazil's main international trading partner. This spillover from Brazil's crisis induced Argentina to contemplate a radical change in its monetary arrangements.

The Prospect of Latin American Dollarization

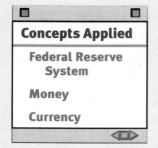

Concepts Applied

Federal Reserve System

Money

Currency

The change that Argentina's leaders considered was *dollarization.* This would entail abandoning Argentina's peso in favor of the U.S. dollar as a medium of exchange, unit of accounting, store of value, and standard of deferred payment. To implement dollarization, Argentina would have to import sufficient U.S. currency for people to use in hand-to-hand transactions. It also would have to convert all Argentine financial accounts and contracts to dollars at the prevailing fixed rate of exchange. Such a conversion would not be too difficult for Argentina, however, because it already has a *currency board* system, in which Argentina issues pesos on a one-to-one basis with the number of U.S. dollars it has on reserve. Thus Argentina's monetary system is already closely linked to that of the United States.

Since Argentina's leaders floated the dollarization proposal, several Latin American nations have revealed that they have been considering the same idea. Dollarization of part of Latin America would have both costs and benefits for the United States. It would simplify efforts by U.S. companies to do business with Latin America, which accounts for about a fifth of U.S. trade. Greater use of the dollar outside the United States could also create a financial windfall for the U.S. government, because Argentina would purchase dollars, giving the U.S. government interest-bearing securities in exchange. The U.S. government would earn the interest on those securities, but as usual, it would not pay interest on its currency. The worldwide return of about $15 billion per year that the U.S. government earns overseas on use of the dollar would undoubtedly increase.

Nevertheless, Federal Reserve and U.S. Treasury officials have expressed concerns about dollarization. Fed policy actions consistent with stabilizing the U.S. economy could have negative consequences outside the United States, fostering resentment and encouraging policymakers in dollarized countries to deflect blame onto U.S. policymakers. This could give governments of dollarized countries political cover for dodging tough decisions regarding appropriate economic policies.

A North American Monetary Union?

So far, Latin American nations, except for Ecuador, have not pursued the dollarization idea any further. Nevertheless, it has now moved north of U.S. borders. Recently, a Toronto-based think tank released a study proposing "North American currency integration" by establishing the U.S. dollar as the single circulating currency in Canada. The authors of the Canadian proposal were not quite as willing as Latin Americans to contemplate unilateral dollarization, however. Their proposal called for the Federal Reserve's Board of Governors to have one Canadian member.

So far the United States has expressed little interest in sharing control of its central bank, but many Canadians seem to be coming around to the idea. After watching the value of the Canadian dollar fall from about 0.90 Canadian dollar per U.S. dollar in 1991 to about 0.65 Canadian dollar per U.S. dollar today, more than a third of Canadians surveyed in public opinion polls indicated support for abolishing the Canadian currency altogether. Three-fourths of Canadians polled said they expected to see a common dollar for the United States and Canada by 2020.

FOR CRITICAL ANALYSIS

1. What would Argentina and Canada give up by dollarizing their economies?

2. Do you see any merit to the arguments by critics of dollarization proposals, who argue that unilateral dollarization in Latin America and Canada would lead to "taxation without representation"?

SUMMARY DISCUSSION OF LEARNING OBJECTIVES

1. **The Key Functions of Money:** Money has four functions. It is a medium of exchange, which means that people use money to make payments for goods, services, and financial assets. It is also is a unit of accounting, meaning that prices are quoted in terms of money values. In addition, money is a store of value, so that people can hold money for future use in exchange. Furthermore, money is a standard of deferred payment, so that the lenders make loans and buyers repay those loans with money.

2. **Important Properties of Goods That Serve as Money:** A good will successfully function as money only if people are widely willing to accept the good in exchange for other goods and services. People must have confidence that others will be willing to trade their goods and services for the good used as money. In addition, while people may continue to use money even if inflation erodes its real purchasing power, they will do so only if the value of money is relatively predictable.

3. **Official Definitions of the Quantity of Money in Circulation:** The narrow definition of the quantity of money in circulation, called M1, focuses on money's role as a medium of exchange. It includes only currency, checkable deposits, and traveler's checks. A broader definition, called M2, stresses money's role as a temporary store of value. M2 is equal to M1 plus near-money assets such as savings deposits, small-denomination time deposits, money market deposit accounts, overnight repurchase agreements and Eurodollars, and noninstitutional holdings of money market mutual fund balances.

4. **Why Financial Intermediaries Such as Banks Exist:** Financial intermediaries help reduce problems stemming from the existence of asymmetric information in financial transactions. Asymmetric information can lead to adverse selection, in which uncreditworthy individuals and firms seek loans, and moral hazard problems, in which an individual or business that has been granted credit begins to engage in riskier practices. Financial intermediaries may also permit savers to benefit from economies of scale, which is the ability to reduce the costs and risks of managing funds by pooling funds and spreading costs and risks across many savers.

5. **The Basic Structure of the Federal Reserve System:** The central bank of the United States is the Federal Reserve System, which consists of 12 district banks with 25 branches. The governing body of the Federal Reserve System is the Board of Governors, which is based in Washington, D.C. Decisions about the quantity of money in circulation are made

by the Federal Open Market Committee, which is composed of the Board of Governors and five Federal Reserve bank presidents.

6. **Major Functions of the Federal Reserve:** The main functions of the Federal Reserve System are supplying the economy with fiduciary currency, providing a system for check collection and clearing, holding depository institutions' reserves, acting as the government's fiscal agent, supervising banks, acting as a lender of last resort, regulating the money supply, and intervening in foreign exchange markets.

Key Terms and Concepts

Adverse selection (337)

Assets (338)

Asymmetric information (337)

Barter (328)

Capital controls (339)

Central bank (336)

Certificate of deposit (CDs) (335)

Checkable deposits (333)

Depository institutions (335)

Eurodollar deposits (335)

The Fed (342)

Fiduciary monetary system (331)

Financial intermediaries (337)

Financial intermediation (337)

International financial diversification (339)

Liabilities (338)

Liquidity (330)

Liquidity approach (332)

M1 (333)

M2 (335)

Medium of exchange (328)

Money (328)

Money Market Deposit Account (MMDAs) (335)

Money market mutual funds (336)

Money supply (332)

Moral hazard (337)

Near moneys (334)

Repurchase Agreement (REPO, or RP) (335)

Savings deposits (335)

Standard of deferred payment (330)

Store of value (329)

Thrift institutions (333)

Time deposit (335)

Transactions accounts (331)

Transactions approach (332)

Traveler's checks (333)

Unit of accounting (329)

Universal banking (341)

World index fund (339)

Problems

Answers to the odd-numbered problems appear at the back of the book.

14-1. On the island of Yap, natives until 1946 used large doughnut-shaped stones as financial assets. Although prices of goods and services were not quoted in terms of the stones, the stones were often used in exchange for particularly large purchases, such as payments for livestock. To make the transaction, several individuals would place a large stick through a stone's center and carry it to its new owner. A stone was difficult for any one person to steal, so an owner typically would lean it against the side of his or her home as a sign to others of accumulated purchasing power that would hold value for later use in exchange. Loans would often be repaid using the stones. In what ways did these stones function as money?

14-2. During the late 1970s, prices quoted in terms of the Israeli currency, the shekel, rose so fast that grocery stores listed their prices in terms of the U.S. dollar and provided customers with dollar-shekel conversion tables that they updated daily. Although people continued to buy goods and services and make loans using shekels, many Israeli citizens converted shekels to dollars to avoid a reduction in their wealth due to inflation. In what way did the U.S. dollar function as money in Israel during this period?

14-3. During the 1945–1946 Hungarian hyperinflation, when the rate of inflation reached 41.9 *quadrillion* percent per month, the Hungarian government discovered that the real value of its tax receipts was falling dramatically. To keep real tax income more stable, it created a good called a "tax pengö," in which all bank deposits were denominated for purposes of taxation. Nevertheless, payments for goods and services were made only in terms of the real Hungarian currency, whose value tended to fall rapidly even though the value of a tax pengö remained stable. Prices were quoted only in terms of the regular currency also. Lenders, however, began denominating loan payments in terms of tax pengös. In what ways did the tax pengö function as money in Hungary in 1945 and 1946?

14-4. Considering the following data (expressed in billions of U.S. dollars), calculate M1 and M2.

Currency	450
Savings deposits and money market deposit accounts	1,400
Small-denomination time deposits	1,000
Traveler's checks	10
Overnight repurchase agreements	100
Total money market mutual funds	500
Institution-only money market mutual funds	200
Overnight Eurodollars	50
Demand deposits	450
Other checkable deposits	490

14-5. Identify whether the following item is counted in M1, M2, or neither:
  a. A $1,000 balance in a checking account at a mutual savings bank
  b. A $100,000 certificate of deposit issued by a New York bank
  c. A $10,000 time deposit an elderly widow holds at her credit union
  d. A Eurodollar deposit that matures in three months
  e. A $50,000 money market deposit account balance

14-6. In the early 1990s, many pension funds and mutual funds began offering U.S. savers special portfolios composed only of financial instruments issued by companies and governments located in other nations. In 1997 and 1998, many of those savers who held these portfolios earned very low, and sometimes negative, returns. By way of contrast, most people who allocated 100 percent of their savings only to U.S. financial instruments earned higher returns. Does this experience mean that international financial diversification is a mistake? Explain your reasoning.

14-7. A few years ago, a Florida county commissioner and her husband, a Washington lobbyist, were indicted for securities laws violations. Allegedly, they sought to improve the terms under which the county could issue new municipal bonds. Suppose this information had not come to light and had made the municipal bonds more risky than they otherwise might have seemed to potential buyers. Would this have been an example of adverse selection or of moral hazard? Explain your reasoning.

14-8. In what sense is currency a liability of the Federal Reserve System?

14-9. In what respects is the Fed like a private banking institution? In what respects is it more like a government agency?

14-10. Take a look at the map of the locations of the Federal Reserve districts and their headquarters in Figure 14-7. Today, the U.S. population is centered just west of the Mississippi River—that is, about half of the population is either to the west or the east of a line running roughly just west of this river. Can you reconcile the current locations of Fed districts and banks with this fact? Why do you suppose the Fed has its current geographic structure?

Economics on the Net

What's Happened to the Money Supply? Deposits at banks and other financial institutions comprise a portion of the U.S. money supply. This application gives you the chance to see how changes in these deposits influence the Fed's measures of money.

Internet URL: www.stls.frb.org/fred/

Title: FRED (Federal Reserve Economic Data)

Navigation: Go directly to the URL, or start at the Web page of the Federal Reserve Bank of St. Louis (www.stls.frb.org), and then click on FRED.

Application

1. Select the data series for demand deposits (either seasonally adjusted or not). Scan through the data. Do you notice any recent trend? (Hint: Compare the growth in the figures before 1993 with their growth after 1993.) In addition, take a look at the data series for currency and for other checkable deposits. Do you observe similar recent trends in these series?

2. Now take a look at the M1 series (again, either seasonally adjusted or not). Does it show any recent trend (pre-1993 versus post-1993)?

Fog Group Study and Analysis   FRED contains considerable financial data series. Assign individual members or groups of the class the task of examining data on assets included in M1, M2, and M3. Have each student or group look for big swings in the data. Then ask the groups to report to the class as a whole. When did clear changes occur in various categories of the monetary aggregates? Were there times that people appeared to shift funds from one aggregate to another? Are there any other noticeable patterns that may have had something to do with economic events during various periods?

MONEY CREATION, PAYMENT SYSTEMS, AND DEPOSIT INSURANCE

Federal Reserve notes are part of the money supply. But they constitute only a small part of the legal reserves that depository institutions keep. In what form are most legal reserves held?

In the early 1990s, banks and other depository institutions held about $30 billion in funds on deposit with Federal Reserve Banks — funds known as *depository institution reserves.* Today, that amount has declined to about $9 billion. In the late 1990s, Federal Reserve Board Chair Alan Greenspan expressed his concern that this development "could adversely affect the ability of the Federal Reserve to gauge the supply of reserves consistent with the Federal Open Market Committee's intended policy stance." Translated, this means that the Fed is worried that the big decline in depository institution reserves at Federal Reserve banks may make it hard for the Fed to control the money supply. Why have banks cut back so much on their reserves on deposit with Federal Reserve banks? What does this have to do with the money supply? In this chapter, you will learn about the concepts you must understand in order to answer these questions.

LEARNING OBJECTIVES

After reading this chapter, you should be able to:

1. Describe how the Federal Reserve assesses reserve requirements on banks and other depository institutions

2. Understand why the money supply is unaffected when someone deposits in a depository institution a check drawn on another depository institution

3. Explain why the money supply changes when someone deposits in a depository institution a check drawn on the Federal Reserve System

4. Determine the maximum potential extent to which the money supply will change following a Federal Reserve purchase or sale of government securities

5. Describe the structure of the U.S. payment system and the associated risks it poses for individual depository institutions and the banking system as a whole

6. Explain the essential features of federal deposit insurance

Did You Know That... virtually overnight, Nick Leeson, a 27-year-old manager in the Singapore branch of Barings Bank, was able to inflict losses of several billion dollars on the institution? Barings was founded in 1762. In 1803, it helped the United States purchase the Louisiana Territory from France. It provided credit to the British government during the Napoleonic Wars (1803–1815). When Barings collapsed in the mid-1990s—as a result of Leeson's actions—it was bought by former competitors, thereby ending the life of one of the longest-running financial institutions in the world. Could the collapse of such an important bank lead to serious problems in the world's banking sector? A lot depends on whether the losses suffered by Barings's depositors would cause other banks to shrink. That in turn depends on the relationship between deposits in different banks.

If you were to attend a luncheon of local bankers and ask the question, "Do you as bankers create money?" you would get a uniformly negative response. Bankers are certain that they do not create money. Indeed, *by itself* no individual bank can create money. But through actions initiated by a central bank such as the Federal Reserve, depository institutions *together* do create money; they determine the total deposits outstanding. In this chapter, we will examine the money multiplier process, which explains how an injection of new money into the banking system leads to an eventual multiple expansion in the total money supply. We will also take a look at our payment system and how it creates risks for depository institutions, including the potential for widespread bank failures. Then we shall examine federal deposit insurance and its role in provoking the 1980s crisis in the savings and loan industry.

LINKS BETWEEN CHANGES IN THE MONEY SUPPLY AND OTHER ECONOMIC VARIABLES

How fast the money supply grows or does not grow is important because no matter what model of the economy is used, theories link the money supply growth rate to economic growth or to business fluctuations. There is in fact a long-standing relationship between changes in the money supply and changes in GDP. Some economists use this historical evidence to argue that money is an important determinant of the level of economic activity in the economy.

Another key economic variable in our economy is the price level. As you learned in Chapter 10, both the quantity of money and the price level have risen since the 1950s, and at least one theory attributes changes in the rate of inflation to changes in the growth rate of money in circulation. Figure 15-1 shows the relationship between the rate of growth of the money supply and the inflation rate. There seems to be a loose, long-run, direct relationship between changes in the money supply and changes in the rate of inflation. Increases in the money supply growth rate seem to lead to increases in the inflation rate, after a time lag.

THE ORIGINS OF FRACTIONAL RESERVE BANKING

As early as 1000 B.C., uncoined gold and silver were being used as money in Mesopotamia. Goldsmiths weighed and assessed the purity of those metals; later they started issuing paper notes indicating that the bearers held gold or silver of given weights and purity on deposit with the goldsmith. These notes could be transferred in exchange for goods and became the first paper currency. The gold and silver on deposit with the goldsmiths were

FIGURE 15-1

Money Supply Growth Versus the Inflation Rate

These time-series curves indicate a loose correspondence between money supply growth and the inflation rate. Actually, closer inspection reveals a direct relationship between changes in the growth rate of money and changes in the inflation rate *in a later period*. This relationship seemed to hold well into the 1990s, when it became less strong.

Sources: Economic Report of the President; Federal Reserve Bulletin; Economic Indicators, various issues.

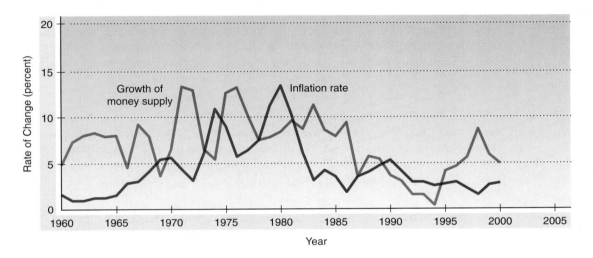

the first bank deposits. Eventually, goldsmiths realized that the amount of gold and silver on deposit always exceeded the average amount of gold and silver withdrawn at any given time—often by a predictable ratio. These goldsmiths started making loans by issuing to borrowers paper notes that exceeded in value the amount of gold and silver they actually kept on hand. They charged interest on these loans. This constituted the earliest form of what is now called **fractional reserve banking.** We know that goldsmiths operated this way in Delphi, Didyma, and Olympia in Greece as early as the seventh century B.C. In Athens, fractional reserve banking was well developed by the sixth century B.C.

Fractional reserve banking
A system in which depository institutions hold reserves that are less than the amount of total deposits.

DEPOSITORY INSTITUTION RESERVES

In a fractional reserve banking system, banks do not keep sufficient reserves on hand to cover 100 percent of their depositors' accounts. And the reserves that are held by depository institutions in the United States are not kept in gold and silver, as they were with the early goldsmiths, but rather in the form of deposits on reserve with Federal Reserve district banks and in vault cash. Depository institutions are required by the Fed to maintain a specified percentage of their customer deposits as **reserves.** There are three distinguishable types of reserves: legal, required, and excess.

Reserves
In the U.S. Federal Reserve System, deposits held by Federal Reserve district banks for depository institutions, plus depository institutions' vault cash.

Legal Reserves

For depository institutions, **legal reserves** constitute anything that the law permits them to claim as reserves. Today, that consists only of deposits held at the Federal Reserve district bank plus vault cash. Government securities, for example, are not legal reserves, even

Legal reserves
Reserves that depository institutions are allowed by law to claim as reserves—for example, deposits held at Federal Reserve district banks and vault cash.

though the owners and managers of the depository institutions may consider them such because they can easily be turned into cash, should the need arise, to meet unusually large net withdrawals by customers. Economists refer to all legal reserves that banks hold with the Federal Reserve or keep in their vaults as their *total reserves.*

Required Reserves

Required reserves The value of reserves that a depository institution must hold in the form of vault cash or deposits with the Fed.

Required reserve ratio The percentage of total deposits that the Fed requires depository institutions to hold in the form of vault cash or deposits with the Fed.

Required reserves are the minimum amount of legal reserves that a depository institution must have to "back" checkable deposits. They are expressed as a ratio of required reserves to total checkable deposits (banks need hold no reserves on noncheckable deposits). The **required reserve ratio** for almost all checkable deposits is 10 percent (except for roughly the first $50 million in deposits at any depository institution, which is subject to only a 3 percent requirement). The general formula is

$$\text{Required reserves} = \text{checkable deposits} \times \text{required reserve ratio}$$

Take a hypothetical example. If the required level of reserves is 10 percent and the bank* has $1 billion in customer checkable deposits, it must hold at least $100 million as reserves. As we shall discuss later in this chapter, during the 1990s banks discovered a novel way to reduce the amounts of reserves that they are required to hold.

Excess Reserves

Excess reserves The difference between legal reserves and required reserves.

Depository institutions often hold reserves in excess of what is required by the Fed. This difference between actual (legal) reserves and required reserves is called **excess reserves.** (Excess reserves can be negative, but they rarely are. Negative excess reserves indicate that depository institutions do not have sufficient reserves to meet their required reserves. When this happens, they borrow from other depository institutions or from a Federal Reserve district bank, sell assets such as securities, or call in loans.) Excess reserves are an important potential determinant of the rate of growth of the money supply, for as we shall see, it is only to the extent that depository institutions have excess reserves that they can make new loans. Because reserves produce no income, profit-seeking financial institutions have an incentive to minimize excess reserves, disposing of them either to purchase income-producing securities or to make loans with which they earn income through interest payments received. In equation form, we can define excess reserves in this way:

$$\text{Excess reserves} = \text{legal reserves} - \text{required reserves}$$

In the analysis that follows, we examine the relationship between the level of reserves and the size of the money supply. This analysis implies that factors influencing the level of the reserves of the banking system as a whole will ultimately affect the size of the money supply, other things held constant. We show first that when someone deposits in one depository institution a check that is written on another depository institution, the two depository institutions involved are individually affected, but the overall money supply does not change. Then we show that when someone deposits in a depository institution a check that is written on the Fed, a multiple expansion in the money supply results.

CONCEPTS IN BRIEF

● Ours is a fractional reserve banking system in which depository institutions must hold only a percentage of their deposits as reserves, either on deposit with a Federal Reserve district bank or as vault cash.

*The term *bank* will be used interchangeably with the term *depository institution* in this chapter because distinctions among financial institutions are becoming less and less meaningful.

● Required reserves are usually expressed as a ratio, in percentage terms, of required reserves to total deposits.

THE RELATIONSHIP BETWEEN RESERVES AND TOTAL DEPOSITS

To show the relationship between reserves and depository institution deposits, we first analyze a single bank (existing alongside many others). A single bank is able to make new loans to its customers only to the extent that it has reserves above the level legally required to cover the new deposits. When an individual bank has no excess reserves, it cannot make loans.

How a Single Bank Reacts to an Increase in Reserves

To examine the **balance sheet** of a single bank after its reserves are increased, let's make the following assumptions:

1. The required reserve ratio is 10 percent for all checkable deposits.
2. Checkable deposits are the bank's only liabilities; reserves at a Federal Reserve district bank and loans are the bank's only assets. Loans are promises made by customers to repay some amount in the future; that is, they are IOUs and as such are assets to the bank.
3. An individual bank can lend as much as it is legally allowed.
4. Every time a loan is made to an individual (consumer or business), all the proceeds from the loan are put into a checkable deposit account; no cash (currency or coins) is withdrawn.
5. Depository institutions seek to keep zero excess reserves because reserves do not earn interest. (Depository institutions are run to make profits; we assume that all depository institutions wish to convert excess reserves that do not pay interest into interest-bearing loans.)
6. Depository institutions have zero **net worth.** (In reality, all depository institutions are required to have some positive owners' equity, or capital, which is another name for net worth. It is usually a small percentage of the institutions' total assets.)

Balance sheet
A statement of the assets and liabilities of any business entity, including financial institutions and the Federal Reserve System. Assets are what is owned; liabilities are what is owed.

Net worth
The difference between assets and liabilities.

Look at the simplified initial position of Typical Bank in Balance Sheet 15-1. Liabilities consist of $1 million in checkable deposits. Assets consist of $100,000 in reserves and $900,000 in loans to customers. Total assets of $1 million equal total liabilities of $1 million. With a 10 percent reserve requirement and $1 million in checkable deposits, the bank has required reserves of $100,000 and therefore no excess reserves.

ASSETS			LIABILITIES	
Total reserves		$100,000	Checkable deposits	$1,000,000
Required reserves	$100,000			
Excess reserves	0			
Loans		900,000		
Total		$1,000,000	Total	$1,000,000

Balance Sheet 15-1
Typical Bank

Assume that a depositor deposits in Typical Bank a $100,000 check drawn on another depository institution. Checkable deposits in Typical Bank immediately increase by $100,000, bringing the total to $1.1 million. Once the check clears, total reserves of Typical Bank increase to $200,000. A $1.1 million total in checkable deposits means that required reserves will have to be 10 percent of $1.1 million, or $110,000. Typical Bank now has excess reserves equal to $200,000 minus $110,000, or $90,000. This is shown in Balance Sheet 15-2.

Balance Sheet 15-2
Typical Bank

ASSETS			LIABILITIES	
Total reserves		$200,000	Checkable deposits	$1,100,000
Required reserves	$110,000			
Excess reserves	90,000			
Loans		900,000		
Total		$1,100,000	Total	$1,100,000

Effect on Typical Bank's Balance Sheet.   Look at excess reserves in Balance Sheet 15-2. Excess reserves were zero before the $100,000 deposit, and now they are $90,000—that's $90,000 worth of assets not earning any income. By assumption, Typical Bank will now lend out this entire $90,000 in excess reserves in order to obtain interest income. Loans will increase to $990,000. The borrowers who receive the new loans will not leave them on deposit in Typical Bank. After all, they borrow money to spend it. As they spend it by writing checks that are deposited in other banks, actual reserves will fall to $110,000 (as required), and excess reserves will again become zero, as indicated in Balance Sheet 15-3.

Balance Sheet 15-3
Typical Bank

ASSETS			LIABILITIES	
Total reserves		$110,000	Checkable deposits	$1,100,000
Required reserves	$110,000			
Excess reserves	0			
Loans		990,000		
Total		$1,100,000	Total	$1,100,000

In this example, a person deposited a $100,000 check drawn on another bank. That $100,000 became part of the reserves of Typical Bank. Because that deposit immediately created excess reserves in Typical Bank, further loans were possible for Typical Bank. The excess reserves were lent out to earn interest. A bank will not lend more than its excess reserves because, by law, it must hold a certain amount of required reserves.

Effect on the Money Supply.   A look at the balance sheets for Typical Bank might give the impression that the money supply increased because of the new customer's $100,000 deposit. Remember, though, that the deposit was a check written on *another* bank. Therefore, the other bank suffered a *decline* in its checkable deposits and its reserves. While total assets and liabilities in Typical Bank have increased by $100,000, they have *decreased* in the other bank by $100,000. The total amount of money and credit in the economy is unaffected by the transfer of funds from one depository institution to another.

The thing to remember is that new reserves are not created when checks written on one bank are deposited in another bank. The Federal Reserve System can, however, create new reserves; that is the subject of the next section.

THE FED'S DIRECT EFFECT ON THE OVERALL LEVEL OF RESERVES

Now we shall examine the Fed's direct effect on the level of reserves, showing how a change in the level of reserves causes a multiple change in the total money supply. Consider the Federal Open Market Committee (FOMC), whose decisions essentially determine the level of reserves in the monetary system.

Federal Open Market Committee

Open market operations are the purchase and sale of existing U.S. government securities in the open market (the private secondary U.S. securities market in which people exchange government securities that have not yet matured) by the FOMC in order to change the money supply. If the FOMC decides that the Fed should buy or sell bonds, it instructs the New York Federal Reserve Bank trading desk to do so.*

Open market operations
The purchase and sale of existing U.S. government securities (such as bonds) in the open private market by the Federal Reserve System.

A Sample Transaction

Assume that the trading desk at the New York Fed has determined that in order to comply with the latest directive from the FOMC, it must purchase $100,000 worth of U.S. government securities.† The Fed pays for these securities by writing a check on itself for $100,000. This check is given to the bond dealer in exchange for the $100,000 worth of bonds. The bond dealer deposits the $100,000 check in its checkable account at a bank, which then sends the $100,000 check back to the Federal Reserve. When the Fed receives the check, it adds $100,000 to the reserve account of the bank that sent it the check. The Fed has created $100,000 of reserves. The Fed can create reserves because it has the ability to add to the reserve accounts of depository institutions whenever it buys U.S. securities. When the Fed buys a U.S. government security in the open market, it initially expands total reserves by the amount of the purchase.

Using Balance Sheets. Consider the balance sheets of the Fed and of the depository institution receiving the check. Balance Sheet 15-4 on page 360 shows the results for the Fed after the bond purchase and for the bank after the bond dealer deposits the $100,000 check.‡ The Fed' balance sheet (which here reflects only account changes) shows that after the purchase, the Fed's assets have increased by $100,000 in the form of U.S. government securities. Liabilities have also increased by $100,000 in the form of an increase in the reserve account of the bank. The balance sheet for the bank shows an increase in assets of

---

*Actually, the Fed usually deals in Treasury bills that have a maturity date of one year or less.

†In practice, the trading desk is never given a specific dollar amount to purchase or to sell. The account manager uses personal discretion in determining what amount should be purchased or sold in order to satisfy the FOMC's latest directive.

‡Strictly speaking, the balance sheets that we are showing should be called the *consolidated balance sheets* for the 12 Federal Reserve district banks. We will simply refer to these banks as the Fed, however.

$100,000 in the form of reserves with its Federal Reserve district bank. The bank also has an increase in its liabilities in the form of a $100,000 deposit in the checkable account of the bond dealer; this is an immediate $100,000 increase in the money supply.

Balance Sheet 15-4
Balance Sheets for the Fed and the Bank When a U.S. Government Security is Purchased by the Fed, Showing Changes Only in Assets and Liabilities

The Fed		Bank	
ASSETS	LIABILITIES	ASSETS	LIABILITIES
+$100,000 U.S. government securities	+$100,000 depository institution's reserves	+$100,000 reserves	+$100,000 checkable deposit owned by bond dealer

Sale of a $100,000 U.S. Government Security by the Fed

The process is reversed when the account manager at the New York Fed trading desk sells a U.S. government security from the Fed's portfolio.

Sale of a Security by the Fed.   When the individual or institution buying the security from the Fed writes a check for $100,000 and the check clears, the Fed reduces the reserves and deposits of the bank on which the check was written. The $100,000 sale of the U.S. government security leads to a reduction in reserves in the banking system and a reduction in checkable deposits. Hence the money supply declines.

Using Balance Sheets Again.   Balance Sheet 15-5 shows the results for the sale of a U.S. government security by the Fed. When the $100,000 clears, the Fed reduces by $100,000 the reserve account of the bank on which the check is written. The Fed's assets are also reduced by $100,000 because it no longer owns the U.S. government security. The bank's checkable deposit liabilities are reduced by $100,000 when that amount is deducted from the account of the bond purchaser, and the money supply is thereby reduced by that amount. The bank's assets are also reduced by $100,000, because the Fed has reduced its total reserves by that amount.

Balance Sheet 15-5
Balance Sheets After the Fed Has Sold $100,000 of U.S. Government Securities, Showing Changes Only in Assets and Liabilities

The Fed		Bank	
ASSETS	LIABILITIES	ASSETS	LIABILITIES
−$100,000 U.S. government securities	−$100,000 depository institution's reserves	−$100,000 reserves	−$100,000 checkable deposit balances

CONCEPTS IN BRIEF

● If a check is written on one depository institution and deposited in another, there is no change in total deposits or in the total money supply. No additional reserves in the banking system have been created.

● The Federal Reserve, through its Federal Open Market Committee (FOMC), can directly increase depository institutions' reserves and the money supply by purchasing U.S. government securities from bond dealers in the open market; it can decrease depository institutions' reserves and the money supply by selling U.S. government securities to bond dealers in the open market.

MONEY EXPANSION BY THE BANKING SYSTEM

Consider now the entire banking system. For practical purposes, we can look at all depository institutions taken as a whole. To understand how money is created, we must understand how depository institutions respond to Fed actions that increase reserves in the entire system.

Fed Purchases of U.S. Government Securities

Assume that the Fed purchases a $100,000 U.S. government security from a bond dealer. The bond dealer deposits the $100,000 check in Bank 1, which prior to this transaction is in the position depicted in Balance Sheet 15-6. The check, however, is not written on another depository institution; rather, it is written on the Fed itself.

ASSETS			LIABILITIES	
Total reserves		$100,000	Checkable deposits	$1,000,000
Required reserves	$100,000			
Excess reserves	0			
Loans		900,000		
Total		$1,000,000	Total	$1,000,000

Balance Sheet 15-6
Bank 1

Now look at the balance sheet for Bank 1 shown in Balance Sheet 15-7. Reserves have been increased by $100,000 to $200,000, and checkable deposits have also been increased by $100,000. Because required reserves on $1.1 million of checkable deposits are only $110,000, the depository institution has $90,000 in excess reserves.

ASSETS			LIABILITIES	
Total reserves		$200,000	Checkable deposits	$1,100,000
Required reserves	$110,000			
Excess reserves	90,000			
Loans		900,000		
Total		$1,100,000	Total	$1,100,000

Balance Sheet 15-7
Bank 1

Effect on the Money Supply. The purchase of a $100,000 U.S. government security by the Federal Reserve from the public (a bond dealer, for example) increases the money supply immediately by $100,000 because checkable deposits held by the public—the bond dealers are members of the public—are part of the money supply, and no other bank has lost deposits.

The process of money creation does not stop here. Look again at Balance Sheet 15-7. Bank 1 has excess reserves of $90,000. No other depository institution (or combination of depository institutions) has negative excess reserves of $90,000 as a result of the Fed's bond purchase. (Remember, the Fed simply created the reserves to pay for the bond purchase.)

Bank 1 will not wish to hold non-interest-bearing excess reserves. Assume that it will expand its loans by $90,000. This is shown in Balance Sheet 15-8.

Balance Sheet 15-8
Bank 1

ASSETS			LIABILITIES	
Total reserves		$110,000	Checkable deposits	$1,100,000
Required reserves	$110,000			
Excess reserves	0			
Loans		990,000		
Total		$1,100,000	Total	$1,100,000

The individual or business that has received the $90,000 loan will spend these funds, which will then be deposited in other banks. For the sake of simplicity, concentrate only on the balance sheet *changes* resulting from this new deposit, as shown in Balance Sheet 15-9. For Bank 2, the $90,000 deposit, after the check has cleared, becomes an increase in reserves as well as an increase in checkable deposits and hence the money supply. Because the reserve requirement is 10 percent, required reserves increase $9,000, so Bank 2 will have excess reserves of $81,000. But of course, excess reserves are not income producing, so by assumption Bank 2 will reduce them to zero by making a loan of $81,000 (which will earn interest income). This is shown in Balance Sheet 15-10.

Balance Sheet 15-9
Bank 2 (Changes Only)

ASSETS			LIABILITIES	
Total reserves		+$90,000	New checkable deposits	+$90,000
Required reserves	+$9,000			
Excess reserves	+81,000			
Total		+$90,000	Total	+$90,000

Balance Sheet 15-10
Bank 2 (Changes Only)

ASSETS			LIABILITIES	
Total reserves		+$9,000	Checkable deposits	+$90,000
Required reserves	+$9,000			
Excess reserves	+0			
Loans		+81,000		
Total		+$90,000	Total	+$90,000

Remember that in this example, the original $100,000 deposit was a check issued by a Federal Reserve bank to the bond dealer. That $100,000 constituted an immediate increase in the money supply of $100,000 when deposited in the bond dealer's checkable account. The deposit creation process (in addition to the original $100,000) occurs because of the fractional reserve banking system, coupled with the desire of depository institutions to maintain a minimum level of excess reserves. Under fractional reserve banking, banks must only hold a portion of new deposits as reserves, and in their quest to earn profits they seek to transform excess reserves into holdings of loans and securities.

Continuation of the Deposit Creation Process.   Look at Bank 3's simplified account in Balance Sheet 15-11, where again only *changes* in the assets and liabilities are shown. Assume that the firm borrowing from Bank 2 writes a check for $81,000 that is deposited in Bank 3; checkable deposits and the money supply increase by $81,000. Legal reserves of Bank 3 rise by that amount when the check clears.

ASSETS		LIABILITIES	
Total reserves	+$81,000	New checkable deposits +$81,000	
Required reserves +$8,100			
Excess reserves +72,900			
Total	+$81,000	Total	+$81,000

Balance Sheet 15-11
Bank 3 (Changes Only)

Because the reserve requirement is 10 percent, required reserves rise by $8,100, and excess reserves therefore increase by $72,900. We assume that Bank 3 will want to lend all of those non-interest-earning assets (excess reserves). When it does, loans (and newly created checkable deposits) will increase by $72,900. This bank's legal reserves will fall to $8,100, and excess reserves become zero as checks are written on the new deposit. This is shown in Balance Sheet 15-12 on page 364.

ASSETS		LIABILITIES	
Total reserves	+$8,100	Checkable deposits	+$81,000
Required reserves +$8,100			
Excess reserves 0			
Loans	+72,900		
Total	+$81,000	Total	+$81,000

Balance Sheet 15-12
Bank 3 (Changes Only)

Progression to Other Banks. This process continues to Banks 4, 5, 6, and so forth. Each bank obtains smaller and smaller increases in deposits because 10 percent of each deposit must be held in required reserves; therefore, each succeeding depository institution makes correspondingly smaller loans. Table 15-1 shows the new deposits, possible loans, and required reserves for the remaining depository institutions in the system.

Effect on Total Deposits. In this example, deposits (and the money supply) increased initially by the $100,000 that the Fed paid the bond dealer in exchange for a bond. Deposits (and the money supply) were further increased by a $90,000 deposit in Bank 2, and they were again increased by an $81,000 deposit in Bank 3. Eventually, total deposits and the money supply will increase by $1 million, as shown in Table 15-1. The $1 million consists of the original $100,000 created by the Fed, plus an extra $900,000 generated by deposit-creating bank loans. The money multiplier process is portrayed graphically in Figure 15-2 on page 364.

Increase in Total Banking System Reserves

Even with fractional reserve banking, if there are zero excess reserves, deposits cannot expand unless total banking system reserves are increased. The original new deposit in Bank 1, in our example, was in the form of a check written on a Federal Reserve district bank. It therefore represented new reserves to the banking system. Had that check been written on Bank 3, by contrast, nothing would have happened to the total amount of checkable deposits; there would have been no change in the total money supply. To repeat: Checks written on banks within the system, without any expansion of overall reserves within the banking system, represent transfers of reserves and deposits among depository

TABLE 15-1

Maximum Money Creation with 10 Percent Required Reserves

This table shows the maximum new loans plus investments that banks can make, given the Fed's deposit of a $100,000 check in Bank 1. The required reserve ratio is 10 percent. We assume that all excess reserves in each bank are used for new loans or investments.

Bank	New Deposits	New Required Reserves	Maximum New Loans
1	$100,000 (from Fed)	$10,000	$90,000
2	90,000	9,000	81,000
3	81,000	8,100	72,900
4	72,900	7,290	65,610
·	·	·	·
·	·	·	·
·	·	·	·
All other banks	656,100	65,610	590,490
Totals	$1,000,000	$100,000	$900,000

FIGURE 15-2

The Multiple Expansion in the Money Supply Due to $100,000 in New Reserves When the Required Reserve Ratio Is 10 Percent

The banks are all aligned in decreasing order of new deposits created. Bank 1 receives the $100,000 in new reserves and lends out $90,000. Bank 2 receives the $90,000 and lends out $81,000. The process continues through banks 3 to 19 and then the rest of the banking system. Ultimately, assuming no leakages, the $100,000 of new reserves results in an increase in the money supply of $1 million, or 10 times the new reserves, because the required reserve ratio is 10 percent.

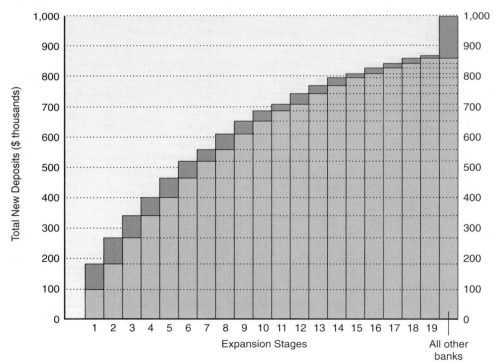

institutions that do not affect the money supply. Only when additional new reserves and deposits are created by the Federal Reserve System does the money supply increase.

You should be able to work through the foregoing example to show the reverse process when there is a decrease in reserves because the Fed sells a $100,000 U.S. government security. The result is a multiple contraction of deposits and therefore of the total money supply in circulation.

CONCEPTS IN BRIEF

● When the Fed increases reserves through a purchase of U.S. government securities, the result is a multiple expansion of deposits and therefore of the supply of money.

● When the Fed reduces the banking system's reserves by selling U.S. government securities, the result is a multiple contraction of deposits and therefore of the money supply.

THE MONEY MULTIPLIER

In the example just given, a $100,000 increase in excess reserves generated by the Fed's purchase of a security yielded a $1 million increase in total deposits; deposits increased by a multiple of 10 times the initial $100,000 increase in overall reserves. Conversely, a $100,000 decrease in excess reserves generated by the Fed's sale of a security will yield a $1 million decrease in total deposits; they will decrease by a multiple of 10 times. The initial $100,000 decrease in overall reserves.

We can now make a generalization about the extent to which the money supply will change when the banking system's reserves are increased or decreased. The **money multiplier** gives the change in the money supply due to a change in reserves. If we assume that no excess reserves are kept and that all loan proceeds are deposited in depository institutions in the system, the following equation applies:

$$\text{Potential money multiplier} = \frac{1}{\text{required reserve ratio}}$$

Money multiplier
The reciprocal of the required reserve ratio, assuming no leakages into currency and no excess reserves. It is equal to 1 divided by the required reserve ratio.

That is, the maximum possible value of the money multiplier is equal to 1 divided by the required reserve ratio for checkable deposits. The *actual* change in the money supply—currency plus checkable account balances—will be equal to the following:

Actual change in money supply = actual money multiplier × change in total reserves

Now we examine why there is a difference between the potential money multiplier—1 divided by the required reserve ratio—and the actual multiplier.

Forces That Reduce the Money Multiplier

We made a number of simplifying assumptions to come up with the potential money multiplier. In the real world, the actual money multiplier is considerably smaller. Several factors account for this.

Leakages. The entire loan (check) from one bank is not always deposited in another bank. At least two leakages can occur:

- *Currency drains.* When deposits increase, the public may want to hold more currency. Currency that is kept in a person's wallet remains outside the banking system and

Putting Economics in Action to Work

Get additional experience thinking through how a change in overall depository institution reserves affects the total quantity of deposits in the banking system. Start the *EIA* CD, click on "Money and Banking," and then click on "Depository Institution Reserves."

cannot be held by banks as reserves from which to make loans. The greater the amount of cash leakage, the smaller the actual money multiplier.

- *Excess reserves.* Depository institutions may wish to maintain excess reserves greater than zero. For example, they may wish to keep them because they want to be able to make speedy loans when good deals arise unexpectedly. To the extent that they want to keep positive excess reserves, the money multiplier will be smaller. The greater the excess reserves that banks maintain, the smaller the actual money multiplier.

Empirically, the currency drain is more significant than the effect of desired positive excess reserves.

Real-World Money Multipliers.   The maximum potential money multiplier is the reciprocal of the required reserve ratio. The maximum is never attained for the money supply as a whole because of currency drains and excess reserves. Also, each definition of the money supply, M1 or M2, will yield different results for money multipliers. For several decades, the M1 multiplier has varied between 2.5 and 3.0. The M2 multiplier, however, has shown a trend upward, ranging from 6.5 at the beginning of the 1960s to over 12 in the 2000s.

Ways in Which the Federal Reserve Changes the Money Supply

As we have just seen, the Fed can change the money supply by directly changing reserves available to the banking system. It does this by engaging in open market operations. To repeat: The purchase of a U.S. government security by the Fed results in an increase in reserves and leads to a multiple expansion in the money supply. A sale of a U.S. government security by the Fed results in a decrease in reserves and leads to a multiple contraction in the money supply.

The Fed changes the money supply in two other ways, both of which will have multiplier effects similar to those outlined earlier in this chapter.

Borrowed Reserves and the Discount Rate.   If a depository institution wants to increase its loans but has no excess reserves, it can borrow reserves. One place it can borrow reserves is from the Fed itself. The depository institution goes to the Federal Reserve and asks for a loan of a certain amount of reserves. The Fed charges these institutions for any reserves that it lends them. The interest rate that the Fed charges is the **discount rate.** When newspapers report that the Fed has decreased the discount rate from 5 to 4 percent, you know that the Fed has decreased its charge for lending reserves to depository institutions. Borrowing from the Fed increases reserves and thereby enhances the ability of the depository institution to engage in deposit creation, thus increasing the money supply.

Often the Federal Reserve System makes changes in the discount rate not necessarily to encourage or discourage depository institutions from borrowing from the Fed but rather as a signal to the banking system and financial markets that there has been a change in the Fed's monetary policy. We discuss monetary policy in more detail in Chapter 17.

Depository institutions actually do not often go to the Fed to borrow reserves because the Fed will not lend them all they want. In fact, the Fed can even refuse to lend reserves when the depository institutions need the reserves to make their reserve accounts meet legal requirements. Since the early 1990s, the Fed has been much more restrictive in lending to depository institutions than it was in the 1970s and 1980s. There are, however, alternative sources for the banks to tap when they want to expand their reserves or when they need reserves to meet a requirement. The primary source is the **federal funds market.** The

Discount rate
The interest rate that the Federal Reserve charges for reserves that it lends to depository institutions. It is sometimes referred to as the *rediscount rate* or, in Canada and England, as the *bank rate.*

Federal funds market
A private market (made up mostly of banks) in which banks can borrow reserves from other banks that want to lend them. Federal funds are usually lent for overnight use.

federal funds market is an interbank market in reserves, with one bank borrowing the excess reserves of another. The generic term *federal funds market* refers to the borrowing or lending reserve funds that are usually repaid within the same 24-hour period.

Depository institutions that borrow in the federal funds market pay an interest rate called the **federal funds rate.** Because the federal funds rate is a ready measure of the price that banks must pay to raise funds, the Federal Reserve often uses it as a yardstick by which to measure the effects of its policies. Consequently, the federal funds rate is a closely watched indicator of the Fed's anticipated intentions.

Federal funds rate
The interest rate that depository institutions pay to borrow reserves in the interbank federal funds market.

Reserve Requirement Changes.   In principle, another method by which the Fed can alter the money supply is by changing the reserve requirements it imposes on all depository institutions. Earlier we assumed that reserve requirements were fixed. Actually, these requirements are set by the Fed within limits established by Congress. The Fed can vary reserve requirements within these broad limits.

What would a change in reserve requirements from 10 to 20 percent do (if there were no excess reserves and if we ignore currency leakages)? We already discovered that the maximum money multiplier was the reciprocal of the required reserve ratio. If the required reserve ratio is 10 percent, then the maximum money multiplier is the reciprocal of $\frac{1}{10}$ or 10 (assuming no leakages). If, for some reason, the Fed decided to increase reserve requirements to 20 percent, the maximum money multiplier would equal the reciprocal of $\frac{1}{5}$, or 5. The maximum money multiplier is therefore inversely related to the required reserve ratio. If the Fed decides to increase reserve requirements, there will be a decrease in the maximum money multiplier. With any given level of legal reserves already in existence, the money supply will therefore contract.

In practice, open market operations allow the Federal Reserve to control the money supply much more precisely than changes in reserve requirements do, and they also allow the Fed to reverse itself quickly. In contrast, a small change in reserve requirements could, at least initially, result in a very large change in the money supply. Reserve requirement changes also impose costs on banks by restricting the portion of funds that they can lend, thereby inducing them to find legal ways to evade reserve requirements. That is why the Federal Reserve does not change reserve requirements very often.

CONCEPTS IN BRIEF

● The maximum potential money multiplier is equal to the reciprocal of the required reserve ratio.

● The actual multiplier is smaller than the maximum money multiplier because of currency drains and excess reserves voluntarily held by banks.

● The Fed can change the money supply in three ways: It can change reserves and hence the money supply through open market operations in which it buys and sells existing U.S. government securities (open market operations are the primary form of monetary policy), it can encourage change in reserves by changing the discount rate, and it can change the amount of deposits created from reserves by changing reserve requirements.

PAYMENT SYSTEMS, THEIR RISKS, AND DEPOSIT INSURANCE

The word *bank* derives from the Italian merchant's bench, or *banco,* across which bankers and borrowers exchanged funds in medieval Europe. In today's electronic trading environments, however, the word has become truly antiquated. Increased electronic trading has also complicated the lives of central bank policymakers, including those at the Fed.

Financial Trading Systems

Financial trading system
A mechanism linking buyers and sellers of stocks and bonds.

Key terms in the vocabulary of bankers and other financial market traders are acronyms such as MATIF and CORES, which refer to automated **financial trading systems.** These are mechanisms linking buyers and sellers of government securities and corporate bonds and stocks. MATIF, the Marché à Terme International de France, is located in Paris, and CORES, the Computer-Assisted Order Routing and Execution System, is a trading system based in Tokyo. Most developed nations have similar systems. These and other trading systems in locales such as Germany, Singapore, Switzerland, and the United Kingdom permit traders to place orders for purchases and sales of securities via computers.

For some time now, the U.S. Chicago Mercantile Exchange (CME) has operated a system known as Globex. People make trades on Globex via computer terminals. A trader uses Globex software programs to access data on market prices of financial contracts. The trader then can interact with the system to initiate and complete financial transactions.

Automated trading permits people to engage in financial transactions at any time of the day or night. For example, a trader who logs on to the Globex system at 10 P.M. Central Time may see a profit opportunity and initiate a transaction on the system. If the trader can transact business at 10 P.M., however, there is no reason to confine trading only to an exchange open during the day. It is also possible, after all, to trade electronically via an exchange in Tokyo, where 10 P.M. in the middle portion of the United States is late morning in Australia, Hong Kong, Japan, and Singapore.

Payment Systems and Payment Intermediaries

Payment system
An institutional structure by which consumers, businesses, governments, and financial institutions exchange payments.

Payment intermediary
An institution that facilitates the transfer of funds between buyer and seller during the course of any purchase of goods, services, or financial assets.

Financial trading systems allow people to conduct financial transactions. Actual transferals of *funds,* however, take place on **payment systems,** which are institutional structures through which people, businesses, governments, and financial institutions transmit payments of funds for goods, services, or financial assets. In most nations, people continue to use coins and currency to conduct transactions. For instance, U.S. residents use coin and currency to make over three-fourths of their exchanges. When a person buys something using coins and currency, the exchange is final at the moment that it occurs. By way of contrast, check transactions are final only after banks transfer funds from the account of the purchaser to the seller. Hence using checks requires people to rely on banks as **payment intermediaries,** or go-betweens in clearing payments that arise from exchanges of goods, services, or financial assets. Not all countries use checks as much as we do in the United States, though.

INTERNATIONAL EXAMPLE

Other Countries Are Not So Fond of Checks

Table 15-2 shows that U.S. residents use paper-based, *nonelectronic* (check) transactions much more than people in other countries. A typical U.S. resident makes over 200 check transactions a year. This is at least three times more—and in comparison with a few nations as much as 100 times more—than the numbers of check transactions made by people outside the United States. Other forms of noncash, nonelectronic payments conducted via payment intermediaries include credit card, money order,

and paper-based *giro* transactions, which are payment order transmittals between banks and other financial institutions. Nonelectronic giro systems are common in both Europe and Asia and link a number of payment intermediaries besides banks, such as post offices.

For Critical Analysis
Why do Americans still write so many checks when credit cards are so easy to use?

| Country | Number of Transactions per Person | | |
	Paper-Based	Electronic	Electronic Share of All Transactions
Switzerland	2	65	97%
Netherlands	19	128	87%
Belgium	16	85	84%
Denmark	24	100	81%
Japan	9	31	78%
Germany	36	103	74%
Sweden	24	68	74%
Finland	40	81	67%
United Kingdom	57	58	50%
France	86	71	45%
Canada	76	53	41%
Norway	58	40	41%
Italy	23	6	20%
United States	234	59	20%

TABLE 15-2
Annual Noncash Transactions per Person in Selected Countries
In comparison with Italy and the United States, other developed nations use more electronic means of payment.

Source: Data from David Humphrey, Lawrence Pulley, and Jukka Vesala, "Cash, Paper, and Electronic Payments: A Cross-Country Analysis," *Journal of Money, Credit, and Banking,* 28 (November 1996, p. 2), pp. 914–939.

Electronic Payment Systems: The Electronic Giro. Table 15-2 indicates that people in other nations use electronic means of payment to a greater extent than U.S. and Italian residents. For instance, many Europeans commonly use *electronic giro* systems, in which banks, post offices, and other payment intermediaries transfer funds over the telephone lines or other electronic pathways.

The closest U.S. counterpart to the electronic giro system is the **automated clearing house (ACH),** which is a computer-based clearing and settlement facility for the transmittal of funds via electronic messages instead of checks. Typical ACH transfers are automatic payroll deposits, in which businesses make wage and salary payments directly into employees' deposit accounts within one or two business days. The U.S. government distributes Social Security benefits via ACH direct-deposit mechanisms and disperses an increasing percentage of welfare and food stamp payments using an *electronic benefits transfer (EBT)* system. The EBT system functions much like an ACH, but to a welfare and food stamp recipient it works much like an ATM, because EBT machines disperse welfare funds or food stamps just as an ATM machine disperses cash.

POS and ATM Networks. Since the 1970s, technology has permitted the development of **point-of-sale (POS) networks,** which are systems allowing consumers to make immediate payments via direct deductions from their deposit accounts at depository institutions. POS networks have not caught on very quickly in the United States, perhaps because U.S. residents so commonly use **automated teller machine (ATM) networks.** These are systems linking more than 90,000 depository institution computer terminals activated by magnetically encoded bank cards. An average U.S. ATM machine is used

Automated clearinghouse (ACH)
A computer-based clearing and settlement facility that replaces check transactions by interchanging credits and debits electronically.

Point-of-sale (POS) network
System in which consumer payments for retail purchases are made by means of direct deductions from their deposit accounts at depository institutions.

Automated teller machine (ATM) network
A system of linked depository institution computer terminals that are activated by magnetically encoded bank cards.

For an overview of the various issues associated with payment systems, start the *EIA* CD-ROM and click on "Electronic Banking and Payments." Then click on "Payment Systems."

for about 100,000 transactions each year, most of which are cash withdrawals. Such ready access to cash helps reduce the extent to which U.S. residents might use POS networks.

By contrast, in places such as the Scandinavian countries, POS networks have caught on quickly, leaving ATM networks much less developed. Current trends toward higher U.S. consumer use of on-line banking via the Internet could lead to greater worldwide interest in POS networks in the future. At present, however, even though a growing number of U.S. retailers make POS systems available to their customers, consumer-oriented electronic payment systems process a negligible percentage of the value of U.S. electronic payments. This may be because the U.S. check-clearing system remains relatively more cost-efficient. Nonetheless, as discussed in greater detail in Chapter 16, most economists believe that ultimately POS networks will become more widespread in the United States.

Large-Value Payment Systems

Large-value wire transfer system
A payment system that permits the electronic transmission of large dollar sums.

Although U.S. consumers have been slow to adopt electronic payment systems for retail transactions, over 80 percent of the total *dollar value* of annual U.S. payments take place via **large-value wire transfer systems.** These are payment systems that banks, other financial institutions, and multinational corporations uses to transmit sizable payment transactions. Large-value wire transfer systems are also commonplace in other developed nations and handle the bulk of the value of total payments in those countries. Table 15-3 lists the world's major large-value payment systems and provides data on annual transactions and flows of funds on these systems. The largest of these outside the United States is the Bank of Japan's BOJ-NET system. Japan has another private system, and Germany and the United Kingdom both have major large-value payment systems.

TABLE 15-3
Transactions and Payment Flows in Major National Payment Systems
The world's major large-value payment systems are in Europe, Japan, and the United States.

Country and Payment System	Transactions (millions)	Value ($ trillions)
Germany		
ELS	13.5	22.4
EAF	22.5	107.0
Japan		
FEYCS	11.2	81.6
BOJ-NET	5.3	329.2
United Kingdom		
CHAPS	18.0	68.8
United States		
Fedwire	98.1	328.7
CHIPS	59.1	350.4

Source: Bank for International Settlements, 2000.

To find out more about large-value payment systems in other nations, go to **www.bis.org**, click on "Publications," and then click on "Committee on Payment and Settlement Systems."

Fedwire.   In the United States, there are two key large-value wire transfer systems. One is **Fedwire,** which is owned and operated by the Federal Reserve System. All financial institutions that must hold reserves at Federal Reserve banks may transmit payments using Fedwire. They pay fees to the Fed to use the system. Financial institutions commonly use Fedwire to make *book-entry securities transactions,* which are electronic payments for U.S. Treasury securities, and to process interbank payments, such as payments for federal funds market loans. The average Fedwire payment is more than $3 million, and the average daily payment volume on the Fedwire system now is well over $1 trillion.

CHIPS. The other major U.S. large-value wire transfer system is the **Clearing House Interbank Payments System (CHIPS).** This is a privately owned system managed by the New York Clearing House Association, which has about 100 member banks. These banks use CHIPS primarily to transfer funds for foreign exchange and Eurocurrency transactions. The average value of a CHIPS transaction is about $6 million, and the average daily payment flow on the CHIPS system now also exceeds $1 trillion.

Payment System Risks

Even before the advent of electronic trading, there was some element of risk inherent in any financial transaction. For instance, when a nineteenth-century frontier store accepted coins from a fur trader, there was a remote possibility that the customer's payment might be counterfeit. A Wal-Mart store faces the same risk today every time its clerks accept a cash payment from a customer. Nonetheless, Wal-Mart and other retailers commonly accept currency and coin payments, because the risk of loss is normally limited to a relatively small payment value. The risk of loss for every multimillion-dollar transfer on a large-value wire transfer system, however, is much greater.

Three types of risk naturally arise in any payment system: *liquidity risk, credit risk,* and *systemic risk.*

Liquidity Risk. You probably know a few people who are not very punctual in keeping scheduled appointments. Some almost seem to be intent on being late for meetings and other engagements. Likewise, people sometimes fail to make payments at promised times, which creates a risk of loss for payment recipients. This risk often is an opportunity cost, because the recipient could have used the funds for other purposes. **Liquidity risk** is the risk that such losses may arise from late receipt of payments.

Before the advent of electronic payment systems, banks and other payment intermediaries had to depend on courier or postal services for hand delivery of paper orders for payment and of currency and coins. Unanticipated delays in these services exposed them to significant liquidity risks. The development of electronic payment systems stems largely from a desire by banks and other payment intermediaries to speed up the process of transferring payments in an effort to reduce these risks. Using large-value wire transfer systems, for instance, banks can initiate payment orders in minutes, and actual transfers take place nearly instantaneously.

Credit Risk. In any exchange, often one person transfers funds before the other party reciprocates with the transfer of a good, service, or financial asset. When this happens, the individual who transfers the funds essentially extends credit to the other party in the transaction. Hence the person who transfers funds first takes on **credit risk,** which is the possibility that the other party in the exchange may ultimately fail to honor the terms of the exchange. Payment intermediaries have developed intricate systems of rules intended to reduce exposure to credit risks. These rules lay out the responsibilities of both parties. They clearly spell out penalties that are assessed if someone fails to settle transactions on a timely basis.

Fedwire
A large-value wire transfer system operated by the Federal Reserve that is open to all depository institutions that legally must maintain required reserves with the Fed.

Clearing House Interbank Payment System (CHIPS)
A large-value wire transfer system linking about 100 banks that permits them to transmit large sums of money related primarily to foreign exchange and Eurodollar transactions.

Learn more about the Clearing House Interbank Payment System at **www.chips.org**

Liquidity risk
The risk of loss that may occur if a payment is not received when due.

Credit risk
The risk of loss that might occur if one party to an exchange fails to honor the terms under which the exchange was to take place.

Systemic risk
The risk that some payment intermediaries may not be able to meet the terms of their credit agreements because of failures by other institutions to settle other transactions.

Systemic Risk.   Liquidity and credit risks are payment system risks that payment intermediaries assume on an individual basis. Because the payment intermediaries that participate in large-value wire transfer systems are all interconnected, however, they share some payment system risks. Payment flows among these intermediaries are interdependent, and that gives rise to **systemic risk**—the risk that some payment intermediaries may not be able to honor financial commitments because of payment settlement breakdowns in otherwise unrelated transactions.

INTERNATIONAL EXAMPLE

Another Risk in the Payment System: Some Customers May Be Crooks!

With the assistance of officials of the Bank of New York, federal investigators spent months tracking wire transfers made by the bank on behalf of Russian clients. The Bank of New York had spent years trying to build customer relationships with these companies because it anticipated big boosts in its profitability when the Russian economy would finally burst into bloom following big privatization efforts. Toward this end, the bank had employed a couple of vice presidents who were originally from Russia and who were well connected with emerging private companies there.

In the summer of 1999, however, the bank's efforts garnered little but unfavorable publicity. It turned out that the vice presidents it had hired may have been well connected with another big Russian private-sector institution: the Russian mafia. Billions of dollars of illegal transactions related to organized crime took place via a complex series of globe-spanning transactions involving Russian clients of the Bank of New York and other international clearing banks. A number of the transactions originated from the Russian central bank, and as much as $2 billion (or perhaps even more—we may never know the actual amounts) transferred from the central bank's accounts were funds that it had received via loans from the International Monetary Fund. Thus funds provided by taxpayers in the United States and other nations that contribute to the IMF may have been "laundered" for ultimate use by criminal elements in Russian society.

Officials at the Bank of New York were asked why they had not done more to monitor the billions of dollars that the bank had transferred on behalf of Russian companies. They replied that these transfers were only a drop in the bucket compared with all the funds they transmit each year. They also pointed out that all they can do is report suspicious activities to federal authorities and cooperate with government investigations, as they had done in this case. For its part, the IMF said that it traditionally relies on governments that borrow its funds to put them to use as promised. It rarely follows up to make sure that this actually happens.

For Critical Analysis
Which of the various parties involved in all these Russian-related wire transfers—clearing banks such as the Bank of New York, Russian companies, the Russian mafia, the Russian government, the people of Russia, and U.S. and other IMF-supporting taxpayers—incurred the largest payment system risks?

Federal Deposit Insurance

Federal Deposit Insurance Corporation (FDIC)
A government agency that insures the deposits held in banks and most other depository institutions; all U.S. banks are insured this way.

Central banks and governments worry about systemic risk in banking because systemic breakdowns can cause widespread bank failures. When businesses fail, they create hardships for creditors, owners, and customers. But when a depository institution fails, an even greater hardship results because many individuals and businesses depend on the safety and security of banks. Figure 15-3 indicates that during the 1920s, an average of about 600 banks failed each year. In the 1930s, during the Great Depression, that average soared to 2,000 failures each year.

In 1933, at the height of such bank failures, the **Federal Deposit Insurance Corporation (FDIC)** was founded to insure the funds of depositors and remove the reason for

FIGURE 15-3
Bank Failures
During the Great Depression, a tremendous number of banks failed. Federal deposit insurance
was created in 1933. Thereafter, bank failures were few until around 1984. Failures peaked at
over 200 in 1989 and are now fewer than a dozen per year.
Source: Federal Deposit Insurance Corporation.

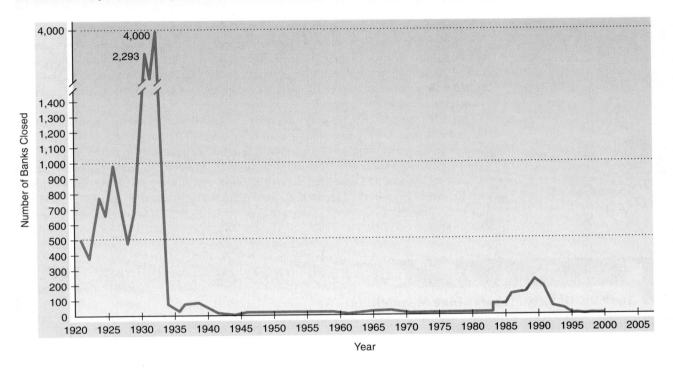

ruinous runs on banks. In 1934, the Federal Savings and Loan Insurance Corporation
(FSLIC) was installed to insure deposits in savings and loan associations and mutual
savings banks. In 1971, the National Credit Union Share Insurance Fund (NCUSIF) was
created to insure deposits in credit unions. In 1989, the FSLIC was dissolved and the
Savings Association Insurance Fund (SAIF) was established to protect the deposits of
those institutions.

As can be seen in Figure 15-3, a tremendous drop in bank failure rates occurred after
passage of the early federal legislation. The long period from 1935 until the 1980s was relatively quiet. From World War II to 1984, fewer than nine banks failed per year. From 1985
until the beginning of 1993, however, 1,065 commercial banks failed—an annual average
of nearly 120 bank failures per year, more than 10 times the average for the preceding
years! We will examine the reasons shortly. But first we need to understand how deposit
insurance works.

The Rationale for Deposit Insurance

The FDIC, FSLIC, and NCUSIF were established to mitigate the primary cause of bank
failures, **bank runs**—the simultaneous rush of depositors to convert their demand deposits
or time deposits into currency.

Putting
Economics in Action
to Work

Use *EIA* to gain further under-
standing of deposit insurance.
Click on "Money and Banking."
Then click on "Federal Deposit
Insurance."

Bank runs
Attempts by many of a bank's
depositors to convert checkable
and time deposits into currency
out of fear for the bank's
solvency.

Consider the following scenario. A bank begins to look shaky; its assets may not seem sufficient to cover its liabilities. If the bank has no deposit insurance, depositors in this bank (and any banks associated with it) will all want to withdraw their money from the bank at the same time. Their concern is that this shaky bank will not have enough money to return their deposits to them in the form of currency. Indeed, this is what happens in a bank failure when insurance doesn't exist. Just as with the failure of a regular business, the creditors of the bank may not all get paid, or if they do, they will get paid less than 100 percent of what they are owed. Depositors are creditors of a bank because their funds are on loan to the bank. In a fractional reserve banking system, banks do not hold 100 percent of their depositors' money in the form of reserves. Consequently, all depositors cannot withdraw all their money simultaneously. It would be desirable to assure depositors that they can have their deposits converted into cash when they wish, no matter how serious the financial situation of the bank.

Keep up with the latest
issues in deposit insurance
and banking issues at
www.fdic.gov

The FDIC (and later the FSLIC, NCUSIF, and SAIF) provided this assurance. They charged insurance premiums to depository institutions based on their total deposits, and these premiums went into funds that would reimburse depositors in the event of depository institution failures. By insuring deposits, the FDIC bolstered depositors' trust in the banking system and provided depositors with the incentive to leave their deposits with the bank, even in the face of widespread talk of bank failures. In 1933, it was sufficient for the FDIC to cover each account up to $2,500. The current maximum is $100,000.

POLICY EXAMPLE

The FDIC Quietly Prepares for a Megafailure

The 1990s and 2000s have witnessed numerous record-breaking bank mergers. The days of $100 billion-asset banks seem to be here to stay. What might happen if one of these megabanks were to fail? The FDIC is quietly preparing for such a possibility. It has formed what has become known as the Mega-Merger Committee, which is trying to answer the following questions:

- When should the government pledge to refund uninsured deposits in order to avoid system-wide chaos?
- Who would manage such a failed megabank's loans and securities until it could be auctioned off?
- How much new staff would the downsized FDIC need to hire in case of a megafailure?

- How could the FDIC hire such a staff on short notice?
- Would the FDIC have to send its employees to other countries to monitor the failed bank's foreign branches?

It would not be easy for the FDIC to sell a $100 billion-asset bank. Consequently, the Mega-Merger Committee has determined that it would break a failed megabank into smaller pieces. The FDIC could, for example, break the bank up along geographic lines or along business lines.

For Critical Analysis
Would U.S. banking authorities have the legal ability to shut down a failed megabank's foreign branches?

How Deposit Insurance Causes Increased Risk Taking by Bank Managers

Until very recently, all insured depository institutions paid the same small fee for coverage. (In 1996, the fee was reduced to zero for most banks.) The fee that they paid was completely unrelated to how risky their assets were. A depository institution that made loans to companies such as General Motors and Microsoft Corporation paid the same deposit insurance premium as another depository institution that made loans (at higher interest rates) to the governments of developing countries that were teetering on the brink of financial collapse. Although deposit insurance premiums for a while were adjusted somewhat in response to the riskiness of a depository institution's assets, they never reflected all of the relative risk. This can be considered a flaw in the deposit insurance scheme.

Because bank managers do not have to pay higher insurance premiums when they make riskier loans, they have an incentive to invest in more assets of higher yield, and therefore higher risk, than they would if there were no deposit insurance. The insurance premium rate is artificially low, permitting institution managers to obtain deposits at less than full cost (because depositors will accept a lower interest payment on insured deposits). Consequently, depository institution managers can increase their profits using lower-cost insured deposits to purchase higher-yield, higher-risk assets. The gains to risk taking accrue to the managers and stockholders of the depository institutions; the losses go to the deposit insurer (and, as we will see, ultimately to taxpayers).

To combat the inherent flaws in the financial industry and in the deposit insurance system, a vast regulatory apparatus was installed. The FDIC was given regulatory powers to offset the risk-taking temptations to depository institution managers; those powers included the ability to require higher capital investment; the ability to regulate, examine, and supervise bank affairs; and the ability to enforce its decisions. Still higher capital requirements were imposed in the early 1990s and then adjusted somewhat beginning in 2000, but the basic flaws in the system remain.

Deposit Insurance, Adverse Selection, and Moral Hazard

As a deposit insurer, the FDIC effectively acts as a government-run insurance company. This means that the FDIC's operations expose the federal government to the same kinds of asymmetric information problems that other financial intermediaries face.

Adverse Selection in Deposit Insurance.   One of these problems, as discussed in Chapter 14, is *adverse selection,* which arises when there is asymmetric information before a transaction takes place. Adverse selection is often a problem when insurance is involved because people or firms that are relatively poor risks are sometimes able to disguise that fact from insurers. It is instructive to examine the way this works with the deposit insurance provided by the FDIC. Deposit insurance shields depositors from the potential adverse effects of risky decisions and so makes depositors willing to accept riskier investment strategies by their banks. Clearly, this encourages more high-flying, risk-loving entrepreneurs to become managers of banks. Moreover, because depositors have so little incentive to monitor the activities of insured banks, it is also likely that the insurance actually encourages outright crooks—embezzlers and con artists—to enter the industry. The consequences for the FDIC—and for the taxpayer—are larger losses.

Moral Hazard in Deposit Insurance and the U.S. Savings and Loan Debacle.   As you learned in Chapter 14, *moral hazard* arises as the result of information asymmetry after a transaction has occurred. Moral hazard is also an important phenomenon in the presence of insurance contracts, such as the deposit insurance provided by the FDIC. Insured depositors know that they will not suffer losses if their bank fails. Hence they have little incentive to monitor their bank's investment activities or to punish their bank by withdrawing their funds if the bank assumes too much risk. This means that insured banks have incentives to take on more risks than they otherwise would—and with those risks come higher losses for the FDIC and for taxpayers.

For a variety of reasons, by the mid-1980s, the savings and loan (S&L) industry in the United States was facing disaster. What was occurring at that time was a perfect example of the perverse incentives that occur when government-provided deposit insurance exists. S&L institution managers undertook riskier actions than they otherwise would have because of the existence of deposit insurance. Moreover, because of the existence of deposit insurance, depositors in savings and loan associations had little incentive to investigate the financial dealings and stability of those institutions. After all, deposits were guaranteed by an agency of the federal government, so why worry? Hence there was little incentive for households and firms to monitor savings and loan institutions or even to diversify their deposits across institutions. From an S&L manager's point of view, as long as deposit insurance protected depositors, the manager could feel confident to "go for the gold." One result was an increase in the amount of high-risk, high-yielding assets purchased by many savings and loan associations.

The first year of the S&L crisis, 135 institutions failed. Over the next two years, another 600 went bankrupt. By the end of the crisis, 1,500 thrift institutions had gone under. Politicians chose to solve the crisis by passing the Financial Institutions Reform, Recovery and Enforcement Act (FIRREA), popularly known as the Thrift Bailout Act of 1989. The estimated cost to American taxpayers was about $200 billion. Congress followed up in 1991 by passing the FDIC Improvement Act (FDICIA). This law toughened regulatory standards and required the FDIC to close weak depository institutions promptly, rather than letting their managers continue to roll the dice with taxpayers' dollars at stake.

POLICY EXAMPLE

Letting the Market Do the Regulators' Work

Some observers contend that there should be less regulation of banks. They argue that markets could do the regulators' work. Indeed, two top Federal Reserve officials have argued just that. The first one was Federal Reserve Bank of Richmond President J. Alfred Broaddus, Jr. The other was Federal Reserve Governor Laurence H. Meyer, who presented a detailed approach to how such a system would work.

Mayer argued that "large, internationally active banks" should be required to issue a minimum amount of "subordinated debt"—such as bonds that are redeemed only after bank depositors and other claimants are repaid following a default—to investors. Such debt would provide an extra cushion of protection for taxpayers. In addition, however, the market price that investors would pay for such subordinated bank debt would depend on how investors evaluate the management strategy of each particular bank. Any subordinated debt holder could lose everything if the bank failed. Thus owners of such debt have an incentive to monitor closely any issuer's activities. This is exactly the type of monitoring that the FDIC currently does on behalf of the insurance funds.

The risk premium a bank's subordinated debt carried would give a signal to the FDIC. Indeed, the FDIC could use the observed risk premiums as a simple way to determine how much an insured bank should be charged in premiums. Imagine a situation in which a certain bank's subordinated debt could be sold only at a very high interest rate. This would be an early warning to regulators that this bank was encountering financial trouble.

For Critical Analysis
Why is it more important to worry about "large internationally active banks" than small banks?

● Banks and other financial institutions function as payment intermediaries, transferring funds used to pay for goods, services, or finanicial assets between the payers and receivers of the funds.

● In most countries, people use nonelectronic payment mechanisms, such as currency, checks, and paper-based giro systems, for the largest portion of their daily payment transactions. The bulk of the total *value* of payments, however, is processed on large-value payment systems. In the United States, Fedwire and the Clearing House Interbank Payment System (CHIPS) are the two key large-value payment systems.

● Their role as payment intermediaries exposes banks to liquidity, credit, and systemic risks. The last of these risks exposes the entire banking system to the threat of bank runs.

● To limit the fallout from systemic failures and bank runs, Congress created the Federal Deposit Insurance Corporation (FDIC) in 1933. Since the advent of federal deposit insurance, there have been no true bank runs at federally insured banks.

● Because of the way deposit insurance is set up in the United States, it encourages bank managers to invest in riskier assets to make higher rates of return.

Are Reserve Requirements on the Way Out or In?

To many economists, reserve requirements are an outdated relic. They argue that reserve requirements might prove useful as a stabilizing tool if central banks really sought to achieve targets for the quantity of money in circulation, but they note that most central banks today pay little attention to variations in money growth. Hence, they contend, reserve requirements around the world should be reduced or even eliminated.

Table 15-4 shows that banks in many industrialized countries face lower required reserve ratios than they did a decade ago. Relative to the required reserve ratios of other nations in the table, the official 10 percent ratio for transactions deposits in the United States stands out. This is misleading, however, because the *effective* U.S. required reserve ratio has been much lower than this since the mid-1990s.

The Great Reserve-Requirement Loophole: Sweep Accounts

A key simplifying assumption in our example of the money creation process was that checkable deposits were the only bank liability system that changes when total reserves change. Of course, banks also issue savings and time deposits. In addition, they offer *automatic transfer accounts*. In these accounts, which banks have offered since the 1970s, funds are automatically transferred from savings deposits to checkable deposits whenever the account holder writes a check that would otherwise cause the balance of checkable deposits to become negative. Automatic transfer accounts thereby protected individuals and businesses from overdrawing their checking accounts.

Concepts Applied

Reserve Requirements

Money Creation

TABLE 15-4
Required Reserve Ratios in Selected Nations
Several nations have reduced their required reserve ratios in recent years.

Required Reserve Ratio	1989	2000
Checkable Deposits		
Canada	10.0%	0%
European Monetary Union*	—	2.0%
Japan	1.75%	1.2%
New Zealand	0%	0%
United Kingdom	.45%	.35%
United States	12.0%	10.0%
Noncheckable Deposits		
Canada	3.0%	0%
European Monetary Union*	—	2.0%
Japan	2.5%	1.3%
New Zealand	0%	0%
United Kingdom	.45%	.35%
United States	3.0%	0%

*The European Monetary Union was formed in 1999.
Sources: Gordon Sellon Jr. and Stuart Weiner, "Monetary Policy Without Reserve Requirements: Analytical Issues," Federal Reserve Bank of Kansas City *Economic Review,* 81 (Fourth Quarter 1996), pp. 5–24; Bank for International Settlements.

FIGURE 15-4

Sweep Accounts and Reserves of U.S. Depository Institutions at Federal Reserve Banks

Panel (a) depicts the growth of sweep accounts, which shift funds from transactions deposits subject to reserve requirements to savings deposits with no legal required reserve ratios. Panel (b) shows that the effect of the existence of sweep accounts has been a steady decline in reserve balances that depository institutions hold with Federal Reserve Banks.

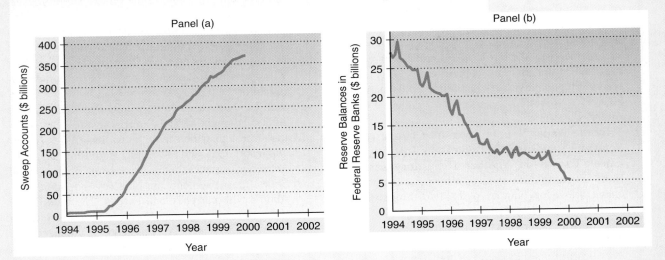

Beginning in 1993, several U.S. banks discovered a way to use automatic transfer accounts to reduce their required reserves. This permitted the banks to shift funds *out of* their customers' checkable deposit accounts, which are subject to reserve requirements, and *into* the customers' savings deposits—mainly money market deposit accounts—which are *not* subject to reserve requirements. Automatic transfer accounts with provisions permitting banks to shift funds from checkable deposits to savings deposits to avoid reserve requirements are called **sweep accounts.** Banks gave the accounts this name because they effectively used them to "sweep" funds from one deposit to another.

As panel (a) of Figure 15-4 shows, total funds in U.S. sweep accounts (and hence total funds exempt from the 10 percent required reserve ratio) have increased dramatically since June 1995. Panel (b) indicates that the result has been a significant decline in the reserves that U.S. banks hold at Federal Reserve banks.

Reserve Requirements on an Upswing in Europe

Even as the United States has joined the movement toward significant reductions in effective reserve requirements, however, European central bank officials successfully imposed *higher* reserve requirements on many banks in European Union countries. When the European Monetary Union began in 1999, the European System of Central Banks established a 2 percent reserve requirement ratio that applies to nearly all bank deposits, including saving and time deposits as well as checkable deposits. Their rationale for this proposal is simple: If European banks have to hold more reserves with central banks, then the central banks can earn interest on the funds, which is a steady source of income to fund their operations. This justification for higher reserve requirements relies on their usefulness as a tax on banks and their customers. It has nothing to do with issues of monetary, financial, or economic stability.

Sweep account
A depository institution account that entails regular shifts of funds from transaction deposits that are subject to reserve requirements to savings deposits that are exempt from reserve requirements.

FOR CRITICAL ANALYSIS

1. What incentive do banks have to establish sweep accounts, and how might bank customers benefit from sweep accounts?

2. What actions, short of forbidding sweep accounts, can the Federal Reserve take to keep reserve changes caused by the growth of sweep accounts from affecting the money supply?

SUMMARY DISCUSSION OF LEARNING OBJECTIVES

1. **How the Federal Reserve Assesses Reserve Requirements:** The Federal Reserve establishes a required reserve ratio, which is currently 10 percent of nearly all checkable deposits at depository institutions. Legal reserves that depository institutions may hold to satisfy their reserve requirements include deposits they hold at Federal Reserve district banks and as cash in their vaults. Any legal reserves that a depository institution holds over and above its required reserves are called excess reserves.

2. **Why the Money Supply Does Not Change When Someone Deposits in a Depository Institution a Check Drawn on Another Depository Institution:** When an individual or a business deposits a check drawn on another party, two things occur. First, the depository institution on which the check was drawn experiences a reduction in its total deposits when the check clears. Second, the depository institution that receives the deposit experiences an equal-sized increase in its total deposits. For the banking system as a whole, therefore, total deposits remain unchanged. Thus the money supply is unaffected by the transaction.

3. **Why the Money Supply Does Change When Someone Deposits in a Depository Institution a Check Drawn on the Federal Reserve System:** When an individual or a business (typically a bond dealer) deposits a check drawn on the Federal Reserve System, the depository institution that receives the deposit experiences an equal-sized increase in its total deposits. Consequently, there is an immediate increase in total deposits in the banking system as a whole, and the money supply increases by the amount of the initial deposit. Furthermore, the depository institution that receives this deposit can lend any reserves in excess of requires reserves, which will generate a rise in deposits at another bank. This process continues as each bank receiving a deposit has additional funds over and above required reserves that it can lend.

4. **The Maximum Potential Change in the Money Supply Following a Federal Reserve Purchase or Sale of U.S. Government Securities:** When the Federal Reserve buys or sells securities, the maximum potential change in the money supply occurs when there are no leakages of currency or excess reserves during the process of money creation. The amount of the maximum potential change is equal to the amount of reserves that the Fed injects or withdraws from the banking system times the reciprocal of the required reserve ratio.

5. **The U.S. Payment System and Payment System Risks:** Payment systems are the institutional structures through which individuals, businesses, financial institutions, and governments transmit payments for goods, services, or financial assets. In the United States, most payments are made by individual consumers with currency and checks. The bulk of the dollar value of payments, however, is transmitted in large-value payment systems handling payments that average millions of dollars each. Any payment system exposes its users to liquidity, credit, and systemic risks. Systemic risk exposes more than one financial institution to the potential for failure, which can give rise to bank runs.

6. **Features of Federal Deposit Insurance:** To help prevent runs on banks, the U.S. government in 1933 established the Federal Deposit Insurance Corporation (FDIC). This government agency provides deposit insurance by charging depository institutions premiums based on the value of their deposits, and it places these funds in accounts for use in closing failed banks and reimbursing their depositors. One difficulty associated with providing deposit insurance is the problem of adverse selection, because the availability of deposit insurance can potentially attract risk-taking individuals into the banking business. Another difficulty is the moral hazard problem. This problem arises when deposit insurance premiums fail to reflect the full extent of the risks taken on by depository institution managers and when depositors who know they are insured have little incentive to monitor the performance of the institutions that hold their deposit funds.

Key Terms and Concepts

Automated clearing house (ACH) (369)

Automated teller machine (ATM) networks (369)

Balance sheet (357)

Bank runs (373)

Clearing House Interbank Payments System (CHIPS) (371)

Credit risk (371)

Discount rate (366)

Excess reserves (356)

Federal Deposit Insurance Corporation (FDIC) (372)

Federal funds market (366)

Federal funds rate (367)

Fedwire (371)

Financial trading systems (368)

Fractional reserve banking (355)

Large-value wire transfer systems (370)

Legal reserves (355)

Liquidity risk (371)

Money multiplier (365)

Net worth (357)

Open market operations (359)

Payment intermediaries (368)

Payment systems (368)

Point-of-sale (POS) networks (369)

Required reserve ratio (356)

Required reserves (356)

Reserves (355)

Sweep accounts (379)

Systemic risk (372)

Problems

Answers to the odd-numbered problems appear at the back of the book.

15-1. A bank's only liabilities are $15 million in checkable deposits. The bank currently meets its reserve requirement, and it holds no excess reserves. The required reserve ratio is 10 percent. Assuming that its only assets are legal reserves, loans, and securities, what is the value of loans and securities held by the bank?

15-2. Draw an empty bank balance sheet, with the heading "Assets" on the left-hand side and the heading "Liabilities" on the right-hand side. Then place the following items on the proper side of the balance sheet:
   a. Loans to a private company
   b. Borrowings from a Federal Reserve district bank
   c. Deposits with a Federal Reserve district bank
   d. U.S. Treasury bills
   e. Vault cash
   f. Loans to other banks in the federal funds market
   g. Checkable deposits

15-3. Suppose that the total liabilities of a depository institution are checkable deposits equal to $2 bil-

lion. It has $1.65 billion in loans and securities, and the required reserve ratio is .15. Does this institution hold any excess reserves? If so, how much?

15-4. A bank has $120 million in total assets, which are composed of legal reserves, loans, and securities. Its only liabilities are $120 million in checkable deposits. The bank exactly satisfies its reserve requirement, and its total legal reserves equal $6 million. What is the required reserve ratio?

15-5. The Federal Reserve purchases $1 million in U.S. Treasury bonds from a bond dealer, and the dealer's bank credits the dealer's account. The required reserve ratio is .15, and the bank typically lends any excess reserves immediately. Assuming that no currency leakage occurs, how much will the bank be able to lend to its customers following the Fed's purchase?

15-6. A depository institution holds $150 million in required reserves and $10 million in excess reserves. Its remaining assets include $440 million in loans and $150 million in securities. If the institution's only liabilities are checkable deposits, what is the required reserve ratio?

15-7. Suppose that the value of the maximum potential money multiplier is equal to 4. What is the required reserve ratio?

15-8. Why is it that you cannot induce any net multiple deposit expansion in the banking system by buying a U.S. government security, yet the Federal Reserve can do so?

15-9. Consider a world in which there is no currency and depository institutions issue only checkable deposits and desire to hold no excess reserves. The required reserve ratio is 20 percent. The central bank sells $1 billion in government securities. What happens to the money supply?

15-10. Assume a 1 percent required reserve ratio, zero excess reserves, and no currency leakages. What is the maximum potential money multiplier? How will total deposits in the banking system change if the Federal Reserve purchases $5 million in U.S. government securities?

Economics on the Net

Statistics on Payment Systems in the Group of Ten Countries   Every nation's overall payment system is different. This application gives you the opportunity to evaluate just how different national payment systems can be.

Internet URL: http://www.bis.org

Title: Bank for International Settlements

Navigation: Begin at http://www.bis.org. Click on Publications. In the margin, click on Committee on Payment and Settlement Systems. Scan down the list and click Statistics on Payment Systems in the Group of Ten Countries (most recent year). Download the entire PDF file, which contains tables displaying payment system data for G-10 countries listed in alphabetical order; then answer the application questions.

Application   You can use the data in this report to make a number of cross-country comparisons. Here let's focus on comparing the relative use of checks and automated teller machines (ATMs) in Belgium and the United States.

1. Look at Table 1 ("Basic Statistical Data") for Belgium (the first country in the report) and the United States (the last country in the report). On a separate sheet of paper, write down each nation's population in the latest available year and the average exchange rate for the Belgian franc, or BEF (given in francs per dollar), for that year. Next scroll to Table 13 ("Indicators of Use of Various Cashless Payment Instruments: Values of Transactions") for each country. What was the *dollar value* of total checks (spelled *cheques* in the tables) issued in each nation during this year? (Use the average BEF exchange rate for the year to convert the Belgian value of checks issued into dollars.) What was the average *per capita dollar value* of checks issued in each nation? (Divide each nation's dollar value of checks issued by its population.) Based on your per capita figures, in which of the two nations are checks a more important means of payment for the average resident?

2. Now consider Table 6 ("Cash Dispensers, ATMs, and EFTPOS Terminals") for each nation. For the most recent year, what was the total *dollar value* of all transactions on ATMs in each country? What was the average *per capita dollar value* of ATM transactions in each nation? Based on your per capita figures, in which of the two nations are ATM transactions a more common means of transferring funds?

For Group Study and Analysis   Assign each student or group to repeat the exercise for other countries included in this report.

ELECTRONIC BANKING

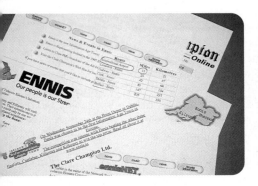

The village of Ennis, Ireland, became Europe's first Internet-age town. All 6,000 Ennis households are now equipped with voice mail, Internet access, and "smart cards." Many more electronic commerce solutions are in the works. Will wider use of digital cash eliminate our banking system?

Recently, the village of Ennis, in County Clare, became Ireland's "Information Age Town." About 6,000 Ennis households were equipped with voice mail, personal computers, and Internet access. They also received *smart cards,* which can store data, process computer messages, and communicate with cell phones, screen phones, personal computers, parking meters, and vending machines.

Department stores, supermarkets, gas stations, taxicabs, and pubs were also equipped with smart-card devices. Participating banks deployed card-accessible, cash-loading stations in parking lots, shopping centers, schools, and bank branches. All this was designed to find out what aspects of "smart-card technology" would and would not work in an ordinary community.

Why are so many banks and companies around the world striving to decide how much, and how quickly, they should invest in the kinds of technologies available to residents of Ennis? What is the expected payoff? To help you to contemplate these questions, let's look at the various forms of electronic payment, including smart cards, and their uses in the emerging world of *e-money* (electronic money) and *cyberbanking.*

383

Digital cash
Funds contained on computer software, in the form of secure programs stored on microchips and other computer devices.

Did You Know That... the Treasury Department estimates that the total annual cost of handling physical cash throughout the United States is approximately $60 billion? This includes all the costs of replacing worn-out currency, printing hard-to-counterfeit currency and minting new coins, and transporting boxes and bags full of currency and coins between banks and retailers. It also includes the cost of sorting and counting billions of coins every day. Since the nation's founding, the Treasury has searched for ways to reduce the costs of producing and handling money. After all, society could direct funds not spent on shuffling cash to a number of alternative uses.

Today, the use of **digital cash,** which consists of funds contained on the computer software stored on microchips and other computer devices, promises to drastically reduce the nation's costs of transferring funds. The reason is that people can store and instantaneously transmit digital cash along preexisting electronic networks. People can keep digital cash on diskettes, compact disks, and hard drives. They can send digital cash payments along telephone lines, between cell phones, or over fiber-optic cables. Certainly, digital cash is in its early stages of experimentation and adoption. Nevertheless, the use of digital cash promises to change the nature of money. It is also beginning to transform the world of banking.

In this chapter, you will find out about the new world of smart cards and digital cash, efforts by bank regulators to try to keep up with the explosion in cyberbanking, and ways in which the use of digital cash may affect the money supply.

CURRENT ELECTRONIC MEANS OF PAYMENT

The idea of electronic payments is not new. Most Americans use paper checks to pay for groceries and other items. The checks we write have magnetic ink encryptions that special machines use to sort and distribute checks automatically. Increasingly, the information on paper checks is transformed into digital information to permit computers to credit and debit accounts electronically. This large-scale automation of check sorting, accounting, and distribution has kept the per-check cost of clearing checks very low. Today, banking institutions clear millions of checks each day—a total of more than 70 billion per year. It was not always this way, however. Fifty years ago, checking accounts were offered primarily to higher-income and upper-middle-income individuals, and bank employees cleared checks by hand using paper accounting ledgers. Because checking accounts were so expensive to maintain, most other people made their purchases using cash or money orders.

Today, most U.S. consumers have experience using automated teller machine (ATM) networks. As noted in Chapter 15, many consumers regularly use ATM networks to make deposits, withdraw cash from their accounts, transfer funds among accounts, and pay bills. Even though all these ATM functions are commonplace today, three decades ago about all an ATM machine could do was dispense cash. Furthermore, banks had to work hard to convince many skeptical customers to trust ATMs to handle even this simple function.

Without knowing it, many of us have used the services of automated clearing house (ACH) systems, as also noted in Chapter 15. Banks began to put ACH payment-clearing and settlement systems into place back in the days when the only computers were mainframes. Anyone who has received a direct deposit, such as an automatic payroll deposit, has taken advantage of the services of an ACH. So has a person who has arranged for a regular monthly insurance or mortgage payment to be debited automatically from a checking account. This is yet another example of an electronic means of payment that did not exist all that long ago. Nevertheless, many of us commonly use them today.

Clearly, various forms of electronic payments have been with us for some time. What is new and different is the potential to replace *physical* cash—coins and paper currency—with *virtual* cash in the form of electronic impulses. This is the unique promise of digital cash.

THE PRECURSOR TO E-MONEY: STORED-VALUE CARDS

According to the Bank for International Settlements, an international institution operated by major central banks, U.S. residents make more than 300 billion cash transactions (or nearly 1,100 per person) every year. Of these, 270 billion are in amounts of less than $2. It is easy to see why people use paper currency and coins to purchase a soft drink, a candy bar, or a magazine. Why would they use e-money, however, instead of currency and coins?

To understand why people might use e-money instead of physical cash, let's begin by thinking about the simplest kind of e-money system, one that uses **stored-value cards.** These are plastic cards embossed with magnetic stripes containing magnetically encoded data. Using a stored-value card, a person purchases specific goods and services offered by the card issuer. For example, a number of college and university libraries have copy machines that students operate by inserting a stored-value card. Each time a student makes copies, the copy machine deducts the per-copy fee. When the balance on the student's card runs low in the middle of copying a news article, the student can replenish the balance by placing the card in a separate machine and inserting physical cash. The machine stores the value of the cash on the card. Then the student can go back to a copy machine, reinsert the card, and finish copying the article.

Some stored-value cards are disposable. The cardholder throws away the card after spending the value stored on it. But many banks and other issuers prefer reusable stored-value cards. Bearers of these cards may use them to purchase goods and services offered by any participating merchant.

Stored-value card
A card bearing magnetic stripes that hold magnetically encoded data, providing access to stored funds.

FROM STORED-VALUE CARDS TO DEBIT CARDS

Plastic cards used in *open* funds transfer systems are called **debit cards.** These cards essentially adapt the technology of stored-value cards to permit authorization of direct funds transfers. People can use them to authorize transfers of funds from their accounts to those of merchants.

Debit card
A plastic card that allows the bearer to transfer funds to a merchant's account, provided that the bearer authorizes the transfer by providing personal identification.

Debit Cards as Electronic Checking

Figure 16-1 on page 386 illustrates a sample transaction flow in a debit card system. A card issuer, Bank A, provides cards to its customers, who use their cards to make purchases from retailers. The retailers' electronic cash registers record the value of the purchases and the routing numbers of the issuing banks. The retailers then submit the recorded data to their own bank, Bank B. This bank then forwards claims for funds to the system operator. The operator transmits these claims to each issuing bank, including Bank A. Once Bank A honors its obligations to Bank B by debiting your checking account, the latter bank credits the deposit accounts of the retailers.

Note that Figure 16-1 could just as easily show the workings of a system of paper checks. Instead of using debit cards to buy goods and services, bank customers could use checks to make their purchases. Then the retailers could send the checks on to their own banks. The banks could then submit them to a clearinghouse, which could then process the

Putting Economics in Action to Work

Use *EIA* to gain further understanding of stored-value, debit, and smart cards. Click on "Electronic Banking and Payments," and then click on "Stored-Value and Debit Cards" or "Smart Cards."

FIGURE 16-1

A Debit Card System

Holders of cards issued by Bank A can automatically authorize payments directly to retailers, who in turn transmit claims to Bank B. This bank then transmits payment claims to the operator of the system, which then transmits the claims to Bank A.

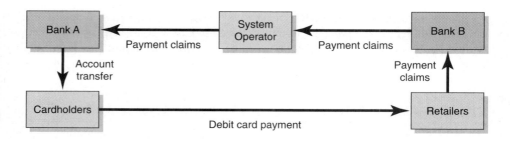

interbank payments required for the retailers to receive final payment of funds. Thus a fully electronic debit card system effectively amounts to electronic checking. As with check clearing, behind-the-scenes interbank clearing must take place to finalize a transaction.

The Trouble and Expense of Debit Cards

The security features of debit card systems make them somewhat cumbersome. When a cardholder presents a typical debit card to a retailer, the retailer's electronic cash register routes a request for authorization to the issuing bank. The bank's computer checks the cardholder's account number against a file of lost or stolen cards. It also verifies that funds are available in the customer's account. Then the bank sends confirmation of payment authorization.

This authorization system helps reduce the chance that someone who stole the card can use it. The thief would have to steal the customer's authorization codes as well as the card. Thus the authorization procedure enhances the security of the system for the legitimate cardholder. In addition, the system guarantees that the retailer will receive final payment. Nevertheless, the telecommunication costs of standard on-line authorizations range from 8 cents to 15 cents per transaction. This is typically much higher than the per-transaction cost of paper currency and coins. In addition, retailers such as fast-food restaurants are not enthused about the slow speed of this kind of authorization system. After all, employees awaiting payment authorizations for customers they have already served cannot start serving customers who are waiting in line.

For these reasons, debit cards represent a purely technical innovation in retail payments. Unless debit card systems become speedier and more cost-effective, they are unlikely to alter fundamentally the nature of retail payments.

SMART CARDS AND DIGITAL CASH

Smart card

A card containing a microprocessor that permits storage of funds via security programming, can communicate with other computers, and does not require on-line authorization for funds transfers.

A more dramatic innovation has been the development of **smart cards;** plastic cards containing minute computer microchips that can hold far more information than a magnetic stripe. Thanks to microchip technology, a smart card can do much more than maintain a running cash balance in its memory or authorize the transfer of funds.

Smart Cards

A smart card carries and processes security programming. This capability of smart cards gives them a technical advantage over stored-value cards. Magnetic stripe cards fail to communicate a transaction correctly about 250 times in every million transactions. Smart cards fail to communicate properly less than 100 times per million transactions. Furthermore, smart cards are no more expensive to produce than standard stored-value cards or debit cards. Many smart cards are designed to be disposable.

The microprocessors on smart cards can also authenticate the validity of transactions. Retailers can program electronic cash registers to confirm the authenticity of the smart card by examining a unique "digital signature" stored on its microchip. The digital signature is created by software called a *cryptographic algorithm.* This is a secure program loaded onto the microchip of the card. The digital signature guarantees to the retailer's electronic cash register that the information on the smart card's chip is genuine. Figure 16-2 shows how digital encryption helps guarantee the security of electronic payments.

In a smart-card-based system for e-money transfers, the user of a smart card can remain anonymous. There is also no need for on-line authorization using expensive telecommunication services. Each time a cardholder uses a smart card, the amount of a purchase is deducted automatically and credited to a retailer. The retailer can in turn store its electronic cash receipts in specially adapted point-of-sale terminals and transfer accumulated balances to its bank at the end of the day via telephone links. This permits payments to be completed within seconds. Effectively, smart cards can do anything that paper currency and coins can do.

Visit the "Smart Card Cybershow at" **www.cardshow.com**

The Convenience of Digital Cash

What does a smart card have that paper currency and coins do not? The answer is potentially greater convenience. Smart cards' microchips can communicate with any computing device equipped with the appropriate software. ATMs and retailers' electronic cash registers are examples, but so are desktop and laptop computers.

People cannot use paper currency and coins, checks, or stored-value cards to complete transactions over the Internet. Instead, they usually provide credit card numbers and finalize payments to credit card issuers when they pay their monthly bills. Using smart cards or other microchip-bearing devices, however, they can send cash directly across cyberspace and finalize a transaction instantly, just as they could by handing over physical cash in person.

FIGURE 16-2
Digital Encryption and Electronic Payment Security
An electronic payment instruction starts out in a form readable by a human being, called "plaintext." When this instruction is entered into a computer, it is secured, or encrypted, using an "encryption key," which is a software code. In computer-readable form, the payment instruction is called "ciphertext," which the computer transmits to another location. A computer at the other location uses another software code, called a "decryption key," to read the data and turn it back into a plaintext form that a human operator can read.

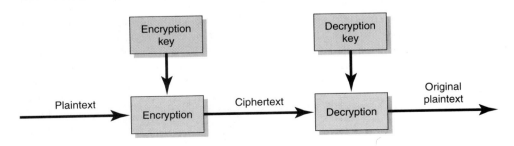

For instance, it is now technologically feasible for someone to use smart card technology to make a digital cash purchase of a service from an Internet-based retailer. Suppose that a student who likes classical music wishes to hear the latest rendition of a Mozart concerto by a favorite set of performers. The student can do this by using a smart-card-reading device connected to her personal computer—hardware manufacturers began introducing these devices at retail prices between $80 and $140 in the late 1990s—or she can load digital cash onto a program located on the hard drive of the computer. As long as the performer's recording company also has the necessary software, the student can enter a designated location on the recording company's Web site, point, click, and download the music as a digital file. The student's computer automatically sends digital cash as payment for this service. Then the student can listen to the latest concerto recording on her computer's speakers.

CYBERPAYMENT INTERMEDIARIES

Of course, the fact that people have the ability to adopt a technology does not mean that they actually will. After all, the basic technology for stored-value cards has been available since the 1970s. Only recently, however, have people made widespread use of stored-value cards to purchase such items as telephone calls and gasoline.

The Shaky Start of On-line Payments

Some initial experiments with on-line payments did not encourage consumers to adopt the new technology. Consider the 1996 experience of a woman in California who thought she had arranged to use financial software to pay her electric bill on the Internet. In fact, what she did when she clicked her computer's mouse was send a pay order to the software company's computers in Illinois. The company automatically wired instructions to a Utah location, where a clerk printed a paper check and sent it by surface mail to the San Francisco power company that provided the woman's electricity. The utility customer learned of this tangled payment chain after power to her home was shut off. The power company had rejected the check after it arrived from Utah because it was missing a payment stub.

Naturally, customers have been unwilling to adopt cyberpayment technologies until they are convinced that their payments are secure from transmission errors, fraud, and theft. They also want to know that technologies such as smart cards will be accepted by many other consumers and merchants before going to the trouble of learning to use them. At the same time, retailers do not want to install systems for

---

FAQ

Are smart cards too hard for the average person to use?

No, because even children can use them. A big fear of banks and companies interested in introducing smart cards and digital cash systems has been the supposedly unsophisticated U.S. consumer. Since the late 1990s, however, elementary school children in Westport, Connecticut, have been using smart cards to buy lunch at the school cafeteria. Each child has an account set up by the school. At the end of each month, parents receive a statement of purchases. Whenever funds are low, a computer generates a letter sent automatically to the parent. Each cafeteria cash register is equipped with a computer, software, printer, external floppy drive, scanner, and digital camera. Each pupil's photo is stored on a host computer for verification purposes. So even though fraud is not completely impossible, the probability of fraudulent card use has been significantly diminished. Today, most Westport schoolchildren—kids as young as 5 years old—use smart cards every day. Clearly, it doesn't take grown-up smarts to use smart cards.

reading smart cards and processing digital cash payments until more customers are willing to use them.

Convincing People That Digital Cash Is "Real Money"

As you learned in Chapter 15, banks have traditionally served as payment intermediaries. Today, many banks have memberships in such credit card industry groups as Visa International, MasterCard, and American Express. As a result, many banks are indirectly members of the Global Chipcard Alliance, an industry trade group that has promoted the standardization of smart card technology. An example is so-called smart card dial tones, which are sophisticated computer programs that allow any smart card to be accepted by any card-reading terminal.

Such standardization is necessary before widespread—indeed, worldwide—adoption of smart cards will be feasible. Today, U.S. videotapes cannot work on European videocassette players. In future years, will U.S. residents who travel to Europe find that their smart cards do not work in European equipment or with European software? Will they find that their smart cards will not function in on-line systems installed in Japan, China, or South Africa? Closer to home, will a New Orleans resident discover that his smart card doesn't work in Des Moines?

At present, every smart card system has a digital cash **certificate authority.** This is a designated payment intermediary that administers and regulates the terms under which people legitimately engage in e-money transactions. A certificate authority's key job is to approve and implement standards for digital signatures of smart cards, thereby enabling smartcard systems to connect all users. Because the security of their funds and the unrestricted ability to spend them when they wish are so important to people, a lot of effort is currently being devoted to standardizing the functions and interactions among certificate authorities. Once this is accomplished, smart cards should work in most locales.

Nearly all economists agree that there is likely to be an incentive for people to shift a portion of their paper-based transactions to exchanges using digital cash. No one can say for sure, however, if people will make this shift quickly or only gradually, perhaps over a period spanning a decade or more. In addition, it is impossible to estimate exactly what portion of retail transactions will ultimately be settled using digital cash. One thing is certain, however: Worldwide distribution of funds transfer cards such as debit cards and smart cards is growing rapidly. In 1989, there was one such card for every 100 people in the world. Today, the ratio is closer to one card for every eight people in the world.

Certificate authority
A group charged with supervising the terms governing how buyers and sellers can legitimately make digital cash transfers.

CONCEPTS IN BRIEF

- Stored-value cards are capable of storing computer-accessible data. They do not process data, so they are most often used in closed systems operated by a single business.

- Debit cards permit transfers of funds among accounts. They essentially perform the same functions as checks, but without paper.

- Smart cards contain microprocessors that can tabulate data, process security programs, and communicate directly with other computers. Smart cards or any other computing device can store and transmit digital cash, which consists of funds in the form of secure software programs.

- Digital cash transactions between different cyberpayment systems can be accomplished only if digital signatures used in one system can be recognized by the other system. This has induced software companies and payment intermediaries to develop digital certification techniques in an effort to make digital cash more widely acceptable.

ON-LINE BANKING

Banks were initially hesitant to jump into cyberspace. But they now recognize that they have an interest in seeing smart cards catch on. The reason is that widespread smart card adoption holds the promise of significant profits. Funds stored on customers' bank-issued smart cards are still, technically speaking, on deposit with their banks. Thus just as with traditional checking accounts, banks can earn profits by lending out unused balances of excess reserves on cards to other customers.

Banks also see the promise of fees that they will be able to charge retailers who accept the cards. They also anticipate getting to keep any spare change that customers leave on a card if they decide to throw it away. For instance, suppose that a bank finds that during a given week, a "typical" customer using a disposable smart card has 21 cents in "spare change" left on the card that the customer does not think worth the effort to spend before throwing away the card. If 10,000 customers are "typical," then each week a bank will get to keep a total amount of $2,100. Over the course of a year, this "spare change" will accumulate to $109,200!

Before most people become comfortable about sending digital cash to retailers across cyberspace, they must be sure that they can have secure on-line dealings with their own banks. This process is further along than the development of digital cash.

The Development of On-Line Banking

On-line banking began through the efforts of home financial management software developers, such as Quicken. These businesses wanted to include attractive features to induce people to buy their software, so they started offering to help software users consolidate bills and initiate payments over the Internet. Bill payments are typically issued from bank accounts, so ultimately the financial software companies formed alliances with banks.

Soon banks realized that they might be able to earn fee income by providing these kinds of services themselves. By 2000, nearly 1,000 U.S. banks offered on-line banking services via the Internet. A survey indicated that about a third of the more than 8,000 U.S. banks were implementing on-line banking and that more than another third were in the planning stages for offering such services.

Most on-line bank customers use three kinds of services. One of the most popular is still bill consolidation and payment. Another is transferring funds among accounts. This on-line service eliminates the need to make trips to a bank branch or ATM. The third is applying for loans, which many banks now permit customers to do over the Internet. Customers typically have to appear in person to finalize the terms of a loan. Nonetheless, they can save some time and effort by starting the process at home.

The Chicken-or-Egg Problem of On-Line Banking

There are two important banking activities generally not available on-line: depositing and withdrawing funds. This, of course, is where smart cards can come into the picture. With smart cards, people could transfer funds on the Internet, thereby effectively transforming their personal computers into home ATMs. This, in turn, would give them more incentive to bank from home via the Internet. Yet many observers believe that on-line banking is the way to introduce people to e-money and to induce them to think about using smart cards.

Putting
Economics in Action
to Work

To learn more about developments in on-line banking, open the *EIA* CD-ROM and click on "Electronic Banking and Payments." Then click on "The Emergence of Online Banking."

This raises the potential for a chicken-or-egg problem to develop. Bank customers may wait for widespread acceptability of smart cards before exploring home banking options. At the same time, banks may wait for more customers to choose on-line banking before making big investments in smart card technology.

Nevertheless, many bankers have decided that there are two very good reasons to promote on-line banking irrespective of smart cards. One is that once in place, on-line banking is less expensive for the bank. Banks require fewer employees to maintain automated systems, so on-line banking saves banks from incurring significant expenses associated with large systems of branch offices. The potential cost savings of on-line banking are hard to quantify. This has not stopped some banks from seeking to convert customers to Internet-based banking services, however. A number of banks have adopted explicit targets for portions of their customers that they wish to entice into on-line banking within the next few years. Many are aiming to convince more than half their customers to bank on-line by before 2010.

Find out about the latest on-line banking options by going to **www.onlinebanking report.com** and clicking on "Finding an Online Bank."

Competitive Pressures for On-Line Banking

Another key rationale that bankers have for developing on-line services is the threat of competition. Many banks worry that if they do not figure out how to provide services on-line, someone else will—and steal away many of their best customers.

Since the late 1990s, several banks have operated exclusively on the Internet. These "virtual banks" have no physical branch offices. Because few people are equipped to send virtual banks funds via smart card technologies, the virtual banks have accepted deposits through physical delivery systems, such as the U.S. Postal Service or Federal Express. This saves the expense of maintaining a costly branch network with buildings and tellers, which sharply reduced the costs that virtual banks incur relative to traditional banks. These Internet-only banks pass on part of the cost savings to customers in the form of lower banking fees and lower interest rates on loans. Some even offer free checking with very low minimum deposits, such as $100, and no-fee money market accounts with average monthly balances of $2,500 or more.

Virtual banks have not been the only on-line competition faced by traditional banks. Today, there are several Internet loan brokers, such as QuickenMortgage, E-Loan, GetSmart, Lending Tree, and Microsoft's HomeAdviser. Each of these broker systems uses software that matches consumers with appropriate loans. The consumer supplies information to the program. The program then searches among available loan products for the best fit. The loans are available from lenders with whom the broker has a contractual relationship.

Internet loan brokers' biggest forays into banks' turf have been in the credit card and mortgage markets. In the credit card business, Internet brokers have been especially successful in providing credit card debt consolidation services. They do not always compete with banks; often they act as marketers for traditional credit-card-issuing banks. Credit card issuers pay the brokers fees to match with new customers. This saves the issuers from having to create lists of potential prospects and to develop and mail card offers.

In the mortgage market, however, the competition is more direct. When mortgage rates fell in the late 1990s, people who wished to refinance flooded the telephone lines of traditional banking institutions. Many experienced busy signals, long waits on hold, and slow responses from loan officers. This induced them to turn to the Internet. One Internet broker reported that visitors to its Web site increased from about 35,000 per month to over

500,000 per month. Some real estate experts estimate that within a few years, at least 10 percent of U.S. mortgage loan refinancings will be initiated through the Internet.

REGULATING E-MONEY AND INTERNET BANKING

Electronic banking technologies make some people nervous. Some people hesitate to adopt digital cash for the same kinds of reasons that have slowed adoption of other new technologies: Until they have time to evaluate what's new, people often begin by assuming the worst.

The Security of Digital Cash

As we all know, from time to time airplanes crash. In the years following the introduction of commercial air passenger service, many people refused to fly. Over time, however, it became clear that flying was often much more convenient than other forms of transportation. Air travel eventually turned out to be safer, too, as reflected by lower average injury and death rates compared to other forms of transportation.

It remains to be seen whether people will find digital cash more convenient than other means of payment. A big issue in the minds of most potential users of smart cards or on-line banking services is the security of the e-money payments they make. For bank regulators, the security of digital cash is one of two key issues raised by electronic banking. The other concerns the potential for an upsurge of fraudulent banking practices.

Potential Security Concerns

Just because smart cards can be equipped with authentication software does not mean they are 100 percent secure. Criminals can be ingenious. There are a number of ways that one could imagine them stealing or otherwise interfering with digital cash. To thwart such efforts, banks and crime enforcement officials must anticipate them and develop ways to hinder potential criminals.

Digital Counterfeiting.   One possible way that a crook could pilfer digital money is old-fashioned but potentially lucrative: counterfeiting. The most obvious way to counterfeit would be to produce smart cards that look, feel, and function just like legitimate smart cards.

Issuers of smart cards have already undertaken a number of defensive measures aimed at preventing such counterfeiting efforts from succeeding. One is to make counterfeit smart cards easier to recognize. Smart card issuers typically place holographic images on their own legitimate cards, just as credit card issuers do. Issuers also place special features in the computer code on smart card microprocessor that complicate efforts to access data stored in memory. They place these features in a portion of the microprocessor's memory that can be changed only by altering its internal functions. Issuers also equip smart cards with physical barriers intended to inhibit optical or electrical analysis of the microprocessor's memory. Most smart card chips are also coated with several layers of wiring, making it difficult to remove the chip without damaging it beyond repair.

Stealing Digital Cash Off-Line and On-Line.   One of the most common types of bank robbery today entails driving a pickup truck through the front window of a bank branch or supermarket containing an automated teller machine. Two or three people quickly lift the ATM into the bed of the truck, drive to their hideout, and remove the cash from the machine. An *off-line theft* of digital cash is only slightly more sophisticated. Thieves break into a merchant's establishment, physically remove electronic devices used to store value from customers' smart cards, and download these funds onto their own cards. The threat of this kind of off-line theft is likely to be a bigger problem for small retailers that do not wish to incur the expense required to process all smart card transactions immediately.

More sophisticated thieves might attempt to engage in *on-line thefts.* They could try to intercept payment messages as they are transmitted from smart cards and other electronic funds storage devices to host computers. For instance, thieves might learn the times of day that a large upscale department store transmits its receipts to a central computer. Then they could attempt to tap into the store's transmission line and steal the funds. These kinds of on-line theft are most likely to be "inside jobs," in which employees pilfer their own companies' funds using their knowledge of internal systems for transmitting digital cash.

Making E-Money "Catch a Cold." A key feature of digital cash is its dependence on smoothly functioning microprocessors and software. This exposes electronic money to special security dangers, such as computer viruses that could damage the input-output mechanisms of smart card microprocessors.

Malfunctioning Money. Paper currency can wear out. Magnetic-ink-scanning devices can misread checks. But people can still exchange physical units of money during electricity outages. Power failures or other equipment breakdowns can bring e-money transactions to a grinding halt.

The widespread use of digital cash could also contribute to a problem that is already well known to today's law enforcement officials. Many people already try to move funds from place to place to avoid reporting the funds to tax authorities or to hide illegalities associated with the funds. These activities could become even more common in a world of digital cash.

Learn about the U.S. government's efforts to prevent money laundering at **www.ustreas.gov/fincen**

POLICY EXAMPLE

E-Cash and Money Laundering

Tax evaders, drug traffickers, and others seek to "launder" money every day. That is, they try moving funds around the world without their actions being traced. Estimates are that about $500 billion is "laundered" worldwide every year. Congress has passed several laws aimed at minimizing money laundering, including the Money Laundering Control Act of 1986 and the Money Laundering Suppression Act of 1994.

A U.S. Treasury Department division, the Financial Crimes Enforcement Network (FinCEN), seeks to fight money laundering. Every year, FinCEN receives 11 million reports covering everything from casino earnings to foreign bank accounts maintained by U.S. citizens. Money launderers today invest in bars, restaurants, travel agencies, jewelry stores, and construction companies—virtually any business through which they can channel cash earned illegally.

The Financial Action Taskforce, a group of 26 countries fighting money laundering, believes that the speed, security, and anonymity of new Internet payment systems will lead to massive additional money laundering. Drug traffickers in particular will no longer need to smuggle currency across borders—they will be able to move funds through the Internet. Technology will permit anonymous transactions outside the regulated banking sector. Consequently, all restrictions on the banking system to make money laundering riskier and costlier will be for naught. Even when digital cash enters the banking system, it will have already bounced among numerous intermediaries, making the funds hard to trace. By definition, e-cash will be heavily encrypted. Thus law enforcement authorities will not be able to reconstruct transactions, nor will private providers of e-cash. DigiCash, a major European electronic money provider, indicates that it cannot track how its customers spend their money.

For Critical Analysis

Imagine yourself as a FinCEN employee trying to hinder money-laundering activities, and you know that banks that transfer cash into digital money systems have a limit of a few hundred dollars per transfer. How might money launderers overcome this constraint?

CONCEPTS IN BRIEF

- ◉ Key factors spurring on-line banking have been banks' interest in earning fee income and their concerns about competition from other banks and nonbanking firms that offer financial services over the Internet.

- ◉ In some respects, the potential security problems of digital cash, such as counterfeiting and outright theft, are simply high-tech versions of security concerns people already experience when they use physical currency and coins.

- ◉ In other ways, however, digital cash has its own special security difficulties. Unlike physical money, digital cash can potentially be infected by computer viruses. In addition, during periods of hardware breakdowns or power failures, digital cash transactions may be hindered or halted. On-line banking and the provision of digital cash also expose bank customers to new types of fraudulent practices on the part of unscrupulous virtual banks.

DIGITAL CASH AND THE MONEY MULTIPLIER

How is digital cash likely to affect the process by which the amount of money in circulation is determined? To address this question, the first thing to do is to recognize that the broad adoption of smart cards and other mechanisms for using digital cash will undoubtedly require redefining measures of the money supply. Because digital cash will function as a medium of exchange, it will ultimately be included in the M1 definition of money. In turn, M1 is included within the broader money measures, so M2 and M3 will also include digital cash. Thus the money multiplier will link changes in reserves in the banking system to measures of money that include digital cash.

Immediate Effects of Digital Cash on the Money Supply Process

To envision the most likely immediate effect of digital cash on the deposit expansion process, suppose that the Fed in a cybereconomy of the not-so-distant future buys $1 million in government securities. Naturally, transactions deposits initially increase by $1 million. The recipient of these funds, however, allocates a portion of the $1 million to both government-issued currency *and* digital cash. The recipient's bank can lend out the remaining deposits less an amount that it must hold to meet its reserve requirement. This generates a deposit at another institution, and the depositor will allocate some of these funds to government currency *and* to digital cash. Thus allocations of funds to digital cash holdings constitute "leakages" from transactions deposits at each stage of the deposit expansion process.

Funds held as digital cash are included in our revised definition of the money supply, however. At every stage of the deposit expansion process, therefore, new digital cash is "created" and included in M1 and other money measures. When the Fed injects more reserves into the banking system, a multiple increase in deposits results, and this causes an increase in digital cash holdings as individuals shift a desired portion of funds from deposit accounts to smart cards and other digital cash storage devices. Unlike government currency holdings, which together with reserves are constrained by the government and the Federal Reserve, privately issued digital cash will vary directly with the extent of transactions deposit expansion. On balance, therefore, the overall quantity of money *increases* with the addition of digital cash. Consequently, the multiplier linking this measure of money to bank reserves must also rise in value. The immediate effect of digital cash, therefore, is likely to be a rise in the value of the money multiplier.

Indirect Effects of Digital Cash on the Money Supply Process

Our reasoning indicates that, other things being equal, the near-term effect of a widespread adoption of digital cash will be an increase in the quantity of money and a rise in the value of the money multiplier. Over time, however, we would not expect that other things will remain equal. For this reason, the money multiplier implications of digital cash will not be so clear-cut in the more distant future.

Substitution of Private Digital Cash for Government Currency. For instance, if many people begin to prefer digital cash to government-provided currency as a means of payment, digital cash could begin to displace government currency. This would have the direct effect of decreasing the government currency component of M1 and other money measures. Although this also would reduce the extent of currency drains—as you learned in Chapter 15, other things being equal, currency drains tend to raise the size of the money multiplier somewhat—the direct effect would dominate. Thus declining use of government-provided currency as people switch to increased use of digital cash will tend to reduce the money multiplier and the money supply.

On-line Banking and the Money Supply Process. What if on-line banking permits people to make payments directly from their checking accounts without the need to write checks? Will this affect the money supply process?

By transferring transactions deposit funds electronically from their accounts via debit cards, automated bill payments, or Internet-based on-line payment mechanisms, people simply avoid writing paper checks. The money multiplier implications of the transactions are the same as those that arise if paper checks change hands, however, provided that the funds are redeposited in another depository institution. So if normal redepositing occurs, all that changes is the nature of the transactions that lie behind the normal deposit expansion process. Even if many of these are electronic, effects on balance sheets are unchanged. Thus on-line transmission of checking funds by itself has no fundamental effect on the money supply process.

This is true, however, only if all transactions deposits from which people can transmit funds on-line are maintained at depository institutions and are subject to reserve requirements. If other, nondepository institutions find ways to issue transactions deposits via on-line mechanisms such as the Internet, these deposits will also function as money, yet they will not be subject to reserve requirements. In that event, the money multiplier will rise, potentially by a sizable amount. At present, any such activities are illegal, because only government-regulated banking institutions have the legal authority to issue transactions deposits accessible either by check or via the Internet. If nonbanking institutions find a way to get around this restriction, however, the money multiplier could increase dramatically.

Putting
Economics in Action
to Work

For additional practice thinking through how digital cash may affect the money supply process, start *EIA*, click on "Electronic Banking and Payments," and then click on "Digital Cash and the Money Multiplier."

CONCEPTS IN BRIEF

● If digital cash is included in M1 and other money measures, widespread adoption of digital cash will have the immediate effect of raising the money multiplier and the amount of money in circulation.

● An offsetting effect that can take place over the longer term is the gradual displacement of government-provided currency by digital cash, which would tend to reduce the money multiplier and money supply somewhat.

● On-line banking services involving transactions deposits will not fundamentally affect the money multiplier. Nevertheless, if nonbanking institutions find ways to offer such deposits while avoiding reserve requirements, the money multiplier could increase significantly.

NETNOMICS

What Will Digital Cash Replace?

If people start to use smart cards, personal computers, and cellular phones to store and transmit digital cash, presumably they will have less desire to use other forms of money. To understand why, consider Table 16-1, which lists the key characteristics of checks, government-issued currency, and digital cash.

In comparing currency with checks, it is clear that people must trade off features that each offers. Checks promise greater security, because if a thief steals a woman's handbag containing cash and checks, she can contact her depository institution to halt payment on all checks in the handbag. Currency payments are final, however, so the thief can spend all the cash he has taken from her. She can send checks through the mail, but using currency requires face-to-face contact. In addition, currency transactions are anonymous, which may be desirable under some circumstances. Nevertheless, not everyone will accept a check in payment for a transaction, and a check payment is not final until the check clears. Check transactions are also more expensive. After evaluating these features of currency and checks, people typically choose to hold both payment instruments.

People will likewise compare the features that digital cash offers with the features currently offered by government-provided currency and checking accounts available from depository institutions. As Table 16-1 indicates, the acceptability of digital cash is uncertain at present. Nonetheless, we are contemplating an environment with wide acceptability, and in such an

TABLE 16-1

Features of Alternative Forms of Money
Digital cash tends to overshadow government-issued currency.

Feature	Checks	Currency	Digital Cash
Security	High	Low	High(?)
Per-Transfer Cost	High	Medium	Low
Payment Final, Face-to-face	No	Yes	Yes
Payment Final, Non-Face-to-Face	No	No	Yes
Anonymity	No	Yes	Yes
Acceptability	Restricted	Wide	Uncertain at present

Source: Aleksander Berentsen, "Monetary Policy Implications of Digital Money," *Kyklos,* 51 (1998), p. 92.

environment, digital cash would be nearly as acceptable as government-provided currency. Digital cash held on smart cards without special security features such as personal identification numbers will be as susceptible to theft as government currency. Some digital cash, however, may be held on devices, such as laptop computers or even wristwatches (Swiss watch manufacturers have already developed watches with microchips for storing digital cash), requiring an access code before a microchip containing digital cash can be accessed. Overall, therefore, digital cash is likely to be somewhat more secure than government-provided currency, though not as secure as check transactions.

Digital cash transactions are likely to be less costly to undertake, because people will not have to go to depository institution branches or automated teller machines to obtain digital cash (although they will be able to do this if they wish). They will also be able to access digital cash at home on their personal computers. In addition, they will be able to send digital cash from remote locations using the Internet, and digital cash transactions will be instantaneously final. Unlike transactions using currency, therefore, digital cash transactions need not be conducted face to face. Like currency transactions, however, most digital cash transfers will be anonymous.

In most respects, therefore, digital cash looks like a better means of payment than government-provided currency. Certainly, for some time to come, a number of items—canned beverages and candy in vending machines, for example—will be easiest to purchase using government-provided currency. Many economists, however, believe that widespread adoption of privately issued digital cash will ultimately tend to crowd out government-provided currency. On many college campuses, vending machines already accept stored-value cards. Eventually, vending machines on street corners are likely to have smart card readers.

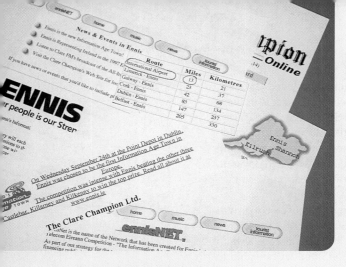

Investing in Digital Cash Systems

Security and standardization are not the only issues that payment intermediaries such as banks must confront when trying to develop e-money systems. Companies invested millions of dollars in Ennis, Ireland, to make cyberpayments a reality for a few thousand households. How much would it cost for the United States to permit widespread use of digital cash?

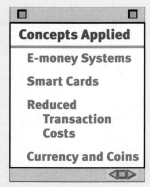

Concepts Applied

E-money Systems

Smart Cards

Reduced Transaction Costs

Currency and Coins

The High Cost of Setting Up Digital Cash Systems

The initial setup costs of e-money systems will likely be very high. Banks will have to provide smart cards to their customers at an estimated cost of $2 to $10 apiece. If 100 million U.S. residents use smart cards, this implies a total investment of between $200 million and $1 billion. Some banks have already begun to work to reduce the initial costs of distributing smart cards by turning credit cards into smart cards. Beginning in 1998, for instance, First USA began issuing credit cards with both stripes and microchips with limited e-money capabilities. Other banks and American Express since have followed the same strategy.

In addition, banks will have to replace the nation's 150,000 automated teller machines with new ATMs that can communicate with smart cards. Depending on the level of sophistication, the purchase price of a typical ATM ranges from $7,000 to $50,000. Thus the aggregate investment that banks will have to undertake solely to make their ATMs part of a digital cash network is somewhere between $1 billion and $7.5 billion.

Although large retailers have sophisticated electronic cash registers, most do not. Current estimates are that to function in a fully digital cash environment, retailers will have to purchase a total of 25 to 35 million new cash registers. The prices of these machines range from $500 to $2,000 apiece. This implies a likely total investment expense for retailers of between $10 billion and $15 billion.

Balancing Costs Against Benefits

Banks and retailers will be willing to undertake capital investments totaling somewhere between $12 billion and $23 billion if e-money systems for digital cash exchange generate cost savings at least as large. As noted at the beginning of the chapter, the U.S. Treasury has estimated that the total cost of handling paper currency and coins amounts to about $60 billion per year. Thus if the use of digital cash becomes sufficiently widespread to reduce this cost by only 10 percent, the cost savings will be $6 billion per year, which will justify the aggregate investment by banks and retailers within a two- to six-year horizon.

The wide ranges in these rough estimates illustrate the degree of uncertainty surrounding the speed at which e-money trading will catch on in the United States. Nevertheless, nearly all economists agree that there is likely to be an incentive for people to shift at least a portion of their paper-based transactions to exchanges using digital cash.

FOR CRITICAL ANALYSIS

1. When must a bank make the decision to invest in electronic banking?

2. Why do U.S. citizens persist in using currency and coins so much?

SUMMARY DISCUSSION OF LEARNING OBJECTIVES

1. **The Distinction Between Stored-Value Cards, Debit Cards, and Smart Cards:** Consumers can use stored-value cards to maintain balances of electronic money that they can use to purchase specific goods or service. Stored-value cards are most often used in closed systems operated by a single business or institution, but in an open, on-line system, they can function as debit cards. Debit cards permit individuals to authorize direct transfers of funds from their bank accounts to retailers, effectively transforming paper-based checking accounts into electronic checking deposits. Smart cards contain computer microchips that permit them to communicate directly with other computers to process software containing programs that store and transmit digital cash. In contrast to stored-value cards, transferring funds with smart cards can be done anonymously.

2. **Digital Certification and the Acceptability of Digital Cash:** Widespread use of digital cash via smart cards and other cybertechnologies will arise only if people have confidence that digital cash payments will be widely accepted by others. For this reason, banks and other payment intermediaries are working to establish digital certification authorities. These groups will develop standards for digital certification, or official recognition that digital cash payments are genuine. This will permit people to transmit digital cash between different payment systems and across national boundaries.

3. **The Security of Digital Cash:** Counterfeiting and theft are potential problems with digital cash, just as they are with physical currency and coins. Special security problems of digital cash are the threat of infection by computer viruses and the potential for monetary breakdowns caused by power outages or hardware malfunctions.

4. **On-Line Banking and Its Regulation:** Banks first offered on-line banking services in conjunction with marketers of home financial software packages. Today, they seek to earn fee income from offering bill consolidation services, providing the capability to transfer funds among accounts via home computers, and processing loan applications. Some observers argue that unique security concerns and an increased potential for bank fraud justify special care in regulating virtual banks that specialize in on-line banking. A few recent cases of on-line banking fraud have heightened the concerns of regulators.

5. **Digital Cash and the Money Supply:** If the use of digital cash becomes sufficiently widespread that digital cash is included in M1 and other money measures, the immediate effect is likely to be a rise in the money multiplier and an increase in the quantity of money in circulation. Over the longer term, if digital cash begins to displace government-provided currency, there may be an offsetting effect as the amount of government-provided currency in circulation declines. If nonbanking institutions find ways to get around current prohibitions on their ability to issue on-line transactions deposits not subject to reserve requirements, the money multiplier could rise dramatically in the future.

Key Terms and Concepts

Certificate authority (389)	Digital cash (384)	Stored-value card (385)
Debit card (385)	Smart card (386)	

Problems

Answers to the odd-numbered problems appear at the back of the book.

16-1. A bank is contemplating issuing smart cards to its 10,000 household customers this year. Producing and distributing the smart cards will cost $2.50 per card. The bank has estimated that the cards will bring in $50 in additional revenues per customer during the year. It will have to pay five people to supervise an existing system for processing transfers and payments generated by the cards, and the average salary of each employee is

$75,000. If there are no other costs or benefits for the bank, and if it only cares about being sure that it will at least break even on smart cards during the current year, should it issue the cards?

16-2. After the bank discussed in Problem 16-1 has made a tentative decision, the head of its legal department convinces the bank's overall management team that it should install devices that provide both audio and video assistance for disabled customers who use smart cards. The cost of installing these devices is $80,000. Should the bank change its original decision?

16-3. As discussed in Chapter 5, an *externality* is a consequence of production or consumption activities in a market that spills over to affect third parties. Some economists argue that payment systems are subject to positive externalities called *network externalities*. Essentially, their argument is that a person who is not currently using a means of payment is more likely to switch to using it if others already use it. Could the existence of network externalities help explain why the average American does not yet carry a smart card?

16-4. In Chapter 15, you learned that there are also some potential *negative* externalities that can arise in payment systems. Based on this chapter's overview of smart cards and on-line banking, can you think of any potential negative externalities associated with digital cash and on-line banking?

16-5. Suppose that FinCEN discovers that individuals and companies seeking to avoid paying taxes on legitimately earned income laundered $100 million in funds using on-line transfers of digital cash during the latest year. FinCEN determines that it can capture one-half of all launderers and force them to pay taxes and penalties. The average rate of taxes and penalties that the government assesses against apprehended money launderers is 50 percent of the laundered funds. Suppose that FinCEN's records indicate that the agency spends $20 million each year investigating these laundering activities and bringing the perpetrators to justice. Ignoring all other factors except recovered taxes and penalties and enforcement costs (that is, abstracting from the issue of whether FinCEN should try to stop all money laundering because it

is morally wrong), were FinCEN's activities justified during this year?

16-6. Some bankers have become concerned that their biggest competition for customers of on-line financial services might come from software companies and Internet service providers. What competitive advantages might the latter firms have over banks in providing on-line financial services? What advantages might banks have in providing such services?

16-7. In terms of the effects on the money multiplier and the money supply, if all transactions deposits are issued by banks that must meet legal reserve requirements, does it matter if their customers make payments from transactions account deposits using paper checks, debit cards, or on-line transfers directly from their checking accounts via the Internet?

16-8. Does your answer to Problem 16-7 change if nonbanking institutions not subject to reserve requirements also offer transfers from transactions deposits using paper checks, debit cards, or on-line transactions?

16-9. Suppose that the Federal Reserve is authorized by Congress to subject any firm that issues transactions-deposit-type liabilities over the Internet to reserve requirements. At the same time, Congress decides to follow the free banking laws of the nineteenth century by allowing any firm to offer such accounts, as long as it submits to the Fed's reserve requirements and meets other minimal standards to operate as a bank. The Fed immediately imposes the same required reserve ratio on firms that enter the on-line banking business that it imposes on traditional banks. What is the implication for the money multiplier?

16-10. Imagine a future world in which both banks and other nonbanking firms find a way to offer transactions deposits on-line while evading all reserve requirements. In this world, nearly all funds are digital cash in bank computer files and on consumers' personal computing equipment and smart cards. What is the potential money multiplier in such a world? What factors are likely to constrain the money multiplier to a lower value?

Economics on the Net

Digital Cash Versus E-Checks In this chapter, we focused on the potential for smart card technology to allow people to purchase goods and services over the Internet and other electronic delivery systems without the need to provide identification codes. The same technology, however, may permit people to write electronic checks that they could also use in this manner.

Internet URL: www.echeck.org/kitprint/index.html

Title: What Is Echeck?

Navigation: First, go to the Echeck homepage (www.echeck.org). Along the left-hand margin, click on *What Is Echeck?*

Application Read the explanation of Echeck, and then answer the following questions.

1. People are likely to use digital cash in place of government-issued currency and coins. Would people be more likely to use e-checks in place of traditional paper checks?

2. Based on the discussion in the article, who are likely to be the main providers of e-check technology? In light of the answer to this question, do e-checks pose the same fundamental questions for monetary policy that arise from the use of digital cash?

For Group Study and Analysis The article indicates that consumer acceptance of e-check technology could set the stage for more widespread consumer use of other electronic delivery systems. As a group, review the arguments in favor of this view. Identify some arguments that run counter to this perspective. Does the banking industry have a vested interest in e-checks' catching on?

DOMESTIC AND INTERNATIONAL MONETARY POLICY

The so-called Group of Seven, or G-7, meets informally and attempts to coordinate monetary and fiscal policies among their governments. Do their decisions have the force of law in these countries?

Security is tight. The heads of the departments of treasury or finance of some of the most powerful economies throughout the world are meeting again. These are usually called the meetings of the Group of Seven (G-7) large industrials world economies. It used to be the G-5, sometimes it's the G-8 if Russia is included, and sometimes it's referred to as the G-10 if other nations are asked to send their ministers of finance. The goal is always the same—to coordinate macroeconomic policies and, more specifically, monetary policies. Can monetary policy be coordinated throughout the world? This is a complex question. Before you can attempt to understand it, though, you must learn about the ins and outs of monetary policy at home.

Did You Know That... you can now purchase the securities of the United States government in amounts as low as $1,000? The program is called Treasury Direct. Through Treasury Direct, you can buy Treasury bills, which have maturities of 3, 6, or 12 months; Treasury notes, with maturities of 1 to 10 years; and Treasury bonds, with maturities of 10 years or more. All you have to do is open an account with Treasury Direct and then call (800)-943-6864 to buy government securities. Or alternatively, you can do it all via the Bureau of Public Debt's Web site at http://www.publicdebt.treas.gov/sec/sec.htm by clicking on "Treasury Direct." What all this means is that you don't need to be a superrich person who flies off to the Federal Reserve to buy U.S. Treasury securities. As you'll see in this chapter, when the Federal Reserve itself buys and sells U.S. Treasury securities (it usually deals in Treasury bills on a daily basis), it is engaging in monetary policy.

Monetary policy is the Fed's changing of the supply of money or the rate at which it grows in order to achieve national economic goals. When you were introduced to aggregate demand in Chapter 10, you discovered that the position of the aggregate demand curve is determined by the willingness of firms, individuals, governments, and foreigners to purchase domestically produced goods and services. Monetary policy works in a variety of ways to change this willingness, both directly and indirectly.

Think about monetary policy in an intuitive way: An increase in the money supply adds to the amount of money that firms and individuals have on hand and so increases the amount that they wish to spend. The result is an increase in aggregate demand. A decrease in the money supply reduces the amount of money that people have on hand to spend and so decreases aggregate demand.

WHAT'S SO SPECIAL ABOUT MONEY?

By definition, monetary policy has to do, in the main, with money. But what is so special about money? Money is the product of a "social contract" in which we all agree to do two things:

1. Express all prices in terms of a common unit of account, which in the United States we call the dollar
2. Use a specific medium of exchange for market transactions

These two features of money distinguish it from all other goods in the economy. As a practical matter, money is involved on one side of every nonbarter transaction in the economy—and trillions of them occur every year. What this means is that something that changes the amount of money in circulation will have some effect on many transactions and thus on elements of GDP. If something affects the number of snowmobiles in existence, probably only the snowmobile market will be altered. But something that affects the amount of money in existence is going to affect *all* markets.

Holding Money

All of us engage in a flow of transactions. We buy and sell things all of our lives. But because we use money—dollars—as our medium of exchange, all *flows* of nonbarter transactions involve a *stock* of money. We can restate this as follows:

To use money, one must hold money.

Given that everybody must hold money, we can now talk about the *demand* to hold it. People do not demand to hold money just to look at pictures of past leaders. They hold it to be able to use it to buy goods and services.

The Demand for Money: What People Wish to Hold

People have a certain motivation that causes them to want to hold money balances. Individuals and firms could try to have zero non-interest-bearing money balances. But life is inconvenient without a ready supply of money balances. There is a demand for money by the public, motivated by several factors.

The Transactions Demand.   The main reason why people hold money is that money can be used to purchase goods and services. People are paid at specific intervals (once a week, once a month, and so on), but they wish to make purchases more or less continuously. To free themselves from making expenditures on goods and services only on payday, people find it beneficial to hold money. The benefit they receive is convenience: They willingly forgo interest earnings in order to avoid the inconvenience and expense of cashing in such nonmoney assets as bonds every time they wish to make a purchase. Thus people hold money to make regular, *expected* expenditures under the **transactions demand.** As national income rises, people will want to hold more money because they will be making more transactions.

The Precautionary Demand.   The transactions demand involves money held to make *expected* expenditures. People also hold money for the **precautionary demand** to make *unexpected* purchases or to meet emergencies. When people hold money for the precautionary demand, they incur a cost in forgone interest earnings that they balance against the benefit that having cash on hand provides. The higher the rate of interest, the lower the money balances people wish to hold for the precautionary demand.

The Asset Demand.   Remember that one of the functions of money is a store of value. People can hold money balances as a store of value, or they can hold bonds or stocks or other interest-earning assets. The desire to hold money as a store of value leads to the **asset demand** for money. People choose to hold money rather than other assets for two reasons: its liquidity and the lack of risk. Moreover, if deflation is expected, money balances can yield an extra return by rising in real value as prices fall.

The disadvantage of holding money balances as an asset, of course, is the interest earnings forgone. Each individual or business decides how much money to hold as an asset by looking at the opportunity cost of holding money. The higher the interest rate—which is the opportunity cost of holding money—the lower the money balances people will want to hold as assets. Conversely, the lower the interest rate offered on alternative assets, the higher the money balances people will want to hold as assets.

The Demand for Money Curve

Assume that the amount of money demanded for transactions purposes is fixed, given a certain level of income. That leaves the precautionary and asset demands for money, both determined by the opportunity cost of holding money. If we assume that the interest rate represents the cost of holding money balances, we can graph the relationship between the interest rate and the quantity of money demanded. In Figure 17-1, the demand for money curve shows a familiar downward slope. The horizontal axis measures the quantity of

Putting
Economics in Action
to Work

For more exposure to the concept of the demand for money, start the *EIA* CD and click on "Money and Banking." Then click on "The Demand for Money."

Transactions demand
Holding money as a medium of exchange to make payments. The level varies directly with nominal national income.

Precautionary demand
Holding money to meet unplanned expenditures and emergencies.

Asset demand
Holding money as a store of value instead of other assets such as certificates of deposit, corporate bonds, and stocks.

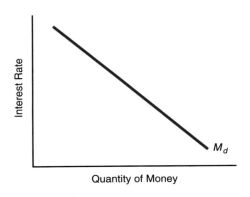

FIGURE 17-1
The Demand for Money Curve
If we use the interest rate as a proxy for the opportunity cost of holding money balances, the demand for money curve, M_d, is downward sloping, similar to other demand curves.

money demanded, and the vertical axis is the interest rate. In this sense, the interest rate is the price of holding money. At a higher price, a lower quantity of money is demanded, and vice versa.

Imagine two scenarios. In the first one, you can earn 20 percent a year if you put your cash into purchases of U.S. government securities. In the other scenario, you can earn 1 percent if you put your cash into purchases of U.S. government securities. If you have $1,000 average cash balances in a non-interest-bearing checking account, in the second scenario over a one-year period, your opportunity cost would be 1 percent of $1,000, or $10. In the first scenario, your opportunity cost would be 20 percent of $1,000, or $200. Under which scenario would you hold more cash instead of securities?

CONCEPTS IN BRIEF

● To use money, people must hold money. Therefore, they have a demand for money balances.

● The determinants of the demand for money balances are the transactions demand, the precautionary demand, and the asset demand.

● Because holding money carries with it an opportunity cost—the interest income forgone—the demand for money curve showing the relationship between money balances and the interest rate slopes downward.

THE TOOLS OF MONETARY POLICY

The Fed seeks to alter consumption, investment, and aggregate demand as a whole by altering the rate of growth of the money supply. The Fed has three tools at its disposal as part of its policymaking action: open market operations, discount rate changes, and reserve requirement changes.

Open Market Operations

The Fed changes the amount of reserves in the system by its purchases and sales of government bonds issued by the U.S. Treasury. To understand how the Fed does this, you must first start out in an equilibrium in which everybody, including the holders of bonds, is satisfied with the current situation. There is some equilibrium level of interest rate (and bond prices). Now if the Fed wants to conduct open market operations, it must somehow induce individuals, businesses, and foreigners to hold more or fewer U.S. Treasury bonds. The inducement must be in the form of making people better off. So if the Fed wants to buy bonds, it is going

Learn about the Federal Reserve's current policy stance regarding openmarket operations, by going to
www.federalreserve.gov /fomc
and clicking on "Minutes" for the most recent month.

FIGURE 17-2

Determining the Price of Bonds
In panel (a), the Fed offers more bonds for sale. The price drops from P_1 to P_2. In panel (b), the Fed purchases bonds. This is the equivalent of a reduction in the supply of bonds available for private investors to hold. The price of bonds must rise from P_1 to P_3 to clear the market.

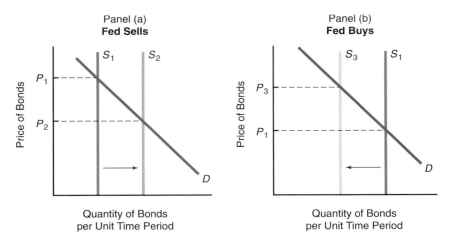

to have to offer to buy them at a higher price than exists in the marketplace. If the Fed wants to sell bonds, it is going to have to offer them at a lower price than exists in the marketplace. Thus an open market operation must cause a change in the price of bonds.

Graphing the Sale of Bonds. The Fed sells some of the bonds in its portfolio. This is shown in panel (a) of Figure 17-2. Notice that the supply of bonds is shown here as a vertical line with respect to price. The demand for bonds is downward-sloping. If the Fed offers more bonds for sale, it shifts the supply curve from S_1 to S_2. It cannot induce people to buy the extra bonds at the original price of P_1, so it must lower the price to P_2.

The Fed's Purchase of Bonds. The opposite occurs when the Fed purchases bonds. In panel (b) of Figure 17-2, the original supply curve is S_1. The new supply curve of outstanding bonds will end up being S_3 because of the Fed's purchases of bonds. You can view this purchase of bonds as a reduction in the stock of bonds available for private investors to hold. To get people to give up these bonds, the Fed must offer them a more attractive price. The price will rise from P_1 to P_3.

Relationship Between the Price of Existing Bonds and the Rate of Interest. There is an inverse relationship between the price of existing bonds and the rate of interest. Assume that the average yield on bonds is 5 percent. You decide to purchase a bond. A local corporation agrees to sell you a bond that will pay you $50 a year forever. What is the price you are willing to pay for the bond? It is $1,000. Why? Because $50 divided by $1,000 equals 5 percent, which is as good as the best return you can earn elsewhere. You purchase the bond. The next year something happens in the economy, and you can now obtain bonds that have effective yields of 10 percent. (In other words, the prevailing interest rate in the economy is now 10 percent.) What has happened to the market price of the existing bond that you own, the one you purchased the year before? It will have fallen. If you try to sell it for $1,000, you will discover that no investors will buy it from you. Why should they when they can obtain the same $50-a-year yield from someone else by paying only $500? Indeed, unless you offer your bond for sale at a price of $500, no buyers will be forthcoming. Hence an increase in the prevailing interest rate in the economy has caused the market value of your existing bond to fall.

The important point to be understood is this:

The market price of existing bonds (and all fixed-income assets) is inversely related to the rate of interest prevailing in the economy.

Changes in the Discount Rate

When the Fed was founded in 1913, the most important tool in its monetary policy kit was changes in the discount rate, discussed in Chapter 15. The Fed originally relied on the discount rate to carry out monetary policy because it had no power over reserve requirements. More important, its initial portfolio of government bonds was practically nonexistent and hence insufficient to conduct open market operations. As the Fed has come increasingly to rely on open market operations, it has used the discount rate less frequently as a tool of monetary policy—especially since the end of World War II.

Recall that the discount rate is the interest rate the Fed charges depository institutions when they borrow reserves directly from the Fed. An increase in the discount rate increases the cost of funds for depository institutions that seek loans from the Fed. That means that the price of one of their major lending inputs—the cost of money—has just gone up. Depository institutions pass at least part of this increased cost on to their borrowing customers by raising the interest rates they charge on loans.

Conversely, a reduction in the discount rate lowers depository institutions' cost of funds. It enables them to lower the rates they charge their customers for borrowing.

Changes in Reserve Requirements

Although the Fed rarely uses changes in reserve requirements as a form of monetary policy, most recently it did so in 1992, when it decreased reserve requirements on checkable deposits to 10 percent. In any event, here is how changes in reserve requirements affect the economy.

If the Fed increases reserve requirements, this makes it more expensive for banks to meet their reserve requirements. They must replenish their reserves by reducing their lending. They induce potential borrowers not to borrow so much by raising the interest rates they charge on the loans they offer.

Conversely, when the Fed decreases reserve requirements, as it did in 1992, some depository institutions attempt to lend their excess reserves out. To induce customers to borrow more, depository institutions cut interest rates.

---

* Monetary policy consists of open market operations, discount rate changes, and reserve requirement changes undertaken by the Fed.

* When the Fed sells bonds, it must offer them at a lower price. When the Fed buys bonds, it must pay a higher price.

* There is an inverse relationship between the prevailing rate of interest in the economy and the market price of existing bonds.

CONCEPTS IN BRIEF

EFFECTS OF AN INCREASE IN THE MONEY SUPPLY

To understand how monetary policy works in its simplest form, we are going to run an experiment in which you increase the money supply in a very direct way. Assume that the government has given you hundreds of millions of dollars in just-printed bills that you load into a helicopter. You then fly around the country, dropping the money out of the window. People pick it up and put it in their billfolds. Some deposit the money in their checking accounts. The first thing that happens is that they have too much money—not in the sense that they want to throw it away but rather in relation to other things that they own. There are a variety of ways to dispose of this "new" money.

Direct Effect

The simplest thing that people can do when they have excess money balances is to go out and spend it on goods and services. Here we have a direct impact on aggregate demand. Aggregate demand rises because with an increase in the money supply at any given price level, people now want to purchase more output of real goods and services.

Indirect Effect

Not everybody will necessarily spend the newfound money on real output. Some people may wish to deposit some or all of this excess cash in banks. The recipient banks now discover that they have higher reserves than they need to hold. As you learned in Chapter 15, one thing that banks can do to get interest-earning assets is to lend out the excess reserves. But banks cannot induce people to borrow more money than they were borrowing before unless the banks lower the interest rate that they charge on loans. This lower interest rate encourages people to take out those loans. Businesses will therefore engage in new investment with the money loaned. Individuals will engage in more consumption of such durable goods as housing, autos, and home entertainment centers. Either way, the increased loans have created a rise in aggregate demand. More people will be involved in more spending, even those who did not pick up any of the money that was originally dropped out of your helicopter.

Putting
Economics in Action
to Work

Get more experience thinking about how monetary policy affects the price level and real output in the short run and in the long run. Start the *EIA* CD, and click on "Aggregate Demand and Supply." Then click on "Monetary Policy."

Graphing the Effects of an Expansionary Monetary Policy

Look at Figure 17-3. We start out in a situation in which the economy is operating at less than full employment. You see a recessionary gap in the figure, which is measured as the difference between *LRAS* and the current equilibrium. Short-run equilibrium is at E_1, with a price level of 120 and real GDP of $9.5 trillion. The long-run aggregate supply curve is

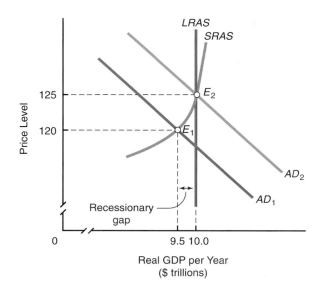

FIGURE 17-3
Expansionary Monetary Policy with Underutilized Resources
If we start out with equilibrium at E_1, expansionary monetary policy will shift AD_1 to AD_2. The new equilibrium will be at E_2.

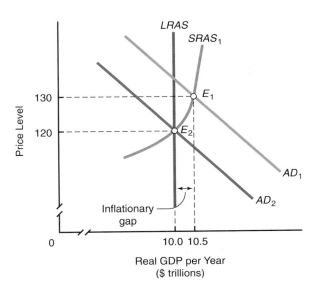

FIGURE 17-4

**Contractionary Monetary
Policy with Overutilized
Resources**
If we begin at an equilibrium at
point E_1, contractionary monetary
policy will shift the aggregate
demand curve from AD_1 to AD_2.
The new equilibrium will be at
point E_2.

at $10 trillion. Assume now that the money supply is increased by the Fed. Because of the direct and indirect effects of this increase in the money supply, aggregate demand shifts outward to the right to AD_2. The new equilibrium is at an output rate of $10 trillion of real GDP per year and a price level of 125. Here expansionary monetary policy can move the economy toward its *LRAS* sooner than otherwise.

Graphing the Effects of Contractionary Monetary Policy

Assume that there is an inflationary gap as shown in Figure 17-4. There you see that the short-run average supply curve, $SRAS_1$, intersects aggregate demand, AD_1, at E_1. This is to the right of the *LRAS* of real GDP per year of $10 trillion. Contractionary monetary policy can eliminate this inflationary gap. Because of both the direct and indirect effects of monetary policy, the aggregate demand curve shifts inward from AD_1 to AD_2. Equilibrium is now at E_2, which is at a lower price level, 120. Equilibrium real GDP has now fallen from $10.5 trillion to $10 trillion.

Note that contractionary monetary policy involves a reduction in the money supply, with a consequent decline in the price level (deflation). In the real world, contractionary monetary policy normally involves reducing the *rate of growth* of the money supply, thereby reducing the rate of increase in the price level (inflation). Similarly, real-world expansionary monetary policy typically involves increasing the rate of growth of the money supply.

CONCEPTS
IN BRIEF

● The direct effect of an increase in the money supply arises because people desire to spend more on real goods and services when they have excess money balances.

● The indirect effect of an increase in the money supply works through a lowering of the interest rates, which encourages businesses to make new investments with the money loaned to them. Individuals will also engage in more consumption (on consumer durables) because of lower interest rates.

OPEN ECONOMY TRANSMISSION OF MONETARY POLICY

For links to other banks around the globe, go to **www.bis.org** and click on "Central Banks."

So far we have discussed monetary policy in a closed economy. When we move to an open economy, in which there is international trade and the international purchase and sale of all assets including dollars and other currencies, monetary policy becomes more complex. Consider first the effect on exports of any type of monetary policy.

The Net Export Effect

When we examined fiscal policy, we pointed out that deficit financing can lead to higher interest rates. Higher (real, after-tax) interest rates do something in the foreign sector—they attract foreign financial investment. More people want to purchase U.S. government securities, for example. But to purchase U.S. assets, people first have to obtain U.S. dollars. This means that the demand for dollars goes up in foreign exchange markets. The international price of the dollar therefore rises. This is called an *appreciation* of the dollar, and it tends to reduce net exports because it makes our exports more expensive in terms of foreign currency and imports cheaper in terms of dollars. Foreigners demand fewer of our goods and services, and we demand more of theirs. In this way, expansionary fiscal policy that creates deficit spending financed by U.S. government borrowing can lead to a reduction in net exports.

But what about expansionary monetary policy? If expansionary monetary policy reduces real, after-tax U.S. interest rates, there will be a positive net export effect because foreigners will want fewer U.S. financial instruments, demanding fewer dollars and thereby causing the international price of the dollar to fall. This makes our exports cheaper for the rest of the world, which then demands a larger quantity of our exports. It also means that foreign goods and services are more expensive in the United States, so we therefore demand fewer imports. We come up with two conclusions:

1. Expansionary fiscal policy may cause interest rates to rise and thereby attract international flows of financial capital. The resulting appreciation of the dollar causes net exports to decline, which reduces the effectiveness of fiscal policy to some extent.
2. Expansionary monetary policy may cause interest rates to fall. Such a fall will induce international outflows of financial capital, thereby lowering the value of the dollar and making American goods more attractive. The net export effect of expansionary monetary policy will be in the same direction as the monetary policy effect, thereby enhancing the effect of such policy.

Contractionary Monetary Policy

Now assume that the economy is experiencing inflation and the Federal Reserve wants to pursue a contractionary monetary policy. In so doing, it may cause interest rates to rise. Rising interest rates will cause financial capital to flow into the United States. The demand for dollars will increase, and their international price will go up. Foreign goods will now look cheaper to Americans, and imports will rise. Foreigners will not want our exports as much, and exports will fall. The result will be a reduction in our international trade balance, that is, a decline in net exports. Again, the international consequences reinforce the domestic consequences of monetary policy.

Globalization of International Money Markets

On a broader level, the Fed's ability to control the rate of growth of the money supply may be hampered as U.S. money markets become less isolated. With the push of a computer button, billions of dollars can change hands halfway around the world. In the world dollar market, the Fed finds an increasing number of dollars coming from *private* institutions. If the Fed reduces the growth of the money supply, individuals and firms in the United States can increasingly obtain dollars from other sources. People in the United States who want more liquidity can obtain their dollars from foreign residents. Indeed, it is possible that as world markets become increasingly integrated, U.S. residents may someday conduct transactions in *foreign* currencies.

● Monetary policy in an open economy has repercussions for net exports.

● If expansionary monetary policy reduces U.S. interest rates, there is a positive net export effect because foreigners will demand fewer U.S. financial instruments, thereby demanding fewer dollars and hence causing the international price of the dollar to fall. This makes our exports cheaper for the rest of the world.

● When contractionary monetary policy causes interest rates to rise, foreign residents will want more U.S. financial instruments. The resulting increase in the demand for dollars will raise the dollar's value in foreign exchange markets, leading to a decline in net exports.

MONETARY POLICY AND INFLATION

Most theories of inflation relate to the short run. The price index in the short run can fluctuate because of events such as oil price shocks, labor union strikes, or discoveries of large amounts of new natural resources. In the long run, however, empirical studies show a relatively stable relationship between excessive growth in the money supply and inflation.

Simple supply and demand can explain why the price level rises when the money supply is increased. Suppose that a major oil discovery is made, and the supply of oil increases dramatically relative to the demand for oil. The relative price of oil will fall; now it will take more units of oil to exchange for specific quantities of non-oil products. Similarly, if the supply of money rises relative to the demand for money, it will take more units of money to purchase specific quantities of goods and services. That is merely another way of stating that the price level has increased or that the purchasing power of money has fallen. In fact, the classical economists referred to inflation as a situation in which more money is chasing the same quantity of goods and services.

The Equation of Exchange and the Quantity Theory

A simple way to show the relationship between changes in the quantity of money in circulation and the price level is through the **equation of exchange,** developed by Irving Fisher:

$$M_s V \equiv PY$$

where

M_s = actual money balances held by the nonbanking public
V = **income velocity of money,** or the number of times, on average, each monetary unit is spent on final goods and services
P = price level or price index
Y = real national output (real GDP)

Equation of exchange
The formula indicating that the number of monetary units times the number of times each unit is spent on final goods and services is identical to the price level times output (or nominal national income).

Income velocity of money
The number of times per year a dollar is spent on final goods and services; equal to GDP divided by the money supply.

Consider a numerical example involving a one-commodity economy. Assume that in this economy, the total money supply, M_s, is $5 trillion; the quantity of output, Y, is $10 trillion (in base-year dollars); and the price level, P, is 1.5 (150 in index number terms). Using the equation of exchange,

$$M_s V \equiv PY$$
$$\$5 \text{ trillion} \times V \equiv 1.5 \times \$10 \text{ trillion}$$
$$\$5 \text{ trillion} \times V \equiv \$15 \text{ trillion}$$
$$V \equiv 3$$

Thus each dollar is spent an average of three times a year.

The Equation of Exchange as an Identity.   The equation of exchange must always be true—it is an *accounting identity*. The equation of exchange states that the total amount of money spent on final output, $M_s V$, is equal to the total amount of money *received* for final output, PY. Thus a given flow of money can be seen from either the buyers' side or the producers' side. The value of goods purchased is equal to the value of goods sold.

If Y represents real national output and P is the price level, PY equals the dollar value of national output, or *nominal* national income. Thus

$$M_s V \equiv PY \equiv \text{nominal national income}$$

The Crude Quantity Theory of Money and Prices.   If we now make some assumptions about different variables in the equation of exchange, we come up with the simplified theory of why prices change, called the **crude quantity theory of money and prices.** If we assume that the velocity of money, V, is constant and that real national output, Y, is basically stable, the simple equation of exchange tells us that a change in the money supply can lead only to a proportionate change in the price level. Continue with our numerical example. Y is 50 units of the good. V equals 5. If the money supply increases to 200, the only thing that can happen is that the price index, P, has to go up from 10 to 20. Otherwise the equation is no longer in balance.

Crude quantity theory of money and prices
The belief that changes in the money supply lead to proportional changes in the price level.

INTERNATIONAL EXAMPLE

Hyperinflation in Belarus: The "Bunny" Breeds Rapidly!

In Belarus, formerly part of the Soviet Union, the national currency is called the *zaichik*, or little hare. People in that country count their currency in "bunnies." The government there is fond of letting the bunnies breed rapidly, that is, printing more and more of them. Not long ago, the government announced that it would issue more bunnies to pay for the fall harvest. Not surprisingly, Belarus's domestic currency dropped in value. In one five-month period, it lost half of its purchasing power. In one week alone, it lost more than 10 percent. Foreign investors simply disappeared.

Officially, there is no inflation in Belarus. The government has instituted price controls while increasing the rate of growth of the money supply. The only country that Belarus has much trade with now is Russia, and most of that trade is through barter.

For Critical Analysis
How might price controls work in a situation in which the money supply is growing rapidly?

Empirical Verification.   There is considerable evidence of the empirical validity of the relationship between monetary growth and high rates of inflation. Figure 17-5 tracks the

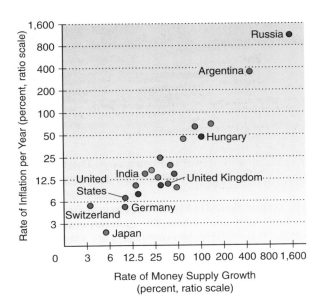

FIGURE 17-5
The Relationship Between Money Supply Growth Rates and Rates of Inflation
If we plot rates of inflation and rates of monetary growth for different countries, we come up with a scatter diagram that reveals an obvious direct relationship. If you were to draw a line through the "average" of the points in this figure, it would be upward-sloping, showing that an increase in the rate of growth of the money supply leads to an increase in the rate of inflation.
Source: International Monetary Fund. Data are for latest available periods.

correspondence between money supply growth and the rates of inflation in various countries around the world.

● The equation of exchange states that the expenditures by some people will equal income receipts by others, or $M_sV \equiv PY$ (money supply times velocity equals nominal national income).

● Viewed as an accounting identity, the equation of exchange is always true, because the amount of money spent on final output must equal the total amount of money received for final output.

● The crude quantity theory of money and prices states that a change in the money supply will bring about an equiproportional change in the price level.

MONETARY POLICY IN ACTION: THE TRANSMISSION MECHANISM

At the start of this chapter, we talked about the direct and indirect effects of monetary policy. The direct effect is simply that an increase in the money supply causes people to have excess money balances. To get rid of these excess money balances, people increase their expenditures. The indirect effect occurs because some people have decided to purchase interest-bearing assets with their excess money balances. This causes the price of such assets—bonds—to go up. Because of the inverse relationship between the price of existing bonds and the interest rate, the interest rate in the economy falls. This lower interest rate induces people and businesses to spend more than they otherwise would have spent.

The Keynesian Transmission Mechanism

One school of economists believes that the indirect effect of monetary policy is the more important. This group, typically called Keynesian because of its belief in Keynes's work, asserts that the main effect of monetary policy occurs through changes in the interest rate.

FIGURE 17-6
The Keynesian Money Transmission Mechanism

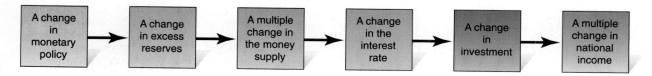

The Keynesian money transmission mechanism is shown in Figure 17-6. There you see that the money supply changes the interest rate, which in turn changes the desired rate of investment.

This transmission mechanism can be seen explicitly in Figure 17-7. In panel (a), you see that an increase in the money supply reduces the interest rate. The economywide demand curve for money is labeled M_d in panel (a). At first, the money supply is at M_s, a vertical line determined by our central bank, the Federal Reserve System. The equilibrium interest rate is r_1. This occurs where the money supply curve intersects the money demand curve. Now assume that the Fed increases the money supply, say, via open market operations. This will shift the money supply curve outward to the right to M_s'. People find themselves with too much cash (liquidity). They buy bonds. When they buy bonds, they bid up the prices of bonds, thereby lowering the interest rate. The interest rate falls to r_2, where the new money supply curve M_s' intersects the money demand curve M_d. This reduction in the interest rate

FIGURE 17-7
Adding Monetary Policy to the Keynesian Model

In panel (a), we show a demand for money function, M_d. It slopes downward to show that at lower rates of interest, a larger quantity of money will be demanded. The money supply is given initially as M_s, so the equilibrium rate of interest will be r_1. At this rate of interest, we see from the planned investment schedule given in panel (b) that the quantity of planned investment demanded per year will be I_1. After the shift in the money supply to M_s', the resulting increase in investment from I_1 to I_2 shifts the aggregate demand curve in panel (c) outward from AD_1 to AD_2. Equilibrium moves from E_1 to E_2, at $10 trillion real GDP per year.

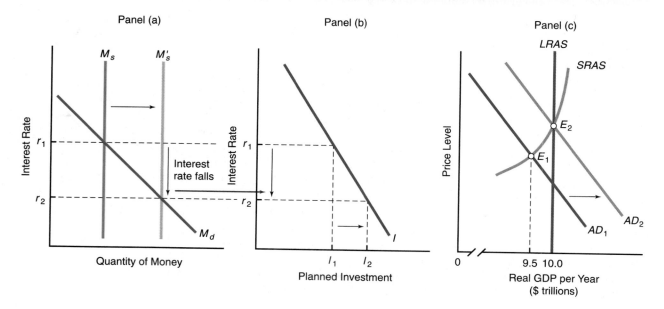

from r_1 to r_2 has an effect on planned investment, as can be seen in panel (b). Planned investment per year increases from I_1 to I_2. An increase in investment will increase aggregate demand, as shown in panel (c). Aggregate demand increases from AD_1 to AD_2. Equilibrium in the economy increases from real GDP per year of \$9.5 trillion, which is not on the *LRAS*, to equilibrium real GDP per year of \$10 trillion, which is on the *LRAS*.

The Monetarists' Transmission Mechanism

Monetarists, economists who believe in a modern quantity theory of money and prices, contend that monetary policy works its way more directly into the economy. They believe that changes in the money supply lead to changes in nominal GDP in the same direction. An increase in the money supply because of expansionary open market operations (purchases of bonds) by the Fed leads the public to have larger money holdings than desired. This excess quantity of money supplied induces the public to buy more of everything, especially more durable goods such as cars, stereos, and houses. If the economy is starting out at its long-run equilibrium rate of output, there can only be a short-run increase in real GDP. Ultimately, though, the public cannot buy more of everything; it simply bids up prices so that the price level rises.

Monetarists
Macroeconomists who believe that inflation is always caused by excessive monetary growth and that changes in the money supply affect aggregate demand both directly and indirectly.

Putting
Economics in Action
to Work

For additional practice thinking through the monetary policy transmission mechanism, start the *EIA* CD, and click on "Money and Banking." Then click on "Monetary Policy and Interest Rates."

Monetarists' Criticism of Monetary Policy

The monetarists' belief that monetary policy works through changes in desired spending does not mean that they consider such policy an appropriate government stabilization tool. According to the monetarists, although monetary policy can affect real GDP (and employment) in the short run, the length of time required before money supply changes take effect is so long and variable that such policy is difficult to conduct. For example, an expansionary monetary policy to counteract a recessionary gap may not take effect for a year and a half, by which time inflation may be a problem. At that point, the expansionary monetary policy will end up making the then current inflation worse. Monetarists therefore see discretionary monetary policy as a *destabilizing* force in the economy.

According to the monetarists, policymakers should consequently follow a **monetary rule:** Increase the money supply *smoothly* at a rate consistent with the economy's long-run potential growth rate. *Smoothly* is an important word here. Increasing the money supply at 20 percent per year half the time and decreasing it at 17 percent per year the other half of the time would average out to about a 3 percent increase, but the results would be disastrous, say the monetarists. Instead of permitting the Fed to use its discretion in setting monetary policy, monetarists would force it to follow a rule such as "Increase the money supply smoothly at 3.5 percent per year" or "Abolish the Fed and replace it with a computer program allowing for a steady rise in the money supply."

Monetary rule
A monetary policy that incorporates a rule specifying the annual rate of growth of some monetary aggregate.

FED TARGET CHOICE: INTEREST RATES OR MONEY SUPPLY?

It is not possible to stabilize the money supply and interest rates simultaneously. The Federal Reserve has often sought to achieve an *interest rate target*. There is a fundamental tension between targeting interest rates and controlling the money supply, however. Interest rate targets force the Fed to abandon control over the money supply; money stock growth targets force the Fed to allow interest rates to fluctuate.

Figure 17-8 on page 416 shows the relationship between the total demand for money and the supply of money. Note that in the short run (in the sense that nominal national

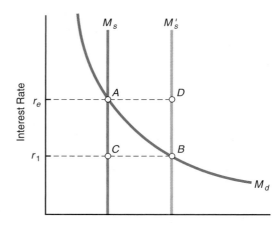

FIGURE 17-8
Choosing a Monetary Policy Target
The Fed, in the short run, can select an interest rate or a money supply target but not both. It cannot, for example, choose r_e and M'_s; if it selects r_e, it must accept M_s; if it selects M'_s, it must allow the interest rate to fall to r_1. The Fed can obtain point A or B. It cannot get to point C or D. It must therefore choose one target or the other.

income is fixed), the demand for money is constant; short-run money supply changes leave the demand for money curve unaltered. In the short run, the Fed can choose either a particular interest rate (r_e or r_1) or a particular money supply (M_s or M'_s).

If the Fed wants interest rate r_e, it must select money supply M_s; if it desires a lower interest rate in the short run, it must increase the money supply. Thus by targeting an interest rate, the Fed must relinquish control of the money supply. Conversely, if the Fed wants to target the money supply at, say, M'_s, it must allow the interest rate to fall to r_1.

But which should the Fed target, interest rates or monetary aggregates? (And which interest rate or which money stock?) It is generally agreed that the answer depends on the source of instability in the economy. If the source of instability is variations in private or public spending, monetary aggregate (money supply) targets should be set and pursued, because with a fixed interest rate, spending variations cause maximum volatility of real national income. However, if the source of instability is an unstable demand for (or perhaps supply of) money, interest rate targets are preferred, because the Fed's effort to keep the interest rate stable automatically offsets the effect of the money demand (or supply) change.

One perennial critic of the Federal Reserve, Milton Friedman, argues that no matter what, "the idea that a central bank can target interest rates is utterly false. Interest rates are partly a real magnitude, partly a nominal magnitude. The Federal Reserve cannot target real interest rates and has done great damage by trying to do so." Here Friedman is referring to the concept of the nominal rate of interest being comprised of the real interest rate plus the future expected inflation rate.

Consider the case in which the Fed wants to maintain the present level of interest rates. If actual market interest rates in the future rise persistently above the present (desired) rates, the Fed will be continuously forced to increase the money supply. The initial increase in the money supply will only temporarily lower interest rates. The increased money stock will eventually induce inflation, and inflationary premiums will be included in nominal interest rates. To pursue its low-interest-rate policy, the Fed must *again* increase the money stock because interest rates are still rising. Note that to attempt to maintain an interest rate target (stable interest rates), the Fed must abandon an independent money stock target.

To find out about the Fed's latest monetary policy actions, go to **www.federalreserve.gov** and click on "Press Releases."

- In the Keynesian model, monetary transmission operates through a change in interest rates, which changes investment, causing a multiple change in the equilibrium level of national income.

- Monetarists believe that changes in the money supply lead to changes in nominal GDP in the same direction. The effect is both direct and indirect, however, as individuals spend their excess money balances on cars, stereos, houses, and other items.

- Monetarists argue in favor of a monetary rule—increasing the money supply smoothly at a rate consistent with the economy's long-run potential growth rate. Monetarists do not believe in discretionary monetary (or fiscal) policy.

- The Fed can choose to stabilize interest rates or to change the money supply but not both.

THE WAY FED POLICY IS CURRENTLY ANNOUNCED

No matter what the Fed is actually targeting, it only announces an interest rate target. You should not be fooled, however. When the chair of the Fed states that the Fed is lowering "the" interest rate from, say, 5.75 percent to 5.25 percent, he really means something else. In the first place, the interest rate referred to is the federal funds rate, or the rate at which banks can borrow excess reserves from other banks. In the second place, even if the Fed talks about changing interest rates, it can do so only by actively entering the market for federal government securities (usually Treasury bills). So if the Fed wants to lower "the" interest rate, it essentially must engage in expansionary open market operations. That is to say, it must buy more Treasury securities than it sells, thereby increasing the money supply. This tends to lower the rate of interest. Conversely, when the Fed wants to increase "the" rate of interest, it engages in contractionary open market operations, thereby decreasing the money supply (or the rate of growth of the money supply).

What is the correct interest rate policy for the Fed to pursue? This is a question being answered by some young people across the country today.

POLICY EXAMPLE

Predict Monetary Policy Correctly and Win a $10,000 Scholarship

Every year since 1995, there has been a "Fed Challenge." This is a contest sponsored by the Federal Reserve Board and Citibank (now a division of Citigroup). More than 200 high schools throughout the country participate. Each school has a five-member team. Each team recommends whether the Fed ought to raise interest rates, keep them the same, or reduce them.

The vice-chair of the Federal Reserve Board and two colleagues judge the national finals at the beginning of May each year. The finalists give presentations of their models reflecting what they think should happen at meetings of the Federal Reserve's Open Market Committee. The winning team members each get a $10,000 scholarship, and their school receives a $50,000 grant to establish an "economics laboratory."

For Critical Analysis
What criteria do you think the judges should use to determine which team has presented the best monetary policy recommendations?

NETNOMICS

Will Digital Cash Weaken Monetary Policy?

In Chapter 16 you learned about digital cash, or e-money. In this chapter, you learned that monetary policy usually works through a process that involves changes in the money supply, which then affect interest rates and nationwide economic activity.

Whether money takes the form of coins, paper, or deposits makes little difference to officials who are charged with conducting monetary policy, as long as it does not interfere with their ability to control the total *quantity* of money in circulation. It is this issue that makes policymakers nervous about digital cash.

If the Federal Reserve and other central banks desire to control, or at least influence, the quantity of money in circulation, it is helpful for them to have direct or indirect oversight over the process by which money is placed into circulation.

It is conceivable that traditional banking institutions, such as commercial banks, savings institutions, and credit unions, may not be the only ones that choose to issue digital cash. To a central bank such as the Federal Reserve, this is the *fundamental* monetary policy issue posed by the development of e-money. Like banks and their customers, the Federal Reserve does not particularly care what form money takes. Nevertheless, it does have some reason to be concerned about who has the power to issue money.

In principle, anyone can issue digital cash accounts. Even if the government were to decide that only traditional banking institutions that fall under the Federal Reserve's regulatory umbrella can issue smart cards, what is to stop other firms from setting up e-money accounts over the Internet? That is, what is to stop firms that technically are not banks from issuing Internet-based digital checking accounts that effectively function as money? Presumably, one answer is that Congress could pass laws prohibiting such accounts, and the Federal Reserve and other bank regulators would have to police the Internet to ensure that only traditional banks issue such accounts.

Another possible answer, however, is that ultimately nothing may be able to stop a host of firms from pecking away at legal loopholes and eventually finding a way to enter the banking business by issuing e-money accounts. Balances stored in these digital cash accounts would be as much a part of the nation's quantity of circulating money as government currency and checkable deposits at traditional banks. As a result, the Fed's central-banking task of measuring and regulating this quantity would become much more complicated.

This is one way in which the new electronic banking systems have the potential to alter profoundly monetary affairs in the United States and worldwide. This potential development, more than any other, may be the *truly* fundamental change brought about by the use of digital cash.

ISSUES & APPLICATIONS

Can Monetary Policy Be Coordinated Worldwide?

For years now, high-level officials, usually from the departments of treasury or finance or the central banks of major industrialized nations, have been meeting on an irregular basis. Every time they do so, the world waits with bated breath to see what has been decided on a global level. Will the G-7 (representatives from the Group of Seven industrialized nations) decide to lower interest rates? Will they decide to increase interest rates? Will they decide to prop up the dollar or some other currency? Will they decide to stop the dollar from increasing in foreign exchange value?

The Asian Financial Meltdown and the G-7 Meetings

A few years ago, many Asian nations experienced a sort of financial meltdown. These economies saw their stock markets drop precipitously, along with the value of their domestic currencies in foreign currency markets. This was referred to at the time as the Asian disease or the Asian contagion, out of fear that other nations, including the United States, would catch it.

While it was happening, then U.S. President Clinton called for a global meeting to deal with the crisis. This caused a major rally in the U.S. stock market. Some analysts argue that this reaction was entirely rational. It is a variant on what military historians call the "mask of command": If one can give the impression that everything is under control, it may be possible to restore confidence and prevent panic from spreading.

A Dose of Reality

The Asian contagion was contained—but not by the G-7. The reality is that every country acts in its own best interest, not the world's. So no matter how often top officials from the G-7 meet, they are all beholden to their own constituents. Thus ideas that sound promising at a G-7 meeting may fall on deaf ears back home.

Furthermore, the Fed is not the world's central bank. Important as it is as an engine of economic policymaking, its impact beyond U.S. borders should not be overstated. The Fed can change the rate of growth of the money supply in the United States. But it cannot change the rate of growth of the money supply in Japan or Europe, and if Japan or Europe is having economic problems, a slight change in monetary policy in the United States is not going to make much difference anyway.

Even in a country that does business in dollars and whose currency is pegged to the dollar, the Fed's actions have little impact. If investors in Argentina, for example, believe, for whatever reason, that their loans will not be paid back in that country, they will simply move their capital somewhere else.

So What About a Global Central Bank?

Some observers have argued that to regulate the world's economies, or at least the world's currencies and rates of inflation, a global central bank should be created. Realistically, this would require a single global currency. The countries in Europe that are switching to a single currency, the euro, and a single central bank, the European Central Bank, took decades to do so. For the rest of the world to follow suit on a global scale is highly—nay, completely—improbable.

Concepts Applied

Monetary Policy

Coordination

Contractionary Policies

Expansionary Policies

Interest Rate Changes

FOR CRITICAL ANALYSIS

1. If meetings of the G-7 cannot make much of a difference, why does the press pay so much attention to them?

2. Why shouldn't the world just adopt the U.S. dollar as its only currency and let the Fed run monetary policy?

SUMMARY DISCUSSION OF LEARNING OBJECTIVES

1. **Key Factors that Influence the Quantity of Money That People Desire to Hold**: People generally make more transactions when real national income rises, and they require more money to make these transactions. Consequently, they desire to hold more money when real national income increases. People also hold money as a precaution against unexpected expenditures they may wish to make, and the interest rate is the opportunity cost of holding money for this purpose. In addition, money is a store of value that people may hold alongside bonds, stocks, and other interest-earning assets, and the opportunity cost of holding money as an asset is again the interest rate. Thus the quantity of money demanded declines as the market interest rate increases.

2. **How the Federal Reserve's Monetary Policy Tools Influence Market Interest Rates:** An open market purchase of government securities, a reduction in the discount rate, or a decrease in the required reserve ratio are all ways that the Federal Reserve can bring about an increase in total reserves in the banking system and an increase in the money supply. The rise in reserve levels that banks have available to lend leads them to bid down interest rates on loans. Thus market interest rates tend to fall in response to any of these changes in the Fed's tools of monetary policy.

3. **How Expansionary and Contractionary Monetary Policies Affect Equilibrium Real GDP and the Price Level in the Short Run:** By pushing up the money supply and inducing a fall in market interest rates, an expansionary monetary policy action causes total planned expenditures to rise at any given price level. Hence the aggregate demand curve shifts rightward, which can eliminate a short-run recessionary gap in real GDP. In contrast, a contractionary monetary policy action reduces the money supply and causes an increase in market interest rates, there-

by generating a fall in total planned expenditures at any given price level. This results in a leftward shift in the aggregate demand curve, which can eliminate a short-run inflationary gap in real GDP.

4. **The Equation of Exchange and the Crude Quantity Theory of Money and Prices:** The equation of exchange is a truism that states that the quantity of money in circulation times the average number of times a unit of money is used in exchange—the income velocity of money—must equal nominal national income, or the price level times real national output. According to the crude quantity theory of money and prices, we can regard the income velocity of money as constant and real GDP as relatively stable. Thus a rise in the quantity of money must lead to a proportionate increase in the price level.

5. **Keynesian and Monetarist Views on the Transmission Mechanism of Monetary Policy:** The Keynesian approach to the monetary policy transmission mechanism operates through effects of monetary policy actions on market interest rates, which bring about changes in desired investment and thereby affect equilibrium real national income via the Keynesian multiplier effect. By contrast, monetarists propose a transmission mechanism in which money supply changes influence total desired expenditures on goods and services.

6. **Why the Federal Reserve Cannot Stabilize the Money Supply and the Interest Rate Simultaneously:** To target a market interest rate, the Federal Reserve must be willing to adjust the money supply as necessary when there are variations in the demand for money. Hence stabilizing the interest rate typically requires variations in the money supply. To target the money supply, however, the Federal Reserve must be willing to let the market interest rate vary whenever the demand for money rises or falls. Consequently, stabilizing the money supply usually entails some degree of interest rate volatility.

Key Terms and Concepts

Asset demand (404)

Crude quantity theory of money and
    prices (412)

Equation of exchange (411)

Income velocity of money (411)

Monetarists (415)

Monetary rule (415)

Precautionary demand (404)

Transactions demand (404)

Problems

Answers to the odd-numbered problems appear at the back of the book.

17-1. Let's denote the price of a nonmaturing bond (called a consol) as P_b. The equation that indicates this price is $= I/r$, where I is the annual net income the bond generates and r is the market nominal interest rate.

   a. Suppose that a bond promises the holder $500 per year forever. If the market nominal interest rate is 5 percent, what is the bond's current price?

   b. What happens to the bond's price if the market interest rate rises to 10 percent?

17-2. Based on Problem 17-1, imagine that initially the market interest rate is 5 percent and at this interest rate you have decided to hold half of your financial wealth as bonds and half as holdings of non-interest-bearing money. You notice that the market interest rate is starting to rise, however, and you become convinced that it will ultimately rise to 10 percent.

   a. In what direction do you expect the value of your bond holdings to go when the interest rate increases?

   b. If you wish to prevent the value of your financial wealth from declining in the future, how should you adjust the way you split your wealth between bonds and money? What does this imply about the demand for money?

17-3. You learned in Chapter 11 that if there is an inflationary gap in the short run, then in the long run a new equilibrium arises when input prices and expectations adjust upward, causing the aggregate supply curve to shift upward and to the left and pushing equilibrium real GDP back to its long-run potential value. In this chapter, however, you learned that the Federal Reserve can eliminate an inflationary gap in the short run by undertaking a policy action that reduces aggregate demand.

   a. Outline one monetary policy action that could eliminate an inflationary gap in the short run.

   b. In what way might society gain if the Fed implements the policy you have proposed instead of simply permitting long-run adjustments to take place?

17-4. In addition, you learned in Chapter 11 that if there is a recessionary gap in the short run, then in the long run a new equilibrium arises when input prices and expectations adjust downward, causing the aggregate supply curve to shift downward and to the right and pushing equilibrium real GDP back to its long-run potential value. In this chapter, however, you learned that the Federal Reserve can eliminate a recessionary gap in the short run by undertaking a policy action that raises aggregate demand.

   a. Outline a monetary policy action that could eliminate a contractionary gap in the short run but uses a different tool of monetary policy than the one you considered in Problem 17-3.

   b. In what way might society gain if the Fed implements the policy you have proposed instead of simply permitting long-run adjustments to take place?

17-5. Explain why the net export effect of a contractionary monetary policy reinforces the usual impact that monetary policy has on equilibrium real GDP in the short run.

17-6. Use a chart to illustrate how the Fed can reduce inflationary pressures by conducting open market sales of U.S. government securities.

17-7. Suppose that the quantity of money in circulation is fixed but the income velocity of money doubles. If real GDP remains at its long-run potential level, what happens to the equilibrium price level?

17-8. Suppose that following the events described in Problem 17-7, the Federal Reserve implements policies that cut the money supply in half. How does the price level now compare with its value before the income velocity of money and the money supply both changed?

17-9. Consider the following data: The money supply is equal to $1 trillion, the price level equals 2, and real output of goods and services is $5 quadrillion in base-year dollars. What is the income velocity of money for this economy?

17-10. Suppose that the Federal Reserve wishes to keep the nominal interest rate at a target level of

6 percent. Draw a money supply and demand diagram in which the current equilibrium interest rate is 6 percent. Explain a specific policy action that the Fed, using one of its three tools of monetary policy, could take to keep the interest rate at its target level if the demand for money suddenly declines.

Economics on the Net

The Fed's Policy Report to Congress   Congress requires the Fed to make periodic reports on the scope of its recent policymaking activities. In this application, you will study recent reports to learn about what factors affect Fed decisions.

Internet URL: www.federalreserve.gov/boarddocs/hh/

Title: Federal Reserve Humphrey-Hawkins Report

Navigation: Begin at the homepage of the Federal Reserve's Board of Governors (http://www.federal-reserve.gov). Click on Monetary Policy, followed by Humprey-Hawkins Report. Then click on Report for the most recent date. Finally, click on Monetary Policy and the Economic Outlook.

Application: Read the report; then answer the following questions:

1. According to the report, what economic events played the most important role in shaping recent monetary policy actions?

2. Based on the report, what are the Fed's current monetary policy goals?

For Group Study and Analysis   Divide the class into "domestic" and "foreign" groups. Have each group read the past four Humphrey-Hawkins reports and then explain to the class how domestic and foreign factors, respectively, appear to have influenced recent Fed monetary policy decisions. Which of the two types of factors seem to have mattered most during the past year?

MONETARY POLICY: A KEYNESIAN PERSEPCTIVE

According to the traditional Keynesian approach to monetary policy, changes in the money supply can affect the level of aggregate demand only through their effect on interest rates. Moreover, interest rate changes act on aggregate demand solely by changing the level of investment spending. Finally, the traditional Keynesian approach argues that there exist plausible circumstances under which monetary policy may have little or no effect on interest rates and thus on aggregate demand.

Figure D-1 measures real national income along the horizontal axis and total planned expenditures (aggregate demand) along the vertical axis. The components of aggregate demand are consumption (C), investment (I), government spending (G), and net exports (X). The height of the schedule labeled $C + I + G + X$ shows total planned expenditures (aggregate demand) as a function of income. This schedule slopes upward because consumption depends positively on income. Everywhere along the line labeled $Y = C + I + G + X$, planned spending equals income. At point Y^*, where the $C + I + G + X$ line intersects this 45-degree reference line, planned spending is consistent with income. At any income less than Y^*, spending exceeds income, so income and thus spending will tend to rise. At any level of income greater than Y^*, planned spending is less than income, so income and thus spending will tend to decline. Given the determinants of C, I, G, and X, total spending (aggregate demand) will be Y^*.

INCREASING THE MONEY SUPPLY

According to the Keynesian approach, an increase in the money supply pushes interest rates down. This reduces the cost of borrowing and thus induces firms to increase the level of investment spending from I to I'. As a result, the $C + I + G + X$ line shifts upward in Figure D-1 by the full amount of the rise in investment spending, thus yielding the line $C + I' + G + X$. The rise in investment spending causes income to rise, which in turn causes consumption spending to rise, which further increases income. Ultimately, aggregate demand rises to Y^{**}, where spending again equals income. A key conclusion of the

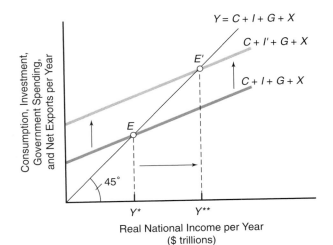

FIGURE D-I

An Increase in the Money Supply

An increase in the money supply increases income by lowering interest rates and thus increasing investment from I to I'.

Keynesian analysis is that total spending rises by *more* than the original rise in investment spending because consumption spending depends positively on income.

DECREASING THE MONEY SUPPLY

Not surprisingly, contractionary monetary policy works in exactly the reverse manner. A reduction in the money supply pushes interest rates up, which increases the cost of borrowing. Firms respond by reducing their investment spending, and this starts income downward. Consumers react to the lower income by scaling back on their consumption spending, which further depresses income. Thus the ultimate decline in income is larger than the initial drop in investment spending. Indeed, because the change in income is a multiple of the change in investment, Keynesians note that changes in investment spending (similar to changes in government spending) have a *multiplier* effect on the economy.

ARGUMENTS AGAINST MONETARY POLICY

It might be thought that this multiplier effect would make monetary policy a potent tool in the Keynesian arsenal, particularly when it comes to getting the economy out of a recession. In fact, however, many traditional Keynesians argue that monetary policy is likely to be relatively ineffective as a recession fighter. According to their line of reasoning, although monetary policy has the potential to reduce interest rates, changes in the money supply have little actual impact on interest rates. Instead, during recessions, people try to build up as much as they can in liquid assets to protect themselves from risks of unemployment and other losses of income. When the monetary authorities increase the money supply, individuals are willing to allow most of it to accumulate in their bank accounts. This desire for increased liquidity thus prevents interest rates from falling very much, which in turn means that there will be virtually no change in investment spending and thus little change in aggregate demand.

Problem

The answer to this problem appears at the back of the book.

D-1. Assume that the following conditions exist:

  a. All banks are fully loaned up—there are no excess reserves, and desired excess reserves are always zero.

  b. The money multiplier is 3.

  c. The planned investment schedule is such that at a 7 percent rate of interest, investment is $200 billion; at 6 percent, investment is $225 billion.

  d. The investment multiplier is 3.

  e. The initial equilibrium level of national income is $2 trillion.

  f. The equilibrium rate of interest is 7 percent.

Now the Fed engages in expansionary monetary policy. It buys $1 billion worth of bonds, which increases the money supply, which in turn lowers the market rate of interest by 1 percent. Indicate by how much the money supply increased, and then trace out the numerical consequences of the associated reduction in interest rates on all the other variables mentioned.

STABILIZATION IN AN INTEGRATED WORLD ECONOMY

At the start of the 2000s, unemployment had dropped to around 4 percent, but the rate of inflation had not budged for several years. So where did economists get the idea that low unemployment can cause higher rates of inflation?

At one time, it was a concept of central importance to economic policymakers. Many economists devoted their careers to trying to understand it. The concept is something known as the *Phillips curve*—a potential policy trade-off between the inflation rate and the unemployment rate arising from a proposed inverse relationship between the two. Today, however, a number of economists regard the idea of a Phillips curve as an anachronism. After all, in recent years inflation and unemployment have been *positively* related. As the unemployment rate declined from the 1990s into the early 2000s, so did the inflation rate. Why did anyone ever suggest that an inverse relationship between the inflation rate and the unemployment was the norm? Why do some economists continue to believe that it is, in spite of the experience of the past decade? You will learn the answers to these questions in this chapter.

LEARNING OBJECTIVES

After reading this chapter, you should be able to:

1. Explain why the actual unemployment rate might depart from the natural rate of unemployment

2. Describe why economic theory implies that there may be an inverse relationship between the inflation rate and the unemployment rate, reflected by the Phillips curve

3. Evaluate how expectations affect the relationship between the actual inflation rate and the unemployment rate

4. Understand the fundamental hypotheses of the new classical theory and their implications for economic policymaking

5. Identify the central features and predictions of real business cycle theory

6. Distinguish among alternative new Keynesian theories of business fluctuations

Did You Know That... since November 1948, Congress has passed at least a dozen bills aimed at fighting recession with fiscal policy? In the mid-1990s, in one 17-month period, the Fed increased short-term interest rates seven times and cut them once. And over a longer period, the Fed has even changed its basic operating targets.

ACTIVE VERSUS PASSIVE POLICYMAKING

All of these actions constitute part of what is called **active (discretionary) policymaking.** At the other extreme is **passive (nondiscretionary) policymaking,** in which there is no deliberate stabilization policy at all. You have already been introduced to one nondiscretionary policymaking idea in Chapter 17—the *monetary rule,* by which the money supply is allowed to increase at a fixed rate per year. In the fiscal arena, passive (nondiscretionary) policy might be simply to balance the federal budget over the business cycle. Recall from Chapter 13 that there are lags between the time when the national economy enters a recession or a boom and the time when that fact becomes known and acted on by the economy. Proponents of passive policy argue strongly that such time lags often render short-term stabilization policy ineffective or, worse, procyclical.

To take a stand on this debate concerning active versus passive policymaking, you first need to know what the potential trade-offs are that policymakers believe they face. Then you need to see what the data actually show. The most important policy trade-off appears to be between price stability and unemployment. Before exploring that, however, we need first to look at the economy's natural, or long-run, rate of unemployment.

THE NATURAL RATE OF UNEMPLOYMENT

Recall from Chapter 7 that there are different types of unemployment: frictional, cyclical, structural, and seasonal. Frictional unemployment arises because individuals take the time to search for the best job opportunities. Except when the economy is in a recession or a depression, much unemployment is of this type.

Note that we did not say that frictional unemployment was the *sole* form of unemployment during normal times. *Structural unemployment* is caused by a variety of "rigidities" throughout the economy. Structural unemployment results from factors such as these:

1. Union activity that sets wages above the equilibrium level and also restricts the mobility of labor
2. Government-imposed licensing arrangements that restrict entry into specific occupations or professions
3. Government-imposed minimum wage laws and other laws that require all workers to be paid union wage rates on government contract jobs
4. Welfare and unemployment insurance benefits that reduce incentives to work
5. A mismatch of worker training and skills with available jobs

In each case, these factors reduce individuals' abilities or incentives to choose employment rather than unemployment.

Consider the effect of unemployment insurance benefits on the probability of an unemployed person's finding a job. When unemployment benefits run out, according to economists Lawrence Katz and Bruce Meyer, the probability of an unemployed person's finding a job doubles. The conclusion is that unemployed workers are more serious about finding a job when they are no longer receiving such benefits.

Active (discretionary) policymaking
All actions on the part of monetary and fiscal policymakers that are undertaken in response to or in anticipation of some change in the overall economy.

Passive (nondiscretionary) policymaking
Policymaking that is carried out in response to a rule. It is therefore not in response to an actual or potential change in overall economic activity.

Frictional unemployment and structural unemployment both exist even when the economy is in long-run equilibrium—they are a natural consequence of costly information (the need to conduct a job search) and the existence of rigidities such as those noted. Because these two types of unemployment are a natural consequence of imperfect and costly information and rigidities, they are related to what economists call the natural rate of unemployment. As we discussed in Chapter 7, this is defined as the rate of unemployment that would exist in the long run after everyone in the economy fully adjusted to any changes that have occurred. Recall that national output tends to return to the level implied by the long-run aggregate supply curve (*LRAS*). Thus whatever rate of unemployment the economy tends to return to can be called the natural rate of unemployment.

EXAMPLE

The U.S. Natural Rate of Unemployment

At the end of World War II, the unemployment rate was below 4 percent. By the early 1990s, it was above 6 percent. These two endpoints for half a cycle of unemployment rates prove nothing by themselves. But look at Figure 18-1. There you see not only what has happened to the unemployment rate over that same time period but an estimate of the natural rate of unemployment. The solid line labeled "Natural rate of unemployment" is esti-

FIGURE 18-1

Estimated U.S. Natural Rate of Unemployment
As you can see in this figure, the actual rate of unemployment has varied widely in the United States in recent decades. If we estimate the natural rate of unemployment by averaging unemployment rates from five years earlier to five years later at each point in time, we get the heavy solid line so labeled. It rose from the 1950s until the mid-1980s and seems to be gradually descending since then.

Sources: Economic Report of the President; Economic Indicators, various issues.

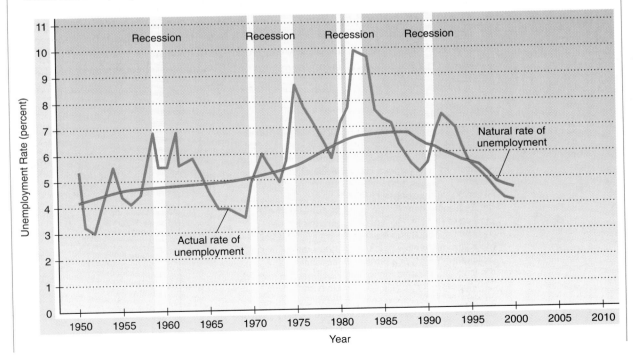

mated by averaging unemployment rates from five years earlier to five years later at each point in time. This computation reveals that until about 1983, the natural rate of unemployment was rising. But since then, a downward trend appears to have taken hold.

For Critical Analysis

Of the various factors that create structural unemployment, which ones do you think explained the gradual trend upward in the natural rate of unemployment from the late 1940s until the 1990s in the United States?

Departures from the Natural Rate of Unemployment

Even though the unemployment rate has a strong tendency to stay at and return to the natural rate, it is possible for fiscal and monetary policy to move the actual unemployment rate away from the natural rate, at least in the short run. Deviations of the actual unemployment rate from the natural rate are called *cyclical unemployment* because they are observed over the course of nationwide business fluctuations. During recessions, the overall unemployment rate exceeds the natural rate; cyclical unemployment is positive. During periods of economic booms, the overall unemployment rate can go below the natural rate; at such times, cyclical unemployment is in essence negative.

To see how departures from the natural rate of unemployment can occur, let's consider two examples. Referring to Figure 18-2, we begin in equilibrium at point *E*, with the associated price level P_1 and real GDP per year of level Y_1.

The Impact of Expansionary Policy.   Now imagine that the government decides to use fiscal or monetary policy to stimulate the economy. Further suppose, for reasons that will soon become clear, that this policy surprises decision makers throughout the economy in the sense that they did not anticipate that the policy would occur. The aggregate demand curve shifts from AD_1 to AD_2 in Figure 18-2, so both the price level and real GDP rise to P_2 and Y_2, respectively. In the labor market, individuals would find that conditions had improved markedly relative to what they expected. Firms seeking to expand output will want to hire more workers. To accomplish this, they will recruit more actively and possibly ask workers to work overtime, so that individuals in the labor market will find more job openings and more possible hours they can work. Consequently, as you learned in Chapter 7, the average duration of unemployment will fall so that the unemployment rate falls. This

FIGURE 18-2

Impact of an Increase in Aggregate Demand on Output and Unemployment

If the economy is operating at E_1, it is in both short-run and long-run equilibrium. Here the actual rate of unemployment is equal to the natural rate of unemployment. Subsequent to expansionary monetary or fiscal policy, the aggregate demand curve shifts outward to AD_2. The price level rises to P_2; real GDP per year increases to Y_2. The new short-run equilibrium is at E_2. The unemployment rate is now below the natural rate of unemployment. We are at a temporary equilibrium at E_2. In the long run, expectations of input owners are revised. The short-run aggregate supply curve shifts from $SRAS_1$ to $SRAS_2$ because of higher prices and higher resource costs. Real GDP returns to the $LRAS$ level of Y_1 per year. The price level increases to P_3.

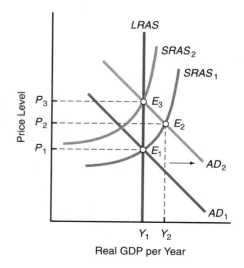

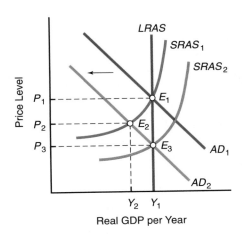

FIGURE 18-3

Impact of a Decline in Aggregate Demand on Output and Unemployment
Starting from equilibrium at E_1, a decline in aggregate demand to AD_2 leads to a lower price level, P_2, and real GDP declines to Y_2. The unemployment rate will rise above the natural rate of unemployment. Equilibrium at E_2 is temporary, however. At the lower price level, the expectations of input owners will be revised. $SRAS_1$ will shift to $SRAS_2$. The new equilibrium will be at E_3, with real GDP equal to Y_1 and a price level of P_3.

unexpected increase in aggregate demand simultaneously causes the price level to rise to P_2 and the unemployment rate to fall. The *SRAS* curve will not stay at $SRAS_1$, however. A change in the expectations of input owners, such as workers and owners of capital and raw materials, will be revised. The short-run aggregate supply curve shifts to $SRAS_2$ as input prices rise. We find ourselves at a new equilibrium at E_3, which is on the *LRAS*. Long-run real GDP per year is Y_1 again, but at a higher price level, P_3.

The Consequences of Contractionary Policy. Instead of expansionary policy, the government could have decided to engage in contractionary (or deflationary) policy. As shown in Figure 18-3, the sequence of events would have been in the opposite direction of those in Figure 18-2. Again, beginning from an initial equilibrium E_1, an unanticipated reduction in aggregate demand puts downward pressure on both prices and real GDP; the price level falls to P_2, and real GDP declines to Y_2. Fewer firms will be hiring, and those that are hiring will offer fewer overtime possibilities. Individuals looking for jobs will find that it takes longer than predicted. As a result, unemployed individuals will remain unemployed longer. The average duration of unemployment will rise, and so will the rate of unemployment. The unexpected decrease in aggregate demand simultaneously causes the price level to fall to P_2 and the unemployment rate to rise. This is a short-run situation only at E_2. $SRAS_1$ will shift to $SRAS_2$ with a change in the expectations of input owners about future prices, and input prices fall. The new equilibrium will be at E_3, which is on the long-run aggregate supply curve, *LRAS*. The price level will have fallen to P_3.

The Phillips Curve: A Trade-Off?

Let's recap what we have just observed. An *unexpected* increase in aggregate demand causes the price level to rise and the unemployment rate to fall. Conversely, an *unexpected* decrease in aggregate demand causes the price level to fall and the unemployment rate to rise. Moreover, although not shown explicitly in either diagram, two additional points are true:

1. The greater the unexpected increase in aggregate demand, the greater the amount of inflation that results, and the lower the unemployment rate.
2. The greater the unexpected decrease in aggregate demand, the greater the deflation that results, and the higher the unemployment rate.

The Negative Relationship Between Inflation and Unemployment.   Figure 18-4 summarizes these findings. The inflation rate (*not* the price level) is measured along the vertical axis, and the unemployment rate is measured along the horizontal axis. Point *A* shows an initial starting point, with the unemployment rate at the natural rate, U^*. Note that as a matter of convenience, we are starting from an equilibrium in which the price level is stable (the inflation rate is zero). Unexpected increases in aggregate demand cause the price level to rise—the inflation rate becomes positive—and cause the unemployment rate to fall. Thus the economy moves up to the left from *A* to *B*. Conversely, unexpected decreases in aggregate demand cause the price level to fall and the unemployment rate to rise above the natural rate—the economy moves from point *A* to point *C*. If we look at both increases and decreases in aggregate demand, we see that high inflation rates tend to be associated with low unemployment rates (as at *B*) and that low (or negative) inflation rates tend to be accompanied by high unemployment rates (as at *C*).

Americans say they are working more hours than ever before. Is that true?

Well, it seems to be true if you ask American workers. Survey after survey shows that full-time workers say they are working more than they were in the 1960s. A more telling examination of 10,000 workers' diaries collected by Professor John Robinson of the University of Maryland tells another story, however. It turns out that Americans today have an average of 40 hours of leisure a week, which is five hours more than their counterparts enjoyed in the 1960s. It is true that Americans still work more hours each year than virtually all Europeans, but they are not working more than previous generations of Americans.

Phillips curve
A curve showing the relationship between unemployment and changes in wages or prices. It was long thought to reflect a trade-off between unemployment and inflation.

Is There a Trade-Off?   The apparent negative relationship between the inflation rate and the unemployment rate shown in Figure 18-4 has come to be called the **Phillips curve,** after A. W. Phillips, who discovered that a similar relationship existed historically in Great Britain. Although Phillips presented his findings only as an empirical regularity, economists quickly came to view the relationship as representing a *trade-off* between inflation and unemployment. In particular, policymakers believed that they could *choose* alternative combinations of unemployment and inflation (or worse, that the trade-off was inevitable because you could not get more of one without giving up the other). Thus it seemed that a government that disliked unemployment could select a point like *B* in Figure 18-4, with a positive inflation rate but a relatively low unemployment rate. Conversely, a government that feared inflation could choose a stable price level at *A,* but only at the expense of a higher associated unemployment rate. Indeed, the Phillips curve seemed to suggest that it was possible for policymakers to fine-tune the economy by selecting the

FIGURE 18-4
The Phillips Curve
Unanticipated changes in aggregate demand produce a negative relationship between the inflation rate and unemployment. *U* * is the natural rate of unemployment.

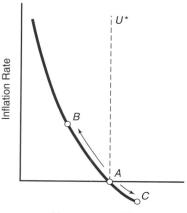

policies that would produce the exact mix of unemployment and inflation that suited current government objectives. As it turned out, matters are not so simple.

The NAIRU. If we accept that a trade-off exists between the rate of inflation and the rate of unemployment, then the notion of "noninflationary" rates of unemployment seems appropriate. In fact, some economists have proposed what they call the **nonaccelerating inflation rate of unemployment (NAIRU).** The NAIRU is therefore the rate of unemployment that corresponds to a stable rate of inflation. When the unemployment rate is less than the NAIRU, the rate of inflation tends to increase. When the unemployment rate is more than the NAIRU, the rate of inflation tends to decrease. When the rate of unemployment is equal to the NAIRU, inflation continues at an unchanged rate. If the Phillips curve trade-off exists and if the NAIRU can be estimated, that estimate will define the short-run trade-off between the rate of unemployment and the rate of inflation. Economists who have estimated the NAIRU for the world's 24 richest industrial countries claim that it has been steadily rising since the 1960s. Critics of the NAIRU concept argue that inflationary expectations must be taken into account.

Nonaccelerating inflation rate of unemployment (NAIRU)
The rate of unemployment below which the rate of inflation tends to rise and above which the rate of inflation tends to fall.

The Importance of Expectations

The reduction in unemployment that takes place as the economy moves from *A* to *B* in Figure 18-4 occurs because the wage offers encountered by unemployed workers are unexpectedly high. As far as the workers are concerned, these higher *nominal* wages appear, at least initially, to be increases in *real* wages; it is this fact that induces them to reduce their duration of search. This is a sensible way for the workers to view the world if aggregate demand fluctuates up and down at random, with no systematic or predictable variation one way or another. But if policymakers attempt to exploit the apparent trade-off in the Phillips curve, according to some macroeconomists, aggregate demand will no longer move up and down in an *unpredictable* way.

The Effects of an Unanticipated Policy. Consider Figure 18-5, for example. If the Federal Reserve attempts to reduce the unemployment rate to U_1, it must increase the money

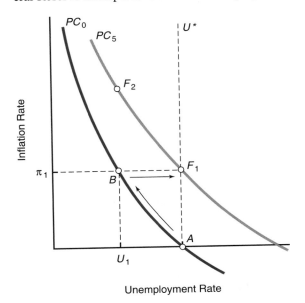

FIGURE 18-5
A Shift in the Phillips Curve
When there is a change in the expected inflation rate, the Phillips curve (*PC*) shifts to incorporate the new expectations. PC_0 shows expectations of zero inflation; PC_5 reflects an expected inflation rate of 5 percent.

supply enough to produce an inflation rate of π_1. If this is an unexpected one-shot affair in which the money supply is first increased and then held constant, the inflation rate will temporarily rise to π_1 and the unemployment rate will temporarily fall to U_1; but as soon as the money supply stops growing, the inflation rate will return to zero and unemployment will return to U^*, its natural rate. Thus an unexpected one-shot increase in the money supply will move the economy from point A to point B, and the economy will move of its own accord back to A.

If the authorities wish to prevent the unemployment rate from returning to U^*, some macroeconomists argue that the Federal Reserve must keep the money supply growing fast enough to keep the inflation rate up at π_1. But if the Fed does this, all of the economic participants in the economy—workers and job seekers included—will come to *expect* that inflation rate to continue. This, in turn, will change their expectations about wages. For example, suppose that π_1 equals 5 percent per year. When the expected inflation rate was zero, a 5 percent rise in nominal wages meant a 5 percent expected rise in real wages, and this was sufficient to induce some individuals to take jobs rather than remain unemployed. It was this perception of a rise in real wages that reduced search duration and caused the unemployment rate to drop from U^* to U_1. But if the expected inflation rate becomes 5 percent, a 5 percent rise in nominal wages means *no* rise in *real* wages. Once workers come to expect the higher inflation rate, rising nominal wages will no longer be sufficient to entice them out of unemployment. As a result, as the *expected* inflation rate moves up from 0 percent to 5 percent, the unemployment rate will move up also.

The Role of Expected Inflation.   In terms of Figure 18-5, as authorities initially increase aggregate demand, the economy moves from point A to point B. If the authorities continue the stimulus in an effort to keep the unemployment rate down, workers' expectations will adjust, causing the unemployment rate to rise. In this second stage, the economy moves from B to point F_1: The unemployment rate returns to the natural rate, U^*, but the inflation rate is now π_1 instead of zero. Once the adjustment of expectations has taken place, any further changes in policy will have to take place along a curve such as PC_5, say, a movement from F_1 to F_2. This new schedule is also a Phillips curve, differing from the first, PC_0, in that the actual inflation rate consistent with any given unemployment rate is higher because the expected inflation rate is higher.

Not surprisingly, when economic policymakers found that economic participants engaged in such adjustment behavior, they were both surprised and dismayed. If decision makers can adjust their expectations to conform with fiscal and monetary policies, then policymakers cannot choose a permanently lower unemployment rate of U_1, even if they are willing to tolerate an inflation rate of π_1. Instead, the policymakers would end up with an unchanged unemployment rate in the long run, at the expense of a permanently higher inflation rate.

Initially, however, there did seem to be a small consolation, for it appeared that in the short run—before expectations adjusted—the unemployment rate could be *temporarily* reduced from U^* to U_1, even though eventually it would return to the natural rate. If an important national election were approaching, it might be possible to stimulate the economy long enough to get the unemployment rate low enough to assure reelection. However, policymakers came to learn that not even this was likely to be a sure thing.

The U.S. Experience with the Phillips Curve

In separate articles in 1968, Milton Friedman and E. S. Phelps published pioneering studies suggesting that the apparent trade-off suggested by the Phillips curve could not be exploited by policymakers. Friedman and Phelps both argued that any attempt to reduce

To try using the Phillips curve as a guide for policymaking in the United Kingdom, go to **http://bized.ac.uk/virtual/ economy/policy** click on "Outcomes," and then click on "Unemployment."

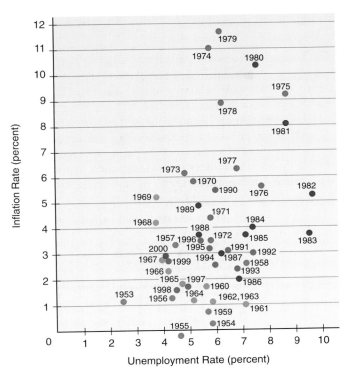

FIGURE 18-6

The Phillips Curve: Theory Versus Data

If you plot points representing the rate of inflation and the rate of unemployment for the United States from 1953 to the present, there does not appear to be any Phillips curve trade-off between the two variables.

Sources: Economic Report of the President; Economic Indicators, various issues.

unemployment by inflating the economy would soon be thwarted by economic participants' incorporating the new higher inflation rate into their expectations. The Friedman-Phelps research thus implies that for any given unemployment rate, *any* inflation rate is possible, depending on the actions of policymakers. As reflected in Figure 18-6, the propositions of Friedman and Phelps were to prove remarkably accurate.

When we examine the data for unemployment and inflation in the United States over the past half century, we see virtually no clear relationship between them. Although there seemed to have been a Phillips curve trade-off between unemployment and inflation from the mid-1950s to the mid-1960s, apparently once people in the economy realized what was happening, they started revising their forecasts accordingly. So once policymakers attempted to exploit the Phillips curve, the presumed trade-off between unemployment and inflation disappeared.

CONCEPTS IN BRIEF

● The natural rate of unemployment is the rate that exists in long-run equilibrium, when workers' expectations are consistent with actual conditions.

● Departures from the natural rate of unemployment can occur when individuals encounter unanticipated changes in fiscal or monetary policy. An unexpected rise in aggregate demand will reduce unemployment below the natural rate, whereas an unanticipated decrease in aggregate demand will push unemployment above the natural rate.

● The Phillips curve exhibits a negative relationship between the inflation rate and the unemployment rate that can be observed when there are *unanticipated* changes in aggregate demand.

● It was originally believed that the Phillips curve represented a trade-off between inflation and unemployment. In fact, no trade-off exists because workers' expectations adjust to any systematic attempts to reduce unemployment below the natural rate.

RATIONAL EXPECTATIONS AND THE NEW CLASSICAL MODEL

You already know that economists assume that economic participants act *as though* they were rational and calculating. We think of firms that rationally maximize profits when they choose today's rate of output and consumers who rationally maximize utility when they choose how much of what goods to consume today. One of the pivotal features of current macro policy research is the assumption that rationality also applies to the way that economic participants think about the future as well as the present. This relationship was developed by Robert Lucas, who won the Nobel Prize in 1995 for his work. In particular, there is widespread agreement among a growing group of macroeconomics researchers that the **rational expectations hypothesis** extends our understanding of the behavior of the macroeconomy. There are two key elements to this hypothesis:

Rational expectations hypothesis
A theory stating that people combine the effects of past policy changes on important economic variables with their own judgment about the future effects of current and future policy changes.

1. Individuals base their forecasts (or expectations) about the future values of economic variables on all available past and current information.
2. These expectations incorporate individuals' understanding about how the economy operates, including the operation of monetary and fiscal policy.

In essence, the rational expectations hypothesis holds that Abraham Lincoln was correct when he said, "You may fool all the people some of the time; you can even fool some of the people all of the time; but you can't fool *all* of the people *all* of the time."

If we further assume that there is pure competition in all markets and that all prices and wages are flexible, we obtain the **new classical model** (referred to in Chapter 13 when discussing the Ricardian equivalence theorem). To see how rational expectations operate within the context of this model, let's take a simple example of the economy's response to a change in monetary policy.

New classical model
A modern version of the classical model in which wages and prices are flexible, there is pure competition in all markets, and the rational expectations hypothesis is assumed to be working.

The New Classical Model

Consider Figure 18-7, which shows the long-run aggregate supply curve (*LRAS*) for the economy, as well as the initial aggregate demand curve (AD_1) and the short-run aggregate supply curve ($SRAS_1$). The money supply is initially given by $M = M_1$, and the price level and real GDP are shown by P_1 and Y_1, respectively. Thus point *A* represents the initial equilibrium.

FIGURE 18-7

Response to an Unanticipated Rise in Aggregate Demand
Unanticipated changes in aggregate demand have real effects. In this case, the rise in demand causes real output to rise from Y_1 to Y_2.

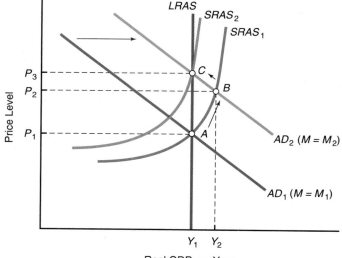

Suppose now that the money supply is unexpectedly increased to M_2, thereby causing the aggregate demand curve to shift outward to AD_2. Given the location of the short-run aggregate supply curve, this increase in aggregate demand will cause output and the price level to rise to Y_2 and P_2, respectively. The new short-run equilibrium is at B. Because output is *above* the long-run equilibrium level of Y_1, unemployment must be below long-run levels (the natural rate), and so workers will soon respond to the higher price level by demanding higher nominal wages. This will cause the short-run aggregate supply curve to shift upward vertically, moving the economy to the new long-run equilibrium at C. The price level thus continues its rise to P_3, even as real GDP declines back down to Y_1 (and unemployment returns to the natural rate). So as we have seen before, even though an increase in the money supply can raise output and lower unemployment in the short run, it has no effect on either variable in the long run.

The Response to Anticipated Policy. Now let's look at this disturbance with the perspective given by the rational expectations hypothesis, as it is embedded in the new classical model. Suppose that workers (and other input owners) know ahead of time that this increase in the money supply is about to take place. Assume also that they know when it is going to occur and understand that its ultimate effect will be to push the price level from P_1 to P_3. Will workers wait until after the price level has increased to insist that their nominal wages go up? The rational expectations hypothesis says that they will not. Instead, they will go to employers and insist on nominal wages that move upward in step with the higher prices. From the workers' perspective, this is the only way to protect their real wages from declining due to the anticipated increase in the money supply.

The Policy Irrelevance Proposition. As long as economic participants behave in this manner, when we draw the *SRAS* curve, we must be explicit about the nature of their expectations. This we have done in Figure 18-8. In the initial equilibrium, the short-run

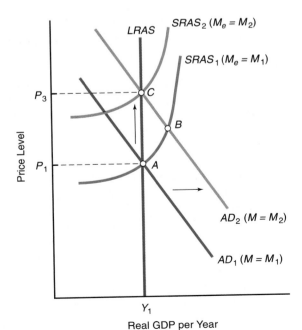

FIGURE 18-8
Effects of an Anticipated Rise in Aggregate Demand
When policy is fully anticipated, a rise in the money supply causes a rise in the price level from P_1 to P_3, with no change in real output.

aggregate supply curve is labeled to show that the expected money supply (M_e) and the actual money supply (M_1) are equal ($M_e = M_1$). Similarly, when the money supply changes in a way that is anticipated by economic participants, the aggregate supply curve shifts to reflect this expected change in the money supply. The new short-run aggregate supply curve is labeled ($M_e = M_2$) to reveal this. According to the rational expectations hypothesis, the short-run aggregate supply will shift upward *simultaneously* with the rise in aggregate demand. As a result, the economy will move directly from point A to point C in Figure 18-8 without passing through B: The *only* response to the rise in the money supply is a rise in the price level from P_1 to P_3; neither output nor unemployment changes at all. This conclusion—that fully anticipated monetary policy is irrelevant in determining the levels of real variables—is called the **policy irrelevance proposition:**

> Under the assumption of rational expectations on the part of decision makers in the economy, anticipated monetary policy cannot alter either the rate of unemployment or the level of real GDP. Regardless of the nature of the anticipated policy, the unemployment rate will equal the natural rate, and real GDP will be determined solely by the economy's long-run aggregate supply curve.

Policy irrelevance proposition
The new classical and rational expectations conclusion that policy actions have no real effects in the short run if the policy actions are anticipated and none in the long run even if the policy actions are unanticipated.

What Must People Know?   There are two important matters to keep in mind when considering this proposition. First, our discussion has assumed that economic participants know in advance exactly what the change in monetary policy is going to be and precisely when it is going to occur. In fact, the Federal Reserve does not announce exactly what the future course of monetary policy (down to the last dollar) is going to be. Instead, the Fed tries to keep most of its plans secret, announcing only in general terms what policy actions are intended for the future. It is tempting to conclude that because the Fed's intended policies are not freely available, they are not available at all. But such a conclusion would be wrong. Economic participants have great incentives to learn how to predict the future behavior of the monetary authorities, just as businesses try to forecast consumer behavior and college students do their best to forecast what their next economics exam will look like. Even if the economic participants are not perfect at forecasting the course of policy, they are likely to come a lot closer than they would in total ignorance. The policy irrelevance proposition really assumes only that *people don't persistently make the same mistakes in forecasting the future.*

What Happens If People Don't Know Everything?   This brings us to our second point. Once we accept the fact that people are not perfect in their ability to predict the future, the possibility emerges that some policy actions will have systematic effects that look much like the movements A to B to C in Figure 18-7. For example, just as other economic participants sometimes make mistakes, it is likely that the Federal Reserve sometimes make mistakes—meaning that the money supply may change in ways that even the Fed does not predict. And even if the Fed always accomplished every policy action it intended, there is no guarantee that other economic participants would fully forecast those actions. What happens if the Fed makes a mistake or if firms and workers misjudge the future course of policy? Matters will look much as they do in panel (a) of Figure 18-9, which shows the effects of an unanticipated increase in the money supply. Economic participants expect the money supply to be M_1, but the actual money supply turns out to be M_2. Because $M_2 > M_1$, aggregate demand shifts relative to aggregate supply. The result is a rise in real output (real GDP) in the short run from Y_1 to Y_2; corresponding to this rise in real output will be an increase in employment and hence a fall in the unemployment rate. So even under the

FIGURE 18-9

Effects of an Unanticipated Rise in Aggregate Demand

Even with rational expectations, an unanticipated change in demand can affect output in the short run.

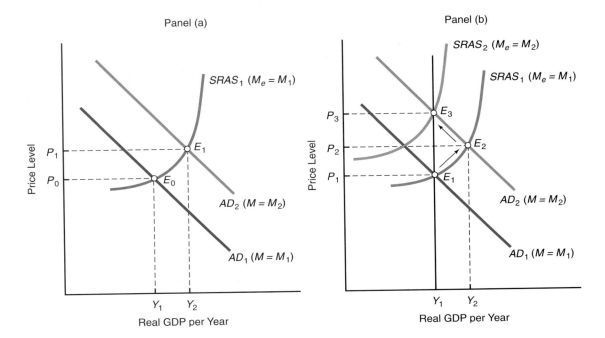

rational expectations hypothesis, monetary policy *can* have an effect on real variables in the short run, but only if the policy is unsystematic and therefore unanticipated.

In the long run, this effect on real variables will disappear because people will figure out that the Fed either accidentally increased the money supply or intentionally increased it in a way that somehow fooled individuals. Either way, people's expectations will soon be revised so that the short-run aggregate supply curve will shift upward. As shown in panel (b) of Figure 18-9, real GDP will return to long-run levels, meaning that so will the employment and unemployment rates.

The Policy Dilemma

Perhaps the most striking and disturbing feature of the new classical model is that it seems to suggest that only mistakes can have real effects. If the Federal Reserve always does what it intends to do and if other economic participants always correctly anticipate the Fed's actions, monetary policy will affect only the price level and nominal input prices. It appears that only if the Fed makes a mistake in executing monetary policy or people err in anticipating that policy will changes in the money supply cause fluctuations in real output and employment. If this reasoning is correct, the Fed is effectively precluded from using monetary policy in any rational way to lower the unemployment rate or to raise the level of real GDP. This is because fully anticipated changes in the money supply will lead to exactly offsetting changes in prices and hence no real effects. Many economists were disturbed at the prospect that if the economy happened to enter a recessionary period, policymakers would be powerless to push real GDP and unemployment back to long-run levels. As a result, they asked, in light of the rational expectations hypothesis, is it *ever* possible for systematic policy to have predictable real effects on the economy? The answer has led to even more developments in the way we think about macroeconomics.

INTERNATIONAL POLICY EXAMPLE

The New Policy Rulebook in a Globalized Economy

Economic events in other countries, such as the financial crises in Eastern Europe and in Asia during the 1990s, have apparently forced the Federal Reserve to take a more global view. This is particularly relevant in how is sets interest rate policies for the United States.

When the economies of Asia suffered severe economic crises, the value of their domestic curriencies fell in international markets. This allowed U.S. companies to buy comodities from these countries at much lower prices in terms of U.S. dollars. These falling commodity prices apparently helped reduce any threat of inflation in the United States during this period. Some observers argue that is why we saw robust economic growth without inflation as well as a surging stock market. Policymakers at the Fed realized that they could continue to increase the money supply at a historically rapid pace without fear of immediate inflation.

At the start of the Asian financial crisis, the U.S. stock market began to falter. The Fed immediately announced several interest rate cuts. Fed policymakers later stated that they wanted to cut rates to avert a credit crunch that could have triggered a global recession.

Clearly, the Fed is taking international developments into account more than ever before when deciding what policy to make for the United States.

For Critical Analysis
In what ways can global events affect the U.S. economy?

CONCEPTS IN BRIEF

- ● The rational expectations hypothesis assumes that individuals' forecasts incorporate all available information, including an understanding of government policy and its effects on the economy.

- ● The new classical economics assumes that the rational expectations hypothesis is valid and also that there is pure competition and that all prices and wages are flexible.

- ● The policy irrelevance proposition says that under the assumptions of the new classical model, fully anticipated monetary policy cannot alter either the rate of unemployment or the level of real GDP.

- ● The new classical model implies that policies can alter real economic variables only if the policies are unsystematic and therefore unanticipated; otherwise people learn and defeat the desired policy goals.

REAL BUSINESS CYCLE THEORY

The modern extension of new classical theory involves reexamining the first principles that assume fully flexible prices.

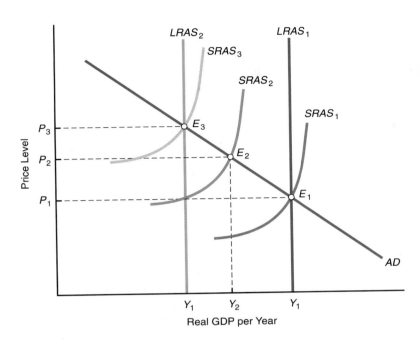

FIGURE 18-10
Effects of a Reduction in the Supply of Resources
The position of the *LRAS* depends on our endowments of all types of resources. Hence a reduction in the supply of one of those resources, such as oil, causes a reduction—an inward shift—in the aggregate supply curve. In addition, there is a rise in the equilibrium price level and a fall in the equilibrium rate of real GDP per year (output).

The Distinction Between Real and Monetary Shocks

The research of the new business cycle theorists differs importantly from that of new classical theorists in that business cycle theorists seek to determine whether real, as opposed to purely monetary, forces might help explain aggregate economic fluctuations. An important stimulus for the development of **real business cycle theory,** as it has come to be known, was the economic turmoil of the 1970s. During that decade, world economies were staggered by two major disruptions to the supply of oil. The first occurred in 1973, the second in 1979. In both episodes, members of the Organization of Petroleum Exporting Countries (OPEC) reduced the amount of oil they were willing to supply and raised the price at which they offered it for sale. Each time, the price level rose sharply in the United States, and real GDP declined. Thus each episode produced a period of "stagflation"—real economic stagnation combined with high inflation. Figure 18-10 illustrates the pattern of events.

We begin at point E_1 with the economy in both short- and long-run equilibrium, with the associated supply curves, $SRAS_1$ and $LRAS_1$. Initially, the level of real GDP is Y_1, and the price level is P_1. Because the economy is in long-run equilibrium, the unemployment rate must be at the natural rate.

A reduction in the supply of oil, as occurred in 1973 and 1979, causes the *SRAS* curve to shift to the left to $SRAS_2$ because fewer goods will be available for sale due to the reduced supplies. If the reduction in oil supplies is (or is believed to be) permanent, the *LRAS* shifts to the left also. This assumption is reflected in Figure 18-10, where $LRAS_2$ shows the new long-run aggregate supply curve associated with the lowered output of oil.

In the short run, two adjustments begin to occur simultaneously. First, the prices of oil and petroleum-based products begin to rise, so that the overall price level rises to P_2. Second, the higher costs of production occasioned by the rise in oil prices induce firms to cut

Real business cycle theory
An extension and modification of the theories of the new classical economists of the 1970s and 1980s, in which money is neutral and only real, supply-side factors matter in influencing labor employment and real output.

back production, so total output falls to Y_2 in the short run. The new temporary short-run equilibrium occurs at E_2, with a higher price level (P_2) and a lower level of real GDP (Y_2).

Impact on the Labor Market

If we were to focus on the labor market while this adjustment from E_1 to E_2 was taking place, we would find two developments occurring. The rise in the price level pushes the real wage rate downward, even as the scaled-back production plans of firms induce them to reduce the amount of labor inputs they are using. So not only does the real wage rate fall, but the level of employment declines as well. On both counts, workers are made worse off due to the reduction in the supply of oil.

Now this is not the full story, because owners of non-oil inputs (such as labor) who are willing to put up with reduced real payments in the short run simply will not tolerate them in the long run. Thus, for example, some workers who were willing to continue working at lower wages in the short run will eventually decide to retire, switch from full-time work to part-time employment, or drop out of the labor force altogether. In effect, there is a reduction in the supply of non-oil inputs, reflected in an upward shift in the $SRAS$ from $SRAS_2$ to $SRAS_3$. This puts additional upward pressure on the price level and exerts a downward force on real GDP. The final long-run equilibrium thus occurs at point E_3, with the price level at P_3 and real GDP at Y_3. (In principle, because the oil supply shock has had no direct effect on labor markets, the natural rate of unemployment does not change when equilibrium moves from E_1 to E_3.)

Generalizing the Theory

Naturally, the focus of real business cycle theory goes well beyond the simple "oil shock" that we have discussed here, for it encompasses all types of real disturbances, including technological changes and shifts in the composition of the labor force. Moreover, a complete treatment of real shocks to the economy is typically much more complex than we have allowed for in our discussion. For example, an oil shock such as is shown in Figure 18-10 would likely also have effects on the real wealth of Americans, causing a reduction in aggregate demand as well as aggregate supply. Nevertheless, our simple example still manages to capture the flavor of the theory.

It is clear that real business cycle theory has improved our understanding of the economy's behavior, but economists agree that it alone is incapable of explaining all of the facets of business cycles that we observe. For example, it is difficult to imagine a real disturbance that could possibly account for the Great Depression in this country, when real income fell more than 30 percent and the unemployment rate rose to 25 percent. Moreover, real business cycle theory continues to assume that prices are perfectly flexible and so fails to explain a great deal of the apparent rigidity of prices throughout the economy.

New Keynesian economics
A macroeconomic approach that emphasizes that the prices of some goods and services adjust sluggishly in response to changing market conditions. Thus an unexpected decrease in the price level results in some firms with higher-than-desired prices. A consequence is a reduction in sales for those firms.

NEW KEYNESIAN ECONOMICS

Although the new classical and real business cycle theories both embody pure competition and flexible prices, a body of research called the **new Keynesian economics** drops both of these assumptions. The new Keynesian economists do not believe that market clearing models of the economy can explain business cycles. Consequently, they argue that macroeconomic models must contain the "sticky" wages and prices assumption that Keynes outlined in his major work (see Chapter 11). Thus the new Keynesian research has as its goal a refinement of the theory of aggregate supply that explains how wages and prices behave in the short run. There are several such theories. The first one relates to the cost of changing prices.

Small Menu Cost Theory

If prices do not respond to demand changes, two conditions must be true: Someone must be consciously deciding not to change prices, and that decision must be in the decision maker's self-interest. One combination of facts that is consistent with this scenario is the **small menu cost theory,** which supposes that much of the economy is characterized by imperfect competition and that it is costly for firms to change their prices in response to changes in demand. The costs associated with changing prices are called *menu costs,* and they include the costs of renegotiating contracts, printing price lists (such as menus), and informing customers of price changes. (But see *Netnomics* on page 444.)

> **Small menu cost theory**
> A hypothesis that it is costly for firms to change prices in response to demand changes because of the cost of renegotiating contracts, printing price lists, and so on.

Many such costs may not be very large in magnitude; that is why they are called *small menu costs.* Some of the costs of changing prices, however, such as those incurred in bringing together business managers from points around the nation or the world for meetings on price changes or renegotiating deals with customers, may be significant.

Firms in different industries have different cost structures. Such differences explain diverse small menu costs. Therefore, the extent to which firms hold their prices constant in the face of changes in demand for their products will vary across industries. Not all prices will be rigid. Nonetheless, new Keynesian theorists argue that many—even most—firms' prices are sticky for relatively long time intervals. As a result, the aggregate level of prices could be very nearly rigid because of small menu costs.

Although most economists agree that such costs exist, there is considerably less agreement on whether they are sufficient to explain the extent of price rigidity that is observed.

Efficiency Wage Theory

An alternative approach within the new Keynesian framework is called the **efficiency wage theory.** It proposes that worker productivity actually *depends on* the wages that workers are paid, rather than being independent of wages, as is assumed in other theories. According to this theory, higher real wages encourage workers to work harder, improve their efficiency, increase morale, and raise their loyalty to the firm. Across the board, then, higher wages tend to increase workers' productivity, which in turn discourages firms from cutting real wages because of the damaging effect that such an action would have on productivity and profitability. Under highly competitive conditions, there will generally be an optimal wage—called the *efficiency wage*—that the firm should continue paying, even in the face of large fluctuations in the demand for its output.

> **Efficiency wage theory**
> The hypothesis that the productivity of workers depends on the level of the real wage rate.

The efficiency wage theory model is a rather simple idea, but it is somewhat revolutionary. All of the models of the labor market adopted by traditional classical, traditional Keynesian, monetarist, new classical, and new Keynesian theorists alike do not consider such real-wage effects on worker productivity.

There are significant, valid elements in the efficiency wage theory, but its importance in understanding national business fluctuations remains uncertain. For example, although the theory explains rigid real wages, it does not explain rigid prices. Moreover, the theory ignores the fact that firms can (and apparently do) rely on a host of incentives other than wages to encourage their workers to be loyal, efficient, and productive.

EXAMPLE

Are the Secretaries of Investment Bankers Overpaid?

Numerous studies have been done to show that secretaries for investment bankers earn considerably more than their counterparts in other sectors of the economy. These studies have taken account of age, education, and length of time on the job. Even when the salary data are corrected for these factors, secretarial pay in the investment banking sector is still much higher than in other sectors. Economist F. R. Mehta of Purdue University suggests that the efficiency wage theory may explain this wage disparity. He argues that in high-productivity industries, managers' time is more valuable. Thus it is more costly for such managers to spend time monitoring employees. To reduce the time highly productive managers (such as investment bankers) spend supervising secretaries, secretaries need additional incentives to keep them working harder and more efficiently. One such incentive is a relatively high rate of pay, one that may seem at an above-market rate. It is therefore rational for highly productive managers as investment bankers to "overpay" their secretaries and others who work under their guidance.

For Critical Analysis
Can you think of other reasons why more profitable firms might pay their secretaries and other workers more than the going wage rate?

Effect of Aggregate Demand Changes on Output and Employment in the Long Run

Some new Keynesian economists argue that a reduction in aggregate demand that causes a recession may affect output and employment even in the long run. They point out that workers who are fired or laid off may lose job skills during their period of unemployment. Consequently, they will have a more difficult time finding new employment later. Furthermore, those who remain unemployed over long periods of time may change their attitudes toward work. They may even have a reduced desire to find employment later on. For these reasons and others, a recession could permanently raise the amount of frictional unemployment.

As yet, little research has been done to quantify this theory.

MACROECONOMIC MODELS AND THEIR IMPLICATIONS FOR STABILIZATION POLICY

Although it is impossible to compare accurately and completely every single detail of the various macroeconomic approaches we have examined, it is useful to summarize and contrast some of their key aspects. Table 18-1 presents features of our five key models: traditional classical, traditional Keynesian, new (modern) classical, new (modern) Keynesian, and modern monetarist. Realize when examining the table that we are painting with a broad brush.

TABLE 18-1
A Comparison of Macroeconomic Models

Issue	Macroeconomic Model				
	Traditional Classical	Traditional Keynesian	New Classical	New Keynesian	Modern Monetarist
Stability of capitalism	Yes	No	Yes	Yes, but can be enhanced by policy	Yes
Price-wage flexibility	Yes	No	Yes	Yes, but imperfect	Yes, but some restraints
Belief in natural rate of employment hypothesis	Yes	No	Yes	Yes	Yes
Factors sensitive to interest rate	Saving, consumption, investment	Demand for money	Saving, consumption, investment	Saving, consumption, investment	Saving, consumption, investment
View of the velocity of money	Stable	Unstable	No consensus	No consensus	Stable
Effect of changes in money supply on economy	Changes aggregate demand	Changes interest rates, which change investment and real output	No effect on real variables if anticipated	Changes aggregate demand	Directly changes aggregate demand
Effects of fiscal policy on the economy	Not applicable	Multiplier changes in aggregate demand and output	Generally ineffective*	Changes aggregate demand	Ineffective unless money supply changes also
Causes of inflation	Excess money growth	Excess real aggregate demand	Excess money growth	Excess money growth	Excess money growth
Stabilization policy	Unnecessary	Fiscal policy necessary and effective; monetary policy ineffective	Too difficult to conduct	Both fiscal and monetary policy may be useful	Too difficult to conduct

*Some fiscal policies affect relative prices (interest rates) and so many have real effects on economy.

CONCEPTS IN BRIEF

● Real business cycle theory holds that even if all prices and wages are perfectly flexible, shocks to the economy (such as technological change and changes in the supply of factors of production) can cause national business fluctuations.

● The new Keynesian economics explains why various features of the economy, such as small menu costs and wage rates that affect productivity, make it possible for monetary shocks to cause real effects.

● Although there remain significant differences between the classical and Keynesian branches of macroeconomics, the rivalry between them is an important source of innovation that helps improve our understanding of the economy.

NETNOMICS

New Keynesian Economics, Sticky Prices, and the Internet

You have read about new Keynesian economics in this chapter. You discovered that new Keynesian economists support the supposition that prices are "sticky." One resulting model is the small menu cost theory. It supposes that much of the economy is characterized by imperfect competition because it is costly for firms to change their prices and respond to changes in demand. Today, many economists believe that the Internet will reduce such supposed price stickiness.

Prices change only when the cost of *not* changing them is greater than the expense of adjusting them. We know that there is virtually no stickiness in prices in financial markets—stocks, bonds, foreign currencies, and so on—because the cost of such price stickiness can be dramatic. The same is true for anyone selling perishable goods. If prices are not reduced downward to eliminate excess quantities supplied, financial losses can be quite great. The existence of the Internet will not change these markets much. Before the Internet, we saw quick movements in prices in response to changing supply and demand in these markets.

Not so elsewhere. Electronic price tags are relatively costless to change. Thus anything that is sold over the Internet can have its price changed instantaneously at the click of a mouse. A travel agency, for example, selling holiday excursions can alter its vacation package prices digitally without any reprinting. Notice also that comparison shopping has become a major activity on the Internet. Any retailer who does not change prices downward in response to an excess quantity supplied will be driven out of the marketplace very quickly. Comparison shopping on the Internet for hotel rooms, airline tickets, CDs, books, and other commodities should cause prices to be far less sticky than just a few years ago. Thus in a sense, the Internet is making competition more intense. Prices will adjust more quickly, thereby undermining macro models that rely on the assumption of price stickiness.

ISSUES & APPLICATIONS

What Happened to the Phillips Curve?

In the 1990s, Dana Mead, the chief executive officer of Tenneco, Inc., quipped, "NAIRU is to economics what the Nehru jacket is to fashion: outdated." (See page 431.) Figure 18-11 provides a rationale for this view. Since 1991, the relationship between inflation and unemployment rates has been shallow and upward-sloping. Through the 1990s, reductions in the unemployment rate were accompanied—to the experts' surprise—by lower, rather than higher, inflation.

Good News and Bad News

This change in the relationship between inflation and unemployment sparked considerable optimism. Many commentators contended that the Internet and other information technologies had transformed the economic landscape. These new sources of economic growth, they claimed, had become self-perpetuating. America had crossed into the territory of a "new economy," and inflation would become a distant memory.

For the Federal Reserve, however, the inverted slope of the Phillips curve posed problems. Fed economists' forecasts of future inflation have been based on Phillips curve models of the inflation process. Starting in the 1990s, the Fed's inflation-forecasting models indicated that inflation was "too low" relative to actual unemployment rates—or, alternatively stated, unemployment was "too low" relative to observed rates of inflation. The Fed's forecasting models consistently indicated that the natural rate of unemployment was close to 6 percent but, as Figure 18-11 indicates, the unemployment rate was consistently 1 to $1\frac{1}{2}$ percent below this level.

Attempting an Explanation

Economists have struggled to explain the shifting inflation-unemployment relationship. Two theories have emerged. One focuses on greater competition in markets for goods and

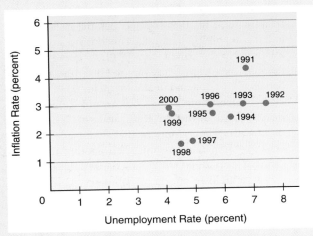

FIGURE 18-11

Inflation and Unemployment Rates Since 1991

During the 1990s, in an apparent contradiction to the standard theory of the short-run Phillips curve, there was an *upward*-sloping relationship between inflation and unemployment rates in the United States.

Sources: Economic Report of the President; Economic Indicators various issues.

1. Can the unemployment rate ever be "too low"?

2. If the age distribution hypothesis concerning the behavior of unemployment rates is correct, when might we expect an upturn in the natural unemployment rate as a result of the "baby boomlet" of the early and mid-1990s, other things being equal?

services following widespread deregulation of many industries, reduced barriers to international trade, and the growth of Internet commerce. This hypothesis proposes that firms in most industries found that the demand for their products was more price-sensitive than it had been before. This left less scope for price changes, which automatically tended to restrain price increases in the face of rising demand. At any given unemployment rate, therefore, increased competition across the economy tends to restrain inflation even as the unemployment rate falls, making the short-run Phillips curve more shallow. In addition, greater competition for goods and services can theoretically reduce the natural rate of unemployment. Both these effects are consistent with the declines in inflation and unemployment depicted in Figure 18-11.

Another theory focuses on the age distribution of the U.S. population. A large fraction of the current population consists of the baby boom generation born between the late 1940s and the late 1950s. This large group reached working age (16) in the 1960s and 1970s. In contrast, fewer people were born between the early 1970s and the early 1980s. These people reached their working years in the late 1980s and 1990s. Unemployment rates for teenagers are always higher than for other groups in the labor force, because most teenagers have only the most rudimentary of skills to offer prospective employers. If we combine this fact with the timing at which different generations reached its teens, we can develop a very simple explanation for why unemployment was higher from the mid-1960s and to the late 1970s: There were a lot of teenagers around, and many of them were unemployed. This factor pushed up the unemployment rate during those years. As the rate of population growth declined, fewer teens were in the labor force, and the unemployment rate naturally fell.

Studies indicate that these two theories can account for 1 to $1\frac{1}{2}$ percentage points of the observed reduction in the U.S. unemployment rate, thereby potentially explaining why unemployment has been "so low" since the early 1990s.

SUMMARY DISCUSSION OF LEARNING OBJECTIVES

1. **Why the Actual Unemployment Rate Might Depart from the Natural Rate of Unemployment:** According to the basic theory of aggregate demand and short- and long-run aggregate supply, an unexpected increase in aggregate demand can cause real GDP to rise in the short run, which results in a reduction in the unemployment rate. Consequently, for a time the actual unemployment rate can fall below the natural rate of unemployment. Likewise, an unanticipated reduction in aggregate demand can push down real GDP in the short run, thereby causing the actual unemployment rate to rise above the natural unemployment rate.

2. **The Phillips Curve:** An unexpected increase in aggregate demand that causes a drop in the unemployment rate also induces a rise in the equilibrium

price level and, consequently, inflation. Thus the basic aggregate demand-aggregate supply model indicates that, other things being equal, there should be an inverse relationship between the inflation rate and the unemployment rate. This downward-sloping relationship is called the Phillips curve, and it implies that there may be a short-run trade-off between inflation and unemployment.

3. **How Expectations Affect the Actual Relationship Between the Inflation Rate and the Unemployment Rate:** Theory only predicts that there will be a Phillips curve relationship when another important factor, expectations, is held unchanged. If people are able to anticipate efforts of policymakers to exploit the Phillips curve trade-off by engaging in inflationary policies to push down the unemployment rate,

then basic theory also suggests that input prices such as nominal wages will adjust more rapidly to an increase in the price level. As a result, the Phillips curve will shift outward, and the economy will adjust more speedily toward the natural rate of unemployment. When plotted on a chart, therefore, the actual relationship between the inflation rate and the unemployment rate will not be a smooth, downward-sloping Phillips curve.

4. **The New Classical Theory and Its Implications for Economic Policymaking:** A key innovation of the new classical approach was the rational expectations hypothesis. According to this hypothesis, people form expectations of future economic variables such as inflation using all available past and current information and based on their understanding of the how the economy functions. A fundamental implication of the new classical theory is that only unanticipated policy actions can induce even short-run changes in real GDP. If people completely anticipate the actions of policymakers, wages and other input prices adjust immediately, so that real GDP remains unaffected. Thus a key implication of new classical theory is the policy irrelevance proposition, which states that the unemployment rate is unaffected by fully anticipated policy actions.

5. **Central Features and Predictions of Real Business Cycle Theory:** The key emphasis of real business cycle theory is on the importance of technological changes and labor market shocks such as variations in the composition of the labor force as factors that can induce business fluctuations. Therefore, this theory focuses on how shifts in aggregate supply curves can cause real GDP to vary over time.

6. **Alternative New Keynesian Views of Business Fluctuations:** New Keynesian approaches to understanding the sources of business fluctuations highlight wage and price stickiness. Small-menu cost theory proposes that imperfectly competitive firms that face costs of adjusting their prices may be slow to change prices in the face of variations in demand, so that real GDP may exhibit greater short-run variability than it otherwise would. Another new Keynesian approach, efficiency wage theory, proposes that worker productivity depends on the real wages that workers earn, which dissuades firms from reducing real wages and thereby leads to widespread wage stickiness. Finally, some new Keynesian theorists propose that short-term downturns in economic activity can affect the natural unemployment rate because people who lose their jobs in the short run also lose the opportunities to develop skills while unemployed or may change their attitudes toward work.

Key Terms and Concepts

Active (discretionary) policymaking (426)

Efficiency wage theory (441)

New classical model (434)

New Keynesian economics (440)

Nonaccelerating Inflation Rate of Unemployment (NAIRU) (431)

Passive (nondiscretionary) policymaking (426)

Phillips curve (430)

Policy irrelevance proposition (436)

Rational expectations hypothesis (434)

Real business cycle theory (439)

Small menu cost theory (441)

Problems

Answers to the odd-numbered problems appear at the back of the book.

18-1. Suppose that the government were to alter the computation of the unemployment rate by including people in the military as part of the labor force.

a. How would this affect the actual unemployment rate?

b. How would such a change affect estimates of the natural rate of unemployment?

c. If this computational change were made, would it in any way affect the logic of the short-run and long-run Phillips curve analysis and its implications for policymaking? Why might the government wish to make such a change?

18-2. When Alan Greenspan was nominated for his third term as chair of the Federal Reserve's Board of Governors, a few senators held up his nomination. One of them acted as spokesperson in explaining their joint action to hinder his approval, saying, "Every time growth starts to go up, they [the Federal Reserve] push on the brakes, robbing working families and businesses of the benefits of faster growth." Evaluate this statement in the context of short-run and long-run perspectives on the Phillips curve.

18-3. Economists have not reached agreement on how lengthy the time horizon for "the long run" is in the context of analysis of the Phillips curve. Would you anticipate that this period is likely to have been shortened or extended by the advent of more sophisticated computer and communications technology? Explain your reasoning.

18-4. The natural rate of unemployment depends on factors that affect the behavior of both workers and firms. Make lists of possible factors affecting both workers and firms that you believe are likely to influence the natural rate of unemployment.

18-5. People called "Fed watchers" earn their living by trying to forecast what policies the Federal Reserve will implement within the next few weeks and months. Suppose that Fed watchers discover that the current group of Fed officials is following very systematic and predictable policies intended to reduce the unemployment rate, and they sell this information to firms, unions, and others in the private sector. If the new classi-

cal theory is correct, are the Fed's policies likely to have their intended effects on the unemployment rate?

18-6. Evaluate the following statement: "In an important sense, the term *policy irrelevance proposition* is misleading because even in the new classical model, economic policy actions can have significant effects on real GDP and the unemployment rate."

18-7. Real business cycle theory attributes even short-run increases in real GDP largely to changes in aggregate supply. Rightward shifts in aggregate supply tend to push down the equilibrium price level. How, then, could a real business cycle theorist explain the low but persistent inflation that the United States has experienced in recent years?

18-8. Does the Federal Reserve have any role in real business cycle theory? If so, what is it?

18-9. Use an aggregate demand and aggregate supply diagram to illustrate why the existence of widespread stickiness in prices established by businesses throughout the economy would be extremely important to predicting the potential effects of policy actions on real GDP.

18-10. Economists have also established that higher productivity due to technological improvements tends to push up real wages. Now suppose that the economy experiences a host of technological improvements. If the efficiency wage theory is correct, meaning that worker productivity responds positively to higher real wages, will this effect tend to add to or subtract from the economic growth initially induced by the improvements in technology?

Economics on the Net

The Inflation-Unemployment Relationship

According to the basic aggregate demand and aggregate supply model, the unemployment rate should be inversely related to changes in the inflation rate, other things being equal. This application allows you to take a direct look at unemployment and inflation data to judge for yourself whether or not the two variables appear to be related.

Internet URL: http://stats.bls.gov/eag.table.html

Title: Bureau of Labor Statistics: Economy at a Glance

Navigation: Begin at the home page of the Bureau of Labor Statistics (http://stats.bls.gov). Then click on Economy at a Glance.

Application Perform the indicated operations, and then answer the following questions.

1. Click on Economy at a Glance. Then scan down to Prices, and click on Consumer Price Index. Take a look at the solid line showing inflation in the graph box. How much has inflation varied in recent years? Compare this with previous years, especially the mid-1970s to mid-1980s.

2. Back up to Economy at a Glance, and now click on Unemployment Rate. Take a look at the graph box. During what recent years was the unemployment rate approaching and at its peak value? Do you note any appearance of an inverse relationship between the unemployment rate and the inflation rate?

For Group Study and Analysis Divide the class into groups, and have each group search through the Economy at a Glance site to develop an explanation for the key factors accounting for the recent behavior of the unemployment rate. Have each group report on its explanation. Is there any one factor that best explains the recent behavior of the unemployment rate?

Case Background

The year is 2029. A special Federal Reserve task force is gathered around the huge mahogany table in the Federal Reserve Board's headquarters meeting room in its building on Constitution Avenue in Washington, D.C. The mission of the task force is to chart the Federal Reserve System's long-term future. At the moment, that future is not bright.

More than a Decade of Change The senior economist whom the task force has charged with researching the current situation summarizes the findings of the Board's economic staff. Estimates indicate that 75 percent of all Americans conduct their financial affairs on-line directly from home. Roughly 95 percent use smart cards to make cash purchases on-line, either from their homes or using kiosks in a wide variety of locations. Only in pockets of rural America is physical cash still the predominant means of payment.

Furthermore, there are now literally tens of thousands of issuers of digital cash accounts that people access using the FinNet, the nationwide on-line financial services network. Any business can issue what once were called transactions deposits (some old-fashioned economists at the Fed still use this term, but *smart accounts* is the more common name for these accounts). The many firms that offer smart accounts settle their payments obligations using private payment intermediaries based on the FinNet. Smart cards and debit cards became indistinguishable a decade ago. Retailers commonly add surcharges to the purchase prices of goods and services when people use paper checks, so even the stodgiest of retired baby boomers have given up on using checks.

These changes have already had significant effects on the Federal Reserve. Its retail product office in Atlanta, which once processed many millions of checks each day, is now a cavernous shell with a handful of employees. The wholesale product office in New York continues to serve as a central conduit for trillions of dollars of daily "interbank" payments, but it now specializes in providing these clearing services on-line in competition with a dozen private providers.

Sharpening the Fed's Mission The Fed has already undergone some major downsizing. Employment at the Fed has shrunk by 70 percent since the turn of the century, and half of current employees do work related to payment clearing, compared to about 80 percent 20 years ago. Many of these work as financial "cyberpolice," seeking to protect the FinNet from hackers, scam artists, and money launderers. Fed examiners also audit the virtual accounting ledgers of the conglomerates that provide financial services, a task assigned to it since the Gramm-Leach-Bliley Act was passed at the end of the last century.

Nevertheless, concludes the senior economist in her briefing of the Fed's task force, it may be time to contemplate additional steps. She proposes that the task force consider the following possibilities for a new Fed of the mid-twenty-first century:

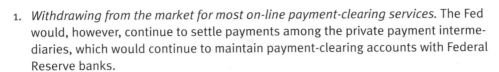

1. *Withdrawing from the market for most on-line payment-clearing services.* The Fed would, however, continue to settle payments among the private payment intermediaries, which would continue to maintain payment-clearing accounts with Federal Reserve banks.

2. *Continuing to supervise the activities of financial services conglomerates.* The Fed has long-standing expertise in this area. Other agencies of the U.S. government would be hard-pressed to duplicate this function.

3. *Ceding the Fed's current cyberpolicing role to the Treasury's Secret Service and to the Federal Bureau of Investigation.* This would eliminate wasteful duplication within the government that has attracted the ire of several powerful members of the Senate and House of Representatives, who also complain that the Fed has sometimes come close to violations of Net privacy laws enacted early in the century.

Points to Analyze

1. In what ways is this Fed of the not-so-distant future much different from today's Federal Reserve System?

2. In what ways is this Fed of the not-so-distant future very much like today's Federal Reserve System?

3. Should this future Fed, or other government agencies, act as a cyberpolice force? Why or why not?

4. Should this future Fed—or, for that matter, today's Fed—"worry" about volatility of interest rates? Why?

Casing the Internet

1. Go to the Web site of *Netbanker* at www.netbanker.com.
   a. What progress are Internet banks making in the marketplace?
   b. Read a free sample issue of Netbanker, and explore some of the links to Internet banks and credit unions. What are some similarities and differences among current approaches to Internet banking?

2. Visit the eCash Technologies, Inc., Web site at www.ecashtechnologies.com.
   a. How do digital cash transactions work?
   b. View on-line demonstrations by clicking on "eCash demonstration." What factors do you believe currently stand in the way of widespread adoption of digital cash by the average account holder?

3. Learn more about the evolution of and newest innovations in smart card technology at www.cardshow.com/guide/index.html.
   a. Explore this Web site. In our scenario for the world of 2029, digital cash and smart cards are commonplace. Nevertheless, smart cards have not yet caught on in the United States. Based on what you have learned in this text and your review of the Cardshow Web site, why do you think that people are not yet rushing to use smart cards?
   b. Should the U.S. government use taxpayer funds to promote the use of smart cards in the interest of the greater good? Take a stand, and support your answer.

Part 8
Global Economics

COMPARATIVE ADVANTAGE AND THE OPEN ECONOMY

These cars built in Japan are being unloaded in Baltimore. Who would lose and who would gain if imports of Japanese cars were outlawed?

LEARNING OBJECTIVES

After reading this chapter, you should be able to:

1. **Discuss the worldwide importance of international trade**

2. **Explain why nations can gain from specializing in production and engaging in international trade**

3. **Distinguish between comparative advantage and absolute advantage**

4. **Understand common arguments against free trade**

5. **Describe ways that nations restrict foreign trade**

6. **Identify key international agreements and organizations that adjudicate trade disputes among nations**

An American businessman visiting an emerging economy came upon a team of about 100 workers using shovels to move earth next to a stream. His guide told him that several days earlier, a local government agency had assigned the people to build a dam. Later, the businessman told a local official about a U.S. company that was offering discounts on earth-moving machines. "With such a machine," the businessman boasted, "one worker could build that dam in a single afternoon." The official replied, "Of course. But think of all the unemployment that importing such a machine would create." The businessman then said, "Oh, I thought you were building a dam. If it's jobs you want to create, take away the workers' shovels and give them spoons!"

In this chapter, you will learn that U.S. exports to other nations do not necessarily cause workers in those nations to lose their jobs or earn lower pay. Nor do American imports of goods from other nations necessitate *net* job losses or pay cuts in the United States. Nevertheless, workers in certain industries often unite with owners and managers to oppose free trade. In this chapter, you will learn the elements of international trade, as well as the arguments for and against free trade.

Did You Know That... most U.S. imports come from a few developed countries? In fact, about two-thirds of imported goods and services are produced in nations that economists classify as high-wage countries. Only 10 percent of U.S. imports come from countries classified as low-wage nations. The remainder of U.S. imports are produced in middle-income countries located mainly in Latin America and Southeast Asia.

The workers residing in nations from which Americans import most of their goods earn relatively high wages. Recent studies indicate that manufacturing wages paid to workers who live and work in twenty-five nations that engage in the most trade with the United States have have risen steadily. In 1975, manufacturing workers in these top U.S. trading partners earned 65 percent of the U.S. compensation level. Today, the wages of these workers have reached 95 percent of the U.S. compensation level.

Without international trade, many people who work to produce goods for sale to other nations would have to find other employment. Some might even have trouble finding work. Nevertheless, other people in these countries would undoubtedly stand to gain from restricting international trade. Learning about international trade will help you understand why this is so.

THE WORLDWIDE IMPORTANCE OF INTERNATIONAL TRADE

Look at panel (a) of Figure 32-1. Since the end of World War II, world output of goods and services (world gross domestic product, or GDP) has increased almost every year until the present, when it is almost six times what it was. Look at the top line in panel (a). World trade has increased to more than 13 times what it was in 1950.

The United States figured prominently in this expansion of world trade. In panel (b) of Figure 32-1, you see imports and exports expressed as a percentage of total annual yearly income (GDP). Whereas imports added up to barely 4 percent of annual national income in 1950, today they account for over 12 percent. International trade has definitely become more important to the economy of the United States. Trade may become even more important in the United States as other countries start to loosen their trade restrictions.

For the most recent data on world trade, go to **www.wto.org** and click on "Statistics."

INTERNATIONAL EXAMPLE

The Importance of International Trade in Various Countries

Whereas both imports and exports in the United States each account for more than 10 percent of total annual national income, in some countries the figure is much greater (see Table 32-1). Consider that Luxembourg must import practically everything!

Another way to understand the worldwide importance of international trade is to look at trade flows on the world map in Figure 32-2 on page 786. You can see that the United States trades more with Europe than with other parts of the world.

For Critical Analysis
How can Luxembourg have a strong economy if it imports so many goods and services?

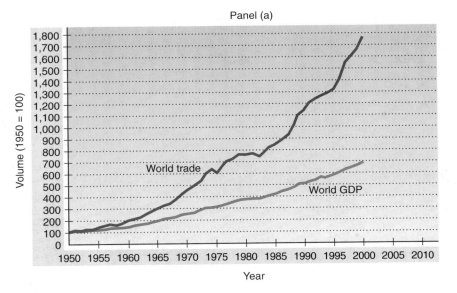

Panel (a)

Panel (b)

FIGURE 32-1
The Growth of World Trade
In panel (a), you can see the growth in world trade in relative terms because we use an index of 100 to represent real world trade in 1950. By the early 2000s, that index had increased to over 1,700. At the same time, the index of world GDP (annual world income) had gone up to only around 700. World trade is clearly on the rise: Both imports and exports, expressed as a percentage of annual national income (GDP) in panel (b), have been rising.

Sources: Steven Husted and Michael Melvin, *International Economics,* 3d ed. (New York: HarperCollins, 1995), p. 11, used with permission; World Trade Organization; Federal Reserve System; U.S. Department of Commerce.

Country	Imports as a Percentage of Annual National Income
Luxembourg	95.0
Netherlands	58.0
Norway	30.0
Canada	23.5
Germany	23.0
United Kingdom	21.0
China	19.0
France	18.4
Japan	6.8

Source: International Monetary Fund.

TABLE 32-1
Importance of Imports in Selected Countries
Residents of some nations spend much of their incomes on imported goods and services.

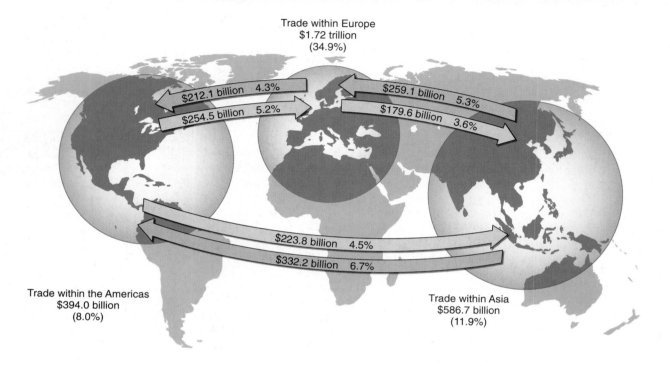

FIGURE 32-2
World Trade Flows
International merchandise trade amounts to over $3 trillion worldwide. The percentage figures show the proportion of trade flowing in the various directions.
Source: World Trade Organization (data are for 2000).

WHY WE TRADE: COMPARATIVE ADVANTAGE AND MUTUAL GAINS FROM EXCHANGE

You have already been introduced to the concept of specialization and mutual gains from trade in Chapter 2. These concepts are worth repeating because they are essential to understanding why the world is better off because of more international trade. The best way to understand the gains from trade among nations is first to understand the output gains from specialization between individuals.

The Output Gains from Specialization

Suppose that a creative advertising specialist can come up with two pages of ad copy (written words) an hour or generate one computerized art rendering per hour. At the same time, a computer artist can write one page of ad copy per hour or complete one computerized art rendering per hour. Here the ad specialist can come up with more pages of ad copy per hour than the computer specialist and seemingly is just as good as the computer specialist at doing computerized art renderings. Is there any reason for the creative specialist and the computer specialist to "trade"? The answer is yes, because such trading will lead to higher output.

Consider the scenario of no trading. Assume that during each eight-hour day, the ad specialist and the computer whiz devote half of their day to writing ad copy and half to computerized art rendering. The ad specialist would create eight pages of ad copy (4 hours × 2) and four computerized art renderings (4 × 1). During that same period, the computer specialist would create four pages of ad copy (4 × 1) and four computerized art renderings (4 × 1). Each day, the combined output for the ad specialist and the computer specialist would be 12 pages of ad copy and eight computerized art renderings with no decline in art renderings.

If the ad specialist specialized only in writing ad copy and the computer whiz specialized only in creating computerized art renderings, their combined output would rise to 16 pages of ad copy (8 × 2) and eight computerized art renderings (8 × 1). Overall, production would increase by four pages of ad copy per day.

The creative advertising employee has a comparative advantage in writing ad copy, and the computer specialist has a comparative advantage in doing computerized art renderings. **Comparative advantage** derives from the ability to produce something at a lower opportunity cost than other producers, as we pointed out in Chapter 2.

For data on U.S. trade with all other nations of the world go to **www.census.gov/foreign-trade/balance/index.html**

Comparative advantage
The ability to produce a good or service at a lower opportunity cost than other producers.

Specialization Among Nations

To demonstrate the concept of comparative advantage for nations, let's take the example of France and the United States. In Table 32-2, we show the comparative costs of production of wine and beer in terms of worker-days. This is a simple two-country, two-commodity world in which we assume that labor is the only factor of production. As you can see from the table, in the United States, it takes one worker-day to produce 1 liter of wine, and the same is true for 1 liter of beer. In France, it takes one worker-day to produce 1 liter of wine but two worker-days for 1 liter of beer. In this sense, Americans appear to be just as good at producing wine as the French and actually have an **absolute advantage** in producing beer.

Trade will still take place, however, which may seem paradoxical. How can trade take place if we can seemingly produce both goods at least as cheaply as the French can? Why don't we just produce both ourselves? To understand why, let's assume first that there is no trade and no specialization and that the workforce in each country consists of 200 workers. These 200 workers are, by assumption, divided equally in the production of wine and beer. We see in Table 32-3 on the next page that 100 liters of wine and 100 liters of beer are produced per day in the United States. In France, 100 liters of wine and 50 liters of beer are produced per day. The total daily world production in our two-country world is 200 liters of wine and 150 liters of beer.

Now the countries specialize. What can France produce more cheaply? Look at the comparative costs of production expressed in worker-days in Table 32-2. What is the cost of producing 1 liter more of wine? One worker-day. What is the cost of producing 1 liter more of beer? Two worker-days. We can say, then, that in terms of the value of beer given up, in France the opportunity cost of producing wine is lower than in the United States. France will specialize in the activity that has the lower opportunity cost. In other words, France will specialize in its comparative advantage, which is the production of wine.

Absolute advantage
The ability to produce more output from given inputs of resources than other producers can.

Product	United States (worker-days)	France (worker-days)
Wine (1 liter)	1	1
Beer (1 liter)	1	2

TABLE 32-2
Comparative Costs of Production

TABLE 32-3
Daily World Output Before Specialization
It is assumed that 200 workers are available in each country.

Product	United States		France		World Output (liters)
	Workers	Output (liters)	Workers	Output (liters)	
Wine	100	100	100	100	200
Beer	100	100	100	50	150

According to Table 32-4, after specialization, the United States produces 200 liters of beer and France produces 200 liters of wine. Notice that the total world production per day has gone up from 200 liters of wine and 150 liters of beer to 200 liters of wine and 200 liters of beer per day. This was done without any increased use of resources. The gain, 50 "free" liters of beer, results from a more efficient allocation of resources worldwide. World output is greater when countries specialize in producing the goods in which they have a comparative advantage and then engage in foreign trade. Another way of looking at this is to consider the choice between two ways of producing a good. Obviously, each country would choose the less costly production process. One way of "producing" a good is to import it, so if in fact the imported good is cheaper than the domestically produced good, we will "produce" it by importing it. Not everybody, of course, is better off when free trade occurs. In our example, U.S. wine makers and French beer makers are worse off because those two *domestic* industries have disappeared.

TABLE 32-4
Daily World Output After Specialization
It is assumed that 200 workers are available in each country.

Product	United States		France		World Output (liters)
	Workers	Output (liters)	Workers	Output (liters)	
Wine	—	—	200	200	200
Beer	200	200	—	—	200

Some people are worried that the United States (or any country, for that matter) might someday "run out of exports" because of overaggressive foreign competition. The analysis of comparative advantage tells us the contrary. No matter how much other countries compete for our business, the United States (or any other country) will always have a comparative advantage in something that it can export. In 10 or 20 years, that something may not be what we export today, but it will be exportable nonetheless because we will have a comparative advantage in producing it.

Other Benefits from International Trade: The Transmission of Ideas

Beyond the fact that comparative advantage results in an overall increase in the output of goods produced and consumed, there is another benefit to international trade. International trade bestows benefits on countries through the international transmission of ideas. According to economic historians, international trade has been the principal means by which new goods, services, and processes have spread around the world. For example, coffee was initially grown in Arabia near the Red Sea. Around A.D. 675, it began to be roasted

Putting
Economics in Action to Work

For more practice applying the concepts of comparative and absolute advantage, start the *EIA* CD and click on "Trade and Exchange Rates." Then click on "HRI Evaluates Gains from Trade."

and consumed as a beverage. Eventually, it was exported to other parts of the world, and the Dutch started cultivating it in their colonies during the seventeenth century and the French in the eighteenth century. The lowly potato is native to the Peruvian Andes. In the sixteenth century, it was brought to Europe by Spanish explorers. Thereafter, its cultivation and consumption spread rapidly. It became part of the American agricultural scene in the early eighteenth century.

All of the *intellectual property* that has been introduced throughout the world is a result of international trade. This includes new music, such as rock and roll in the 1950s and hip-hop and grunge in the 1990s. It includes the software applications that are common for computer users everywhere.

New processes have been transmitted through international trade. One of those involves the Japanese manufacturing innovation that emphasized redesigning the system rather than running the existing system in the best possible way. Inventories were reduced to just-in-time levels by reengineering machine setup methods. Just-in-time inventory control is now common in American factories.

INTERNATIONAL EXAMPLE

International Trade and the Alphabet

Even the alphabetic system of writing that appears to be the source of most alphabets in the world today was spread through international trade. According to some scholars, the Phoenicians, who lived on the long, narrow strip of Mediterranean coast north of Israel from the ninth century B.C. to around 300 B.C., created the first true alphabet. Presumably, they developed the alphabet to keep international trading records on their ships rather than having to take along highly trained scribes.

For Critical Analysis
Before alphabets were used, how might have people communicated in written form?

THE RELATIONSHIP BETWEEN IMPORTS AND EXPORTS

The basic proposition in understanding all of international trade is this:

In the long run, imports are paid for by exports.*

The reason that imports are ultimately paid for by exports is that foreigners want something in exchange for the goods that are shipped to the United States. For the most part, they want goods made in the United States. From this truism comes a remarkable corollary:

Any restriction of imports ultimately reduces exports.

This is a shocking revelation to many people who want to restrict foreign competition to protect domestic jobs. Although it is possible to protect certain U.S. jobs by restricting foreign competition, it is impossible to make *everyone* better off by imposing import restrictions. Why? Because ultimately such restrictions lead to a reduction in employment in the export industries of the nation.

View the most recent trade statistics for the United States at **www.census.gov/indicator/ www/ustrade.html**

---

*We have to modify this rule by adding that in the short run, imports can also be paid for by the sale (or export) of real and financial assets, such as land, stocks, and bonds, or through an extension of credit from other countries.

INTERNATIONAL EXAMPLE

The Importation of Priests into Spain

Imports affect not only goods but also services and the movement of labor. In Spain, some 3,000 priests retire each year, but barely 250 young men are ordained to replace them. Over 70 percent of the priests in Spain are now over the age of 50. The Spanish church estimates that by 2005, the number of priests will have fallen to half the 20,441 who were active in Spain in 1990. The Spanish church has had to seek young seminarians from Latin America under what it calls Operation Moses. It is currently subsidizing the travel and training of an increasing number of young Latin Americans to take over where native Spaniards have been before.

For Critical Analysis
How might the Catholic church in Spain induce more native Spaniards to become priests?

INTERNATIONAL COMPETITIVENESS

"The United States is falling behind." "We need to stay competitive internationally." These and similar statements are often heard in government circles when the subject of international trade comes up. There are two problems with this issue. The first has to do with a simple definition. What does "global competitiveness" really mean? When one company competes against another, it is in competition. Is the United States like one big corporation, in competition with other countries? Certainly not. The standard of living in each country is almost solely a function of how well the economy functions *within that country,* not relative to other countries.

Another problem arises with respect to the real world. According to the Institute for Management Development in Lausanne, Switzerland, the United States continues to lead the pack in overall productive efficiency, ahead of Japan, Germany, and the rest of the European Union. According to the report, America's top-class ranking is due to the sustained U.S. economic recovery following its 1990–1991 recession, widespread entrepreneurship, and a decade of economic restructuring. Other factors include America's sophisticated financial system and large investments in scientific research.

 FAQ

Don't productivity improvements in other countries erode the competitive position of the United States?

International trade is not a zero-sum game: If China becomes more productive, this does not mean that the United States is now less productive. A more productive China will certainly have more products to market to American consumers. It will also have higher-quality products to sell at lower prices than before, which benefits consumers in the United States who buy Chinese goods. Furthermore, China's national income will rise as a result of its productivity improvement. Consequently, it will become a bigger potential market for U.S. exports. Thus other nations can experience economic success without in any way reducing the ability of U.S. firms to produce efficiently and compete with foreign producers.

CONCEPTS IN BRIEF

- Countries can be better off materially if they specialize in producing goods for which they have a comparative advantage.

- It is important to distinguish between absolute and comparative advantage; the former refers to the ability to produce a unit of output with fewer physical units of input; the latter refers to producing output that has the lowest opportunity cost for a nation.

- Different nations will always have different comparative advantages because of differing opportunity costs due to different resource mixes.

ARGUMENTS AGAINST FREE TRADE

Numerous arguments are raised against free trade. They mainly point out the costs of trade; they do not consider the benefits or the possible alternatives for reducing the costs of free trade while still reaping benefits.

The Infant Industry Argument

A nation may feel that if a particular industry were allowed to develop domestically, it could eventually become efficient enough to compete effectively in the world market. Therefore, if some restrictions were placed on imports, domestic producers would be given the time needed to develop their efficiency to the point where they would be able to compete in the domestic market without any restrictions on imports. In graphic terminology, we would expect that if the protected industry truly does experience improvements in production techniques or technological breakthroughs toward greater efficiency in the future, the supply curve will shift outward to the right so that the domestic industry can produce larger quantities of each and every price. National policymakers often conclude that this **infant industry argument** has some merit in the short run. They have used it to protect a number of industries in their infancy around the world.

    Such a policy can be abused, however. Often the protective import-restricting arrangements remain even after the infant has matured. If other countries can still produce more cheaply, the people who benefit from this type of situation are obviously the stockholders (and specialized factors of production that will earn economic rents) in the industry that is still being protected from world competition. The people who lose out are the consumers, who must pay a price higher than the world price for the product in question. In any event, it is very difficult to know beforehand which industries will eventually survive. In other words, we cannot predict very well the specific infant industries that policymakers might deem worthy of protection. Note that when we speculate about which industries "should" be protected, we are in the realm of *normative economics*. We are making a value judgment, a subjective statement of what *ought to be*.

Infant industry argument
The contention that tariffs should be imposed to protect from import competition an industry that is trying to get started. Presumably, after the industry becomes technologically efficient, the tariff can be lifted.

EXAMPLE

An Infant Industry Blossoms Due to Protection from Foreign Imports: Marijuana

Marijuana was made illegal in the United States in the 1930s, but just as for many other outlawed drugs, a market for it remained. Until about 25 years ago, virtually all the marijuana consumed in the United States was imported. Today, earnings from the burgeoning and increasingly high-tech "pot" industry are estimated at $35 billion a year, making it the nation's biggest cash crop (compared to corn at $15 billion). Starting with President Richard Nixon in the 1970s, the federal government has ended up protecting the domestic marijuana industry from imports by declaring a war on drugs. Given virtually no foreign competition, the American marijuana industry expanded and invested millions in developing both more productive and more potent seeds as well as more efficient growing technologies. Domestic marijuana growers now dominate the high end of a market in which consumers pay $300 to $500 an ounce for a reengineered home-grown product. New growing technologies allow domestic producers, using high-intensity sodium lights, carbon dioxide, and advances in genetics, to produce a kilogram of the potent sinsemilla variety every two months in a space no bigger than a phone booth.

For Critical Analysis
What has spurred domestic producers to develop highly productive indoor growing methods?

For a review of antidumping actions in the United States and around the world, go to **www.cbo.gov/showdoc. cfm?index=439&sequence= 0&from=1**

Dumping
Selling a good or a service abroad below the price charged in the home market or at a price below its cost of production.

Countering Foreign Subsidies and Dumping

Another strong argument against unrestricted foreign trade has to do with countering other nations' subsidies to their own producers. When a foreign government subsidizes its producers, our producers claim that they cannot compete fairly with these subsidized foreigners. To the extent that such subsidies fluctuate, it can be argued that unrestricted free trade will seriously disrupt domestic producers. They will not know when foreign governments are going to subsidize their producers and when they are not. Our competing industries will be expanding and contracting too frequently.

The phenomenon called *dumping* is also used as an argument against unrestricted trade. **Dumping** is said to occur when a producer sells its products abroad below the price that is charged in the home market or at a price below its cost of production. When a foreign producer is accused of dumping, further investigation usually reveals that the foreign nation is in the throes of a recession. The foreign producer does not want to slow down its production at home. Because it anticipates an end to the recession and doesn't want to hold large inventories, it dumps its products abroad at prices below home prices. U.S. competitors may also allege that it sells its output at prices below its costs in an effort to cover at least part of its variable costs of production. Dumping does disrupt international trade. It also creates instability in domestic production and therefore may impair commercial well-being at home.

INTERNATIONAL POLICY EXAMPLE

Who's Dumping on Whom?

Claims of dumping are handled on a case-by-case basis under international rules. Only a few firms in an industry have to lodge a claim to justify a dumping investigation. Under international law, antidumping rules permit governments to impose *duties*—special taxes on imported goods—on the products sold by firms of offending nations. Take a look at Figure 32-3. As you can see, in the early 1990s, developed nations filed an

FIGURE 32-3

Claims to the World Trade Organization for Antidumping Relief
In recent years, developing nations have filed at least as many claims seeking antidumping relief as the number filed by developed nations.

Source: World Trade Organization.

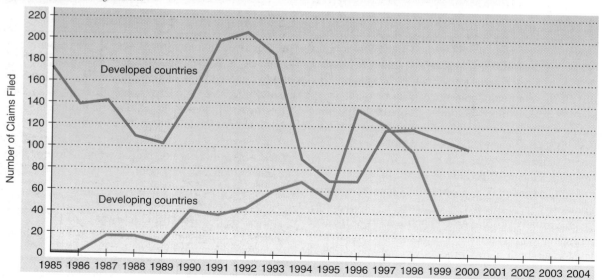

increasing number of claims seeking antidumping relief. The biggest filer of dumping claims during this period was the United States, which launched cases mainly against companies based in South America and Asia. The United States began to cut back on dumping claims beginning in the mid-1990s. Nevertheless, dumping claims by emerging economies—notably Argentina, Brazil, Mexico, and South Africa—rose precipitously. Whom did these emerging economies accuse of dumping? Firms in the United States, of course.

For Critical Analysis

Why did dumping claims by emerging nations fall as their economies expanded after the early 1990s?

Protecting American Jobs

Perhaps the argument used most often against free trade is that unrestrained competition from other countries will eliminate American jobs because other countries have lower-cost labor than we do. (Less restrictive environmental standards in other countries might also lower their private costs relative to ours.) This is a compelling argument, particularly for politicians from areas that might be threatened by foreign competition. For example, a representative from an area with shoe factories would certainly be upset about the possibility of constituents' losing their jobs because of competition from lower-priced shoe manufacturers in Brazil and Italy. But of course this argument against free trade is equally applicable to trade between the states.

 In the long run, aren't workers who have to leave their jobs because of foreign competition the biggest losers from free trade?

Some economists would argue that this is the opposite of the truth. Americans who leave their jobs rather than take wage cuts to match lower labor costs of new foreign competitors are presumably the ones who cared the least about their jobs in the first place. From this perspective, the biggest losers in the U.S. workplace are the Americans who value their jobs highly enough to keep them and absorb the full effects of the wage cuts. Because these workers presumably lack skills that they need to switch to jobs in industries with a comparative advantage over foreign producers, they are more likely to be "stuck" in low-paying jobs.

Economists David Gould, G. L. Woodbridge, and Roy Ruffin examined the data on the relationship between increases in imports and the rate of unemployment. Their conclusion was that there is no causal link between the two. Indeed, in half the cases they studied, when imports increased, unemployment fell.

Another issue has to do with the cost of protecting American jobs by restricting international trade. The Institute for International Economics examined just the restrictions on foreign textiles and apparel goods. U.S. consumers pay $9 billion a year more to protect jobs in those industries. That comes out to $50,000 a year for each job saved in an industry in which the average job pays only $20,000 a year. Similar studies have yielded similar results: Restrictions on the imports of Japanese cars have cost $160,000 *per year* for every job saved in the auto industry. Every job preserved in the glass industry has cost $200,000 each and every year. Every job preserved in the U.S. steel industry has cost an astounding $750,000 per year.

Emerging Arguments Against Free Trade

In recent years, two new antitrade arguments have been advanced. One of these focuses on environmental concerns. For instance, many environmentalists have raised concerns that genetic engineering of plants and animals could lead to accidental production of new diseases. These worries have induced the European Union to restrain trade in such products.

Another argument against free trade arises from national defense concerns. Major espionage successes by China in the late 1990s led some U.S. strategic experts to propose sweeping restrictions on exports of new technology.

Learn about the domestic costs of trade restrictions at **www.cbo.gov/showdoc. cfm?index= 1133&sequence= 0&from=1**

Free trade proponents counter that at best these are arguments for the judicial regulation of trade. They continue to argue that by and large, broad trade restrictions mainly harm the interests of the nations that impose them.

● The infant industry argument against free trade contends that new industries should be protected against world competition so that they can become technologically efficient in the long run.

● Unrestricted foreign trade may allow foreign governments to subsidize exports or foreign producers to engage in dumping—selling products in other countries below their cost of production. To the extent that foreign export subsidies and dumping create more instability in domestic production, they may impair our well-being.

WAYS TO RESTRICT FOREIGN TRADE

There are many ways in which international trade can be stopped or at least stifled. These include quotas and taxes (the latter are usually called *tariffs* when applied to internationally traded items). Let's talk first about quotas.

Quotas

Quota system
A government-imposed restriction on the quantity of a specific good that another country is allowed to sell in the United States. In other words, quotas are restrictions on imports. These restrictions are usually applied to one or several specific countries.

Under the **quota system,** individual countries or groups of foreign producers are restricted to a certain amount of trade. An import quota specifies the maximum amount of a commodity that may be imported during a specified period of time. For example, the government might not allow more than 50 million barrels of foreign crude oil to enter the United States in a particular year.

Consider the example of quotas on textiles. Figure 32-4 presents the demand and the supply curves for imported textiles. In an unrestricted import market, the equilibrium quantity imported is 900 million yards at a price of $1 per yard (expressed in constant-quality units). When an import quota is imposed, the supply curve is no longer S. Rather, the supply

Putting
*Economics in Action
to Work*

See how trade restrictions work by loading the *EIA* CD and clicking on "Trade and Exchange Rates." Then click on "Trade Restrictions and Their Effects."

FIGURE 32-4
The Effect of Quotas on Textile Imports
Without restrictions, 900 million yards of textiles would be imported each year into the United States at the world price of $1.00 per yard. If the federal government imposes a quota of only 800 million yards, the effective supply curve becomes vertical at that quantity. It intersects the demand curve at a new equilibrium price of $1.50 per yard.

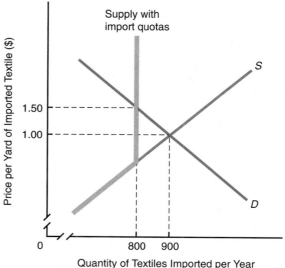

curve becomes vertical at some amount less than the equilibrium quantity—here, 800 million yards per year. The price to the American consumer increases from $1.00 to $1.50. Thus the output restriction induced by the textile quota also has the effect of influencing the price that domestic suppliers can charge for their goods. This benefits domestic textile producers by raising their revenues and therefore their profits.

INTERNATIONAL POLICY EXAMPLE

The U.S. Textile Industry: A Quota Agency of Its Very Own

Recently, American textile companies decided that they did not want so much foreign competition. Under normal circumstances, an industry might have to band together with others to lobby Congress for new laws imposing tariffs or quotas. Since the 1970s, however, the U.S. textile industry has had a special arrangement known as CITA—the Committee for the Implementation of Textile Agreements. CITA is comprised of appointees from the U.S. departments of Commerce, Labor, State, and Treasury, along with the chief textile negotiator of the Office of the President.

CITA holds no open meetings. Yet in a recent four-year period, CITA reduced or threatened to reduce quotas on specific types of textile imports. For instance, it placed limits on men's underwear from the Dominican Republic, cotton nightwear from Jamaica, and wool coats from Honduras. The annual benefit of CITA quotas for U.S. textile firms has been estimated to be as high as $12 billion in additional profits. In 2005, the United States is committed to international treaties that will phase out most textile quotas. Until then, however, CITA's quotas will be the law of the land.

For Critical Analysis
How are CITA quotas on textile imports likely to affect the prices that American consumers pay for underwear, nightwear, and coats?

Voluntary Quotas. Quotas do not have to be explicit and defined by law. They can be "voluntary." Such a quota is called a **voluntary restraint agreement (VRA).** In the early 1980s, the United States asked Japan voluntarily to restrain its exports to the United States. The Japanese government did so, limiting itself to exporting 2.8 million Japanese automobiles. Today, there are VRAs on machine tools and textiles.

The opposite of a VRA is a **voluntary import expansion (VIE).** Under a VIE, a foreign government agrees to have its companies import more foreign goods from another country. The United States almost started a major international trade war with Japan in 1995 over just such an issue. The U.S. government wanted Japanese automobile manufacturers voluntarily to increase their imports of U.S.-made automobile parts. Ultimately, Japanese companies did make a token increase in the imports of U.S. auto parts.

Voluntary restraint agreement (VRA)
An official agreement with another country that "voluntarily" restricts the quantity of its exports to the United States.

Voluntary import expansion (VIE)
An official agreement with another country in which it agrees to import more from the United States.

Tariffs

We can analyze tariffs by using standard supply and demand diagrams. Let's use as our commodity laptop computers, some of which are made in Japan and some of which are made domestically. In panel (a) of Figure 32-5 on the next page, you see the demand and supply of Japanese laptops. The equilibrium price is $1,000 per constant-quality unit, and the equilibrium quantity is 10 million per year. In panel (b), you see the same equilibrium price of $1,000, and the *domestic* equilibrium quantity is 5 million units per year.

Now a tariff of $500 is imposed on all imported Japanese laptops. The supply curve shifts upward by $500 to S_2. For purchasers of Japanese laptops, the price increases to $1,250. The quantity demanded falls to 8 million per year. In panel (b), you see that at the

Take a look at the U.S. State Department's reports on economic policy and trade practices at **www.state.gov/www/ issues/economic/ trade_reports**

FIGURE 32-5

The Effect of a Tariff on Japanese-Made Laptop Computers

Without a tariff, the United States buys 10 million Japanese laptops per year at an average price of $1,000, as shown in panel (a). American producers sell 5 million domestically made laptops, also at $1,000 each, as shown in panel (b). A $500-per-laptop tariff will shift the Japanese import supply curve to S_2 in panel (a), so that the new equilibrium is at E_2, with price $1,250 and quantity sold reduced to 8 million per year. The demand curve for American-made laptops (for which there is no tariff) shifts to D_2 in panel (b). Domestic sales increase to 6.5 million per year.

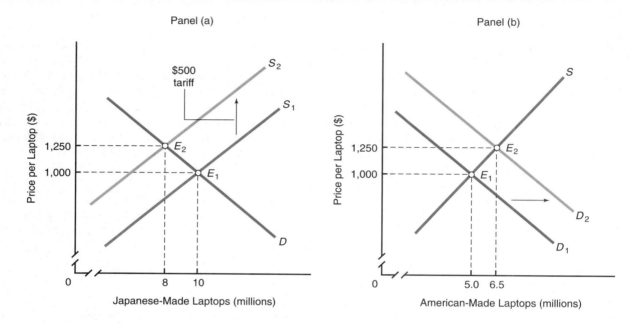

higher price of imported Japanese laptops, the demand curve for American-made laptops shifts outward to the right to D_2. The equilibrium price increases to $1,250, but the equilibrium quantity increases to 6.5 million units per year. So the tariff benefits domestic laptop producers because it increases the demand for their products due to the higher price of a close substitute, Japanese laptops. This causes a redistribution of income from American consumers of laptops to American producers of laptops.

Tariffs in the United States. In Figure 32-6, we see that tariffs on all imported goods have varied widely. The highest rates in the twentieth century occurred with the passage of the Smoot-Hawley Tariff in 1930.

POLICY EXAMPLE

Did the Smoot-Hawley Tariff Worsen the Great Depression?

By 1930, the unemployment rate had almost doubled in a year. Congress and President Hoover wanted to do something that would help stimulate U.S. production and reduce unemployment. The result was the Smoot-Hawley Tariff, which set tariff schedules for over 20,000 products, raising duties on imports by an average of 52 percent. This attempt to improve the domestic economy at the expense of foreign economies backfired. Each trading partner of the United States in turn imposed its own high tariffs, including the United Kingdom, the Netherlands, France, and Switzerland. The result was a massive reduction in international trade by an incredible 64 percent in three years. Some believe that the ensuing world Great Depression was partially caused by such tariffs.

For Critical Analysis

The Smoot-Hawley Tariff has been labeled a "beggar thy neighbor" policy. Explain why.

Current Tariff Laws. The Trade Expansion Act of 1962 gave the president the authority to reduce tariffs by up to 50 percent. Subsequently, tariffs were reduced by about 35 percent. In 1974, the Trade Reform Act allowed the president to reduce tariffs further. In 1984, the Trade and Tariff Act resulted in the lowest tariff rates ever. All such trade agreement obligations of the United States were carried out under the auspices of the **General Agreement on Tariffs and Trade (GATT),** which was signed in 1947. Member nations of GATT account for more

General Agreement on Tariffs and Trade (GATT)

An international agreement established in 1947 to further world trade by reducing barriers and tariffs.

FIGURE 32-6

Tariff Rates in the United States Since 1820

Tariff rates in the United States have bounced around like a football; indeed, in Congress, tariffs are a political football. Import-competing industries prefer high tariffs. In the twentieth century, the highest tariff we had was the Smoot-Hawley Tariff of 1930, which was almost as high as the "tariff of abominations" in 1828.

Source: U.S. Department of Commerce.

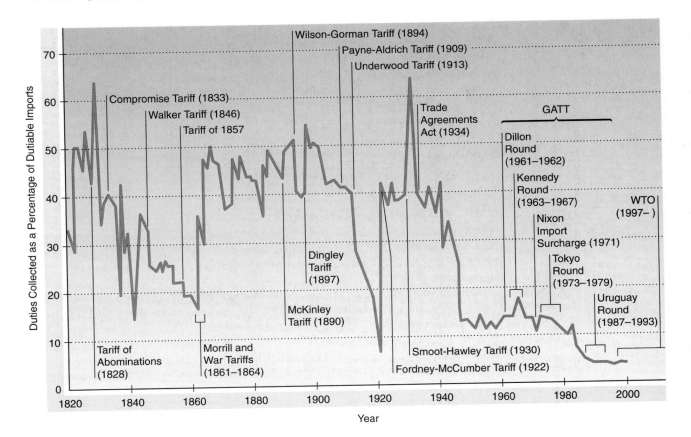

than 85 percent of world trade. As you can see in Figure 32-6 on page 797, there have been a number of rounds of negotiations to reduce tariffs since the early 1960s. The latest round was called the Uruguay Round because that is where the meetings were held.

The World Trade Organization (WTO)

World Trade Organization (WTO)
The successor organization to GATT, it handles all trade disputes among its 135 member nations.

The Uruguay Round of the General Agreement on Tariffs and Trade (GATT) was ratified by 117 nations at the end of 1993. A year later, in a special session of Congress, the entire treaty was ratified. On January 1, 1995, the new **World Trade Organization (WTO)** replaced GATT. As of 2000, the WTO had 135 member nations, plus 32 observer governments, all but two of which have applied for membership. WTO decisions have concerned such topics as the European Union's "banana wars," in which the EU's policies were determined to favor unfairly many former European colonies in Africa, the Caribbean, and the Pacific at the expense of banana-exporting countries in Latin America. Now those former colonies no longer have a privileged position in European markets.

On a larger scale, the WTO fostered the most important and far-reaching global trade agreement ever covering financial institutions, including banks, insurers, and investment companies. The more than 100 signatories to this new treaty have legally committed themselves to giving foreigners more freedom to own and operate companies in virtually all segments of the financial services industry.

CONCEPTS IN BRIEF

- ● One means of restricting foreign trade is a quota system. Beneficiaries of quotas are the importers who get the quota rights and the domestic producers of the restricted good.
- ● Another means of restricting imports is a tariff, which is a tax on imports only. An import tariff benefits import-competing industries and harms consumers by raising prices.
- ● The main international institution created to improve trade among nations is the General Agreement on Tariffs and Trade (GATT). The latest round of trade talks under GATT, the Uruguay Round, led to the creation of the World Trade Organization.

NETNOMICS

WTO: "Wired Trade Organization"?

Across the span of human history, technological change has helped advance international trade. Speedier transoceanic transport fed the growth of cross-border trade in the eighteenth and nineteenth centuries. Air transport played a key role in spurring trade among nations in the twentieth century.

Likewise, the telecommunications revolution promises to provide a big boost in the twenty-first century. Books and compact disks are easier to locate and purchase from afar using the Internet. In addition to increasing cross-border trade in such physical goods, however, the Internet also promises to be an avenue for increased trade in services. Anything that is tradable in digital form is fair game. Examples include architectural designs, information about new medical treatments and surgical techniques, and banking, insurance, and brokerage services.

Electronic commerce is emerging as a big problem for the WTO. WTO rules work differently for tariffs versus quotas. In most nations, goods are subjected to tariffs. By contrast, many nations have chosen to apply quotas to services by placing restrictions on access to national markets.

The Internet and digital technology are blurring the distinctions between traded goods and traded services, however. Under current interpretation, a recording by a top rap artist that crosses a national border while resident on a CD is a good subject to tariffs. Is the same recording sent over the Internet in digital form a service under WTO rules? Or is it no different from a CD and thus subject to the WTO's tariff guidelines? Likewise, if an architectural firm ships detailed drawings to a customer in another country, the drawings are treated as goods, and tariffs apply. But what if the firm sends the drawings to its client in the form of an e-mail attachment?

These examples illustrate how WTO rules concerning how to define goods and services might exert significant effects on the choice between physical and digital methods of trade. National authorities are already having trouble keeping track of the proliferation of Internet-based service offerings. If quotas on cross-border Internet services are difficult for national authorities to enforce, people will have a strong incentive to shift even more trade to the Internet.

ISSUES & APPLICATIONS

Does Importing Goods Hurt Low-Wage Workers at Home?

Once the U.S. economy got past the 1990–1991 recession, it entered a lengthy period of simultaneous low inflation and low unemployment. For many Americans, the 1990s were a time of higher real wages, increased fringe benefits, and soaring stock values.

Concepts Applied

International Trade

Imports

Comparative Advantage

Rising Earnings Inquality

Not all Americans shared in these gains, however. Since the 1970s, the real pay of male workers among the 10 percent at the top of the U.S. income distribution has risen by over 10 percent, but the real compensation received by the 10 percent at the bottom has not increased by much. Female workers in the bottom 10 percent of the U.S. income distribution have done a little better than their male counterparts: Their earnings have risen by just under 5 percent. Women in the top 10 percent have made considerable strides, however. These high-income women have seen their earnings increase by nearly 30 percent.

Some politicians and union leaders blamed this growing U.S. earnings inequality on international trade. In the early 1970s, they point out, only one-sixth of U.S. imports of manufactured goods came from emerging economies. Today, the proportion is about one-third. There must be a simple line of causation, they claim. Extrapolating from these data, they conclude that to keep from losing his job to foreign workers, the pay of an "average Joe" is falling. The "average Jane," they contend, has barely been holding her own in the face of this same competition from abroad.

FIGURE 32-7

U.S. Manufacturing Wages and Trade with Developing Countries

In recent decades, wages earned by workers in manufacturing in nations that trade with the United States have increased relative to the wages of U.S. manufacturing workers. Some observers argue that the implied relative decline in U.S. manufacturing wages is due in part to increased trade with developing countries.

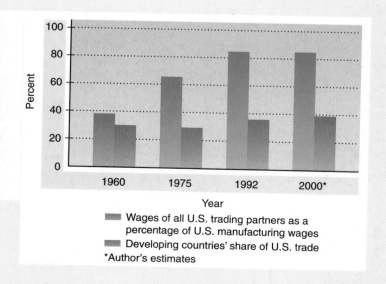

Wages of all U.S. trading partners as a percentage of U.S. manufacturing wages
Developing countries' share of U.S. trade
*Author's estimates

Is Free Trade the Culprit?

Take a look at Figure 32-7. It shows that American consumers have slightly increased the share of products they buy from developing countries. It also shows that the wages of all U.S. trading partners, including emerging economies, have increased relative to the wages of American manufacturing workers. One interpretation of these data is that the politicians and union leaders are correct: By purchasing more goods from emerging nations, American consumers end up reducing the wages of American workers relative to low-wage workers in those countries. Thus, goes the argument, Americans are losing out from freer trade, and the United States should put up barriers against imports from emerging nations.

As you have learned in this chapter, however, the story is not nearly this simple. The whole point of free trade is that it induces nations to specialize in producing goods for which they have a comparative advantage. Thus when trade barriers are removed—as many of them were in the United States during the 1970s and 1980s—resources naturally shift into industries in nations with a comparative advantage. They shift away from industries that lack a comparative advantage. Although this change undoubtedly works in favor of the U.S. economy as a whole, in the short run it can also work to the disadvantage of people with fewer marketable skills. One result can be a relative decline in the real earnings of lower-paid workers, at least in the near term.

SUMMARY DISCUSSION OF LEARNING OBJECTIVES

1. **The Worldwide Importance of International Trade:** Total trade among nations has been growing faster than total world GDP. The growth of U.S. exports and imports relative to U.S. GDP parallels this global trend. Exports and imports now equal more than 10 percent of total national production. In some countries, trade accounts for much higher shares of total economic activity.

2. **Why Nations Can Gain from Specializing in Production and Engaging in Trade:** A country has a comparative advantage in producing a good if it can produce that good at a lower opportunity cost, in terms of forgone production of a second good, than another nation. If the other nation has a comparative advantage in producing the second good, both nations can gain by specializing in producing the goods in which they have a comparative advantage and engaging in international trade. Together they can then produce and consume more than they would

have produced and consumed in the absence of specialization and trade.

3. **Comparative Advantage Versus Absolute Advantage:** Whereas a nation has a comparative advantage in producing a good when it can produce the good at lower opportunity cost relative to the opportunity cost of producing the good in another nation, a nation has an absolute advantage when it can produce more output with a given set of inputs than can be produced in the other country. Nevertheless, trade can still take place if both nations have a comparative advantage in producing goods that they can agree to exchange. The reason is that it can still benefit the nation with an absolute advantage to specialize in production.

4. **Arguments Against Free Trade:** One argument against free trade is that temporary import restrictions might permit an "infant industry" to develop to the point where it could compete without such

restrictions. Another argument concerns dumping, in which foreign companies allegedly sell some of their output in domestic markets at prices below the prices in the companies' home markets or even below the companies' costs of production. In addition, some environmentalists contend that nations should restrain foreign trade to prevent exposing their countries to environmental hazards to plants, animals, or even humans. Finally, some contend that countries should limit exports of technologies that could pose a threat to their national defense.

5. **Ways That Nations Restrict Foreign Trade:** One way to restrain trade is to impose a quota, or a limit on imports of a good. This action restricts the supply of

the good in the domestic market, thereby pushing up the equilibrium price of the good. Another way to reduce trade is to place a tariff on imported goods. This reduces the supply of foreign-made goods and increases the demand for domestically produced goods, which brings about a rise in the price of the good.

6. **Key International Agreements and Organizations That Adjudicate Trade Disputes:** From 1947 to 1995, nations agreed to abide by the General Agreement on Trades and Tariffs (GATT), which laid an international legal foundation for relaxing quotas and reducing tariffs. Since 1995, the World Trade Organization (WTO) has adjudicated trade disputes that arise between or among nations.

Key Terms and Concepts

Absolute advantage   (787)

Comparative advantage   (787)

Dumping   (792)

General Agreement on Tariffs and Trade (GATT)   (797)

Infant industry argument   (791)

Quota system   (794)

Voluntary import expansion (VIE)   (795)

Voluntary restraint agreement (VRA)   (795)

World Trade Organization (WTO)   (798)

Problems

Answers to the odd-numbered problems appear at the back of the book.

32-1. The following hypothetical example depicts the number of calculators and books that Norway and Sweden can produce with one unit of labor.

Country	Calculators	Books
Norway	2	1
Sweden	4	1

If each country has 100 workers and the country splits its labor force evenly between the two industries, how much of each good can the nations produce individually and jointly? Which nation has an absolute advantage in calculators, and which nation has an absolute advantage in books?

32-2. Suppose that the two nations in Problem 32-1 do not trade.

a. What would be the price of books in terms of calculators for each nation?

b. What is the opportunity cost of producing one calculator in each nation?

c. What is the opportunity cost of producing one book in each nation?

32-3. Consider the nations in Problem 32-1 when answering the following questions.

a. Which has a comparative advantage in calculators and which in books?

b. What is total or joint output if the two nations specialize in the good for which they have a comparative advantage?

32-4. Illustrate the production possibilities frontiers for the two nations in Problem 32-1 in a graph with books depicted on the vertical axis and calculators on the horizontal axis. What is the significance of the differing slopes of the PPFs for these two nations?

32-5. Suppose that the two nations in Problem 32-1 trade with each other at a rate where one book exchanges for three calculators. Using this rate of exchange, explain, in economic terms, whether their exchange is a zero-sum game, a positive-sum game, or a negative-sum game. (Hint: Review Chapter 25 if necessary to answer this question.)

32-6. The marginal physical product of a worker in an advanced nation (MPP_A) is 100 and the wage (W_A) is $25. The marginal physical product of a worker in a developing nation (MPP_D) is 15 and the wage (W_D) is $5. As a cost-minimizing business manager in the developing nation, would you be enticed to move your business to the developing nation to take advantage of the lower wage?

32-7. You are a policymaker of a major exporting nation. Your main export good has a price elasticity of demand of $-.50$. Is there any economic reason why you would voluntarily agree to export restraints?

32-8. The following table depicts the bicycle industry before and after a nation has imposed quota restraints.

	Before Quota	After Quota
Quantity imported	1,000,000	900,000
Price paid	$50	$60

Draw a diagram illustrating conditions in the imported bicycle market before and after the quota, and answer the following questions.

a. What are the total expenditures of consumers before and after the quota?

b. What is the price elasticity of demand for bicycles?

c. Who benefits from the imposition of the quota?

32-9. The following diagrams illustrate the markets for imported Korean-made and U.S. manufactured televisions before and after a tariff is imposed on imported TVs.

a. What was the amount of the tariff?

b. What was the total revenue of Korean television exports before the tariff? After the tariff?

c. What is the tariff revenue earned by the U.S. government?

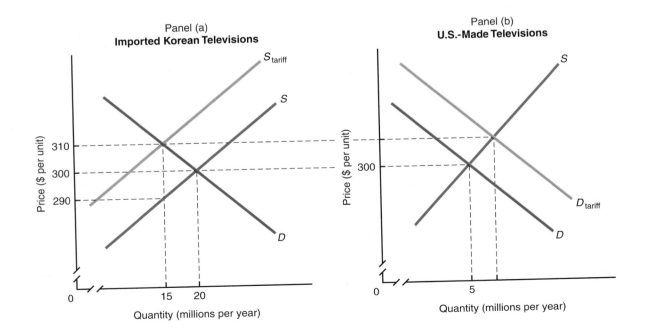

Panel (a)
Imported Korean Televisions

Panel (b)
U.S.-Made Televisions

32-10. Base your answers to the following questions on the graph accompanying Problem 32-9.

   a. What was the revenue of U.S. television manufacturers before the tariff was imposed?

   b. What is their total revenue after the tariff?

   c. Who has gained from the tariff and who has it made worse off?

Economics on the Net

How the World Trade Organization Settles Trade Disputes   A key function of the WTO is to adjudicate trade disagreements that arise among nations. This application helps you learn about the process that the WTO follows when considering international trade disputes.

Internet URL: www.wto.org/wto/about/dispute0.htm

Title: The World Trade Organization: Settling Trade Disputes

Navigation: Begin at the WTO's homepage (www.wto.org). Then click on Dispute Settlement, and click on How Does the WTO Settle Disputes?

Application Read the article, which you can scroll through by clicking on the right arrow at the bottom of the page. Then answer the following questions.

1. As the article discusses, settling trade disputes often takes at least a year. What aspects of the WTO's dispute settlement process take the longest time?

2. Does the WTO actually "punish" a country it finds has broken international trading agreements? If not, who does impose sanctions?

For Group Study and Analysis The Summary section on the last page of this report lists areas that the WTO is currently exploring for future action. Have a class discussion of the pros and cons of WTO involvement in each of these areas. Which are most important for promoting world trade? Which are least important?

EXCHANGE RATES AND THE BALANCE OF PAYMENTS

LEARNING OBJECTIVES

After reading this chapter, you should be able to:

1. **Distinguish between the balance of trade and the balance of payments**

2. **Identify the key accounts within the balance of payments**

3. **Outline how exchange rates are determined in the markets for foreign exchange**

4. **Discuss factors that can induce changes in equilibrium exchange rates**

5. **Understand how policymakers can go about attempting to fix exchange rates**

6. **Explain alternative approaches to limiting exchange rate variability**

During the Asian currency crisis, the Thai government launched a campaign to keep the national currency, the baht, from falling in value. The government asked Thais to turn in their foreign currencies in exchange for baht. Why?

In 1997, an international payments crisis swept Southeast Asia. Investors from around the world began selling off their holdings of bonds and stocks denominated in the Thai baht, Indonesian rupiah, and Malaysian ringgit. The prime minister of Malaysia, Mahathir Mohamad, said that the crisis was caused by currency speculators—individuals and firms that seek to profit solely from the activity of buying currencies at low values and selling them at higher values. During the summer of 1997, a number of currency speculators earned sizable profits by conjecturing that Southeast Asian nations, including Malaysia, could not maintain the value of their currencies. According to Mahathir, these were ill-gotten gains. Speculative currency trading, Mahathir contended, "is unnecessary, unproductive, and immoral." Are currency speculators really unproductive individuals engaged in an unnecessary and immoral business? To evaluate this question, you must first learn more about international payments and exchange rates.

Did You Know That... every day, around the clock, over $1 trillion in foreign currencies is traded? Along with that trading come news headlines, such as "The dollar weakened today," "The dollar is clearly overvalued," "The dollar is under attack," and "Members of the Group of Seven acted to prevent the dollar from rising." If you are confused by such newspaper headlines, join the crowd. Surprisingly, though, if you regard the dollar, the pound, the euro, the yen, and the baht as assets that are subject to the laws of supply and demand, the world of international finance can be quickly demystified. Perhaps the first step is to examine the meaning of the terms used with respect to U.S. international financial transactions during any one-year period.

THE BALANCE OF PAYMENTS AND INTERNATIONAL CAPITAL MOVEMENTS

Governments typically keep track of each year's economic activities by calculating the gross domestic product—the total of expenditures on all newly produced final domestic goods and services—and its components. In the world of international trade also, a summary information system has been developed. It relates to the balance of trade and the balance of payments. The **balance of trade** refers specifically to exports and imports of goods as discussed in Chapter 32. When international trade is in balance, the value of exports equals the value of imports. When the value of imports exceeds the value of imports, we are running a deficit in the balance of trade. When the value of exports exceeds the value of imports, we are running a surplus.

The **balance of payments** is a more general concept that expresses the total of all economic transactions between a nation and the rest of the world, usually for a period of one year. Each country's balance of payments summarizes information about that country's exports, imports, earnings by domestic residents on assets located abroad, earnings on domestic assets owned by foreign residents, international capital movements, and official transactions by central banks and governments. In essence, then, the balance of payments is a record of all the transactions between households, firms, and the government of one country and the rest of the world. Any transaction that leads to a *payment* by a country's residents (or government) is a deficit item, identified by a negative sign (−) when we examine the actual numbers that might be in Table 33-1. Any transaction that leads to a *receipt* by a country's residents (or government) is a surplus item and is identified by a plus sign (+) when actual numbers are considered. Table 33-1 gives a listing of the surplus and deficit items on international accounts.

Balance of trade
The difference between exports and imports of goods.

Balance of payments
A system of accounts that measures transactions of goods, services, income, and financial assets between domestic households, businesses, and governments and residents of the rest of the world during a specific time period.

Accounting Identities

Accounting identities—definitions of equivalent values—exist for financial institutions and other businesses. We begin with simple accounting identities that must hold for families and then go on to describe international accounting identities.

If a family unit is spending more than its current income, such a situation necessarily implies that the family unit must be doing one of the following:

1. Reducing its money holdings, or selling stocks, bonds, or other assets
2. Borrowing
3. Receiving gifts from friends or relatives

Accounting identities
Values that are equivalent by definition.

Surplus Items (+)	Deficit Items (−)	
Exports of merchandise	Imports of merchandise	**TABLE} 33-1**
Private and governmental gifts from foreigners	Private and governmental gifts to foreigners	**Surplus (+) and Deficit (−) Items on the International Accounts**
Foreign use of domestically owned transportation	Use of foreign-owned transportation	
Foreign tourists' expenditures in this country	Tourism expenditures abroad	
Foreign military spending in this country	Military spending abroad	
Interest and dividend receipts from foreign entities	Interest and dividends paid to foreigners	
Sales of domestic assets to foreigners	Purchases of foreign assets	
Funds deposited in this country by foreigners	Funds placed in foreign depository institutions	
Sales of gold to foreigners	Purchases of gold from foreigners	
Sales of domestic currency to foreigners	Purchases of foreign currency	

4. Receiving public transfers from a government, which obtained the funds by taxing others (a transfer is a payment, in money or in goods or services, made without receiving goods or services in return)

We can use this information to derive an identity: If a family unit is currently spending more than it is earning, it must draw on previously acquired wealth, borrow, or receive either private or public aid. Similarly, an identity exists for a family unit that is currently spending less than it is earning: It must be increasing its money holdings or be lending and acquiring other financial assets, or it must pay taxes or bestow gifts on others. When we consider businesses and governments, each unit in each group faces its own identities or constraints. Ultimately, net lending by households must equal net borrowing by businesses and governments.

Disequilibrium. Even though our individual family unit's accounts must balance, in the sense that the identity discussed previously must hold, sometimes the item that brings about the balance cannot continue indefinitely. *If family expenditures exceed family income and this situation is financed by borrowing, the household may be considered to be in disequilibrium because such a situation cannot continue indefinitely.* If such a deficit is financed by drawing on previously accumulated assets, the family may also be in disequilibrium because it cannot continue indefinitely to draw on its wealth; eventually, it will become impossible for that family to continue such a lifestyle. (Of course, if the family members are retired, they may well be in equilibrium by drawing on previously acquired assets to finance current deficits; this example illustrates that it is necessary to understand circumstances fully before pronouncing an economic unit in disequilibrium.)

Equilibrium. Individual households, businesses, and governments, as well as the entire group of households, businesses, and governments, must eventually reach equilibrium. Certain economic adjustment mechanisms have evolved to ensure equilibrium. Deficit households must eventually increase their income or decrease their expenditures. They will find that they have to pay higher interest rates if they wish to borrow to finance their deficits. Eventually, their credit sources will dry up, and they will be forced into equilibrium. Businesses, on occasion, must lower costs or prices—or go bankrupt—to reach equilibrium.

TABLE 33-2
U.S. Balance of Payments Account, 2000 (in billions of dollars)

Current Account		
(1) Exports of goods	+711.6	
(2) Imports of goods	−1,135.3	
(3) Balance of trade		−423.7
(4) Exports of services	+311.2	
(5) Imports of services	−213.4	
(6) Balance of services		+97.8
(7) Balance on goods and services [(3) + (6)]		−325.9
(8) Net unilateral transfers	−34.2	
(9) Balance on current account		−360.1
Capital Account		
(10) U.S. private capital going abroad	−642.2	
(11) Foreign private capital coming into the United States	+987.1*	
(12) Balance on capital account [(10) + (11)]		+344.9
(13) Balance on current account plus balance on capital account [(9) + (12)]		−15.2
Official Reserve Transactions Account		
(14) Official transactions balance		+15.2
(15) Total (balance)		.00

Sources: U.S. Department of Commerce, Bureau of Economic Analysis; U.S. Department of the Treasury.
*Includes a $26 billion statistical discrepancy, probably unaccounted capital inflows, many of which relate to the illegal drug trade.

An Accounting Identity Among Nations.   When nations trade or interact, certain identities or constraints must also hold. Nations buy goods from people in other nations; they also lend to and present gifts to people in other nations. If a nation interacts with others, an accounting identity ensures a balance (but not an equilibrium, as will soon become clear). Let's look at the three categories of balance of payments transactions: current account transactions, capital account transactions, and official reserve account transactions.

Current Account Transactions

During any designated period, all payments and gifts that are related to the purchase or sale of both goods and services constitute the current account in international trade. The four major types of current account transactions are the exchange of merchandise, the exchange of services, unilateral transfers, and net investment income.

Merchandise Trade Exports and Imports.   The largest portion of any nation's balance of payments current account is typically the importing and exporting of merchandise goods. During 2000, for example, as can be seen in lines 1 and 2 of Table 33-2, the United States exported $711.6 billion of merchandise and imported $1,135.3 billion. The balance of merchandise trade is defined as the difference between the value of merchandise exports and the value of merchandise imports. For 2000, the United States had a balance of merchandise trade deficit because the value of its merchandise imports exceeded the value of its merchandise exports. This deficit amounted to $423.7 billion (line 3).

Service Exports and Imports.   The balance of (merchandise) trade has to do with tangible items—you can feel them, touch them, and see them. Service exports and imports have to do with invisible or intangible items that are bought and sold, such as shipping, insurance, tourist expenditures, and banking services. Also, income earned by foreigners on U.S. investments and income earned by U.S. residents on foreign investments are part of service imports and exports. As can be seen in lines 4 and 5 of Table 33-2, in 2000, service exports were $311.2 billion and service imports were $213.4 billion. Thus the balance of services was about $97.8 billion in 2000 (line 6). Exports constitute receipts or inflows into the United States and are positive; imports constitute payments abroad or outflows of money and are negative.

When we combine the balance of merchandise trade with the balance of services, we obtain a balance of goods and services equal to −$325.9 billion in 2000 (line 7).

Unilateral Transfers.   U.S. residents give gifts to relatives and others abroad, the federal government grants gifts to foreign nations, foreigners give gifts to U.S. residents, and some foreign governments have granted money to the U.S. government. In the current account, we see that net unilateral transfers—the total amount of gifts given by U.S. residents minus the total amount received by U.S. residents from abroad—came to −$34.2 billion in 2000 (line 8). The fact that there is a minus sign before the number for unilateral transfers means that U.S. residents gave more to foreigners than foreigners gave to U.S. residents.

Balancing the Current Account.   The balance on current account tracks the value of a country's exports of goods and services (including military receipts plus income on investments abroad) and transfer payments (private and government) relative to the value of that country's imports of goods and services and transfer payments (private and government). In 2000, it was −$360.1 billion.

If the sum of net exports of goods and services plus unilateral transfers plus net investment income exceeds zero, a current account surplus is said to exist; if this sum is negative, a current account deficit is said to exist. A current account deficit means that we are importing more than we are exporting. Such a deficit must be paid for by the export of money or money equivalent, which means a capital account surplus.

For latest U.S. balance-of-payments figures, go to **www.bea.doc.gov** and under "International," click on "Data."

Capital Account Transactions

In world markets, it is possible to buy and sell not only goods and services but also real and financial assets. This is what the capital accounts are concerned with in international transactions. Capital account transactions occur because of foreign investments—either by foreign residents investing in the United States or by U.S. residents investing in other countries. The purchase of shares of stock on the London stock market by a U.S. resident causes an outflow of funds from the United States to Britain. The building of a Japanese automobile factory in the United States causes an inflow of funds from Japan to the United States. Any time foreign residents buy U.S. government securities, that is an inflow of funds from other countries to the United States. Any time U.S. residents buy foreign government securities, there is an outflow of funds from the United States to other countries. Loans to and from foreign residents cause outflows and inflows.

The United States has large trade deficits. Does this mean we have a weak economy?

It is true that the current account in the United States has been in deficit continuously since the early 1980s, but this was also true during the 1880s. So it is not a new phenomenon. (Note also that we were a creditor nation from 1914 to 1985.) Figure 33-1 shows that whenever the United States is in deficit in its current account, it is in surplus in its capital account. The United States does not have a trade deficit because its economy is weak and it cannot compete in world markets. Rather, the United States is a good place to invest capital because we have strong prospects for growth. As long as foreign residents wish to invest more in the United States than U.S. residents wish to invest abroad, there will *always* be a current account deficit. The U.S. is better off, not worse off, because of it.

Line 10 of Table 33-2 indicates that in 2000, the value of private and government capital going out of the United States was −$642.2 billion, and line 11 shows that the value of private and government capital coming into the United States (including a statistical discrepancy) was $987.1 billion. U.S. capital going abroad constitutes payments or outflows and is therefore negative. Foreign capital coming into the United States constitutes receipts or inflows and is therefore positive. Thus there was a positive net capital movement of $344.9 billion into the United States (line 12). This is also called the balance on capital account.

There is a relationship between the current account and the capital account, assuming no interventions by the finance ministries or central banks of nations.

In the absence of interventions by finance ministries or central banks, the current account and the capital account must sum to zero. Stated differently, the current account deficit must equal the capital account surplus when governments or central banks do not engage in foreign exchange interventions. In this situation, any nation experiencing a current account deficit, such as the United States, must also be running a capital account surplus.

Official Reserve Account Transactions

The third type of balance of payments transaction concerns official reserve assets, which consist of the following:

1. Foreign currencies
2. Gold
3. **Special drawing rights (SDRs),** which are reserve assets that the International Monetary Fund created to be used by countries to settle international payment obligations
4. The reserve position in the International Monetary Fund
5. Financial assets held by an official agency, such as the U.S. Treasury Department

Special drawing rights (SDRs)
Reserve assets created by the International Monetary Fund for countries to use in settling international payment obligations.

To consider how official reserve account transactions occur, look again at Table 33-2. The surplus in the U.S. capital account was $344.9 billion. But the deficit in the U.S. current account was −$360.1 billion, so the United States had a net deficit on the combined accounts (line 13) of −$15.2 billion. In other words, the United States obtained less in foreign money in all its international transactions than it used. How is this deficiency made up? By our central bank drawing down its existing balances of foreign moneys, shown by the +$15.2 billion in official transactions shown on line 14 in Table 33-2. There is a plus sign on line 14 because this represents an *inflow* of foreign exchange into our international transactions.

The balance (line 15) in Table 33-2 is zero, as it must be with double-entry bookkeeping. The U.S. balance of payments deficit is measured by the official transactions figure on line 14.

FIGURE 33-1

The Relationship Between the Current Account and the Capital Account

To some extent, the capital account is the mirror image of the current account. We can see this in the years since 1970. When the current account was in surplus, the capital account was in deficit. When the current account was in deficit, the capital account was in surplus. Indeed, virtually the only time foreigners can invest in America is when the current account is in deficit.

Sources: International Monetary Fund; *Economic Indicators.*

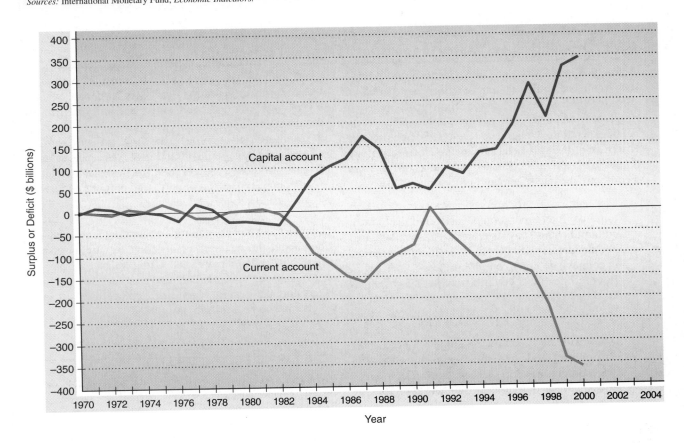

What Affects the Balance of Payments?

A major factor affecting any nation's balance of payments is its rate of inflation relative to that of its trading partners. Assume that the rates of inflation in the United States and in Japan are equal. Now suppose that all of a sudden, the U.S. inflation rate increases. The Japanese will find that U.S. products are becoming more expensive, and U.S. firms will export fewer of them to Japan. At the current exchange rate, U.S. residents will find Japanese products relatively cheaper, and they will import more. The converse will occur if the U.S. inflation rate suddenly falls relative to that of Japan. All other things held constant, whenever the U.S. rate of inflation exceeds that of its trading partners, we expect to see a larger deficit in the U.S. balance of trade and payments. Conversely, when the U.S. rate of inflation is less than that of its trading partners, other things being constant, we expect to see a smaller deficit in the U.S. balance of trade and payments.

Another important factor that sometimes influences a nation's balance of payments is its relative political stability. Political instability causes *capital flight.* Owners of capital in countries anticipating or experiencing political instability will often move assets to countries that are politically stable, such as the United States. Hence the U.S. capital account balance, and so its balance of payments, is likely to increase whenever political instability looms in other nations in the world.

POLICY EXAMPLE

Does "Competitiveness" Apply to Countries as Well as Corporations?

Although a nation's balance of payments bears similarities to the accounting system of a company, deficit or surplus measures in the balance of payments are much different from a corporation's bottom line—that is, its net of expenditures relative to receipts. Economist Paul Krugman of the Massachusetts Institute of Technology argues that a nation's balance of payments differs from a corporate income statement in four important ways:

1. The bottom line for a corporation is truly its bottom line. If a corporation persistently fails to meet commitments to pay its employees, suppliers, and bondholders, it will go out of business. Countries, in contrast, do not go out of business.
2. Bottom lines for a country, such as the merchandise trade balance, do not necessarily indicate "weakness" or "strength." A deficit is not necessarily "good" or "bad."
3. U.S. residents typically consume about 90 percent of the goods and services produced within U.S. borders. Even the largest corporation rarely sells any of its output to its own workers. By way

of contrast, the "exports" of a company such as Microsoft Corporation—its sales to people who do not work for the company—account for virtually all its sales.
4. Countries do not compete the same way that companies do. A negligible fraction of Netscape's sales go to Microsoft Corporation, for instance. Countries may export and import large portions of their goods and services, however.

Thus we must be very cautious about drawing conclusions about the meaning of a deficit or surplus in a nation's balance of payments. Using balance of payments statistics to support an argument that one nation is economically more viable or "competitive" than another may be completely misguided.

For Critical Analysis
Under what circumstances might a nation find a trade deficit to be beneficial?

CONCEPTS IN BRIEF

● The balance of payments reflects the value of all transactions in international trade, including goods, services, financial assets, and gifts.

● The merchandise trade balance gives us the difference between exports and imports of tangible items. Merchandise trade transactions are represented by exports and imports of tangible items.

● Included in the current account along with merchandise trade are service exports and imports relating to commerce in intangible items, such as shipping, insurance, and tourist expenditures. The current account also includes income earned by foreign residents on U.S. investments and income earned by U.S. residents on foreign investments.

● Unilateral transfers involve international private gifts and federal government grants or gifts to foreign nations.

● When we add the balance of merchandise trade and the balance of services and take account of net unilateral transfers and net investment income, we come up with the balance on the current account, a summary statistic.

● There are also capital account transactions that relate to the buying and selling of financial and real assets. Foreign capital is always entering the United States, and U.S. capital is always flowing abroad. The difference is called the balance on capital account.

● Another type of balance of payments transaction concerns the official reserve assets of individual countries, or what is often simply called official transactions. By standard accounting convention, official transactions are exactly equal to a nation's balance of payments but opposite in sign.

● A nation's balance of payments can be affected by its relative rate of inflation and by its political stability relative to other nations.

DETERMINING FOREIGN EXCHANGE RATES

When you buy foreign products, such as a Japanese-made laptop computer, you have dollars with which to pay the Japanese manufacturer. The Japanese manufacturer, however, cannot pay workers in dollars. The workers are Japanese, they live in Japan, and they must have yen to buy goods and services in that country. There must therefore be some way of exchanging dollars for yen that the computer manufacturer will accept. That exchange occurs in a **foreign exchange market,** which in this case specializes in exchanging yen and dollars. (When you obtain foreign currencies at a bank or an airport currency exchange, you are participating in the foreign exchange market.)

The particular **exchange rate** between yen and dollars that prevails—the dollar price of the yen—depends on the current demand for and supply of yen and dollars. In a sense, then, our analysis of the exchange rate between dollars and yen will be familiar, for we have used supply and demand throughout this book. If it costs you 1 cent to buy 1 yen, that is the foreign exchange rate determined by the current demand for and supply of yen in the foreign exchange market. The Japanese person going to the foreign exchange market would need 100 yen to buy 1 dollar.

We will continue our example in which the only two countries in the world are Japan and the United States. Now let's consider what determines the demand for and supply of foreign currency in the foreign exchange market.

Foreign exchange market
A market in which households, firms, and governments buy and sell national currencies.

Exchange rate
The price of one nation's currency in terms of the currency of another country.

Demand for and Supply of Foreign Currency

You wish to purchase a Japanese-made laptop computer direct from the manufacturer. To do so, you must have Japanese yen. You go to the foreign exchange market (or your U.S. bank). Your desire to buy the Japanese laptop computer therefore causes you to offer (supply) dollars to the foreign exchange market. Your demand for Japanese yen is equivalent to your supply of U.S. dollars to the foreign exchange market.

Every U.S. transaction involving the importation of foreign goods constitutes a supply of dollars and a demand for some foreign currency, and the opposite is true for export transactions.

In this case, the import transaction constitutes a demand for Japanese yen.

In our example, we will assume that only two goods are being traded, Japanese laptop computers and U.S. microprocessors. The U.S. demand for Japanese laptop computers creates a supply of dollars and demand for yen in the foreign exchange market. Similarly, the Japanese demand for U.S. microprocessors creates a supply of yen and a demand for dollars in the foreign exchange market. Under a system of **flexible exchange rates,** the supply of and demand for dollars and yen in the foreign exchange market will determine the

Flexible exchange rates
Exchange rates that are allowed to fluctuate in the open market in response to changes in supply and demand. Sometimes called *floating exchange rates*.

equilibrium foreign exchange rate. The equilibrium exchange rate will tell us how many yen a dollar can be exchanged for—that is, the dollar price of yen—or how many dollars (or fractions of a dollar) a yen can be exchange for—the yen price of dollars.

The Equilibrium Foreign Exchange Rate

To determine the equilibrium foreign exchange rate, we have to find out what determines the demand for and supply of foreign exchange. We will ignore for the moment any speculative aspect of buying foreign exchange. That is, we assume that there are no individuals who wish to buy yen simply because they think that their price will go up in the future.

The idea of an exchange rate is no different from the idea of paying a certain price for something you want to buy. If you like coffee, you know you have to pay about 75 cents a cup. If the price went up to $2.50, you would probably buy fewer cups. If the price went down to 5 cents, you might buy more. In other words, the demand curve for cups of coffee, expressed in terms of dollars, slopes downward following the law of demand. The demand curve for yen slopes downward also, and we will see why.

Let's think more closely about the demand schedule for yen. Let's say that it costs you 1 cent to purchase 1 yen; that is the exchange rate between dollars and yen. If tomorrow you had to pay $1\frac{1}{4}$ cents ($.0125) for the same yen, the exchange rate would have changed. Looking at such an increase with respect to the yen, we would say that there has been an **appreciation** in the value of the yen in the foreign exchange market. But another way to view this increase in the value of the yen is to say that there has been a **depreciation** in the value of the dollar in the foreign exchange market. The dollar used to buy 100 yen; tomorrow, the dollar will be able to buy only 80 yen at a price of $1\frac{1}{4}$ cents per yen. If the dollar price of yen rises, you will probably demand fewer yen. Why? The answer lies in looking at the reason you and others demand yen in the first place.

Appreciation and Depreciation of Japanese Yen.   Recall that in our example, you and others demand yen to buy Japanese laptop computers. The demand curve for Japanese laptop computers, we will assume, follows the law of demand and therefore slopes downward. If it costs more U.S. dollars to buy the same quantity of Japanese laptop computers, presumably you and other U.S. residents will not buy the same quantity; your quantity demanded will be less. We say that your demand for Japanese yen is *derived from* your demand for Japanese laptop computers. In panel (a) of Figure 33-2, we present the hypothetical demand schedule for Japanese laptop computers by a representative set of U.S. consumers during a typical week. In panel (b), we show graphically the U.S. demand curve for Japanese yen in terms of U.S. dollars taken from panel (a).

An Example of Derived Demand.   Let us assume that the price of a Japanese laptop computer in Japan is 100,000 yen. Given that price, we can find the number of yen required to purchase up to 500 Japanese laptop computers. That information is given in panel (c) of Figure 33-2. If one laptop computer requires 100,000 yen, 500 laptop computers require 50 million yen. Now we have enough information to determine the derived demand curve for Japanese yen. If 1 yen costs 1 cent, a laptop computer would cost $1,000 (100,000 yen per computer × 1 cent per yen = $1,000 per computer). At $1,000 per computer, the representative group of U.S. consumers would, we see from panel (a) of Figure 33-2, demand 500 laptop computers.

From panel (c), we see that 50 million yen would be demanded to buy the 500 laptop computers. We show this quantity demanded in panel (d). In panel (e), we draw the derived demand curve for yen. Now consider what happens if the price of yen goes up to $1\frac{1}{4}$ cents

For recent data on the exchange value of the U.S. dollar relative to the major currencies of the world, go to **www.stls.frb.org/fred/ data/exchange.html**

Appreciation
An increase in the exchange value of one nation's currency in terms of the currency of another nation.

Depreciation
A decrease in the exchange value of one nation's currency in terms of the currency of another nation.

Panel (a)
Demand Schedule for Japanese Laptop Computers in the United States per Week

Price per Unit	Quantity Demanded
$1,500	100
1,250	300
1,000	500
750	700

Panel (b)
American Demand Curve for Japanese Laptop Computers

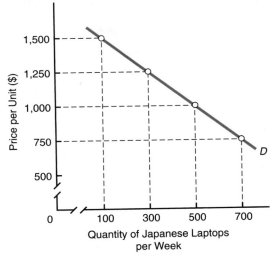

Panel (c)
Yen Required to Purchase Quantity Demanded (at P = 100,000 yen per computer)

Quantity Demanded	Yen Required (millions)
100	10
300	30
500	50
700	70

Panel (d)
Derived Demand Schedule for Yen in the United States with Which to Pay for Imports of Laptops

Dollar Price of One Yen	Dollar Price of Computers	Quantity of Computers Demanded	Quantity of Yen Demanded per Week (millions)
$ .0150	$1,500	100	10
.0125	1,250	300	30
.0100	1,000	500	50
.0075	750	700	70

Panel (e)
American Derived Demand for Yen

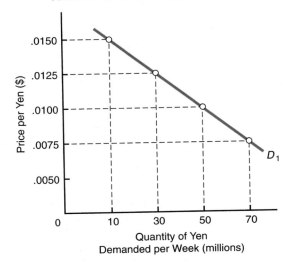

FIGURE 33-2

Deriving the Demand for Yen

In panel (a), we show the demand schedule for Japanese laptop computers in the United States, expressed in terms of dollars per computer. In panel (b), we show the demand curve, *D*, which slopes downward. In panel (c), we show the number of yens required to purchase up to 700 laptop computers. If the price per laptop computer in Japan is 100,000 yen, we can now find the quantity of yen needed to pay for the various quantities demanded. In panel (d), we see the derived demand for yen in the United States in order to purchase the various quantities of computers given in panel (a). The resultant demand curve, D_1, is shown in panel (e). This is the American derived demand for yen.

FIGURE 33-3

The Supply of Japanese Yen

If the market price of a U.S.-produced microprocessor is $200, then at an exchange rate of $.0100 per yen (1 cent per yen), the price of the microprocessor to a Japanese consumer is 20,000 yen. If the exchange rate rises to $.0125 per yen, the Japanese price of the microprocessor falls to 16,000 yen. This induces an increase in the quantity of microprocessors demanded by Japanese consumers and consequently an increase in the quantity of yen supplied in exchange for dollars in the foreign exchange market. By contrast, if the exchange rate falls to $.0075 per yen, the Japanese price of the microprocessor rises to 26,667 yen. This causes a decrease in the quantity of microprocessors demanded by Japanese consumers. As a result, there is a decline in the quantity of yen supplied in exchange for dollars in the foreign exchange market.

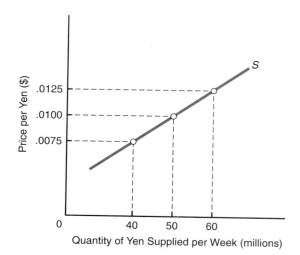

($.0125). A Japanese laptop computer priced at 100,000 yen in Japan would now cost $1,250. From panel (a), we see that at $1,250 per computer, 300 laptop computers will be imported from Japan into the United States by our representative group of U.S. consumers. From panel (c), we see that 300 computers would require 30 million yen to be purchased; thus in panels (d) and (e), we see that at a price of $1\frac{1}{4}$ cents per yen, the quantity demanded will be 30 million yen.

We continue similar calculations all the way up to a price of $1\frac{1}{2}$ cents ($.0150) per yen. At that price, a Japanese laptop computer costing 100,000 yen in Japan would cost $1,500, and our representative U.S. consumers would import only 100 laptop computers.

Downward-Sloping Derived Demand.   As can be expected, as the price of yen rises, the quantity demanded will fall. The only difference here from the standard demand analysis developed in Chapter 3 and used throughout this text is that the demand for yen is derived from the demand for a final product—Japanese laptop computers in our example.

Supply of Japanese Yen.   Assume that Japanese laptop manufacturers buy U.S. microprocessors. The supply of Japanese yen is a derived supply in that it is derived from the Japanese demand for U.S. microprocessors. We could go through an example similar to the one for laptop computers to come up with a supply schedule of Japanese yen in Japan. It slopes upward. Obviously, the Japanese want dollars to purchase U.S. goods. Japanese residents will be willing to supply more yen when the dollar price of yen goes up, because they can then buy more U.S. goods with the same quantity of yen. That is, the yen would be worth more in exchange for U.S. goods than when the dollar price for yen was lower.

An Example.   Let's take an example. Suppose a U.S.-produced microprocessor costs $200. If the exchange rate is 1 cent per one yen, a Japanese resident will have to come up with 20,000 yen (= $200 at $.0100 per yen) to buy one microprocessor. If, however, the exchange rate goes up to $1\frac{1}{4}$ cents for yen, a Japanese resident must come up with only 16,000 yen (= $200 at $.0125 per yen) to buy a U.S. microprocessor. At a lower price (in yen) of U.S. microprocessors, the Japanese will demand a larger quantity. In other words, as the price of Japanese yen goes up in terms of dollars, the quantity of U.S. microprocessors demanded will go up, and hence the quantity of Japanese yen supplied will go up.

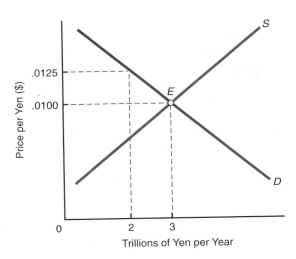

FIGURE 33-4
Total Demand for and Supply of Japanese Yen
The market supply curve for Japanese yen results from the total demand for U.S. microprocessors. The demand curve, *D*, slopes downward like most demand curves, and the supply curve *S*, slopes upward. The foreign exchange price, or the U.S. dollar price of yen, is given on the vertical axis. The number of yen is represented on the horizontal axis. If the foreign exchange rate is $.0125—that is, if it takes $1\frac{1}{4}$ cents to buy 1 yen—Americans will demand 2 trillion yen. The equilibrium exchange rate is at the intersection of *D* and *S*. The equilibrium exchange rate is $.0100 (1 cent). At this point, 3 trillion yen are both demanded and supplied each year.

Therefore, the supply schedule of yen, which is derived from the Japanese demand for U.S. goods, will slope upward.*

We could easily work through a detailed numerical example to show that the supply curve of Japanese yen slopes upward. Rather than do that, we will simply draw it as upward-sloping in Figure 33-3 on the previous page. In our hypothetical example, assuming that there are only representative groups of laptop computer consumers in the United States and microprocessor consumers in Japan, the equilibrium exchange rate will be set at 1 cent per yen, or 100 yen to 1 dollar.

Total Demand for and Supply of Japanese Yen. Let us now look at the total demand for and supply of Japanese yen. We take all demanders of Japanese laptop computer and U.S. microprocessors and put their demands for and supplies of yen together into one diagram. Thus we are showing the total demand for and total supply of Japanese yen. The horizontal axis in Figure 33-4 represents a quantity of foreign exchange—the number of yen per year. The vertical axis represents the exchange rate—the price of foreign currency (yen) expressed in dollars (per yen). The foreign currency price of $.0125 per yen means it will cost you $1\frac{1}{4}$ cents to buy 1 yen. At the foreign currency price of $.0100 per yen, you know that it will cost you 1 cent to buy 1 yen. The equilibrium is again established at 1 cent for 1 yen.

This equilibrium is not established because U.S. residents like to buy yen or because the Japanese like to buy dollars. Rather, the equilibrium exchange rate depends on how many microprocessors the Japanese want and how many Japanese laptop computers U.S. residents want (given their respective incomes, their tastes, and the relative price of laptop computers and microprocessors).[†]

---

*Actually, the supply schedule of foreign currency will be upward-sloping if we assume that the demand for U.S. imported microprocessors on the part of the Japanese is price elastic. If the demand schedule for microprocessors is inelastic, the supply schedule will be negatively sloped. In the case of unit elasticity of demand, the supply schedule for yen will be a vertical line. Throughout the rest of this chapter, we will assume that demand is price elastic. Remember that the price elasticity of demand tells us whether or not total expenditures by microprocessor purchasers in Japan will rise or fall when the Japanese yen drops in value. In the long run, it is quite realistic to think that the price elasticity of demand for imports is numerically greater than 1 anyway.

[†]Remember that we are dealing with a two-country world in which we are considering only the exchange of U.S. microprocessors and Japanese laptop computers. In the real world, more than just goods and services are exchanged among countries. Some U.S. residents buy Japanese financial assets; some Japanese residents buy U.S. financial assets. We are ignoring such transactions for the moment.

A Shift in Demand.   Assume that a successful advertising campaign by U.S. computer importers has caused U.S. demand for Japanese laptop computers to rise. U.S. residents demand more laptop computers at all prices. Their demand curve for Japanese laptop computers has shifted outward to the right.

The increased demand for Japanese laptop computers can be translated into an increased demand for yen. All U.S. residents clamoring for laptop computers will supply more dollars to the foreign exchange market while demanding more Japanese yen to pay for the computers. Figure 33-5 presents a new demand schedule, D_2, for Japanese yen; this demand schedule is to the right of the original demand schedule. If the Japanese do not change their desire for U.S. microprocessors, the supply schedule for Japanese yen will remain stable.

A new equilibrium will be established at a higher exchange rate. In our particular example, the new equilibrium is established at an exchange rate of $.0120 per yen. It now takes 1.2 cents to buy 1 Japanese yen, whereas formerly it took 1 cent. This will be translated into an increase in the price of Japanese laptop computers to U.S. residents and as a decrease in the price of U.S. microprocessors to the Japanese. For example, a Japanese laptop computer priced at 100,000 yen that sold for $1,000 in the United States will now be priced at $1,200. Conversely, a U.S. microprocessor priced at $50 that previously sold for 5,000 yen in Japan will now sell for 4,167 yen.

A Shift in Supply.   We just assumed that the U.S. demand for Japanese laptop computers had shifted due to a successful ad compaign. Because the demand for Japanese yen is a derived demand by U.S. residents for laptop computers, this is translated into a shift in the demand curve for yen. As an alternative exercise, we might assume that the supply curve of Japanese yen shifts outward to the right. Such a supply shift could occur for many reasons, one of which is a relative rise in the Japanese price level. For example, if the price of all Japanese-manufactured computer components went up 100 percent in yen, U.S. microprocessors would become relatively cheaper. That would mean that Japanese residents would want to buy more U.S. microprocessors. But remember that when they want to buy more U.S. microprocessors, they supply more yen to the foreign exchange market.

Thus we see in Figure 33-6 that the supply curve of Japanese yen moves from S to S_1. In the absence of restrictions—that is, in a system of flexible exchange rates—the new

FIGURE 33-5

A Shift in the Demand Schedule
The demand schedule for Japanese laptop computers shifts to the right, causing the derived demand schedule for yen to shift to the right also. We have shown this as a shift from D_1 to D_2. We have assumed that the Japanese supply schedule for yen has remained stable—that is, Japanese demand for American microprocessors has remained constant. The old equilibrium foreign exchange rate was $.0100 (1 cent). The new equilibrium exchange rate will be E_2; it will now cost $.0120 (1.2 cents) to buy 1 yen. The higher price of yen will be translated into a higher U.S. dollar price for Japanese laptop computers and a lower Japanese yen price for American microprocessors.

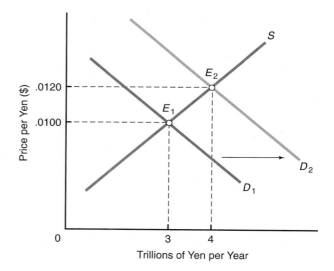

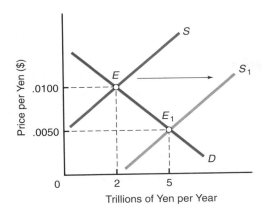

FIGURE 33-6
A Shift in the Supply of Japanese Yen
There has been a shift in the supply curve for Japanese yen. The new equilibrium will occur at E_1, meaning that $.0050 ($\frac{1}{2}$ cent), rather than $.0100 (1 cent), will now buy 1 yen. After the exchange rate adjustment, the amount of yen demanded and supplied will increase to 5 trillion per year.

equilibrium exchange rate will be 1 yen equals $.0050, or $\frac{1}{2}$ cent equals 1 yen. The quantity of yen demanded and supplied will increase from 2 trillion per year to 5 trillion per year. We say, then, that in a flexible international exchange rate system, shifts in the demand for and supply of foreign currencies will cause changes in the equilibrium foreign exchange rates. Those rates will remain in effect until supply or demand shifts.

Market Determinants of Exchange Rates

The foreign exchange market is affected by many other variables in addition to changes in relative price levels, including the following:

1. *Changes in real interest rates.* If the United States interest rate, corrected for people's expectations of inflation, abruptly increases relative to the rest of the world, international investors elsewhere will increase their demand for dollar-denominated assets, thereby increasing the demand for dollars in foreign exchange markets. An increased demand for dollars in foreign exchange markets, other things held constant, will cause the dollar to appreciate and other currencies to depreciate.

2. *Changes in productivity.* Whenever one country's productivity increases relative to another's, the former country will become more price competitive in world markets. At lower prices, the quantity of its exports demanded will increase. Thus there will be an increase in the demand for its currency.

3. *Changes in consumer preferences.* If Germany's citizens suddenly develop a taste for U.S.-made automobiles, this will increase the derived demand for U.S. dollars in foreign exchange markets.

4. *Perceptions of economic stability.* As already mentioned, if the United States looks economically and politically more stable relative to other countries, more foreign residents will want to put their savings into U.S. assets than in their own domestic assets. This will increase the demand for dollars.

● The foreign exchange rate is the rate at which one country's currency can be exchanged for another's.

● The demand for foreign exchange is a derived demand; it is derived from the demand for foreign goods and services (and financial assets). The supply of foreign exchange is derived from foreign residents' demands for domestic goods and services.

CONCEPTS IN BRIEF

- ● The demand curve of foreign exchange slopes downward, and the supply curve of foreign exchange slopes upward. The equilibrium foreign exchange role occurs at the intersection of the demand and supply curves for a currency.

- ● A shift in the demand for foreign goods will result in a shift in the demand for foreign exchange, thereby changing the equilibrium foreign exchange rate. A shift in the supply of foreign currency will also cause a change in the equilibrium exchange rate.

THE GOLD STANDARD AND THE INTERNATIONAL MONETARY FUND

The current system of more or less freely floating exchange rates is a recent development. We have had, in the past, periods of a gold standard, fixed exchange rates under the International Monetary Fund, and variants of these two.

The Gold Standard

Until the 1930s, many nations were on a gold standard. The value of their domestic currency was tied directly to gold. Nations operating under this gold standard agreed to redeem their currencies for a fixed amount of gold at the request of any holder of that currency. Although gold was not necessarily the means of exchange for world trade, it was the unit to which all currencies under the gold standard were pegged. And because all currencies in the system were linked to gold, exchange rates between those currencies were fixed. Indeed, the gold standard has been offered as the prototype of a fixed exchange rate system. The heyday of the gold standard was from about 1870 to 1914.

There was (and always is) a relationship between the balance of payments and changes in domestic money supplies throughout the world. Under a gold standard, the international financial market reached equilibrium through the effect of gold flows on each country's money supply. When a nation suffered a deficit in its balance of payments, more gold would flow out than in. Because the domestic money supply was based on gold, an outflow of gold to foreign residents caused an automatic reduction in the domestic money supply. This caused several things to happen. Interest rates rose, thereby attracting foreign capital and reducing any deficit in the balance of payments. At the same time, the reduction in the money supply was equivalent to a restrictive monetary policy, which caused national output and prices to fall. Imports were discouraged and exports were encouraged, thereby again improving the balance of payments.

Two problems plagued the gold standard. One was that by varying the value of its currency in response to changes in the quantity of gold, a nation gave up control of its domestic monetary policy. Another was that the world's commerce was at the mercy of gold discoveries. Throughout history, each time new veins of gold were found, desired expenditures on goods and services increased. If production of goods and services failed to increase, however, prices of goods and services increased, so inflation resulted.

International Monetary Fund (IMF)
An international agency, founded to administer the Bretton Woods agreement and to lend to member countries that experienced significant balance of payments deficits, that now functions primarily as a lender of last resort for national governments.

Bretton Woods and the International Monetary Fund

In 1944, as World War II was ending, representatives from the world's capitalist countries met in Bretton Woods, New Hampshire, to create a new international payment system to replace the gold standard, which had collapsed during the 1930s. The Bretton Woods Agreement Act was signed on July 31, 1945, by President Harry Truman. It created a new permanent institution, the **International Monetary Fund (IMF)**, to administer the agreement and to lend to member countries that were experiencing significant balance of payments deficits. The arrangements thus provided are now called the old IMF system or the Bretton Woods system.

Member governments were obligated to intervene to maintain the value of their currencies in foreign exchange markets within 1 percent of the declared **par value**—the officially determined value. The United States, which owned most of the world's gold stock, was similarly obligated to maintain gold prices within a 1 percent margin of the official rate of $35 an ounce. Except for a transitional arrangement permitting a onetime adjustment of up to 10 percent in par value, members could alter exchange rates thereafter only with the approval of the IMF.

On August 15, 1971, President Richard Nixon suspended the convertibility of the dollar into gold. On December 18, 1971, the United States officially devalued the dollar—that is, lowered its official value—relative to the currencies of 14 major industrial nations. Finally, on March 16, 1973, the finance ministers of the European Economic Community (now the European Union) announced that they would let their currencies float against the dollar, something Japan had already begun doing with its yen. Since 1973, the United States and most other trading countries have had either freely floating exchange rates or managed ("dirty") floating exchange rates, in which their governments or central banks intervene from time to time to try to influence market exchange rates.

Par value
The officially determined value of a currency.

FIXED VERSUS FLOATING EXCHANGE RATES

The United States went off the Bretton Woods system of fixed exchange rates in 1973. As Figure 33-7 indicates, many other nations of the world have been less willing to permit the values of their currencies to vary in the foreign exchange markets.

Fixing the Exchange Rate

How did nations fix their exchange rates in years past? How do many countries accomplish this today? Figure 33-8 on the next page shows the market for baht, the currency of Thailand. At the initial equilibrium point E_1, U.S. residents had to give up $0.40 to obtain 1 baht. Suppose now that there is an increase in the supply of baht for dollars, perhaps because Thai residents wish to buy more U.S. goods. Other things being equal, the result would be a movement to point E_2 in Figure 33-8. The dollar value of the baht would fall to $0.30.

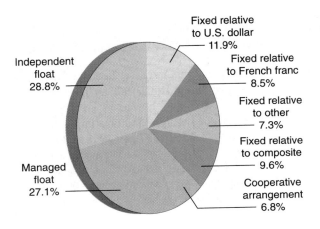

Independent float 28.8%

Fixed relative to U.S. dollar 11.9%

Fixed relative to French franc 8.5%

Fixed relative to other 7.3%

Fixed relative to composite 9.6%

Managed float 27.1%

Cooperative arrangement 6.8%

FIGURE 33-7
Current Foreign Exchange Rate Arrangements
Currently, 56 percent of the member nations of the International Monetary Fund have an independent float or managed float exchange rate arrangement. Among countries with a fixed exchange rate, nearly one in three uses a fixed U.S. dollar exchange rate. Fixing the exchange rate relative to a composite or basket of currencies is the next most common arrangement.
Source: International Monetary Fund.

FIGURE 33-8

A Fixed Exchange Rate

This figure illustrates how the Bank of Thailand could fix the dollar-baht exchange rate in the face of an increase in the supply of baht caused by a rise in the demand for U.S. goods by Thai residents. In the absence of any action by the Bank of Thailand, the result would be a movement from point E_1 to point E_2. The dollar value of the baht would fall from $0.40 to $0.30. The Bank of Thailand can prevent this exchange rate change by purchasing baht with dollars in the foreign exchange market, thereby raising the demand for baht. At the new equilibrium point E_3, the baht's value remains at $0.40.

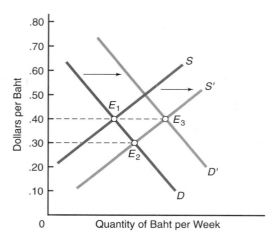

To prevent a baht depreciation from occurring, however, the Bank of Thailand, the central bank, could increase the demand for baht in the foreign exchange market by purchasing baht with dollars. The Bank of Thailand can do this using dollars that it had on hand as part of its *foreign exchange reserves.* All central banks hold reserves of foreign currencies. Because the U.S. dollar is a key international currency, the Bank of Thailand and other central banks typically hold billions of dollars in reserve so that they can, if they wish, make transactions such as the one in this example. Note that a sufficiently large purchase of baht could, as shown in Figure 33-8, cause the demand curve to shift rightward to achieve the new equilibrium point E_3, at which the baht's value remains at $0.40. Provided that it has enough dollar reserves on hand, the Bank of Thailand could maintain—effectively fix—the exchange rate in the face of the sudden fall in the demand for baht.

This is the manner in which the Bank of Thailand fixed the dollar-baht exchange rate until 1997. This basic approach—varying the amount of the national currency demanded at any given exchange rate in foreign exchange markets when necessary—is also the way that *any* central bank seeks to keep its nation's currency value unchanged in light of changing market forces.

> Central banks can keep exchange rates fixed as long as they have enough foreign exchange reserves available to deal with potentially long-lasting changes in the demand for or supply of their nation's currency.

INTERNATIONAL POLICY EXAMPLE

Can Foreign Exchange Rates Be Fixed Forever?

Trying to keep the exchange rate fixed in the face of foreign exchange market volatility can be a difficult policy to pursue. Consider Thailand's experience. At the beginning of 1997, the Bank of Thailand was holding $40 billion in foreign exchange reserves. Within 10 months, those reserves had fallen to $3 billion. Whatever the Bank of Thailand promised about not devaluing, it no longer had credibility. Not surprisingly, the baht's value relative to the dollar fell by more than 25 percent in July 1997 alone.

The Thai experience was repeated on a larger scale throughout Southeast Asia in 1997 and 1998 as efforts by the central banks of Indonesia, Malaysia, South Korea, and Vietnam to fix exchange rates ultimately collapsed, leading to sizable devaluations. Even the previously stalwart exchange rate arrangements of

Singapore, Taiwan, and Hong Kong became increasingly less credible. These nations learned an old lesson: Trying to protect residents from foreign exchange risks works only as long as foreign exchange market traders believe that central banks have the financial wherewithal to keep exchange rates unchanged. Otherwise, a fixed exchange rate policy can ultimately prove unsustainable.

For Critical Analysis

Why do you think governments attempt to maintain the foreign exchange value of their domestic currencies?

Pros and Cons of a Fixed Exchange Rate

Why might a nation such as Thailand wish to keep the value of its currency from fluctuating? One reason is that changes in the exchange rate can affect the market values of assets that are denominated in foreign currencies. This can increase the financial risks that a nation's residents face, thereby forcing them to incur costs to avoid these risks.

Foreign Exchange Risk. The possibility that variations in the market value of assets can take place as a result of changes in the value of a nation's currency is called the **foreign exchange risk** that residents of a country face because their nation's currency value can vary. For instance, if companies in Thailand had many loans denominated in dollars but earned nearly all their revenues in baht from sales within Thailand, a decline in the dollar value of the baht would mean that Thai companies would have to allocate a larger portion of their earnings to make the same *dollar* loan payments as before. Thus a fall in the baht's value would increase the operating costs of these companies, thereby reducing their profitability and raising the likelihood of eventual bankruptcy.

Limiting foreign exchange risk is a classic rationale for adopting a fixed exchange rate. Nevertheless, a country's residents are not defenseless against foreign exchange risk. They can **hedge** against such risk, meaning that they can adopt strategies intended to offset the risk arising from exchange rate variations. For example, a company in Thailand that has significant euro earnings from sales in Germany but sizable loans from U.S. investors could arrange to convert its euro earnings into dollars via special types of foreign exchange contracts called *currency swaps*. The Thai company could thereby avoid holdings of baht and shield itself—*hedge*—against variations in the baht's value.

Foreign exchange risk
The possibility that changes in the value of a nation's currency will result in variations in market values of assets.

Hedge
A financial strategy that reduces the chance of suffering losses arising from foreign exchange risk.

The Exchange Rate as a Shock Absorber. If fixing the exchange rate limits foreign exchange risk, why do so many nations allow the exchange rates to float? The answer must be that there are potential drawbacks associated with fixing exchange rates. One is that exchange rate variations can actually perform a valuable service for a nation's economy. Consider a situation in which residents of a nation speak only their own nation's language, which is so difficult that hardly anyone else in the world takes the trouble to learn it. As a result, the country's residents are very *immobile:* They cannot trade their labor skills outside of their own nation's borders.

Now think about what happens if this nation chooses to fix its exchange rate. Imagine a situation in which other countries begin to sell products that are close substitutes for the products its people specialize in producing, causing a sizable drop in worldwide demand for the nation's goods. Over a short-run period in which prices and wages cannot adjust, the result will be a sharp decline in production of goods and services, a fall-off in national income, and higher unemployment. Contrast this situation with one in which the exchange rate floats. In this case, a sizable decline in outside demand for the nation's products will cause it to experience a trade deficit, which will lead to a significant drop in the demand for the nation's currency. As a result, the nation's currency will experience a sizable depreciation, making the goods that the nation offers to sell abroad much less expensive in other countries. People abroad who continue to consume the nation's products will increase their purchases, and the nation's exports will increase. Its production will begin to recover somewhat, as will its residents' incomes. Unemployment will begin to fall

This example illustrates how exchange rate variations can be beneficial, especially if a nation's residents are relatively immobile. It can be much more difficult, for example, for a Polish resident who has never studied Portuguese to make a move to Lisbon, even if she is highly qualified for available jobs there. If many residents of Poland face similar linguistic or cultural barriers, Poland could be better off with a floating exchange rate even if its residents must incur significant costs hedging against foreign exchange risk as a result.

Splitting the Difference: Dirty Floats and Target Zones

In recent years, national policymakers have tried to soften the choice of either adopting a fixed exchange rate or allowing exchange rates full flexibility in the foreign exchange markets by "splitting the difference" between the two extremes.

A Dirty Float.   One way to split the difference is to let exchange rates float most of the time but "manage" exchange rate movements part of the time. U.S. policymakers have occasionally engaged in what is called a **dirty float,** the management of flexible exchange rates. The management of flexible exchange rates has usually come about through international policy cooperation. For example, the Group of Five (G-5) nations—France, Germany, Japan, the United Kingdom, and the United States—and the Group of Seven (G-7) nations—the G-5 nations plus Italy and Canada—have for some time shared information on their economic policy objectives and procedures. They do this through regular meetings between economic policy secretaries, ministers, and staff members. One of their principal objectives has been to "smooth out" foreign exchange rates.

Is it possible for these groups to "manage" foreign exchange rates? Some economists do not think so. For example, economists Michael Bordo and Anna Schwartz studied the foreign exchange intervention actions coordinated by the Federal Reserve and the U.S. Treasury during the second half of the 1980s. Besides showing that such interventions were sporadic and variable, Bordo and Schwartz came to an even more compelling conclusion: Exchange rate interventions were trivial relative to the total trading of foreign exchange on a daily basis. For example, in April 1989, total foreign exchange trading amounted to $129 billion per day, yet the American central bank purchased only $100 million in deutsche marks and yen during that entire month (and did so on a single day). For all of 1989, Fed purchases of marks and yen were only $17.7 billion, or the equivalent of less than 13 percent of the amount of an average day's trading in April of that year. Their conclusion is that neither the U.S. central bank nor the central banks of the other G-7 nations can influence exchange rates in the long run.

Crawling Pegs.   Another approach to splitting the difference between fixed and floating exchange rates is called a **crawling peg.** This is an automatically adjusting target for the

Dirty float
Active management of a floating exchange rate on the part of a country's government, often in cooperation with other nations.

Crawling peg
An exchange rate arrangement in which a country pegs the value of its currency to the exchange value of another nation's currency but allows the par value to change at regular intervals.

value of a nation's currency. For instance, a central bank might announce that it wants the value of its currency relative to the U.S. dollar to decline at an annual rate of 5 percent, a rate of depreciation that it feels is consistent with long-run market forces. The central bank would then try to buy or sell foreign exchange reserves in sufficient quantities to be sure that the currency depreciation takes place gradually, thereby reducing the foreign exchange risk faced by the nation's residents.

In this way, a crawling peg functions like a floating exchange rate in the sense that the exchange rate can change over time. But it is like a fixed exchange rate in the sense that the central bank always tries to keep the exchange rate close to a target value. In this way, a crawling peg has elements of both kinds of exchange rate systems.

Target Zones. A third way to try to split the difference between fixed and floating exchange rates is to adopt an exchange rate **target zone.** Under this policy, a central bank announces that there are specific upper and lower *bands,* or limits, for permissible values for the exchange rate. Within those limits, which define the exchange rate target zone, the central bank permits the exchange rate to move flexibly. The central bank commits itself, however, to intervene in the foreign exchange markets to ensure that its nation's currency value will not rise above the upper band or fall below the lower band. For instance, if the exchange rate approaches the upper band, the central bank must sell foreign exchange reserves in sufficient quantities to prevent additional depreciation of its nation's currency. If the exchange rate approaches the lower band, the central bank must purchase sufficient amounts of foreign exchange reserves to halt any further currency appreciation.

Starting in 1999, officials from the European Union attempted to get the United States, Japan, and several other countries' governments to agree to target zones for the exchange rate between the newly created euro and the dollar, yen, and some other currencies. Officials in the United States were not in favor. So far no target zones have been created, and the euro has floated freely—mostly downward.

Target zone
A range of permitted exchange rate variations between upper and lower exchange rate bands that a central bank defends by selling or buying foreign exchange reserves.

CONCEPTS IN BRIEF

- The International Monetary Fund was developed after World War II as an institution to maintain fixed exchange rates in the world. Since 1973, however, fixed exchange rates have disappeared in most major trading countries. For these nations, exchange rates are largely determined by the forces of demand and supply in foreign exchange markets.

- Many other nations, however, have tried to fix their exchange rates, with varying degrees of success. Although fixing the exchange rate helps protect a nation's residents from foreign exchange risk, this policy makes less mobile residents susceptible to greater volatility in income and employment. It can also expose the central bank to sporadic currency crises arising from unpredictable changes in world capital flows.

- Countries have experimented with exchange rate systems between the extremes of fixed and floating exchange rates. Under a dirty float, a central bank permits the value of its nation's currency to float in foreign exchange markets but intervenes from time to time to influence the exchange rate. Under a crawling peg, a central bank tries to push its nation's currency value in a desired direction. Pursuing a target zone policy, a central bank aims to keep the exchange rate between upper and lower bands, intervening only when the exchange rate approaches either limit.

NETNOMICS

Making Foreign Exchange Markets More Efficient

The buying and selling of foreign exchange can involve considerable transaction costs. This is particularly true for companies that do not engage in large orders. The Internet has allowed for increased efficiency in this market, at least measured by real-time access and lower implicit commission rates for such transactions.

Back in 1993, a company called E-FOREX was founded to take advantage of Internet technology to develop a new marketplace for foreign exchange. In October 1995, E-FOREX completed its first Internet-based foreign exchange trade. Initially, E-FOREX was conceived as an on-line brokerage company, similar to E*Trade for stocks. Starting in 1996, though, E-FOREX began to license its Internet platforms to other financial institutions. Banks, brokers, and asset managers, for companies, pension plans, and governments, are using E-FOREX to trade today.

Consider a client that wishes to convert U.S. dollars to pay a 13 million yen invoice from its Japanese parts supplier. Even though a foreign exchange trading company would charge only a $50 commission on such a trade, it would also impose a large "spread" between the buying and selling price of yen. E-FOREX charges no commission but makes its profit on a small spread. In this transaction, the savings would be over $500 to the client. Throughout a year's worth of transactions, these savings might become considerable.

With large quantities of dollars, yen, euros, baht, and other currencies being traded over the Internet, security is a major issue. E-FOREX incorporates the latest 128-bit encryption technology and uses digital certificates from Versign as well as firewalls, which prevent outsiders from entering the secure system.

To avoid disaster, if one computer system fails, E-FOREX, similar to other Internet-based brokerage companies, operates two or more systems for routers and database servers. In addition, a remote backup data center supports those systems redundantly. In the event of a service interruption at any facility, no data are lost.

Finally, E-FOREX provides so-called 100 percent double-blind dealing. The party who takes the other side of a client's trade does not know who the client is, and vice versa. This increases foreign exchange efficiency because no clients can guess at the direction of trades and skew rates to earn trading profits in excess of a normal profit.

ISSUES & APPLICATIONS

Are Currency Speculators Unproductive?

When the exchange value of the pound sterling plummeted more than 30 years ago, British politicians blamed the fall on "gnomes of Zurich"—currency speculators based in Switzerland. More recently, when Mahathir Mohamad, the Malaysian prime minister, decried currency speculators as "immoral," he particularly had in mind a speculator named George Soros, the chief executive of Quantum Fund, a firm that sought to earn speculative trading profits for its clients.

Speculative Attacks

In Mahathir's view, Quantum Fund reaped millions of dollars in trading profits at the expense of Malaysia when Soros correctly speculated that Malaysia could not maintain a fixed exchange rate for the Malaysian ringgit relative to the U.S. dollar. Quantum Fund and other individuals and firms conducted large numbers of currency trades with an aim to profit from a decline in the ringgit's value, thereby engaging in what economists call a *speculative attack* on the Malaysian currency.

Perhaps not surprisingly, Mahathir has argued that speculative currency trading is "excessive." He points to the trend highlighted in Figure 33-9: The growth of total foreign exchange trading has far outpaced the growth of total world trade in goods and services. Much of the growth in foreign exchange trading arises from increased purchases and sales of currencies by speculators. Much of this trading, Mahathir concludes, is "unnecessary" and "unproductive."

Some economists and policymakers agree with this assessment. They worry that foreign exchange markets may experience excessive volatility because of the activities of currency

---

Concepts Applied

Exchange Rates

Foreign Exchange Market Equilibrium

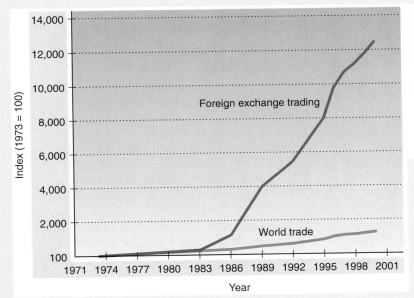

FIGURE 33-9

Foreign Exchange Trading and World Trade Since 1973

This figure displays index measures (1973 = 100) of the dollar volumes of total world trade and foreign exchange trading. At least a portion of the much faster growth of foreign exchange trading undoubtedly reflects an increase in speculative currency trading.

Sources: Bank for International Settlements; World Trade Organization.

speculators. To address this concern, Nobel laureate James Tobin has proposed taxing foreign exchange transactions to reduce the incentive to engage in currency speculation. In 1999, a United Nations study proposed imposing this "Tobin tax" and transferring the proceeds to the less developed nations of the world.

The Economic Role of Currency Speculators

There are, however, reasons to argue that the activities of currency speculators have social value. Firms such as Quantum Fund devote considerable time to studying the economic and political factors that play a fundamental role in determining exchange rates. This helps the firms seek out economic imbalances that are ultimately likely to force exchange rates to move into line with these fundamental factors at some point in the future. For currency speculators, such imbalances—such as, in the case of Malaysia in 1997, a fixed exchange rate that conflicts with the nation's economic policies—offer profitable opportunities. It is arguable that these imbalances could eventually pose serious economic problems in nations that experience them. By forcing countries to deal with imbalances sooner rather than later, speculative attacks may help prevent national policymakers from following misguided policies.

Speculative currency trading also plays an important economic role by making foreign exchange markets more liquid. Suppose that currency speculation were inhibited, for instance, by high taxes on foreign exchange transactions or by regulations requiring anyone who buys a foreign-currency-denominated asset to keep it for a specified period, regardless of changes in economic conditions. In such a situation, there might not be a strong incentive to hold the currency at all. This could make it hard for someone who wants to engage in the cross-border exchange of a real good or service to find willing buyers or sellers of currency required to finance the transaction. Thus the activities of currency speculators may contribute to the liquidity of foreign exchange markets and thereby contribute to the growth of world trade in goods and services. Stopping currency speculation could hinder or even reverse global growth of international trade.

FOR CRITICAL ANALYSIS

1. Why might it be desirable for a country's government to alter policies that are contributing to national economic imbalances sooner rather than later?

2. If defenders of currency speculators are correct, does Figure 33-9 indicate that foreign exchange markets have become more or less liquid in recent years?

SUMMARY DISCUSSION OF LEARNING OBJECTIVES

1. **The Balance of Trade Versus the Balance of Payments:** The balance of trade is the difference between exports of goods and imports of goods during a given period. The balance of payments is a system of accounts for all transactions between a nation's residents and the residents of other countries of the world. In addition to exports and imports, therefore, the balance of payments includes cross-border exchanges of services, income, and financial assets within a given time interval.

2. **The Key Accounts Within the Balance of Payments:** There are three important accounts within the balance of payments. The current account measures net exchanges of goods and services, transfers, and income flows across a nation's borders. The capital account measures net flows of financial assets. The official reserve transactions account tabulates cross-border exchanges of financial assets involving the home nation's governments and central bank as well as foreign governments and central banks. Because each international exchange generates both an inflow and an outflow, the sum of the balances on all three accounts must equal zero.

3. **Exchange Rate Determination in the Market for Foreign Exchange:** From the perspective of the United States, the demand for a nation's currency by U.S. residents is derived largely from the demand for imports from that nation. Likewise, the supply of a

nation's currency is derived mainly from the supply of U.S. exports to that country. The equilibrium exchange rate is the rate of exchange between the dollar and the other nation's currency at which the quantity of the currency demanded is equal to the quantity supplied.

4. **Factors That Can Induce Changes in Equilibrium Exchange Rates:** The equilibrium exchange rate changes in response to changes in the demand for or supply of another nation's currency. Changes in desired flows of exports or imports, real interest rates, productivity in one nation relative to productivity in another nation, tastes and preferences of consumers, and perceptions of economic stability are key factors that can affect the positions of the demand and supply curves in foreign exchange markets. Thus changes in these factors can induce variations in equilibrium exchange rates.

5. **How Policymakers Can Attempt to Keep Exchange Rates Fixed:** If the current price of another nation's currency in terms of the home currency

starts to fall below the level where the home country wants it to remain, the home country's central bank can use reserves of the other nation's currency to purchase the home currency in foreign exchange markets. This raises the demand for the home currency and thereby pushes up the currency's value in terms of the other nation's currency. In this way, the home country can keep the exchange rate fixed at a desired value, as long as it has sufficient reserves of the other currency to use for this purpose.

6. **Alternative Approaches to Limiting Exchange Rate Variability:** Today, many nations permit their exchange rates to vary in foreign exchange markets. Others pursue policies that limit the variability of exchange rates. Some engage in a dirty float, in which they manage exchange rates, often in cooperation with other nations. Some establish crawling pegs, in which the target value of the exchange rate is adjusted automatically over time. And some establish target zones, with upper and lower limits on the extent to which exchange rates are allowed to vary.

Key Terms and Concepts

Accounting identities (806)

Appreciation (814)

Balance of payments (806)

Balance of trade (806)

Crawling peg (824)

Depreciation (814)

Dirty float (824)

Exchange rate (813)

Flexible exchange rates (813)

Foreign exchange market (813)

Foreign exchange risk (823)

Hedge (823)

International Monetary Fund (IMF) (820)

Par value (821)

Special drawing rights (SDRs) (810)

Target zone (825)

Problems

Answers to the odd-numbered problems appear at the back of the book.

33-1. Over the course of a year, a nation tracked its foreign transactions and arrived at the following amounts:

Merchandise exports	500
Service Exports	75
Net unilateral exports	10

Domestic assets abroad (capital outflows)	−200
Foreign assets at home (capital inflows)	300
Changes in official reserves	−35
Merchandise imports	600
Service imports	50

What is this nation's balance of trade, current account balance, and capital account balance?

33-2. Whenever the United States reaches record levels on its current account deficit, Congress flirts with the idea of restricting imported goods. Would trade restrictions like those studied in Chapter 32 be an appropriate response?

33-3. Explain how the following events would affect the market for the Mexican peso.

  a. Improvements in Mexican production technology yield superior guitars, and many musicians desire these guitars.

  b. Perceptions of political instability surrounding regular elections in Mexico make international investors nervous about future business prospects in Mexico.

33-4. On Wednesday, the exchange rate between the euro and the U.S. dollar was $1.07 per euro. On Thursday, it was $1.05. Did the euro appreciate or depreciate against the dollar? By how much?

33-5. On Wednesday, the exchange rate between the euro and the U.S. dollar was $1.07 per euro and the exchange rate between the Canadian dollar and the U.S. dollar was U.S. $.68 per Canadian dollar. What is the exchange rate between the Canadian dollar and the euro?

33-6. Suppose that signs of an improvement in the Japanese economy lead international investors to resume lending to the Japanese government and businesses. Policymakers, however, are worried about how this will influence the yen. How would this event affect the market for the yen? How should the central bank, the Bank of Japan, respond to this event if it wants to maintain the value of the yen?

33-7. Briefly explain the differences between a flexible exchange rate system, a fixed exchange rate system, a dirty float, and a target zone.

33-8. Explain how each of the following would affect Canada's balance of payments.

  a. Canada's rate of inflation falls below that of the United States, its main trading partner.

  b. The possibility of Quebec's separating from the federation frightens international investors.

33-9. Suppose that under a gold standard, the U.S. dollar is pegged to gold at a rate of $35 per ounce and the pound sterling is pegged to gold at a rate of £17.50 per ounce. Explain how the gold standard constitutes an exchange rate arrangement. What is the exchange rate between the U.S. dollar and the pound sterling?

33-10. Suppose that under the Bretton Woods System, the dollar is pegged to gold at a rate of $35 per ounce and the pound sterling is pegged to the dollar at a rate of $2 = £1. If the dollar is devalued against gold and the pegged rate is changed to $40 per ounce, what does this imply for the exchange value of the pound?

Economics on the Net

Daily Exchange Rates   It is an easy matter to keep up with changes in exchange rates every day using the Web site of the Federal Reserve Bank of New York. In this application, you will learn how hard it is to predict exchange rate movements, and you will get some practice thinking about what factors can cause exchange rates to change.

Internet URL:
www.ny.frb.org/pihome/statistics/forex12.shtml

Title: The Federal Reserve Bank of New York: Foreign Exchange 12 Noon Rates

Navigation: Start at the Federal Reserve Bank of New York's homepage (www.ny.frb.org). Select Statistics (www.ny.frb.org/pihome/statistics). Click on Foreign Exchange 12 Noon Rates.

Application

1. For each currency listed, how many dollars does it take to purchase a unit of the currency in the spot foreign exchange market?

2. For each day during a given week (or month), choose a currency from those listed and keep track of its value relative to the dollar. Based on your tabulations, try to predict the value of the currency at the end of the week *following* your data collections. Use any information you may have, or just do your best without any additional information. How far off did your prediction turn out to be?

For Group Study and Analysis Each day, you can also click on a report titled "Foreign Exchange 10 a.m. Rates," which shows exchange rates for a subset of countries listed in the noon report. Assign each country in the 10 A.M. report to a group. Ask the group to determine whether the currency's value appreciated or depreciated relative to the dollar between 10 A.M. and noon. In addition, ask each group to discuss what kinds of demand or supply shifts could have caused the change that occurred during this interval.

Case Background

The president of a small, less developed Latin American nation has big problems. The annual inflation rate is running above 100 percent, the value of the country's currency is dropping like a rock, and foreign savers are rushing to sell off their shares in investment within the country. The president has appointed a working group of economists to study alternative approaches to achieving the president's goal of fixing the nation's exchange rate relative to the U.S. dollar.

A Currency Board Versus Dollarization It does not take long for the working group to narrow down the choices. One means of establishing a truly fixed rate of exchange for a nation's currency is by establishing a currency board. This is an institution that issues currency fully backed by reserves of a foreign currency. That is, the currency board pledges to redeem its domestic currency for a foreign "hard currency," such as the U.S. dollar, at a fixed rate of exchange. With full backing of outstanding currency, the government board can fulfill this pledge.

Establishing a currency board would preclude a couple of activities associated with central banking. Most obviously, this nation could no longer conduct an independent monetary policy if it cannot vary the quantity of its currency that is in circulation. In the event of unexpected outflows of funds—such as the one the country has recently experienced—there would be pressure for the nation's currency to depreciate. To prevent this from occurring, the currency board would simply sell some of its foreign reserves. The second central-banking activity that a currency board often cannot undertake is lending to liquidity-constrained banks and other financial institutions to thwart a bank run or similar financial crisis. Some nations, such as Argentina, have preserved this central-banking role for their currency boards by permitting the currency board to hold some domestic securities. In the event of a liquidity crunch, the currency board can lend financial institutions funds from that available pool of domestic assets.

In addition, there can be an explicit cost of operating a currency board. Financial instruments of developing nations often yield higher returns than those of a developed country such as the United States. Because a currency board would hold dollar-denominated reserves instead of domestic securities, the government of this Latin American country would have to forgo some interest earnings that it normally could use to help fund public expenditures.

An even more dramatic way to achieve a permanently fixed exchange rate is dollarization, which entails the abandonment of the nation's own currency in favor of making the U.S. dollar the country's only legal currency. In this event, there really would be no exchange rate, of course; the currency circulating in the Latin American nation would be the U.S. currency. But the rate of exchange of home currency for U.S. currency would be, as the president wishes, one for one, so in this sense dollarization is the most extreme form of a fixed exchange rate.

In a fully dollarized economy, the nation's monetary policymaker's job would simply be to facilitate the replacement of worn-out dollars. To get to the point of complete dollarization, the nation would obtain the dollars by issuing dollar-denominated debts, and the interest it would have to pay on these debts would be an explicit cost of dollarization. As with a currency board, this forgone interest income could be used to help fund public expenditures. Another cost would be the expense of transporting new dollars and coins from the United States when setting up the system and when old U.S. currency eventually wears out and has to be replaced.

1. What is the fundamental difference between a fixed-exchange-rate policy as implemented by a central bank as compared with a fixed exchange rate policy as pursued by a currency board? Why might foreign savers perceive that the latter is less risky than the former?

2. Is there any point in retaining a central bank if there is a currency board? If the economy is dollarized?

3. Why might adopting a currency board or dollarization help stabilize cross-border flows of funds and international trade in goods and services?

4. Why are foreign savers likely to believe that dollarization is a more credible commitment to stable terms of international exchange than a currency board would be?

5. Suppose that the nation decides to dollarize its economy. Who in this country would pay for this change? (Hint: Who pays for the public expenditures that in the past have been partly funded with government revenues from interest on domestic security holdings?)

6. Is an irrevocably fixed exchange rate more desirable than a floating exchange rate? Why?

1. To learn more about how currency boards have functioned, go to **www.erols.com/kurrency**, and click on "Introduction." Read the article, and then answer the following questions:
   a. What are the key features of an "orthodox" currency board?
   b. In what ways have Argentina and Bulgaria's currency board arrangements differed from those of an orthodox currency board?
   c. The article lists a number of countries that have used currency board arrangements in the past and present. Make a list of nations that have had either good or poor experience with currency boards. What factors appear to influence how well a currency board works?

2. Go to the Web site of the Hong Kong Monetary Authority (**www.info.gov.hk/hkma/**), and answer the following questions:
   a. Click on "Establishment," and after you read the page, in the left-hand margin click on "Exchange Fund Advisory Committee." In the context of our case description of a currency board, what exactly is the Hong Kong "Exchange Fund"?
   b. Back up to the homepage, and click on "Currency Board System." Read the paragraphs on this page, and then click on "Linked Exchange Rate System." Why does the Hong Kong Monetary Authority refer to its system by this latter name?

CHAPTER 1

1-1. This issue involves choice and therefore can be approached using the economic way of thinking. In the case of health care, an individual typically has an unlimited desire for good health. The individual has a limited budget and limited time, however. She must allocate her budget across other desirable goods, such as housing and food, and must allocate their time across waiting in the doctor's office, work, leisure, and sleep. Hence choices must be made in light of limited resources.

1-3. Sally is displaying rational behavior if all of these activities are in her self-interest. For example, Sally likely derives intrinsic value from volunteer and extracurricular activities and may believe that these activities, along with good grades, improve her prospects of finding a job after she completes her studies. Hence these activities are in her self-interest even though they take away some study time.

1-5. Suppose that you desire to earn an A (90 percent) in economics and merely to pass (60 percent) in French. If your model indicates that you earn 15 percentage points on each exam for every hour you spend studying, you would spend 6 hours ($6 \times 15 = 90$) studying economics and 4 hours ($4 \times 15 = 60$) studying French.

1-7. Positive economic analysis deals with the outcome of economics models, whereas normative analysis includes social values in the choice as well.

1-9. a. An increase in the supply of laptop computers, perhaps because of the entry of new computer manufacturers into the market, pushes their price back down.
   b. Another factor, such as higher hotel taxes at popular vacation destinations, makes vacation travel more expensive.

c. Some other factor, such as a fall in wages that workers earn, discourages people from working additional hours.

APPENDIX A

A-1. a. Independent: price; dependent: quantity
   b. Independent: work-study hours; dependent: credit hours
   c. Independent: hours of study; dependent: economics grade

A-3. a. Above x axis; left of y axis
   b. Below x axis; right of y axis
   c. Above x axis; on y axis

A-5.

y	x
-20	-4
-10	-2
0	0
10	2
20	4

A-7. 5

A-9. a. Positive
b. Positive
c. Negative

CHAPTER 2

2-1. Each additional 10 points earned in economics costs 10 additional points in biology, so this PPC illustrates *constant* opportunity costs.

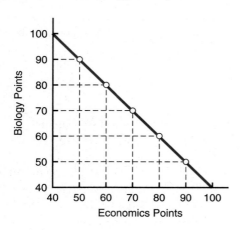

2-3. The $4,500 paid for tuition, room and board, and books consists of explicit costs, not opportunity costs. The $3,000 in lost wages is a forgone opportunity, as is the 3 percent interest that could have been earned on the $4,500. Hence the total opportunity cost is equal to $3,000 + ($4,500 × 0.03) = $3,000 + $135 = $3,135.

2-5.

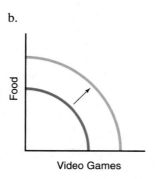

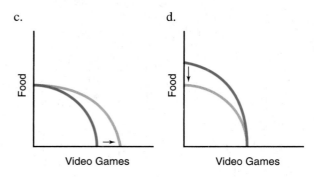

2-7. Because it takes you less time to do laundry, you have an absolute advantage in laundry. Neither you nor your roommate has an absolute advantage in meal preparation. You require two hours to fold a basket of laundry, so your opportunity cost of folding a basket of laundry is two meals. Your roommate's opportunity cost of folding a basket of laundry is three meals. Hence you have a comparative advantage in laundry, and your roommate has a comparative advantage in meal preparation.

2-9. If countries produce the goods for which they have a comparative advantage and trade for those for which they are at a comparative disadvantage, the distribution of resources is more efficient in each nation, yielding gains for both. Artificially restraining trade that would otherwise yield such gains thereby imposes social losses on the residents of both nations.

2-11. a. If the two nations have the same production possibilities, they face the same opportunity costs of producing consumption goods and capital goods. Thus at present neither has a comparative advantage in producing either good.
b. Because country B produces more capital goods today, it will be able to produce more of both goods in the future. Consequently, country B's PPC will shift outward by a greater amount next year.
c. Country B now has a comparative advantage in producing capital goods, and country A now has a comparative advantage in producing consumer goods.

CHAPTER 3

3-1. The equilibrium price is $11 per CD, and the equilibrium quantity is 80 million CDs. At a price of $10 per CD, the quantity of CDs demanded is 90 million, and the quantity of CDs supplied is 60 million. Hence there is a shortage of 30 million CDs at a price of $10 per CD.

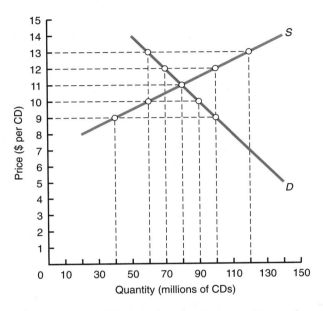

3-3. a. This fall in the price of an input used to produce rock music CDs causes the supply of these CDs to increase. The results are a decline in the market price of rock music CDs and an increase in the equilibrium quantity of rock music CDs.

b. Because CD players and CDs are complements in consumption, a decrease in the price of CD players causes the demand for rock music CDs to increase. This results in an increase in the market price of rock music CDs and an increase in the equilibrium quantity of these CDs.

c. Because cassette tapes and CDs are substitutes in consumption, an increase in the price of cassette tapes increases the demand for rock music CDs. This causes an increase in the market price of rock music CDs and an increase in the equilibrium quantity of rock music CDs.

d. As long as a CD is a normal good, an increase in the income of the typical rock music CD consumer results in an increase in the demand for rock music CDs, which causes the market price of rock music CDs to rise and the equilibrium quantity of these CDs to increase.

e. This shift in preferences would cause a decrease in the demand for rock music CDs, so the market price of these CDs would decline, and the equilibrium quantity of rock music CDs would decrease.

3-5. The imposition of this tax would decrease the supply of Roquefort cheese, which would cause the supply curve to shift leftward. The market price would increase, and equilibrium quantity would fall.

3-7. a. Because memory chips are an input in the production of laptop computers, a decrease in the price of memory chips causes an increase in the supply of laptop computers. The market supply curve shifts to the right, causing the market price to fall and the equilibrium quantity to increase.

b. A decrease in the price of memory chips used in desktop personal computers causes the supply of desktop computers to increase, thereby bringing about a decline in the market price of desktop computers, which are substitutes for laptop computers. This causes a decrease in the demand for laptop computers. The market demand curve shifts leftward, which causes declines in the market price and equilibrium quantity of laptop computers.

c. An increase in the number of manufactures of laptop computers causes an increase in the supply of laptop computers. The market supply curve shifts rightward. The market price of laptop computers declines, and the equilibrium quantity of laptop computers increases.

d. Because computer peripherals are complements, decreases in their prices induce an increase in the demand for laptop computers. Thus the market demand curve shifts to the right, and the market price and equilibrium quantity of laptop computers increase.

3-9. a. The demand for tickets declines, and there will be a surplus of tickets.

b. The demand for tickets rises, and there will be a shortage of tickets.

c. The demand for tickets falls, and there will be a surplus of tickets.

d. The demand for tickets increases, and there will be a shortage of tickets.

CHAPTER 4

4-1. To the band, its producer, and consumers, the market price of the CD provides an indication of the popularity of the band's music; for instance, if the market price rises relative to other CDs, this signals that the band should continue to record its music for sale.

4-3. The market rental rate is $500 per apartment, and 2,000 apartments are rented at this price. At a ceiling price of $450 per month, students wishing to live off campus wish to rent 2,500 apartments, but apartment owners are willing to supply only 1,800 apartments. Thus there is a shortage of 700 apartments at the ceiling price.

4-5. At the above-market price of sugar in the U.S. sugar market, U.S. businesses that use sugar as an input in their products (such as chocolate manufacturers) face higher costs, which shifts the market supply curve leftward. This pushes up the market price of chocolate products and reduces the equilibrium quantity. U.S. sugar producers also sell surplus sugar in foreign sugar markets, which causes the supply curve to shift rightward in foreign markets. This reduces the market price of foreign sugar and raises the equilibrium quantity in the international market.

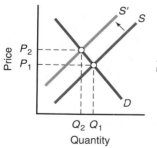

U.S. Chocolate Market

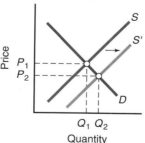

Foreign Sugar Market

4-7. The market price is $400, and the equilibrium quantity of seats is 1,600. If airlines cannot sell tickets to more than 1,200 passengers, passengers are willing to pay $600 per seat, but airlines are willing to sell each ticket for $200.

4-9. Before the price support program, total revenue for farmers was $5 million. After the program, total revenue is $10 million. The cost of the program for taxpayers is $5 million.

CHAPTER 5

5-1. a. As shown in the figure, if the social costs associated with groundwater contamination were reflected in the costs incurred by pesticide manufacturers, the supply schedule would be S' instead of S, and the market price would be higher. The equilibrium quantity of pesticides produced would be lower.

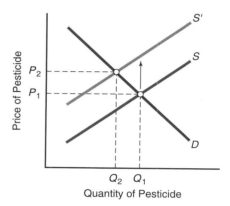

Quantity of Pesticide

b. The government could tax the production and sale of pesticides, thereby shifting the supply curve upward and to the left.

5-3 a. As shown in the figure, if the social benefits associated with bus ridership were taken into account, the demand schedule would be D' instead of D, and the market price would be higher. The equilibrium quantity of bus rides would be higher.

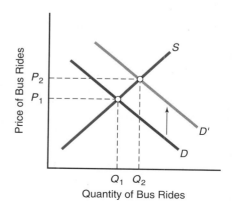

Quantity of Bus Rides

b. The government could pay commuters a subsidy to ride the bus, thereby shifting the demand curve upward and to the right. This would increase the market price and equilibrium number of bus rides.

5-5. The problem is that although most people around the lighthouse will benefit from its presence, there is no incentive for people to contribute voluntarily if they believe that others ultimately will pay for it. That is, the city is likely to face a free-rider problem in its efforts to raise its share of the funds required for the lighthouse.

5-7. Because the marginal tax rate increases as workers' earnings decline, this tax system is regressive.

5-9. Seeking to increase budget allocations in future years and to make workers' jobs more interesting is similar to the goals of firms in private markets. Achieving these goals via majority rule and regulatory coercion, however, are aspects that are specific to the public sector.

CHAPTER 6

6-1. 50 percent

6-3. No more than $9 per hour

6-5. a. Equilibrium price = $500; society's total expense = $40 million
b. 100,000 tests
c. Producers' per-unit cost = $700; society's total expense = $70 million
d. Government's per-unit subsidy = $600; total subsidy = $60 million

CHAPTER 7

7-1. By the time you would begin employment with employer B, the purchasing power of the salary you would earn from that job would have dropped by 5 percent. Thus a year from now, the purchasing power of the $25,000 salary will have dropped to $25,000/1.05 = $23,809.52. Furthermore, additional inflation during the following year will continue to erode the salary's purchasing power. In contrast, you anticipate that the purchasing power of the job offer from employer A will remain

unchanged at $24,000. Because you are indifferent between the jobs in other respects, you should accept job A.

7-3. a. 3 percent
b. 5 percent
c. 6 percent
d. 8 percent

7-5. a. 5 percent
b. One month
c. Two months
d. 10 percent

7-7. 105.0

7-9. a. The homeowner gains; the savings bank loses.
b. The tenants gain; the landlord loses.
c. The auto buyer gains; the bank loses.
d. The employer gains; the pensioner loses.

CHAPTER 8

8-1. a. GDP = $14.6 trillion; NDP = $13.3 trillion; NI = $12.5 trillion.
b. GDP in 2006 will equal $13.5 trillion.
c. If the value of depreciation were to exceed gross private domestic investment in 2006, the nation's capital stock would decline. Because capital is a productive resource, the nation's future productivity likely would decline, and this decline would worsen if the situation were to continue beyond 2006.

8-3. a. Gross domestic income = $14.6 trillion; GDP = $14.6 trillion.
b. Gross private domestic investment = $2 trillion.
c. Personal income = $12 trillion; personal disposable income = $10.3 trillion.

8-5. a. Measured GDP declines.
b. Measured GDP increases.
c. Measured GDP does not change (the firearms are not newly produced).

8-7. a. Nominal GDP for 1997 is $2,300; for 2002, $2,832.
b. Real GDP for 1997 is $2,300; for 2002, $2,229.

8-9. The market transactions included in GDP would be the $15 million paid to construction companies and the $5 million paid to salvage companies, for a total of $20 million included in real GDP. Any lost market value of existing homes not reclaimed would be a wealth loss not captured in GDP, because it is a loss in the value of a *stock* of resources. In addition, the $3 million in time that some devote to the reconstruction of their homes would be nonmarket transactions not included in GDP. Also not included would be the reduction in the general state of happiness-which is not valued in the marketplace-for everyone affected by the hurricane.

CHAPTER 9

9-1. a. *B*
   b. *C*

9-3. 1.77 times higher after 20 years; 3.16 times higher after 40 years

9-5. Five years

9-7. 4 percent

CHAPTER 10

10-1. Unemployment would consist of only frictional and structural unemployment.

10-3. $2 trillion

10-5. There are three effects of a rise in the price level. First, there is a real-balance effect, because the rise in the price level reduces real money balances, inducing people to cut back on their spending. In addition, there is an interest rate effect as a higher price level pushes up interest rates, thereby reducing the attractiveness of purchasing autos, houses, and business assets. Finally, there is an open economy effect as home residents respond to the higher price level by reducing purchases of domestically produced goods in favor of foreign-produced goods, while foreign residents cut back on their purchases of home-produced goods. All three effects entail a reduction in purchases of goods and services, so the aggregate demand curve slopes downward.

10-7. a. At the price level P_2 above the equilibrium price level P_1, the total quantity of real output that people plan to consume is less than the total quantity that is consistent with firms' production plans. One reason is that at the higher-than-equilibrium price level, real money balances are lower, which reduces real wealth and induces lower planned consumption. Another is that interest rates are higher at the higher-than-equilibrium price level, which generates a cutback in consumption spending. Finally, at the higher-than equilibrium price level P_2, people tend to cut back on purchasing domestic goods in favor of foreign-produced goods, and foreign residents reduce purchases of domestic goods. As unsold inventories of output accumulate, the price level drops toward the equilibrium price level P_1, which ultimately causes planned consumption to rise toward equality with total production.

   b. At the price level P_3 below the equilibrium price level P_1, the total quantity of real output that people plan to consume exceeds the total quantity that is consistent with firms' production plans. One reason is that at the lower-than-equilibrium price level, real money balances are higher, which raises real wealth and induces higher planned consumption. Another is that interest rates are lower at the higher-than-equilibrium price level, which generates an increase in consumption spending. Finally, at the lower-than equilibrium price level P_2, people tend to raise their purchases of domestic goods and cut back on buying foreign-produced goods, and foreign residents increase purchases of domestic goods. As inventories of output are depleted, the price level begins to rise toward the equilibrium price level P_1, which ultimately causes planned consumption to fall toward equality with total production.

10-9. Unexpected inflation transfers resources. For example, unanticipated inflation harms creditors but benefits debtors. Unpredictable nonstationarity of the price level results in such transfers.

CHAPTER 11

11-1. a. Because saving increases at any given interest rate, the desired saving curve shifts rightward. This causes the equilibrium interest rate to decline.

b. There is no effect on current output, however, because in the classical model the vertical long-run aggregate supply curve always applies.

c. A change in the saving rate does not directly affect the demand for labor or the supply of labor in the classical model, so equilibrium employment does not change.

d. The decrease in the equilibrium interest rate generates a rightward and downward movement along the demand curve for investment. Consequently, desired investment declines.

e. The fall in current investment implies lower capital accumulation. Other things being equal, this will imply lower future production.

11-3. Because there is full information and speedy adjustment of wages and prices in the classical model, the aggregate demand curve shifts leftward along the vertical long-run aggregate supply curve. The equilibrium price level decreases, but there is no change in equilibrium national output.

11-5. a. A decline in nominal wages is one factor. A decrease in the cost of any other important input, such as energy, is another.

b. A technological improvement is one factor. Greater capital accumulation or increased labor force participation are others.

11-7. At this point, the actual unemployment rate is below the natural rate of unemployment. The reason is that the economy is producing a level of output per year that exceeds its long-run capability, which entails employing workers that in normal times would be frictionally or structurally unemployed.

11-9. This will make it relatively more expensive for businesses to purchase inputs from abroad, thereby pushing up their operating costs. Thus the short-run aggregate supply curve will shift leftward. Although it also makes home-produced products cheaper to foreign residents and foreign-produced products more expensive for home residents, the amount of trade is said to be low, so aggregate demand does not shift rightward by much. On net, therefore, the equilibrium price level is likely to fall, and the equilibrium level of real output is likely to decline.

CHAPTER 12

12.1 a, b.

Disposable Income	Saving	Consumption	APS	APC
$ 200	$-40	$240	-0.20	1.20
400	0	400	0.00	1.00
600	40	560	0.07	0.93
800	80	720	0.10	0.90
1,000	120	880	0.12	0.88
1,200	160	1,040	0.13	0.87

c. MPS = 40/200 = 0.20; MPC = 120/200 = 0.8.

12-3. a. Yes, because the rate of return on the investment exceeds the market interest rate

b. No, because the rate of return on the investment is now less than the market interest rate

12-5. a.

Real Income	Consumption	Saving	Investment
$ 2,000	$ 2,000	$ 0	$ 1,200
4,000	3,600	400	1,200
6,000	5,200	800	1,200
8,000	6,800	1,200	1,200
10,000	8,400	1,600	1,200
12,000	10,000	2,000	1,200

MPC = 1,600/2000 = 0.8; MPS = 400/2,000 = 0.2.

b, c.

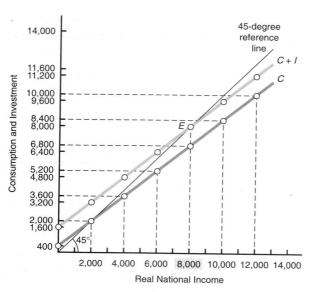

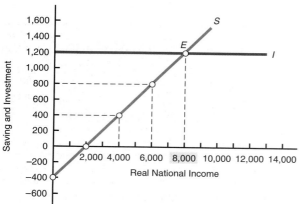

Equilibrium real national income on both graphs equals $8,000.

d. 5

e. 0.15

f. If autonomous consumption were to rise by $100, equilibrium real national income would increase by $100 × 5, or $500.

CHAPTER 13

13-1. a. A key factor that could help explain why the actual multiplier effect may turned out to be lower is the crowding-out effect. Some government spending may have directly crowded out private expenditures on a dollar-for-dollar basis. In addition, indirect crowding out may have occurred. Because the government did not change taxes, it probably sold bonds to finance its increased expenditures, and this action likely pushed up interest rates, thereby discouraging private investment. Furthermore, the increase in government spending likely pushed up aggregate demand, which may have caused a short-run increase in the price level. This may in turn have induced foreign residents to reduce their expenditures on U.S. goods. It could also have reduced real money holdings sufficiently to discourage consumers from spending as much as before. On net, therefore, real GDP rose in the short run but not by the full multiple amount.

b. In the long run, as the increased spending raised aggregate demand, wages and other input prices likely increased in proportion to the resulting increase in the price level. Thus in the long run, the aggregate supply schedule was vertical, and the increase in government spending induced only a rise in the price level.

13-3. Because of the recognition time lag entailed in gathering information about the economy, policymakers may be slow to respond to a downturn in real national income. Congressional approval of policy actions to address the downturn may be delayed, causing an action time lag. Finally, there is an effect time lag, because policy actions take time to exert their full effects on the economy. If these lags are sufficiently long, it is possible that by the time a policy to address a downturn has begun to have its effects, real national income might already be rising. If so, the policy action might push real GDP up faster than intended, thereby making real national income less stable.

13-5. b, d

13-7. One possibility would be a government spending decrease of just the right amount to shift the aggregate demand curve leftward to a new equilibrium point on the long-run aggregate supply curve. Another would be a tax increase designed to achieve the same outcome.

13-9. A cut in the tax rate should induce a rise in consumption and consequently a multiple increase in equilibrium real income. In addition, however, a tax rate reduction reduces the automatic stabilizer properties of the tax system, so equilibrium real income would be less stable in the face of changes in autonomous spending.

APPENDIX C

C-1. a. The marginal propensity to consume is equal to $1 - MPS$, or $\frac{6}{7}$.
   b. Investment or government spending must increase by $50 billion.
   c. The government would have to cut taxes by $58.33 billion.

C-3. a. The aggregate expenditure curve shifts upward by $1 billion; equilibrium real income increases by $5 billion.
   b. The aggregate expenditures curve shifts downward by the MPC times the tax increase, or 0.8 $\times$ $1 billion = 0.8 billion; equilibrium real income falls by $4 billion.
   c. The aggregate expenditures curve shifts upward by $(1 - MPC) \times$ $1 billion = 0.8 billion. Equilibrium real income rises by $1 billion.
   d. No change; no change.

CHAPTER 14

14-1. Medium of exchange; store of value; standard of deferred payment

14-3. Store of value; standard of deferred payment

14-5. a. Both
   b. Neither
   c. M2
   d. M2
   e. M2

14-7. This is an example of adverse selection, in which a prospective borrower had information not possessed by potential lenders.

14-9. It provides banking services such as check clearing for other banks and for the U.S. Treasury, just as a private bank provides such services for its customers. Unlike a private bank, however, the Federal Reserve serves as a lender of last resort, a regulator, and a policymaker.

CHAPTER 15

15-1. $13.5 million

15-3. Yes, the bank holds $50 million in excess reserves.

15-5. $850,000

15-7. 25 percent (or 0.25)

15-9. The money supply declines by $5 billion.

CHAPTER 16

16-1. The bank's total costs from issuing smart cards are $400,000, and its expected revenues will $500,000, so the bank will anticipate profiting and should issue the smart cards.

16-3. Yes. Unless many people carry and use smart cards, retailers will be less likely to accept them, which reduces any given individual's incentive to carry one.

16-5. If FinCEN discovers half of $100 million in laundered funds each year, or $50 million, it can bring in half that amount, or $25 million, in taxes and penalties. If it spends $20 million each year investigating laundering activities and bringing perpetrators to justice, on net it earns $5 million for the government. Ignoring any other factors, this would give FinCEN a rationale for conducting these activities.

16-7. The money supply implications are the same no matter which mechanism people use to make payments.

16-9. The maximum potential value of the money multiplier would remain unchanged at 1 divided by the required reserve ratio. If new on-line banking institutions hold excess reserves in the same proportion to checkable deposits that they issue on-line and if their customers hold the same relative quantities of currency or digital cash that regular bank customers hold, the actual money multiplier also would be the same.

CHAPTER 17

17-1. a. $10,000
     b. Its price falls to $5,000.

17-3. a. One possible policy action would be an open market sale of securities, which would reduce the money supply and shift the aggregate demand curve leftward.
     b. In principle, the Fed's action would reduce inflation more quickly.

17-5. Because a contractionary monetary policy causes interest rates to increase, financial capital begins to flow into the United States. This causes the demand for dollars to rise, which pushes up the value of the dollar and makes U.S. exports more expensive to foreign residents. They cut back on their purchases of U.S. products, which tends to reduce U.S. real national income.

17-7. The price level doubles.

17-9. 10

APPENDIX D

D-1. By its purchase of $1 billion in bonds, the Fed increased excess reserves by $1 billion. This ultimately caused a $3 billion increase in the money supply after full multiple expansion. The 1 percent drop in the interest rate, from 10 to 9 percent, caused investment to rise by $25 billion, from $200 billion to $225 billion. An investment multiplier of 3 indicates that equilibrium national income rose by $75 billion to $2,075 trillion.

CHAPTER 18

18-1. a. The actual unemployment rate would decline.
     b. Natural unemployment rate estimates would also be lower.
     c. The logic of the short- and long-run Phillips curves would not be altered. The government might wish to make this change if it feels that members of the military do "hold jobs" and should therefore be counted as employed persons in the U.S. economy.

18-3. The "long run" is an interval sufficiently long that input prices fully adjust and people have full infor-mation. Adoption of more sophisticated computer and communications technology provides people with more immediate access to information, which can reduce this interval.

18-5. No, because then the new classical theory indicates that workers and firms will speedily adjust nominal wages and other input prices when the price level changes in response to Fed policy actions. As a result, real GDP will not change, so the actual unemployment rate will remain unaltered.

18-7. The explanation would be that aggregate demand has increased at a faster pace than the rise in aggregate supply caused by economic growth. On net, therefore, the price level has risen during the past few years.

18-9. If there is widespread price stickiness, the short-run aggregate supply curve would be horizontal (see Chapter 11), and real GDP would respond strongly to a policy action that affects aggregate demand. By contrast, if prices are highly flexible, the short-run aggregate supply curve slopes upward, and real GDP is less responsive to the change in aggregate demand.

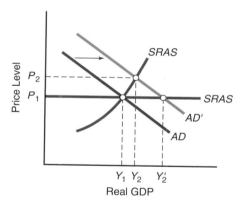

APPENDIX E

E-1. The indifference curve is convex to the origin because of a diminishing marginal rate of substitution. That is, as an individual consumes more and more of an item, the less they are willing to forgo of the other item. The diminishing marginal rate of substitution is due to a diminishing marginal utility.

E-3. Sue's marginal rate of substitution is calculated as follows:

Combination of Bottled Water and Soft Drinks	Bottled Water per Month	Soft Drinks Per Month	MRS
A	5	11	
B	10	7	5:4
C	15	4	5:3
D	20	2	5:2
E	25	1	5:1

The diminishing marginal rate of substitution of soft drinks for water shows Sue's diminishing marginal utility of bottled water. She is willing to forgo fewer and fewer soft drinks to get an additional five bottles of water.

E-5. Given that water is on the horizontal axis and soft drinks on the vertical axis, the slope of Sue's budget constraint is the price of water divided by the price of soft drinks, $P_W/P_S = \frac{1}{2}$. The only combination of bottled water and soft drink that is on Sue's indifference curve and budget constraint is at point C, where total expenditures on water and soft drink total $23.

E-7. Given that water is on the horizontal axis and soft drinks on the vertical axis, the slope of Sue's budget constraint is the price of water divided by the price of soft drinks, $P_W/P_S = 1$. The only combination of bottled water and soft drink that is on Sue's indifference curve and budget constraint is at point C, where total expenditures on water and soft drink total $23.

E-9. Yes, Sue's revealed preferences indicate that her demand for soft drinks obeys the law of demand. As the price of soft drinks declines from $2 to $1, her quantity demanded rises from 4 to 8.

CHAPTER 32

32-1. Norway can produce 100 calculators and 50 books, while Sweden can produce 200 calculators and 50 books. Their total output, therefore, is 300 calculators and 100 books. Sweden has an absolute advantage in calculators. Neither country has an absolute advantage in books.

32-3. a. Norway has a comparative advantage in the production of books and Sweden has a comparative advantage in the production of calculators.
   b. If they specialize, total production is 400 calculators and 100 books.

32-5. Without trade, Norway would have to forgo 1/2 book to obtain 1 calculator. With trade, however, Norway can obtain 1 calculator for 1/3 book. Without trade, Sweden would have to forgo 4 calculators to obtain 1 book. With trade, however, Sweden can obtain 1 book for 3 calculators. By trading, both nations can obtain the good at a price that is less than the opportunity cost of producing it. They are both better off with trade, so this is a positive-sum game.

32-7. A price elasticity of demand less than unity indicates inelastic demand, and therefore price and total revenue move in the same direction. If the nation restricts its exports, the price of the product rises and so does total revenue, even though the nation is selling fewer units.

32-9. a. Because the supply curve shifts by the amount of the tariff, the diagram indicates that the tariff is $20 per television.
   b. Total revenue was $6 billion before the tariff and $4.35 billion after the tariff.
   c. The tariff revenue earned by the U.S. government is $20 × 15 million, or $300 million.

CHAPTER 33

33-1. The trade balance is a deficit of 100, the current account balance is a deficit of 65, and the capital account balance is a surplus of 100.

33-3. a. The increase in demand for Mexican-made guitars increases the demand for the Mexican peso, and the peso appreciates.
   b. International investors will move their capital out of Mexico. The increase in the supply of the peso in the foreign exchange market will cause the peso to depreciate.

33-5. The Canadian dollar–euro rate is found by dividing the U.S. dollar–euro rate by the U.S. dollar–Canadian dollar rate. Thus the Canadian dollar–euro rate = 1.07/0.68 = 1.57.

33-7. A flexible exchange rate system allows the exchange value of a currency to be determined freely in the foreign exchange market with no intervention by the government. A fixed exchange rate pegs the value of the currency, and the authorities responsible for the value of the currency intervene in foreign exchange markets to maintain this value. A dirty float involves occasional intervention by the exchange authorities. A target zone allows the exchange value to fluctuate, but only within a given range of values.

33-9. When the U.S. dollar is pegged to gold at a rate of $35 and the pound sterling at a rate of $17.50, an implicit value between the dollar and the pound is established. The exchange value is $35/£17.50 = $2 per pound.

Glossary

Absolute advantage The ability to produce more units of a good or service using a given quantity of labor or resource inputs. Equivalently, the ability to produce the same quantity of a good or service using fewer units of labor or resource inputs. *Can also be viewed as the ability to produce more output from given inputs of resources than other producers can.*

Accounting identities Values that are equivalent by definition.

Accounting profit Total revenues minus total explicit costs.

Action time lag The time between recognizing an economic problem and implementing policy to solve it. The action time lag is quite long for fiscal policy, which requires congressional approval.

Active (discretionary) policymaking All actions on the part of monetary and fiscal policymakers that are undertaken in response to or in anticipation of some change in the overall economy.

Adverse selection The likelihood that individuals who seek to borrow money may use the funds that they receive for unworthy, high-risk projects.

Age-earnings cycle The regular earnings profile of an individual throughout his or her lifetime. The age-earnings cycle usually starts with a low income, builds gradually to a peak at around age 50, and then gradually curves down until it approaches zero at retirement.

Aggregate demand The total of all planned expenditures for the entire economy.

Aggregate demand curve A curve showing planned purchase rates for all final goods and services in the economy at various price levels, all other things held constant.

Aggregate demand shock Any shock that causes the aggregate demand curve to shift inward or outward.

Aggregates Total amounts or quantities; aggregate demand, for example, is total planned expenditures throughout a nation.

Aggregate supply The total of all planned production for the economy.

Aggregate supply shock Any shock that causes the aggregate supply curve to shift inward or outward.

Anticipated inflation The inflation rate that we believe will occur; when it does, we are in a situation of fully anticipated inflation.

Antitrust legislation Laws that restrict the formation of monopolies and regulate certain anticompetitive business practices.

Appreciation An increase in the exchange value of one nation's currency in terms of the currency of another nation.

Asset demand Holding money as a store of value instead of other assets such as certificates of deposit, corporate bonds, and stocks.

Assets Amounts owned; all items to which a business or household holds legal claim.

Asymmetric information Possession of information by one party in a financial transaction but not by the other party.

Automated clearinghouse (ACH) A computer-based clearing and settlement facility that replaces check transactions by interchanging credits and debits electronically.

Automated teller machine (ATM) network A system of linked depository institution computer terminals that are activated by magnetically encoded bank cards.

Automatic, or built-in, stabilizers Special provisions of certain federal programs that cause changes in desired aggregate expenditures without the action of Congress and the president. Examples are the federal tax system and unemployment compensation.

Autonomous consumption The part of consumption that is independent of (does not depend on) the level of disposable income. Changes in autonomous consumption shift the consumption function.

Average fixed costs Total fixed costs divided by the number of units produced.

Average physical product Total product divided by the variable input.

Average propensity to consume (APC) Consumption divided by disposable income; for any given level of income, the proportion of total disposable income that is consumed.

Average propensity to save (APS) Saving divided by disposable income; for any given level of income, the proportion of total disposable income that is saved.

Average tax rate The total tax payment divided by total income. It is the proportion of total income paid in taxes.

Average total costs Total costs divided by the number of units produced; sometimes called average per-unit total costs.

Average variable costs Total variable costs divided by the number of units produced.

Balance of payments A system of accounts that measures transactions of goods, services, income, and financial assets between domestic households, businesses, and governments and residents of the rest of the world during a specific time period.

Balance of trade The difference between exports and imports of goods.

Balance sheet A statement of the assets and liabilities of any business entity, including financial institutions and the Federal Reserve System. Assets are what is owned; liabilities are what is owed.

Bank runs Attempts by many of a bank's depositors to convert checkable and time deposits into currency out of fear for the bank's solvency.

Barter The direct exchange of goods and services for other goods and services without the use of money.

Base year The year that is chosen as the point of reference for comparison of prices in other years.

Bilateral monopoly A market structure consisting of a monopolist and a monopsonist.

Black market A market in which goods are traded at prices above their legal maximum prices or in which illegal goods are sold.

Bond A legal claim against a firm, usually entitling the owner of the bond to receive a fixed annual coupon payment, plus a lump-sum payment at the bond's maturity date. Bonds are issued in return for funds lent to the firm.

Budget constraint All of the possible combinations of goods that can be purchased (at fixed prices) with a specific budget.

Business fluctuations The ups and downs in overall business activity, as evidenced by changes in national income, employment, and the price level.

Capital consumption allowance Another name for depreciation, the amount that businesses would have to save in order to take care of the deterioration of machines and other equipment.

Capital controls Legal restrictions on the ability of a nation's residents to hold and trade assets denominated in foreign currencies.

Capital gain The positive difference between the purchase price and the sale price of an asset. If a share of stock is bought for $5 and then sold for $15, the capital gain is $10.

Capital goods Producer durables; nonconsumable goods that firms use to make other goods.

Capital loss The negative difference between the purchase price and the sale price of an asset.

Capture hypothesis A theory of regulatory behavior that predicts that the regulators will eventually be captured by the special interests of the industry being regulated.

Cartel An association of producers in an industry that agree to set common prices and output quotas to prevent competition.

Central bank A banker's bank, usually an official institution that also serves as a country's treasury's bank. Central banks normally regulate commercial banks.

Certificate authority A group charged with supervising the terms governing how buyers and sellers can legitimately make digital cash transfers.

Certificate of deposit (CD) A time deposit with a fixed maturity date offered by banks and other financial institutions.

Ceteris paribus **[KAY-ter-us PEAR-uh-bus] assumption** The assumption that nothing changes except the factor or factors being studied.

Checkable deposits Any deposits in a thrift institution or a commercial bank on which a check may be written.

Clearing House Interbank Payment System (CHIPS) A large-value wire transfer system linking about 100 banks that permits them to transmit large sums of money related primarily to foreign exchange and Eurodollar transactions.

Closed shop A business enterprise in which employees must belong to the union before they can be hired and must remain in the union after they are hired.

Collateral An asset pledged to guarantee the repayment of a loan.

Collective bargaining Bargaining between the management of a company or of a group of companies and the management of a union or a group of unions for the purpose of setting a mutually agreeable contract on wages, fringe benefits, and working conditions for all employees in all the unions involved.

Collective decision making How voters, politicians, and other interested parties act and how these actions influence nonmarket decisions.

Common property Property that is owned by everyone and therefore by no one. Air and water are examples of common property resources.

Comparable-worth doctrine The belief that women should receive the same wages as men if the levels of skill and responsibility in their jobs are equivalent.

Comparative advantage The ability to produce a good or service at a lower opportunity cost compared to other producers.

Complements Two goods are complements if both are used together for consumption or enjoyment—for example, coffee and cream. The more you buy of one, the more you buy of the other. For complements, a change in the price of one causes an opposite shift in the demand for the other.

Concentration ratio The percentage of all sales contributed by the leading four or leading eight firms in an industry; sometimes called the *industry concentration ratio*.

Constant dollars Dollars expressed in terms of real purchasing power using a particular year as the base or standard of comparison, in contrast to current dollars.

Constant returns to scale No change in long-run average costs when output increases.

Constant-cost industry An industry whose total output can be increased without an increase in long-run per-unit costs; an industry whose long-run supply curve is horizontal.

Consumer optimum A choice of a set of goods and services that maximizes the level of satisfaction for each consumer, subject to limited income.

Consumer Price Index (CPI) A statistical measure of a weighted average of prices of a specified set of goods and services purchased by wage earners in urban areas.

Consumption Spending on new goods and services out of a household's current income. Whatever is not consumed is saved. Consumption includes such things as buying food and going to a concert. *Can also be viewed as* the use of goods and services for personal satisfaction.

Consumption function The relationship between amount consumed and disposable income. A consumption function tells us how much people plan to consume at various levels of disposable income.

Consumption goods Goods bought by households to use up, such as food, clothing, and movies.

Contraction A business fluctuation during which the pace of national economic activity is slowing down.

Cooperative game A game in which the players explicity cooperate to make themselves better off. As applied to firms, it involves companies colluding in order to make higher than competitive rates of return.

Corporation A legal entity that may conduct business in its own name just as an individual does; the owners of a corporation, called shareholders, own

shares of the firm's profits and enjoy the protection of limited liability.

Cost-of-living adjustments (COLAs) Clauses in contracts that allow for increases in specified nominal values to take account of changes in the cost of living.

Cost-of-service regulation Regulation based on allowing prices to reflect only the actual cost of production and no monopoly profits.

Cost-push inflation Inflation caused by a continually decreasing short-run aggregate supply curve.

Craft unions Labor unions composed of workers who engage in a particular trade or skill, such as baking, carpentry, or plumbing.

Crawling peg An exchange rate arrangement in which a country pegs the value of its currency to the exchange value of another nation's currency but allows the par value to change at regular intervals.

Creative response Behavior on the part of a firm that allows it to comply with the letter of the law but violate the spirit, significantly lessening the law's effects.

Credit risk The risk of loss that might occur if one party to an exchange fails to honor the terms under which the exchange was to take place.

Cross price elasticity of demand (E_{xy}) The percentage change in the demand for one good (holding its price constant) divided by the percentage change in the price of a related good.

Crowding-out effect The tendency of expansionary fiscal policy to cause a decrease in planned investment or planned consumption in the private sector; this decrease normally results from the rise in interest rates.

Crude quantity theory of money and prices The belief that changes in the money supply lead to proportional changes in the price level.

Cyclical unemployment Unemployment resulting from business recessions

that occur when aggregate (total) demand is insufficient to create full employment.

Debit card A plastic card that allows the bearer to transfer funds to a merchant's account, provided that the bearer authorizes the transfer by providing personal identification.

Decreasing-cost industry An industry in which an increase in output leads to a reduction in long-run per-unit costs, such that the long-run industry supply curve slopes downward.

Deflation The situation in which the average of all prices of goods and services in an economy is falling.

Demand A schedule of how much of a good or service people will purchase at any price during a specified time period, other things being constant.

Demand curve A graphical representation of the demand schedule; a negatively sloped line showing the inverse relationship between the price and the quantity demanded (other things being equal).

Demand-pull inflation Inflation caused by increases in aggregate demand not matched by increases in aggregate supply.

Demerit good A good that has been deemed socially undesirable through the political process. Heroin is an example.

Dependent variable A variable whose value changes according to changes in the value of one or more independent variables.

Depository institutions Financial institutions that accept deposits from savers and lend those deposits out at interest.

Depreciation Reduction in the value of capital goods over a one-year period due to physical wear and tear and also to obsolescence; also called *capital consumption allowance. Can also be viewed as* a decrease in the exchange value of one nation's currency in terms of the currency of another nation.

Depression   An extremely severe recession.

Deregulation   The elimination or phasing out of regulations on economic activity.

Derived demand   Input factor demand derived from demand for the final product being produced.

Development economics   The study of factors that contribute to the economic development of a country.

Digital cash   Funds contained on computer software, in the form of secure programs stored on microchips and other computer devices.

Diminishing marginal utility   The principle that as more of any good or service is consumed, its extra benefit declines. Otherwise stated, increases in total utility from the consumption of a good or service become smaller and smaller as more is consumed during a given time period.

Direct expenditure offsets   Actions on the part of the private sector in spending income that offset government fiscal policy actions. Any increase in government spending in an area that competes with the private sector will have some direct expenditure offset.

Direct relationship   A relationship between two variables that is positive, meaning that an increase in one variable is associated with an increase in the other and a decrease in one variable is associated with a decrease in the other.

Dirty float   Active management of a floating exchange rate on the part of a country's government, often in cooperation with other nations.

Discounting   The method by which the present value of a future sum or a future stream of sums is obtained.

Discount rate   The interest rate that the Federal Reserve charges for reserves that it lends to depository institutions. It is sometimes referred to as the rediscount rate or, in Canada and England, as the bank rate.

Discouraged workers   Individuals who have stopped looking for a job because they are convinced that they will not find a suitable one.

Diseconomies of scale   Increases in long-run average costs that occur as output increases.

Disposable personal income (DPI)   Personal income after personal income taxes have been paid.

Dissaving   Negative saving; a situation in which spending exceeds income. Dissaving can occur when a household is able to borrow or use up existing assets.

Distribution of income   The way income is allocated among the population.

Dividends   Portion of a corporation's profits paid to its owners (shareholders).

Division of labor   The segregation of a resource into different specific tasks; for example, one automobile worker puts on bumpers, another doors, and so on.

Dominant strategies   Strategies that always yield the highest benefit. Regardless of what other players do, a dominant strategy will yield the most benefit for the player using it.

Dumping   Selling a good or a service abroad below the price charged in the home market or at a price below its cost of production.

Durable consumer goods   Consumer goods that have a life span of more than three years.

Economic goods   Goods that are scarce, for which the quantity demanded exceeds the quantity supplied at a zero price.

Economic growth   Increases in per capita real GDP measured by its rate of change per year.

Economic profits   Total revenues minus total opportunity costs of all inputs used, or the total of all implicit and explicit costs. *Can also be viewed as the* difference between total revenues and the opportunity cost of all factors of production.

Economic rent   A payment for the use of any resource over and above its opportunity cost.

Economics   The study of how people allocate their limited resources to satisfy their unlimited wants.

Economies of scale   Decreases in long-run average costs resulting from increases in output.

Effect time lag   The time that elapses between the onset of policy and the results of that policy.

Efficiency wage theory   The hypothesis that the productivity of workers depends on the level of the real wage rate.

Efficiency   The case in which a given level of inputs is used to produce the maximum output possible. Alternatively, the situation in which a given output is produced at minimum cost.

Efficiency wages   Wages set above competitive levels to increase labor productivity and profits by enhancing the efficiency of the firm through lower turnover, ease of attracting higher-quality workers, and better efforts by workers.

Effluent fee   A charge to a polluter that gives the right to discharge into the air or water a certain amount of pollution. Also called a *pollution tax.*

Elastic demand   A demand relationship in which a given percentage change in price will result in a larger percentage change in quantity demanded. Total expenditures and price changes are inversely related in the elastic region of the demand curve.

Empirical   Relying on real-world data in evaluating the usefulness of a model.

Endowments   The various resources in an economy, including both physical resources and such human resources as ingenuity and management skills.

Entrepreneurship   The factor of production involving human resources that perform the functions of raising capital, organizing, managing, assembling other factors of production, and making basic business policy decisions. The entrepreneur is a risk taker.

Entry deterrence strategy Any strategy undertaken by firms in an industry, either individually or together, with the intent or effect of raising the cost of entry into the industry by a new firm.

Equation of exchange The formula indicating that the number of monetary units times the number of times each unit is spent on final goods and services is identical to the price level times output (or nominal national income).

Equilibrium The situation when quantity supplied equals quantity demanded at a particular price.

Eurodollar deposits Deposits denominated in U.S. dollars but held in banks outside the United States, often in overseas branches of U.S. banks.

Excess reserves The difference between legal reserves and required reserves.

Exchange rate The price of one nation's currency in terms of the currency of another country.

Exclusion principle The principle that no one can be excluded from the benefits of a public good, even if that person hasn't paid for it.

Expansion A business fluctuation in which overall business activity is rising at a more rapid rate than previously or at a more rapid rate than the overall historical trend for the nation.

Expenditure approach A way of computing national income by adding up the dollar value at current market prices of all final goods and services.

Explicit costs Costs that business managers must take account of because they must be paid; examples are wages, taxes, and rent.

Externality A consequence of an economic activity that spills over to affect third parties. Pollution is an externality. *Can also be viewed as* a situation in which a private cost (or benefit) diverges from a social cost (or benefit); a situation in which the costs (or benefits) of an action are not fully borne (or gained) by the two parties engaged in exchange or by an individual engaging in a scarce-resource-using activity.

Featherbedding Any practice that forces employers to use more labor than they would otherwise or to use existing labor in an inefficient manner.

The Fed The Federal Reserve System; the central bank of the United States.

Federal Deposit Insurance Corporation (FDIC) A government agency that insures the deposits held in banks and most other depository institutions; all U.S. banks are insured this way.

Federal funds market A private market (made up mostly of banks) in which banks can borrow reserves from other banks that want to lend them. Federal funds are usually lent for overnight use.

Federal funds rate The interest rate that depository institutions pay to borrow reserves in the interbank federal funds market.

Fedwire A large-value wire transfer system operated by the Federal Reserve that is open to all depository institutions that legally must maintain required reserves with the Fed.

Fiduciary monetary system A system in which currency is issued by the government and its value is based uniquely on the public's faith that the currency represents command over goods and services.

Final goods and services Goods and services that are at their final stage of production and will not be transformed into yet other goods or services. For example, wheat is not ordinarily considered a final good because it is usually used to make a final good, bread.

Financial capital Money used to purchase capital goods such as buildings and equipment.

Financial intermediaries Institutions that transfer funds between ultimate lenders (savers) and ultimate borrowers.

Financial intermediation The process by which financial institutions accept savings from businesses, households, and governments and lend the savings to other businesses, households, and governments.

Financial trading system A mechanism linking buyers and sellers of stocks and bonds.

Firm A business organization that employs resources to produce goods or services for profit. A firm normally owns and operates at least one plant in order to produce.

Fiscal policy The discretionary changing of government expenditures or taxes to achieve national economic goals, such as high employment with price stability.

Fixed costs Costs that do not vary with output. Fixed costs include such things as rent on a building. These costs are fixed for a certain period of time; in the long run, they are variable.

Fixed investment Purchases by businesses of newly produced producer durables, or capital goods, such as production machinery and office equipment.

Flexible exchange rates Exchange rates that are allowed to fluctuate in the open market in response to changes in supply and demand. Sometimes called *floating exchange rates.*

Flow A quantity measured per unit of time; something that occurs over time, such as the income you make per week or per year or the number of individuals who are fired every month.

Foreign exchange market A market in which households, firms, and governments buy and sell national currencies.

Foreign exchange rate The price of one currency in terms of another.

Foreign exchange risk The possibility that changes in the value of a nation's currency will result in variations in market values of assets.

45-degree reference line The line along which planned real expenditures equal real national income per year.

Fractional reserve banking A system in which depository institutions hold reserves that are less than the amount of total deposits.

Free-rider problem A problem that arises when individuals presume that others will pay for public goods so that, individually, they can escape paying for their portion without causing a reduction in production.

Frictional unemployment Unemployment due to the fact that workers must search for appropriate job offers. This takes time, and so they remain temporarily unemployed.

Full employment An arbitrary level of unemployment that corresponds to "normal" friction in the labor market. In 1986, a 6.5 percent rate of unemployment was considered full employment. Today, it is assumed to be 5 percent or possibly even less.

Game theory A way of describing the various possible outcomes in any situation involving two or more interacting individuals when those individuals are aware of the interactive nature of their situation and plan accordingly. The plans made by these individuals are known as *game strategies*.

GDP deflator A price index measuring the changes in prices of all new goods and services produced in the economy.

General Agreement on Tariffs and Trade (GATT) An international agreement established in 1947 to further world trade by reducing barriers and tariffs.

Goods All things from which individuals derive satisfaction or happiness.

Government, or political, goods Goods (and services) provided by the public sector; they can be either private or public goods.

Gross domestic income (GDI) The sum of all income—wages, interest, rent, and profits—paid to the four factors of production.

Gross domestic product (GDP) The total market value of all final goods and services produced by factors of production located within a nation's borders.

Gross private domestic investment The creation of capital goods, such as factories and machines, that can yield production and hence consumption in the future. Also included in this definition are changes in business inventories and repairs made to machines or buildings.

Gross public debt All federal government debt irrespective of who owns it.

Hedge A financial strategy that reduces the chance of suffering losses arising from foreign exchange risk.

Horizontal merger The joining of firms that are producing or selling a similar product.

Human capital The accumulated training and education of workers.

Implicit costs Expenses that managers do not have to pay out of pocket and hence do not normally explicitly calculate, such as the opportunity cost of factors of production that are owned; examples are owner-provided capital and owner-provided labor.

Import quota A physical supply restriction on imports of a particular good, such as sugar. Foreign exporters are unable to sell in the United States more than the quantity specified in the import quota.

Incentive-compatible contract A loan contract under which a significant amount of the borrower's assets are at risk, providing an incentive for the borrower to look after the lender's interests.

Incentives Rewards for engaging in a particular activity.

Incentive structure The system of rewards and punishments individuals face with respect to their own actions.

Income approach A way of measuring national income by adding up all components of national income, including wages, interest, rent, and profits.

Income elasticity of demand (E_i) The percentage change in demand for any good, holding its price constant, divided by the percentage change in income; the responsiveness of demand to changes in income, holding the good's relative price constant.

Income in kind Income received in the form of goods and services, such as housing or medical care; to be contrasted with money income, which is simply income in dollars, or general purchasing power, that can be used to buy *any* goods and services.

Income velocity of money The number of times per year a dollar is spent on final goods and services; equal to GDP divided by the money supply.

Income-consumption curve The set of optimum consumption points that would occur if income were increased, relative prices remaining constant.

Increasing-cost industry An industry in which an increase in industry output is accompanied by an increase in long-run per-unit costs, such that the long-run industry supply curve slopes upward.

Independent variable A variable whose value is determined independently of, or outside, the equation under study.

Indifference curve A curve composed of a set of consumption alternatives, each of which yields the same total amount of satisfaction.

Indirect business taxes All business taxes except the tax on corporate profits. Indirect business taxes include sales and business property taxes.

Industrial unions Labor unions that consist of workers from a particular industry, such as automobile manufacturing or steel manufacturing.

Industry supply curve The locus of points showing the minimum prices at which given quantities will be forthcoming; also called the *market supply curve.*

Inefficient point Any point below the production possibilities curve at which resources are being used inefficiently.

Inelastic demand A demand relationship in which a given percentage change in price will result in a less than proportionate percentage change in the quantity demanded. Total expenditures and price are directly related in the inelastic region of the demand curve.

Infant industry argument The contention that tariffs should be imposed to protect from import competition an industry that is trying to get started. Presumably, after the industry becomes technologically efficient, the tariff can be lifted.

Inferior goods Goods for which demand falls as income rises.

Inflation The situation in which the average of all prices of goods and services in an economy is rising.

Inflation-adjusted return A rate of return that is measured in terms of real goods and services, that is, after the effects of inflation have been factored out.

Inflationary gap The gap that exists whenever the equilibrium level of real national income per year is greater than the full-employment level as shown by the position of the long-run aggregate supply curve.

Innovation Transforming an invention into something that is useful to humans.

Inside information Information that is not available to the general public about what is happening in a corporation.

Insider-outsider theory A theory of labor markets in which workers who are already employed have an influence on wage bargaining in such a way that outsiders who are willing to work for lower real wages cannot get a job.

Interest The payment for current rather than future command over resources; the cost of obtaining credit. Also, the return paid to owners of capital.

Interest rate effect One of the reasons that the aggregate demand curve slopes downward is that higher price levels increase the interest rate, which in turn causes businesses and consumers to reduce desired spending due to the higher price of borrowing.

Intermediate goods Goods used up entirely in the production of final goods.

International financial diversification Financing investment projects in more than one country.

International Monetary Fund (IMF) An international agency, founded to administer the Bretton Woods agreement and to lend to member countries that experienced significant balance of payments deficits, that now functions primarily as a lender of last resort for national governments.

Inventory investment Changes in the stocks of finished goods and goods in process, as well as changes in the raw materials that businesses keep on hand. Whenever inventories are decreasing, inventory investment is negative; whenever they are increasing, inventory investment is positive.

Inverse relationship A relationship between two variables that is negative, meaning that an increase in one variable is associated with a decrease in the other and a decrease in one variable is associated with an increase in the other.

Investment Any use of today's resources to expand tomorrow's production or consumption. *Can also be viewed as* the spending by businesses on things such as machines and buildings, which can be used to produce goods and services in the future. The investment part of total output is the portion that will be used in the process of producing goods in the future.

Job leaver An individual in the labor force who quits voluntarily.

Job loser An individual in the labor force whose employment was involuntarily terminated.

Jurisdictional dispute A dispute involving two or more unions over which should have control of a particular jurisdiction, such as a particular craft or skill or a particular firm or industry.

Keynesian short-run aggregate supply curve The horizontal portion of the aggregate supply curve in which there is unemployment and unused capacity in the economy.

Labor Productive contributions of humans who work, involving both mental and physical activities.

Labor force Individuals aged 16 years or older who either have jobs or are looking and available for jobs; the number of employed plus the number of unemployed.

Labor force participation rate The percentage of noninstitutionalized working-age individuals who are employed or seeking employment.

Labor productivity Total real domestic output (real GDP) divided by the number of workers (output per worker).

Labor unions Worker organizations that seek to secure economic improvements for their members; they also seek to improve the safety, health, and other benefits (such as job security) of their members.

Land The natural resources that are available from nature. Land as a resource includes location, original fertility and mineral deposits, topography, climate, water, and vegetation.

Large-value wire transfer system A payment system that permits the electronic transmission of large dollar sums.

Law of demand The observation that there is a negative, or inverse, relationship between the price of any good or service and the quantity demanded, holding other factors constant.

Law of diminishing (marginal) returns The observation that after some point, successive equal-sized increases in a variable factor of production, such as labor, added to fixed factors of production, will result in smaller increases in output.

Law of increasing relative cost The observation that the opportunity cost of additional units of a good generally increases as society attempts to produce more of that good. This accounts for the bowed-out shape of the production possibilities curve.

Law of supply The observation that the higher the price of a good, the more of that good sellers will make available over a specified time period, other things being equal.

Leading indicators Factors that economists find to exhibit changes before changes in business activity.

Legal reserves Reserves that depository institutions are allowed by law to claim as reserves—for example, deposits held at Federal Reserve district banks and vault cash.

Lemons problem The situation in which consumers, who do not know details about the quality of a product, are willing to pay no more than the price of a low-quality product, even if a higher-quality product at a higher price exists.

Liabilities Amounts owed; the legal claims against a business or household by nonowners.

Limited liability A legal concept whereby the responsibility, or liability, of the owners of a corporation is limited to the value of the shares in the firm that they own.

Limit-pricing model A model that hypothesizes that a group of colluding sellers will set the highest common price that they believe they can charge without new firms seeking to enter that industry in search of relatively high profits.

Liquidity The degree to which an asset can be acquired or disposed of without much danger of any intervening loss in *nominal* value and with small transaction costs. Money is the most liquid asset.

Liquidity approach A method of measuring the money supply by looking at money as a temporary store of value.

Liquidity risk The risk of loss that may occur if a payment is not received when due.

Long run The time period in which all factors of production can be varied.

Long-run aggregate supply curve A vertical line representing real output of goods and services after full adjustment has occurred. *Can also be viewed as* representing the real output of the economy under conditions of full employment—the full-employment level of real GDP.

Long-run average cost curve The locus of points representing the minimum unit cost of producing any given rate of output, given current technology and resource prices.

Long-run industry supply curve A market supply curve showing the relationship between prices and quantities forthcoming after firms have been allowed the time to enter into or exit from an industry, depending on whether there have been positive or negative economic profits.

Lorenz curve A geometric representation of the distribution of income. A Lorenz curve that is perfectly straight represents complete income equality. The more bowed a Lorenz curve, the more unequally income is distributed.

Lump-sum tax A tax that does not depend on income or the circumstances of the taxpayer. An example is a $1,000 tax that every family must pay, irrespective of its economic situation.

M1 The money supply, taken as the total value of currency plus checkable deposits plus traveler's checks not issued by banks.

M2 M1 plus (1) savings and small-denomination time deposits at all depository institutions, (2) overnight repurchase agreements at commercial banks, (3) overnight Eurodollars held by U.S. residents other than banks at Caribbean branches of member banks, (4) balances in retail money market mutual funds, and (5) money market deposit accounts (MMDAs).

Macroeconomics The study of the behavior of the economy as a whole, including such economywide phenomena as changes in unemployment, the general price level, and national income.

Majority rule A collective decision-making system in which group decisions are made on the basis of more than 50 percent of the vote. In other words, whatever more than half of the electorate votes for, the entire electorate has to accept.

Marginal cost pricing A system of pricing in which the price charged is equal to the opportunity cost to society of producing one more unit of the good or service in question. The opportunity cost is the marginal cost to society.

Marginal costs The change in total costs due to a one-unit change in production rate.

Marginal factor cost (MFC) The cost of using an additional unit of an input. For example, if a firm can hire all the workers it wants at the going wage rate, the marginal factor cost of labor is the wage rate.

Marginal physical product The physical output that is due to the addition of one more unit of a variable factor of production; the change in total product occurring when a variable input is increased and all other inputs are held constant; also called *marginal product* or *marginal return*.

Marginal physical product (MPP) of labor The change in output resulting from the addition of one more worker. The MPP of the worker equals the change in total output accounted for by hiring the worker, holding all other factors of production constant.

Marginal propensity to consume (MPC) The ratio of the change in consumption to the change in disposable income. A marginal propensity to consume of 0.8 tells us that an additional $100 in take-home pay will lead to an additional $80 consumed.

Marginal propensity to save (MPS) The ratio of the change in saving to the change in disposable income. A marginal propensity to save of 0.2 indicates that out of an additional $100 in take-home pay, $20 will be saved. Whatever is not saved is consumed. The marginal propensity to save plus the marginal propensity to consume must always equal 1, by definition.

Marginal revenue The change in total revenues resulting from a change in output (and sale) of one unit of the product in question.

Marginal revenue product (MRP) The marginal physical product (MPP) times marginal revenue. The MRP gives the additional revenue obtained from a one-unit change in labor input.

Marginal tax rate The change in the tax payment divided by the change in income, or the percentage of additional dollars that must be paid in taxes. The marginal tax rate is applied to the highest tax bracket of taxable income reached.

Marginal utility The change in total utility due to a one-unit change in the quantity of a good or service consumed.

Market All of the arrangements that individuals have for exchanging with one another. Thus we can speak of the labor market, the automobile market, and the credit market.

Market clearing, or **equilibrium, price** The price that clears the market, at which quantity demanded equals quantity supplied; the price where the demand curve intersects the supply curve.

Market demand The demand of all consumers in the marketplace for a particular good or service. The summing at each price of the quantity demanded by each individual.

Market failure A situation in which an unrestrained market operation leads to either too few or too many

resources going to a specific economic activity.

Market share test The percentage of a market that a particular firm supplies, used as the primary measure of monopoly power.

Median age The age that divides the older half of the population from the younger half.

Medical savings account (MSA) A tax-exempt health care account into which individuals would pay on a regular basis and out of which medical care expenses could be paid.

Medium of exchange Any asset that sellers will accept as payment.

Merit good A good that has been deemed socially desirable through the political process. Museums are an example.

Microeconomics The study of decision making undertaken by individuals (or households) and by firms.

Minimum efficient scale (MES) The lowest rate of output per unit time at which long-run average costs for a particular firm are at a minimum.

Minimum wage A wage floor, legislated by government, setting the lowest hourly rate that firms may legally pay workers.

Models, or **theories** Simplified representations of the real world used as the basis for predictions or explanations.

Monetarists Macroeconomists who believe that inflation is always caused by excessive monetary growth and that changes in the money supply affect aggregate demand both directly and indirectly.

Monetary rule A monetary policy that incorporates a rule specifying the annual rate of growth of some monetary aggregate.

Money Any medium that is universally accepted in an economy both by sellers of goods and services as payment for those goods and services and by creditors as payment for debts.

Money illusion Reacting to changes in money prices rather than relative prices. If a worker whose wages double when the price level also doubles thinks he or she is better off, the worker is suffering from money illusion.

Money market deposit accounts (MMDAs) Accounts issued by banks yielding a market rate of interest with a minimum balance requirement and a limit on transactions. They have no minimum maturity.

Money market mutual funds Funds of investment companies that obtain funds from the public that are held in common and used to acquire short-maturity credit instruments, such as certificates of deposit and securities sold by the U.S. government.

Money multiplier The reciprocal of the required reserve ratio, assuming no leakages into currency and no excess reserves. It is equal to 1 divided by the required reserve ratio.

Money price The price that we observe today, expressed in today's dollars. Also called the *absolute* or *nominal price.*

Money supply The amount of money in circulation.

Monopolist A single supplier that comprises its entire industry for a good or service for which there is no close substitute.

Monopolistic competition A market situation in which a large number of firms produce similar but not identical products. Entry into the industry is relatively easy.

Monopolization The possession of monopoly power in the relevant market and the willful acquisition or maintenance of that power, as distinguished from growth or development as a consequence of a superior product, business acumen, or historical accident.

Monopoly A firm that has great control over the price of a good. In the extreme case, a monopoly is the only seller of a good or service.

Monopsonist A single buyer.

Monopsonistic exploitation Exploitation due to monopsony power. It leads to a price for the variable input that is less than its marginal revenue product. Monopsonistic exploitation is the difference between marginal revenue product and the wage rate.

Moral hazard The possibility that a borrower might engage in riskier behavior after a loan has been obtained.

Multiplier The ratio of the change in the equilibrium level of real national income to the change in autonomous expenditures; the number by which a change in autonomous investment or autonomous consumption, for example, is multiplied to get the change in the equilibrium level of real national income.

National income (NI) The total of all factor payments to resource owners. It can be obtained by subtracting indirect business taxes from NDP.

National income accounting A measurement system used to estimate national income and its components; one approach to measuring an economy's aggregate performance.

Natural monopoly A monopoly that arises from the peculiar production characteristics in an industry. It usually arises when there are large economies of scale relative to the industry's demand such that one firm can produce at a lower average cost than can be achieved by multiple firms.

Natural rate of unemployment The rate of unemployment that is estimated to prevail in long-run macroeconomic equilibrium, when all workers and employers have fully adjusted to any changes in the economy.

Near moneys Assets that are almost money. They have a high degree of liquidity; they can be easily converted into money without loss in value. Time deposits and short-term U.S. government securities are examples.

Negative-sum game A game in which players as a group lose at the end of the game.

Net domestic product (NDP) GDP minus depreciation.

Net investment Gross private domestic investment minus an estimate of the wear and tear on the existing capital stock. Net investment therefore measures the change in capital stock over a one-year period.

Net public debt Gross public debt minus all government interagency borrowing.

Net worth The difference between assets and liabilities.

New classical model A modern version of the classical model in which wages and prices are flexible, there is pure competition in all markets, and the rational expectations hypothesis is assumed to be working.

New entrant An individual who has never held a full-time job lasting two weeks or longer but is now seeking employment.

New growth theory A theory of economic growth that examines the factors that determine why technology, research, innovation, and the like are undertaken and how they interact.

New Keynesian economics A macroeconomic approach that emphasizes that the prices of some goods and services adjust sluggishly in response to changing market conditions. Thus an unexpected decrease in the price level results in some firms with higher-than-desired prices. A consequence is a reduction in sales for those firms.

Nominal rate of interest The market rate of interest expressed in today's dollars.

Nominal values The values of variables such as GDP and investment expressed in current dollars, also called money values; measurement in terms of the actual market prices at which goods are sold.

Nonaccelerating inflation rate of unemployment (NAIRU) The rate of unemployment below which the rate

of inflation tends to rise and above which the rate of inflation tends to fall.

Noncooperative game A game in which the players neither negotiate nor cooperate in any way. As applied to firms in an industry, this is the common situation in which there are relatively few firms and each has some ability to change price.

Nondurable consumer goods Consumer goods that are used up within three years.

Nonincome expense items The total of indirect business taxes and depreciation.

Nonprice rationing devices All methods used to ration scarce goods that are price-controlled. Whenever the price system is not allowed to work, nonprice rationing devices will evolve to ration the affected goods and services.

Normal goods Goods for which demand rises as income rises. Most goods are considered normal.

Normal rate of return The amount that must be paid to an investor to induce investment in a business; also known as the *opportunity cost of capital*.

Normative economics Analysis involving value judgments about economic policies; relates to whether things are good or bad. A statement of what ought to be.

Number line A line that can be divided into segments of equal length, each associated with a number.

Oligopoly A market situation in which there are very few sellers. Each seller knows that the other sellers will react to its changes in prices and quantities.

Open economy effect One of the reasons that the aggregate demand curve slopes downward is that higher price levels result in foreigners' desiring to buy fewer American-made goods while Americans now desire more foreign-made goods, thereby reducing net exports. This is equivalent to a reduction in the amount of real goods and services purchased in the United States.

Open market operations The purchase and sale of existing U.S. government securities (such as bonds) in the open private market by the Federal Reserve System.

Opportunistic behavior Actions that ignore the possible long-run benefits of cooperation and focus solely on short-run gains.

Opportunity cost The highest-valued, next-best alternative that must be sacrificed to obtain something or to satisfy a want.

Opportunity cost of capital The normal rate of return, or the available return on the next-best alternative investment. Economists consider this a cost of production, and it is included in our cost examples.

Optimal quantity of pollution The level of pollution for which the marginal benefit of one additional unit of clean air just equals the marginal cost of that additional unit of clean air.

Origin The intersection of the y axis and the x axis in a graph.

Par value The officially determined value of a currency.

Partnership A business owned by two or more joint owners, or partners, who share the responsibilities and the profits of the firm and are individually liable for all of the debts of the partnership.

Passive (nondiscretionary) policymaking Policymaking that is carried out in response to a rule. It is therefore not in response to an actual or potential change in overall economic activity.

Patent A government protection that gives an inventor the exclusive right to make, use, or sell an invention for a limited period of time (currently, 20 years).

Payment intermediary An institution that facilitates the transfer of funds between buyer and seller during the

course of any purchase of goods, services, or financial assets.

Payment system An institutional structure by which consumers, businesses, governments, and financial institutions exchange payments.

Payoff matrix A matrix of outcomes, or consequences, of the strategies available to the players in a game.

Perfect competition A market structure in which the decisions of individual buyers and sellers have no effect on market price.

Perfectly competitive firm A firm that is such a small part of the total industry that it cannot affect the price of the product it sells.

Perfectly elastic demand A demand that has the characteristic that even the slightest increase in price will lead to zero quantity demanded.

Perfectly elastic supply A supply characterized by a reduction in quantity supplied to zero when there is the slightest decrease in price.

Perfectly inelastic demand A demand that exhibits zero responsiveness to price changes; no matter what the price is, the quantity demanded remains the same.

Perfectly inelastic supply A supply for which quantity supplied remains constant, no matter what happens to price.

Personal income (PI) The amount of income that households actually receive before they pay personal income taxes.

Phillips curve A curve showing the relationship between unemployment and changes in wages or prices. It was long thought to reflect a trade-off between unemployment and inflation.

Physical capital All manufactured resources, including buildings, equipment, machines, and improvements to land that is used for production.

Planning curve The long-run average cost curve.

Planning horizon The long run, during which all inputs are variable.

Plant size The physical size of the factories that a firm owns and operates to produce its output. Plant size can be defined by square footage, maximum physical capacity, and other physical measures.

Point-of-sale (POS) network System in which consumer payments for retail purchases are made by means of direct deductions from their deposit accounts at depository institutions.

Policy irrelevance proposition The new classical and rational expectations conclusion that policy actions have no real effects in the short run if the policy actions are anticipated and none in the long run even if the policy actions are unanticipated.

Positive economics Analysis that is strictly limited to making either purely descriptive statements or scientific predictions; for example, "If A, then B." A statement of what is.

Positive-sum game A game in which players as a group are better off at the end of the game.

Precautionary demand Holding money to meet unplanned expenditures and emergencies.

Present value The value of a future amount expressed in today's dollars; the most that someone would pay today to receive a certain sum at some point in the future.

Price ceiling A legal maximum price that may be charged for a particular good or service.

Price controls Government-mandated minimum or maximum prices that may be charged for goods and services.

Price differentiation Establishing different prices for similar products to reflect differences in marginal cost in providing those commodities to different groups of buyers.

Price discrimination Selling a given product at more than one price, with the price difference being unrelated to differences in cost.

Price elasticity of demand (E_p) The responsiveness of the quantity demanded of a commodity to changes in its price; defined as the percentage change in quantity demanded divided by the percentage change in price.

Price elasticity of supply (E_s) The responsiveness of the quantity supplied of a commodity to a change in its price; the percentage change in quantity supplied divided by the percentage change in price.

Price floor A legal minimum price below which a good or service may not be sold. Legal minimum wages are an example.

Price index The cost of today's market basket of goods expressed as a percentage of the cost of the same market basket during a base year.

Price leadership A practice in many oligopolistic industries in which the largest firm publishes its price list ahead of its competitors, who then match those announced prices. Also called *parallel pricing*.

Price searcher A firm that must determine the price-output combination that maximizes profit because it faces a downward-sloping demand curve.

Price system An economic system in which relative prices are constantly changing to reflect changes in supply and demand for different commodities. The prices of those commodities are signals to everyone within the system as to what is relatively scarce and what is relatively abundant.

Price taker A competitive firm that must take the price of its product as given because the firm cannot influence its price.

Price war A pricing campaign designed to capture additional market share by repeatedly cutting prices.

Price-consumption curve The set of consumer optimum combinations of

two goods that the consumer would choose as the price of one good changes, while money income and the price of the other good remain constant.

Principal-agent problem The conflict of interest that occurs when agents—managers of firms—pursue their own objectives to the detriment of the goals of the firms' principals, or owners.

Principle of rival consumption The recognition that individuals are rivals in consuming private goods because one person's consumption reduces the amount available for others to consume.

Principle of substitution The principle that consumers and producers shift away from goods and resources that become priced relatively higher in favor of goods and resources that are now priced relatively lower.

Prisoners' dilemma A famous strategic game in which two prisoners have a choice between confessing and not confessing to a crime. If neither confesses, they serve a minimum sentence. If both confess, they serve a maximum sentence. If one confesses and the other doesn't, the one who confesses goes free. The dominant strategy is always to confess.

Private costs Costs borne solely by the individuals who incur them. Also called *internal costs*.

Private goods Goods that can be consumed by only one individual at a time. Private goods are subject to the principle of rival consumption.

Private property rights Exclusive rights of ownership that allow the use, transfer, and exchange of property.

Producer durables, or **capital goods** Durable goods having an expected service life of more than three years that are used by businesses to produce other goods and services.

Producer Price Index (PPI) A statistical measure of a weighted average of prices of commodities that firms produce and sell.

Product differentiation The distinguishing of products by brand name, color, and other minor attributes. Product differentiation occurs in other than perfectly competitive markets in which products are, in theory, homogeneous, such as wheat or corn.

Production Any activity that results in the conversion of resources into products that can be used in consumption.

Production function The relationship between inputs and maximum physical output. A production function is a technological, not an economic, relationship.

Production possibilities curve (PPC) A curve representing all possible combinations of total output that could be produced assuming (1) a fixed amount of productive resources of a given quality and (2) the efficient use of those resources.

Profit-maximizing rate of production The rate of production that maximizes total profits, or the difference between total revenues and total costs; also, the rate of production at which marginal revenue equals marginal cost.

Progressive taxation A tax system in which as income increases, a higher percentage of the additional income is taxed. The marginal tax rate exceeds the average tax rate as income rises.

Property rights The rights of an owner to use and to exchange property.

Proportional rule A decision-making system in which actions are based on the proportion of the "votes" cast and are in proportion to them. In a market system, if 10 percent of the "dollar votes" are cast for blue cars, 10 percent of the output will be blue cars.

Proportional taxation A tax system in which regardless of an individual's income, the tax bill comprises exactly the same proportion. Also called a *flat-rate tax*.

Proprietorship A business owned by one individual who makes the business decisions, receives all the profits, and is legally responsible for all the debts of the firm.

Public goods Goods to which the principle of rival consumption does not apply; they can be jointly consumed by many individuals simultaneously at no additional cost and with no reduction in quality or quantity.

Purchasing power The value of money for buying goods and services. If your money income stays the same but the price of one good that you are buying goes up, your effective purchasing power falls, and vice versa.

Purchasing power parity Adjustment in exchange rate conversions that takes into account differences in the true cost of living across countries.

Quota system A government-imposed restriction on the quantity of a specific good that another country is allowed to sell in the United States. In other words, quotas are restrictions on imports. These restrictions are usually applied to one or several specific countries.

Random walk theory The theory that there are no predictable trends in securities prices that can be used to "get rich quick."

Rate of discount The rate of interest used to discount future sums back to present value.

Rate of return An economic system in which relative prices are constantly changing to reflect changes in supply and demand for different commodities. The prices of those commodities are signals to everyone within the system as to what is relatively scarce and what is relatively abundant.

Rate-of-return regulation Regulation that seeks to keep the rate of return in the industry at a competitive level by not allowing excessive prices to be charged.

Rational expectations hypothesis A theory stating that people combine the effects of past policy changes on important economic variables with their own judgment about the future effects of current and future policy changes.

Rationality assumption The assumption that people do not intentionally make decisions that would leave them worse off.

Reaction function The manner in which one oligopolist reacts to a change in price, output, or quality made by another oligopolist in the industry.

Real-balance effect The change in expenditures resulting from the real value of money balances when the price level changes, all other things held constant. Also called the wealth effect.

Real business cycle theory An extension and modification of the theories of the new classical economists of the 1970s and 1980s, in which money is neutral and only real, supply-side factors matter in influencing labor employment and real output.

Real-income effect The change in people's purchasing power that occurs when, other things being constant, the price of one good that they purchase changes. When that price goes up, real income, or purchasing power, falls, and when that price goes down, real income increases.

Real rate of interest The nominal rate of interest minus the anticipated rate of inflation.

Real values Measurement of economic values after adjustments have been made for changes in the average of prices between years.

Recession A period of time during which the rate of growth of business activity is consistently less than its long-term trend or is negative.

Recessionary gap The gap that exists whenever the equilibrium level of real national income per year is less than the full-employment level as shown by the position of the long-run aggregate supply curve.

Recognition time lag The time required to gather information about the current state of the economy.

Recycling The reuse of raw materials derived from manufactured products.

Reentrant An individual who used to work full time but left the labor force and has now reentered it looking for a job.

Regressive taxation A tax system in which as more dollars are earned, the percentage of tax paid on them falls. The marginal tax rate is less than the average tax rate as income rises.

Reinvestment Profits (or depreciation reserves) used to purchase new capital equipment.

Relative price The price of one commodity divided by the price of another commodity; the number of units of one commodity that must be sacrificed to purchase one unit of another commodity.

Rent control The placement of price ceilings on rents in particular cities.

Repricing, or menu, cost of inflation The cost associated with recalculating prices and printing new price lists when there is inflation.

Repurchase agreement (REPO, or RP) An agreement made by a bank to sell Treasury or federal agency securities to its customers, coupled with an agreement to repurchase them at a price that includes accumulated interest.

Required reserve ratio The percentage of total deposits that the Fed requires depository institutions to hold in the form of vault cash or deposits with the Fed.

Required reserves The value of reserves that a depository institution must hold in the form of vault cash or deposits with the Fed.

Reserves In the U.S. Federal Reserve System, deposits held by Federal Reserve district banks for depository institutions, plus depository institutions' vault cash.

Resources Things used to produce other things to satisfy people's wants.

Retained earnings   Earnings that a corporation saves, or retains, for investment in other productive activities; earnings that are not distributed to stockholders.

Ricardian equivalence theorem   The proposition that an increase in the government budget deficit has no effect on aggregate demand.

Right-to-work laws   Laws that make it illegal to require union membership as a condition of continuing employment in a particular firm.

Saving   The act of not consuming all of one's current income. Whatever is not consumed out of spendable income is, by definition, saved. *Saving* is an action measured over time (a flow), whereas *savings* are a stock, an accumulation resulting from the act of saving in the past.

Savings deposits   Interest-earning funds that can be withdrawn at any time without payment of a penalty.

Say's law   A dictum of economist J. B. Say that supply creates its own demand; producing goods and services generates the means and the willingness to purchase other goods and services.

Scarcity   A situation in which the ingredients for producing the things that people desire are insufficient to satisfy all wants.

Seasonal unemployment   Unemployment resulting from the seasonal pattern of work in specific industries. It is usually due to seasonal fluctuations in demand or to changing weather conditions, rendering work difficult, if not impossible, as in the agriculture, construction, and tourist industries.

Secondary boycott   A boycott of companies or products sold by companies that are dealing with a company being struck.

Secular deflation   A persistent decline in prices resulting from economic growth in the presence of stable aggregate demand.

Securities   Stocks and bonds.

Separation of ownership and control   The situation that exists in corporations in which the owners (shareholders) are not the people who control the operation of the corporation (managers). The goals of these two groups are often different.

Services   Mental or physical labor or help purchased by consumers. Examples are the assistance of doctors, lawyers, dentists, repair personnel, housecleaners, educators, retailers, and wholesalers; things purchased or used by consumers that do not have physical characteristics.

Share of stock   A legal claim to a share of a corporation's future profits; if it is *common stock*, it incorporates certain voting rights regarding major policy decisions of the corporation; if it is *preferred stock*, its owners are accorded preferential treatment in the payment of dividends.

Share-the-gains, share-the-pains theory   A theory of regulatory behavior in which the regulators must take account of the demands of three groups: legislators, who established and who oversee the regulatory agency; members of the regulated industry; and consumers of the regulated industry's products or services.

Short run   The time period when at least one input, such as plant size, cannot be changed.

Short-run aggregate supply curve   The relationship between aggregate supply and the price level in the short run, all other things held constant. If prices adjust gradually in the short run, the curve is positively sloped.

Short-run break-even price   The price at which a firm's total revenues equal its total costs. At the break-even price, the firm is just making a normal rate of return on its capital investment. (It is covering its explicit and implicit costs.)

Short-run shutdown price   The price that just covers average variable costs. It occurs just below the intersection of the marginal cost curve and the average variable cost curve.

Shortage   A situation in which quantity demanded is greater than quantity supplied at a price below the market clearing price.

Signals   Compact ways of conveying to economic decision makers information needed to make decisions. A true signal not only conveys information but also provides the incentive to react appropriately. Economic profits and economic losses are such signals.

Slope   The change in the y-value divided by the corresponding change in the x value of a curve; the "incline" of the curve.

Small menu cost theory   A hypothesis that it is costly for firms to change prices in response to demand changes because of the cost of renegotiating contracts, printing price lists, and so on.

Smart card   A card containing a microprocessor that permits storage of funds via security programming, can communicate with other computers, and does not require on-line authorization for funds transfers.

Social costs   The full costs borne by society whenever a resource use occurs. Social costs can be measured by adding private, or internal, costs to external costs.

Social Security contributions   The mandatory taxes paid out of workers' wages and salaries. Although half are supposedly paid by employers, in fact the net wages of employees are lower by the full amount.

Special drawing rights (SDRs)   Reserve assets created by the International Monetary Fund for countries to use in settling international payment obligations.

Specialization   The division of productive activities among persons and regions so that no one individual or one area is totally self-sufficient. An individual may specialize, for example, in law or medicine. A nation may specialize in the production of coffee, computers, or cameras.

Standard of deferred payment A property of an asset that makes it desirable for use as a means of settling debts maturing in the future; an essential property of money.

Stock The quantity of something, measured at a given point in time—for example, an inventory of goods or a bank account. Stocks are defined independently of time, although they are assessed at a point in time.

Store of value The ability to hold value over time; a necessary property of money.

Stored-value card A card bearing magnetic stripes that hold magnetically encoded data, providing access to stored funds.

Strategic dependence A situation in which one firm's actions with respect to price, quality, advertising, and related changes may be strategically countered by the reactions of one or more other firms in the industry. Such dependence can exist only when there are a limited number of major firms in an industry.

Strategy Any rule that is used to make a choice, such as "Always pick heads"; any potential choice that can be made by players in a game.

Strikebreakers Temporary or permanent workers hired by a company to replace union members who are striking.

Structural unemployment Unemployment resulting from a poor match of workers' abilities and skills with current requirements of employers.

Subsidy A negative tax; a payment to a producer from the government, usually in the form of a cash grant.

Substitutes Two goods are substitutes when either one can be used for consumption to satisfy a similar want—for example, coffee and tea. The more you buy of one, the less you buy of the

other. For substitutes, the change in the price of one causes a shift in demand for the other in the same direction as the price change.

Substitution effect The tendency of people to substitute cheaper commodities for more expensive commodities.

Supply A schedule showing the relationship between price and quantity supplied for a specified period of time, other things being equal.

Supply curve The graphical representation of the supply schedule; a line (curve) showing the supply schedule, which generally slopes upward (has a positive slope), other things being equal.

Supply-side economics The notion that creating incentives for individuals and firms to increase productivity will cause the aggregate supply curve to shift outward.

Surplus A situation in which quantity supplied is greater than quantity demanded at a price above the market clearing price.

Sweep account A depository institution account that entails regular shifts of funds from transaction deposits that are subject to reserve requirements to savings deposits that are exempt from reserve requirements.

Sympathy strike A strike by a union in sympathy with another union's strike or cause.

Systemic risk The risk that some payment intermediaries may not be able to meet the terms of their credit agreements because of failures by other institutions to settle other transactions.

Target zone A range of permitted exchange rate variations between upper and lower exchange rate bands that a central bank defends by selling or buying foreign exchange reserves.

Tariffs Taxes on imported goods.

Tax bracket A specified interval of income to which a specific and unique marginal tax rate is applied.

Tax incidence The distribution of tax burdens among various groups in society.

Technology Society's pool of applied knowledge concerning how goods and services can be produced.

Terms of exchange The terms under which trading takes place. Usually the terms of exchange are equal to the price at which a good is traded.

Theory of contestable markets A hypothesis concerning pricing behavior that holds that even though there are only a few firms in an industry, they are forced to price their products more or less competitively because of the ease of entry by outsiders. The key aspect of a contestable market is relatively costless entry into and exit from the industry.

Theory of public choice The study of collective decision making.

Third parties Parties who are not directly involved in a given activity or transaction. For example, in the relationship between caregivers and patients, fees may be paid by third parties (insurance companies, government).

Thrift institutions Financial institutions that receive most of their funds from the savings of the public; they include mutual savings banks, savings and loan associations, and credit unions.

Time deposit A deposit in a financial institution that requires notice of intent to withdraw or must be left for an agreed period. Withdrawal of funds prior to the end of the agreed period may result in a penalty.

Tit-for-tat strategic behavior In game theory, cooperation that continues so long as the other players continue to cooperate.

Total costs The sum of total fixed costs and total variable costs.

Total income The yearly amount earned by the nation's resources (factors of production). Total income therefore includes wages, rent, interest payments, and profits that are received, respectively, by workers, landowners, capital owners, and entrepreneurs.

Total revenues   The price per unit times the total quantity sold.

Transaction costs   All of the costs associated with exchanging, including the informational costs of finding out price and quality, service record, and durability of a product, plus the cost of contracting and enforcing that contract.

Transactions accounts   Checking account balances in commercial banks and other types of financial institutions, such as credit unions and mutual savings banks; any accounts in financial institutions on which you can easily write checks without many restrictions.

Transactions approach   A method of measuring the money supply by looking at money as a medium of exchange.

Transactions demand   Holding money as a medium of exchange to make payments. The level varies directly with nominal national income.

Transfer payments   Money payments made by governments to individuals for which in return no services or goods are concurrently rendered. Examples are welfare, Social Security, and unemployment insurance benefits.

Transfers in kind   Payments that are in the form of actual goods and services, such as food stamps, subsidized public housing, and medical care, and for which in return no goods or services are rendered concurrently.

Traveler's checks   Financial instruments purchased from a bank or a non-banking organization and signed during purchase that can be used as cash upon a second signature by the purchaser.

Unanticipated inflation   Inflation at a rate that comes as a surprise, either higher or lower than the rate anticipated.

Unemployment   The total number of adults (aged 16 years or older) who are willing and able to work and who are actively looking for work but have not found a job.

Union shop   A business enterprise that allows the hiring of nonunion members, conditional on their joining the union by some specified date after employment begins.

Unit elasticity of demand   A demand relationship in which the quantity demanded changes exactly in proportion to the change in price. Total expenditures are invariant to price changes in the unit-elastic region of the demand curve.

Unit of accounting   A measure by which prices are expressed; the common denominator of the price system; a central property of money.

Universal banking   Environment in which banks face few or no restrictions on their power to offer a full range of financial services and to own shares of stock in corporations.

Unlimited liability   A legal concept whereby the personal assets of the owner of a firm can be seized to pay off the firm's debts.

Util   A representative unit by which utility is measured.

Utility   The want-satisfying power of a good or service.

Utility analysis   The analysis of consumer decision making based on utility maximization.

Value added   The dollar value of an industry's sales minus the value of intermediate goods (for example, raw materials and parts) used in production.

Variable costs   Costs that vary with the rate of production. They include wages paid to workers and purchases of materials.

Vertical merger   The joining of a firm with another to which it sells an output or from which it buys an input.

Voluntary exchange   An act of trading, done on a voluntary basis, in which both parties to the trade are subjectively better off after the exchange.

Voluntary import expansion (VIE)   An official agreement with another country in which it agrees to import more from the United States.

Voluntary restraint agreement (VRA)   An official agreement with another country that "voluntarily" restricts the quantity of its exports to the United States.

Wants   What people would buy if their incomes were unlimited.

Wealth   The stock of assets owned by a person, household, firm, or nation. For a household, wealth can consist of a house, cars, personal belongings, stocks, bonds, bank accounts, and cash.

World index fund   A portfolio of bonds issued in various nations whose yields generally move in offsetting directions, thereby reducing the overall risk of losses.

World Trade Organization (WTO)   The successor organization to GATT, it handles all trade disputes among its 135 member nations.

x axis   The horizontal axis in a graph.

y axis   The vertical axis in a graph.

Zero-sum game   A game in which any gains within the group are exactly offset by equal losses by the end of the game.

Index